FREEDOM'S CHILDREN

FREEDOM'S CHILDREN

The 1938 Labor Rebellion

and the Birth of Modern Jamaica

COLIN A. PALMER

THE UNIVERSITY OF NORTH CAROLINA PRESS | *Chapel Hill*

© 2014 THE UNIVERSITY OF NORTH CAROLINA PRESS
All rights reserved.
Designed by Sally Scruggs and set in Charter by codeMantra.

The paper in this book meets the guidelines for permanence and durability of the Committee on Production Guidelines for Book Longevity of the Council on Library Resources.

Library of Congress Cataloging-in-Publication Data
Palmer, Colin A., 1944–
Freedom's children : the 1938 labor rebellion and the birth of modern Jamaica / Colin A. Palmer.
pages cm
Includes bibliographical references and index.
ISBN 978-1-4696-1169-3 (pbk : alk. paper)
ISBN 978-1-4696-1170-9 (ebook)
1. Jamaica—Politics and government—To 1962. 2. Labor—Jamaica—History—20th century. 3. Labor unions—Political activity—Jamaica—History—20th century. 4. Jamaica—History—To 1962. I. Title.
F1886.P35 2014
320.97292'0904—dc23
2013028648

CONTENTS

Acknowledgments | ix   *Jamaican Currency in 1938* | xi

Introduction | 1

ONE   Jamaica in 1938 | 7

TWO   The Labor Rebellion | 28

THREE   Race and the Colonial Imagination | 64

FOUR   Looking Back, Moving Forward | 87

FIVE   Bustamante, Unionism, and the Politics of Performance | 115

SIX   Bustamante and the Politics of Power | 179

SEVEN   Challenging Power and Facing the Consequences | 230

EIGHT   Constitutional Change | 280

NINE   Party Politics | 309

Conclusion | 357

Notes | 363   *Selected Bibliography* | 393   *Index* | 399

ILLUSTRATIONS, TABLES, AND MAP

Illustrations

Norman Manley, ca. 1938 | 54

Alexander Bustamante and striking workers, June 1, 1938 | 62

Tables

1. Population Classified by Racial Origin and Sex Showing Numerical and Percent Distribution, 1943 | 14

2. Percentage Distribution of Certain Racial Origin Groups, Jamaica, 1881–1943 | 15

3. Racial Origins and Literacy, Seven Years of Age and Older, 1943 | 16

4. Gross Annual Incomes in Jamaica, 1935 | 17

5. Ordinary Workers' Estimated Monthly Minimum Budget | 18

6. Distribution of Landholdings, 1938 | 22

7. The West Indies Sugar Company, Ltd., Scale of Pay Prior to May 3, 1938 | 34

8. The West Indies Sugar Company, Ltd., Cultivation Rates | 35

9. Membership of Unions in Jamaica, 1943 | 169

Map

Jamaica | 8

ACKNOWLEDGMENTS

I would like to thank several persons for their kind assistance as I conducted the research for this book. The staffs of the Jamaica Archives; the Institute of Jamaica; the National Archives in College Park, Maryland; the British Archives; and the Schomburg Center for Research in Black Culture deserve my gratitude. Nora Strudwich of the Bustamante Museum was particularly helpful. I also want to thank Jobert Bienvenue and Maristela Perez for typing the manuscript. My good friends and colleagues Franklin Knight, Patrick Bryan, Nicole Burrowes-Caserly, and Sean Greene read the entire manuscript and provided me with trenchant criticisms and useful suggestions for its improvement. The manuscript also benefited enormously from the criticisms of the two readers for the University of North Carolina Press. I thank these six scholars for their selfless and priceless contributions to the preparation of this volume.

JAMAICAN CURRENCY IN 1938

1 farthing (1/4d) = lowest denomination
4 farthings = 1 penny (1d)
6 farthings = 1 penny and a half (1 ½)
12 pennies = 1 shilling (1/–)
18 pennies = one shilling and sixpence (1/6)
4 shillings = 1 dollar
20 shillings = 1 pound (£)

INTRODUCTION

This book is the third in a series that began with the publication in 2006 of *Eric Williams and the Making of the Modern Caribbean*. That volume was primarily a study of the important role that the brilliant scholar and statesman from Trinidad and Tobago played in imagining and working to construct a politically and economically integrated Anglophone Caribbean. Williams was the most outstanding personage that his country produced in the twentieth century, serving as head of its government from 1956 to 1981. The book was, in a larger sense, also a study of Trinidad and Tobago's quest for self-determination and Williams's attempts to call a new and modern Caribbean into being.

Published in 2010, the second volume in the trilogy examined British Guiana's tumultuous struggle to achieve nationhood. The Guyanese nation in formation was damaged by the corrosive politics of race, the self-serving and destructive machinations of the British and the Americans, and the mediocrity of its elected leaders. Entitled *The Politics of Power: Cheddi Jagan and the Struggle for British Guiana's Independence*, the book was a case study of a colonial tragedy.

More positive in tone, this volume is concerned with the labor rebellion that occurred in Jamaica in 1938 and how it helped to create a new polity. Beginning in the mid-1930s, workers in many colonies of the Anglophone Caribbean rejected the appalling conditions that had imprisoned them, challenging an oppressive status quo. Predominantly of African descent, these descendants of enslaved peoples did not experience a fundamental change in their life chances since the abolition of slavery in 1838. The worldwide economic depression of the 1930s exacerbated their dire circumstances, and so would World War II. Jamaican workers were no strangers to abuse, exploitation, and economic deprivation. But some of them were starting to realize their collective power and their ability to force the barons of capital to change, or at least to alter, the texture of their relationship with labor.

This is the story of Jamaican workers who forged a class consciousness in contestation with capital. Workers began to draw psychological strength and energy from one another, despite their variegated jobs, skills, age, gender, and residential location. This book describes the dynamism that emanated from below and discusses the social unrest that engulfed the island in May and June of that fateful year, 1938. Neither the colonial state nor the elite groups were prepared for the ubiquity of these challenges to the status quo, their fervor, and their frightening urgency. They began on the West Indies Sugar Company's estate in Frome on May 2, 1938, spreading to Kingston's waterfront and elsewhere three weeks later. These streams of protest were the result of numerous tributaries of discontent that had been eroding the island's workplaces, awaiting the moment when they would coalesce into one mighty river.

This spontaneous outpouring of discontent initially lacked leadership, direction, strategy, or even a coherent series of objectives. The workers' inchoate but passionate and irrepressible demands for change could not be contained, tempered, ignored, or diverted. Although a modern trade union, the Jamaica Workers and Tradesmen Union, had been founded a year earlier by Allan George St. Claver Coombs, the workers did not consult him before they began their strikes. Coombs had invited a self-identified wealthy man and usurer to assist him in the union, but the relationship was acrimonious and short-lived. William Alexander Bustamante, a charismatic personality, had no experience as a labor leader before he enlisted with Coombs, but he would develop into the most celebrated trade unionist that Jamaica has produced.

Born William Alexander Clarke in Blenheim in the parish of Hanover in 1884, he formally changed his surname to Bustamante in 1944 after using that name for a decade or more. Of mixed racial ancestry, young Clarke received an elementary school education. He migrated to Cuba in 1905, joining the ranks of many thousands of Jamaicans seeking their fortunes in that island. Clarke worked as a tramway operator in Cuba before relocating to Panama. He returned to Cuba either in 1919 or 1920, procuring a job with the Special Police Force. Clarke visited Jamaica three times between 1922 and 1932, eventually settling in New York, where he obtained a job in a hospital, probably as an attendant.

Clarke's/Bustamante's overseas sojourns are shrouded in mystery. The veracity of the narrative he recounted when he returned to Jamaica cannot be established, as he invented and reinvented his past. Bustamante claimed that he made a fortune in the stock market in the United States of America, but there is no independent corroboration of his story.[1] Returning to Jamaica permanently in 1934, he became a usurer with a mostly impoverished clientele.

Although Bustamante's association with Coombs was short and bitter, he remained committed to labor's cause, building a reputation as a friend of and advocate for the island's working people. When the workers on Kingston's waterfront began to protest against their condition in May 1938, they invited Bustamante to assume the leadership of the developing rebellion. His acceptance of that invitation not only changed the trajectory of his life but fundamentally altered Jamaica's history. The still-unseasoned leader founded seven unions in 1938, each one directed at particular occupational groups of workers. Known as the Bustamante unions, they would coalesce in 1939 into the Bustamante Industrial Trade Union (BITU), which became the second modern trade union to exist in the island. In 1943 Bustamante founded the Jamaica Labour Party (JLP), which was really the union's progeny. The workers had created Bustamante and provided the space for his emergence as a political leader and their most passionate advocate, but he was not always their most rational, visionary, and sagacious chieftain.

The workers' rebellion also produced another leader of distinction: Norman Washington Manley. He was Bustamante's cousin but followed a different career path. Born in the parish of Manchester in 1893, the brilliant young student attended Jamaica College, distinguishing himself as an athlete and winning the prestigious Rhodes Scholarship, tenable at Oxford University. Manley took leave from Oxford to serve in World War I. Resuming his studies at war's end, he graduated as a barrister-at-law in 1922. Returning to Jamaica, he pursued an enormously successful legal career, becoming a respected counsel for the elite. Manley received the highly coveted appointment as a King's Counsel in 1932.

Prior to the rebellion that began in May 1938, Norman Manley eschewed any involvement in the political life of Jamaica. He experienced an epiphany during the turmoil, however, offering his services as a mediator between capital and labor. Manley emerged from the conflict with his prestige enhanced and with a commitment to pursue a political career. Along with others, he founded the People's National Party (PNP) in September 1938, ultimately embracing socialism as its ideology. Manley led an aggressive movement for self-government in the island, making a significant contribution to the politicization of the people through his speeches before various audiences.[2]

Bustamante and Manley, the two brown-skinned cousins, dominated Jamaica's political life after the rebellion, but they did not stand alone. There were others who played important roles, as this book will show. But the new Jamaica was called into being not by members of the elite but by those workers who rejected their oppression in 1938, became members of the trade unions that emerged, and provided Bustamante in particular with much popular support. Recognizing that the rebellion created the moment for widespread changes in the society, Norman Manley and his allies demanded constitutional reforms that would give the Jamaican people more control over their own affairs. But it was the workers who had unleashed the creative energies in the society. The new and modern Jamaica that emerged was their monumental achievement.

This book describes the rebellion and the changes it wrought in Jamaican society between 1938, when it began in earnest, and 1944, when the island elected its first legislature under the aegis of universal adult suffrage. It is organized thematically and attempts to capture the dynamism of those years as the workers, their allies, and leaders engaged in the task of imagining and constructing a new Jamaica. The book privileges their voices, sometimes extensively, but it does not engage in hagiography. It is a critical assessment of a people's travail, their struggles, their successes and failures, and their human foibles too.

The book's documentation is grounded in manuscripts located in the British National Archives, the National Archives of the United States, the Jamaica Archives, and the Bustamante Museum. The Jamaican newspapers, particularly the *Daily Gleaner*, were also invaluable resources. *Freedom's Children* is based almost entirely on these records, many of which have hitherto remained unexamined. This new documentation allowed me to make a more-trenchant analysis of the labor rebellion and its aftermath and to underscore my argument that the events of 1938 were as much an assault on the barons of capital as they were a racial conflict.

This study is an exercise in labor, political, and social history. While it is organized thematically, each of its chapters includes a chronological discussion of the issues addressed. Inevitably, this methodological approach involves some overlap since it is sometimes necessary to refer briefly to previously discussed events. Although the period covered coincides roughly with the outbreak and duration of World War II, I reject any assertion that the principal developments in the island were initiated, influenced, and shaped by the war. The major exceptions to this claim were the persecution and detention of some of the war's critics by Governor Arthur Richards and the increase in the price of some imported and scarce consumer items. The labor rebellion preceded the outbreak of the war and was primarily the product of local conditions.

The book is divided into nine chapters. Conceptually, the first four chapters focus on the origin and course of the rebellion. Chapter 1 provides a brief discussion of the evolution of Jamaica's history under British suzerainty up to 1938. But more important, it focuses on the social and economic conditions that existed in the 1930s and that produced the fuel for the rebellion. Chapter 2 is a discussion of the labor rebellion of May and June 1938, the rise of Alexander Bustamante to the leadership of the workers, and Norman Manley's emergence as a mediator. The third chapter addresses the volatile issue of race in Jamaica, the racist narrative that some English people constructed, and the growing assault on racial and color discrimination in the wake of the rebellion. Chapter 4 concludes the first half of the book with an account of the Royal Commission that the Colonial Office dispatched to the colonies in the Caribbean to investigate the conditions that fed the rebellions and make appropriate recommendations to redress the people's grievances.

The second half of the book is concerned principally with the actualization of the rebellion. Chapter 5 is a detailed discussion of the development of trade unionism in the island and Bustamante's frequently unsteady but charismatic leadership of the workers. Governor Arthur Richards's internment of Bustamante for seventeen months in 1940 for allegedly inciting a worker-led race war and the labor leader's split with Norman Manley and the People's National Party are examined in chapter 6. Chapter 7 discusses the governor's suppression of political dissent during wartime and the opposition it spawned in the island. Chapter 8 analyses the struggle to achieve constitutional changes in the island in the wake of the rebellion. It addresses the emergence of a nascent Jamaican nationalism and the denial of self-government in the new constitution that was promulgated in 1944. The concluding chapter focuses on the introduction of party politics in the island, providing a comprehensive account of the formation of the People's National Party in 1938, the subsequent founding of other parties, and the first election conducted under the aegis of universal adult suffrage in 1944.

Modern scholars maintain that "race" is a social construct. I use the word in this book in the way it would have been understood at the time. The appellation "Bustamante unions" refers to the seven unions that bore the labor chieftain's name and that existed between June 1938 and January 1939. They were replaced in the latter month by the umbrella Bustamante Industrial Trade Union. Thereafter, most of the extant manuscripts employ the singular "union" instead of the plural "unions," although not consistently. In researching and writing this book, I have tried to respect the admonition of Dr. Roy Augier, a historian at the University College of the West Indies (later the University of the West Indies), that "the first law of history is to tell the whole truth about the past."[3] Many aspects of the story I tell in this book are being addressed for the first time and are likely to be controversial, and the veracity of my account likely will be questioned, especially by general readers. Consequently, I include in the narrative copious excerpts from the sources that I consulted. This is particularly the case in the extensive discussions of the activities and roles of Alexander Bustamante, Norman Manley, and Arthur Richards. In order to add some levity to the narrative, I include a humorous episode or comment at times.

Freedom's Children excavates the history of the people at the societal margins who provided the catalyst for the making of modern Jamaica. A hundred years after the end of slavery, the peoples of African descent remained the exploited and marginalized denizens of their homeland. Slavery's physical shackles had been removed, but the majority of the island's people still bore the scars. The labor rebellion did not destroy all the wrongs that bedeviled Jamaican society, but it was surely a good beginning.

ONE

Jamaica in 1938

"The spectacle of bonfires on the hills, fireworks at the National Stadium and other centres, dancing in the streets, donkey races, treats for school children and the aged, regattas, parties galore, brought Jamaicans of all races, all classes, and colours and creeds together to celebrate their independence and to symbolize the motto, *Out of many, one people*," reported the *Daily Gleaner*, Jamaica's principal daily newspaper. It was describing the scene on August 6, 1962, when Jamaica gained its independence from Britain. Twenty thousand Jamaicans had gathered in the National Stadium at midnight to witness the lowering of the Union Jack, the hoisting of the new nation's flag, and the singing of its national anthem for the first time. In saluting his fellow Jamaicans, Sir Alexander Bustamante, the first prime minister, declared his "faith in my people" and conviction that "you all will respond to the challenge of this new era on which we now enter and to the difficult task and heavy responsibilities ahead of us."[1]

Jamaica had a long history as a colony. It began in 1494 when Christopher Columbus disembarked on the island, encountered the indigenous peoples, and proclaimed it the property of Spain. The Spanish presence led to a decline in the population of the native peoples as a consequence of violence and disease. In 1501, nine years after Columbus's first arrival in the hemisphere, the Spanish crown authorized the importation of enslaved Africans to Hispaniola, inaugurating the Atlantic slave trade to the Americas. The institution of slavery spread to Jamaica in 1511, permanently altering the demographic configuration of the island. The English took possession of it in 1655 after a military conflict with the Spanish. Under English suzerainty, Jamaica experienced a significant expansion of the plantation system, with sugarcane as the principal crop, and a tremendous increase in the trade in enslaved Africans. Overall, as many as 900,000 African peoples were purchased in the island and became human property. Many of these enslaved Africans rejected their condition by escaping to the mountainous areas of the island. Their flights enabled them to claim a precarious freedom, demonstrating

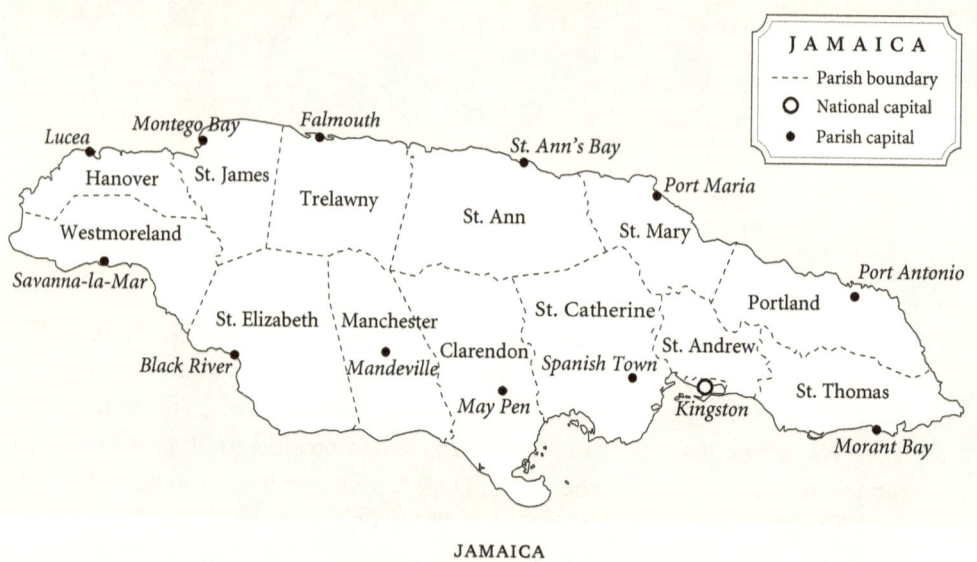

JAMAICA

independence from the existing economic and political structures of oppression. Mostly African born, these people were not seeking to destroy or even to control the colonial state whose armed might protected the system of property in persons. Seen through their optic, they were escaping from an alien society that both defined and treated them as property. They wanted to live as free people in communities of their own making. These communities of freedom invited reprisals from the colonial state. But neither the state nor those who held property in persons could stanch the hemorrhaging of unfree laborers from the sites of their oppression.

In spite of frequent military assaults on them, these communities of freedom were never annihilated. In 1739 the colonial state was forced to sign a treaty recognizing the freedom of those who had rejected their enslavement and acquiescing to the ownership of the land they occupied. The state was humiliated by having to sign such a treaty, effecting a fragile modus vivendi with those who were previously defined as human property.

These maroons, as they were called, did not constitute a part of the Jamaican polity since they governed themselves. But they were the pioneers in the struggle for political autonomy and self-determination by the peoples of African descent in the island. After 1655, political power in the English colony of Jamaica was the preserve of a very small white minority. The colony was awarded its first constitution in 1663. There was a governor, a legislative upper chamber nominated by the governor, and an elected House of Assembly. The franchise was restricted to men who owned freehold with a minimum value of £10, and membership in the Assembly was open to those men with freehold worth £300 or more. The Assembly enjoyed the power of the purse, but the governor could veto any bill of which he disapproved.

This constitution lasted until 1865, although there were important changes in it over time. It was substantially reformed in 1854 with the introduction of an Executive Committee that was designed to play a principal role in formulating policy and in the administration of the government. The composition of the upper house or Legislative Council was changed, with the number of official members limited to four. Planters would be privileged in the governor's selection of unofficial members. Not surprisingly, the vast majority of the peoples of African descent remained disenfranchised. In fact, the Franchise Act of 1859 severely restricted the franchise by imposing a poll tax of ten shillings on voters, a requirement beyond the reach of most black and formerly enslaved people. The smoldering discontent of the peoples of African descent with their economic and political condition ignited a rebellion in Morant Bay in October 1865. The violence, loss of several hundred lives, and fears for the future forced the white power elite to surrender the constitution and with it the representative government the island possessed. The imposition of Crown colony government was the result. Political power reverted to the governor. In 1866 the imperial government issued an Order in Council creating a single-chamber Legislative Council consisting of six official members and an equal number of unofficial ones, all appointed by the governor.

Responding to a petition from the local elite, the Colonial Office issued another Order in Council in 1884, permitting the election of nine members of the Legislative Council. The island received a new constitution in 1895, providing for a Legislative Council presided over by the governor with five ex officio members, no more than ten members appointed by the governor, and fourteen elected members. There was also a Privy Council consisting of the governor, the senior military officer, the colonial secretary, the attorney general, and a maximum of eight additional members appointed by the governor. This body advised the governor on matters relating to policy. The governor could veto any legislation he opposed and had the power to implement any bill that the legislature rejected after declaring it of "paramount importance" to the welfare of the colony. The votes of nine of the elected members of the Legislative Council could secure the rejection of any financial measure, and the votes of all fourteen could cause the rejection of any other proposal.

The franchise remained severely restricted. In order to qualify, male voters had to pay taxes amounting to ten shillings per annum or enjoy an annual income of £50. Women had to pay taxes of £2 per annum. Men were eligible for the vote at age twenty-one and women at age twenty-five. Only the wealthy could stand for election to the Legislative Council. The candidates had to own land producing an income of £150 annually. They could also qualify by earning £200 each year derived from business and the land. Candidates had to show an income of £300 if it came from other sources.[2]

Jamaica's constitution was structured to protect and advance the interests of the colonial state and the privileged members of society. The vast majority of adult Jamaicans could not qualify for the franchise. In 1935, for example, there were only 68,637 registered voters, constituting 5.5 percent of an estimated population of 1.25 million. Only 27,545, or 40 percent, of these voters participated in the general election of that year. Facing such a small electorate, the fourteen elected members of the Council could usually ignore the needs of the majority of the country's people with electoral impunity.

Freedom's Children did not accept their official neglect passively. Building upon a culture of resistance pioneered by their enslaved ancestors, disgruntled sugar-estate workers struck in various parts of the island in 1867, 1868, 1878, and 1901. These disturbances did not imperil the colonial state.[3] Still, they were an expression of the discontent of the people and a clear indication that challenges to an oppressive economic and social order could occur at any time.

The elected members of the Legislative Council were frequently derided for their mediocre performance in office. Governor Arthur Richards (1938–43) was one of their harshest, albeit partisan, critics. Richards did not welcome their criticism of the colonial state and the administration over which he presided, having little respect for the men who offered themselves for election to the Council. "The class of politicians now elected to the Council," he complained, "is with one or two exceptions the professional who can talk with superficial fluency on any subject, tethered to no fixed principles other than a desire to benefit his own parish." These men were inclined to give lengthy speeches in the Council in order to gain publicity in the *Daily*

Gleaner, the governor asserted. "In a country where gossip is supreme and where the value of an elected member is apt to be rated by the length and frequency of his speeches and by a generally critical attitude towards Government," Richards wrote, "the influence of such timely publicity is very great."[4]

Local critics would have agreed that the elected members were skilled practitioners of the politics of rhetoric. But the cruel truth was that the constitution accorded them no power other than to criticize, and if necessary to obstruct the administration's policy by voting against it. This was frequently an exercise in frustration, since the governor could override such negative votes by declaring the measure to be of "paramount importance" and implement it. Elected members possessed the power to irritate the administration by their rhetoric and their votes, but not to make policy for their country.

The governor was assisted in his administration of the island by a system of Parochial Boards. The island was divided into fourteen parishes, excluding Port Royal, which was designated a subsidiary division of Kingston, which served as the capital city. Kingston was only nominally a parish, being deemed so for the purpose of municipal administration. The governor was represented in each parish by a custos, who was usually a prominent and wealthy white man. The parishes of Kingston and St. Andrew were managed by a corporation, while the remaining twelve parishes were governed by the Parochial Boards, which were similar in their functions to the English councils that administered local services.

The members of the Parochial Boards were elected by the voters that met the aforementioned property and income qualifications. Each board elected its chairman, and the custos and the member of the Legislative Council for the parish served as ex officio members. The principal administrative officer for each board was called the clerk, and his terms of service and remuneration were determined by the elected officials. These Parochial Boards were characterized by their inefficiency. Richards was caustic in his criticism of them, reporting that "there is not on any Parochial Board any trained Civil Servants; there is no one with any knowledge of administration and there is no certainty of the Board having any financial sense. They have neither prestige nor tradition nor experience to guide them. It is not surprising that they are in general inefficient and dilatory."[5]

Governor Richards was appalled by the poor quality of the colonial administration in the island. "In Jamaica," he reported to his superiors in London, "there is no administrative service. There is no district administration in the ordinary Colonial sense and, so far as I know, the history of general administration in Jamaica is one of neglect.... There is little likelihood of the ordinary wants of the people receiving the personal attention and investigation which is a common place elsewhere."[6] Richards wrote this unflattering commentary on the conditions he found in the island about nine months after he assumed the office of governor. He had previously served in Malaya and Fiji, colonies where the colonial administration must have been superior to that which he found in Jamaica, hence his sharp criticisms.

Richards emphasized that the failure of the administration in Jamaica was "no new condition. It has always been so." Outraged by the conditions he observed, the governor's tone was uncharacteristically blunt for someone in his official position. "Disguised under the pseudo-democracy of the Parochial Board system, camouflaged under the cries of Elected Members," he reported, "the administration of Jamaica is, and always has been, a sham."[7] The new governor was not engaging in hyperbole. He had recognized that the colonial state lacked the administrative machinery and capacity to provide services to the people and to respond to their grievances. Britain had governed Jamaica for almost 300 years but had failed to introduce an effective administrative apparatus in the island, if only to avoid challenges to the imperial regime. Governor Richards drew upon his experiences in the colony to dramatize his point:

> It is my own personal experience that wherever I stay in the parishes I am overwhelmed with the minor needs of the people, some reasonable, some unreasonable but all such a District Officer or an Asst. District Officer could and would deal with satisfactorily in the ordinary course of his work. Ask the people why they do not approach the Parochial Board?—they smile at the idea, or the Elected Member?—they only interest him in detail at Election time; or the Custos?—it is not his business and he has no power or legal standing. Ask the people how they think the Governor can go into every detail himself?—they reply, "To whom else can we go?" There is no adequate reply. Jamaica has not and never has had an administration. It has a Governor and a Colonial Secretary who have to choose between the alternatives of cultivating a cynical indifference or of facing an ultimate breakdown from overwork.[8]

Arthur Richards had spoken an unpleasant truth. It had come from a governor who would later demonstrate that he was no great admirer of the

Jamaican people. But he was a colonial administrator sworn to promote and advance the interests of the British Empire. He knew that administrative sloppiness hindered the successful execution of this objective. Richards had no patience with bureaucratic incompetence. Nor did he take kindly to the criticism of the status quo by an increasingly aggressive and confident group of Jamaican leaders. The governor had come to the island at a time of social and political ferment, and he was determined to consolidate and strengthen the imperial presence.

When African slavery officially ended in 1838, the British government imported thousands of Indians and Chinese to work as indentured laborers in British Guiana, Trinidad and Tobago, and Jamaica. Syrians began to arrive in Jamaica in 1891. By the turn of the twentieth century, the island was characterized by the presence of a large number of "racial" groups and their various admixtures. The stunning diversity of peoples led the *Daily Gleaner* to proclaim in March 1939 that "there is no such thing as a Jamaica race." But it conceded that "there is a distinctly Jamaica people." The Jamaican people, the newspaper maintained, "have been coming into existence" since the island became an English possession in 1655, "but we cannot today speak of a Jamaica race though that may be possible another three hundred years hence."[9]

The term "race" lacked precision in usage and meaning until recent times. It was frequently conflated with "ethnicity" and national origin. The 1943 Jamaica census, for example, employed the classification "race" to mean "descendants of a common ancestor." Thus, it identified "English and Welsh" races, "Scottish" races, "Syrian" races, "black" races, and so on. It used "coloured" to mean persons of "mixed African and European blood." Such designations as "Chinese coloured," "East Indian coloured," and "Syrian coloured" included persons whose "racial origins have been mixed with 'Coloured' or 'Black' racial origins." According to the 1943 census, people of "Black and Coloured" origins constituted 95.6 percent of the population, East Indians 2.1 percent, White 1.1 percent, Chinese 1 percent, and other "races" .2 percent.[10] Table 1 shows the composition of the population according to "race."

A review of the 1943 census data also indicates a steady growth in the size of the "black" population since 1881, increasing from 76.5 percent to 78.1 percent of the total population. The "white" population, on the other hand, declined from 2.5 percent of the total population to 1.1 percent.

TABLE 1. Population Classified by Racial Origin and Sex Showing Numerical and Percent Distribution, 1943

RACIAL ORIGIN	NUMERICAL DISTRIBUTION			PERCENT DISTRIBUTION		
	Total	Male	Female	Total	Male	Female
All races	1,237,063	598,267	638,796	100	48.4	51.6
Black	965,960	472,348	493,612	100	48.9	51.1
Colored	216,348	98,272	118,076	100	45.4	54.6
White	4,803	2,219	2,584	100	46.2	53.8
English and Welsh	3,837	1,777	2,060	100	46.3	53.7
Irish	472	212	260	100	44.9	55.1
Scottish	1,077	529	548	100	49.1	50.9
German	581	290	291	100	49.9	50.1
Italian	287	88	199	100	30.7	69.3
Jewish	1,067	508	559	100	47.6	52.4
Portuguese	130	52	78	100	40.0	60.0
Spanish	1,139	378	761	100	33.2	66.8
Chinese	6,886	4,343	2,543	100	63.1	36.9
Chinese colored	5,508	2,580	2,928	100	46.8	53.2
East Indian	21,393	10,924	10,469	100	51.1	48.9
East Indian colored	5,114	2,478	2,636	100	48.5	51.5
Syrian	834	455	379	100	54.6	45.4
Syrian colored	171	82	89	100	48.0	52.0
Other races and not specified	1,456	732	724	100	50.3	49.7

Sources: *Eighth Census of Jamaica and Its Dependencies, 1943* (Kingston: Government Printer, 1945), LXIX; "What the Census Tells," *Daily Gleaner*, February 10, 1944, 1, 4.

Table 2 reveals the demographic changes in the island between 1881 and 1943.

The peoples of African descent were dominant demographically, but political and economic power and social prestige resided elsewhere. According to the 1943 census, and as table 3 shows, 28.1 percent of "Black" Jamaicans were illiterate, compared with 3.2 percent of "Whites," 1.3 percent of "British Isle Races," and 8.4 percent of "European Races." The latter groups, by virtue of tradition, privilege, and education, dominated the professional services and public administration. Similarly, the tiny "white" minority, whether local or foreign born, occupied all the important and

TABLE 2. Percentage Distribution of Certain Racial Origin Groups, Jamaica, 1881–1943

CENSUS YEAR	ALL RACES	RACIAL ORIGIN						
		Black	Colored	White	Chinese	East Indian	Other Races	Not Specified
1881	100.0	76.5	18.9	2.5	.0	1.9	—	.2
1891	100.0	76.4	19.1	2.3	.1	1.6	—	.5
1911	100.0	75.8	19.6	1.9	.3	2.1	—	.3
1921	100.0	77.0	18.3	1.7	.4	2.2	—	.4
1943	100.0	78.1	17.5	1.1	1.0	2.1	.2	—

Source: *Eighth Census of Jamaica and Its Dependencies, 1943* (Kingston: Government Printer, 1945), LXIX, L.

powerful positions in the government, including that of governor, colonial secretary, attorney general, and so on. The peoples of European descent disproportionately controlled the commanding heights of the economy, although by 1938 the Syrians and the Chinese were beginning to claim a larger share.

The largest number of Jamaicans lived in the parish of St. Andrew, with 10.36 percent, followed by Clarendon with 9.78 percent and Kingston and Port Royal with 8.90 percent.[11] The overwhelming majority of the Jamaican people were unquestionably poor. In 1935, for example, 184,150, or 92 percent, of those who were employed earned less than 25 shillings per week. Of this number, 71 percent received an average of 14 shillings per week. On the other hand, 466 persons earned over £1,000 per annum. Table 4 shows the range of gross annual incomes compiled for 1935 and the number of individuals who fell into each category.

The gross national income of the island in 1942 was around £33 million to £34 million. This was the equivalent of £26 per year, or ten shillings per week, per head of population. In comparison, Britain's per capita income stood at £110 in 1940.[12]

These statistics do not capture the degree of human deprivation that existed in the island. In order to do this, it is necessary to compare the cost of living with the per capita weekly income of a Jamaican worker. Two comparisons of this nature exist for 1938. The first was prepared by Alexander Bustamante, the labor leader who would later found the Bustamante Industrial Trade Union. The second was prepared by Robert Kirkwood, who

TABLE 3. Racial Origins and Literacy, Seven Years of Age and Older, 1943

Racial Origins	Illiterate	Literate
All races	25.6	74.4
Black	28.1	71.9
Colored	13.8	86.2
White	3.2	96.8
British Isles races	1.3	98.7
European races	8.4	91.6
Chinese and Chinese colored	13.9	86.1
East Indian and East Indian colored	48.6	51.4
Syrian and Syrian colored	5.6	94.4
Others and not specified	20.7	79.3

Source: *Eighth Census of Jamaica and Its Dependencies, 1943* (Kingston: Government Printer, 1945), LII.

was the managing director of the West Indies Sugar Company, Ltd., one of the major employers of labor in the island. Bustamante estimated that the average worker needed to earn at least £4 13s 8d to cover his monthly expenses. Kirkwood, the voice of capital, had a competing estimate of £2 8s 8d. When it is recalled that the typical employed worker earned an average of ten shillings per week, or £2 per month, it is clear that he was engaged in deficit financing. These estimates did not take into account the cost of supporting a family of four or more or one that was dependent on just one wage earner. Kirkwood's estimate was somewhat lower than that submitted by Bustamante because the sugar company provided the workers with housing and medical care, and it made no provision for the cost of recreation, union dues, contributions to their church, and so on. The two estimates, reproduced in table 5, are instructive.

These estimates by Bustamante and Kirkwood were abstract calculations of the wages and expenditures of the "typical" worker. But a deeper appreciation of the workers' economic condition can be obtained by examining the frequency of their employment and the purchasing power of their daily wage. Many workers, if not the majority, were offered employment at an average of three days per week. This was a strategy used by some employers to ensure that as many persons as possible would obtain work, albeit for a portion of the workweek. Major G. St. J. Orde Browne, an expert on labor relations, was dispatched by the Colonial Office to the Caribbean in 1938

TABLE 4. Gross Annual Incomes in Jamaica, 1935

Range of Income	Total Number of Incomes
Between £1,500 and £20,000	259
Between £1,000 and £1,500	207
Between £750 and £1,000	346
Between £500 and £750	843
Between £400 and £500	916
Between £200 and £400	1,847
About £200	1,900
About £80	9,900
Between £26 and £65	147,750
Under £26	36,400

Source: "Nutrition in Jamaica," *Daily Gleaner*, October 22, 1937, 7.

to study and report on the conditions he found. Reporting on Jamaica in July 1939, Orde Browne did not attribute the poor economic condition of the workers primarily to low wages. "The main evil is not the low wage," he wrote, "but the intermittent employment, and particularly the pernicious system of rotational engagement, whereby a man is only in work for half the time, and is therefore really required to live on half the nominal wage."[13]

Orde Browne was partially correct. Underemployment was just as ubiquitous in the island as unemployment. But the workers were also woefully underpaid. Orde Browne knew that some workers received 1/6 or less per day. In fact, he concluded that a single man who lived in Kingston required between 11/– and 17/– to cover his weekly expenses. Orde Browne did not address the wages earned by women in his memorandum, but it was well known that some were paid as little as 9d to 10 ½d per day, or 3/9 to 4/4 ½d per week.[14] A worker who earned 1/6 per day could use that money to purchase twelve copies of the *Daily Gleaner*, or six cakes of palmolive soap, or eighteen eggs, or twelve pounds of rice, or twelve pounds of brown sugar. Similarly, someone who earned 9d per day could purchase 50 percent of those individual items. Viewed in the context of the purchasing power of the daily wage of many workers, the gathering storm of protest became understandable.

Many Jamaicans, to be sure, were not wage earners. A significant number were jobless. In 1936, for example, a government-appointed commission reported that there were 5,000 "genuinely" unemployed adults in

TABLE 5. Ordinary Workers' Estimated Monthly Minimum Budget

	BUSTAMANTE			AN ALTERNATIVE (KIRKWOOD)		
	£	Shillings	Pennies	£	Shillings	Pennies
Food	1	4	0	1	4	0
Clothing	1	0	0	0	5	0
Fuel and matches	0	2	8	0	2	8
Rent	0	12	0	Free	—	—
Doctor	0	10	0	Free	—	—
Toothpaste	0	1	0	0	1	0
Washing materials		Not allowed for		0	4	0
Necessities of life	3	9	0	1	16	8
per week	0	17	3	0	9	2
Rum	0	0	6	—		
Church	0	1	0	—		
Hairdressing	0	1	0	—		
Newspaper	0	2	0	0	12	0
Recreation	0	4	0			
per week				0	3	0
Cinema	0	6	0	—		
Union Fee	0	1	6	—		
Smokes	0	1	6	—		
TOTAL	4	13	8	2	8	8
per week	1	3	5	0	12	2

Source: "The Ordinary Worker's Budget," *Daily Gleaner*, December 2, 1938, 5.

Kingston, out of an estimated population of 90,000. This was a surprisingly low estimate of the number of unemployed people in the capital city. The report did not provide any indication of the size of the potential labor force as opposed to the total population, so it was impossible to determine the percentage that could not find jobs. It maintained, optimistically, that "there is an appearance of more unemployment than actually exists," due in part to "the large number of casual wharf-laborers who although working two or three days a week appear most of the time, to be unemployed."

Appointed by Governor Edward Denham (1933–38), the commission attributed the swelling ranks of the unemployed in the island to several factors, including migration from the rural areas to the cities, the paucity of sites for emigration, the return of approximately 31,000 emigrants to the colony between 1930 and 1934, the scarcity of industries based upon agriculture, and the failure of the educational system to equip students with the skills that the economy needed, particularly vocational training. The commission concluded that there was a "large number of persons" who were "unemployable," and that there was a "considerable" number of people in the Kingston area "who have a regrettable preference for the precarious existence of the itinerant labourer, jobber, vendor, etc., rather than the ordered life of a regular employee, and who would not alter their present mode of existence even if regular employment was available."[15] This insensitive comment essentially blamed the workers for their economic condition, providing a questionable cultural explanation for it. The influential *Daily Gleaner* promoted a similar erroneous explanation for the high rate of unemployment in the urban areas: it attributed its existence to the migration of rural residents. These people moved, the *Gleaner* said, "not so much because they cannot live in the country, but because they prefer urban conditions and excitement." The "unemployment problem," the newspaper declared, "is therefore to a certain extent self created. And for those who suffer from conditions thus created it is not easy to feel real sympathy."[16]

The commission's report did not identify any systemic factors that helped to explain the high incidence of unemployment throughout the island. Nor did it capture the festering anger of the unemployed and its threatening implications for the societal status quo. Emphasizing that unemployment was not confined to Kingston, the commission identified "a serious condition" in Portland, parts of St. Mary, southern Manchester, and St. Elizabeth.

The 1943 census reported that Jamaica had a workforce of 732,675, aged fifteen to sixty-four. Of this number, only 484,300 persons were actually working, leaving an estimated deficit of almost 250,000.[17] When it is recognized that many of the employed worked seasonally or were offered jobs only intermittently, the extent of the people's economic deprivation can be appreciated. Unemployment and economic deprivation, its progeny, constituted a volatile combination in a colony where the hope for a better life remained a luxury for many people. Lucius Watson, a port worker, captured the plight of Freedom's Children, their desperate competition for scarce jobs, and the pain of their frequent disappointments:

> Unemployment was bad, bad, bad. It was terrible! . . . I don't know how to put it to you but the workers was suffering bad. The Depression was

on. Everything was tight and when one ship come you would have three, four hundred [men] waiting on the ship when it could only take on four gang of men for the ship and four gang for the dock. But the condition of work was very bad. It was one bone to a dozen lion. That was the kind of condition. Men was just grabbing and scraping to get a little work. And the men them was forced to the conditions, for nobody ever thinking about the workers.[18]

Frank Gordon echoed these sentiments. "Economic conditions," he recalled, "were very bad." He remembered that the people "used to march and go to prison to Mr. Shillingford, the Director of Prisons, asking to give them work in prison." They pleaded with Shillingford using the words of a song: "Birds have nest, foxes have hole, but the son of man have no where to lay his weary head."[19] Speaking more generally of those appalling conditions, Gladys Longbridge reminisced: "A lot of people went barefooted. The people used to [journey] from the hills down to the plains, where the estates are, to seek work in [the sugar harvest]. No preparations were made for them. They slept under the tree and I have pictures to show you to prove that—not dead but sleeping (laugh). They used to sleep on banana trash, coconut trash and box and board shacks. Plenty of them I will tell you. [Others] came up and stayed with relatives and if they got a job, they got a job."[20]

Women found it more difficult than the men to obtain jobs, except in domestic service. Winsburg Grubb, who was employed as a proofreader in 1938, noted that "the greatest jobs for women you could think of was domestic work. They were just mere domestics. That is the truth."[21] Women who found employment on the sugar estates were not only underpaid but labored under the most trying circumstances. Donald Byfield described the conditions that prevailed:

Women had to do the most menial things in their day to day work more so in the cane field. You could see the women in the cane field with an old pair of stocking covering from the finger tip to the shoulder. Their feet covered with bandages like they were sick. And in many cases you could see the women going out in the mornings with babies one month, three weeks, two weeks old in the cane fields. They had to find a cool spot, lay the baby down there, and go out to do the trash turning, the grass weeding and in some case loading the "gona gonas." The "gona gonas" is a sort of trailer thing that moves the cut cane from the field to the factory.[22]

Jamaican workers were long familiar with the problems and vicissitudes of the labor market. Some of them actually welcomed the opportunity to work only a few days each week, or even seasonally. Possessed of an area of about 4,450 square miles, the island had 67,023 farms of one acre or more, according to the 1943 census. The total acreage of these farms amounted to 1,793,840. The number of parcels of land of less than one acre that were employed either as very small farms or gardens or that had fruit trees was 147,000.[23] The census identified a farm as any tract of land "of one acre or more in extent," in one or more parcels, and under cultivation or used as pasturage. It avoided the use of the mostly pejorative appellation "peasant," an imported nomenclature that lacked both cultural meaning and legitimacy in the island. Depending on the size of their acreage, Jamaicans self-identified as large farmers, small farmers, or cultivators. The census preferred the term "farm operator," which it used to designate "the person who directly worked the farm whether as owner, hired manager, tenant, or cropper." It found that in 1943, 44 percent of Jamaica's working population, or 221,376 persons, were engaged in agriculture.[24]

Enterprising Jamaicans cultivated a wide variety of crops on their plots of land for their own subsistence, selling any surplus. Some plots were too small to be self-sufficient, much less to produce surpluses. This would have been particularly true of many of the 118, 143 plots of land of less than five acres that existed in 1938 and are identified in table 6. At the other extreme, there were only 146 farms of 2,000 acres or more.

Although many people owned land, regardless of their small acreage, there were others who were not that fortunate. Beginning in the aftermath of emancipation, an insatiable land hunger stoked the fires of resistance, legitimizing in the eyes of the landless the seizure of unoccupied holdings. Known pejoratively as "squatters," these people risked the retaliatory violence of those whose lands they "captured." Stanley Reid did not approve of the land seizures, but he described one such incident that occurred in the parish of St. Thomas: "Wid de lan' problem. Now Mr. Pringle [land owner] 'ave a lan' called Garden Wood. De people dem waan it fe work an' dem try to capture de lan'. Well Mr. Pringle go to Kingston an' [got] some soldier[s] was going to come up an' to shot down who goin' capture the lan' [and the capturers said] everybody mus' come togedder. Well dem a gadder [gather] axe an' machete. An me sey I don't inna dat because the lan' nuh fe we."[25] These land seizures were generally spontaneous and leaderless. In early 1938, however, Robert E. Rumble sought to give organizational expression to the pervasive land hunger. Returning to the island after

Jamaica in 1938 | 21

TABLE 6. Distribution of Landholdings, 1938

	Number of Landowners	Estimated Acreage	Average Acreage
½ to 5 acres	118,143	262,688	2.2
5 to 10 acres	22,819	154,559	6.8
10 to 50 acres	12,933	260,800	20.1
50 to 100 acres	1,107	78,377	70.8
100 to 200 acres	650	95,449	146.8
200 to 500 acres	573	185,093	323.0
500 to 1,000 acres	392	283,507	723.2
1,000 to 2,000 acres	269	378,629	1,407.5
Above 2,000 acres	146	466,552	3,195.6
TOTAL	157,092	2,165,654	

Source: Ken Post, *Arise Ye Starvelings: The Jamaica Labour Rebellion of 1938 and Its Aftermath* (The Hague: Martinus Nijhoff, 1978), 115.

having emigrated to Cuba, Rumble founded the Poor Man's Improvement Land Settlement and Labour Association (PMILSLA) to promote the interest of tenants and "squatters." Headquartered in Clarendon, it may have had as many as 800 members. The organization was short-lived, however. The labor rebellion of May and June 1938 would force the government to launch an ambitious land-settlement scheme, legally satisfying some of the yearnings for land.[26]

Those Jamaicans who described themselves as cultivators or as small farmers frequently had to seek outside employment to supplement whatever income, if any, they derived from their plots. Some sought seasonal employment with the large sugar plantations, others worked for the better-off local residents, and many flocked to Kingston and other urban areas seeking jobs. The Jamaican economy was never robust enough to absorb all of the job seekers at any one time, creating a condition of permanent unemployment or underemployment for many of the island's people. The low wages that many of those fortunate enough to procure jobs received helped to fuel the irrepressible movement for change in 1938 and after.

Beginning in 1934, disgruntled workers in many Anglophone colonies in the Caribbean engaged in strikes and other forms of social protest. They started in British Honduras and continued in Trinidad and British Guiana. In succeeding years, strikes and other forms of social unrest occurred in St. Kitts, St. Vincent, St. Lucia, Barbados, the Bahamas, and Antigua. Jamaica also experienced strikes in Oracabessa and Falmouth, but the rest of the island remained calm. Jamaicans had varying degrees of familiarity with the social unrest in their sister colonies and were not immune to their impact and example. Still, the labor rebellion that would engulf the island in 1938 stemmed from local conditions.

Coincidentally, the rebellion occurred on the centenary of the abolition of slavery in the island. Emancipation had not brought fundamental economic change to most West Indians of African descent. As a people, they had weathered the challenges of freedom. There was a small but growing middle class, although most people remained mired in poverty. As proud members of the British Empire, they revered the distant monarch. But their mostly black skins confined them to secondary roles and spaces in a society where political, economic, and social power wore white faces.

There were visible signs, however, that Freedom's Children were beginning to rediscover and reinvent themselves racially in the two decades or so prior to 1938. Race had been the single most important determinant of an individual's social and economic status and life chances and was deeply imbedded in the island's psychology and cultural DNA. It did not lend itself to any easy exorcism, but this did not mean that Jamaicans would continue to be wounded and imprisoned by an immutable and pernicious racist ideology. Freedom's Children never remained in a state of psychological stasis or paralysis. By 1900 emancipation had occurred sixty-two years earlier, and few people then alive had been enslaved. Born in freedom, these new people had, for the most part, life experiences that were different from those of their parents or grandparents, who had been defined as human property.

This new generation of African Jamaicans was becoming quite receptive to criticisms of the prevailing unequal racial status quo. Alexander Bedward (1859–1931), a Christian revivalist preacher, led a movement for religious and racial regeneration in the island in the 1890s and the first two decades of the twentieth century. A man of little formal education, he fused his religious message with an assault on white power and privilege in the country from his headquarters in August Town: "Brethren! Hell will be your position if you do not rise up and crush the white man. The time is coming! There will be a white wall and a black wall, but now the black wall is becoming bigger than the white, and we must knock the white wall down. The white wall has oppressed us for years: now we must oppress the white wall. The government passes laws that oppress black people. They take their money out of their pockets, rob them of their bread, and they do nothing for it."²⁷ Bedward was arrested and tried for such incendiary utterances. Pleading insanity, he avoided conviction and punishment by the colonial state. The Bedwardite movement continued to grow, however, attracting the support of thousands of Jamaica's dispossessed peoples. It had its denouement in 1921 when the government remanded Bedward to an asylum. It is not entirely clear whether Bedward had lost his mental balance or whether the state was silencing a severe critic.²⁸

Bedward's racially inspired comments were a call to African Jamaicans to stage an attack on the "white wall" of oppression. The embrace and nurturing of a healthy, confident, and pugnacious racial consciousness by Freedom's Children was certainly prerequisites for the success of Bedward's challenge. Marcus Mosiah Garvey (1887–1940), was one who understood the imperative of developing race pride among a people who had been denigrated because of their skin color and ancestral heritage. Such an internal rebirth, Garvey said, should presage the emergence of a collective proud black self that is able to protect its "manhood rights . . . at all costs." Born in the parish of St. Ann, Garvey founded the Universal Negro Improvement Association (UNIA) in 1914 to promote the uplift of the peoples of African descent everywhere. Its defining philosophy of "race first" had a special meaning for them. Garvey left Jamaica for New York in 1916; the transplanted UNIA eventually attracted some 6 million adherents worldwide. Promulgated in 1920, the organization's principal policy statement, the Declaration of Rights of the Negro Peoples of the World, affirmed its support for self-determination for the peoples of African descent. It proclaimed "Africa for the Africans at home and abroad," denounced racial discrimination and segregation, and condemned violence directed at black people. The declaration adopted the colors red, black, and green as "the colors of the Negro Race."²⁹

Garvey was deported to Jamaica in 1927 after his conviction in the United States for alleged mail fraud. Two years later, he founded the People's Political Party to promote the ideas he espoused in electoral politics. Garvey was elected to the Kingston and St. Andrew Corporation in 1930 but failed in his later bid to become a member of the Legislative Council. Garvey's departure for London in 1935 did not end his influence in the island. Although he was denounced by some for raising the race question, Garvey's pugnacious assertion of the philosophy of race pride had much resonance among the island's black poor and to some extent among the black middle class. His intervention in the politics of race in Jamaica created the space for others to articulate their views on the issue. Speaking in the Legislative Council in 1935, for example, D. T. Wint, the member for St. Ann, complained that "effort is made to make it convincing, that there is no colour prejudice in Jamaica, and certainly none in government. . . . [I]t is a tremendous lie which deceives . . . those who want to be deceived."[30]

Garvey not only forced reluctant Jamaicans to recognize the salience of race in the polity, but he also brought Africa, and Ethiopia in particular, into their consciousness. The UNIA had adopted the anthem "Ethiopia, Thou Land of Our Fathers" as the "anthem of the Negro race":

Ethiopia, thou land of our fathers,
Thou land where the gods loved to be,
As storm cloud at night suddenly gathers
Our armies come rushing to thee.
We must in the fight be victorious
When swords are thrust outward to gleam;
For us will the vict'ry be glorious
When led by the red, black and the green.
[CHORUS]
Advance, advance to victory,
Let Africa be free;
Advance to meet the foe
With the might
Of the red, the black and the green.[31]

This invocation and celebration of Ethiopia by Africans and peoples of African descent can be traced to the late eighteenth century. Deriving its legitimacy from the biblical verse "Princes shall come out of Egypt; Ethiopia shall soon stretch forth its hands unto God," many black people believed that Africa's travail would be "redeemed" by Ethiopia. This belief, known as Ethiopianism, gathered strength in Jamaica when Ras Tafari was crowned as the Emperor Haile Selassie of Ethiopia in 1930. Based upon their interpretation of prophecies in the Bible, some Jamaicans proclaimed Ras Tafari to be divine, paving the way for the emergence of Rastafarianism as a religious movement with secular flavors such as the opposition to colonialism. Three men played significant roles in its founding, the most prominent and renowned being Leonard Howell, who had his headquarters in the parish of St. Thomas. The Italian invasion of Ethiopia in 1935 also strengthened the developing emotional identification that some Jamaicans had with Africa in general and Ethiopia in particular. Unlike African Americans, Jamaicans did not form organizations to support the Ethiopians. But the widespread feeling that the African nation was being mistreated by a European power fueled antiwhite, anti-European, and anti-imperial sentiment in the island.[32]

Garvey, the Rastafarians and their adherents, and the Italo-Ethiopian War had introduced the race question and Africa into Jamaica's societal and psychological consciousness. It was not a development that many people welcomed, finding much discomfort in the public ventilation of matters relating to race. They preferred to ignore the presence of the sleeping racial giant, fearing that its arousal would produce unpredictable consequences. These attitudes were generally associated with whites and the rising middle class, particularly those members of mixed racial ancestry. Thirsty for knowledge about Africa and receptive to exhortations about racial uplift and pride, however, many working people flocked to meetings in Kingston's parks where racial issues were unabashedly addressed. Their developing racial consciousness helps to explain their participation in the imminent rebellion.

There were other signs of political energy and protest. Politically conscious Jamaicans reflecting a variety of ideological stripes founded organizations to help shape the new Jamaica they imagined. They joined such existing groups as Marcus Garvey's UNIA and the Jamaica Imperial Association, which was founded in 1917 to promote the interests of the large landowners and businesses. In mid-1937 Allan George St. Claver Coombs, a contractor, former policeman, and member of the West India Regiment, founded the Jamaica Workers and Tradesmen Union, the first modern trade union in the island. Kenneth Hill, a journalist, organized the National Reform Association in that year. Its purpose was to promote political reform in the island. Founded in 1937 by Norman Manley and others, the Jamaica Welfare League pledged "to build a new Jamaica." The organization promoted rural development and the provision of social services, particularly for young people. The 1930s also saw the founding of a plethora of citizens' organizations dedicated to fostering civic consciousness. Located in both rural and urban areas, they coalesced into the Federation of Citizens' Associations in 1936.[33]

These societal motions were being manifested in diverse ways. But their larger meanings were not the subject of general discussion, nor were their long-term implications recognized. Jamaican society had never been quiescent, whether in slavery or freedom, but the 1930s saw a quickening of the people's energy. These stirrings were not all inspired by the same imperatives, nor did they emanate from the same sources. The people who formed civic associations were imagining and promoting an orderly and respectable societal change over which they would preside. Others expended their energies opposing any disruption of the economic and social systems that served their narrow interests. Seething with rage on occasion and at other times accommodating themselves to the blows administered by Jamaica's arsenal of oppression, the working people were beginning to discover themselves and their power to build the island anew.

The labor rebellion that occurred in May and June 1938 was the creation of these Jamaican workers. It was a spontaneous assault on an exploitative status quo that kept them trapped in poverty. They had no voice in the government and no effective institutions through which to express their grievances. A hundred years after slavery ended, almost all workers remained at the mercy of capital. Nor did the government offer them any protection nor demonstrate any serious and sustained interest in improving their condition. Jamaica's dispossessed, its throw-away people, would soon call a modern society into being.

TWO

The Labor Rebellion

Newly released from jail in May 1938, Alexander Bustamante addressed "a vast gathering of labourers" at Trench Pen, Kingston. The labor leader had come to announce to the cheering crowd that the government had agreed to increase the wages of those who worked for the Public Works Department by 25 percent. "I have given proof I am willing to suffer for your cause," he declared as the excited crowd "waved their hands high and cheered." Continuing, Bustamante boasted, "I have suffered," promising that "if more should come, I am willing to accept it with a smile." He told the people that he expected them "to accept my advice as you would that of a good and faithful father." Bustamante saw himself, he said, "as your father, your protector." "And our saviour!" shouted a voice from the rear of the crowd.[1]

Alexander Bustamante must have been very pleased when someone called him "our saviour." This was not an indication of his deification but rather an expression of gratitude and a recognition of the special place he was beginning to occupy in the hearts of many Jamaican workers. It was a meteoric ascent from skepticism to affection, from mistrust to blind faith. The brown-skinned usurer who had spent most of his adult days away from his homeland had, in a matter of days, become the repository of the dreams for a better life for black Jamaican workers.

Bustamante's identification with the plight of Jamaica's poor began shortly after his return to the island from the United States in 1934. As he recalled: "I discovered something radically wrong—there were too many barefooted, half-naked and hungry people around. They seemed hopeless, friendless."[2] By 1937 he had embraced their cause and trade unionism as well. At first, Bustamante served as an officer of the Jamaica Workers and Tradesmen Union (JWTU), founded by Allan Coombs. The partnership was a rocky one, and the two men went their separate ways in November of that year. Bustamante's break with the union did not mean his withdrawal from labor's cause. Since he had no legally sanctioned official standing, however, employers were not required to give him a hearing.

Bustamante's identification with Jamaica's underclass was dramatically captured in a series of letters that he wrote to British officials in early 1938. Not since 1865, when Dr. E. B. Underhill sent a letter to the secretary of states for the colonies, had British officials received such a ferocious criticism of their regime in Jamaica. Underhill's letter, written in January 1865, was a catalog of the economic deprivations that many Jamaicans endured. "The people," he wrote, "are starving." Underhill reported that "there is not sufficient employment for the people; there is neither work for them, nor the capital to employ them." Underhill blamed the policies of the colonial government for the disgraceful conditions and proposed a series of reforms.

The Colonial Office forwarded the letter to Edward Eyre, the local governor. Eyre dismissed Underhill's charges, blaming the Jamaicans for their condition. Their laziness and moral turpitude explained their condition, the governor asserted. The mostly white elites supported the governor's position when the Underhill letter became the subject of popular discourse. Concerned members of the colonial middle class held meetings throughout the island to discuss Underhill's letter. Known as the Underhill meetings, the attendees passed resolutions supporting the Baptist missionary's conclusions. The public, as a whole, was also actively engaged in debates on the contents of the letter, leading one contemporary to observe that "since the date of emancipation, no subject had so seriously agitated the public opinion of Jamaica, or called forth more acrimonious discussion."[3] The seething discontent with the status quo produced the great Morant Bay rebellion in October, the loss of 893 lives, and the cruel repression of the protest.[4]

It is very likely that Bustamante was aware of the Underhill letter and its connection to the Morant Bay rebellion. He was born in 1884, nineteen years after the rebellion occurred, and it was conceivably still a part of the popular consciousness. Bustamante was probably also introduced to the events of 1865 in school. In any event, Bustamante's letters to sympathetic British officials echoed that written by Underhill. Bustamante also sent copies of these letters to the British press to ensure widespread publicity. He sent his first letter on January 26, 1938, to George Griffiths, a Labour member of the House of Commons. He noted in that letter that the Jamaican government was not providing the Colonial Office with sufficient information about the conditions in the island, making it "almost impossible for you or anyone else to be able to grasp the dreadful and distressing economical and social conditions that exist amongst the masses—the workers of Jamaica where we are blessed—I should say cursed—with a callous Government as far as the workers are concerned and a government whose bound duty it would appear is to keep away the facts of the conditions of the island from the Home Government."

Bustamante spoke of the "low wages" paid to the workers, calling their work "sweated labour." He assured Griffiths that "the Poor House, the Mad House, and the Prisons are overcrowded through dire need and poverty, while the streets and villages are overrun with beggars who were once respectable people." Bustamante painted an alarming picture of conditions in the island, observing that "thousands upon thousands of able bodied men and women willing to work, overrun the towns and districts hungry and ragged from the want of employment, thousands of children run the villages not being able to go to school from the lack of food and clothing, some are weak-legged and bow-legged from the want of nourishment."[5]

Bustamante reported that the people who were demanding redress of their grievances were being intimidated by the government. "If the people dared to stage a hunger demonstration," he declared, "they face rifles glittering with bayonets in the hands of the police menacing these unfortunate, peaceful citizens, whilst police clubs are splintered on their heads and limbs." He accused "the capitalists" of being "oppressive" and faulted the local government for "taking little or no interest in labour." The Jamaican government, he said, "is a mockery to good government." Bustamante noted that the "consensus" in the island was that it was futile to appeal to the imperial country for justice, "for if Governor Denham should tell the Secretary of State for the Colonies that a horse was a cow, he might be quite likely to say 'yes.'" He had no respect for the governor's leadership, charging that "the captain" of the Jamaican ship "never seem[s] to have sufficient control of the rudder . . . the situation is critical, it needs a specialist, there is none in Jamaica."[6]

Approximately two weeks after writing to Griffiths, Bustamante took his complaints to Clement Attlee, the leader of the Labour Party. Writing to him on February 11, he charged the Jamaican government with the repression of critics. To give his charges weight, he described himself as a person of an "irreproachable character, sound mind." He was writing to Attlee "in the interest of the masses of my people." Bustamante complained that Jamaicans were "surrounded with misery, poverty, and sickness through low wages and unemployment." The governor was a failure and most Jamaicans would like to see him leave, he asserted. Bustamante claimed that his advocacy of the workers' cause had led "high government officials" to question his sanity. This was a "despicable" government, he said. There were individuals in it "who have expressed the desire that I should be medically examined with a view to rail road me to the Lunatic Asylum or that the police should endeavour to nab me for stirring up trouble amongst the workers . . . but when one is fighting for a righteous cause, fear if any must be dominated."[7]

Bustamante wrote a second letter to Attlee on March 16, repeating his allegations. He hinted at social disturbances if there was no relief "for the masses" since "human nature can only stand a certain amount of endurance." Bustamante pointed to labor unrest in Trinidad, where the "endurance of the workers . . . had ceased."[8] Led by Uriah Butler, the workers in southern Trinidad struck in 1937, paralyzing the oil industry. When the strikes spread to the sugar estates, the colonial authorities ordered Butler's arrest, jailing him for two years on a charge of inciting to riot.

Bustamante took his cause directly to the English people in a letter he wrote to the *Manchester Guardian* in April. His charges were the familiar ones, but this time he cited some questionable statistics to support them. "According to one estimate," Bustamante wrote, about "fifty thousand children were roaming the country parts not being able to go to school chiefly because of lack of food and clothing. . . . There are at least seventy-five thousand unemployed, and the majority of those who are employed are very little better off, for they work on empty stomachs." He reported that on one occasion, "hundreds of ragged men, women, and children marched to the doors of the prison in Kingston pleading for admittance so that they might get food." Bustamante thought that the local government was only interested in enacting "oppressive laws" and in extracting "even the blood out of our pores for taxes." When strikes occurred, he said, the government was only concerned with giving police protection to "capitalists." The workers, on the other hand, "are being treated as if they have no rights in this island."[9]

Bustamante's letters caused a sensation in England and in Jamaica. Their exaggerated truths embarrassed the Colonial Office as much as they found a resonance among the Jamaican workers. Members of Parliament began to take an interest in the condition of the Jamaican people, directing probing questions to the colonial secretary. In response to enquiries from the Colonial Office, Governor Denham called Bustamante's allegations "exaggerated" and denied that thousands of children were unable to go to school because of their economic condition. He said that "record expenditures on new schools [are] now being incurred to meet record attendances." The governor refuted Bustamante's statement that desperate workers had recently marched to the prison in Kingston demanding admission. He thought Bustamante was referring to a demonstration in June 1936 "where some 200 persons marched to [the] General Penitentiary in search of work and food though when offered work outside Kingston none were prepared to accept." Governor Denham reported that the government had budgeted £170,000 for relief programs for the unemployed.[10]

Denham dismissed Bustamante as a "well known agitator," adding that he had been holding meetings throughout the island. Attended by as many as 2,000 to 3,000 persons, these meetings attracted "the labouring classes and the unemployed." Denham was convinced that the meetings were also attended by criminals and other "irresponsible elements." Bustamante's speeches, the governor reported, "are at times of an inflammatory character." He was having the situation carefully watched with the possibility of taking legal action against the labor leader. Governor Denham described Bustamante as possessing "a vain and unbalanced temperament, which at times reaches a degree almost of madness[.] [H]is knowledge of the labour problem in Jamaica appears to be but superficial while his efforts and criticisms of Government lack any constructive merit and are directed to promoting feelings of general unrest and dissatisfaction among the unemployed and labouring classes."[11]

Denham gave grudging credence to some of Bustamante's allegations, admitting that "undoubtedly a certain amount of hardship and poverty exist and may be increasing in certain areas." In a letter to the secretary of state, he conceded that the children were experiencing "a considerable amount of malnutrition," and that conditions "are bad and there are five thousand children in the colony either in Industrial Homes or receiving Outdoor Relief." Ignoring the systemic factors that helped to explain the poverty of the majority of Jamaicans, the governor attributed its existence and exacerbation "to poor markets resulting in low prices for certain products, notably sugar and citrus," as well as increases in the price of some imported goods.[12]

The Jamaican press contested Bustamante's allegations, accusing him of gross exaggerations. The *Jamaica Times* reluctantly admitted that "all allegations contain a core of truth, and this one has underlined two things—unemployment amongst adults and insufficient food amongst children." The *Daily Gleaner* tried to poke fun at Bustamante's allegations of children's nudity but admitted that "there is much poverty in Jamaica." The *Jamaica Standard* was particularly upset, denouncing Bustamante for being intemperate "in speech and writing." Mr. Bustamante, the editorial observed, "is warm hearted to the extent of hot headedness."[13]

In order to determine the accuracy of Bustamante's allegations regarding the starvation of children and their lack of clothes to attend school, the *Gleaner* sent its correspondents to several parishes to investigate. The headmaster of the Four Paths School supported the allegations, adding that fifty school-age children were employed at a nearby estate. Similar reports came from Annotto Bay, Port Maria, Morant Bay, and Pear Tree Grove.[14]

As in the case of the Underhill letter, the Bustamante letters generated considerable discussion in the island. Bustamante was almost demonized by the elite for sullying the island's reputation overseas. The letters, along with his fiery rhetoric at his regularly scheduled public meetings, began to earn him the trust, affection, and adulation of some workers. Although he exaggerated the degree of economic distress, Bustamante had dramatically focused attention on the plight of the poor in Jamaica. Their condition had obtained the attention of the British Parliament, generating the expectation that the Colonial Office would introduce ameliorative measures.

Bustamante had predicted that social unrest would occur if the people's grievances remained unredressed. There was a certain urgency to his description of the condition of the island's poor because, as he said, the "the pot" was boiling. Although some people thought that these fears were groundless, and the governor insisted that the island's problems were being addressed, the sugar industry and waterfront workers had other ideas about their condition and future prospects. Even so, the authorities were surprised when the workers at the Frome estate in the parish of Westmoreland rebelled on May 2, 1938.

The Frome sugar estate was acquired by the London-based Tate and Lyle sugar firm in 1937. Its Jamaican subsidiary was known as the West Indies Sugar Company (WISCO). The new company soon initiated a program to improve the facilities on the estate and to expand the acreage under cultivation as well. In 1938, for example, it planned to spend £500,000 on various projects, including an increase in wages for the workers. The number of workers the company employed rose from 10 to 20 in November 1937, to 327 in January 1938, and to 911 by the end of April of that year.[15]

Although the company had no difficulty attracting workers, the pay scales produced some discontent. The workers who were employed as "general labourers" to construct the new factory, for example, received a daily wage of 1/9 to 2/−. In real terms, this could purchase fourteen or sixteen copies of the daily newspaper or fourteen to sixteen pounds of brown or unrefined sugar. Table 7 shows the pay scales that existed prior to May 3, 1938. These people worked ten hours daily Monday through Friday, from

TABLE 7. The West Indies Sugar Company, Ltd., Scale of Pay Prior to May 3, 1938

DAILY	
General Labor	1/9 to 2/–
Sand washing	2/– to 2/3
Concrete mixing	2/– to 2/3
Riggers	2
Riggers' helpers	3/–/6 to 3/–
MECHANICS	Depending on experience
Apprentices	1/– and up
Carpenters	3/– and up
ELECTRICIAN MECHANICS	3/6 and up
Helpers	2/6 and up
MASONS	3/6 and up
Helpers	2/3 and up
BLACKSMITHS	3/6 and up
Helpers	2/–

Source: "Report to the Governor," October 15, 1938, Records of the Colonial Office, Commonwealth and Foreign and Commonwealth Offices, British National Archives, London, 137/826/9.

6:45 A.M. to 11:30 A.M. and again from 12:30 P.M. to 5:30 P.M. They worked on Saturdays from 6:45 A.M. to 11:30 A.M.

The workers who planted, weeded, and harvested the canes also received appallingly low wages, as table 8 shows. Those who planted canes received 1/– for 14 chains, or 26/6 per acre. Weeders and forkers were paid 1/– for every 14 chains, and cane cutters earned 1/– for each ton. These tasks were all tedious and backbreaking, and the remuneration was far below that which fairness should have dictated. A worker who received 1/– for his hard work could use it to purchase 3 quarts of milk or 4 pounds of salted codfish, or 3 pounds of beef or 3 pounds of pork. Seen in this light, the workers were virtually donating their labor. Table 8 shows the wages that the workers were being paid by WISCO.

TABLE 8. The West Indies Sugar Company, Ltd., Cultivation Rates (Cost per Acre on Four-Foot Rows)

Class of Work	Old Rates
Cutlassing	6d to 1/3 per square chain
Lining cane holes	2/6 per acre
Digging cane hole	6 chains for 1/−; 26/6 per acre
Cutting seed	6d per 1,000
Dressing tops for seed	4d per 1,000
Planting	14 chains for 1/−; 11/9 per acre
Weeding 1st	14 chains for 1/−; 11/9 per acre
Weeding 2nd	16 chains for 1/−; 10/4 per acre
Weeding 3rd	18 chains for 1/−; 9/1 per acre
Weeding and turning trash	24 chains for 1/−; 7/− per acre
Turning trash	—
Forking	—
Draining	14 chains for 1/−; 11/9 per acre
	Old drains: 5d per square foot
	New drains: 6d per square foot
	Spading: 1/9
	Axemen: 1/6
	Cutlassmen: 1/3
Day work	Women: 9d
Breaking stones	6d per box
Wire fences	4 ½d per strand per chain
Tradesmen	—
Cane cutting	Plants: 1/− per ton
Tying and heading out	Ratoons: 1/5 per ton
Cane cutting without tying or heading out	—
Carting canes (including loading)	Mule carts: 4d to 6d per ton
	Cattle carts: 6d to 8d per ton

Source: "Report to the Governor," October 15, 1938, Records of the Colonial Office, Commonwealth and Foreign and Commonwealth Offices, British National Archives, London, 137/826/9.

Despite these low wages, WISCO enjoyed a better reputation in the island than many of its counterparts. It was, for example, engaged in the building of cottages for its workers. By mid-May 1938 the company had constructed twenty-three six-room cottages, fourteen three-room cottages, and twelve one-room cottages for them. Between September 1937 and May 1938, it spent £8,010 on housing for the workers, but the demand still exceeded the supply. The company was also making a serious attempt to meet the medical needs of the workers. It reported that the medical staff had 1,458 "attendancies" in April and 942 in May 1938.[16] When it was rumored in the spring of 1938 that the company intended to pay its workers a daily wage of one dollar or four shillings, hundreds of unemployed workers from across the island hurried to the estate to seek employment, mostly unsuccessfully. These disappointed and disillusioned workers remained in Frome, hoping that their fortunes would change. But they constituted a group of people with a seething anger that awaited an opportunity to explode in unpredictable ways.

The workers who were employed in construction on the estate were reported to be the ones most unhappy with their wages. But it cannot be maintained that the poorly paid workers in the cane fields accepted their exploitation. Some feared that any protest would invite reprisals from management and the loss of their jobs. Accustomed to being respectful of authority, Jamaican workers were never easily given to expressing their displeasure at their working conditions, often tolerating them with stoicism. But the accumulated wrongs they had endured could precipitate a violent reaction if they perceived that a moral boundary had been transgressed and a seemingly intolerable situation had become worse.

The workers on the WISCO estate at Frome did not have a history of overt resistance to their condition. They had remained tranquil in 1937 when strikes erupted on the waterfront and on estates and plantations in various parts of the island. The situation changed dramatically in May 1938, however, surprising the governor and others. Governor Denham reported to the secretary of state that "the rioting" that took place surprised the "agitators" as "much I believe as it did Government."[17]

The surface calm on the estate at Frome was broken by the construction workers on April 29. It was a Friday afternoon, and the workers had gathered at the pay office to receive their wages for the week's work. They had begun to arrive at 5:00 P.M., but hours later, many were still waiting to be paid. Some noticed a reduction in their rate of pay, receiving no persuasive explanation when they protested. The *Gleaner* reported that "every passing minute swelled the noise of protest until a veritable tumult held sway."

Swearing and taking oaths, some of the angry workers hurled stones at the pay office's windows, shattering thirteen panes of glass. Feeling besieged, the pay clerks responded with revolver fire, but they did not hit anyone. They bolted the windows and doors as the angry workers "applied sticks to the walls of the office." "You want to kill we on top o' we money! It's going to be he[ll] here today," they screamed, as many men "armed with machetes, stones, and fat clubs battered the Pay Office." The police soon appeared on the scene, and order was restored. The pay clerks resumed their work, but closed their offices at 10:00 P.M. It seemed that some workers had begun to talk about a strike, but it was late in the day. Still angry, however, the workers proceeded to the home of the WISCO general manager, L. A. Grant, "but advanced information reached its occupants who decamped before the angry mob arrived."[18]

The anger festered throughout the night. By Saturday morning. the majority of the workers had decided to strike, intimidating those who wanted to work. "The comparatively small number of men who would have started work Saturday morning," the *Gleaner* reported, "were terrorized by the strikers and warned to keep off the estate." The number of strikers swelled to 1,000, and by nightfall some had set fire to cane fields.[19] An eyewitness, Morvel Price, recalled that "all you could si [see] was bare fiyah [fire]. You turn to the east—fiyah. Yu turn to the west, fiyah."[20] The fire ravaged thirty acres of cane before it was extinguished. The razed cane fields would have yielded an estimated 700 tons of cane. The *Gleaner* noted that "the workers know that canes when burnt must be ground early or be lost. Hence the fire is a move to force the hands of the company."[21]

Finding strength in their numbers, the workers began to voice a catalog of grievances. They disliked being treated in "a domineering and overbearing manner" by their employers and resented being referred to as "natives." Other complaints included poor living conditions, the introduction of labor-saving machinery on the estate, low wages and changes in the wage scale, and the work regimen. The workers alleged that they were being forced to work every day, a requirement that prevented them from having any time to cultivate their own provision grounds.[22]

The workers' anger simmered over the weekend, and by Monday morning, leaders had emerged. Their rallying cry had become "A Dollar a Day." "There is no maybe about it, we will have to get a dollar a day," a newly minted leader enjoined the crowd. "If they don't decide now or in a few hours' time, today is going to be a day," he threatened. "It is going to be serious here today: it is going to be death," the leader proclaimed. Continuing, he denounced anyone who would accept a wage of less than a dollar per day, declaring that "if it is even my father, I will bear the gallows for him."[23]

Rhetoric such as this stoked the passions of the workers. By 10:00 A.M., the *Gleaner* reported, "widespread violence stalked the little square at Frome, the crowd hurling missiles, breaking windows, and doors, wielding dangerous weapons, causing officials of the estate to take cover, and even injuring a policeman."[24] Inspector L. O'Donoghue of the Westmoreland police station said there were "3,000 labourers (strikers) armed with large sticks and pieces of iron piping, marching up and down the factory yard, brandishing their sticks and irons." When the crowd subsequently "rushed" toward the police, "throwing stones and sticks" and injuring three of them, O'Donoghue ordered "10 men of the front rank to open fire." The crowd then retreated to the cane fields, setting fire to various parts. The blaze continued, burning eighty acres of cane until a shower of rain extinguished it. Before the melee ended, the police had killed four persons, including a pregnant woman, and wounded seventeen others. In addition, the police arrested 100 persons.[25]

The violence unleashed by the police had the desired effect. An uneasy calm returned to the estate. Reinforcements from nearby police stations arrived to help maintain tranquility. Hearing of the violence, Alexander Bustamante rushed to the scene on Tuesday morning to meet with the general manager of the estate in an effort to create better understanding between management and labor. He would later report that he was "satisfied" that the company was serious about improving the conditions under which its employees worked. His visit became the subject of much embellishment as it was told and retold in later years. Morvel Price, who was present at Frome throughout the unrest, was accurate in noting that "when it comes to Monday down at Frome, Busta wasn't dere at all. (It's a lie that he had taken off his coat and given it to the pregnant lady dat was shot). Dat is a lie. Busta wasn't down dere at all."[26]

Allan Coombs, the president of the Jamaica Tradesmen and Workers Union, also motored from Montego Bay to Frome to show his support for the workers. The two men, Bustamante and Coombs, were the most prominent public personages who identified with the workers' cause. Alarmed by the violence that occurred, Governor Denham warned the workers that he would not tolerate outbreaks of disorder, telling them that "there can be nothing more detrimental to their interests than demonstrations which result in acts of violence, loss of life and destruction of property."[27] He was particularly worried, he told the secretary of state, because "a Negro mob can be very dangerous. They completely lose their heads."[28]

The rebellion had immediate and positive financial consequences for the construction workers who had led it. Speaking to 1,000 workers on Saturday, the first full day of the strike, general manager Grant assured them: "I am in sympathy with you, but you must realize that I must be allowed time to consider such adjustments in your rates of pay as may be necessary."[29] The following day, he announced increases in pay for several categories of workers, ranging from 3d to 6d per day. The length of the work day was reduced by thirty minutes, and the workers were allowed one hour for lunch on weekdays. These were hardly generous concessions, but they were acceptable to the workers, at least for awhile. Fearing that unemployed workers in Kingston might initiate their own protests, Governor Denham hastily announced a construction program on May 3. It included the provision of work on a number of highways and at the airport.[30]

Governor Denham also announced the appointment of a commission to inquire into the rebellion at Frome. It was empowered to investigate the causes of the rebellion, the wages and terms of employment of the workers on the estate, and the conduct of the police in quelling the unrest. The three-member commission included two prominent white Jamaicans, Sir Henry Brown and Sir Charles Doorly. The third member was Harold Allan, a respected black member of the Legislative Council representing the parish of Portland. The governor may have appointed Allan for public-relations purposes, judging by his failure to mention him in a letter to the new secretary of state, Malcolm McDonald. "I had realised that enquiries were necessary," he wrote, "and fortunately in our two commissioners—Sir Henry Brown and Sir Charles Doorly—we have two of the best men anywhere to make such investigations."[31]

The news of the rebellion received considerable attention in England. In response to a question about it in the House of Commons on May 4, the colonial secretary stressed that the event was "local in character."[32] He was trying to calm fears that the island was experiencing widespread unrest. The rebellion was also covered extensively in the London and provincial press. Representatives of Tate and Lyle defended their company's record in Jamaica, pointing to their provision of better housing for the workers at Frome and wage increases that had "stirred up excitement among the workers." The city editor of the *Daily Herald*, with a circulation of 2 million, minced no words in his criticism of the company and the government of Jamaica:

> Once again it seems we are confronted with a great concern which can well afford to pay high wages, but which finds difficulty in having

the courage entirely to abandon the principle [of paying] the competitive wages prevailing in a primary area. A great responsibility rests on the British administration in Jamaica, which has allowed a deplorably low standard of living to persist in the island; but a similar responsibility rests on Tate and Lyle, as a great combine, making high profits and holding a privileged position in the British market. The company is plainly under an obligation to use its vast resources to improve the condition of the natives.[33]

This and similar criticisms in the English press severely damaged Tate and Lyle's reputation. The most devastating criticism, however, came from the pen of Lord Sydney Olivier, who had served as the governor of Jamaica from 1907 to 1913. Highly respected, he was regarded as the greatest living authority in England on the British West Indies in general and Jamaica in particular. Commenting on the unrest at Frome and on conditions in the Caribbean as a whole, Lord Olivier identified the low price that the British public paid for sugar as the principal cause of the poor wages the workers received. He emphasized that "at the present prices of sugar in England, no sugar labourer can be paid living wages, and no sugar producing enterprise can afford to pay any appreciable increase of wages. Until British consumers are prepared to pay a half penny per pound more for their sugar, such disturbance as this [Frome] riot are bound to occur."[34]

Sir Leonard Lyle, the chairman of Messers Tate and Lyle, objected to these criticisms of his company's treatment of its Caribbean workers. There were fundamental differences, he maintained, between the English worker and his Caribbean counterpart. "We must be careful to remember," Sir Leonard said, "that the West Indian labourer does not even remotely resemble the English labourer, either in his mode of living or mentality." He knew that "in the most favourable circumstances it will be a very long time before West Indian labour can be educated up to the English standard." Lord Olivier rejected this assertion in a subsequent interview with the press.[35] But Leonard Lyle had already defamed the West Indian worker, upon whose sweat the fortunes of his company partly depended.

Governor Denham had been in the island for almost four years before the rebellion at Frome. Tired, he was looking forward to a brief respite from his responsibilities. The rebellion had forced a change in his plans, and he assured the colonial secretary that he had "no intention of leaving until I was satisfied that any serious trouble was over and that everything was quiet." He was confident that "these agitations die down very often as quickly as they arise." Writing his letter on May 21, the governor was hoping that "conditions" would improve, allowing him "to get some leave this summer."[36] Approximately two weeks later, the exhausted governor was buried at sea.

The rebellion at Frome was barely over when Governor Denham confronted another crisis. He had not yet developed a sympathetic understanding of the economic plight of the majority of the Jamaican people. Denham saw unemployment as a "serious menace" in the island. But he explained that it was confined to the towns and not "in the country, where planters tell me they are continually in need of employees." He recognized that wages were low, "but it was very difficult to raise these owing to the present state of the cultivations and the fact that if wages were doubled it might merely result in half the number of people being employed." Incredibly, the governor was making his comment about unemployment being an urban phenomenon three weeks after the rebellion at Frome.

Governor Denham denied that there was any "real starvation" in the island, although he admitted that there was "a considerable amount of malnutrition, especially amongst the children." This malnutrition, he maintained, was "due largely to a comparatively enormous infantile [sic] population, the result largely of illegitimacy." There was, to be sure, a high percentage of out-of-wedlock births, but the incidence of malnourished children was a function of the acute economic condition of the parents. Denham did not have a high opinion of the people he governed in the name of His Imperial Majesty. "It is very important," the governor wrote, "in a country like this that everything should not be done for the people but only something supplementary to their efforts. If all children were given free meals as all poor people here [London] are given free medicine the gift would only be abused and the expenditure could neither be borne nor justified."[37]

The truth, of course, was that Jamaicans were hard workers if given the opportunity to work. The century following the end of slavery in 1838 had posed enormous challenges for them, and few had the option of inertia. Most struggled to overcome poverty and deprivation, constituting for the most part a law-abiding citizenry that stoically accepted adversity but also never lost faith in the elusive promise of freedom. The rapid return to a degree of normalcy at Frome belied the depth of the fury that animated the unrest. Contrary to the assessment of the governor, it was not a local phenomenon. Frome was the signifier, the pulse, the exemplar of the entire

The Labor Rebellion | 41

island. Jamaicans were facing common problems; Frome was Jamaica, and Jamaica was Frome.

Although the overt tensions at Frome quickly abated, pockets of serious unrest surfaced in various parts of the island. In Kingston on May 11, for example, 100 unemployed persons marched to the site of the legislature, Headquarters House, and the offices of the Kingston and St. Andrew Corporation, demanding jobs at Trench Pen. The *Gleaner* described them as "resolute, and grimly determined, yet . . . orderly and peaceful." The men asserted that "we are not out to make any trouble. But things are hard. We want work." Promised work, and with their numbers swelling to 350, they returned to Trench Pen the following day, only to be disappointed. "There must be some mistake," the leaders said. "We do not think the government would deliberately make fools of us."[38] Their demand for work was serious and urgent. There would be limits to their forbearance as the days wore on.

There was trouble on May 17, when the dreams for employment remained unmet. According to a news report, "hundreds of unemployed men in threatening and violent mood halted work at Trench Pen." Forty men had been hired by a contractor, but those who failed to procure work forced them to cease working. Two men received injuries, and others fled for their lives. Appearing on the scene, Alexander Bustamante urged the workers to maintain the peace, telling them that the government was very anxious to relieve unemployment.[39] This was little comfort to those who had no lifeline, whose developing rage could not and would not be easily contained.

The acid test of the workers' mood occurred when those employed at the United Fruit Company's wharf in Kingston staged a general walkout on May 19. Demanding improved working conditions, the men refused to unload the cargo vessel *Harboe Jensen*. Other vessels were similarly treated over the next several days. The men complained about verbal abuse by management, a shift system that allowed them to work only one day per week, being forced to work at excessive speeds, and inadequate personnel to help with very heavy weights. They were prepared, they said, to "suffer hunger and deprivation" rather than return to work at less than one shilling per hour.[40]

The strike was spontaneous, and the workers soon realized that they needed a leader. According to Lucius Watson, he and five other workers said "well we don't have no leader, let us go call St William Grant."[41] Although he was not working on the wharves, Grant was an obvious choice. An ardent Garveyite, Grant had spent time in New York. Deported to Jamaica in the 1930s, he gave lectures on Sunday nights in one of Kingston's parks.

Evon Blake, a journalist and former policeman, recalled that "St William Grant mostly talked race, mostly talked Garveyism. He was a race man. He was first and last [a race man]. He was more race than labour, because he was one of Garvey's lieutenants in Harlem. His ideology was black racism. St William Grant was a 'leftist.' You can't be a black man and not be a leftist, unless you fool"![42]

Short in stature, Grant shaved his head and dressed in a military uniform similar to that worn by the Italian fascist Benito Mussolini. Evon Blake noted that he had "a voice that rang like a bell." One had to listen to Grant, Blake recalled, "whether he was talking damn nonsense or talking sense."[43] Alexander Bustamante, Watson said, "always go out to Grant meeting. And Grant always project him as a rich man come from Spain and dis and dat, blah, blah, blah, you know. But there was nutten like that. He was just a brag on us."[44]

When Lucius Watson and his colleagues turned up at Grant's home to invite him to lead the workers, they saw him "leaning on a broom, in the yard, and without any shirt on, and merino [undershirt] on." Greeting Grant, the men said: "Mr. Grant, is you we come to." Grant inquired as to the purpose of their visit. "We say there is a strike down the waterfront and we want somebody to come and talk to us," the men responded. "Alright," Grant said, "oonu [all of you] wait on me. Wait deh [there], a coming." He dressed hurriedly, and as the men followed him on foot, he told them: "I'm just going to call on somebody."[45]

Grant's destination was Alexander Bustamante's home on Beeston Street. He knocked on Bustamante's door, and a familiar voice inquired:

"Who dat?" Im sey, "[M]e, Mr. Bustamante, me Chief." "What you want, Grant?" Im sey, "[M]e have something here, Sir." And Busta just push 'im head out and sey "What is it Grant?" [A]nd he said, "These men strike on the waterfront and they come and call me to come and talk for them down there." Busta sey, "Alright, Alright, I'll come!" Same time Busta shut back the door, go in and 'im put on his clothes and get ready to come out.[46]

Bustamante recalled that the delegation "told me they definitely wanted me to be their leader and to take up their grievances with the employers." He readily accepted the invitation, receiving the support of his young secretary, Gladys Longbridge. Bustamante said she "backed me up and assured me she would stick by me through thick and thin because the workers' cause was a just one."⁴⁷ Born in 1912 in Ashton, the parish of Westmoreland, Miss Longbridge studied commercial subjects in Kingston and worked briefly as a cashier, typist, and clerk before becoming Bustamante's secretary in 1936. Bustamante had made a momentous decision, one that would change the course of his life and Jamaica's history. St William Grant had played the major role in Bustamante's elevation to the role of labor leader at the most challenging time in the history of labor in the island since 1838. "If there was no St William Grant, there would be no Bustamante," Evon Blake concluded.⁴⁸ Vivian Durham, an eyewitness to the rebellion and an admirer and supporter of the new labor chief, was certain that "Grant was to Bustamante what St. Peter was to our Divine Lord."⁴⁹

Grant's choice of Bustamante to lead the workers did not immediately win their support. When Bustamante addressed the workers at Church and North Streets, the crowd was at first very skeptical of him. Blake recalled that "when this tall white man rose to speak, people said, 'we no wan' no white man! We no wan' no white man yah!' St William Grant said: 'Listen to him! He have sense. If you don't listen to him, the meeting is over.' . . . [T]he crowd was uneasy at the start. But when he was finished, they almost lifted him off the platform. They never heard a white man talk like that."⁵⁰

Blake believed that St William Grant promoted Bustamante as the workers' leader because they would not have accepted a black man serving in that capacity. Elaborating, he said: "You see, Jamaica has never accepted a black man as a maximum leader. Jamaica didn't accept Garvey. The followers that Garvey should have had in Jamaica he didn't have. Black and white and brown ridiculed him. If St William Grant had taken the lead, he wouldn't have had a great following. Because black don't trust black. When they see this tall, handsome white man, call himself the leader, your leader, they felt better."⁵¹

Vivian Durham described Bustamante as a "brown" man. Bustamante, he said, "was quite an enigma." A tall man, "his hair was heavy and unruly," and "he had a pair of eyes that looking back now, one could see it was the eyes that were looking into the future." Bustamante, Durham recalled, always sat in one of the parks "discussing the deplorable social and economic conditions of the time—low, desperately low wages, infant mortality, lack of good health service[, wearing] pitchy-patchy pants like Joseph's coat of many colours." Children liked Bustamante, calling him "Daddy Long Legs." Durham described him as "good looking, very charming, with an infectious disposition." Brown men, Durham noted, did not "condescend to sit in the park," but Bustamante crossed those boundaries. He "psychologically identified himself with the humble people." Bustamante was "the only brown man who talked the language of the exploited, downtrodden black people of Jamaica."⁵²

Lawrence McKenzie remembered his excitement at seeing Bustamante for the first time during the unrest in Kingston. He was particularly struck by the labor leader's color. "To be quite honest," McKenzie said, "I thought it was Christ came when I saw Bustamante, since his picture was white. Christ picture was always white."⁵³ By associating Bustamante's phenotype with that which Christ was portrayed to possess, McKenzie was giving the labor leader greater respect and credibility. Bustamante's apparent whiteness was an important factor in his attracting attention. The color "white" had enormous symbolic power in a society that had revered white people for so long.

Bustamante's skin color was never a neutral factor in his ascent to the leadership of the workers. But as a source of his appeal or disfavor, racial ancestry did not function independently of other variables. In addition to his noticing Bustamante's "whiteness," for example, Lawrence McKenzie was impressed by "de courage dat I saw in him. He was never at the back, he was never in the middle, up FRONT."⁵⁴ Most Jamaicans would not have considered Bustamante a white man, identifying him as "a brown man" despite his pale complexion. Bustamante never seemed to wear his racial ancestry on his sleeve, although he was accused of distancing himself from any African roots. McKenzie recalled "listening to 'im one night, when he said that there was not one drop of negro blood in his vein and people cheer. He goes on to say dat he would be [was] born in Ireland because his father is an Irish man and his mother is a Spanish woman, and I held down my head in shock and shame. While people was cheering, I was able to say to myself that this man can't be for the people if he is saying dat."⁵⁵

Bustamante was "for the people," but such utterances, if true, revealed much about Bustamante's tendency to invent and reinvent himself. Phenotypically black, most Jamaicans did not have the dubious satisfaction of falsifying their racial roots, even if they wanted to do so. In fact, the volatile social environment of the 1930s was due, in part, to Marcus Garvey's efforts to promote the gospel of a pugnacious black identity and consciousness. The Universal Negro Improvement Association (UNIA) that he created politicized the workers, paving the way for the emerging labor movement. "The whole impact of the working class leadership," observed Frank Gordon, "came out of the Garvey movement. . . . The UNIA was the basic organization that united black people throughout Jamaica."⁵⁶ Joseph

Kennedy shared the view that Garvey "united the people," so "Bustamante and others inherited the unity that Garvey laid."[57] A third contemporary, Lucius Watson, maintained that "Garvey and de whole a de Garvey people dem, had an impact, great impact on de people. Garvey laid the foundation in educating the workers—the masses of this country."[58] This developing black consciousness, whether articulated or not, was a necessary prerequisite for the contest against the mostly white barons of capital.

Bustamante, it must be stressed, did not hold any official position in a union or any other organization in May 1938. Consequently, he identified himself to the management of the wharves as an intermediary between capital and labor. His initial meetings with management achieved nothing since their representatives insisted that there would be no negotiation before the workers resumed their work. Bustamante spent much of May 22 addressing crowds and leading marches consisting of workers, their supporters, and the unemployed. At one meeting at Duke Street and Harbour Street, he proclaimed himself the leader of the developing rebellion. According to Evon Blake, an eyewitness, Bustamante "mounted one of the cassia trees" to deliver his exhortation to the crowd. "Follow me!" he ordered, "From this day on I am your leader." As Bustamante spoke, Blake remembered, the cassia tree's branch broke "and Busta fell on his two feet right beside me."[59] The crowd's reaction to this dramatic event was not recorded.

But this was merely one of several dramatic events that occurred that day. Led by inspector William Orrett, the police singled out Bustamante for special harassment. As Bustamante led the marchers, Orrett blocked them at several points, yelling: "Turn back, Bustamante, turn back." Blake recalled that at one stage, "Orrett pulled his gun from the holster and pushed it in Busta's throat. He said: 'Turn back or I'll shoot!' I was there. Busta said: 'Shoot us! Then go home and tell your wife and children that you have shot your brothers who are fighting for you!' Not a policeman move. Orrett became discomforted. He didn't know what to do with himself and his gun. He put the gun back into the holster, then marched his men back to the station."[60]

Vivian Durham remembered the incident slightly differently. He said that when inspector Orrett "ordered his people to fire on Bustamante, Grant was there, beside him and Busta said, 'Orrett, you damn coward! You dare shoot me!' It was fixed bayonets. It was no joke. Grant was there and people ran up John's Lane [shouting] 'Lawd God! Dem gwine kill the

Chief now!' And Busta held his ground and defied Orrett. The guns dropped and Busta was made immortal."[61]

In a brief recollection of the rebellion, Bustamante wrote that at Georges Lane and Harbour Street, he had to "draw my gun to prevent what would have been an ugly situation as the Inspector of the Police in charge was hell bent on shooting these unfortunate hungry, friendless people." At the Queen Victoria statue in downtown Kingston, Bustamante displayed the kind of flamboyance that would endear him to the workers. "Just as I alighted from the statue," he remembered, "there arrived forty policemen with bayonets fixed in battle form, headed by Inspector Orrett. I heard a voice [saying] 'shoot' and the rattling of rifles. I turned to the policemen, bared my chest, and said 'Shoot me, but leave those unfortunate hungry people alone.' I dispersed the crowd and told them to be calm.'"[62] Bustamante's reputation for bravery, flamboyance, and dramatic flair was being constructed.

Tensions increased over the weekend as the employed and unemployed alike gathered on the waterfront to hear Bustamante speak at various times. Bustamante, the *Gleaner* reported, was received with "thunderous rounds of applause and boisterous demonstrations." Meeting with the workers early Sunday morning, he called for a vote to determine if they wanted to strike. "Every hand in the crowd flashed sky-high for an immediate strike," the *Gleaner* said. To the individual worker, this was a searing act of psychological liberation, a thrilling embrace of the agency of self, and a passionate belief in the possibility of positive change in his material circumstances. Although he seemed pleased by the decision, the labor leader declared: "I did not call this strike. If I ever cause a strike[,] . . . I will cause it in every parish in this country. I would tie up every plantation and works—and that's the strike I am going to pull off one day. I am not going to start any terrible revolution, but I will organize from Negril to St. Thomas. . . . I am deeply sorry for the people—the masses—of this country."[63]

Bustamante urged the crowd to remain peaceful but warned against strikebreakers. "It must be understood that this strike must not be broken," he admonished. Advocating unity among the workers, Bustamante asserted: "[T]his is war and you cannot expect to win a war if the soldiers are divided and against the other."[64]

Bustamante's address to the waterfront workers on that Sunday morning was the defining and watershed moment in his long life. The workers had proclaimed him their leader, and he had accepted the challenge and the responsibility. They had converted the brown-faced usurer into a labor leader, giving him the legitimacy he had long sought. It was a stunning rise to respectability, a triumph of blind faith and charisma over a credible record of performance. Neither the workers present at the meeting nor Bustamante himself could have predicted the role he would play in his country's history over time.

But this was May 22, 1938, and the principal concern of the waterfront workers was to resolve their dispute with the owners of the wharves. Their objective was a limited one; it had not yet become the grand and larger conflict between capital and labor over the fundamentals of the workplace, such as working conditions, the rewards structure, and the machinery for the resolution of grievances. Bustamante brought neither a strategy nor a set of proposals to the table. But he did bring his energy, indefatigability, and passion to the workers' cause. The newly anointed leader held discussions throughout the day with management, addressing several public meetings and talking to the workers. He even got into a verbal tussle with Erasmus E. A. Campbell, a prominent Kingston lawyer and civic leader. Campbell had denounced "inflammatory talk or inflammatory action" by the leaders of the workers. Bustamante interpreted this as an attack on him. When he encountered Campbell later that day, he "jumped" out of his car, threatening to throw his critic into the sea. "Listen Campbell," Bustamante warned, "if you came here to say anything against me, I am going to throw you in the sea. I will hold you and switch you and flog you properly."[65]

Bustamante did not execute his threat. But there was a feeling of dark foreboding in the city, an uncanny and perverse expectancy. "The day was fine," the daily newspaper reported, adding that "the weather [was] splendid and in the gathering dusk a cry pierced the troubled atmosphere." The police immediately "cleared for action" as one man in a crowd screamed, "[T]hey are bringing men from the country to break the strike." The workers were vowing "to kill" strikebreakers, and some had actually attacked persons who were taking food to those who were still working aboard the ship, the *Jamaica Planter*. By nightfall, the waterfront had become eerily quiet as the crowds dispersed, but the police were everywhere, alert to any threat to societal peace.[66]

The passions did not cool overnight. Bustamante called "a monster" meeting of the workers at daybreak on the 23rd at the corner of Duke and Harbour Streets, presumably to maintain their élan. Trouble ensued as the crowd dispersed, clashing with the police. Finding strength in their number, the people forced businesses to close, and by eleven o'clock only a few grocery stores remained open. The crowd targeted establishments owned by the Chinese and "rough handled" those who resisted an order to close. Some demonstrators yelled, "This is black man day." One man ordered a Chinese businessman who was in his store on Princess Street to "come out mek we beat you." Others in the crowd shouted, "All Chinamen's shop must close and black men shop must open."[67] Years later, Mrs. U. Gordon, a black woman who owned a shop at Pink Lane and Charles Street, recalled that she resisted the urging of her customers to close as the insurgents approached: "[D]em say: 'Crowd coming! Close up!' I sey: 'No! I not closing.' So dey come right on Charles Street an' dey look an' see me behind the counter, an' dey sey 'Oh! Black man open! Your time, you open.... All de Chinese dem close, [but] the black people dem open up.'... [A]s long as you black dem sey you can open up. But Chinese mus' close."[68]

The assault on the oppressive status quo became overtly racialized in a physical sense with these assaults on Chinese enterprises. But the Chinese were not a part of the power elite and had no history of institutional mistreatment of black Jamaicans. They were, however, sharp entrepreneurs, and some people looked askance at their success and seeming lack of respect for their customers. Lucius Watson, a port worker and eyewitness to the rebellion in Kingston, observed: "The Chinese use' to live amongst the low class people, till they start to grow up. Chinese start to come up, and come up. Hear what the Chinese use' to do when dey come here. They use' to laundry, use' to do cultivation, cash crop and laundry an open shop. Dat was dere trade and dey build deyself right up and up and dey lef' us [blacks] same place."[69] Years of acute resentment against the Chinese, their upward mobility, and their entrepreneurial successes were now finding a violent expression.

The *Gleaner* reported that "strikers virtually seized the city of Kingston Monday morning, invaded St. Andrew around noon." The disorder forced "all workers, particularly those employed in public buildings to quit their jobs." In response, the government called out 400 police officers, 80 troops, 250 special constables, and 100 members of the militia. The mayhem continued throughout the day as the protesters blocked streets, destroyed street lamps, and attacked cars and their occupants. Miraculously, only a few persons were injured. But the *Gleaner* observed that "it was a day of anxiety and dirt and loss for the Corporate Area." It was, the newspaper continued, "a fruitless day, as no attempt at arbitration could be made with thousands patrolling the streets and keeping the armed forces on the move."

The crowds reassembled on Tuesday the 24th, but on a smaller scale. Ironically, it was Empire Day, a public holiday devoted to honoring British rule. This day of leisure may have kept some people home. Others may have been intimidated by the ubiquitous presence of law-enforcement officials. Still, there was a continuation of the mayhem that characterized the city the previous day. Tragedy struck early, however. The police opened fire on Matthews Lane around ten o'clock, killing Sarah Thomas and her eleven-year-old son, Stanley. A second son, six-year-old Henry, was gravely wounded. The mother and her dead son were both shot in their heads. The police claimed that missiles were being hurled at them from various homes and they retaliated, hitting the victims as they were entering their gate. Predictably, the horror exacerbated the prevailing tensions, unleashing raw emotions. Family members were reported to be "screaming hysterically." Acting most insensitively, the police "clubbed men and women who assembled in the lane." Daniel, the dead woman's husband and father of the boy who was killed, "paced up and down Matthews Lane crying inconsolably."[70]

The news of the Matthews Lane horror was bad enough for the workers and demonstrators, but they were outraged by the arrest of Bustamante and Grant on that day. The two men were holding a public meeting on Sutton Street when Inspector Orrett arrested them. Lucius Watson provided a graphic account of the event:

> When we went [to] Sutton Street, Orrett and a police squad came out and stop Busta and tell Busta, well you under arrest. By the time 'im come out and tell Busta 'im under arrest (Orrett walk beside Busta wid 'im gun in hand). Dem lick [hit] the police! 'Bout five police tumble down. Mi Dear Sah, police start to lick lef, right and centre, and police tumble down 'pon Grant wid de big stick, wid the big long staff and lawd, dem start to beat Grant! And dem give Grant one beating! Them never touch Busta. The black man dem beat you, you know. Dem beat him you see? Bloodup! Nearly kill him. . . . Grant nuh du nutten, you know. Dem neva touch Busta far 'im was the cousin of Norman Manley. 'Im was a brown man. They only arrest Busta.[71]

Eyewitness accounts of the incident vary in the details, but they tell a similar story. Roderick Francis, a ship's pilot, recalled that "Grant was hit on his testicles by the police and I think Grant suffered from that right through his life." He speculated that the police did not hit Bustamante "maybe because he was a brown man." Francis reported that "our police those days were afraid of brown people. But they took a chance and lick the black man. Black man licking black man all the while. Bustamante was never ill treated."[72]

Bustamante may have avoided physical abuse by the police because of his brown skin, but his color did not spare him and Grant from being arrested. He gave a much less dramatic account of his arrest than did those who witnessed the incident. According to him, he was addressing some firemen who were contemplating going on strike when Inspector Orrett and "two or three officers" arrived on the scene. Orrett "pushed a gun in my side and addressed me thus: '[Y]ou are under arrest.' I said '[O]k.' 'Come along!'"[73] Bustamante was charged with inciting people to assemble unlawfully and with sedition.

Grant was charged with sedition (an offense that he allegedly committed on May 4 at North Parade in Kingston), with inciting people to assemble unlawfully, and with failing to obey a policeman's orders to move and to keep moving. The two men were denied bail by the presiding judge, S. T. B. Sanguinetti. He explained that if bail were granted, the crowd would not allow the two men to appear for trial.[74] This was not a credible explanation, and it was unacceptable to the workers. Bustamante and Grant's arrest may have been ordered by the governor, but there is no evidence to support this speculation. The arrest was a blatant attempt, however, to silence the two leaders, intimidate the strikers, and crush the strike itself. Ill conceived and a naked expression of state power, the arrests may have found favor with capital, but the workers were angered. Bustamante and Grant would emerge from their ordeal with greater prestige and as martyrs for the cause of labor.

Bustamante reported that when he arrived at the jail, "I took out my 38 revolver and holster and delivered same to one Cpl. Thompson. I said, 'Cpl. Thompson, your Inspector did not have any [the] sense to disarm me.' I also took out a wad of money I had on me and delivered same to the Corporal in charge. (One British soldier was heard to say Goddam it! That bloke has a whole bank on him)." Bustamante recalled that he was "stripped of every piece of clothing except my B.V.D. (underpants) and left to sleep on the cold concrete. The slab of board which other persons had to sleep on was taken out."[75]

A defiant Bustamante went on a hunger strike after he was arrested. "They took me to the police station," he recalled. "I refused to eat for two days. I'd have lasted until death if they'd kept me there but they moved me to a penitentiary." He tried to maintain the peace while he languished in jail. "I was told 3,000 people were ready to march on the prison to release me. 'We are going to burn Kingston down' was the message I received." He said he responded, "No my friends, you must be patient."[76]

The longshoremen did not stand alone in their conflict with their employers. Jamaican workers were snapping at the heels of their employers with increasing vigor, so it is not surprising that they would not remain distanced from the struggles of their brethren on the waterfront. This nascent class consciousness did not necessarily mean that these workers withdrew their labor in solidarity with those on the waterfront. Rather, they were articulating their own local and specialized grievances and demands. Frank Gordon, who witnessed the unrest, observed that the working people "were working together, [but] there was no ideological conception at that time. It was groups of separate people doing their own thing."[77] Nor did those who were emerging as leaders propose general principles designed to regulate the relations between capital and labor that transcended specific workplaces. The strikes that took place in tandem with that on the waterfront and in its aftermath drew attention to the conditions at particular workplaces, paralyzing them for a time. They provided the necessary space, however, for the honing of negotiating skills and strategies for capital and labor alike, the nurturing of a working-class consciousness, and ultimately the emergence of a responsible trade-union movement.

That said, the pulse of the workers was quickened by the events on the waterfront, as an epidemic of strikes occurred in their wake. The sanitation workers, pejoratively known as "city scavengers," struck for higher wages on May 22. They were soon joined by the tram car operators, the bus operators, the city cleaners, and the shirt manufacturers. Occurring in rapid succession and in the disruptive milieu of street demonstrations, they created the image of a city in turmoil and ruled by a threatening "mob."

There was a dramatic turn in the crisis when Norman Manley, the country's most eminent barrister, offered his services on May 24 as a mediator between capital and labor. Unlike Bustamante or Allan Coombs, Manley had no prior identification with labor's cause. In fact, Manley had held a retainer with the West Indies Sugar Company since November 1937. When the workers at Frome who were arrested during the rebellion faced the courts, Manley was watching the proceedings on behalf of the sugar company. He was invited to appear for the workers but had to decline because of his retainer with their employer. This association did not help Manley's reputation among the island's workers. His detractors, a category of persons that would eventually include Bustamante, used it to great effect to question his credibility as a friend of labor.[78]

But in those tumultuous days in May 1938, Manley emerged as a voice of caution, sanity, and reason. His legal eminence gave him the stature that his self-appointed role as mediator demanded. The crisis provided Manley with an opportunity to establish a credible reputation as an advocate and friend of labor. It was a defining moment for him, as it was for Bustamante. His life's work as a politician and public servant was being launched.

As a member of Jamaica's elite, Manley was horrified by the mayhem that occurred on Monday, May 23. Although he was sympathetic to labor's strivings, Manley condemned their modus operandi, particularly that which was on display on that fateful Monday. "The workers themselves," he advised, "will have to recognize that . . . the putting of garbage in the streets, pulling up of trees, the smashing of windows and being shot and killed is [sic] not going to give them better wages or better hours or better conditions of employment."[79] This was certainly a reasonable observation, but the workers and their sympathizers were using the weapons at their disposal to dramatize their grievances and the urgency of their redress. Lacking institutions to represent their interests and denied the franchise for the most part, they had no voice in the legislature. By taking to the streets and shattering the disinterested complacency of the island's elite, they had achieved a victory of sorts.

Manley was also not pleased with the caliber of the leadership that the workers were experiencing. He knew that recent events "have proved how necessary it is today that the people of the country should have good leadership and good advice in putting forward their grievances and making their demands for their betterment." Manley said he was placing his services at the disposal of the workers, conveying their grievances to their employers. "I hope that any group of labourers," he said, "who wish some concrete good to come out of the trouble of the past two days will take some advantage of this offer and will understand that their interest will be served to the best of my ability along legitimate lines."[80] A beleaguered governor Denham welcomed Manley's offer with enthusiasm, publicly calling him "one of the most distinguished sons of Jamaica." Manley had already earned the governor's respect and trust. A year earlier, Denham had praised him in a letter that he wrote to the Colonial Office. Manley was "the ablest Jamaican of today," the governor confided, "very helpful, sane and conservative . . . not a controversialist nor a politician, though a man of strong—but I believe loyal—views."[81] The workers, however, had no formal mechanism to express their acceptance of the barrister's offer, but his enormous national prestige sufficed. The employers certainly accorded him respect and credibility, recognized him as the representative of the workers, and negotiated with him accordingly.

Norman Manley, ca. 1938
(Photo courtesy of the Jamaica Archives and Records Department, Kingston, Jamaica)

Manley spent Wednesday, May 25, in negotiation with the owners of the wharves. He called a meeting of the dockworkers at four o'clock that day to provide them with a preliminary report on his activities. It was attended by thousands of men, "leaderless and willing to be led," the *Daily Gleaner* reported. The newspaper observed that "all they want is a square deal and a fair chance to make an honest living. . . . [T]he men gave Mr. Manley a significantly splendid reception." Manley told the crowd that he regretted the "riot" that had occurred, absolving the workers of any responsibility for it and blaming "the rabble." He invited "genuine workers" to a meeting the following morning, asking them "to help to see that idlers who have no concern in the business do not come to interfere with the proceedings."[82] Manley was new to the business of dealing with the folks from below, hence his use of pejorative terms such as "rabble" and "idlers."

Norman Manley's developing role as a mediator of the conflict helped to calm the unsettled nerves of the elite groups. A nervous Legislative Council voted on May 25 to give the governor the power to declare a state of emergency by proclamation. Governor Denham hastily created a Board of Conciliation, charged with the responsibility to settle existing disputes, avert future ones, and propose social legislation. Although the violence in Kingston subsided rapidly, the incidence of strikes continued. The list included hospital workers, banana carriers, shop assistants, railway men, and others. There were strikes in Spanish Town as well. Strikers at the Caymanas Sugar Estate in St. Catherine had a violent confrontation with the representatives of the management on May 25, resulting in the shooting of four workers. The following day, eight persons were injured in Spanish Town during a violent conflict between law-enforcement officials and people protesting against the shootings at the Caymanas Sugar Estate. The injured included four civilians, one police officer, two special constables, and a member of the militia.[83]

These conflicts revealed the widespread grievances of the workers and the ubiquity of their protests. Writing in the *Daily Gleaner* on May 27, Hugh S. Burns observed that the workers' "gaining of Mr. Manley as leader remains their biggest gain." Continuing, Burns noted: "It is a great compliment to him [Manley] and also a positive proof of his popularity and of the people's trust in him that his momentous, generous, and inspired offer to become advocate and champion of workers has been hailed with joy on all sides."[84] Acutely cognizant of the need to provide leadership for the inchoate labor movement, Manley proposed the formation of a Labour Committee. It would "represent the different groups of workers before the Conciliation Board and to negotiate on their behalf. Secondly, to deal with the organization of Trade Unions, and thirdly, to propose and advocate a programme for the general improvement of labour conditions." This was a bold and creative attempt to give direction to the energies of the workers and provide the institutional machinery to advance their cause. Manley's lens was focused on laying the foundation for a better future for the working people of the island. "Now is the opportunity for labour to organise itself, and to secure fullest consideration of its problems and to strengthen its position forever," he declared. Manley warned that "there may never be such an opportunity again for many years to come and it is for all the workers to recognize that this is their day and their chance."[85]

Manley's articulation of a new vision for labor earned him the respect but not the deep affection of the workers. Their hearts were with Bustamante, and Manley was the new, but not completely trusted, suitor. In fact, when Manley addressed 3,000 dockworkers on May 27, he denounced a pamphlet that attacked him and Erasmus Campbell, who was assisting him in his mediation efforts. "Workers," the pamphlet read, "Do not trust Manley and Campbell. They are the tools of 'capitalists.' Support Bustamante and Grant." This was not exactly an expression of confidence in the self-appointed mediator. Although the workers who attended the meeting applauded Manley's announcement that there were discussions under way to form a trade union, they said they would not sign a document pledging their support for it. "They were unanimous in their resolve," the *Gleaner* reported, to do nothing until Bustamante and Grant were released. Shouting "No work: We want Bustamante," the workers rejected wage increases that Manley had negotiated. "We don't want 1/− an hour. We want Bustamante," they said as they refused to follow Manley's instruction to return to work.[86]

Bustamante and Grant were released on bail on Saturday, May 28, five days after their arrest. The Crown withdrew its opposition to their release after it received affidavits, including one from Manley, guaranteeing their good conduct. The authorities must have realized that there would be no return to some degree of normalcy in Kingston if the two labor leaders remained in custody. Bustamante addressed 7,000 jubilant supporters at the pier immediately after his release. He announced pay increases for the workers and proclaimed an end to the strike. "I am asking you all unanimously to go back to work," he added. "Are you prepared to unload those ships tomorrow?" Bustamante asked. The crowd "went hoarse in its joyous efforts," the *Gleaner* observed. Bustamante would later issue a statement expressing his confidence that "a better day is in store for the great body of toilers in our land."[87]

Bustamante's speech at the pier provided a clue to his future relationship with Manley and his leadership style. "Yes, my friends," Bustamante said, "Mr. Manley meant well, and he came at a time when I did not ask him to come but when I really needed his services." Manley volunteered, Bustamante admitted, "to help in getting me out of the penitentiary and I appreciate it sincerely. If he had waited until I asked him, I would not have appreciated it." Bustamante said he was gratified that Manley had "tried" to help the workers, but "I was more glad that you all refused to work. When you did this, you gave definite proof that you respect your leader and you accept but one leadership." Bustamante was warning Manley, not so subtly, that he would accept no competition for the leadership of the workers. Two weeks later, he could not resist alluding to Manley's association with capital. The wily labor leader complimented his "dear friend" Manley for securing his release from jail, adding: "Manley spoke at one of my meetings. Edna [Manley's wife] spoke. Edna has been so kind. She has been feeding the strikers so that they could win their fight, although her husband's clients are the employers the strikers have been fighting."[88]

Bustamante's release ended the dockworkers' strike, but other workers continued to assert their growing militancy throughout the island. On Tuesday, May 31, the *Daily Gleaner* characterized Jamaica as "a land of strikes."

It reported that there were strikes on almost all the banana plantations in St. Thomas, Portland, St. Mary, and parts of St. Catherine. In Montego Bay, "all classes of workers" struck, and telegraph services were "crippled" in three parishes. Construction workers left their jobs in St. Ann, St. Elizabeth, and elsewhere. This epidemic of strikes reached their peak on June 6, with work stoppages and general disorder in St. Catherine, Clarendon, Manchester, St. Elizabeth, Westmoreland, St. James, Trelawny, St. Ann, Portland, and St. Thomas. Thereafter, the island-wide unrest subsided as the strikes were settled and passions cooled.

The work stoppages were often accompanied by street demonstrations and violence, or the threat of it. Some workers and their allies were frequently armed with sticks and cutlasses to intimidate those who resisted demands to strike. Strikers blocked roads, cut telephone wires, and looted shops, particularly those belonging to the Chinese. Police reinforcements tried, sometimes unsuccessfully, to restore order with their guns and bayonets. On Friday, June 3, the police fired into a crowd at Islington, St. Mary, killing four persons and wounding three others. The police shot three persons at Worthy Park, St. Catherine, on June 6 and killed two persons at Tryall estate in St. James on the same day. They also killed one man and wounded two others at Ulster Spring in Trelawny. Three policemen received injuries in the melee.[89]

Understandably, the labor rebellion generated much introspection in Jamaica and in England. The Colonial Office, for example, received letters diagnosing the causes of the labor crisis and proposing remedial measures. Marcus Garvey, the prominent black nationalist and founder of the UNIA, blamed the deplorable conditions in Jamaica on the inattention of the governors:

> Governors in Jamaica do not understand the situation of the common people, in that after they are well settled in the Island, they accept thoroughly the representations made to them by the associates of the aristocracy and become positively deaf to the cries of the struggling masses. . . . [T]he common people are really without a friend and anyone attempting to speak honestly in the interest of these people becomes locally tabooed, and in financial and other circles he is harassed to the point where he either retires into silence or ultimately leaves the island.[90]

Garvey was speaking about himself as well, since he had left the island for England after an experiment with electoral politics. Garvey described

Jamaica to the Colonial Office as an "Island Poor House." It was "a country of social inhumanity where the class that is above shows no interest in the class below." Jamaicans, Garvey said, "do not want to be bad or riotous but there is no other way to express themselves than in this manner." P. W. Peat, another Jamaican, blamed the discontent in the island on the "barriers which are created by those who possess skins of lighter hue." The laborer, Peat said, "is made to feel that because he is black he is little better than an animal . . . [and] that it is a disgrace to be black." These people are now "awake" to the fact that their condition "is deplorable," he declared.[91]

R. F. Glanville Richards had a different point of view. An Englishman who had lived and worked in Jamaica, he admitted that when he left the island, "conditions" in the sugar industry "for both staff and labourer, was [sic] little short of slavery itself." Still, Richards claimed that the labor rebellion had been caused by workers who had returned from Cuba and elsewhere. "They have been spoilt in other lands," he wrote to the secretary of state, "and become agitators of the worst kind."[92] James Gibb, another Englishman, censured the Colonial Office for ignoring his advice and offer to help the colonial administration in the West Indies. He charged the colonial bureaucrats with casting a blind eye on the condition of the Jamaican people and the loss of lives there "possibly and presumably" because they were "Niggers."[93] The Colonial Office was not particularly bothered by these and other criticisms, although it was beginning to develop plans to address the social and economic conditions of the people in the colonies.

The rebellion also commanded the attention of various political groups and organizations. The Jamaica Progressive League in New York quickly passed a resolution denouncing the "inexcusable killing and wounding of underpaid and mistreated workers of the island." Similarly, the London Scots Self-Government Committee, an organization that promoted self-government for the colonies, passed a resolution supporting the struggles of the Jamaican and other West Indian workers for better working conditions. The Oxford University League of Nations Society and the London District Committee of the Communist Party of Great Britain, among others, voiced their support as well.[94]

The widespread unrest that wracked the island in late May and early June was unprecedented in the century since slavery ended. But to those who had not shared their experiences of want and deprivation, these protestors were publicly dismissed as "hooligans," "the mob," "the rabble," "the agitators."

They were probably called more abusive names in private discourse. When a number of persons who were arrested for participating in the disturbances in St. Catherine appeared before the resident magistrate, J. M. Nethersole, he took the opportunity to admonish them "to have patience and keep out of disturbances." The justice emphasized that "those of the criminal classes, hooligans, have no place in this community. Every branch of the community is determined that they should make no disorders. All hooliganism and ruffianism will be suppressed."[95]

Justice Nethersole said that he had seen women act "in such a manner in Kingston's disturbance that they could never expect any mercy from me." The justice was sworn to uphold and administer the law, but his rhetoric demonstrated no sympathetic understanding of the social and economic milieus that shaped these peoples' behavior and worldview and limited and circumscribed their human possibilities as well. These were Justice Nethersole's fellow Jamaicans. But they were also the Jamaicans who Bustamante characterized as "oppressed" and "living in misery and poverty."[96] Their conduct, so condemned and abhorred by those of a more privileged status in society, was certainly justified in their own eyes. The sweat of those with agricultural and industrial jobs had built the island, but their reward was niggardly and unacceptably exploitative. Those without jobs were sharing not at all in the country's economic promise; they were seething and receptive to the possibilities of change, through their own energies or by whatever means.

The sticks, stones, and cutlasses they employed were the weapons they possessed, terrifying to some but hardly as effective as the guns and bayonets of the defenders and protectors of the colonial status quo. Bustamante, Manley, and others urged behavioral restraint, but the passions of the crowd sometimes defied any boundaries. In the aftermath of Bustamante's release from custody, he traveled with Manley to various parts of the country, calming passions and negotiating settlements with management. Allan Coombs played a similar role, especially in St. James, where he enjoyed popular esteem. Acting quickly, the newly appointed Conciliation Board agreed upon rates for employees in the banana industry in volatile St. Mary, expecting the scale to serve as a model for the rest of the country. The intervention of the labor leaders, the redress of the grievances of some of the workers, the efforts of the Conciliation Board, and the combat weariness of the workers all helped to produce a respite in the unrest in June.[97]

The government did not remain inactive during the labor rebellion and its aftermath. Governor Denham, who was beginning to develop an understanding of the roots of the crisis, died unexpectedly on June 3. He had, on May 26, announced the appointment of the Conciliation Board to mediate labor disputes. Its members included the chief justice; the island's treasurer; a former assistant colonial secretary; the member of the Legislative Council for Manchester; a former official of the United Fruit Company, a major banana exporter; the mayor of Kingston; and H. P. Jacobs, an English-born public intellectual. Surprisingly, there was no representative of labor on the board, an indication of its obvious pro-employer bias. Attempting to implement a plan to address the people's other grievances, the acting governor, C. C. Woolley, hastily announced a £500,000 land-settlement scheme on June 5. The government was convinced that the country's economic growth and the solution to its unemployment problem depended on the intensive development of agriculture. The *Gleaner* reacted by praising the administration's "stupendous plan."[98] Woolley's announcement represented a major turning point in the rebellion. Its tantalizing promise of land for the landless tempered the intensity of the rebellion, largely contributing to its cessation.

The new governor, Sir Arthur Richards, appointed a Commission of Enquiry in August to report on the causes of the rebellion and the responses to it. The three-member body included Claud Ramsay Seton, a justice of the High Court; Charles Archibald Reid, the member of the Legislative Council for the parish of Manchester; and Horace Somerville Sewell, brigadier general and custos of the parish of Trelawny. The commission held sessions in Kingston, Mandeville, Montego Bay, Port Maria, and Port Antonio.

The Commission of Enquiry reported that eight persons were killed during the disturbances, thirty-two were wounded by gunshot, and 139 were "otherwise injured." The "crown forces," it said, did not have any fatalities, but 109 men were injured. Its statistics were incomplete, but the commission calculated that 745 persons were arrested, of whom 480 were convicted and 265 were found not guilty. Those declared guilty were either "admonished and discharged" or sentenced to up to nine months of hard labor. The police were deemed to be justified in the killing of the eight persons. At least twenty persons were reported as being robbed and assaulted by crowds, and thirty-six shopkeepers, principally Chinese, had their businesses looted. The commission praised the police for discharging their "onerous duties with courage and discretion." It observed that the "small number of casualties" was "a tribute alike to the good temper of the labouring classes of Jamaica and to the forbearance and humanity of those whose duty it was to preserve order."[99]

The commission was "inclined to the view" that the disturbances in the rural areas had not been organized by a "central authority" in Kingston. It was effusive in its praise of Norman Manley's role in the rebellion:

> Perhaps no man in the Island did more to re-establish confidence and restrict the growth of the disorders than Mr. N. W. Manley, K.C., who came forward almost immediately after the beginning of the disturbances, placed himself unreservedly at the disposal of the working classes and undertook to submit, on their behalf, their claims for better pay and better working conditions to the proper authorities. He appreciated that what was desired could only be obtained by constitutional means and that if the disturbances were to continue, the chief sufferers would be the labouring classes themselves. Both sides were gainers by his intervention. Employers had someone with whom to negotiate, who understood conditions in the island, and who knew what demands could reasonably be made and what could not. On the other hand, the labourers had at their disposal and working wholeheartedly on their behalf one of the best brains in the country and one of the most disinterested. Mr. Manley toiled unceasingly for almost a month addressing meetings throughout the Island, negotiating with employers, conferring with various groups of labour on the subject of their demands and finally representing them before the Board of Conciliation. We think that his services to the community as a whole were invaluable.[100]

The report had described accurately Manley's extraordinary role in mediating the crisis. It enhanced his image in the island as a man of outstanding ability, balance, and good sense. In contrast, the report was silent on the role of Alexander Bustamante, declining to even mention his name. Interestingly, six years after the publication of the report, Bustamante sought to discredit Manley and his role in the events. By 1943 the two men had become bitter political foes. Writing to "the people of Jamaica" on November 17, 1944, Bustamante charged that Manley refused to defend the workers who were arrested at Frome "even though I offered to pay him. Will Manley tell the public why he refused to defend these workers and why he has become so suddenly in love with them?" he challenged. Manley, as has been already noted, held a retainer from the West Indies Sugar Company, so he was not free to accept an invitation to defend the workers. He seemed to have ignored Bustamante's accusation, thereby avoiding a public brawl.

Alexander Bustamante and striking workers, June 1, 1938
(© Bettmann/CORBIS)

Bustamante never abandoned the charge, and in 1947 Manley sent a letter to the *Gleaner* denying it and defending himself. Bustamante, he wrote, "now says that it was in 1938 that he asked me to defend the Frome prisoners. That is another lie. The first time I spoke to Bustamante in the year 1938 was towards the end of May when I saw him with a view to securing his release from arrest. The Frome matter took place months [weeks] before that and was at that time entirely at an end."

Manley was not usually given to hurling wild accusations at his cousin and political foe. He was too reserved for such idle utterances and too circumspect to contemplate, much less engage in besmirching the character of those with whom he fought political battles. His weapon of first resort was the use of the language he commanded so well to belittle and demolish his target. "But does Bustamante seriously think that anybody believes what he says[?]" Manley asked as he denied Bustamante's charge. "This lying is a current disease and very infectious," he asserted. "Alexander [Bustamante] should be put in moral quarantine. It is foot and mouth disease. Put your foot in it, use your mouth to lie to get it out."[101]

Bustamante also alleged that Manley had left him to suffer in jail for five days before visiting him, finally doing so only after the workers rejected Manley's recommendation to return to work. "We will leave it to the public to decide who is the unworthy character, Manley or me," Bustamante declared. Bustamante, to be sure, was being ably defended by King's Counsel J. A. G. Smith and Ross Livingston, his solicitor, after his arrest. Manley was playing the larger role of mediator, for which the Commission of Enquiry had applauded him. Six years earlier, as described in these pages, Bustamante had complimented Manley for his role in effecting his release.[102]

The rebellion of May and June 1938 inaugurated modern Jamaica. It set in motion a series of developments that transformed the island's political trajectory. The Crown responded to that rebellion by appointing a Royal Commission that made important recommendations for the island's future course. Implemented in 1944, Jamaica's new constitution was one of the direct consequences of the workers' challenge to the status quo. But for many of Freedom's Children, the illusory expectation of a societal nirvana remained largely unmet. "The 1938 riots gave way to new thinking," observed Donald Byfield, who was a young man at the time, "but as far as practice is concerned, it was slow to become what the riot really should have done to Jamaica."[103]

Still, the labor rebellion had another significant consequence. The workers of Jamaica undertook their journey of self-discovery in May 1938 as individuals who defined themselves by their particular jobs and workplaces. As the strikes spread, and as they joined other workers in the epidemic of protests, experiencing the official threats, arrests, injuries, loss of lives, victories, and defeats, they were becoming a people with an identity larger than their individual selves and workplaces. They were beginning to form, in fits and starts, a *working class*.

THREE

Race and the Colonial Imagination

"The situation," the letter to Malcolm MacDonald, the secretary of state read, "is further complicated by the fact that an issue between Capital and Labour, or property owners and Labour, takes on added gusto according to colour."[1] The writer, presumably Robert Kirkwood, an Englishman and the new managing director of the West Indies Sugar Company, was discussing the 1938 labor rebellion and its aftermath in the island. Discontented workers had challenged their oppression, displaying their agency and asserting their right to social justice. Overwhelmingly, if not totally, of African descent, they confronted the mostly white barons of capital, contesting their power. The rebellion was, in part, a class conflict. But in another and equally significant sense, it represented a racial confrontation. Black workers were carrying on their shoulders the weight of a racialized oppression and centuries of European denigration of African peoples. The rebellion was a cathartic experience; an act of exorcism and a discovery of the possibilities of self. History had been their enemy; their future was now theirs to make.

Burdened by slavery and its legacy, black Jamaicans remained the people of unmet promise, sleeping giants awaiting their moment of arousal to claim their place at the center of their homeland. Not only had their ancestors been reduced to the rank of human property, but the perpetrators of their oppression had developed an elaborate intellectual justification for white supremacy. This influential body of racist literature helped to shape colonial policy during slavery and in its aftermath. Europeans and Americans, too, were fed a steady diet of racially pejorative views about Africans and peoples of African descent. Not surprisingly, these racially inspired conclusions, exercises in ethnocentrism, cultural misunderstandings, and prejudices had an enduring and pernicious impact on the general public.

British colonial officials were not immune to being influenced by the prevailing racial *weltanschauung*. But by the first decades of the twentieth century, they had begun to sanitize their official language of racist phraseology as well as their policy formulations and assumptions that were rooted in notions of white supremacy. They were not entirely successful, to be sure. The governors who were sent to Jamaica in the twentieth century did not usually make racially insensitive comments in public. Their private but official comments, however, betrayed racist conclusions about black Jamaicans, frequently conflating class and race in their pejorative references to the colonial subjects. England had not codified racial segregation as had the United States of America. But a color bar existed and was replicated with varying degrees of rigor in the colonies. Jamaica was no exception, as a white phenotype signified privilege, social prestige, and superior human worth. The mayor of Kingston, Dr. Oswald Anderson, observed in 1938 that "race hatred is being fostered and conditions here tend to develop this." Supporting his claim, the mayor wrote that "there is a clique formed by Government officials who are sent there, and whose one desire is to do what they feel, and in so many cases little regard is given to the coloured people, and the only reason that is evident is colour. This clique and their families receive every protection that the clique can give, and in short they are likened to kings—as they can do no wrong. This clique is enlarged by certain types of people in the island and they also can do no wrong."[2]

This kind of attitude and behavior bred resentment among black Jamaicans. They helped to fuel the rebellion and some hostility to whites in general. But the society functioned well enough without the kind of racially inspired daily indignities that had come to characterize the lives of African Americans, particularly those in the southern United States. Nonetheless, black Jamaicans were trapped at the bottom of their homeland's social and economic order.

Marcus Garvey had admonished Jamaicans to reclaim and proudly affirm their human worth and dignity. The celebrated writer, playwright, broadcaster, and feminist Una Marson (1905–60) also drew attention to the absence of race consciousness among many Jamaicans of African descent. She bemoaned the fact that many distanced themselves from any identification with their African past. Writing in 1937, this eminent Jamaican observed that "educated Jamaicans spend their whole lives thinking they are not coloured, and it is an insult to call them 'Negro' because one or two generations back they had some white ancestor of the male sex. Now we can never be free from inhibitions, complexes, indecision and lack of confidence until we accept ourselves for what we are. We may boast of the white blood in us but to the white people it is an affront. While we worship at the shrine of colour the intelligent whites despise us for lack of loyalty to our own."[3]

Una Marson understood that this rejection of their black selfhood was not unique to Jamaicans. But she maintained that "it reached its zenith" in the island. "Jamaicans have told me," Marson wrote, that "I regret the coloured blood in me" or "I regret to be called a Negro." She believed that progress in the island depended on the people's acceptance of their racial identity. As she put it:

> If by some miracle all the people in Jamaica including those with one drop of coloured blood could be made to realize that they are a racial entity and all their first loyalties lie within the race, then in the next twenty years Jamaica would make more progress than she has done in the past hundred years. If all the energies we spend in discussions and contemplations of "raising our colour" and turning up our nose at black people, were spent in a united effort to pull Jamaica out of her social and economic rut, we would witness the birth of a new Jamaica.[4]

Marson believed that a profound change in the black Jamaican people's psychology and perception of themselves was a prerequisite for the social and economic transformation of the society. As Garvey had done before her, she noted the deleterious effect of a European-derived racial ideology on them. Marson remained optimistic, however, that the subordinate worldwide condition of the peoples of African descent would change. She maintained that "it is a truism that the Negro has been so long placed with his back to the wall that he has not had much chance for the development of the finer things of life. It is also true that he has hitherto been solely occupied in providing wealth, not for himself, but for his masters, by the sweat of his brow. But no race can remain in the same condition through the ages. There must be growth, change, and decay."[5]

This was a perspicacious observation. But as discussed in chapter 1, during the middle and late 1930s, some Jamaicans had begun to challenge an oppressive status quo through sporadic strikes, by forming a plethora of reform organizations, and by becoming receptive to the black-consciousness ideas promoted by the Universal Negro Improvement Association. There were signs that black Jamaicans were beginning to reject the leadership of white politicians. George Seymour Seymour, the white member of the Legislative Council for the parish of St. Andrew, recalled that when he campaigned in Jones Pen, Whitfield Pen, Spanish Town Road, and elsewhere in the election of 1935, the people told him that "we don't want a white man to represent us, we want our own colour." Three years later, he observed that "the colour question is becoming more acute every day," a fact that persuaded him not to seek reelection to the council.[6]

Not only was Jamaica infected by a racist virus, but intense prejudices based upon economic status and class position existed as well. There was, to be sure, a marked intersection of class, status, and race in the island, with wealthy and professional people of European descent ranked at the top of the social and racial hierarchies. But the peoples of African descent who enjoyed financial and professional success could also harbor prejudices against those mired at the bottom of the society that were as crass as those manifested by the Europeans. Those who were "coloured," as defined by the 1943 census, were wont to practice a form of color or shade prejudice that diminished their fellow Jamaicans of a darker hue. These people lived throughout the island, but a disproportionate number resided in the suburban areas of the parish of St. Andrew.

Mindful of his constituency of black working people, Alexander Bustamante spoke the language of racial and class uplift. He was aggressive in his assault on the demons of racial and class prejudices. Gladys Longbridge, who stressed that "the white people were taking advantage of black people," recalled that "Busta fought for everything. He didn't distinguish between black, Chinese, or anything. . . . Those people who lived in St. Andrew felt that they were better off. But Busta brought them to their senses and let everybody know they are all the same people under God. You see, he did not agree with any class or race situation."[7]

Mrs. Euphey Josephs, who was between twenty and twenty-one years old in 1938, remembered Bustamante's speeches on the cancerous issues of race and class in the island. According to her, he told his audiences that he wanted them to "take pride in themselves, realize that they are somebody, and stop calling St. Andrew people Missus and Massa. He was telling them that he wanted them to have pride in themselves so that they could bring up their children, that a black girl could go in King Street and work, a Chinese girl could be there, an Indian could be there. Because in those days it was only white faces." "The people up in St. Andrew," Euphey Josephs said, "were oppressing the poor people, because you see when Busta began to talk like that, people started to get wise."[8]

The rebellion had a cathartic effect on those people who were quietly bearing their class and racially inspired grievances. They had got "wise," as Euphey Josephs put it, and some acted on their impulses as soon as the rebellion gathered steam on May 23, 1938. Carmelita James witnessed one telling example of the challenge to the racial and class etiquettes that had hitherto determined the seating arrangements on the public tramcars. She related that on "the tram in those days, the white people, you'd call them, or the dress people sit [on one side], you that wasn't properly dressed or the people taking their baskets couldn't sit that side, you have to go to the back, the rear, of the tram. That morning, the people got between those dress people. All some dirty boys (laughter) got between them and shuffle them up and sit down."[9]

Actions such as these meant that the existing social order was crumbling. They were small motions, but Freedom's Children had started to "shuffle" the entrenched seats of prejudice, placing themselves at the center of the society to which they had just claims. These heady moments of individual and collective physical and psychological liberation in 1938 constituted a second emancipation, with all of its tantalizing promise of fundamental change in the Jamaica they had inherited.

While black Jamaicans were anxious to call a new racial order into being, the white residents were apprehensive about their future in the island. Many of them had become psychologically unhinged by the social ferment of the time, attributing the unrest to fundamental defects in the character of the black people. These stereotypical constructs were not new and were the staples of the Europeans' imagination of Africa and African peoples for centuries.[10] The Colonial Office received much unsolicited advice from former and current residents of the island, all seeking to influence and shape future policy based upon the presumed incapacities of African Jamaicans.

Frederick Davies was one such person. He had lived in Jamaica and was extremely troubled by the events of 1938. Davies had no great respect for black Jamaicans, questioning why funds were being used to build "schools and more schools" for their children. He feared, however, that "an uneducated Black Majority" would "flock into Kingston and swell the unemployed and hooligan army, refusing to work on the land." Such an unpalatable situation, Davies surmised, could produce a revolution similar to that which began in Haiti in the 1790s. White people, he alleged, did not "feel secure" in the island because of the turmoil created by Bustamante. The labor leader, he said, "is in the employ of the communists." It was obvious, Davies maintained, that "a rich money lender would not put aside such a lucrative business without having more than the welfare of Negroes to work for." Bustamante "evidently did not appreciate the childlike mentality of the average labourer," having "influenced that low mentality to stir up trouble and cause mob violence." Davies quoted approvingly from a letter he had recently received from Jamaica: "If only someone from Downing Street could spend a week in Jamaica, they would realize how very necessary it is for Bustamante and his colleagues to be silenced forever by the use of Gun Powder and lead. The sooner the 'Bust up' comes the better for all."[11]

These were harsh recommendations indeed, an unthinking mixture of fear, irrationality, and racial intolerance. Living in a fool's paradise, Frederick Davies believed that "the average labourer" in Jamaica "was perfectly content and happy until Bustamante appeared on the scene." His solution to the Bustamante menace was to "send a regiment of troops, put up a good demonstration of Force (especially Aircraft) and deport Bustamante with his Agents." Davies proceeded to inform the Colonial Office how he once attempted to give Bustamante "a good scare" by sending him a sketch of a cross and writing underneath: "Bustamante you have now been warned by the KKK." He imagined that his racist stunt would keep Bustamante "within bounds" by making him think that "at any moment he is likely to be shot."[12]

Davies was not entirely representative of English opinion on Jamaica and Jamaicans. But he was not exceptional in his positions. By 1938 Helen P. Hyatt-Shortt had lived in Morant Bay for thirteen years with her husband. She had served in France during World War I as a nurse and in the Censorship Department of the War Office. In 1926 the couple accepted a job in Jamaica, and "we have now been muddling along which is the only thing it seems possible to do in this island where at every turn one's best efforts are hamstrung by someone's laziness and inefficiency." They had, by 1938, "grasped the negro mentality." Mrs. Hyatt-Shortt saw the "Jamaican Negro as vain, which leads him to try to conceal his ignorance and mistakes by lying. He is a boaster, and credulous especially of the incredible." She continued: "The kindness and generosity of strangers as he considers 'white people' does not command his respect. He thinks it is weakness and trades on it, but he likes to get a living wage regularly paid. If more is given as is happening now, he decides to work only 3 days a week instead of 5. He is a coward and terribly afraid of being hurt, except when full of rum when he reverts to the total savage, and rape and murder become a past time to him."[13]

Mrs. Hyatt-Shortt was repeating the age-old stereotypes that Europeans held of the peoples of African descent. Residing for thirteen years in Jamaica had not dispelled or even tempered them. She was troubled by the fact that the Jamaican "does not want to live like a European[,] as a matter of fact he would rather be Black than white." In spite of this unfortunate shortcoming, "he is quite happy but he loves to listen to anyone who will get up and talk, and is of course an easy prey to the political agitator." Mrs. Hyatt-Shortt saw a dismal future for whites in the island, with its conflict between capital and labor and the prevailing "race hatred." She feared the prospect of the equality of blacks and whites. "Is the negro with his hastily-acquired top-dressing of civilization [and] half-concealed mass of primitive instincts, whose superstition, uncontrolled sex indulgencies and rage, lying and thieving propensities, there is scarcely any check—to be put in line with the white man now that he has realized his power?" was her anxious question.[14]

The prospect that Jamaica might become self-governing worried Josiah Oldfield of London, who was also a member of the Jamaican Bar. Echoing the racist nonsense about African peoples being perpetual children, he wrote a letter to the secretary of state for the colonies opposing the introduction of universal adult suffrage in the island. Oldfield identified "an aristocracy in Jamaica independent of money or of colour," placing what he called the "Black Nigger" at the bottom of the socioracial hierarchy. The "Black Nigger" was closer to being an "animal," unlike a more "cultured" and presumably more Europeanized person of African descent. As he warned:

> Now if there is one thing which would tend to prevent progress upwards would be to "lump" everybody on one level, and to give the black negroes equality with the white or half caste, or cultured negro types. They are extremely sensitive of the progress they have made, and they all aim to become whiter, not only in skin, but in habit and thoughts. This delicate vibrational movement which is going on steadily throughout the Island would be greatly interfered with and checked if the animal type of negro is able to consider himself, and is to be considered, from a political point of view, as an equal with the white negro type, which is the result of much breeding and much cultured influence.[15]

Oldfield's foray into the realms of racial sociology and developmental psychology led him to conclude that "the lower types of the negro element are not even up to the evolutionary standard of a little white girl at school." To him, "they are charming, they are kindly, but they are children and are incapable of becoming, in one short lifetime, intelligent enough to utilize the Ballot." But he believed that this dismal situation could be improved through a program of miscegenation sponsored by the government. "If, perchance, your predecessor had been able to send to Jamaica 5,000 fine, intelligent, white men, and used them to breed, and had repeated the process every ten years," Oldfield wrote, "then the probability is that in 100 years time you might get a population fully capable of universal franchise."[16]

Oldfield demonstrated a lingering affection for his racist views. Writing to Norman Manley in 1947, he expressed his opposition "to the giving of Universal Suffrage [to Jamaicans] upon the grounds that a considerable portion of the peoples of Jamaica are only Politically and Socially children in their Mental experience." He was convinced that his position was valid because the Jamaicans "have shown that they are carried away first by Mr. Bustamante and secondly by yourself." Manley took this insult with equanimity, using his powerful intellect to turn the tables on the imperious and self-righteous Englishman. "I am quite unconvinced by the Jamaican experience that there is anything wrong with universal suffrage," Manley wrote. He then continued:

> It is true that the electorate are easily influenced and tend to be carried away by personalities but I can never get out of my mind the fact that it is the comparatively educated personality that abuses the simplicity of the electorate. The fault is not in the mass but at the top. . . . [I]t seems to me that the electorate as such is always manipulated by the leadership. . . . I see no basic difference between a successful conspiracy to befuddle the whole mass mind on what is supposed to be an ideological issue and a similar effort based on a personality stunt.

Manley did not use the language of race to assault Oldfield's assertion of superiority; his invocation of the moral failings of the power elite sufficed.[17]

While Mrs. Hyatt-Shortt regretted the fact that the black people preferred to remain black, Oldfield was offering a miscegenation program to rescue them from their color. Seen through Hyatt-Shortt and Oldfield's optic, blackness was a badge of dishonor, a mark of human inferiority. This narrative had not changed since the sixteenth century, when Englishmen first encountered black Africans. The racism articulated and manifested by English peoples in the twentieth century had a long and ignoble tradition.

Most of the English had their image of Jamaicans, and of West Indians in general, shaped by what they read in the popular press. Visitors to the islands and long-term residents as well delighted in describing their experiences in the newspapers, frequently embellishing them with delicious tidbits about the people's culture. These amateur anthropologists conflated race and culture, making gross generalizations about the residents' lifestyles. They seldom recognized differences in class, occupations, educational backgrounds, and so on. The exotic became the norm, and racial essentialism was the unstated assumption. These unscripted accounts betray a high degree of racial condescension, as they depict the experiences of a mostly economically comfortable white expatriate group convinced of its innate superiority. The relationships of white women and their domestic servants, for example, demonstrated the idyllic quality of the lives of privileged whites in the island and the images of black Jamaicans that they constructed and frequently propagated.

Mrs. Aspinall of London had spent several months in Jamaica in the 1930s with her husband, a physician. In reporting on her experiences in the *Western Morning News* of Plymouth, she painted a picture of tropical bliss, stressing that "days to the English mind are strangely planned in the sunshine island of Jamaica. By 6 A.M. the household has stirred to life. The black arm of a native servant appears through the door of Madame's room, and sets the glass of orange juice that displaces the early morning cup of tea of England, just within."[18]

Mrs. Aspinall enjoyed the service. "We became used to the black arm that served our early morning needs so noiselessly," she gushed. After awakening at 6:00 A.M. and having a cup of coffee, Mrs. Aspinall said it was then "time to do the ordering and send the native servants about their daily chores." Whites lived a life of endless leisure in the carefree Jamaican environment: "Ten o'clock brings breakfast, and it is usual to invite friends in for the meal. In an hour the sun becomes unbearable. Songsters [birds] become silent, as do the animals. The whole country takes a siesta until three, even the household pets. Then it is time to take up the social round again. The white community go a-visiting, and it is not at all unusual for friends to arrive for breakfast, stay for 3 o'clock tea and 7 o'clock dinner, and make their farewells in the early morning."[19]

Mrs. Aspinall was creating a portrait of a life that not even the most privileged English person must have enjoyed. But it was also a picture of economically challenged Jamaicans contented with their condition and even enjoying their lot. In an island with limited opportunities for the peoples of African descent, dissemblance in the cause of employment had been elevated to a principle. It was a charade that Mrs. Aspinall missed entirely. She found the butleresses "amusing" because "as soon as a new white woman makes her appearances on the island, she is besieged by obeisant native girls seeking to become butleresses. Deft and nimble these girls are excellent as pantry, kitchen, or parlour-maids, and most make good cooks."[20]

These women, Mrs. Aspinall added, enjoyed the difficult task of fetching water and carrying it on their heads in pails. Not having done it herself, she knew little of the weight of the water or the challenge of balancing the pails while going up and down hills on the dirt paths. "Most girls enjoy this job," observed Mrs. Aspinall. "They run off skipping and jumping to the water catcher. On the way they pause to exchange chaff with their friends. Tins filled, they return to delude their mistresses into the belief that they have not dallied, but are just weary from carrying so heavy a load."[21]

These happy workers imitated the dress and the behavior of white women, observed Mrs. Aspinall. "They look so incongruous and pathetic in spike heels and long white frocks," she said. "Accustomed to go barefoot, the women walk in an ugly stilted way in high heels," she continued in her caricature of Jamaican women. "Ordinarily they walk with perfect poise." She reported that "to these dark-skinned women, the white man is a god: the white woman someone of far less account. . . . [S]ervants flee to do their master's bidding, and ogle them in the most amusing fashion." Mrs. Aspinall was struck by the respect and civility accorded whites. "Women bow when white people pass; greet you as 'master' or 'mistress,'" she said, adding: "When newcomers arrive, black girls will do a special curtsy for them."[22]

Mrs. Aspinall's observations must be placed in the context of her experiences in a rural area of the island. The civility and obsequiousness that she described, albeit embroidered, would not have been evident in Kingston, and certainly not among the growing black middle class. But the English were fed a steady diet of questionable information about the Jamaican people. Speaking of the dress of Jamaican women, Mary Luke, who served as the secretary to Bishop E. W. Sara, the assistant Anglican bishop of Jamaica, in 1939 observed: "One sees some strange sights. The native women wear filthy clothes, usually are in rags. Frequently they go barefoot, a handkerchief shielding their heads from the sun. . . . They sleep in dirty little hovels, whole families together, and live outdoors in the daytime." Miss Luke reported that the women work six days per week, while the men remained idle.[23] When Bishop Sara read his secretary's comments, he hastily contacted the *Western Morning News* of Plymouth disassociating himself from her comments and pointing out that "the word 'native' is used with no effort to explain it. I presume that what is really meant is 'peasant.' There are 'native Jamaicans' of whom I am proud to think of as friends and who are proud of their country. They do important work in all the professions, are cultured and their kindly hospitality is a strange contrast to that which one so often meets with in this country [England]."[24]

Bishop Sara rejected the statement that Jamaican men "idle all the week." He stressed that Jamaican women have "a remarkable flair for dress which makes the Englishwoman look dowdy. The women who are able to do so dress beautifully and the peasant has always amazed me with her ability to dress well, often on an almost nonexistent income."[25] The bishop provided a necessary corrective to his secretary's remarks, but the damage had already been done. He resigned his position a few weeks later, probably because of the embarrassment Miss Luke's comment caused him in the Jamaica diocese.[26]

Englishmen had no qualms about making observations about the psychology of the Jamaican people with great certitude. This was hardly peculiar to them, but in the colonial context, the pejorative and essentialist nonsense that permeated these observations had the potential to help shape public policy. Philip Putnam, who spent eighteen months in Jamaica, concluded that "the natives have a trait in them which makes them highly excitable, that on many occasions amounts very nearly to hysteria."[27] This proclivity for excitability by the Jamaicans was an oft-repeated mantra. G. B. Pease, who had lived in Jamaica for a decade, believed that "the negro's mind is not like our mind, it doesn't function in the same way." The "negro" had "an idea that in some way he is being exploited," Pease complained to the secretary of state. "As an example of this I can tell you that sometime back when the trouble was brewing a friend of mine called some of the more intelligent labourers together and tried to explain that the company was doing a lot of things for their good, such as good houses, churches, schools, looking after their wives etc. and the answer he got was 'But, Busha, that no better than slavery!' Can you follow the curious reasoning?"[28] Continuing, Pease emphasized that "a Negro cannot be hurried mentally, he must be able to think things out slowly. If he is rushed, he immediately comes to the conclusion that he is being 'had' somehow." Pease was convinced, however, that the "ordinary Negro and coloured man is not a rioting, evilly disposed person." He "is naturally law abiding and loyal, but the majority are grossly ignorant with the minds of children and in consequence are easily influenced and like children, when anything is happening, they like to be in it. The chance of riding on a train for nothing or raiding a China man's shop is not to be missed, not because they are really rioters but simply for the fun of it."29

The notion that Jamaicans were "childlike" could be held even by those who professed to respect them and to promote their interests. The Reverend F. Cowell Lloyd was a Baptist minister who had served in the island for many years. He was much beloved and a strong advocate for the island's self-government. When he returned to London for a visit in late 1938, Cowell Lloyd wrote an article about Jamaica for a local religious publication. He informed his English readers that "the average Jamaican is childlike, affectionate, religious, and intensely loyal to the Crown." The congregation of the East Queen Street Baptist Church where Cowell Lloyd pastored may have been surprised by his stereotyping them, and other Jamaicans, as "childlike."30

David Yeo, who visited Jamaica in 1938, wrote an article in the *Daily Despatch* of Manchester. The "Jamaican negro is extremely loyal," he reported. "He thinks of himself not as a 'coloured' person, not as a member of a separate race, but as a free-born British subject." The "atmosphere" in Jamaica was "free, happy-go-lucky," as epitomized by "a gang of Jamaican negresses at work loading a banana boat. Nearly always they are singing or laughing or joking among themselves." Yeo observed that as "they moved forward in a long line each negress with a huge bunch of bananas on her head, they sing in time to their movements. One of their favorite songs is the refrain, 'I sent a letter to my lover,' but hymns are overwhelmingly popular."31

Yeo may not have realized the weight of a bunch of bananas, but he was not insensitive to the low wages the carriers received. "The fact that such a loyal, easy-going and happy-natured individual as the Jamaican negro was forced to strike," he wrote, "proves that reforms are needed." The Jamaican worker, Yeo said, was not "a dangerous potential Bolshevik," as some commentators had alleged. He was "in some ways . . . childishly simple. He loves to possess a little authority, to be in a position to lord it over his fellows." The Jamaican "loves gaiety," his "working clothes are a miracle of patchwork," and he is not "self conscious about it." But, the writer said, "see him in his Sunday best! No peacock ever hatched could give him points in vanity." The *Gleaner* published Yeo's article in its entirety without comment. Nor did it elicit any notice in the letters to the editor section of the newspaper.32

Ernest Platt was a resident of Mandeville and had evidently lived in the island for sometime. In May 1942 he wrote to Arthur Creech Jones, a member of the British Parliament, detailing his opinion of the Jamaican people.

Platt was, he said, concerned about crime in the island and "the manners of the average Kingston nigger." He wanted to assure Creech Jones that he had "no prejudice against the coloured folk [?] in fact I am only too delighted to shake hands with and have them at my table." Platt admitted that he had "come in contact a good deal with the coloured folk here but they are awful liars and bad ones ay [at] that but they have a sense of humour which makes you forgive many of their faults." When he "heard of fools bleating about the equality of white and black," Platt complained, "it makes one wonder [if] they have ever come in contact with [the] Kingston Nigger [since] he would or she who had been assaulted by these gentry would I fancy speedily change his or hers [sic] opinion."[33]

Ernest Platt feared that Jamaica might be "turned into a second Hayti." This catastrophe could be avoided, however. If the island received self-government, it should be "controlled so that they could do no mischief." He maintained that

> sentimentality for the poor does not enter into the argument[.] [O]ne thing is quite clear[:] the Island would not be fit for a White man to live in [and] even if you divide up the big properties you have no guarantee that the peasant owners would produce anything unless heavily subsidised, these people as a whole hate work. . . . I do know something about these people but their real thoughts is [sic] another matter[.] [T]he gulf between the black and white remains and will always be so[.] Whether it is the memories of the old slave days I cannot say.[34]

Platt's diatribe ignored the incessant demands by unemployed Jamaicans for work and the pleas by the would-be cultivators for land. Despite his disavowal of any racist sentiments, Platt's observations invited comparisons with the "lazy nigger" stereotype that informed the writings of nineteenth-century British personages and racists such as Anthony Trollope and James Anthony Froude.[35] A marked sense of amused smugness, titillating voyeurism, and cultural superiority suffuse the writings of Englishmen and -women about the Jamaican people over time. But these writings invariably revealed more about the prejudices of the colonial masters and their perceptions of the people they governed than they illuminated the texture of the lives of Jamaicans. Based significantly upon racist assumptions and flawed understandings of the culture of the people, these observers produced a body of writings and newspaper interviews that reflected the self-congratulatory fantasies of the colonial elite. By depicting the colonized in negative ways, these elites were absolving themselves of any responsibility for their mistreatment of them. The writers seemed not to understand the systemic factors that accounted for the dire economic state of the people that they denigrated with such relish.

The mayor of Kingston, Dr. Oswald E. Anderson, became increasingly exercised as he read an advertisement in the *British Medical Journal* for a health officer in Jamaica. The advertisement listed the usual academic qualifications for the job but stipulated that the successful applicant must be of European parentage. Anderson brought the advertisement to the attention of the *Daily Gleaner*, and its content was discussed at a meeting of the Kingston and St. Andrew Corporation on June 30, 1938. Several members of the corporation's council angrily condemned the racism implied by the advertisement and approved a resolution "to vary the terms set so that Jamaicans who are eligible may be included."[36]

In condemning the advertisement, the mayor told his colleagues that "when such things occurred they could not pass them over in silence. An advertisement of that kind was a distinct insult to the people of this country." He called it "race discrimination of the worst type," predicting that "it is bound to produce race hatred." Mayor Anderson said he had told various government officials and the Chamber of Commerce that "racial feeling existed and was a danger and if that feeling was kept alive in the community it was going to mean 'bloodshed,' it was going to mean conflagration and ruin." He wanted the official responsible for placing the advertisement to know that he "is disloyal to the person of His Majesty the King and he should be withdrawn from the colony immediately. . . . [H]e is reducing the loyalty of a most loyal people."[37]

Mayor Anderson rejected the claim of the director of medical services in Jamaica that he was not responsible for the advertisement. In fact, Jamaican officials maintained that it was conceived and written in England. The acting governor assured Anderson on July 4 that the advertisement followed a formula kept in the Colonial Office. Although this was not explained in the news report of the meeting, the existence of a formula presumably meant that positions such as the one advertised had to be filled by both whites and blacks to ensure racial balance. The secretary of state, however, would later admit in the House of Commons that the governor "in reporting the vacancy stated that there was no suitably qualified officer available in the colony. It was assumed therefore that no useful purpose would be served by inviting applications from Jamaicans." This was not a convincing explanation for this blatant act of racism. After all, the advertisement had excluded applications from all races or ethnicities except Europeans.[38]

Dissatisfied with the explanation he received from the local authorities and outraged by the advertisement, Dr. Anderson hastily dispatched a cable and a letter to Dr. Harold Moody, a Jamaican and the head of the League of Coloured Peoples, in London. He asked Dr. Moody to take up the matter with the Colonial Office and urge it to investigate the condition of the Jamaican people. The mayor said that the Royal Commission that was expected to visit Jamaica "can never tell the story." Dr. Anderson stressed that the situation in Jamaica was "deplorable." He claimed that some officials "assume oligarchic role[s]. Many Government Departments, especially the Medical [are] vile; injecting colour discrimination. Race hatred [is] being fostered." Dr. Moody immediately took up the complaint with the Colonial Office, sending a cable to Dr. Anderson that read: "Send details. Colonial Office to investigate."[39]

Dr. Anderson opened a hornet's nest when he brought the content of the advertisement to the public's attention. Long reluctant to confront the specter of racism in the island, many Jamaicans were embarrassed by the revelation. Racial difference had been at the core of Jamaican life, and white was the dominant color of political power and the measure of social prestige and human worth. Those who presided over the colony's affairs preferred not to recognize the salience of race in the colony, fearing that any public comment on its power and ubiquity might create social unrest and shatter the fragile racial harmony. As Mayor Anderson noted, "the serious state of affairs which began in Kingston on May 23rd was not merely a strike against very poor wages which were being paid; but it was largely based upon a feeling of disgust from a racial standpoint and was noticeable on that day when certain [white] people could not be seen on the highways of Kingston or their lives would be in danger." The mayor observed that "the people have just awakened, and in other words the worm has turned."[40]

The mayor's revelation terrified those black and white elites for whom the public discussion of race was anathema. Entering the developing controversy, the *Daily Gleaner* dismissed the salience of racial prejudice in the island, interpreting Jamaica's problems entirely in economic terms. It agreed "that the situation in Jamaica is deplorable, due to the incidence of unemployment being abnormally high, and other unfavourable conditions—the outcome of inattention over a number of years to the economic, industrial and social well being of the greater portion of the population: we mean Jamaicans."[41]

The *Gleaner*'s editorial did not recognize the racially lubricated systemic conditions that explained the inequities in the society. In fact, it rejected Anderson's charge of racial discrimination in the halls of government. "We are afraid that the charge cannot be sustained," the editorial asserted, "and as for colour discrimination the only evidence that can be adduced to support the assertion is an obnoxious condition included in an advertisement published by the Crown Agents in a London journal."[42]

The editorial was the voice of privileged whites and others unable to recognize or accept the centrality of racial difference in the island's DNA. It was common knowledge that phenotypical or shade prejudice existed as well. Amy Bailey, a prominent social worker, drew attention to the discrimination that "is practiced against the black man or woman, boy or girl, as far as employment in the stores . . . is concerned." Youths of "intelligence and ambition," she said, "were debarred from getting decent jobs simply on account of the pigment of their skin."[43] Una Marson also maintained that "it is a reproach to us that in reality [in] all shops and offices—government service excepted—only lightskinned people are seen. It is a reproach to us that advertisements are continually appearing for workers (fair), (very fair), (or white), in brackets in such advertisements."[44]

Recalling the racial climate of the 1930s, Lucius Hall, a port worker, stressed that in order to join the civil service "you have to be somebody of a white-skin face. . . . If you go to a store in King Street, the only person, only place you see a black man is the man a push up the store window. You go in the bank, is pure red people. Don't care how him [a black man] qualify, as long as somebody with a fair skin [was available] you find him have to migrate before he could make himself into somebody."[45]

Donald Byfield reported that when a person who was phenotypically black gained employment, that person faced a glass ceiling. He explained that "if you go to the quasi government department, however good or efficient that black fellow was, the brown man or the Englishman had to be superintendent. And right through the whole employment service the brown girl or guy sometimes below qualification was always there. And if the black man happen to be there he was never able to reach the head of department, post office, hospital, public works, railway, banks. Everywhere that was the position."[46]

Black women, in particular, faced the scourge of discrimination based upon sex, race, and skin color. Their sex largely accounted for their general confinement to domestic service. Although these jobs carried little social prestige, some employers preferred to have brown or light-skinned women in their employ. "A girl or young woman, coloured (fair) to assist with children, tidy house and mend clothes," read one help-wanted advertisement in the *Jamaica Standard*.[47] The hiring of a black-skinned woman in a job that served the public was an extraordinary event. Spencer B. Soulette recalled that "the first [black] girl that got to work in the Bank of Nova Scotia, they put her in a chair and everybody came and saw her."[48]

Euphey Josephs also painted an ugly picture of the racial discrimination that black Jamaicans were experiencing in 1938. As a resident of Kingston, she remembered that "if a girl even had education, a black girl, and she left school she couldn't get a job in King Street bank or nowhere there. She had to go down in Luke Lane and work with the Syrians who had their stores there. And yet still, a girl from St. Elizabeth that had a white face, and didn't have no education [could get a job] because when the tourist come off the boat and come up Victoria pier, they must see white faces in the stores."[49]

Some employers attempted to absolve themselves of any responsibility for practicing discrimination based upon race and skin color. One employer, whose clerks were all "fair" skinned, told Amy Bailey that they "would not associate with dark girls." Another one said that "the customers, especially the black ones, would object to buying from black clerks."[50] The latter comment was probably self-serving. On the other hand, if it were accurate, it demonstrated the psychological damage that a pernicious racial ideology and its execution brought in their wake.

Since Jamaicans were uncomfortable discussing such unpleasant truths in public, it was not surprising that some members of the Kingston and St. Andrew Corporation's council sought to silence and humiliate their mayor. It was a racially mixed body, a fact that added to the sensitivity of the matter at hand. When the council met for its regular session on July 11, the white custos of St. Andrew, S. R. Cargill, led the charge against the mayor. He moved a motion to censure him for the nature of his statements on the racial question in the island and for his involvement in a matter that was beyond "the scope of the Corporation Council." The motion was seconded by a brown-skinned member, Ernest Rae.[51]

The motion noted that appointments made by the government were "foreign to the business of the Corporation," except those that "directly affect" it. The mayor's statements, it said, "are grossly improper and tend to prejudice the good will which has always existed between the several members of the community resident in the island of Jamaica; in fact, some of the expressions are likely to create class prejudice and inflame the people of Jamaica against government officials." In keeping with the contrived silence on race in the public discourse, the motion feared that the mayor's remarks would inflame class but not racial animus, although Jamaica's race problem stood at the heart of the controversy. Cargill wanted his colleagues to "record their emphatic protest and disapproval of the mayor's action and to disassociate" themselves from it. The motion requested the mayor "to refrain from uttering statements which are on the borderline of sedition and which are likely to incite the people against law and order and thus bring the Corporation into disrepute and contempt." The custos was asserting that Dr. Anderson's pronouncement on race was probably seditious, a clear indication of the nervousness among the white elite about the fragility of the race-based society.[52]

The councillors did not disappoint him. According to the *Daily Gleaner*, they characterized the mayor's remarks variously as "grossly improper," "indiscreet," "very inflammatory," "harsh," and "immoderate." The deputy mayor, himself a white man, pleaded with Dr. Anderson to "withdraw what you have said and express your regret." Councillor E. R. D. Evans, a black man, condemned the advertisement but felt that the mayor "gave utterance to words that just at this time, especially when they are put in the Press, might prove to be inflammatory." He thought that the mayor "would be in good grace" to admit that "those remarks were not meant to be as strong as they were made out to be." Another black man, Councillor T. Duval, believed the mayor should have adopted "a more moderate attitude, a more diplomatic method." His "method," the councillor predicted, "will create an enormous amount of bad feeling among the people here." The Honorable N. B. Livingston, a white man and the custos of Kingston, called the mayor's conduct "indiscreet."[53]

Dr. Anderson, for the most part, listened to the debate on the motion in irritated silence. He gave no ground to his critics when he responded, emphasizing that "in anything . . . I have done, I have acted as a man and I will act as a man anytime. I will not surrender my manhood. But when it comes to taking a stand for the good of the community, if I cannot do it as a member of the Council, if pussy footism is the characteristic of the views of the Council I belong to, I don't want to belong to it."[54]

The gallery applauded the mayor as he asserted his "manhood," his right to protest against injustice. He said that the sending of the cable to London was his "private business . . . no one can dare to say it is not correct." Dr. Anderson was critical of the advocates of moderation as the methodology of change. "Moderation," he said, "has been in existence here all these years, and as a result of the moderation, we had the tidal wave we had here a few weeks ago." He declined to withdraw any of the allegations about discrimination in the medical department of the island. "I know more about it than anyone around this table," the physician told his colleagues. Making a dramatic announcement as he concluded his remarks, the mayor declared that "if my office as mayor prevents me exercising my rights as a man to act as I feel for the good of the country, you can have the office and have the Council and I am going to resign right now from this Council for I don't think I should waste my time here, as a busy man."[55]

That said, Dr. Anderson handed a note, written in pencil, to the town clerk. It read simply: "Mr. Town Clerk, receive my resignation as a member of the Council and as Mayor. I am gone." He then stormed out of the building with the cheering visitors in the gallery in tow. It was an extraordinary act of defiance, at once principled, dramatic, and theatrical.[56] Having demitted his high office, Dr. Anderson proceeded to his sanatorium, where he was interviewed by the *Daily Gleaner*. He admitted that he listened with "little interest" to Mr. Cargill's speech "because when a matter like colour discrimination is being discussed everybody will know what observations to expect from Mr. Cargill." But the former mayor took the two black councillors more seriously. The two councillors made "my blood boil" as they spoke, Dr. Anderson confessed. He was very upset that the two men

> who on the face of it should have but one interest in such a question and that is to fight as strenuously as is possible for the tearing down of what has been keeping down our community for so long, my blood fairly boiled within me. Those councillors should be the last to say that anything in denunciation of this type of discrimination is too strong. They should welcome it, if not for their sakes, for the sake of their children, and when they got up and advised me to withdraw what I had said, I thought the time had come for me to part company with such colleagues.[57]

Dr. Anderson's harsh criticism of his colleagues was calculated to embarrass them, calling into question the two black men's appalling blindness on the question of racial discrimination in Jamaica. He observed that "here in Jamaica we have been behaving like the ostrich, holding our heads and pretending that there is no discrimination. We have been adopting just the attitude that those whose interests are not identical with our own would have us adopt and any attempt to break away from that will arouse universal opposition. But I am prepared to face that, and if discrimination must not be mentioned, it must be abolished."

Dr. Anderson denounced the "display of supineness" by his black colleagues. He would not subordinate his manhood "and the higher principles that dwell within me so as to please any sect in this country whose interests are not the interests of the masses." Ending the interview, the former mayor pledged to continue "standing up for the rights of my people so long as I have life, and so long as I have health."[58]

The mayor's resignation had profound reverberations throughout the island, particularly in Kingston. His admirers quickly formed a committee to organize support for him and to plan for future action. On Friday, July 15, some 4,000 persons attended a meeting at the Kingston Race Course to pass two resolutions of support for the ex-mayor. The speakers included such prominent persons as Alexander Bustamante, Kenneth Hill, and Councillor E. E. McLaughlin, the only member who voted against the censure motion. The first resolution expressed its "complete agreement with and its implicit confidence in Dr. O. E. Anderson." It requested that Dr. Anderson allow himself to be nominated to contest the by-election necessitated by his resignation. The second resolution condemned the councillors who voted to censure Dr. Anderson or had declined to vote. It emphasized the existence of racial discrimination in the island, "despite the views of those who are dishonest in not admitting the truth." Upon the completion of the meeting, the crowd marched to Dr. Anderson's home to present him with the resolutions that had expressed confidence in him. "It was a scene unprecedented in the history of the Corporate Area," the *Gleaner* noted. "Torchbearers held high a dozen or more improvised flames," it reported. Bustamante presented the resolutions to Dr. Anderson when he appeared to greet the crowd. The *Gleaner* described him as being "deeply moved by the unexpected demonstration of public confidence."[59]

The *Daily Gleaner* remained unimpressed by the meeting's censure of the councillors and its approval of the resolution charging that "colour discrimination" existed in the island. The newspaper said that the inclusion of such language in the resolution "was intended to appeal to the passions rather than to reason." It looked askance at those persons who "seek to make capital out of the bogey of colour discrimination in services maintained by the Colony."[60]

Black Jamaicans, in general, did not share the *Gleaner*'s sentiments. When the Kingston Citizens Association held its annual meeting on July 12, members expressed great admiration for Dr. Anderson and endorsed his position on racial discrimination in the island. Miss Amy Bailey observed that racial discrimination in Jamaica was "as old as the hills." C. G. Walker said it was "rife." Dr. W.(?) Duhaney characterized the ex-mayor's comments as "the truth." The *Gleaner* was deluged by so many letters on the matter that it was forced to declare a moratorium on publishing them. Some letter writers named government departments where black faces were absent. "Would you be so good as to tell us young Jamaicans why is it that until now no dark skin Jamaican has ever been attached to the staff of the Colonial Secretary's office?" inquired Rupert Meikle in a letter to the *Gleaner*. Others noted the existence of a color bar in the island. The Jamaica Progressive League of New York congratulated Dr. Anderson on his "self-respecting action." It condemned "councillors and editors" for denouncing "a man for truly describing existing conditions even though the description be painfully exact." Edgar Bradshaw characterized Dr. Anderson as "a man of sterling worth" and "a man with a golden heart." O. Alphonsous Malcolm, the principal of the Tweedside Elementary School, praised Dr. Anderson as "an able man, as conscientious as he is capable, as fearless as he is zealous."[61]

Dr. Anderson, to be sure, had his critics. They were led by the editorial columns of the *Daily Gleaner*. Responding to Rupert Meikle's question about the absence of black faces on the staff of the colonial secretary, the newspaper said that with the exception of the acting colonial secretary, "the staff of the department consists of Jamaicans," and that a "couple of individuals who are distinctly coloured are attached to that staff." This was an artful response from the newspaper, since it skillfully avoided discussing the hue of the employees—an important issue in an island where shade prejudice existed alongside racial discrimination. White remained at the top of the color or shade hierarchy, with black at the bottom and a bewildering variety of shades in between. The *Gleaner* deliberately avoided any discussion of the existence of racial prejudice in the island as a whole, confining its observations to the departments of government. In an editorial that appeared on July 16, the newspaper said it remained "unrepentant" in its claim that racial discrimination did not exist in the public service. Continuing, the editorial claimed that "it is ill conceived, and on the whole vicious, that the colour question should become an issue in the colony. It is ability, not colour that counts. . . . [W]hen Jamaicans of colour seek to make capital out of what is calculated to inflame the public mind, they are playing with fire."[62]

The *Gleaner* appeared to be suggesting that "Jamaicans of colour" had no basis for alleging that racial discrimination existed in the island. Someone using the pseudonym "Rate Payer" went beyond the *Gleaner*'s racial blindness by charging Dr. Anderson with sowing "the seed of race hatred in this country." Dr. Anderson, the writer said, "evidently thinks the creation of race prejudice is more important than the administration of the Municipality." This was ludicrous; Dr. Anderson wanted to eradicate racism, not create it, even if that were within his power. Another contributor to the *Gleaner* asked rhetorically: "[W]hy stir up colour prejudice?" This writer, probably a white person, continued: "Isn't it realized . . . that the black man and woman as a rule are better treated, better liked and gets a squarer deal from the wholly white than the coloured employer?" "Anti-Humbug," the pseudonym for another letter writer, expressed similar sentiments. "It is an indisputable fact," this contributor wrote, "that the ordinary Jamaican labourer infinitely prefers to be ruled by white men, than coloured. The latter, with a little brief authority, domineers it over the worker." Anti-Humbug called Dr. Anderson's cable to London "mischievous" and "ill conceived."[63]

Taken together, these competing statements about racialism in Jamaica revealed the fault lines in the society. The lives of the peoples of African descent and those of the white residents of the island intersected at several points, but they never met. An uneasy modus vivendi had existed since the Morant Bay Rebellion in 1865. The Anderson affair had awakened the racial specter, and whites in particular were nervous about what damage it might do to the fragile social order. When Dr. Anderson contested and won the by-election for the seat that he had vacated, one of his principal supporters, C. G. Walker, emphasized that the contest was not with J. C. Chisholm, the opponent, but with "a well-known autocratic group which has for quite some time used their influence against the interests of the people." He hoped that the election "will prove to them that their influence is at an end." His meaning was clear: Dr. Anderson and the race he represented had triumphed.[64]

The influence of the "autocratic group" that Walker had identified did not disappear immediately, although it began to wane. Spencer B. Soulette was correct, however, in noting that "after 1938, things began to change." He acknowledged that "race was there but it was kept under control." The activist and publisher, Stennet Kerr-Coombs, agreed that "since 1938 dem have more respect fi black people." Interviewed in 1987, Soulette also expressed his pleasure at the positive changes that had occurred in the employment opportunities for the peoples of African descent. "Just take a walk in any office from Half-Way-Tree, and see who are the managers, the accountants, all of the leaders of industry," he advised. "Manager of bank is a black man, absolute reverse to what it was. Blacks now get positions [once] reserved for the Europeans at the time." To him, "the riot was the peak of all that started the epoch we lived in."[65]

Norman Manley, himself a brown-skinned Jamaican, noticed the decline of shade prejudice. "Jamaica is rapidly passing beyond the stage," he wrote in 1946, "where coloured people of any complexion attach importance to differences in shade." This was an exaggeration, but such prejudices were weakening. Manley emphasized that shade prejudice "is one of the things to be completely eradicated before any idea of a real West Indian civilization can be realized."[66] Seven decades later, his observation remains prescient.

There were other signs of change in the island's racial configuration. In 1943, for example, a number of African Jamaicans founded the United Negro Party. Its secretary was Hugh Buchanan, Bustamante's former colleague. The party hoped to build upon the work that had been initiated by the Universal Negro Improvement Association. Buchanan explained that "the Negro cannot fully express himself through parties organized and dominated by other people; as then he would be an accessory—as a tool. . . . This party stands for the good of the country as a whole but has a special interest in matters affecting the Negro, therefore it must be led and financed by Negroes."[67] The United Negro Party was short-lived. But its race-based rhetoric was directly influenced by Marcus Garvey and the 1938 rebellion that his racial philosophy helped to spawn.

Dr. Anderson's electoral victory was not for himself alone. It was a repudiation of officially sponsored racism in the island as a whole. The labor rebellion shook the society, challenged the old order, and gave the black workers a sense of their own power and of their capacity to force fundamental changes in the status quo. It would not be an easy task to destroy the pernicious ideology of white supremacy and its practice in the island. Racially sanctioned inequities had become firmly imbedded in Jamaica's societal fabric, its Zeitgeist, and its psychology and could not be easily exorcised. Anderson had forced the open discussion of an issue that the colonial state and some of the island's people preferred to ignore. But the worm had turned. Jamaicans would have to confront the daunting challenge of constructing a model polity that perceived and celebrated an individual's race and skin color as the fortuitous product of conception and birth, bearing no larger meaning or significance.

FOUR

Looking Back, Moving Forward

The West India Royal Commission's arrival was anxiously awaited in the island. It was only the second time in forty-one years that a commission had been appointed by the imperial government to investigate conditions in the Caribbean colonies. The members of the ten-person commission were excited by the prospect of traveling to the West Indies to do their civic duty. As six members of the commission prepared to depart on October 13, 1938, by boat train from Euston Station in London for Liverpool, where a ship awaited them, no one was bothered by the fearsome reputation of the number 13. "I have no qualms about the number 13 and I don't think any of my colleagues have either," declared one member. "I don't suppose that the voyage—or for that matter—our mission to the West Indies would be any less eventful if it started on any other day of the month." The secretary to the commission confessed that he was looking forward "to a warm, or rather busy, time in the West Indies."[1]

The optimism evinced by these two members of the commission was not misplaced. They needed all the enthusiasm they could muster to confront and report on the awful social and economic conditions they were likely to discover in the colonies. Their mission was occurring on the occasion of the centenary of the emancipation of the enslaved peoples in the British West Indies. Jamaicans had commemorated the event on August 1, approximately three months after the unrest that began in the island the previous May. The revolt from below had starkly dramatized the unfulfilled promise of emancipation.

Given the immediate past history of the island, the authorities were fearful that there would be violence on August 1, Emancipation Day. They had heard the disquieting rumor that the landless were being told that on Emancipation Day they would get land that had been allegedly bequeathed to them by Queen Victoria in 1838. These persons who rented land on the large holdings in Clarendon and elsewhere would demand and get those plots by right. Robert Rumble, the founder of the Clarendon-based Poor

Man's Improvement Land Settlement and Labour Association (PMILSLA), had fed the fears of the island's elite that the landless were in the mood to create social disturbances. After all, Rumble had sent a petition to Governor Edward Denham in April proclaiming: "We are the Sons of slaves who have been paying rent to Landlords for fully many decades[,] we want better wages, we have been exploited for years and we are looking to you to help us. We want a Minimum Wage Law. We want freedom in this the hundredth year of our Emancipation. We are still Economic Slaves, burdened in paying rent to Landlords who are sucking out our vitalities."[2]

As the rumor that Queen Victoria had bequeathed land to the freed people in 1838 gained currency, the acting colonial secretary threatened to prosecute anyone "attempting to interfere with the quiet and peaceful possession of land," emphasizing that the government would not "tolerate trespassing upon other persons' lands." Individuals who were collecting money with the promise to give people land were acting illegally, he stressed. The *Daily Gleaner* added its voice to that of the colonial official, denouncing "the scoundrels" who were misleading the people. These "human leeches," the paper said, were injecting "a dangerous virus into the minds of many tenants to create ill will on the part of the latter against property owners."[3]

Meeting in Old Harbour on June 25, the members of the St. Catherine Federation of Teachers were urged to dispel the rumors. J. H. Loftman, a former president of the Jamaica Union of Teachers, dismissed the content of the rumor as "foolish, stupid, and ignorant," urging his listeners to refute the "silly" idea "which was [being] scattered by mischievous propagandists." Some of these people, Loftman declared, were being told that the land upon which they worked "would automatically fall into their possession," and many people "were making preparations to enter into their supposed heritage."[4] The government continued to take these rumors so seriously that on July 14, the acting colonial secretary asked the elected members of the Legislative Council to help refute what the *Gleaner* called this "land claim delusion among tenants" in the island.[5] A group of concerned citizens who said they were representing the "thinking people of the community" issued a statement on July 21 advising the government to undertake an island-wide campaign to advise "these people to act wisely and orderly, and not commit any breach of the law" in August, particularly on Emancipation Day. It urged the government, however, to refrain from using "arms and force" if the people contravened the law.[6]

The fears of the government and the worried elite were not realized. Emancipation Day passed peacefully as Jamaicans across the island attended church services and participated in various festivities. Political, civic, and religious leaders extolled the progress that the island had experienced since 1838, expressed gratitude to the Crown for ending slavery, and affirmed their loyalty to the empire. A. B. Lowe, the member for St. James in the Legislative Council, praised the "marvellous" progress the island had made since 1838. Alexander Bustamante expressed gratitude to Queen Victoria for ending slavery, and Canon J. C. Swaby told his congregation at the Anglican cathedral in Spanish Town that "it was a matter of thankfulness to be a British citizen." He took comfort in the fact that "the progress of the black man has been remarkable. They are all British subjects by birth; speaking the English language, enjoying English institutions with English literature and English laws. . . . It has been well said that there is no race of people who have responded so admirably to British culture and Gospel . . . than our West Indian people, and that within the space of only a hundred years."[7]

The centenary of emancipation was not only the occasion for an uncritical celebration of the ties with England but also a time for the rewriting of history. G. St. C. Scotter, a columnist in the *Gleaner* and an Englishman, observed that slavery "still exists in full force in every part of Africa," a fantastic claim for anyone to have made in 1938. The African peoples who came to Jamaica, he said, were rescued from "a far worse form of slavery by their own people," a statement not supported by modern historical research.[8] The English, Scotter wrote, delivered the Africans "from slavery to freedom." Since the English presided over slavery in Jamaica from 1655 to 1838, this delivery into freedom had taken them almost 200 years to accomplish. England, Scotter stressed, had played "a great and glorious part" in the abolition of slavery.[9] R. A. Thompson, a teacher, demonstrated his unfamiliarity with Jamaican history by telling his colleagues: "Since we did not fight for emancipation we are supine."[10] Thompson probably did not know that Jamaica had more slave rebellions than any other slave society in the hemisphere. Occurring in western Jamaica in 1831, the Sam Sharpe rebellion had hastened the end of slavery.[11]

Dr. Sylvia Lowe commemorated the centenary by writing an article in the *Daily Gleaner*. Entitled "History of Emancipation," the article invoked in lyrical prose the travail of slavery, the ecstasy of freedom, and the continuing legacy of the institution. Capturing the mood of the newly freed as the clock struck midnight on August 1, 1838, Dr. Lowe reminded the readers of the newspaper that "old men and women, bent with burdens they had had to bear . . . women and children wept and shouted for joy. Mothers held up their babies to William Knibb blessing him for having set them free, and like sweet license their paen of thanksgiving rose to heaven. Liberty trees were planted on the 1st of August, and underneath them were buried a driver's whip, shackles, neck chains, and many other dreadful symbols of slavery."[12]

Dr. Lowe wrote eloquently of the day of freedom:

Through that long day religious services were held. Oh the songs of praise! Oh the sweet music of the bells, pealing out the glad news of Freedom! Freedom!
From East to West ring out ye gladsome bells
of freedom blest, of joy each
sweet chime tells,
O'er hills and valleys hark the
Chorus swells.
Alleluia![13]

Dr. Lowe admitted that, 100 years later, "our race has progressed," but "some of us are still slaves to habits that bind us with chains as terrible as those that bound our forebears. We must break them. Gird your loins like men and be strong. Let us cultivate race consciousness."

Dr. Lowe exhorted Jamaican women to "look back" and "remember that as the purity of those slave women was dragged in the dust, you hold your purity higher, let it be a thing of bounty, a priceless possession of our Race." The men should remember that "even as those slaves left footprints of blood in the sod, so leave your footprints on the sands of time, footprints that those who come after you will deem worthy to follow." And Dr. Lowe ended on a note of prayerful gratitude and with a supplication for humility as the past was remembered and its lessons kept alive:

One hundred years dear Lord:
We thank thee yet
As in Thy house to praise Thee we
Have met,
Keep our hearts humble Lord, lest we forget
Lest we forget.[14]

Dr. Lowe had raised troubling questions about the psychological legacy of slavery and the continuation of the structural forms of oppression. Jamaicans like Dr. Lowe were hardly revolutionaries, and many proudly affirmed their fealty to the king and the empire. But they saw the vestiges of the past in the present and contemplated a different and better future for their homeland. Edwin Allen, the principal of the Leicesterfield primary school, told his countrymen: "We must realize that complete emancipation has not yet taken place and so long as the last vestige of social, mental, moral or economic suppression or depression remains the struggle for freedom must continue. The emblems and paraphernalia were solemnly entombed in 1838 but in many places and in diverse ways the spirit of slavery still stalks abroad. It is the duty of this generation to kill and bury for all time the spirit of slavery."[15] The task that Allen identified had not been accomplished in 100 years, but the island appeared in 1938 to be on the verge of a new beginning.

Many Jamaicans, particularly members of the underclass, were not surprised by the absence of violence on Emancipation Day. There were undoubtedly "vampires in human form," as the *Gleaner* called them, who sought to exploit the landless by spreading rumors about land giveaways and extorting money from the gullible.[16] But most Jamaicans did not believe such tales, in spite of the prevailing land hunger. An insecure officialdom and a hysterical elite attributed the worst intentions to the workers and tenants. Noting the calm that prevailed on Emancipation Day, the editor of the prolabor *Jamaica Labour Weekly* observed that "there are those who are suffering from the pangs of disappointment and frustration because they did not get their eagerly sought opportunity to shoot down the troublemakers." The paper taunted the elite groups, asserting: "So widespread was the belief, so mischievously circulated was the tale that there would be great disorder, looting, arson, seizure of land and all sorts of things, that the 'Jitters' were all hoping to have a 'holiday' at the expense of the unarmed and oppressed masses whose deplorable economic and social conditions are caused by the system which these same Capitalist Jitters uphold."[17]

This was a harsh criticism, but Jamaican elites, in the main, demonstrated a deeply ingrained callousness to the dispossessed in the society. That they harbored such a profound fear of the people who existed at the societal margins was more the product of their insensitivity and less the ill will of those they viewed with incomprehension and contempt. The Rev. J. T. Dillon, a Baptist pastor for forty-five years and a self-described "son of Freedom," wrote perspicaciously about the texture of the relationship between the "employer of labour" and his workers: "It will be . . . found, that there is in us no innate hatred for the rich employer of labour, but a tendency to magnify him, and to honour him because of his superior economic position. But when it is discovered that rich landowners are using their superior economic position, and the high estimate of them by their employees, to deprive the labourers of their hire, then there is at first murmurings and complainings which if not attended to in a sympathetic and just manner beget hatred and malice."[18]

Those people who made lives for themselves from below were never the one-dimensional beings that existed in the imagination of the elites. E. F. Williams, identified as a poet of the people, said it well in the aftermath of Emancipation Day:

> The first of August was a memorable day
> Perfect peace and harmony held sway
> The labourers whom some think would make a row
> Behaved in such a manner that their oppressors wonder how.
>
> Keep on fooling them, you labouring man
> Let them know you were poor but not a fool
> You know when and how to raise "hell"
> You know when your power will tell.[19]

The centenary of emancipation provided Jamaicans with a marvelous moment for societal introspection and an opportunity to imagine the island's future. Dr. Lowe had urged her fellow Jamaicans to "look back" but also to leave "footprints" worthy of emulation. The moment for deep introspection was lost, however, overshadowed by the fears of the recurrence of the social disturbances of the previous months. The people of property and standing were concerned less about introspection and more about protecting a status quo that had benefited them. When the acting governor, C. C. Woolley, sent his message to the Jamaican people on the occasion of the centenary, for example, he said it was a time for "rejoicing" and "thanksgiving" for the island's progress. But the major emphasis in his message was on the need for the maintenance of "law and order."[20]

Embarrassed by the terrible social and economic conditions to which the rebellions called attention, the British government quickly began contemplating the appointment of a commission to investigate and report on them. Inactivity was not an option for the imperial government in view of the public outcry in the West Indies. Lloyd George, a former prime minister and chancellor of the exchequer, described Britain's colonies as belonging to a "slum empire." The *Daily Telegraph* of Northamptonshire maintained that "events in the West Indies have stirred the national conscience." Stuart

Fletcher of the *London Daily Herald* asked his readers "to take a look" at Jamaica, "whose problems are representative of the West Indian problem," observing wryly that "it is a view to which distance does not lend enchantment." In Jamaica, Fletcher said, there are "slums and poverty, cruelty and unhappiness, and recent events of such blood and violence and tears so as to remove the narrow line which divides history from hysteria."[21]

Voices such as these, as well as the stark reality of the conditions in the Caribbean, could not be ignored. The acting governor announced on July 28, 1938, that a Royal Commission had been named and charged to "investigate the social and economic conditions in Barbados, British Guiana, British Honduras, Jamaica, and the Leeward Islands, Trinidad and Tobago, and the Windward Island and matters associated and to make recommendations." The chairman of the ten-person commission was the Right Honorable Lord Moyne, who had been a Conservative member of Parliament and had served in many different capacities in the government. The vice chairman was Sir Edward Stubbs, a former governor of Jamaica. Entering the colonial service in 1900, he served as the colonial secretary of Ceylon and the governor of Hong Kong before being posted to Jamaica in 1926. Sir Walter Citrine, prominent trade unionist, was also appointed a member. A former electrician, Citrine became secretary of the Electrical Trades Union in 1914, rising to the rank of general secretary of the powerful Trades Union Congress twelve years later. Most notably for the time, the commission included two women: Dr. Mary Blacklock, an authority on tropical medicine, and Dame Rachel Crowdy, a social worker.[22]

Although the members of the commission were very accomplished in their fields of endeavor, only Stubbs had a close familiarity with the West Indian colonies and their problems. The all-white composition of the commission invited the criticism of prominent people of African descent in England. The officers of the International African Service Bureau, a pan-Africanist organization, dispatched a letter to the *Manchester Guardian* urging the appointment of a person of African descent to the commission. "In order to inspire confidence," the letter said, "commissions sent out to investigate colonial conditions must never create the impression that His Majesty's Government is judge, jury, plaintiff, and defendant." The signatories included the intellectuals C. L. R. James and George Padmore of Trinidad and Tobago and Jomo Kenyatta of Kenya.[23]

There were many Jamaicans who expressed cynicism about the purpose and utility of the commission. The editor of the *Jamaica Labour Weekly* maintained that "so far as practical results are concerned, the Commission will serve but little purpose." He urged Jamaicans to testify before it, however, because "when the day of reckoning comes . . . within the Empire," the imperial government could not claim ignorance about the conditions that existed.[24] The paper also doubted that "any group or faction of Imperialist Englishmen [would] be able to find the true cause of such a feeling that exist deep down in the breast of every Negro worker."[25] P. W. Sangster of Giddy Hall, St. Elizabeth, spoke for many Jamaicans when he said the appointment of the commission was "a joke . . . and is intended to be a joke on us." Continuing, Sangster asked rhetorically: "[W]hat are the conditions here that the Colonial Office does not know?" He was certain that the officials knew "more about us than most Jamaicans of every class." To Sangster, the commission's appointment represented "pure political manoeuvring" among the British political parties.[26] Other critics were displeased that the commission's terms of reference did not include studying and making recommendations on constitutional changes for the island.[27]

The commission began its deliberations in Kingston on November 3 at the Constant Spring Hotel. Opening the proceedings, Lord Moyne noted that the social and economic conditions in the West Indies were "in no way exceptional under present world conditions," although he knew that the colonies had "certain special problems." He invited Jamaicans to submit memoranda to the commission on their concerns, with that body reserving the right to invite whomever it wished to give oral testimony. It was impossible, he said, for the commission to inquire into "individual grievances" since it was concerned with "the social and economic condition of the whole community."[28]

In order to obtain some familiarity with the peoples' lives and condition, members of the commission visited selected areas of the country on Saturday and Sunday the 5th and 6th of November. Dividing themselves into five groups of two members each, they toured various slums in Kingston, including Salt Lane, Dung Hill, Smith Village, Trench Pen, and Maranga Lane. Sir Edward Stubbs, according to a newspaper report, "went to the worse of all places in the slums, the dung hill where men and women were living in trees and hovels—really pieces of tin and rotten boards kept together by bits of rope or with a single nail." At Kingston Pen, Lord Moyne observed the "miserable shacks" and spoke to the residents, learning about their subhuman existence. He was told that "often there was but one latrine to some 20 people. A place about 3' by 3' and 4' high. Some places were without even this. A kitchen built of the rear part of a motor car's carriage with a wheel barrow's body was shown to them."

Summarizing his impressions, Edward Stubbs, the former governor, recalled: "I knew that there were some very bad places in the slums during my term here, [but] I see that there has been no change at all."[29] The following day, Lord Moyne led three other commissioners on a tour of the conditions on the Low Leighton estate, a short walk from Buff Bay, Portland. As Lord Moyne "picked his way through the bush" to the first house that he inspected, he was struck by the large number of children who lived on the estate. According to the news report: "The first building inspected was a wattle-built hut measuring perhaps eight feet by seven. It was divided into two tiny compartments each containing a bed. Eight people . . . lived in that hut, the children, of whom there are four sleeping on the floor. The four rugged urchins in question stood shyly by while their living quarters were inspected. 'This is the worst, I suppose,' remarked Lord Moyne. 'No sir,' came the answer, 'there is worse than this.'"[30]

The group also visited "dwellings" in the neighboring Orange Bay. These were "mere hovels," the news report concluded. Lord Moyne, it said, "asked many pertinent questions about these dwellings: had they all latrines? (Answer, no). How many of them had latrines? (Answer, very few). Was there a public latrine for them all? (Answer, yes but unusable). How many of them had to use the bush? (Answer, the great majority of them)."[31]

The overcrowded housing conditions that the members of the commission observed were not atypical. The 1943 census revealed that 100,561 Jamaicans lived in dwellings of less than 100 square feet. Each dwelling was home to an average of 2.8 persons, suggesting a considerable degree of overcrowding. The majority of them lacked indoor toilet facilities and running water. The census identified 8.2 percent of the dwellings as tenements. Not surprisingly, the majority, or 28.5 percent, were located in Kingston, followed by St. Andrew with 15.1 percent and St. Catherine with 10.6 percent.[32]

At the end of his tour of Jamaica's underside, Lord Moyne and his team motored to Port Antonio to board his luxurious yacht, *Rosaura*, for the return trip to Kingston. Seeking to temper the impact of the horrendous social conditions that the commission was observing, the editor of the *Daily Gleaner* blamed those in Kingston on rural migrants. "They have to live somewhere and somehow," the paper observed; "they are not very particular as to how they live; indeed it may be said without fear of contradiction that a considerable percentage of them prefer squalor to tidiness, a happy go lucky existence to the maintenance by constant exertion of a decent standard of living."[33] This outrageous comment from the voice of an insensitive elite ignored the historical and systemic factors that largely accounted for the atrocious social and economic situation of the vast majority of Jamaicans. Ironically, the same day's editorial page carried a letter from O. Alphonsous Malcolm, principal of the Tweedside Elementary School, "hoping that the Commissioners will see more than the white sepulchres of Jamaica."[34]

The commission's hearings gave Jamaicans another opportunity to assess their current condition and to contemplate the future. The centenary of emancipation had not produced a deep introspection, nor had it generated any new ideas about the challenges of the next century. But the commission's anticipated presence unleashed much excitement, and Jamaicans, representing different interest groups, began to think seriously about the island's future. The commission received memoranda from organizations such as the Jamaica Imperial Association, the Jamaica Progressive League, the Jamaica Union of Teachers, the Bustamante unions, the churches, the East Indians, the Chinese, and others. It was an impressive list of organizations and a creative number of recipes for the making of a new Jamaica. The commission heard from forty-two witnesses or groups of witnesses in public or in private.

The commission was interested in hearing from government officials to ascertain their views about the condition of the people and the policies they were implementing. The governor did not testify, but his principal lieutenants did, sometimes to their embarrassment. Their testimony often revealed their insensitivity to the social and economic problems that animated the recent rebellion and that continued to fuel the rumblings from below. The commission, however, never heard formally from any of the persons at the societal bottom, choosing to listen to those who spoke in their name. This was not at all unusual; the English lords of the land had never been in the habit of listening to those over whom they ruled, except in times of trouble. The empowerment of the people whose rebellion led to the creation of the commission was not a part of the imperial agenda.

The condition of the working poor and the unemployed, in spite of their not being invited to give testimony, could not be ignored. Sir Walter Citrine, the member of the commission most deeply concerned with questions of labor, was extraordinarily effective in laying bare official inattention to the plight of the workers. When A. W. Grantham, the colonial secretary, testified, Citrine forced him to admit that there was no minimum-wage legislation in the island, despite an order from the Colonial Office in 1932 to that effect. Nor had the local government, in accordance with the 1932 order, appointed advisory boards to fix minimum wages for occupations where they were deemed to be unacceptably low. Citrine told the colonial secretary that Trinidad had passed the recommended labor legislation in 1935, and so had the Leeward and Windward Islands. The dialogue between the two men is instructive.

> SIR WALTER CITRINE: Am I right in saying that there is no legislation or protection by law against exploitation of wages?
>
> MR. GRANTHAM: To the extent there is no minimum wage legislation, yes, there is none.[35]

Citrine also got the colonial secretary to admit that there was no legislation protecting people working in industry, providing for the inspection of factories to ensure the safety of the workers, and safeguarding the health of those working under medically hazardous conditions. The Workmen's Compensation Act that was enacted in December 1937 elicited strong criticism from Citrine. It was passed, Citrine charged, only after the riots in Trinidad had occurred. Lecturing the colonial secretary, he said: "[Y]ou know of course there were many covenants at Geneva, and other places, and you had reminders from the Secretary of State on the question; but you did not do anything until last year, and that was not until there had been some industrial trouble in the neighboring colony."[36]

The assistant colonial secretary, F. L. Brown, denied the charge, but he seemed less than credible given the government's track record. The Workmen's Compensation Act, as Citrine pointed out, excluded domestic servants, clerks and shop assistants, general transport drivers and chauffeurs, and agricultural workers, except those operating power driven plants. Noting that "the great bulk" of the island's population was employed in agriculture, Citrine wanted to know if they would be included in a new act or by amending legislation.

> MR. BROWN: We want to have experience of the working of this Act for about twelve months before we attempt to amend it.
>
> SIR WALTER: But you know perfectly well [that] experience of the working of an Act cannot help you with information about a class that has been excluded. What is the good of delaying when you can't possibly find out anything about the incidence of accidents and the liabilities resulting from those accidents to a class you have excluded from the law.[37]

Mr. Brown gave no response to this comment. The law was transparent, bereft of any substance, and it was antilabor in its conceptualization and intent.

Not only did the laws afford little or no protection to the workers; the colonial authorities also were unfriendly to trade unions. Unlike the British Trade Union Law of 1919, which was intended to serve as a model for Jamaican laws, the island's variant disallowed picketing and allowed unions to be sued by employers for damages in the event of a strike. The latter provision constituted intimidation of the worst sort and was intended to discourage strikes. In order to be registered, Jamaican unions also had to submit their rules to the Crown solicitor for approval as opposed to the keeper of the records, as sanctioned by the British 1919 law. Citrine thought this was a ploy to discourage registration by the unions, since the Crown solicitor "may indeed be employed in prosecuting some of the leading members of the union." "Do you know?" Citrine asked Grantham, "that trade unions are generally suspicious of the courts?" "I think everybody keeps out of the law courts," was the flippant response.[38]

They began arriving at the Constant Spring Hotel early on November 16, 1938. The word had spread that Alexander Bustamante, their leader, would be testifying before the Royal Commission that day. "Labourers in hundreds ascended into the luxurious hotel which, before yesterday," reported the *Gleaner*, "they only saw while they were building it or else, distantly when they passed by to seek municipal employment at Constant Spring and areas north of Kingston." On that November morning, however, "they swarmed unbidden, but unmolested all over the beautiful lawns, bare feet sucked [?] the glazed tile of the vestibule . . . [as they sat] comfortably on the sun-shaded gliders and around mosaic tables under balmy trees and shadowed porticoes," the newspaper continued.[39]

These lowly workers knew their place and kept their distance from the mighty and their social betters. They did not venture inside the hotel and "the Commission room," where "a gathering of the classes which have been attending the daily sittings" occupied all available chairs. The *Gleaner* observed that "around them and in the midst of them stood representatives of the upper proletariat, and on the outskirts of these, stretching out and blocking all approaches, were the labourers in their dishabille." The *Gleaner* did not know how much the "labourers" were able to hear "of what transpired."[40]

It probably did not matter to these exemplars of the underclass how much they heard. Some members of the "upper proletariat" were more fortunate, as they shared the cramped space in the commission room with "society ladies." Those who remained outside, confined by invisible but real boundaries of class, were reenacting their social status: they had never been on the inside anywhere in their own country. Bustamante had promised to change all of that, and they had come to support him as he confronted the representatives of the all-powerful imperial government on their behalf.[41]

Bustamante arrived for the 10:00 A.M. hearing accompanied by five prominent officials of his unions and their solicitor. He had submitted a memorandum to the commission a few days earlier and was prepared to answer questions on it. His appearance gave him the opportunity to delineate his vision for the workers of Jamaica. The seven Bustamante unions had been in existence for about five months, but their founder had never articulated a detailed and coherent set of programs and policies.

The memorandum that the unions submitted to the Royal Commission contained a list of social legislation that they desired, along with the requisite justification. The document proposed that the daily minimum rate of pay for "a labourer or ordinary worker should not be less than 4/−." It claimed that "the general daily pay for the average worker on the Estates of Jamaica at present, ranges from 1/6 to 2/6 for men; and for women 9d to 1/3." In order to support its proposal, the unions provided an estimate of the "minimum average monthly expenditure of an ordinary worker." Such a worker, it claimed, spent £4 13s 8d monthly.

The document pointed out that a worker who received 4/− per day would earn a total of £4 16s 0d per month, an amount that covered his basic expenses. It appears that this estimate reflected the priorities of the urban worker, given the projected expenditures for "pictures" (movies), newspapers, union fees, and rent. Under close questioning from Lord Moyne, Bustamante said 90 percent of all industries were in a position to pay the minimum wage he suggested. He agreed, however, that "there would have to be some modification in certain districts and in certain Industries." The labor leader stressed that in Jamaica, wages "have not been formed on any calculation other than the exploitation of the workers of this island. That is to say there is a feeling in this country . . . that the workers must be kept down into the gutter of poverty or that they must be treated as if they were discarded foot mats or mongrel dogs." These were biting criticisms leveled at big business, with their representatives sitting and listening in the hearing room. But Bustamante was never able to sanitize his language if he felt strongly about an issue.

The Bustamante unions' memorandum also proposed a law that would set "maximum working hours for all workers." It claimed that the majority of the workers "work from 12 to 15 hours per day on Estates and larger properties, Factories, such as Bakeries, Aerated water factories, Soap Factories etc." Bustamante's "agitation" over the last few months had reduced the working week to an average of ten hours, the document asserted. The memorandum also proposed the introduction of an old-age pension scheme. It observed that 80 percent of the "inmates" of the almshouses "have never earned enough, even to buy food and other vital necessities of life, much more to have been able to have a farthing for their support in their declining stages of life." In his testimony, Bustamante told the commission that the provision of an old-age pension scheme was the most important of the social legislation the unions were proposing. He had obviously, however, not given the details of the scheme much thought, suggesting to Lord Moyne that pensions should begin at age fifty, eventually agreeing that age fifty-five was more feasible. Bustamante proposed a payment of ten shillings per week to the 100,000 persons who would qualify, producing the following dialogue:

> THE CHAIRMAN: Ten shillings per week for 100,000 people. That's £25 a year each. That's 2 ¼ million pounds. That's more than the total of your budget. And where could we hope to find increased resources, not only in connection with Old Age Pension but the other services. Have you any views as to how this can be met?
>
> MR. BUSTAMANTE: If we cannot find the money to meet that then there is one thing to do. To cover the entire country with Poor Houses and Mad Houses [asylums].
>
> THE CHAIRMAN: Yes. But you have to pay for those too.

The memorandum also recommended "sick leave with pay for weekly and monthly Employees." It noted that "it is a common experience that an individual worker after working 7, 8, to 10 years as a Servant or worker otherwise, who falls sick is simply thrown out of his job." It urged the passage of a law to protect "the normal moral living of young girls up to the age of 18." The document explained: "We must state this emphatically that the dignity of womanhood in Jamaica at present is as a fact relegated to the bottom of the sea due of course to the uncontrollable desire of these

Employers class, who deem themselves the lords of the land, and the adult male children are following their footsteps."

The memorandum seems to have been alluding to white employers, although they were neither the sole nor the principal offenders. It connected the sexual exploitation of the women to the low wages paid to the men: "We make bold to say that one of the chief reasons why the male Negro worker is so badly underpaid is an intentional and calculative one, based on the fact that the employer class . . . thought it best to adopt such a measure to make the Negro worker male become impotent financially speaking to take care of his daughters; hereby [sic] weakening the regard and the respect of fatherhood and motherhood which subsequently results in their daughters becoming 'easy prey' to the animal desires of this ruling class [meaning the employers]." This amateurish exercise in psychology was not entirely persuasive. It ignored the historical and systemic factors that largely explained the exploitation of the Jamaican workers. The memorandum further alleged that women who worked in stores as clerks "are forced to indulge in immoral practices by their employers after working hours." Those who refuse are either dismissed or "overworked." These women were also blacklisted and unable to obtain work elsewhere, actions the memorandum called "Un-Godly and Un-righteous."

The unions also wanted to obtain legislation protecting workers who were injured on their jobs and an amendment to the Workmen's Compensation Act to include agricultural workers. They recommended that the government provide legal assistance to accused persons who were unable to afford the services of lawyers. These persons, the memorandum argued, "are unable to defend themselves when they are being prosecuted for very trivial things, primarily because their not being able to intelligently express themselves due to the lack of even elementary education which of course is no fault of their own but the fault of the conditions by which their parents had to face, from an economic viewpoint and which made it impossible for them to have been schooled."

The unions had identified a problem that a poor and illiterate person confronted in the halls of justice. This was not, generally speaking, a matter that fell within the purview of a trade union's mission, but the memorandum maintained that workers were sometimes assaulted by their employers, "and if they should retaliate . . . they are victimized." In order to be able to operate effectively, the unions proposed that picketing be legalized and that legal protection should be accorded them in the event of strikes being called. Bustamante admitted to Lord Moyne that until Sir Walter Citrine raised the matter, he was unaware that "the unions could not officially call a strike without having serious consequences."

The unions' memorandum contained a catalog of grievances against employers and descriptions of the appalling conditions under which people worked and the low wages they received. Women who did the difficult work of breaking stones for the roads obtained 6d per day, "and in very exceptional cases where a worker is exceptionally strong she can earn 7 1/2d or 9d" per day. Workers who belonged to unions were discriminated against for work on public projects, the memorandum alleged. "Go to your Bustamante for work," they were admonished. The offenders, the memorandum said, are not "imported whites" but are "brown, coloured, and black Jamaicans." Continuing, it alleged that the workers "have more justice" from the "imported whites" than from "coloured and negro bosses." It further charged that "even in the Police Force you will find that the most reasonable Inspectors are the foreigners."

Lord Moyne was intrigued by these allegations and questioned Bustamante.

> THE CHAIRMAN: Why [is] the Jamaican less friendly and fair to other Jamaicans than imported officials?
>
> MR. BUSTAMANTE: On the whole the Jamaican—I am a Jamaican and I am quite sure I will be criticized for this but nothing hurts me in Jamaica—the Jamaican on the whole cannot stand success and the moment he gets a certain position—I am only referring to the Police Force—the moment our Negroes, coloured people, are promoted to Sergeants Major, excuse me Sir, they are the worse [sic] brutes you ever see towards their own fellowmen.

Bustamante gave the commission graphic descriptions of his hostile encounters with the police and of their brutality toward Jamaicans. He probably embellished his accounts for dramatic effect. But there is no doubt that official violence was a feature of the culture, particularly against the poor. The violence of slavery had left a legacy in the island, and the mistreatment of the politically powerless hardly elicited a backward glance of concern from those who governed the country. The unions' memorandum had denounced the use of "despotic methods" by the government to "handle alleged strikers." It rejected the use of "guns and bayonets," characterizing the government as a "Fascist Government and the present governor a Fascist by his action."

Bustamante elaborated on this charge in his testimony.

> THE CHAIRMAN: Well now you say [you] look upon this Government as a Fascist government. I take it as an objection to the present Constitution and not a personal matter, what do you want to say?
>
> MR. BUSTAMANTE: It is not exactly my Lord, the Constitution. I look upon the present and the former Government, the Governors, as Fascist. They use Fascist methods here. I am referring to the present Governor, shortly before you came the governor had the "nerve" to say that there is no starvation in the country and that the employees are paid favourably and he further stated that I was an alarmist. Of course he did not call my name but he called me a scaremonger.
>
> THE CHAIRMAN: You are not using the term dictatorial government to mean that there is no faith in democracy?
>
> MR. BUSTAMANTE: I complain that there is not enough democracy and I complain that this government has adopted the Fascist method when there is any labour trouble, instead of investigating they surround us with bayonets and try to intimidate. It provokes me and it causes me to attack him and to lose respect for him for I realise that I have more power than this governor has. [Laughter]

This was, to be sure, typical bombast from Bustamante. Under questioning from Sir Walter Citrine, he retreated from his allegation that the government engaged in Fascist behavior. "When you accuse people of being Fascist," Citrine asked, "is your reason for accusing them of being Fascist that they use coercive methods instead of getting cooperation?" "Yes," Bustamante answered. He also clarified his assertion that he exercised more power in the island than the governor.

> SIR WALTER: Now when you made that statement that seemed to create some amusement; that you had more power than the governor of this island.
>
> MR. BUSTAMANTE: I do.
>
> SIR WALTER: Do you mean power over the workers of the island?
>
> MR. BUSTAMANTE: Yes sir.
>
> SIR WALTER: Would it be right to say that if the workers of Jamaica were out on strike in some parts of the island and the governor ordered them to go back to work—

Looking Back, Moving Forward | 103

MR. BUSTAMANTE: I think they would laugh at the Governor. [Laughter]

SIR WALTER: If you and your executive instructed them to go back to work, would they go back to work?

MR. BUSTAMANTE: As I do so they go back.

SIR WALTER: So really what you meant to say is [that] you have more moral authority over workers than the Governor has?

MR. BUSTAMANTE: Yes.

SIR WALTER: The Governor might send the Police and the Military but you can do it by another process?

MR. BUSTAMANTE: Yes. By peace.

SIR WALTER: By persuasion.

MR. BUSTAMANTE: Yes.

SIR WALTER: That is what you meant when you said you had more power.

MR. BUSTAMANTE: Definitely.

Bustamante voiced his annoyance with the government's attempts to intimidate and harass him.

SIR WALTER: When you see police reporters taking down your speeches what effect does that have upon you?

MR. BUSTAMANTE: I lash them with my tongue. [Laughter] I lash government with my tongue.

SIR WALTER: Have you been subjected to any sort of what you might call annoyance from the police?

MR. BUSTAMANTE: They come to our office with a book in their hand as though they are going to arrest a criminal and with this book and pencil ask about unions. Of course I drive them out. . . . That they would send a Police to interview me in the same manner that they would interview a criminal and I resented it and told them to tell the Inspector to mind his own business.

The unions' memorandum and Bustamante's testimony revealed that he had given little thought to issues beyond those directly concerned with the welfare of the workers. The memorandum, for example, proposed the imposition of "heavy duty" on the importation of "corn (raw or canned), canned pineapples, cheap ready made shirts, all ready made dresses, cement, condensed milk, rice." These were "measures," the memorandum said, "to assist economic conditions of the people." These "measures" were obviously designed to protect local industries, but they constituted a relatively small part of the island's imports. Bustamante's suggestion, during his testimony, that the income tax should be increased was quickly challenged by the chairman. Lord Moyne pointed out that the people at the higher income levels were already paying 40 percent of their income in taxes.

The labor leader saw sugarcane as the foundation of the island's prosperity and economic future. "I would like to see Jamaica covered with canes," Bustamante told the commission. Bustamante, at least in 1938, was unable to envisage a Jamaican economy that did not depend primarily on the cultivation of that plant. It is true that the value of sugarcane exports had been increasing. In 1921, for example, it stood at £509,202 (26,837 tons), and it increased to £864,570 (95,776 tons) in 1937. The corresponding figure for bananas was £1,602,000 in 1921 and £2,656,883 in 1937.[42] Seen from a different angle, it must be noted that while the volume of sugar production increased by 256 percent between the years in question, the value rose by only 69 percent. Sugar prices never kept pace with production. In fact, the sugar industry was being kept economically viable by the preferential treatment it enjoyed in the English market. The cultivation of sugarcane in 1938 or any time thereafter did not represent the island's economic future. The banana industry was also facing difficult times. It was dealing with the impact of the incurable Panama disease and the ravages of the equally destructive leaf spot. The two diseases had destroyed Cuba's banana industry, and there was the prospect that the same could happen in Jamaica.

In spite of the enormous land hunger in the island, Bustamante did not propose a land-settlement scheme. Nor did he advocate programs to address the island's illiteracy, which hovered around 30 percent. Bustamante and the unions did not recommend any progressive changes in the Jamaican constitution. He remained silent on the issue of self-government, preferring a return to the representative government that existed at the time of the Morant Bay rebellion in 1865. Bustamante did not advocate universal adult suffrage during his testimony, dismissing the elected members of the Legislative Council as "imbeciles."

Bustamante was a politically conservative leader operating at a potentially revolutionary moment. He expended much of his energy trying to control the behavior of his followers, although his own rhetoric could at times frighten the colonial authorities. Bustamante, as the following dialogue suggests, did not portray himself as a threat to the state:

SIR WALTER: When you are talking to a big crowd... you have to employ what people call the "arts of the orator?" [Laughter]

MR. BUSTAMANTE: I have an enormous amount of psychology and I act on that. [Laughter]

SIR WALTER: And your purpose is to try and persuade your members on certain points?

MR. BUSTAMANTE: My purpose is really to bring my members together and instill in them loyalty and peace amongst themselves and the Government and the employers.

SIR WALTER: Would it be wrong to say that time after time you have publicly proclaimed your readiness to cooperate with the authorities and that you have referred in the highest terms to the present ruler of the British Empire?

MR. BUSTAMANTE: Yes sir.

SIR WALTER: It would be right.

MR. BUSTAMANTE: I don't think I have ever spoken where I did not exhort the people to cooperate with the present Governor and to exalt in their minds loyalty to the head of the Empire.

SIR WALTER: You have neither publicly nor privately, have you, advocated revolution?

MR. BUSTAMANTE: I have no desire. I have never.

The labor leader was not guilty of obfuscation. He was a restraining influence on his more impatient and radical followers, deeply loyal to the Crown but identifying with the grievances that the workers were nursing. Bustamante's testimony underscored his passionate commitment to improving the condition of the underclass, but his program was not designed to effect systemic change or fundamentally alter power relations in the island. The workers, if they were lucky, would see an improvement in their material circumstances, but the political and economic structures that facilitated their oppression would remain in place. Speaking the language of class, Bustamante lambasted the rich, who "in many cases" increased their wealth by "100 percent each year." They "go to England on holidays for three and six months," he alleged, "and they change their motor cars yearly, they bank [bask?] in wealth daily, yet they refuse to allow their workers a reasonable living wage." This was a rhetorically effective charge, but bold and creative ideas to address the structurally determined grievances of the workers were absent from his imagination. Still, despite his inattention to policy details and a marked self-centeredness, Bustamante was a genuine voice of the people in whose name he spoke.[43]

Allan George St. Claver Coombs was anxious to testify before the Royal Commission. A resident of Montego Bay, Coombs prepared a lengthy memorandum detailing the social and economic conditions of the dispossessed and proposing solutions to them. Coombs was founder and president of the Jamaica Workers and Tradesmen Union, numbering some 900 dues-paying members. He had confined his union activity to the parishes of St. Elizabeth, St. James, Westmoreland, St. Ann, and St. Mary, knowing well the circumstances and hopes of the people. His memorandum constituted the most detailed assessment of the prevailing conditions in rural Jamaica that the commission received. It discussed the severe unemployment situation, the terrible housing conditions, the low wages, and the physical mistreatment of the workers. The memorandum said the lives of the workers on the plantation and sugar estates "are so burdensome that they are little [better] off than animals. The owners of these estates in the majority pays [sic] better attention to the cattle on their properties than [to] these unfortunates." Coombs advocated legislation to protect domestic workers from exploitation and abuse, the expansion of the Workmen's Compensation Act "to cover all groups and classes of workers," and the enforcement of the law prohibiting child labor.

Coombs's memorandum emphasized the ways in which the police and other officials abused workers who were demanding their rights. "Any attempt by a courageous labourer of average intelligence to air his grievances or represent those of his fellowmen," the document complained, is "met with the combined hostility of the employers and government." Coombs cited an example of the treatment a group of people received as they were attempting to petition the colonial state. Their abuse

> was glaringly demonstrated on the 30th day of December 1936 when a group of 400 men, women, and children under the auspices of the Jamaica Workers and Tradesmen Union attempted to stage a hunger march Demonstration from the Kingston Race Course to the Governor's residence and Headquarters House. A force of 800 armed constables with several truck loads of ammunitions [sic] was brought out to disperse them. The people all armed were only carrying flags and banners bearing the words "Starvation, Nakedness, Shelterless."

These were destroyed by the police. The Union Jack was torn in pieces. The batons and clubs of the police were brought in play mercilessly on the people, while extra armed men kept the people covered with rifles, bayonets, and pistols, while the poor and unfortunate people received their floggings which necessitated many going to the hospital for treatment. One woman was fleeing away from the wrath of the police and was chased and strucked [sic] down from behind by the policeman's club. The people lived under these conditions from the abolition of slavery.

Of humble background and economic circumstance, Coombs had resided in the island all of his life, a survivor of the thwarted promise of freedom. "I myself," Coombs said, "was not fortunate in getting the opportunity of getting a good education." The rawness of his memorandum gave it a haunting power, its passion conveyed an urgency to its demands, and the conditions it described produced its arresting moral fervor. Bustamante, the wealthy usurer—phenotypically brown skinned, a man who had lived most of his adult life overseas—had identified with and embraced the cause of the dispossessed; but Coombs was the exemplar, the more authentic voice and representative of the descendants of the enslaved.[44]

When Coombs testified before the commission in Montego Bay, the *Gleaner* reported that laborers "thronged their court house to hear him." Interestingly, only three members of the commission had traveled to Montego Bay to conduct the proceedings. Lord Moyne did not attend, but Sir Walter Citrine and the vice president, Sir Edward Stubbs, were present.[45] The absentees had lost the opportunity to listen to the only witness who was not a member of the island's elite either in terms of birth, education, profession, or material circumstance.

Norman Manley's appearance before the commission was its intellectual high point. In contrast to the sparse official attendance at Coombs's hearing, the entire commission was present for Manley. In addition, the room was packed to capacity. The *Gleaner* observed that "it was a remarkable demonstration of the leadership of Mr. Manley, not only by the size of the attendance, but by the variety of classes represented." The outstanding barrister spoke as a representative of the Jamaica Welfare League and was accompanied by eleven distinguished members of Jamaica's professional and intellectual elite. The delegation included Noel Nethersole, Lewis Ashenheim, Philip Sherlock, Edith Clarke, and H. P. Jacobs. The *Gleaner* said they constituted Jamaica's "Brain Trust."[46]

Manley had submitted a memorandum before his appearance, and it became the foundation for the questions that he was asked. The memorandum was the most thoughtful document the commission had received, and it covered a wide range of issues about the island's condition and its future. Manley spoke for all peoples in the island, so the memorandum was comprehensive in its scope, as well as balanced and learned. But it lacked the passion of the one submitted by Coombs, who had shared the experiences about which he wrote. Nor did it possess Bustamante's captivating identification with the dispossessed.

Manley proposed an extensive land-settlement scheme that he predicted would improve the economic conditions of the rural poor. But the plots of land, he stressed, should be large enough to enable the recipients to derive an adequate sustenance from them. This would keep such persons out of the labor market because "if you cannot get the small settler off the labour market, there is no solution to the agrarian problems in Jamaica." Manley advocated a "radical protection" of nascent industries, a decrease in the interest rates charged by the government-assisted loan banks, and an expansion of the coverage of the Workmen's Compensation Act. He proposed improvements in the provision of social services, housing, education, and medical care.

Manley condemned the lack of power accorded to the elected members of the Legislative Council, calling the situation "a major evil." They enjoyed "the evil," he said, "of having no responsibility and having powers that can only be used for destructive criticism." He supported the granting of self-government to the island and the introduction of universal adult suffrage. Manley seemed tentative, however, on the question of whether a literacy test should be required for the suffrage.

> MR. MANLEY: I am all in favour, sir, of the widest possible franchise. I think judging by the results that have been secured from the limited franchise that any change must necessarily be not a change for the worse.
>
> SIR PERRY MARKINNON: Universal suffrage?
>
> MR. MANLEY: I am quite prepared to risk the experiment. Or a literacy test.
>
> SIR WALTER CITRINE: A literacy test?
>
> MR. MANLEY: Yes.
>
> SIR WALTER: In other words the voter must read and write?
>
> MR. MANLEY: Please understand I am giving my individual opinion. I would be quite satisfied to see adult suffrage.

SIR WALTER: Without any test whatsoever?
MR. MANLEY: Without any test.

This was a less-than-enthusiastic endorsement of universal adult suffrage without qualifications by the principal founder of the People's National Party.[47]

The letter—or perhaps more accurately, the memorandum—came from "some labourers" in Spanish Town. The Royal Commission had no plans to hear from people like them in the hallowed rooms of the Constant Spring Hotel. But it was Jamaicans from their ranks who had forced the appointment of the commission by engaging in strikes and other forms of protest. Members of the commission were making on-site inspections of slums and having perfunctory conversations with the residents. But no one from those communities of despair had been scheduled to appear before the commission, in spite of the fact that its raison d'etre was their social and economic condition. They had, however, metaphorically brought the slums with them to the Constant Spring Hotel when Bustamante testified before the commission. The letter from their brethren in Spanish Town was not as dramatic an intervention as theirs had been, but as the letter or memorandum was read to the commission on November 14, none could ignore its emotional impact.

> I was told that it was [advertised] in the *Gleaner* that we the poverty stricken people should explain our grevence, so things is so hard with us that one of us could not afford to rite this letter so it is a small body of us put together last night to send this letter. So I will begin now. Please sir read carefully and look into our condition. I am a man who have three children and a wife. I live in a little room ten shillings a month for it. I have a baby with my wife and sometimes for weeks the child had to live on the dry bread[,] not a penny to bye milk.

Continuing the account of his battle with life, the writer revealed that "sometime I get two days [work] which is fore [four] shillings [and] I have give the land master two and six pence leaving one and six: please sir what is that to a family of five[,] good lord look into it carefully." He then continued:

> There is hundreds of us who would like to rite and explain but a two pence to send this letter they caunt afford it for they had to leave [use]

it to make a meal when they come in. . . . [I]n all ways land owners opres us. What so every little something we have in the house they take it away so we are back up in apression in all ways[.] I really caunt explain everything because it don't look so pleasant[.] I have a little girl start go to school and is going fore [four] mounths now and I caunt send her back to school [because she has] nothing to put on[.] Last week the mother had to cut a old dress to put on her[.] Cloth is selling 4 ½d a yard and so help my God I caunt bye two yards to make her a dress[.] My grevence is like a world without hend [end].⁴⁸

Jamaicans such as this man wanted to work and to earn enough to improve their economic conditions, but this was the proverbial pipe dream. A century after slavery's end, the children of freedom were still struggling in their place at the society's bottom, humbly taking their supplications for succor to the king's representatives sitting at the commission's table.

Not only were the voices of the dispossessed notably absent from the witness table, but women were also not invited to give testimony. This was not an unusual practice. The exclusion of women reflected their subordinate status in the society and their existence at its political margins. Even if women satisfied the property qualifications, for example, they could not exercise the franchise until they attained the age of twenty-five, four years later than men. No woman had ever been elected to political office in Jamaica. The commission was probably insensitive to the sexism that permeated its proceedings and made no effort to include women.

The commission, however, heard directly from several interest groups or received memoranda from them. The Jamaica Progressive League requested for Jamaica "the status of a Dominion with all the rights, privileges and responsibilities appertaining there to." The Jamaican Union of Teachers recommended that elementary education be made available "to every child eligible for it" and urged consideration of the question of compulsory school attendance. Chafing under some discriminatory legislation, the Chinese residents urged the amelioration of restrictions against the immigration of their countrymen to the island. Representing the commercial, business, industrial, and agricultural elite, the Jamaica Imperial Association urged "a radical change" in the fiscal policy of Great Britain whereby colonial produce would receive protection from "the produce and raw material of foreign states."⁴⁹

Carefully prepared, these and other memoranda were studies in societal introspection from the perspective of significant interest groups. Their individual constituencies were small, outnumbered by the poor and the dispossessed. But these groups were the ones that normally commanded the attention of the colonial state, except in times of trouble by the folks from below. Most of them had the governor's ear, as he received delegations from various groups from time to time. But the dispossessed had to create their own pathways for supplication, their own transcripts of protest. The Royal Commission heard, for the most part, from elite men, voices that were not entirely representative of the island as a whole. The multitudes at the societal bottom and at its margins, those who had not participated fully in Jamaica's journey over the past century, were still clamoring for recognition as partners in their country's complex odyssey.

The commission made a major blunder when it approved by majority vote a request by the all-white custodes to give their testimony in camera. Sir Walter Citrine and fellow commissioner Morgan Jones publicly dissented from this decision. It had the effect of denying the public its right to know the views of their appointed leaders on the important social and economic questions of the moment. "It was given the impression," Robert Kirkwood wrote to the secretary of state, "that the majority of the Commission are on the side of the vested interests, and that members [of the commission] favourably disposed towards Labour have been muzzled." Citrine's vigorous support for the rights of the workers earned him the animus of the purveyors of race and color prejudices. "Sir Walter may have won popularity with the blacks," Kirkwood wrote, "but I do not think there is a single white or lightskinned Jamaican who has a good word to say for him."[50]

Walter Citrine did not deserve this hostile reaction to his prolabor stances. He was undoubtedly the principal advocate on the commission for social justice for Jamaican workers. This was a principled position that transcended the imperatives of race and color, a fact that seemed to have eluded the white and light-skinned residents of the island. Citrine was a convenient target upon which to deflect their fears and insecurities. The mistreatment of the workers based upon racial and color differences had been one of the principal causes of the rebellion. Walter Citrine wanted to redress these societal wrongs, not exacerbate them.

The Royal Commission's report was anxiously awaited throughout the British West Indies and in the halls of the Colonial Office. The commission had concluded its site visit to the colonies in Trinidad in late March 1939, but it continued its work in England, taking testimony "on technical points which had arisen during our enquiries in the West Indies."[51] The report and its recommendations were submitted to the Colonial Office in December 1939. Shaken by the report's graphic description of the terrible economic and social conditions in the colonies, His Majesty's Government decided to publish only the recommendations and not the full text. The secretary of state's unpersuasive explanation was that the publication of the entire report would feed enemy propaganda during a time of war. Arthur Creech Jones voiced the sentiments of many people when he said that the failure to publish the entire report was calculated "to arouse enormous suspicion as reflecting very gravely on the administration of the colonial empire."[52]

The Moyne Commission, as it would become known, made some bold proposals to address the social and economic conditions in the colonies. It represented a break with a cardinal principle of British colonialism: the colonies should pay for the services they enjoyed out of their own resources. This principle was not always adhered to, particularly in times of acute economic distress in the colonies or in emergencies of one sort or another. In the previous ten years, for example, the imperial country's Colonial Development Fund had authorized the expenditure of £10,000,000 on various development projects in the empire. This included grants to Jamaica to fight the diseases affecting bananas, to Nigeria for research on sleeping sickness, and to Kenya and Tanganyika for scientific surveys. Impoverished colonies also received grants-in-aid to balance their budgets. Building upon these precedents, the Moyne Commission wanted to establish the principle that financial assistance to the colonies was justified in moments other than those of crises.

The centerpiece of the Moyne Commission's recommendations was a special grant of £1,000,000 yearly for twenty years to the West Indian colonies. The money was to be spent primarily in the areas of education, housing, health services, slum clearance, and land settlement. Known as the "West Indian Welfare Fund," the annual grant would be administered by a "central organization" headed by a comptroller and staffed by technical officers of "the highest qualifications." The commission also recommended the appointment of an inspector general of agriculture for the colonies, with the responsibility to oversee their agricultural development. It wanted to see an emphasis on the "development of peasant farming" and the creation "of an agricultural system of permanent mixed farming."

The commission urged the enactment of laws everywhere to protect trade unions "from actions for damages consequent on strikes," the compulsory registration of unions, and the legalization of picketing. It declined to support "the grant of immediate and complete self government based on universal suffrage, or for a wide increase of the authority of governors which would convert the existing system into a virtual autocracy." The commission's members were divided on constitutional questions, but their failure to make recommendations on them was an abdication of responsibility. It held, however, that political federation should be the ultimate goal of the West Indian colonies.[53]

Since the Royal Commission examined conditions in all of the West Indian colonies, its report was written in general terms. The Colonial Office had the responsibility to work out the details for each colony since the lengthy set of recommendations lacked prescriptions for their implementation. The press gave the report a mixed reception. The *London Express*, for example, observed that "the recommendations appear to offer the colonies doles but not an economic plan." This was true enough. The *Daily Gleaner*, on the other hand, was surprised that the imperial government intended to undertake such an ambitious program involving vast expenditures of funds during wartime. Jamaican nationalists were disappointed that the commission did not recommend self-government for the island, while opponents were relieved.[54]

The Royal Commission was the imperial government's response to the people's grievances. It was a safety valve, a way for the regime to strengthen its authority by reforming the administration of the colonies. There was no expectation at the time that the sun would ultimately set on the British Empire in the West Indies, hence the commission's failure to recommend an expansion of the franchise and placing colonies like Jamaica, Trinidad and Tobago, and British Guiana on the path to self-government. Disappointed by this failure, the proponents of self-government in Jamaica redoubled their efforts to achieve their objective. The Royal Commission had bought the king and his government time, but it could not and did not redress all the grievances that had given it birth.

FIVE

Bustamante, Unionism, and the Politics of Performance

"I had the honour to be responsible for the birth of Trade Unionism in the island of Jamaica," Alexander Bustamante wrote to Secretary of State Oliver Stanley on December 22, 1942. Bustamante was writing to Stanley to urge him to investigate the circumstances under which he had been arrested and placed in Detention Camp as a security risk. This was an erroneous claim and one that was unnecessary, particularly in a letter that was written "in the interest of my honour and my always well guarded and unblemished name."[1] Although Bustamante became by 1942 the best-known and most effective trade unionist Jamaica had yet produced, he stood on the shoulders of other men, principally Allan George St. Claver Coombs.

In contrast to the United States of America or Europe, labor unions made a late appearance in Jamaica. Unions are generally recognized as successors to the craft guilds of medieval Europe, emerging in the wake of the Industrial Revolution. Founded in 1827, the Mechanics Union of Trade Associations became the first modern labor union in the United States, attracting workers from different occupations. Hitherto, these associations of workers were craft based. In comparison, Jamaican workers lacked any protection from their employers in the aftermath of slavery, having neither unions nor guilds.

The first organization of workers in Jamaica was probably the Carpenters, Bricklayers, and Painters Union. It was founded in 1898 and had its headquarters in Kingston. Known also as the Artisans' Union, it became moribund in 1901. It was probably more akin to a European craft guild since its membership seemed to have consisted of people employed in the construction industry. The painters and tobacco workers created guilds in subsequent years, but they were short-lived. In 1918 Alexander Bain Alves founded the Longshoremen's Union No. 1. Four years later, in 1922, the Longshoremen's Union No. 2 appeared. The two organizations belonged to what was called the Jamaica Federation of Labour, constituting the pioneers of a nascent trade-union movement in the island. By May 1938 there were five unions registered with the government. They included the Longshoremen's Union No. 2, the People's Progressive Union No. 1, the Jamaica Workers and Tradesmen's Union, the Jamaica Hotel Employees Association, and the Jamaica United Clerks Association.[2]

Jamaica's first trade-union law was adopted by the Legislative Council in 1919. It was modeled after a similar law passed in England in that year. The law provided for the compulsory registration of unions, but unlike its English counterpart, it did not legalize picketing nor protect strikers from legal action by disgruntled employers. The legislation appeared at a time of increasing labor unrest that came in the aftermath of World War I. Experiencing severe economic distress, dockworkers, firefighters, and workers on the railroads and the banana and sugar plantations walked off their jobs, demanding higher wages. Although the workers continued to be exploited by their employers, the labor movement grew slowly after the passage of the 1919 law.[3]

The first modern trade union in Jamaica was registered on June 29, 1937. Named the Jamaica Workmen and Tradesmen's Union (JWTU), it was founded by Allan Coombs. Unlike its craft-based predecessors and contemporaries, the JWTU was open to all categories of workers in accordance with modern trade-union practice. Coombs had been a police officer, served in the West India Regiment, and worked for the Public Works Department as a contractor. He was not a man of means, a factor that made him identify fully with the workers. Coombs lacked organizational experience and the resources to assist the fledgling union, but this did not temper his energy and enthusiasm.

Aware of his limitations, Coombs invited the usurer and prolific letter writer to the *Daily Gleaner*, Alexander Bustamante, to assume a leadership role in the union. Bustamante brought deeper pockets and boundless energy to the cause. He was named the treasurer. Coombs, Bustamante, and the other officials faced the problem of organizing workers who were unfamiliar with the concept of collective bargaining or even the objectives of a union. Workers, generally speaking, were united primarily by ties arising from kin, friendship, membership in the local cricket club, the conviviality of the neighborhood bar, and religious affiliation. There was a workplace consciousness but not yet a class consciousness in the Marxist sense. They shared a deep sense of identification with their peers at work, but this did not extend to those on the other plantations or at other workplaces, even if their grievances were similar in nature. Many workers were also suspicious of unionization, fearing the reprisals of the employers and the loss of their jobs. Not all workers shared the opposition to unions, but it would take time, education, and a series of epiphanies for them to make the transition from being atomized individual workers to constituting a working class with a shared consciousness.

The opposition to unionization was on dramatic display when Bustamante, Coombs, and other officials of the JWTU attempted to hold a public meeting at Port Antonio on Friday, October 22, 1937. They had come to the town to organize the banana carriers at Boundbrook wharf and the railway pier. The *Gleaner* reported that "memories of Friday's hectic happenings will live for many a day." It described the scene: "In traditional public meeting style, Port Antonio workers broke up the meeting by singing and others tried very effective methods of 'passive resistance,' including the No. 1 declaration of disfavour, the all inclusive, devastating 'away with him,' before which many a speaker has been known to wilt and fade."[4]

Although "sticks were in evidence," there was apparently no violence or "any broken bones," the *Gleaner* reported. The police, according to Bustamante, declined to protect the speakers from the crowd's fury. When Bustamante briefly left the scene to send a telegram of protest to the governor, the crowd "put out lanterns which provided light, and eventually smashed the speakers' stand—a box—and threw it [in] the sea." In spite of the hostility that greeted the officials of the JWTU, Bustamante insisted that there was substantial support for unionization in the crowd. Some men had told him that "they wanted to join the union but they are afraid the police [will] beat them up." The ugly incident was the source of much excitement in Port Antonio. The newspaper reported that the "talk of the town in Port Antonio on Saturday was the affair. A novel sort of 'morning after the night before,' feeling was in the air and wherever two or three were gathered together there was 'Bustamante' in the midst [of] them. If ever a man sprang into town talk overnight it was the labour leader. His name was on everyone's lips."[5]

The "leading citizens" of the town, according to the *Gleaner*, were pleased that the union was not given a hearing. The "union and labour unrest will do Port Antonio not a bit of good," they maintained. It was later revealed, however, that the fracas was not entirely spontaneous. Dr. T. A. Campbell, a prominent dentist, had urged the laborers "not to hear the Unionists, but not to use any violence; just make them know they were not wanted." Bustamante reported that as he and his party proceeded on foot to the meeting, he "saw two men with sticks, one addressed me as follows: you come from Kingston. We have orders to beat up all Kingston people.

You will get no police protection." Reuben Gunter, a cold-drinks vendor said it simply and emphatically: "We want no union here."[6]

The union organizers received a similar reception at Buff Bay. Warned that they would be unwelcome in Manchioneal, the team canceled their visit. When Coombs and other JWTU officials visited the banana workers on the plantations at Amity Hall, Leyden, and Sunderland in St. James to help resolve a dispute with their employers, they received a cool reception. The *Gleaner* reported that 85 percent of the workers "do not belong and have no intention of becoming members of the JWTU."[7] Nor was Bustamante's self-appointed leadership of the nascent labor movement uncritically embraced. When the workers on the Serge Island estate in St. Thomas struck in January 1938, Bustamante hastened there to help resolve the dispute. The workers rejected the terms the owner and Bustamante proposed, refused to listen to him and denounced him as "a traitor," and forced him to leave.[8]

Bustamante would later deny the accuracy of the newspaper report. He admitted, however, that "there were times when a few men whilst I spoke, yelled out: 'you better be careful of that gentlemen' (referring to me), 'he looks like a genal [crook].'" But he claimed that "each time the men said that, they were booed by the great majority who said: 'Don't pay any attention to them Mr. Bustamante, they have no sense.'" Bustamante wanted to restrain the workers from making any wage demands that the employers could not, in his judgment, meet. "And whether the workers want to dislike me for this or not," he said, "it is my duty to instruct them in a sane way so that they might not get up tomorrow and find they have been misled by a few agitators." Elaborating, the aspiring labor leader explained: "My aim in trying to help the workers of this island is to act as a just medium between capital and labour, and if labour cannot even appreciate this, I will still continue to help them, because I am doing so as a labourite at heart without getting any recompense."

The strikes that paralyzed plantations with frequency in the latter part of 1937 and the first half of 1938, the intimidation of fellow workers, and the use of violence occurred because the workers lacked the institutions through which to articulate their grievances. They had to employ a direct, confrontational approach as a substitute for calm and reasoned negotiation. The workers on the Serge Island estate, for example, had no mechanism through which to resolve their dispute in early 1938 when the management rejected their demand for increased wages. Those who remained on the job were intimidated by the others, resulting in the arrest of sixty-four men for "unlawfully, wrongfully and without lawful authority [forcing] . . . persons to depart from their employment by intimidating them." They were tried in two groups. The first group, according to a reporter, "presented a haggard appearance, their manacled hands contributing to the general look of dejection." One policeman testified that "the crowd of non-workers increased daily; they had with them cutlasses and sticks: many of them had both." These people intimidated those who were continuing to work, vowing to "beat their [asses]." The officer said that they "were a most excited, violent crowd, shouting, waving their cutlasses over their heads, insisting that nobody else should work." Others threatened them with death.⁹

Many of the accused men had no attorneys to defend them, being totally at the mercy of the prosecution, the police officers, and the judge. The judge allowed them, however, to pose questions to the policemen who testified. One of the accused, Cecil Russell, provided some comic relief when the judge asked whether he wanted to direct questions to the officer who gave testimony.

> RUSSELL: I will not discommode the witness by asking any questions.
> HIS HONOUR: Your mouth is very sweet. [Laughter]
> RUSSELL: I grow with the Magistrate, Mr. Sharpe at Frankfield, sir. [Laughter]
> HIS HONOUR: There was a lot of excitement at Serge Island that day?
> RUSSELL: Very much so, sir.
> HIS HONOUR: Who caused the excitement?
> RUSSELL: The people who were willing to work. That is what made all the trouble.¹⁰

The judge, after a three-day trial, found sixty-three of the accused men guilty. Three of them, described as "the worst of the lot," were sentenced to one month in prison without the option of a fine. Eight men received fines, and the remainder were admonished and discharged. The angry judge lectured the men not to repeat their behavior at the Duckenfield estate, which would be reaping its canes soon. He wanted "no nonsense" there. "Vehement in voice and manner," the judge "made it quite plain to the men that he was not going to put up with that sort of thing." The judge, Ansel O. Thomson, blamed the men "for being like sheep, easily misled by agitators from outside." Should they have "difficulties" in the future, the men should settle them with their employer in a "sensible manner, but never resort to violence," he advised.¹¹

The arrest and trial of the workers revealed their internal divisions. The intimidation had been directed by one sector of the workers at another sector, indicating that a working class with an identifiable consciousness was still in formation. Judge Thomson's remarks suggested that he was the uncomprehending voice of the elite, blaming the actions of the workers on outside agitators and dismissing their grievances. The judge was guilty of intimidation of another sort: while the workers used the weapons at their disposal—sticks and cutlasses—to intimidate their peers, the judge threatened to use the power of the state to punish those who were demanding justice at the workplace.

Bustamante's brief tenure as an officer of the JWTU provides a window into his philosophy as an emerging labor leader, his leadership style, and his personality. Not content with his job as treasurer of the JWTU, Bustamante demanded that he be named president, threatening to destroy the union if it failed to do so. The union acquiesced, with Coombs later saying that he "voluntarily stood down." Bustamante held that position for only nine days. According to Coombs, Bustamante told his former colleagues that he resigned because he "felt as if he had committed a crime against his conscience and could never hold it [the presidency] any longer because he had taken away my position."[12]

This was the first of many disputes that Bustamante would have with his colleagues and associates. In letters to the press and to Coombs, he accused the union's officers of financial irregularities, of employing "a deceptious method" to "obtain members," and of "jealousy" within its ranks. He was not impressed with the quality of the leadership that the union was providing the workers. "Each day," Bustamante said, "I have more reasons to feel that the present management could do little or no good for the workers." Bustamante accused Hugh Buchanan, the secretary, of undermining his influence in the union. He denounced the "narrow-mindedness" and "unprogressive thinking" that existed in it. He thought "the interest of the masses should be protected by good brain and when I decided to throw my lot in, it was only done so through love for the masses, through a noble heart, a noble mind, and I expected of course greater and better brain in the form of a general secretary."[13] Bustamante's portrayal of Buchanan was harsh, if not self-serving. Born in Clarendon in 1904, Buchanan migrated to Cuba as a young man and became a Garveyite. He also embraced Marxism before he returned to Jamaica in 1929.

Thereafter, he served as a social and political critic and assisted Coombs in establishing the JWTU.

Bustamante used the occasion of his split with the JWTU to explain the nature of his involvement in labor's cause. Writing to Coombs, he said he had "an intense interest in the progress of those who are more unfortunate financially than I am." His role in the union "was only one of nobleness, trying to help others," and he was committed to seeing that the workers "are lifted out of the gutter." Bustamante explained that he had accepted leadership positions in the JWTU "believing I would be in a better position to supervise the interest of the workers" and had "relinquished the posts of treasurer and president chiefly to protect and preserve my honour, dignity, and prestige."

Bustamante made it clear to Coombs that he would not associate himself with "ignorance," an abusive reference to the caliber of the JWTU's leaders. Nor would he do so with those who were "jealous of an outstanding leader," presumably himself. Bustamante was taking his first halting steps as a trade unionist, rhetorically identifying himself with the workers' cause but simultaneously betraying certain qualities that interfered with his ability to work well with others. As he explained to Coombs: "Responsible, intelligent [and] reliable persons will not associate themselves with ignorance unless the latter will submit to training. I shall make it a point of my duty to see that the workers of this country are organized properly not just for wages for a few but chiefly in the interest of the members and the moment I find there is any that is jealous of the ability of an outstanding leader out shall he go."[14]

Alexander Bustamante's most extensive discussion of his views on labor unions, their functions, and relationships with the workers took place in a letter he wrote to the *Daily Gleaner* on November 5, 1937. His limited experience with workers was of recent vintage, and he really had no claim to any accomplishments in the organization of workers, the management of unions, or even the articulation, negotiation, and resolution of their grievances. The principles elucidated in the letter did not emerge from the laboratory of experience or even from a theoretical familiarity with the operation of labor unions internationally. But they would guide his developing work as a trade unionist.

Bustamante's letter was published seven days before he resigned as treasurer of the JWTU and ten days before he left the post of president. His letter urged "workers of all kinds" to join the JWTU to make it "the biggest thing in the history of Jamaica." Betraying his tendency toward inconsistency and unpredictability, he threatened a few days later to "kill" the union if it did not acquiesce to his demands to become president. In the November 5 letter, Bustamante wanted "to explain the objects of Labour unions to the workers of this island as the majority does not seem to know."

According to Bustamante, the "objects" of unions were "to get the people to unite in masses to contribute their little money for cases of emergency so that in the time of this and the time of that, the Union will have money to work for the interest of the workers the way the Executive Committee thinks best; that there should be labour representatives who will represent the cause of labour not alone to their employers but to Government: to work for better wages, better working conditions, and to work in the interest of the unemployed to seek ways and means to obtain them work."

Bustamante stressed that "a labour union is nothing more than the working people's club where they can unite for one common good, for one common cause so that they can bring their grievances to their officers." In addition to their accepting an all-powerful Executive Committee, he admonished the workers to "follow your officers and you must not expect them to follow you, and for that reason the officers should be men of intelligence, honesty, and reliability." "We were not all born to be leaders," Bustamante asserted, "otherwise we would need no clubs nor unions." Since the workers were seeking "justice" from their employers, "they must also measure out justice and fair play to them, however cruel they may be."

Bustamante was unsympathetic to strikes, except as a last resort. Workers, he advised, "should never attempt" strikes against their employers without first voicing their grievances, "and even when capitalists may refuse to do anything, it is your duty to persist in a responsible way to gain your ends before you resort to strikes. Strikes must be the last thing on your minds." Workers, in the end, must be prepared to "die" for their "common cause." Bustamante was dismayed by the number of strikes then occurring in the island, and he urged their cessation. "I know you have reasons to strike" he admitted, "but this is the wrong way to obtain success." When he learned that the clerks and other employers of the steamship companies were planning to form a union, Bustamante hastened to assure them that "they too should know and realize the beauty of unionism and should organize."[15] But he cautioned moderation in their modus operandi. He believed that the employers would "cooperate" with the potential union "provided it is carried on with modification [moderation?]." "Someone may say that the writer is an out and out radical," Bustamante wrote. "Then how can he speak of modification, but if they exercise their power of criticism in this fashion, it would be because they have heard of extreme radicalism, but do not know what it means. I believe in modified radicalism. Extreme radicalism should be only used if that is the only way to conquer, but it should be the last method, if used."[16]

Bustamante's letters were designed to temper the developing militancy of the disgruntled workers. They were also directed at the employers, assuring them that they would not have to contend with frequent strikes. Seen through the optic of the workers, this was hardly in their interest. It sought to neutralize the most effective weapon that a labor union had in its arsenal, a fact that Bustamante would come to realize as he gained greater experience as a trade unionist. Bustamante's comments on governance in a union emphasized an uncritical acceptance of the leadership's decisions by the rank and file. This did not augur well for the development of unions as democratic organizations.

Although Bustamante severed his ties with the JWTU, he continued to advocate labor's cause. The two men, Coombs and Bustamante, threw verbal darts at one another from the pages of the *Gleaner*. Their disagreements were not ideologically based but stemmed from personal rivalry and enormous differences in personality and leadership style. The men were competing for the affection and fealty of the workers. But whereas Coombs voluntarily resigned to make Bustamante the president of the JWTU, Bustamante was beginning to demonstrate an incapacity to work well with his colleagues, unless he were the unquestioned *jefe maximo*.

In spite of its internal difficulties, the JWTU limped along; by the end of 1937, it had about 950 members, constituting less than one-half of 1 percent of the workers in Jamaica. The Jamaica Hotel Employees Association was founded at the end of 1937, bringing to four the number of registered unions in the island. They had a combined membership of 1,050 and assets of £150. The number of the unions and the size of their membership, however, did not accurately reflect the strength of the emerging labor movement.[17]

If 1937 saw an angry awakening of sectors of the working population, the following year constituted a veritable volcanic eruption. This motion from below was not orchestrated by Coombs and the JWTU. The union lacked the organization and power to do so. In fact, the people's dire economic circumstances were the sources of their energy, the engine of their demands. Bustamante was the ubiquitous negotiator, appearing at the scenes of labor unrest whether invited or on his own volition. He was not the creator of the unrest; it needed no such leader. Nor did he give it shape or direction. But he was the loudest voice of protest, the pit bull in the assault on those whom he denounced as "the capitalists." Bustamante brought to labor's cause in these early months his empathy, his angry rhetoric, and his boundless energy. As the months wore on in 1938, he became increasingly accepted as a labor leader, honing his credentials. It was an incredible achievement: a usurer who boasted of his wealth, a near-white man who acquired a Spanish surname, was becoming the widely recognized, if unpredictable, voice of Jamaica's mostly black working people.

Seizing the opportunity created by the 1938 uprising, Bustamante and the people around him conceived the creation of a number of labor unions, each one representing a category of workers. The model seemed to have been that of the European guilds, being occupationally based. Bustamante would serve as the president of each one, providing the link between them. Ten thousand persons had gathered at the Kingston Race Course on June 22, 1938, to hear Bustamante outline his plans to organize all Jamaican workers under his leadership. It was a festive occasion, but it belied the importance of the moment in the history of the labor movement in the colony. St William Grant, the first speaker and a man described by the *Gleaner* as Bustamante's "henchman and watchman," urged the workers to protect their leader from the "czarist regime in the police force," vowing to "die in my tracks for him" in promoting their common cause. In his speech, Hugh Buchanan, the former secretary of the JWTU, explained the constituency of the unions that Bustamante intended to found. Named the Maritime Union, the first union was intended to include dock and ship workers, shipping clerks, banana carriers and stowers, and longshoremen. The Transport Workers Union included railway, tram, and bus workers. It welcomed track men, drivers, mechanics, chauffeurs, and taximen. The third union, the Factory Workers Union, was being created for industrial workers and those who worked where articles or goods were being manufactured. The Municipal Workers Union was directed at individuals who were in the employ of cities, parochial boards, the water commission, and so on. The fifth union, the General Workers Union, was aimed at all agricultural workers and those not falling within the purview of the others. Before long, seven unions emerged. These Bustamante unions, as they were called, were reorganized, combined, and registered as the Bustamante Industrial Trade Union (BITU) in January 1939.[18]

The formation of these unions meant that Bustamante was now prepared to undertake the difficult task of organizing workers and negotiating on their behalf in an institutional context. He was making the transition from the itinerant, ubiquitous, self-identified labor leader to the founder of unions, pledging to work with colleagues. Addressing the large gathering on that afternoon in June, Bustamante asked: "Why have you been giving away your labour for next to nothing? I shall answer it for you. Because you were not organized, because you did not have the right leadership, because you are too suspicious, because you will not confide or trust implicitly in any one [applause]. But the time has come when you must trust someone, when you must leave your destiny in the hands of one who has more thinking faculties than you have [cheers]."

Bustamante was obviously speaking of himself, demonstrating a kind of self-centeredness that characterized his public utterances. He called for unity among the workers and threatened those who intended to form rival unions. "Let me tell them," he shouted, "don't attempt to run any race with me. I will break them into smithereens [loud and prolonged cheers]. I don't want to do them any harm, but I don't want them to harm the people [cheers]. So I will crush them from the very start [cheers]."

Bustamante also warned employers who refused to negotiate, telling them that "we are going to compel them to do so. . . . I will step upon their corns and upon their heads." He criticized the clerks and shop assistants for declining to be members of his unions. Earlier, St William Grant had derided them for believing that they were not "part of labour" because "they get ten shillings a week and have to straighten their hair and wear spike-heel shoes." This was a reference to the divisions in the ranks of labor, a fact that led Bustamante to tell his audience that "every man or woman who works or takes money for his work belongs to labour."[19] Later that night, Bustamante addressed a meeting at the Papine market, where he was hailed as "Bustamante the Great," as "a man sent to the People by Jehovah," and as "the Greatest Worker Jamaica has ever seen."[20]

This was a good start for Bustamante and his unions. But the labor leader's rhetoric invited criticism. His threat to destroy competing unions did not bode well for the future of unionism in the island. Nor was his promise to coerce recalcitrant employers into line suggestive of a deep understanding of the modus operandi of the modern trade-union movement. But the full implications of these statements would not become immediately clear. Bustamante, to be sure, did not stand alone in his effort to unionize the workers island-wide. His assistants included the prominent attorney Ross Livingston; the brilliant young journalist Kenneth Hill; Leslie Rose, a shoemaker from St. Catherine; J. M. Edwards, a railway employee; Hugh

Buchanan; St William Grant; and Gladys Longbridge, his private secretary. Norman Manley served as a general adviser.

Once he created and named his unions, Bustamante confronted the formidable task of recruiting members. Apart from his brief and unsatisfactory relationship with Allan Coombs in 1937, he lacked experience in organizing workers. Bustamante's preferred organizational strategy was to hold public meetings in selected parts of the island, explain to the attendees the mission of trade unions, and invite them to join the ones that bore his name. Thousands of employed and unemployed people generally attended these meetings, many responding positively to the call to be unionized. Bustamante was careful at times not to encourage the unemployed to join, promising in June 1938 that "as soon as we are able, we will devise some means of assisting the unemployed and we will be only too glad to accept them as members. If we take these people's money and can do nothing for them they would be the first ones to call us dishonest."[21] His lieutenants were frequently not as scrupulous, accepting the unemployed as members.

The unemployed, however, nominally swelled the ranks of the union, believing that this would help them to obtain work. That some Jamaican workers embraced this belief was a function of their misunderstanding of the purposes of labor unions. Bustamante, ostensibly, did not feed these illusions, but joblessness and the desperation created by poverty did the job. He established branch offices of the unions in selected towns of the island, each one headed by a secretary who was assisted by one or two other persons. These people were recruited rather quickly, many of them being only marginally literate. "The Union has been organised all in a hurry," Bustamante wrote to Manley. "[H]undreds of secretaries could hardly read." Ten weeks after the foundation of the unions, Bustamante was able to report that "field organisation . . . has been developing so rapidly throughout the island, that we found we could not give sufficient time to [the] work at headquarters."[22] In order to boost membership, Bustamante and the other officials undertook frequent and extensive tours of the island. They visited towns in Portland, St. Thomas, St. James, and the other parishes, where they were warmly received by the working people.

The members of the unions were predominantly male, reflecting the composition of the workplace. Women, to be sure, found employment on the sugar estates and the waterfront, but they seemed to have been in the minority. A few women found employment in the restaurants and as salespersons in businesses. Others performed the difficult task of breaking stones with a hammer for the network of unpaved roads in the island. Most women, however, labored as domestic servants, washerwomen, cooks, and nursemaids. The "help wanted" columns of the newspapers listed these opportunities, describing the qualifications the applicants should possess. Young women, particularly those residing in rural areas, also advertised their availability for these jobs.

Female workers had participated in the labor rebellion. Their number was not as large as that of the men given their low representation in the workforce, with the exception of domestic service. Donald Byfield recalled that "women played a minority role in the riots. One or two women or one or two pockets of women did join the demonstrations and become quite loud and showed their interest to break down what was known as the tyranny of unemployment in Jamaica."[23] Gladys Longbridge, who later became Bustamante's spouse, remembered that "when the riot started, there were many women in the organization. [Women] were part of the waterfront crowd. There were some very strong poor women who used to lift and load bananas. Some women, the women, a few women played a great part supporting the men, cooking for them and all that type of thing. Of course, they weren't [especially prominent], you know. They were just in the crowd."[24]

Two women, in particular, received unanimous acclaim for their supportive roles in the rebellion on the waterfront. Edna Manley, the wife of Norman Manley, raised money to feed the striking workers and assisted in cooking the food. Vivian Durham was effusive in his praise of her work, declaring: "Edna Manley was a grand and splendid woman. She played a noble role. Again, there was a psychological factor because people of Mrs. Manley's power and social position wouldn't normally mix with 'Quashie' at the Waterfront."[25]

Aggie Bernard was the other outstanding woman who contributed to the workers' cause. Vivian Durham described her as "a poor, humble, Jamaican woman, a washerwoman. . . . [S]he washed for the Waterfront men. She shared their mutual burden, and often she shed for them sympathizing tears, and crystallized it into action to help them to maintain their strike."[26] Miss Bernard took the lead in preparing food for the strikers. Evon Blake, a journalist, said she was motivated by "pure humanity: . . . she knew the boys. She knew them. She is the one who should get a statue."[27] Vivian Durham provided a convincing assessment of the roles of these two key women in Jamaica's history. He was certain that "Aggie Bernard played a vital and indispensable role along with Mrs. Edna Manley in the birth and evolution of the Trade Union movement in this country."[28]

Domestic servants constituted a disproportionate share of the general labor force. The 1943 census reported that they numbered 62,792. The majority were located in the parishes of Kingston and St. Andrew. Kingston had 9,500 domestic workers in 1943, and St. Andrew had 11,124. In contrast, there were 1,293 female office clerks, 1,367 waiters, 90 telephone operators, and 31,485 farm laborers in the island. Overall, the census reported 183,455 female workers in Jamaica in 1943. Domestic workers, therefore, constituted approximately one-third of this labor force.[29]

In spite of their numerical strength, these women were ignored entirely by Coombs, Bustamante, and the other labor leaders. Some of them probably employed women in their households as domestic servants. Writing to the *Gleaner* on October 24, 1941, M. O. Spence noted that there were "dozens" of unions in the island but "not even the leaders of these unions seem to think of domestic servants as a form of labour." He called attention to the low wages they received; the long work day; and the "disgraceful" and "unsanitary" baths, rooms, and sewers they had to "endure" where they worked.[30] Spence had made an important point. Domestic work was deemed to be unimportant and lacking in social prestige. The unionists may have thought that the relationship between employers and domestics was so intimate that it was beyond the purview and scrutiny of any organization of workers. Fearing reprisals from their employers, domestics may also have been unwilling to be unionized.

It was undeniable, however, that many of these women worked under the most appalling conditions, laboring from sunup to sundown and frequently much later. Those who lived on the premises generally had no fixed hours of labor, being on call throughout the day and night. These women, particularly those who came to Kingston from the rural parishes, usually had no choice but to accept the accommodations provided by the employers. The wages were low, frequently less than five shillings weekly. Although the *Gleaner* did not support an increase in wages, it admitted that "five shillings a week for a grown woman in this city [Kingston] with fourteen hours of labour per day, is an altogether inadequate remuneration even in a tropical colony like this." The daily newspaper reminded its readers, however, that since some domestics received food and lodging from their employers, they were earning in "real" wages a sum much higher than that which they were actually being paid. The *Gleaner* maintained that members of the middle class were unable to pay higher wages "because of the steadily increasing price of things." These employers, the editorial observed sadly, would have "to do in their own households what they have hitherto employed servants to help in doing." Although the *Gleaner* conceded that these workers were on the job for twelve or fourteen hours daily, it stressed that it was not "continuous" labor. "Most of our servants are leisurely," the paper noted; "most of them have hours of rest; they become in time . . . almost a part of the family." The *Gleaner* returned to this issue twice in two weeks, each time warning that any legislation setting a minimum wage for domestics would harm those it was intended to help.[31]

The *Gleaner*'s views were echoed by one of its columnists, G. St. C. Scotter. He opined that any legislation on behalf of the domestic workers ran the risk of "killing or at least crippling the goose that lays the golden eggs." Given the deplorable conditions most domestics endured, this was an unfortunate choice of words. Scotter believed, however, that the "younger generation of servants" worked less diligently and efficiently than their older counterparts. In contrast, the columnist suggested that "the employers of domestic servants are perhaps more reasonable and fair-minded than any other class of employer."[32] This was a questionable conclusion, and even if it were accurate, it was hardly a positive comment on the state of domestic service in Jamaica.

Reflecting the social conventions of the society in which they operated, the trade unions only had two women in their official hierarchy: Gladys Longbridge and Edith Nelson of the Bustamante unions. The other unions had no women in official positions and seemed not to recognize their invisibility. It cannot be said definitively, however, that these two women articulated and advanced the interests of their sex. To the degree that they wielded any influence in the unions, that was probably a function of their personal relationship with Bustamante and not any other imperative. Gladys Longbridge recalled that "my role [as a woman] was support, support, to support Bustamante and what he fought for. I had a job with him, and I wrote most of his letters and so on."[33] The women's interests were represented by the men, Vivian Durham recalled. "The women," he said, "were taken care of through the [male] union secretaries who would tend to their economic needs."[34] Bustamante, it should be said, championed causes relating to the welfare of women at the workplace around the negotiating table even if his union did not accord them a special place in its ranks.

Encouraged and buoyed by the adulation of the workers and growing in confidence, Bustamante gave speeches and wrote letters that were frequently confrontational in tone. When he visited Port Maria in September

1938, he accused the "capitalists" of "looking for trouble," threatening them with "a continuous march until we bend or break their wicked hearts." Bustamante said he had written "to ask them to do the right thing by the workers, I have written to ask them to alter their ways; but if they refuse, if they try to murder me, to spill my blood, then blood will be spilt in this country so much that it will leave a history in this country for a long time."[35]

Bustamante dramatically told his audience that a plot existed to kill him, but "neither capitalists nor government can intimidate me. They have now concluded that the only way to get me is through assassination." Suggesting that he was incorruptible, he told the workers at the waterfront in Kingston that "the employers had been accustomed to buy[ing] leaders with social position or with money." He assured his listeners that "thank God, he wanted no social position and he had his own money." Then he boasted: "I do not see the man I cannot run out of the country, if he is treating labourers unjustly."[36]

Bustamante's style as a labor leader emerged quite clearly in these early months. His indefatigability was evident as he traveled throughout the island, met countless people, and addressed public meetings late into the nights. By November 1938 he had fallen ill, probably from overwork. As he explained to an interviewer on that occasion: "I am still being besieged, night and day, all with complaints. They little realise what it means to break down under the strain I have been through since May, and before, long before. I wish someone could point out to them that I must have a rest or . . ."

The interviewer added that "I remember the Americanism 'or else.' I was nearly tempted to ask, 'or else what?' But it would have been too trite. It would have been facetious." But, he continued, "Bustamante still needs rest and much more rest or else . . . well there might be no more Bustamante." This restlessness, this desire to be always on the move, would remain one of Bustamante's defining characteristics.[37]

Bustamante's constant travels interfered with his time for introspection or to engage in planning. But he was never known for the articulation of long-term objectives, either for the workers or the colony as a whole. When Sir Stafford Cripps, the distinguished English socialist and legislator, met Bustamante in September 1938, he wanted to know the program he had conceived for his unions. "What is your programme?" Sir Stafford asked Bustamante. After a pause, Bustamante replied: "we are endeavouring to secure for the working man a living wage." Sir Stafford was not satisfied with the response, telling Bustamante, "but that is not a programme." Continuing mercilessly, Cripps admonished Bustamante: "You cannot stir up unrest and leave it there. You must have a programme for the country. What is your objective? Raising wages is not a programme. I suggest that you get together and work out some programme."[38]

Before he could do what Sir Stafford prescribed, Bustamante had to develop a coherent political philosophy that would guide his work as a labor leader and aspiring politician. He had given an indication of his thinking and objectives when he wrote his letters to the *Gleaner* in November 1937 and when he responded to a series of questions from G. St. C. Scotter. Scotter was not very sympathetic to the labor movement and wanted to understand what he called the "Bustamante riddle." Scotter asked, "What is at the back of Bustamante's mind? What are his personal motives? Are they purely altruistic? Does he do what he does simply for the people alone? Are they pecuniary; is any money he may be paid for his labours the motive? Is it personal power?"

Continuing, Scotter said that it would be no exaggeration to maintain that "Bustamante is, in himself, the Unions: that they have no existence, control or function (apart from him or even) in conjunction with him." He observed that "the only action the public has heard of by the Unions independent of Bustamante seems to have been their proposal to put up a statue to him during his life, and endow him with a Rolls Royce."[39]

Scotter had posed questions that were on the lips of many Jamaicans, principally Bustamante's middle-class detractors. Bustamante responded a few days later in a published article entitled "Why I Want Power." He had had time to consider his answers, so they can be given considerable credence. The article was vintage Bustamante, a mixture of braggadocio, bombast, and abusive rhetoric. "I am delighted that Mr. Scotter realises I have a mind. I just wish I could think that of others," he observed. Bustamante then listed his sacrifices in the cause of labor. "Up to now" he said, "I have been living off my own capital, expending excessive energy, perhaps ruining the excellent health I possess to prevent workers of all classes from being trampled upon, as they have been in the past as if they were foot mats belonging to no one, not even the British Government."

Bustamante noted that labor would never be able to pay him adequately for his work, claiming that the unions had become "gigantic organisations admittedly through my personal influence." His private business had suffered because of his devotion to labor, particularly his foreign ventures. Bustamante had, he confessed, "thousands upon thousands of dollars, not hundreds, invested in Jamaica also," and he was losing "much of this money." He found Scotter's "suggestion regarding pecuniary motives" to be "impertinent." Continuing, Bustamante explained why he needed power: "Yes I want power, sufficient power to be able to defend those weaker than I am; those less fortunate, and that's what I have today—POWER. That hurts Scotter and his type." Admitting that he harbored undemocratic tendencies, Bustamante said: "It has been said that I want to be a dictator. Yes, I do want to dictate the policy of the unions in the interest of the people I represent and the only ones who are getting results today are dictators."[40]

Responding to Bustamante's assertions, Scotter observed: "How you can have a dictatorship and a union at one and the same time seems to me an impossibility, a direct contradiction in terms." He called attention to Bustamante's frequent use of the pronoun "I," asking his readers to "note the heading 'Why "I" want Power.' [N]ot 'Why the Union Wants Power . . .' [always] 'I' 'I' 'I.' No mention whatever throughout the entire article of the Union! What can one gather from this? Merely that Mr. Bustamante takes the position that he is the Union—that the Union itself has no voice, no power, no constitution . . . except in so far as he, Bustamante, says so."[41]

Scotter's critique of Bustamante's modus operandi was not underserved. Enjoying the spotlight, Bustamante's egotism was invariably on full display, and his self-serving comments were a regular feature of his speeches. A few days after his exchange with Scotter, Bustamante boasted to a crowd at Edelweiss Park that "all Jamaica and even the civilized world know I fear no man." He was certain that he had the love of the great majority of workers, asserting: "I believe I have the hate of capitalists, but I have their respect too." Bustamante assured his listeners that "the more your number, the greater the strength of your unions, the more I will be respected."[42]

Bustamante seized another opportunity to explain his political philosophy when he addressed a crowd of about 3,000 persons at the Ward Theatre in late August 1938. The occasion was a meeting designed to encourage clerks to join the Bustamante unions. He announced that he was going to contest the 1940 elections for the Legislative Council. "I am going to stand for Kingston in 1940," Bustamante declared. "[N]o matter who come[s] forward labour is going to triumph. . . . [W]e want more radicals in the Council. . . . [W]e must keep out our sissies and send the he-men. And I want to tell you when in the Council unless they treat with labour, they will have to get the fire brigade to cool me down."[43]

Energized by the noisy, enthusiastic crowd, Bustamante promised to help the clerks destroy their "yoke of oppression and the depression too." Elaborating, he denounced those who had "the impertinence to say that I am a Red." "I am not a Communist," he thundered. "I am a Radical Socialist

Republican." He did not say what this meant, and perhaps no explanation was necessary given the temper of the crowd. After Bustamante announced his support for the clerks, the *Gleaner* reported that "the speaker's voice dropped into inaudible tones, his left knee bent and his clenched fists outstretched.... [H]e gazed into the vast spell-bound throng, speechless. Then pandemonium let loose.... [R]oars of almost endless cheering greeted the pronouncements of the leader, while his lithe, rigid figure stood in that pose so characteristic of Bustamante and so beloved by his followers."[44]

Bustamante was the consummate showman, particularly on a public platform. To his admirers, this was an endearing attribute; to his detractors, it signified his intellectual challenges and a frivolous temperament. Bustamante never claimed to be a man of cerebral depth or sober reflection; that was cousin Norman's province. His animating passion was the workers' cause, and it was to their welfare that he had dedicated himself. Despite the fervor of his rhetoric, Bustamante did not seek a radical transformation of the Jamaican political and economic status quo. His advocacy of better treatment for the workers was always tempered by his need to reassure the barons of capital that he was not their foe. In August 1940, for example, he told the secretary of state that his union had endeavored "to steer clear of any attempt at emotionalism or to bully capitalistic interests unduly." This disclaimer notwithstanding, he blamed such "interests" for the low wages and deplorable condition of the workers on the sugar estates. Bustamante condemned the "terrible pay of the workers" and the "long hours of labour which exist to an appalling extent, where in some cases people are paid less than 2d per hour. Task work is given out at the same pitiful price which does not enable the workers to earn more than the same pittance, insufficient for them even to eke out a miserable existence filling up the Poor Houses and other institutions of pity and Crime, whilst another small section of this community, becomes richer and richer—thus the reason for the volcanic discontent existing in the country."[45]

This was the language of class conflict, but Bustamante would never have proclaimed himself a political ideologue or a disloyal citizen of the empire. He was grateful, he assured the secretary of state, for the government-appointed Labour Adviser's role in mediating disputes in the island. Had it not been for that official's work, Bustamante said,

> [t]he country would be brought to a stage where it would be decorated with bayonets from one extreme to another, and then cables would have been sent to England that hooligans and criminals had

caused trouble as was the nature of the cables sent in 1938. And when it was said that the Leader of this Union, Bustamante, was just a "Stir-Up," a "Mischief-Maker," a "Communist" and an "Anarchist from Spain," this was a delusion and a snare—because in truth and in fact it [he] was only a common patriot with honest intent and purposes fighting for justice and fairplay for those less fortunate.[46]

Bustamante and other unionists were certainly not alone in calling attention to what he described as "the shocking and intolerable" wages the workers received, their eleven- or twelve-hour workday and their awful economic circumstances. James A. Armitage, a Roman Catholic priest, was equally outraged by the conditions that existed throughout the island, declaring: "We find poverty, hunger, disease, ignorance, superstition, illegitimacy, prostitution—general wholesale misery. The people are illfed, illclothed, illhoused. They are sunk in abject and degrading pauperism. . . . Our capitalistic civilization hasn't given them a chance. It's the economic system that's at fault, and not the poor people."[47]

The two men spoke an unpalatable truth. Bustamante yearned to achieve respect and power in the island to change the conditions he described so passionately. "I will prove to the entire country that there is one king of labour—Bustamante," he yelled to a cheering audience at the Race Course in July 1939. A month later, he threatened to have Jamaica annexed by the United States if Britain did not pay more attention to the island. "If the British Empire does not give Jamaica a square deal, then I am going to Italy and Germany to expose Great Britain," he declared. Such a threat bordered on sedition in wartime. Clearly not imagining a time when Jamaica would become an independent nation, Bustamante made it known that "if any commoner is going to be governor of Jamaica, it will be Alexander Bustamante and he alone."[48]

This was a premature fantasy; Bustamante was hardly setting the agenda for the restless workers. He had not developed a viable strategy for providing leadership for them. Nor was he bringing much organizational coherence to the labor movement. One critic, self-identified as "a businessman," observed in September 1938 that Bustamante "has never called a strike. He has always come in after and settled it. He is therefore not the leader of the people but the titular head." Consequently, Bustamante was "their tool and their mouthpiece."[49] This was an overly critical assessment. But the modus operandi of labor unions was as new to Bustamante as it was to the workers and to the Jamaican people as a whole. Accustomed to exercising power over their workers without the intervention of a union, employers resented the intrusion and in some cases tried to sabotage and destroy it. For example, Major G. St. J. Orde Browne, the Labour Adviser in the Colonial Office, maintained that "a proportion" of the sugar-estate employers opposed the union's existence "and endeavor to undermine and discredit its influence."[50] Similarly, the workers were unfamiliar with collective bargaining and used strikes as the weapon of first resort. Realizing their awesome power for the first time, they preferred direct action as manifested by strikes as opposed to the more-complicated, slower, and less-dramatic process of negotiation.

The effectiveness of the Bustamante unions was also severely compromised by turmoil and instability in their leadership. The first major crack appeared in mid-August 1938, when St William Grant denounced several officers of the union as "rats, sycophants, crooks, worms." The occasion was a mass meeting at the Pier l, attended by some 5,000 "labourers." Accusing his colleagues of "jealousy, graft and treachery," Grant reportedly "wept as a child." Sobbing, he declared that "my heart is so full, that it could break." Grant spoke for an hour, using profanities. According to the newspaper report, "Grant's temper rose with the seconds. Coat in hand, sweat streaming down his clean-shaven head and, more profanities coming from his lips, he stormed from the platform. . . . [N]ext he climbed the high wall east of the premises, cursing, screaming, accusing."

A stunned Bustamante immediately condemned Grant's conduct, declaring that "his conduct is a disgrace to himself and the Unions. Such conduct can only dig a grave for the Unions. I will not tolerate it—whether from an officer, a man whom I love dearly—or from the lowliest one of you. . . . Much as I would shed blood for Grant because I know he will shed blood for me, I deplore his conduct. . . . This organization must have discipline." Agreeing with Bustamante, the excited crowd demanded that Grant apologize for his outburst. Ignoring the demand, Grant was "seized by another violent fit of temper . . . slung his coat over his shoulder, and with more violent language, departed in the "custody of a stout dark woman."[51]

This was dark comedy, and it was not a good advertisement for the Bustamante unions. Grant had used a public forum to air his grievances and embarrass his colleagues. His conduct suggested the absence of institutional mechanisms to handle his charges on the one hand, or reflected the behavior of a man unfamiliar with the etiquette of responsible union leadership on the other. One plausible conclusion was that Grant's tirade was a function of the two possibilities. It was, in a professional sense, an ugly performance, one not likely to enhance confidence in the unions among their supporters and critics alike.

Bustamante plunged into damage-control mode immediately. Speaking to the press, he revealed that "within the next forty-eight hours I shall come to the most important decision in my eventful life and one which may sadden my heart, perhaps forever, as it may affect the tens of thousands of workers in Jamaica who look to me for guidance."[52] This was classic Bustamante hyperbole. Meanwhile, Grant visited Bustamante several times to settle the dispute, but to no avail. He also appointed a confidante to mediate and to call a public meeting to enable him to "publicly apologize" to Bustamante, the unions, "and its [sic] followers."[53]

The wily Bustamante exploited the incident to consolidate his power and to strengthen his appeal to the workers. The leader did not address the dispute in private but took it directly to the people. Thousands of workers gathered at the Pier 1 on August 17 to listen to four hours of speeches denouncing Grant. The meeting, the *Gleaner* reported, was "a triumph" for the unions. The crowd supported Grant's dismissal, endorsing one speaker's claim that "the scriptures teach that the traitor was always the one next to the leader." Another observed that "the rat has come to cut the bottom from our bread basket."

But it was Alexander Bustamante's show. After affirming his continuing love for Grant, he emphasized that he had a "greater duty to the majority of the people than I have to just one man." He revealed that he had been unhappy with Grant for the previous several weeks because his conduct at Frome was "so damnable, his words so wretchedly bad." Grant was also an unsatisfactory worker who made outrageous demands, such as wanting "his name on all the Union's papers: he wanted the Union to be called the Bustamante and Grant Unions: Grant wanted to sign cheques. Grant wanted his name on everything: Grant wanted to employ the office help: Grant went around and promised people jobs in the office: Grant wanted when he went in the office that everybody should get up and pay attention to him."

Bustamante's scathing criticisms of Grant resonated with the crowd. "Away with Grant," its members roared. Warming to his subject, Bustamante declared that "some people cannot stand success. The moment they get a little success and are able to live above the manner in which they used to live they get fanatical ideas [Applause] and if they are not allowed to carry those ideas through they become the most spiteful people you ever saw. If I did not have so much faith in Grant I would believe that he was hired by one of the companies to break up the unions."

Bustamante then revealed his momentous decision. "It has come to the moment," he said, "when I must decide in favour of the Union, in favour of the people, because it is better to have an enemy out than in [Cheers]. And as leader, as your leader, I don't feel that I should throw that responsibility upon your shoulders. I am supposed to accept responsibility, , , GRANT IS FIRED [Loud and continuing cheering]." To demonstrate his compassion, Bustamante asked the crowd to approve his paying Grant two-thirds of his salary for three months. He wanted the throng to support "this merciful act."[54] Following the imbroglio from his base in Montego Bay, Coombs told a crowd of 1,000 persons that "the other side has fallen into the ditch they dug for us. The Government must show Bustamante he is not God."[55]

Bustamante did not claim he was a deity, nor did he claim divine powers. But this unseemly row and Bustamante's actions demonstrated that he exercised absolute control over the unions, unilaterally dismissing a prominent officer. It was an early demonstration of Bustamante's personalist leadership style, his tendency to play to the crowd and to vilify his antagonists—real or imagined—publicly. Grant's intemperate diatribe was inexcusable, but his leader's handling of the matter on a public platform was inappropriate and an abdication to the politics of the street.

Bustamante's dismissal of Grant was not the termination of the dispute. Grant expressed his contrition and desire to return to the unions' fold. When he attempted to speak with Bustamante at the No. 3 Pier on August 16, the chief declined, emphasizing that he would have nothing to do with anyone who could "perpetrate" such a "scandalous act—just what the capitalists wanted." Humiliated by Bustamante's disdain for him, Grant reminded his supporters that he had been loyal to Bustamante, even going to jail with him. He had kept faith with his leader and the promise he had made when he was hired. "Grant," Bustamante had asked, "will you march always with me and if necessary die for the people and increased wages? Will you go to prison with me?" "Yes" was Grant's unhesitating reply. As the days wore on, Bustamante revisited his decision to dismiss Grant. "We like each other too much to have trouble," the leader said on August 25. "Why punish a man after he has realized he is wrong and has promised to make amends?" Grant was subsequently reinstated, but the rapprochement was not destined to endure.[56]

The union experienced another serious crisis in its hierarchy when Hugh Buchanan, the secretary for organization and propaganda, resigned on

April 17, 1939, complaining about its "method of organization and leadership." He had been displeased with Bustamante's dictatorial style. Kenneth Hill, the young and talented vice president, also resigned. Hill expressed his disappointment "with the lack of management" of the union. It was, he said, without "any policy, a democratic constitution and rational management, in spite of repeated pressure from one and other quarters." Hill was harshly critical of Bustamante's leadership of the newly constituted BITU, the umbrella union that had replaced the seven Bustamante unions in January 1939. He charged that "the management of the Union stands urgently in need of reform, efficiency and knowledge of trade unionism, and that while your leadership is not lacking in vigour and courage, it is wanting in balance, vision, and discipline and should be amenable to the jurisdiction of an executive body elected by the members to ensure democratic representation."[57]

These allegations had considerable merit, but Bustamante responded by accusing the two men of wanting to destroy the BITU. This was a preposterous charge to level against two colleagues who were as committed to the welfare of the workers as was their erstwhile leader. Bustamante publicly alleged that Hill resigned because of a reduction in his salary. This was an inaccurate statement since Hill had "willingly" accepted it in a letter he wrote to the leader. Hill's and Buchanan's resignation was soon followed by that of Stanley Vernon, the organizing secretary of the chauffeur's section, and V. Elliott, one of the representatives of the transport workers section of the union. "I know I will be slated as a traitor but I can stand all of that. It will pass over my head," Vernon ventured. He denounced the "slackness" and the inefficiency at the union's headquarters.[58] Bustamante once more responded to the spate of resignations in the union, particularly that of Hugh Buchanan and Kenneth Hill, when he addressed a public meeting at the Race Course. "Praise God, Alleluia," he exulted, "the traitors within have resigned." He knew that "it is better to have the enemy outside as one can fight him better than inside." Continuing his assaults on the men, Bustamante said: "I am told that £2,000 is being paid to smash the Union up—all kinds of rascality are being used to destroy the Union . . . all kinds of pressures are used on me to surrender to the enemies. . . . [M]y friends if this union is to survive I must have the courage of a Napoleon. . . . [W]e must fight back to destroy and annihilate our enemies."

Bustamante told his audience that he had rejected financial support from foreign communists. Buchanan, the leader said, had resigned from the BITU because he wanted to introduce communism into it.[59] This was not a persuasive argument since Buchanan would certainly have been more effective in that regard if he acted from within the union. Bustamante's claim that the men who resigned were enemies of the union was unfounded. The men were totally dedicated to the workers' cause; their problem was with Bustamante and the nature of his leadership.

Bustamante seemed, in the early months of the existence of the unions, to be modeling his leadership style after that of the political strong men in the Latin American republics, the jefe maximos of popular repute. This was hardly an appropriate model for an organization that should have been less dependent on the personality of one man and more on shared leadership and its constitutional provisions and mechanisms. Bustamante's erraticism and his personalist leadership style were manifested once again when he announced his resignation from the BITU at a public meeting at the Kingston Race Course on August 20, 1939. There were 4,000 people in attendance to listen to Bustamante and St William Grant. Preceding Bustamante at the microphone, Grant criticized the sitting governor and officers of the unions "in his harangue to the crowd." Reprising the incident that occurred almost a year earlier, Bustamante condemned Grant's remarks, angrily declaring: "[Either] you Grant or I will resign. You are fired from this Union." Grant declined to withdraw his remarks, adding: "Bustamante cannot leave the union." Bustamante "yelled" in response: "I resign. I leave the Union now. Grant can run it." Shocked by Bustamante's unexpected announcement, the crowd became "wilder and . . . more disorderly," shouting: "[Y]ou cannot go. You are our leader and we will die for you." Moved by these entreaties, Bustamante withdrew his resignation "amidst great applause." Grant later shook hands with Bustamante "and showed repentance for his action."[60] This was another extraordinary performance by the two men whose juvenile theatrics certainly brought no credit to the union. Actions such as this one were solidifying Bustamante's image as a tempestuous, temperamental, and unpredictable leader.

The Bustamante-Grant public tantrum was symptomatic of deeper problems in the union. It was reported that the officers were "talking back" to their leader. They wanted "a more democratic" constitution for the unions, which would give the members the right to elect the officers rather than having them named by the leader. Some were prepared to see Bustamante execute his frequent threats to resign rather than allow the continuance of what they called "a dictatorship." The disgruntled officers were also critical of "the finances of the union" and were requesting "the calling in of an unbiased auditor."[61] They wanted information on the salary paid to the principal officers, such as the president, secretary, and treasurer, and the policy for the reimbursement for their travel expenses. This was not the first time that questions had been raised about the expenditures of the unions' funds. Coombs, although not a member of the Bustamante unions, had done so as early as August 1938. Speaking at Petersfield, Westmoreland, on August 23, Coombs pleaded with his listeners not to "entrust your money into the hands of one man." Producing some unverified statistics, he charged that the Bustamante unions collected more in membership fees than their accounts indicated.[62] These innuendoes and charges of malfeasance did not abate, gaining greater currency in succeeding months and years.

Bustamante stubbornly resisted any interference in his conduct of the business of the BITU, just as he had done for the seven smaller and more occupationally specialized unions that earlier bore his name. In late October 1939, he suspended Grant after yet another dispute. Rejecting the BITU's undemocratic constitution, Grant demanded that his case be heard by his colleagues and "not by any picked committee." Responding to this request, Bustamante declared that "no officers in this union can tell me when to call a meeting to try any officer because this is my union and I run it." He then ordered Grant to "walk out [of] the office, you are fired." An obdurate Grant challenged the leader: "I am not going to get out of this union until it is straightened up and you stop fooling the people. You are no Czar in this union and everybody must have a right to say something to you, the leader, whilst it is reasonable on behalf of the union."[63]

Grant, as a former insider, now joined those who were questioning the management of the union's money. This was an assault on Bustamante's probity, as well as that of Gladys Longbridge, his private secretary and handpicked treasurer of the union. "I am not out to create any trouble," Grant said, "but I want the members of this union to know that they must not come to meetings, and clap their hands and say hear, hear and have their bodies full of emotion and sentiment and singing 'We will follow Bustamante' and don't look at the financial side of the organization. Because it is not Bustamante the employers are going to laugh at in the future; it is the members of the association who pay their dues who will be called jackasses."[64]

Grant was more explicit in his charges against Bustamante a few days later, when he said that he had told Bustamante that he had been "a secret service operator" in the United States. He reported that Bustamante responded, "Grant, this union is too small for you, and needs no secret service man in it, but you can make money with me if you are alright." Grant said, according to the *Gleaner*, that "he understood what that meant, and from that time his troubles started."[65]

These allegations were read by a public intrigued by the labor leader, his leadership style, and the operation of the union. They provided fodder for those who were inclined to deride Bustamante and to dismiss him as corrupt. Some members of the union declined to pay their dues, but the belief of the majority in Bustamante's credibility was not seriously punctured. Bustamante reacted by firing Grant and J. A. G. Edwards, the union's general secretary. Bustamante would later accuse Edwards of mishandling the union's resources. By the end of the year, Bustamante had also severed his ties with Ross Livingston, the union's attorney, and other lesser-known functionaries.[66]

The continuing squabbles between the labor leaders impeded the progress of trade unionism in Jamaica. But they should not be allowed to obscure the reality that it was the working people who provided the engine for the social ferment that engulfed the island in 1938 and after. They had been the heroes in their own story, setting the pace of their movement. Not restrained by traditional trade-union etiquette, these workers frequently walked off their jobs without the authorization of their union's leadership. These "wildcat" strikes frustrated management and the officials of the unions, but the workers saw them as a direct and immediate form of protest. These strikes were an expression of the workers' growing recognition of their power to disrupt the workplace in pursuit of their objectives.

The workers greeted January 1939 with a series of strikes on the Kingston waterfront, at the Constant Spring Hotel, and on sugar estates in St. Catherine and St. Thomas. Although the waterfront strikes were ordered by Bustamante, the others occurred without his approval. The ranks of the strikers in Kingston were swelled by thousands of unemployed people, according to the *Gleaner*. The flyers they distributed in support of their cause reflected their anger with their condition.

> Vengeance!
> Justice and Judgment.
> It is better to die free than to live this condition. No Work. No Food. No money. Nowhere to sleep. Do it now! It must be hell or heaven. We are

all satisfied to face the guns or bayonets for the better life. Black men arise and seek for your rights for right must beat might.
Death! Death![67]

As the flyer showed, racialism was being openly and publicly invoked by the workers to help legitimize their demands. It was the ubiquitous specter in any contest between capital and labor in the island. Capital almost always wore a white face, and labor was mostly black. It is hardly surprising, therefore, that racialized language would be employed by the workers. Nor would it be surprising if the employers did not use a similar rhetoric in private.

The strikes quickly tied up the Kingston waterfront, prompting the governor to create an arbitration board consisting of representatives of labor and capital to resolve the disputes in the city. Responding quickly, Bustamante called off the waterfront strike. Speaking before a large audience at Victoria Park, he admonished the workers: "Let them know by your actions that you are prepared to follow me as people follow Hitler and Mussolini." Shouting from the bandstand, he ordered: "[G]o back to work immediately everyone of you. Leave the rest to me." The scene at the meeting was vividly described by a reporter after Bustamante issued his order: "The crowd cheered. They forgot the fracas when Police a few minutes before tried to baton listeners from a valuable ornamental tree. How they had surged around the uniform men and rifles were loaded and unloaded in spectacular fashion. How Bustamante himself had sprung catlike from the Bandstand, had struck a characteristic stance and said to the Police: 'Fire at me! But leave them alone.'"[68]

Addressing another meeting of some 5,000 persons on the drama-filled day, Bustamante threatened to fight the employers of the island if they did not accede to the demands of the workers. "No longer are the workers afraid of bayonets," he declared. "[T]hey are prepared to fight for their rights." The workers did not want "bloodshed," he said, "but if it is bloodshed you must all follow me."[69] But not all workers were prepared to follow Bustamante blindly, and some declined to return to work. Confronting this resistance and the prevalence of unauthorized strikes, Bustamante threatened to transport loyal unionists from one area to another to act as strikebreakers. This was certainly a novel approach to unionism—using fellow unionists against one another. It was another indication of the fact that a working class was still in formation.[70]

The January strikes were a demonstration of the agency of the workers, as well as their restlessness and impatience with their condition. Although he expressed his support for labor's cause, Governor Arthur Richards observed that "the entire country is growing heartily sick of the labour troubles in Kingston."[71] The governor was expressing the sentiments of the elite groups in society, but societal peace would not be restored until the unemployed obtained jobs and the workers perceived that they were being justly treated.

There is no doubt that the unfortunate split between Coombs and Bustamante had hurt the labor movement. Unable to resolve a dispute that was more a product of competing ambitions and less the consequences of differences in their goals for the workers, the two men conducted a war of words in the press and on the platform at public meetings. Their supporters took sides, heckling one or the other leader when he addressed crowds.[72] There were those, however, who hoped that Bustamante and Coombs would bury the hatchet and place the interests of the workers above personal advantage. In December 1938, for example, Sir Walter Citrine met with the two men, along with Norman Manley, to mediate their dispute. The discussion was to be kept confidential, but the subsequent publication of the transcript revealed much about the character of the two men, especially Bustamante's tendency to shade the truth.

Bustamante was the first to reveal the substance of the conversation. When he read in the press that Coombs wanted to merge the unions, he quickly announced that he wanted "nothing whatsoever to do with Mr. Coombs." Then he asked derisively:

> What has Mr. Coombs got to merge with the Bustamante Unions? During the conference, Sir Walter asked Mr. Coombs if he believes he is capable of leading the workers as Mr. Bustamante can, Mr. Coombs replied "No." "Do you think," Sir Walter said, "you are tactful as Mr. Bustamante?" He replied "No." "Do you believe you can do as much good for workers of this country as Mr. Bustamante can?" Mr. Coombs replied "No." "You admit that he is the most powerful leader in this country." "Yes." "Have you got anything ill to say of Mr. Bustamante?" Mr. Coombs replied "No," for Mr. Bustamante had always done everything possible for the workers, and when he was president for (Mr. Coombs') organization, he always treated him with courtesy and consideration. But in spite of Mr. Coombs' admission that I am a kind, honest, and capable leader, it must be remembered

that for almost a year up to about three weeks ago, Mr. Coombs was always attacking me in the press.[73]

Coombs was incensed by Bustamante's version of the discussion with Citrine and released a transcript of the conversation. It differed substantially from Bustamante's account.

> SIR WALTER: Will you admit that Mr. Bustamante is the most powerful leader in Jamaica at present Mr. Coombs?
> ANSWER: Yes, but will shortly become the weakest.
> SIR WALTER: Why so?
> ANSWER: Because power in the hands of one who is incapable of using it wisely is dangerous.
> SIR WALTER: Do you mean to say that Mr. Bustamante is using power to destroy himself?
> ANSWER: Yes sir.
> SIR WALTER: In what direction?
> ANSWER: By boasting of being more powerful than the governor; the threatening of wrecking companies and employers; the upholding of outlaw strikes and disturbances.
> SIR WALTER: If this is correct it is regrettable. Will you admit that Mr. Bustamante is a more tactful leader than you are?
> ANSWER: No Sir, tact is different from Threat.
> SIR WALTER: What do you mean?
> ANSWER: Whilst Mr. Bustamante threatens the employers, I bargain with them peacefully.
> SIR WALTER: Now Mr. Bustamante what do you wish to say.
> MR. BUSTAMANTE: I wish to have nothing in the world to do with Mr. Coombs, because in my opinion it will do the workers of Jamaica no good . . .
> SIR WALTER: I see nothing more that I can do then. I will ask you both, as two leading personalities in labour in the island to do everything possible to help Labour from falling; nothing has been done yet, as far as Unions are concerned in Jamaica. One unwise step will spoil all the work done already. No one of you should think of striking for another twelve months, before you lay a foundation. I am unable to see a programme for labour's future. I am unable to see any one else who will make good Leaders besides you two. You should be together. It is dangerous for any one man to be building a Union off his own

personality. When he is dead or the people remove him, what will happen to the Union?

MR. BUSTAMANTE: The people love me.[74]

The transcript revealed the degree to which Bustamante had distorted the conversation. He did not publicly contest its accuracy and seemed to have retreated into silence on the matter. The nature of the dialogue showed the gulf between the two men, their mutual mistrust, and bitter rivalry. Citrine's pointed observation that "it is dangerous for any one man to be building a Union off his own personality" was clearly directed at Bustamante. The labor leader's flippant response that "the people love me," showed that he failed to appreciate the implications of Citrine's rebuke for the institutionalization and future health of the unions he had founded. Bustamante did not change his leadership style, much to the detriment of trade unionism in the island over the long haul.

The 1939 January strike fever had barely abated when the feud between Coombs and Bustamante once more took center stage, reaching its climax when Bustamante called a disastrous strike on February 14. Bustamante had the habit of intimidating employers by threatening to call general strikes. In August 1938, two months after he founded his unions, Bustamante proposed calling a general strike. Writing to Manley on August 24, 1938, he expressed his dissatisfaction with the Conciliation Board that Governor Denham had set up during the rebellion to mediate disputes between capital and labor. "As you know," his letter said, "the Conciliation Board has appealed to me to co-operate with them in every respect, and they would like me to endeavour not to call any strikes before arbitrating with them. This of course is hurting my unions, not because I am not desirous of using up every source of bargaining first, but as the Conciliation Board stands now, even with all its good intention, it is of no use."

Bustamante was unhappy with the slowness with which the board resolved disputes. His unions had unresolved problems with three sugar estates and the Bronstorph Ice Company in Kingston. He charged that the four employers were dismissing workers because they were "unionists." In light of the fact that the Conciliation Board failed to act expeditiously on his complaints, Bustamante threatened to call an island-wide strike. "We can tie up the entire country," he threatened, "and fight these abuses out once and for all, but it [is] not my desire, still, if we can get no help from the Conciliation Board, what else can I do but to protect my members, by stopping cogs of industrial machines. I will not allow such outstanding despotism."[75]

This was not an empty threat. But Bustamante's fledgling unions were unprepared to manage such a giant undertaking and to protect the welfare of the thousands of workers who would be involved. There was also the important question of whether such local disputes justified the initiation of a general strike. Manley responded to Bustamante's letter with alacrity. "At this state of affairs," he wrote, "I think that the general strike would be a fatal move." His opinion was that "action should be taken on the spot with the recalcitrant estate involved." In addition, he conjectured, "a direct move against an estate that could be proved to have acted against men because of Unionism would gather public sympathy behind it." Manley advised his cousin that "a localised show-down with the individual estate at fault is not only the right and the justifiable tactic but will also work a greater lesson of example by showing that a Union can compel respect and fair play in a straight issue between one employer and the local group."[76]

Manley had given Bustamante sound advice, and the labor leader seemed to have accepted the counsel since a general strike was not called, at least not at that time. Bustamante still retained a lingering affection for the efficacy of a general strike, however, issuing a public threat in September to call one. He had become incensed, he said, by plots to assassinate him, the breaking up of his meetings, and the opposition of those whom he called "capitalists." He was prepared, he said, to call an island-wide strike "without so much as two seconds notice." The "capitalists," Bustamante threatened, "are asking for a fight and [they] shall have it." He was determined "to bend capitalistic power in this country if it is the last thing I do before I die."[77]

Bustamante clearly believed his own rhetoric and had an exaggerated sense of his power over the Jamaican workers. He knew he could bend "capitalistic" power because "I can lead and Jamaicans are following me."[78] Bustamante made similar threats about calling a general strike with distressing frequency, but he seemed not to have thought through the economic implications of such a work stoppage for the island or even his ability to organize and execute one successfully. Bustamante had no experience with a task of this magnitude, despite his apocryphal boast that he had led 400,000 workers in Spain. In January 1939 Bustamante once again threatened to call an island-wide strike of longshoremen and agricultural workers. Governor Richards took this latest threat seriously and invited

Bustamante to a meeting. According to Robert Kirkwood, Richards told Bustamante: "I don't mind your going about the island saying that you are the Hitler and Mussolini of Jamaica, and that I am only the Governor, as long as you don't come to believe it yourself. You see, if you were to call the General Strike you keep threatening, I would have to break you and your organisation. I could do it, you know, and I could do it within twenty-four hours."[79]

Kirkwood reported that Bustamante "appeared to agree" with the governor "and promised that he would not call a general strike without first consulting His Excellency."[80] Bustamante broke his word and called a general strike on February 14. His capacity to manage such a strike would be severely tested. It would never have occurred, however, if the Bustamante-Coombs dispute had not intensified.

The circumstances that led to the strike revealed, once again, Bustamante's inexperience with trade unionism, his erratic temperament, and his autocratic management style. According to a police report, the strike grew out of an incident that began on February 12. Early that morning, St William Grant of the BITU was leading a procession in Montego Bay when he was allegedly threatened by George Reid, a member of the JWTU, the union led by Coombs. Grant sought to have Reid arrested, but the police officers declined to do so. Coombs, in his turn, failed to get Grant arrested when he tried to act on Reid's behalf.

Matters took a dramatic turn the following day when Bustamante arrived in Montego Bay. When he was informed that Reid was employed as a boatman by the United Fruit Company, he demanded his dismissal. The company's representative refused. Reacting to Bustamante's intervention, Coombs hastened to the United Fruit Company's office, demanding that Reid be allowed to keep his job or he would call a strike. Seeking to demonstrate that he had greater influence over the workers than did Coombs, Bustamante dispatched a telegram to Thomas Bradshaw, the head of the United Fruit Company in Jamaica. He charged that Reid had threatened to "chop off the heads of Edwards, St William Grant, and myself" and that he supported the refusal of the other employees to work with him. "If needs be," Bustamante threatened, "full force of [the] union at all ports will be used." Bradshaw was caught between the corrosive rivalry between the two labor leaders. As he explained in a telegram to Bustamante:

> The Coombs' union informs us that if we refuse to continue to give this man [Reid] employment they will call a strike of the stevedores.

You [Bustamante] inform us that if we give the man work you will tie up all the work not only in Montego Bay but also in other ports and on the sugar estates. You must agree with me that we are not, and cannot be responsible for acts committed by laborers when not working on the company's premises. . . . In the past we have repeatedly refused the request of other unions that we discharge labourers because they are members of your union, and it is unreasonable of you to ask us to discharge any man on account of some act committed by him as a private citizen, and not as a company employee or because he is not a member of your union.[81]

Alexander Bustamante was not persuaded by Bradshaw's arguments. His actions were driven less by the imperatives of responsible trade unionism than by the bitter rivalry with Allan Coombs for the support of the workers. The George Reid incident should never have become the occasion for a local strike, much less a wider one. There were no trade-union issues involved; it was the intemperate act of a labor leader whose irresponsible action had the potential to destroy the labor movement in the island. Governor Richards had warned Bustamante about the potential negative consequences for his union of any rash and precipitous action.

When the United Fruit Company refused to dismiss George Reid, an angry Bustamante responded by calling a general strike at all three wharves—the United Fruit Company, the Jamaica Banana Producers Association, and the Standard Fruit Company. Bustamante's principal lieutenants would later report that they were never consulted before the leader made his dramatic announcement. Bustamante also placed the sugar workers in the island on strike alert, although there was no connection between them, the waterfront workers, and the reason for the strike. His intention was to extend the strike to all business and commercial ventures in the island. Bustamante sent telegrams to the union's organizing secretaries throughout the island charging that there was a plot to destroy the union and urging unity among the workers. The first workers to strike were the banana carriers, and they were soon joined by stevedores, boatmen, and bakery workers. Excited workers staged marches of support in Kingston, Montego Bay, and Port Antonio. The *Gleaner* reported that thousands of workers assembled in front of the union's headquarters in Kingston and on the waterfront, anxiously awaiting news of developments throughout the island.

The work stoppages and the threat of more created considerable tension throughout the island. Jamaica was unaccustomed to strikes of such island-wide magnitude with the looming possibility of disorder. The suddenness of the strikes tested the loyalty of the workers to the BITU and to the principles of trade unionism. In Montego Bay, the Jamaica Tradesmen and Workers Union broke the strike and loaded the ships waiting for bananas. Bustamante wept as workers in Port Antonio ignored his plea to cease loading the ships. The police were everywhere maintaining order and intimidating strikers and their supporters. Hungry for work, the unemployed were only too willing to take the jobs temporarily vacated by the strikers, acting as unrepentant strikebreakers. The indefatigable Bustamante hastened from place to place, encouraging the strikers but urging respect for law and order. "Be orderly boys and cause no trouble. Abide by instruction," was his constant refrain. There were limits to his rhetoric of civil conduct, however. When the police opened fire on a crowd of some 2,000 people at Port Antonio on February 14, Bustamante told a later meeting that "if any blood is shed tonight, the entire island will be washed in blood." He derided Sergeant Major David Robinson, who reportedly had given an order to fire on the crowd that he was addressing. "If the Sergeant Major is mad," Bustamante exclaimed, "then I will have him examined by a doctor and sent to the asylum. There is not a dam [sic] soul in the country of whom I am afraid." He asserted: "If the Sergeant Major is mad, let him arrest me. I can die tonight. I am prepared to die as a hero rather than to allow you, my people, to suffer."

Such rhetorical bombast did not ease the tension in the island but may have exacerbated it. Alarmed by the wildcat general strike and its potential to damage the island's economy and disturb the peace, Governor Arthur Richards proclaimed an island-wide State of Emergency late on February 14. He acted after consultation with his Privy Council. Operating under the aegis of the Emergency Powers Law of 1938, the governor was empowered to take such action when "it appears to him that any action has been taken or is immediately threatened by any persons or body of persons of such a nature as to be calculated by interfering with the supply or distribution of food, water, fuel or light, or with the means of locomotion, to deprive the community, or any substantial portion of the community, of the essentials of life." The Emergency Order banned any assembly or gathering of ten or more persons "at any time in any street, road, lane, or other public places, in any part of the Island, for the purpose of marching or holding any procession." It prohibited the postal officers from transmitting and delivering letters and telegrams to or from Bustamante and other officials of the union. The order forbade all garages and gas stations to supply petrol or rent cars to the unions' leaders. The press was forbidden to publish news about the strike except that which was authorized by the government. The Emergency Order delivered the coup de grace to the strike since it also prohibited all public meetings and marches with more than ten persons attending. It also allowed strikebreakers to do work unmolested by the unionists.[82]

Robert Kirkwood described these regulations as "brilliant," noting that "Bustamante found himself fluttering like a bird in a cage." Continuing his assault on the strike, the governor called an emergency meeting of the Legislative Council on Thursday, the following day. Addressing its members, Richards declared that the "reasons given" for the strike "are tragically trivial in relation to the attempted paralysis of the commercial life of the community." The governor said that he "found it difficult to appreciate why the sugar estates of St. Thomas and the trade of Kingston and Port Antonio should be sacrificed because of a personal quarrel in Montego Bay, for which the law provides a remedy in court." He described the strike as "the irresponsible will of a few men," asserting that it was his responsibility to maintain essential services in the island. Richards reaffirmed his support for labor's cause but warned that "there can be no settlement and no peace until the orders for a general strike are unconditionally withdrawn."[83]

Faced with the governor's firm response and the success of the strike-breaking efforts, Bustamante sought a face-saving admission of defeat. He hurriedly consulted with the governor, seeking his advice as to how he should proceed. "Call off the strike at once, and send the men back to work," Richards urged. Seeking to calm the public's fears, Bustamante brazenly denied that he had called a general strike, but he ordered workers, other than those employed on the waterfront, to return to their jobs. He was prepared, he said, to submit the waterfront issue to arbitration or conciliation. A day later, on Friday, February 17, Bustamante called off the waterfront strike "in the interest of peace and in an effort to restore the possibility of harmony in labour relations."[84]

There was, to be sure, no issue to be arbitrated since the strike had nothing to do with wages, conditions of work, and so on. It had all along been a matter to be handled by the courts. Bustamante's intemperate act had plunged the labor movement into crisis, threatening to destroy it. His denial that he had called a general strike severely tested his credibility. He had sent instructions to the union's secretaries throughout the island ordering such a strike. This had resulted in sporadic work stoppages but not the complete cessation of work that he wanted.

In calling the strike, Bustamante had misjudged the power that he had over the workers and the degree to which they were sharing a common consciousness. Many workers ignored his order to strike, choosing to work with strikebreakers. They did so because they needed the income in the absence of any financial assistance from the union. The Bustamante unions had existed for less than a year, and the workers were still in the process of developing that consciousness that would define them as a class. In fact, the vast number of unemployed people in the island were only too willing to take the jobs abandoned by the strikers. The Shipping Association boasted that it succeeded in loading 220,000 stems of bananas in Port Antonio, despite Bustamante's opposition. The story was much the same in Montego Bay and Kingston. Commenting on the work of the strikebreakers on the wharves in Kingston, the Shipping Association noted that "the conduct of these men from the country and the expeditious manner in which they handled the cargo in Kingston during the last two days have been a source of wonder and admiration to many. Most of these men had never worked on a ship before . . . yet they handled at least double the quantity of cargo in the time that would have been taken . . . by the regular stevedores in Kingston."[85]

The association complimented these men, whom it called "small cultivators" and "small capitalists," for their work. They had done "their bit to save Jamaica from being ruined by agitators represented as working for the welfare of the country."[86] This was a barely disguised assault on Bustamante and his unions. Needless to say, the barons of capital were pleased that the strike had been aborted and expressed their relief and gratitude to the governor. Kirkwood reported that a "very tired" governor had met with "a deputation of representatives of all the leading vested interests in the Island. They had come to offer him the thanks of the Republic, and to advise him to break Trade Unionism in the island forever. They had argued their points for over three hours, but he remained firm. He told them that he believed in strong well-directed Trade unions, and that he believed tremendously in the rights of Labour."[87]

The failure of the general strike represented the lowest point in the brief history of trade unionism in the island. Norman Manley had remained publicly silent during the strike. Recognizing that the trade-union movement was facing a potential destruction, Manley conceived a plan to save it. He arranged a meeting with Bustamante on the night of February 17 to discuss the future of the labor movement. Manley was acting in his capacity as leader of the newly founded People's National Party (PNP), an acknowledged ally of the unions. The BITU was represented by Bustamante; Edwards, the secretary; and Kenneth Hill, a vice president. Norman Manley; W. A. Domingo, the vice president of the Jamaica Progressive League;

and Dr. E. Campbell represented the PNP. Manley's proposal that a Trades Union Advisory Council be constituted to advise the unions and to help educate the workers was accepted. Bustamante agreed to change the union's constitution to make it more democratic and endorsed the composition of the Advisory Council. Bustamante also accepted some "declarations of principle" in the furtherance of trade-union practice in the island.

Reporting this important development to the governor, Manley said that Bustamante had accepted the principle that strikes should be resorted to only after conciliation had failed, and that a general strike "is not ordinarily an Industrial Weapon to which resort can or should be made." He had also committed himself to "the peaceful settlement" of industrial disputes. The governor enthusiastically endorsed the proposals, reaffirming his support for unionism in the colony.[88]

Bustamante's acceptance of "the declarations of principle" represented a repudiation of his calling of the ill-fated general strike. He knew that the strike was a mistake, and that it had tarnished his reputation and weakened his appeal to and support from the workers.

The crowd was the largest ever seen in Kingston, numbering about 10,000 persons. The people had gathered at the Race Course to hear Bustamante and other leaders. It was the first time that Bustamante spoke from a prepared text so that he would say exactly what he meant. He knew that he had to explain the strike's failure: "Many are wondering why the strike has been called off. Is it because we have been crushed? Is it because we are not numerically strong? Was it on account of the Emergency Act having been employed, or was it because we were wrong? Was it because we lacked resources equal to the occasion? Nay!"

Answering his questions, Bustamante asserted, rather unconvincingly:

> The reason why the strike has been called off, is because I felt that I should have brought the matter personally to the governor's attention, after we had been refused arbitration by the United Fruit Company—Not that I was under any obligation to bring this or any such incident to the attention of the Governor—but on account of the way he had treated me in the past—which treatment has caused a deep seated liking for him—and the respect I have for him through the interest he has demonstrated in the workers, which has forced me to withdraw that which I felt justified in calling—the strike.

Bustamante declared that he had not called off the strike because of "fear," since "no one with a reasonable thinking mentality would accuse me of not being a man of natural courage, and one who is absolutely fearless—to call it off just because it is Governor Richards."

Bustamante's second reason for calling off the strike was equally questionable. He acted, he said, because "my love and regard for the workers is too great for me to do anything which might have caused undue hardships not only of the workers but of small cultivators throughout the country." Continuing, he made this astounding statement: "I personally feel that the Union is a part of the State and when the Governor asked for withdrawal of the strike I felt then I should leave the protection of the workers in his hands for I could never conceive the idea that when His Excellency stated that no arbitration would be allowed until I had called off the strike unconditionally, taken the protective measures for the workers out of my hands, the workers would be left to suffer, when past experiences with His Excellency caused me to regard him as a father of the workers. Now I am confident . . . that he has no desire to let down the workers." Bustamante's claim that unions were a part of the state could not have been articulated by anyone with a sophisticated understanding of trade unions and their need for independence from state power and control. Although Governor Richards proclaimed himself a friend of the workers, he most certainly enjoyed closer ties with capital. Nor was he a credible candidate for the title "father of the workers."

Bustamante announced the names of a distinguished group of people who would constitute the ten-member Advisory Council. Norman Manley was named legal adviser to the unions and Ross Livingston was the solicitor. The members included the Honorable E. E. A Campbell, the member of the Legislative Council for Kingston; W. Adolphe Roberts, president of the Jamaica Progressive League; H. P. Jacobs, intellectual and historian; W. A. Domingo, vice president of the Jamaica Progressive League; J. A. G. Edwards, the secretary of the BITU; Mrs. P. A. Aitken, a civic leader known also as Madam DeMena; Noel Nethersole, a solicitor; Dr. O. E. Anderson, councillor of the Kingston and St. Andrew Corporation; and Dr. G. E. Valentine, prominent physician and political reformer. This was an outstanding group, composed principally of people of independent judgment and not readily susceptible to Bustamante's influence. The problematic, to be sure, was whether the labor chief could work productively with such people.[89]

The public meeting at the Race Course was quickly followed by a meeting of the Advisory Council and representatives of all the unions in the

Island. They included the Bustamante union, the Montego Bay Clerks Association, the Northern Longshoremen's Union, the Jamaica Workers and Tradesmen Union, the Builders and Allied Trades Union, and the Jamaican United Clerks' Association. They all readily became members of the Advisory Council, and elected Noel Nethersole as its secretary.[90]

Sensing that he needed more than a speech at the Race Course to consolidate his influence and burnish his image with the workers, Bustamante wrote a letter to them. It should be read as a testament from a defeated leader fearful that his troops would desert him. Bustamante made a full-throttled defense of his actions in the face of attacks on the union by enemies he identified as the newspapers, the capitalists, and the employers. He claimed that "what happened was a direct attack not only on me, not only on the Union but the whole working class movement in Jamaica."

The chastened leader admitted that the strike's failure was "a severe blow to us." But he understood that he had to soothe the workers' disappointment, cauterize their emotional wounds, and fertilize their drooping spirit. "We know of the big problem which face [sic] the workers in the weeks to come," he wrote, "probably greater than ever before—we shall not flinch." The workers, he urged, should seize the chance "to show your heroism and loyalty; an opportunity to win a crown of renown by showing the Capitalists that in spite of their lies we shall stick together." He advised them to "stand fast in the faith, and by the Grace of God and our whole hearted effort we shall build here in Jamaica a foundation against which the gates of hell shall not prevail."[91]

The gates of hell did not prevail, and the BITU survived. The strike's failure imperiled the labor movement in the island. But the workers did not abandon their leader or the union. Bustamante's invocation of loyalty to him and the union in his letter to the workers, and his ringing call to demonstrate their unity, heroism, and fortitude, had a profound appeal and resonance. The workers threw Bustamante—and unionism in Jamaica—a lifeline. The rebellion of May and June 1938 had been theirs, and Bustamante's missteps would not be allowed to become its denouement. Norman Manley's brainchild, the Trades Union Advisory Council, brought the prospect of rationality, stability, and respect to trade unionism in the island and was welcomed by the friends of labor. Bustamante had been induced to accept it and the potential diminution in his power that came in its wake. But no one was really sure that a new era had dawned in the practice of trade unionism in the colony.

The formation of the Advisory Council brought a brief respite from the dispute between Coombs and Bustamante. Manley was successful in bringing the two men together on a public platform on March 4, when they shook hands and pledged to work together. On March 25 Coombs, Bustamante, Manley, and Edwards met to discuss a potential amalgamation of the two unions they headed. Coombs demanded a more-democratic constitution for the BITU as a prerequisite for an amalgamation. He also wanted the union's name changed since his members did not want to belong to an organization that was Bustamante's "absolute property." Coombs feared that Bustamante would use the absolute power he exercised in his union to the disadvantage of the members of the JWTU, such as "depriving them of certain rights and privileges." Nothing tangible emerged from this discussion, as Bustamante declined to accept Coombs's demands. The members of the JWTU, Coombs later reported, "told me that they were not prepared to affiliate with a person of such a nature who was not prepared to respect the rational opinions of other people."[92]

The attempted rapprochement that Manley initiated was well-intentioned but premature. Bustamante never trusted Coombs, charging that he was taking bribes from the banana growers in Highgate, St. Mary, where the JWTU enjoyed strong support from the workers. Coombs, who had no regular income, was always strapped for money. According to Bustamante, he asked him for £30 to help pay for a car, threatening to obtain the money from the banana growers if Bustamante declined to advance the funds. Coombs, Bustamante wrote to Manley, said "he does not want to continue doing that." Bustamante observed, however, that "once a person had got into the habit of betraying labour to that extent, one can scarcely count on his cooperation, still we must try, but with me it must be honest cooperation or none at all."

Manley was aware of the allegations against Coombs but was unhappy with the continuing divisions in the labor fraternity he was trying to strengthen. "I am most anxious that now you have got unity we should be able to preserve it," he wrote to Bustamante. Alluding to Coombs, Manley said that he "was well aware of some of the difficulties you write about. I believe that if we could get the person in question out of all existing [financial?] troubles that we would be able to make a useful assistant of him. I am hoping that patience will lead to results."

But patience was not Alexander Bustamante's strong suit. Writing to Coombs on March 25, he accused him of collusion with capital and of dishonesty, but not explicitly. First, Bustamante attempted to establish his own probity.

> My close associates and my lawyers can prove the great financial loss that no union in this country could ever replace; the physical loss that only God could remedy. The only feeling that inspired me to give my business up, local and foreign, very profitable ones of nearly £200 net profit per week, and sometimes hundreds maybe thousands of pounds overnight and on my stock exchange is the real love and interest I have not alone in the workers of Jamaica, but the workers of the entire universe. With that love for the people, it will always be impossible for me to serve capitalists and the workers at the same time.

Bustamante was stressing the physical and financial sacrifices that he was allegedly making on behalf of his beloved workers. He accused Coombs of duplicitous conduct without naming him: "In Jamaica, any leader who is willing to break strikes, or to advise the people against their interest for the benefit of the employers are the only ones who can expect benefit from the employers. I want no favour from the employers, and I believe if I were as poor as a church mouse, I still would not betray the people for the sake of any favour from employers."

Developing his subject, Bustamante denounced Coombs as an enemy of labor: "You have promised co-operation, but I do not quite understand your way of co-operating; it is more like an opposition party which can only tend to destroy the workers more and more each day. A man must either be my friend 100% or my enemy, and a leader must be 100% for labour not just in words, but in action, otherwise he too is an enemy of labour, for the man who pretends that he is for labour and still is not serving labour as he should is a greater enemy to labour."

Bustamante condemned Coombs for not honoring his agreement to "amalgamate" the JWTU with the BITU. He was not pleased that Coombs had written to him expressing his desire "to work for us in this union on a salaried basis, that you wanted to be the next man in this organisation." Bustamante was troubled that Coombs joined the representatives of the banana companies in denigrating the workers.

> I was surprised yesterday at the Conciliation Board that before the enemies of organised labour you would have got up and broadly stated that the workers of Montego Bay are the most unbalanced and

undisciplined people you have seen or met. One would think—one would expect you not to confirm such a statement as was made by Mr. Williams of the Jamaica Banana Producers' Association that he did not have one word good to say of the workers of any of the parishes in this country. No wonder that Mr. Williams thanked you, and was so pleased; then you went on to say the people of the Standard Fruit Company are the worst of them all. Mr. Coombs, don't you realise that you are a representative of labour, that your duty is to endeavor to educate your undisciplined people if they [are] undisciplined, your worthless people if they are worthless, but not to help employers to condemn them?

Bustamante was chastising Coombs on a variety of levels. Six days later, he wrote to Manley complaining: "I am not so blind as not to see that Mr. Coombs is using his association with us not in the interest of organised labour, but to continue his usual activities to serve as usual his own selfish end." His words were ominous.

How many hours do you think I am going to allow him or anyone else to use my sincerity as a weapon to further destroy the cause of labour—the cause that is nearest to my breast? To prove that my offer to co-operate is not a pretenceful [sic] one, I open my office to this man; I spent about Thirty Pounds [£30] cash to help him out to prevent him going to Highgate where he said he could get money, but that he did not want to continue that sort of thing anymore, and I suppose that whilst I am bled, others too are bled in secret, and may be still bleeding [because he tells them] that the money could be had from Bustamante, but he doesn't want it, playing a double game upon labour and capital at the same time.

This was a devastating assault on Allan Coombs's probity. Bustamante was accusing him of playing capital against labor and vice versa, reaping financial rewards. There is no independent corroboration of these allegations. But Bustamante made this accusation in two extant letters to Manley. His March 25 letter to Coombs made similar charges, albeit less explicitly. Manley did not dismiss Bustamante's accusations, cautiously admitting that he was familiar with them. The truth cannot be established definitively, but given Manley's admission in particular, the charges against Coombs seemed to have had some merit. Bustamante's mistrust of Coombs was implacable and virulent. Coombs, on the other hand, was willing to be a junior partner in any relationship with Bustamante provided that he was accorded some degree of independence and respect, as well as adequate remuneration.[93]

The gulf between the two men was unbridgeable. Bustamante lost no time in deciding to terminate his fragile relationship with Coombs. On April 6 he made a surprise announcement that Coombs was not connected to the BITU in any way. He did not explain publicly the reasons for his action, prompting angry JWTU officials to once again affirm their commitment to democratic principles and raise the question of alleged financial impropriety in the BITU. The JWTU, the officials said in a statement, "is not a one man concern. No one could be contented with a Union or set of unions which when they are called upon to produce a statement of their working affairs, produce a man who tells of his balance in hand, without even telling one word about his income and expenditures."[94]

These allegations aside, the Bustamante union's reputation for fiscal irresponsibility was not helped when the leader was subsequently fined in a Spanish Town court for failing to submit the union's financial records to the registrar as required by law. Ross Livingston, Bustamante's attorney, hoped that the judge "would realize the magnitudinous task of filing returns from some 70,000 members." Bustamante, he said, maintained that "rather than sending in a cooked account to catch the Registrar's eye . . . decided not to do so but to submit to a penalty." This may well have been an accurate statement, but the case fed continuing and damaging allegations of malfeasance by the union's hierarchy.[95]

The Bustamante-Coombs dispute notwithstanding, there was further trouble ahead for the much-heralded Advisory Council. Recognizing the potential for misunderstanding with Bustamante, Manley had sought to set the record straight in a letter he wrote to him on February 21. Its tone was candid and its content was not likely to have been embraced by Bustamante with equanimity. Manley told Bustamante that he took the lead in founding the Advisory Council because he feared the demise of the unions. "As you are aware," he wrote, "my actions have been dictated by my knowledge, which has every day been more strongly confirmed, that owing to the error made in calling a strike which was not justified and in threatening a General Strike, and in part commencing one, the whole of public opinion was alienated, the forces of the Government were brought in at full strength and the enemies of Unionism in Jamaica and even more particularly your own enemies determined to completely destroy the Movement which you had laboured to build up."

After complimenting Bustamante for his pioneering role in constructing trade unions in the island, Manley said he rejected any organization "which is based on autocratic methods." He believed that people "have to be trained to produce their own leaders and to accept responsibility and to be able to exercise it intelligently." Bustamante's mission, he said, "is to recognize this and to be able to bring it about." Manley wanted Bustamante to

> reorganize . . . your union constitution so as to produce a democratic basis for its operations . . . [so] that officers should be elected by democratic choice. This is the only way in which the movement will ever be able to produce its own leadership and in which you will ever be able to train those leaders; and secondly [exercise] democratic power in the matter of Strikes. Strong corporate [cooperative?] action can never be achieved except by men who have an interest in decisions. . . . It is impossible for any man to be a Dictator in this country, though possible for him to wield an enormous power as you have proven.

Manley also wanted a "cessation of the feud between yourself and Coombs." He decried the disunity in the ranks of labor. Manley hoped that Bustamante would "have the vision and bigness of mind" to resolve the problems. In addition, he proposed a change in the name of the Bustamante union since the "time has come when the attention of everybody must be concentrated on the principles of Unionism and people taught their own responsibility inside the Movement." According to Manley, Bustamante quickly visited him to express his acceptance of the proposals but requested a delay of one month for the union's change of name since the members might think he was deserting the organization.[96]

Bustamante was pleased with the support he was receiving from Manley and Noel Nethersole, the designated secretary of the Advisory Council. Writing to Manley on March 21, Bustamante thanked him and Nethersole for "the very sincere manner" in which they were cooperating with the union. He also pledged his own and his union's assistance to the People's National Party.[97] But cracks soon began to appear in the precarious Manley-Bustamante alliance. Bustamante was once again becoming annoyed with some members of his union who were demanding a more-democratic constitution for their organization. When the Advisory Council made a similar proposal, Bustamante denounced it as a ploy to destroy his union.[98] He was even more incensed when members of the council wanted to make membership on it more egalitarian by giving each union one vote. Bustamante protested against this heresy, arguing that since his union had the majority of the workers, it should have greater representation. This was a defensible position, but it was contrary to the democratic principles that had given the council its life. Believing that the members of the council were conspiring against him and the BITU, an angry Bustamante dispatched a telegram to the secretary, Noel Nethersole, on April 27 conveying his resignation. "There are plotters on the Trade Union Board," he alleged, "jealous of the influence I have with workers, ready to destroy the Union, with a hope that they can reorganize." He challenged any members of the council who wanted to destroy his union "to try." Any such attempt, he stressed, "will bring the people together and closer behind me." In a telegram to the *Gleaner* two days later, Bustamante complained that it was "a bit of impudence and impertinence on the part of the Union Council to attempt to offer any constitution to running of the unions. It is ultra vires and out of order; the ultimate end [is] the destruction of the Unions. . . . I appoint the men of the Trade Council and I can discharge them."[99]

Bustamante's ultimate withdrawal from the council, in effect, gave it the coup de grace. Meeting on May 5, the council dissolved itself but simultaneously formed a new one and invited all existing unions to join it. With the Bustamante union excluding itself, this new body was unrepresentative of the labor movement and was not likely to be effective. Bustamante did not leave the council quietly, lambasting some of its members as communists and, incredibly, as "enemies" of labor. The allegation of communism was bad enough, but Bustamante seemed not to understand that those who embraced that ideology were the acknowledged friends of labor everywhere.[100] Bustamante intensified his vilification of his former colleagues in subsequent weeks and months, singling out Manley, Nethersole, and the PNP for special abuse. The PNP did not immediately respond in kind, fearing that attacks on Bustamante would alienate workers from the party.

Using only his initials, "H.S.B." gave an account in the *Gleaner* of a luncheon meeting he had with Bustamante and Gladys Longbridge. Bustamante was in a jovial mood, taking a perverse delight in his demonization of the PNP and suggesting that any attack on him would create unrest in the island and might be unpatriotic. Wrapping himself in the British flag, Bustamante inquired: "Is stirring up strife such as must come by any attack on me, helping the island, the Empire or the local government in this 'time of difficulty' that they speak of?" He boasted that he had "killed the Party [PNP] in the country parishes and I have seriously maimed it in Kingston." Elaborating, Bustamante said: "I shall play with them now as a rat plays with a mouse." Miss Longbridge interposed: "[C]at . . . cat . . . a cat plays with a mouse." Undeterred, the labor chief continued in his fine theatrical form. "I wrote Manley some time ago," he revealed. "I told him he had not monopolized all the brains in the family. But that I had monopolized the personality. Haven't I?" Bustamante vowed to fight any attempts to "besmirch my honour." He promised to do the same "if one word ever appears against my Secretary." "Honour" is "more [important] to me than life," he exclaimed; "therefore I should attack." He had lived in Spain, he said, "and the blood is in my heart."[101] Despite his boast, Bustamante had not destroyed the PNP, but it was damaged by his unfounded charge that it was a communist organization.

Bustamante's recollection of the history of the Trades Union Advisory Council is at variance with some of the facts. On November 17, 1944, he published a lengthy message "to the people of Jamaica," giving his account of his role in the labor movement and his relationship with Manley. Bustamante denied that he had called a general strike in February 1939, since "only some three wharves, some sugar workers on two estates and a few people here and there struck." He accused Manley of being in collusion with the governor during the strike, saying that Manley "took no part and gave no assistance." Bustamante derided Manley's idea to create a Trades Union Advisory Council, believing that it was a conspiracy against him. After Bustamante "condescended" to join the council, Manley had told him: "Busta you can't be the same fire-cracker now. The Council will control you." Bustamante said he knew, however, that "Manley did not have enough brain to tie me up." Ignoring the fact that he had recommended the members of the council, he dismissed them as "novices" and accused them of needing "counsel themselves, and just as badly today." Bustamante viewed the proposal to democratize the council's board as a "trap," describing the other unions as having "invisible" memberships. He decided that he did not "fit in" and resigned from "this supposed Trade Union Council."[102] This was a self-serving narrative, but it provided an important window into the labor leader's conspiratorial and mental worlds and his capacity for distortion.

The official leadership of the Bustamante Industrial Trade Union seemed to function in a state of dynamic turmoil. As long as absolute power resided in the hands of the founder, this was certain to generate dissension, despoiling the organization's image and undermining of its efficacy. The union had barely recovered from the internal disarray that had bedeviled it in 1939 when it was wracked by fresh disputes, this time between Bustamante and the new general secretary, Oswald Penso. Bustamante had handpicked Penso, a minister of religion, for the job. He soon had disagreements with Bustamante over the union's undemocratic constitution and the management of its finances. Acting in his signature fashion, Bustamante sent a letter to the managing executive committee on February 25, 1940, indicating that he and treasurer Gladys Longbridge would be resigning from the union, effective March 25. The committee accepted the resignation, undoubtedly to Bustamante's surprise.

Bustamante really had no intention of resigning, and after he had supposedly demitted office, he "suspended" and then "fired" Penso. His "fired" general secretary hastily called a public meeting at Liberty Hall on March 28 to form a new managing executive committee, which would be directed to recall Bustamante to the presidency but under new conditions, "reasonable terms[,] and no dictatorship." Penso told the crowd of about 1,000 people that Bustamante "can only come back on our terms and if he draws a single cheque against the Union funds he is doing an unlawful act." Alluding to Bustamante's tendency to arm himself, Penso declared: "The days of brandishing dirty daggers and rusty revolvers are past. That cannot scare me. We want brain and cold reason today."

Intensifying the dispute, Penso filed a suit in the Supreme Court seeking a declaration that Bustamante and Longbridge were no longer officers of the union and could not act on its behalf. They were to be enjoined from spending the union's funds, and from "intermeddling" in its activities. Bustamante was to be ordered to provide an account of his expenditures of the union's funds, and its books were to be audited. Bustamante responded to the suit and the suggestions of financial irregularities by delivering an impassioned address at the Conversorium, declaring that Penso was "a general without any soldiers."

Bustamante believed that Penso had prominent allies in the feud. He wrote a letter to Manley on April 6 claiming: "I have been told that you are the brain behind Penso's dispute." He also implicated Noel Nethersole in the alleged conspiracy, noting that he was being assisted by "a well known firm of lawyers [who] are the ones who have placed heads together to help Penso." Bustamante denied that he had resigned as president of the union, asserting that Penso "has no document to prove that I have, for I have never signed any such document. If my name appears on any document that I have resigned, then someone is going to get trouble." Bustamante was technically correct; he had not signed any official document to that effect, although his letter had clearly expressed his intentions. The letter was a product of Bustamante's intemperance, and he had not expected his colleagues to take its contents seriously. Manley and Nethersole ignored his allegations of conspiracy with Penso to effect his demise. Nor had Bustamante submitted any credible evidence to support them.

This was another messy dispute that did the cause of unionism no good. The ugly charade ended with Bustamante and Longbridge remaining officers of the union and with Penso withdrawing to nurse his wounds. He seemed not to have pursued his suit after an initial hearing, recognizing that he would lose any contest with Bustamante for the support of the unionists, regardless of the merits of his claims or even if he received a favorable court decision.[103]

The leaders of Jamaica's developing trade-union movement did not possess any training in the art of negotiating with employers, nor were the employers any more familiar with trade-union etiquette. Bustamante lacked the temperament for negotiating, often substituting threats, abuse, and intimidation for rational discourse and compromise. Ross Livingston, the union's solicitor, and Kenneth Hill were capable negotiators and provided Bustamante with solid advice and assistance during the unions' formative months, but they ultimately resigned their positions after bitter disputes with their leader.

It is true, however, that Bustamante and his union often faced the intransigent opposition of some employers, a hostility that invited angry responses from the labor leader and fed a disposition to direct action. This reaction included strikes, threats, demonstrations by workers, and verbal abuse. When Bustamante had a labor dispute with the Shippers Association in May 1939, he telegraphed the chairman with a thinly veiled threat of violence. "You fail to realise [the] reason that there has not been bloodshed amongst high and low," he declared, "is because I preach peace."[104]

But he did not always practice what he preached. When he learned that a "Busha," or sugar-estate supervisor, in Little London in the parish of Westmoreland had disparaged him, the labor leader announced that he would "kick" him in retaliation. The Busha subsequently attended one of Bustamante's meetings, remaining discreetly at the rear of the crowd. Upon learning that he was present, Bustamante hurriedly left the speaker's platform, determined to execute his threat. Desperately trying to avoid a physical confrontation, the Busha jumped in his car and fled, with Bustamante and Edwards in hot pursuit. The Busha successfully eluded his pursuers, forcing a disappointed Bustamante to explain that he did so only because he was more familiar with the road.[105] This was a hilarious comedy, and Bustamante had given another fine theatrical performance. But it was also a study in unorthodox trade-union practice.

Bustamante behaved in a similar fashion when he had a dispute with the Public Works Department in Montego Bay in January 1939. He led an angry group of workers to the office of J. G. Young, the acting executive engineer. According to Young: "I went into the main office and there at the door stood Bustamante in his best newspaper photograph pose; shoulders stilted, arms straight down, fists clenched with backs [sic] uppermost. Behind him was a villainous looking crowd. . . . I said 'Good morning. You want to see me?' By way of reply he roared in a most offensive manner. 'I am Bustamante!' I said, 'Well, what about it?' Whereupon he simply yelled at the top of his voice, 'I am only telling you my name.'"

Young reported that he was not "prepared to be insulted in that way in my own office so I said 'Oh no! You can't address me in that fashion. I don't permit that sort of thing here,' and I thereupon went into my room and closed the door." According to Young, Bustamante then left, followed by the crowd he led.[106] This was not atypical behavior by Bustamante. But the labor leader was not all bluster. The tactics that he employed on this occasion failed of their purpose, but Bustamante was using one of the weapons available to him. In the absence of a functioning governmental department to advance and protect the interests of labor, Bustamante had to engage in direct confrontations with some employers, with his army of supporters at his back.

Bustamante's negotiating style, as opposed to his direct confrontation tactic, can also be examined. Four examples typify the labor chief's approach. In August 1942, for example, the women working at the Jamaica Shirt Factory in Kingston went on strike. The details of the dispute are unclear, but Bustamante intervened and secured the return to work of some of the women who had been fired, except those who had played a role in organizing the strike. Bustamante sent a strong letter to Francisco Miret, the manager of the factory, threatening a reopening of the dispute. "Let me tell you mister," he wrote, "there is going to be a fight again . . . not like the last one when I extended sympathy." Intensifying the dispute, the letter demanded "not only the return of those girls but an all-round 25% increase for all there." Bustamante reminded Miret that some time ago, he had threatened to close his factory, but "that's your damned business," he said. "When you go, someone else come and we won't be sorry to see you go." Continuing, he said: "What we are concerned with is that labour is respected in this country." Bustamante was particularly outraged that Miret was a foreigner. "We are not going to allow any of our Natives to ill-abuse our people much more Foreigners," he exclaimed. His language was unrestrained and intimidating: "It's the most barefaced thing I have seen for a long time, stupid, glaring to have picked out the girls who took a prominent part. That won't work in Jamaica and no lawyer is going to help you in this. This is an industrial fight, lawyers won't help you in this, and it is going to be a very peaceful one at that. If any of the merchants who sell your goods or give you goods to make has advise [sic] you to do that, we are going to include his store in the fight. We are getting suspicious of everybody."

Bustamante was threatening businesses that distributed the shirts that Miret's company manufactured. He identified one Mr. Hanna as an offender. "I don't want to hurt him," the labor leader wrote, "unless I have to do it to protect the workers . . . for I will carry it [this dispute] to every end of the Corporate area within my right as a Leader of my people." Further chastising Miret, Bustamante added: "You can't do my women these things man . . . I can't do it to yours in your country, and I am not writing as an individual but as president of the Bustamante Industrial Trade Union, a wide-flung Organization in this country which you have got to respect." Then, he issued his parting shot to Miret: "Perhaps you intend going out of business. This may hurry it up."[107]

This letter clearly went beyond the bounds of responsible trade-union etiquette and practice. A second example also elucidates Bustamante's behavior as a trade unionist. On October 5, 1942, S. G. Fletcher of the Coconut Producers Association wrote to Bustamante, ostensibly reminding him that a strike at the Copra-Dryer Morant Bay "apparently" occurred with his approval. Responding the following day, Bustamante told Fletcher:

> [A]pparently your imagination is too strong. The day that I order a strike either on your factory here [Kingston] or Morant Bay or wherever you may have business[,] there will be no "apparent" action of mine; it will be a definite action; and I do not like your assuming something without any good reason. You understand that your cause is connected with the dismissal of one Davis now fired for good. . . . If this man is fired unjustly, it will not be for good, unless you intend to close your factory down, for as sure as God made Moses, if the man is

Bustamante and the Politics of Performance | 165

wrongly fired, that factory is going to be closed down in St. Thomas. This I assure you, and there won't be any apparent in this.

Bustamante accused Fletcher of being "rude," instructing him that that "will not take you nor your business anywhere." Resorting to threatening language, he told Fletcher that "when anything stirs, my people will not use your soap or oil in no part of this Island. You always look for a fight and you are too slim to fight this organization." Bustamante reminded Fletcher that "when you write to me, you must remember that I'm not a little isolated Manager of a little Oil Company, but the leader of my people." He wanted Fletcher to recognize the differences in their social and political status. The labor leader's language was accusatory, strident, and abusive. He told Fletcher:

> [T]he dispute that exists over there now is on account of the starvation wages that you pay the people, not enough to feed a mongrel dog, for which you as an employer should be ashamed, calling yourself a Jamaican and keeping down your own people; and that's that. The day that I call a strike on you, it won't be just on a [copra] Dryer but on everything you supervise in this country, and in every parish, I may give you but a month and a handful of it, so that bunctiousness [arrogance?] of yours will be smashed once and for all, for you believe you can fight the workers and consumers of this country. You would better take good care of your employers' interest by being not so rude, for after all it is only a job you have.[108]

Letters such as this one exacerbated the relations between capital and labor in the island. The acrimony was not all one-sided to be sure. Employers did not welcome the union's interference in their relationship with the workers, but Bustamante's rhetorical stridency did not help matters. When R. F. Robison of Port Morant continued to employ some headmen on his property to whom Bustamante objected, he sent him an angry letter. "As long as the Headmen are on your property," he threatened, "your property won't run I can assure you; even if you gave 100% raise, I will order the workers not to work with those headmen, and that's that. This is no maybe."[109]

W. E. Powell, the proprietor of a bakery in Kingston, had a similar experience with the labor chieftain. Bustamante's ire was aroused when Powell continued to have nonunionized workers in his employ. Writing to Powell, he demanded that the workers be dismissed: "[E]ven though they have been with you from the days of Methuselah until donkey rope was making Bredda Nancy's nest, we are not going to work with them. It will be a 'blitz.'" He made a series of demands on behalf of the workers, warning Powell that "the time has come to share your profits with the workers." Bustamante said that he understood that "when you started, you had nothing save the Bakery and a few hundred Pounds." He could not resist ridiculing Powell, telling him that "today you are almost wealthy—not as wealthy as I am of course." Then he added: "You see, I played the stock exchange and made money over-night while someone else grinds the workers and make money on it." Powell brought these letters to the attention of Oliver Stanley, the secretary of state, describing Bustamante as a "so called labour leader." He thought the letters revealed "the utter irresponsibility of this man and his so called trade union." Powell denounced "the campaign of terrorism by this man and his followers" for obstructing his delivery trucks. Bustamante, Powell alleged, joined "in threatening shop keepers with dire consequences if they attempted to sell our products." The baker said he had "no objection whatever to properly constituted and properly conducted trade unions, but I most emphatically do object to the racket now masquerading as trade unionism."[110]

These were harsh comments, reflecting the views of a disgruntled employer. But Bustamante must bear some of the responsibility for the antiunion sentiment that existed. His strong-arm tactics alienated those whose understanding and cooperation he needed most, namely, the employers and the representatives of capital. Winning their understanding was no easy task under the best of circumstances. But Bustamante did not possess the temperament to provide the kind of aggressive but steady and rational leadership that the union required. His greatest asset was the support of the majority of the workers and their increasing recognition that their collective power could cripple the operation of capital. Bustamante, however, despite his enormous limitations, was playing the defining role in the forging of a Jamaican working class.

In spite of his tendency to intimidate the employers, Bustamante could exude a calmer and more-controlled demeanor on other occasions. Governor Richards, for example, reported most favorably on a meeting the two men had in September 1938. Bustamante was accompanied by Ross Livingston, who was then his solicitor, and Hugh Buchanan, the union's secretary. Livingston did "a great deal of the talking," with Bustamante "merely assenting," the governor observed. "I found Bustamante and his assistants quiet and reasonable in the main to talk to over a table," Richards noted. "Others have had the same experience, I believe." Richards maintained that Bustamante's "attitude in an interview does not square with the intemperate expression of his views which he finds necessary to appeal to his audience at labour meetings."[111] Bustamante could be charming, rational, and subdued, but an angry, volcanic eruption was never too far away.

In spite of its history of internal turmoil, the Bustamante Industrial Trade Union remained dominant in the island. Governor Richards reported to the Colonial Office in July 1943 that it had an "approximate membership" of 28,700, of whom 18,500 were "paid up" members. The other unions were relatively small, as table 9 shows.

"I'm ready to die today if I can help you," Alexander Bustamante told a crowd of workers in the aftermath of the rebellion at Frome in May 1938. Railing against the governor and the legislators who had dismissed the workers as "agitators," he asked rhetorically, "Who are the agitators?" Answering his own question, he said they were the people "trying to make conditions better for posterity." Then he added with an air of moral superiority: "I am above those who are fighting us." Bustamante was burnishing his credentials as the intrepid labor leader, willing to give his life for the cause of the exploited and the dispossessed. He did not define himself as an agitator, a term that had pejorative connotations. He saw himself as an authentic leader of the workers, their voice, their enabler, and their protector. To his supporters, as one reporter later said, Bustamante was "a Messiah" and "to his opponents a villain."[112]

The search for the authentic Alexander Bustamante is a complex and difficult enterprise. C. V. R. Thompson, a reporter for the *London Daily Express*, observed that there were "two Bustamantes." First, there was Bustamante "the fanatical labour leader, who dashes around town speaking to workers in a seedy old brown suit." The other Bustamante, he said, was a "wealthy money lender who, in a newly pressed tropical suit and immaculate linen, moves in the station to which his wealth entitles him." Thompson's description of Bustamante as a "fanatic" reflected the way in which the members of the elite groups viewed Jamaica's principal spokesperson for the workers and the dispossessed. He was certainly indefatigable in his quest for an improvement in their condition, passionate and boisterous in his espousal of their cause. This was the fanaticism of the committed person in service of the betterment of the life situations of the exploited. The

TABLE 9. Membership of Unions in Jamaica, 1943

Union Name	Approximate Membership	Paid Up
Bustamante Industrial Trade Union	28,700	18,500
Jamaica United Clerks Association	1614	234
Jamaica United Workers Union	766	403
Tramways Transport & General Workers Union	465	93
Jamaica Printers and Allied Workers' Union	344	93
Jamaica Government Railways Employees Union	1,368	1,365
Jamaica War Veterans and Small Planters Trades and Labor Unions	296	142
Water Commission Workers' Union	265	72

Source: Governor Richards to the Secretary of State for the Colonies, July 20, 1943, Records of the Colonial Office, Commonwealth and Foreign and Commonwealth Offices, British National Archives, London, 137/855/11. Allan Coombs had, by 1943, disappeared from the active trade-union scene, and with him the JWTU.

second Bustamante, Thompson reported, was the man of privilege. He had encountered Bustamante sipping "a glass of sparkling burgundy on a verandah of Kingston's Myrtle Bank Hotel." When Thompson asked the labor leader about the prevailing unrest, he reported that "in a second I saw the first Bustamante again. His eyes filled with fire, his white teeth were bared, he gesticulated like a wild man. One moment he shouted, another moment his voice was smooth as honey."[113]

Bustamante's voice could be as smooth as honey; perhaps that helped to explain his hypnotic effect on the Jamaican working people. Carmelita James, a dressmaker, attended a public meeting that Bustamante held in Kingston in 1938 and recalled the people's reaction to him.

> Oh! The people, the people! I wouldn't be able to tell you everything that Bustamante said, because you are so excited that you not even listening. You know that what he is saying is what is right, but the people, Oh Lord! . . . In those days you couldn't say anything about Bustamante before or after those meetings you know, for the people, he came like a God to them for everybody is going to follow Bustamante. He really did something for the people. Bustamante come on and there is a crowd of just small people—we would say the dirty people, barefoot. He just throw his hand around them and maybe he

wouldn't have given a shilling, but just the thought or the mind of him trying to help the poorer people made them love him.[114]

Bustamante's arrest, allegedly for sedition, and his internment without trial from September 1940 to February 1942 became a political boon that he skillfully exploited upon his release. He knew that he commanded the confidence and affection of the workers he led, but he needed to frame his incarceration in such a way that he could be defined and celebrated as a martyr for their cause. Addressing a crowd of 1,500 persons at Duckenfield, St. Thomas, in April 1942, shortly after he regained the right to speak at large public meetings, Bustamante said it was his "duty" to go to prison. As the *Jamaica Times* reported, he declared that "no prison could break his courage, only death could do that. No sacrifice was too great for him to make so that they [the workers] could realize that 'unity is strength.' When he was away he thought of their poverty, of their distress, their nakedness, not of his suffering. Poverty was written all over their faces that night, and whilst he could not see their stomachs, he was sure many of them had not had a square meal that day."

Emphasizing his victimhood status and his sacrifice in the service of the workers, Bustamante told the audience that "for four years he had sacrificed his life and his health for them. His cheeks were now sunken but his spirit was as fiery as ever. . . . [E]ach day he was losing his health more and more. Each day he was nearer to the grave." Not only was his health declining, but he had also confronted the animus of his "adversaries," who wanted a divided labor movement that would be ineffective. Those who were demanding his freedom while he was interned, he claimed, really wanted to keep him behind bars. They knew the governor would be infuriated by their language and would do the opposite of what they were requesting. The newspaper summarized his incredible accusation: "Last year [1941] he would have been released but certain persons made trouble for him. His supposed friends from public platforms demanded that 'Bustamante must be released.' But if anyone 'must' the Governor[,] it simply means a lost cause. His supposed friends were aware of this so when they said that he must be released what they really meant was that he shouldn't be."

Bustamante attributed his release to the efforts of Gladys Longbridge, who, he said, visited the governor five times. The "tears and prayers" of the workers were also efficacious, he declared. When his "adversaries" thought Miss Longbridge's intervention would be successful, "they went to the authorities with the malicious information that she intended to call an island-wide strike to secure his freedom. The intention was that she would also be detained, leaving him without such a sincere worker on the outside."[115]

Bustamante was casting aspersions on the efforts of Manley and others to release him, denying and distorting their roles in the process. The truth was entirely different. In March 1941 the officials who were administering the BITU in Bustamante's absence decided to call a strike of the workers on the sugar estates in order to force management to grant their demands. The strike was planned to begin in St. Thomas and would proceed to other parts of the island in stages. The Sugar Manufacturers Association responded positively to the first series of strikes, making it unnecessary to call the others. The situation was exacerbated when some people began to promote and propagate the view that a continuation of the strikes might force the authorities to release Bustamante. It was also rumored that Bustamante was seriously ill, and that the cessation of the strikes represented a betrayal of their absent leader. These disgruntled workers struck in protest on several estates.

Recognizing the strength of Bustamante's influence over the workers, the union's officials requested that the government grant them permission to visit Bustamante at Detention Camp to obtain his assistance to resolve the impasse. According to Manley's accurate recounting of the event, the officials wanted to ask Bustamante "to issue a personal note to the workers assuring them that it was his will that they should not strike with a view to securing his release." Bustamante complied, and Manley reported that he "and others went out that night and addressed groups of workers and by next morning the whole movement died down and everybody was back at work."[116] Bustamante's pandering speech to the adoring crowd at Duckenfield diminished the goodwill and work of his colleagues, but it unquestionably framed the narrative he wanted his followers to believe, internalize, and disseminate.

Bustamante regaled the crowd with a story about a friend he had come to distrust. This friend, presumably Manley, visited him in detention to tell him that he needed to change the BITU's constitution as a price for his release. Pointing to the gate to the camp, Bustamante dismissed the visitor. "There is the gate," he had said. "It was open when you came in, it is still open, now get out!" Bustamante explained to the crowd that he had "made up his mind to die rather than betray the workers." He was, in what was probably an apocryphal story, expressing his determination to eschew democratic principles in the union that he founded and that bore his name while simultaneously affirming his commitment to the cause of labor. The workers would have little influence over the affairs of an organization they supported with their scarce pennies. It was a theater of the absurd.

In spite of these contradictions, Bustamante wanted the workers to be assured of his love as much as he took comfort in theirs for him. The *Jamaica Times* reported him as saying that "the people loved him and he loved them. . . . He knew that they had more love for him than the rest of the men of Jamaica put together. In pouring rain when they heard that he was passing through the parishes, the people of Trelawny and Hanover had jammed the wayside to hear him, singing 'Our wandering Boy has returned.'"[117]

Bustamante seemed to have needed the adulation of the crowds for his psychological nourishment and sustenance. He craved validation by the people, hence the constant refrain about his sacrifices for them and appreciation for the affection they showed in return. Bustamante imagined enemies everywhere, especially among his colleagues. The people's love was an indispensable antidote, but it had to be constantly renewed and always loudly expressed. The labor leader, still a man learning his new role in life, was apt to substitute bluster, braggadocio, and emotion for deep analysis and reason. His psychological needs were as complex as his challenges. But the crowds also reveled in his frequently articulated expressions of affection for them. It was the first time in the twentieth century that a charismatic, brown-skinned member of the economic elite had championed their cause so passionately and lost his liberty as a consequence.

Bustamante's comfortable material circumstances were an asset in his relationship with the workers. J. H. Hunter, H. Steele, and F. Lazarus, writing to the *Gleaner* in March 1942 on behalf of "hundreds of workers" of Highgate, St. Mary, bemoaned the fact that "we followed the advice of others who said Mr. Coombs could not lead us as he is too poor."[118] These workers had lost their confidence in Bustamante's leadership, expressing their regret at being beguiled by his money and the belief that a rich man would be a better advocate of their cause than a man of modest means who had drunk at their well. A stampede away from Bustamante was not yet taking place in 1942, but the chief was beginning to lose a slice of his charismatic appeal.

Some scholars and contemporary observers have maintained that the workers saw Bustamante as a messianic figure, namely, an individual sent by the Christian deity to lead and liberate them from their societal oppression. Norman Manley was one who articulated this point of view, but he saw messianism as a negative phenomenon in Jamaica's history. "Bustamante," Manley said, "has been made by a dangerous tendency manifested on several occasions in Jamaican history, the danger of social frustrations finding escape in messianic figures or magic men."[119]

It is true that some of the workers supported Bustamante with a religious-like fervor, but this was inspired more by his charisma as a secular leader and less by any messianic appeal. It must be readily conceded, however, that Bustamante's fervent support could have reflected both impulses, given the difficulty of discerning the motivating factors for individual behavior in mass movements. In the absence of specific evidence, absolute claims must be avoided or cautiously advanced. That said, the nature of the ardent support for Bustamante is complicated by the Christian vocabulary that punctuated his public meetings. Those were secular gatherings, flavored with Christian prayers and hymns in the rousing time-honored Jamaican tradition. This blending of the secular and the religious was captured in the rewriting of the 23rd Psalm from the workers' secular perspective. Entitled the "The Labourers' Psalm," it was written by E. F. Williams and published in August 1938.

> Bustamante is my earthly shepherd, I shall not want,
> He maketh me to lie down on Simmons Spring Beds, he
>   leadeth me to better rooms;
> He restoreth my ambition, he leadeth me in the part [path] of
>   better food for my health's sake.
> Yea, though I walk through the valley of the Police batons
>   and steel bullets,
> I will fear no evil for he is with me, his intelligence and
>   good counsel will comfort me,
> Busta prepareest a table before me in the presence of the
>   capitalist,
> He anointeth my palm with more money, my cup will soon
>   run over,
> Surely, better wages and shorter working hours shall follow
>   me all the days of my life,
> And I shall dwell in peace and contentment in this my
>   Island home forever and ever
>   Amen.[120]

Bustamante loved to hear the people sing at his meetings. His favorite hymn was composed by the American Jeremiah Rankin in 1880 and was sung at the close of each meeting:

God be with you till we meet again,
By His counsels guide, uphold you,
With His sheep securely fold you
God be with you till we meet again.

By late 1938 or early 1939, however, the unions had acquired their own anthem. It was composed by S. Bigenoi of the Jamaica Biscuit Factory. Known as the "Bustamante Anthem," it was not intended to replace "God be with you till we meet again," but it celebrated the special place that Bustamante had come to hold in the hearts of the unionists and his other admirers. In time, the anthem became deeply imbedded in the folk culture of the island:

1. Jamaica's Labour Leader
   Is ALEXANDER BUSTAMANTE
   We the Workers of this Island
   We will follow our Leader to the end.

2. In the morning in the evening
   And at midnight when we are dreaming
   We the workers always singing
   We shall follow BUSTAMANTE all the time.

3. In this Island there is colour question
   With the workers not much intention
   We will always be united
   We will follow BUSTAMANTE to the end.

4. From the Mountains from the Valley
   From the seashores of this Country
   All the workers' Voices Shouting
   We will follow BUSTAMANTE to the end.

5. Through the darkness we will follow
   Through the daylight we will follow

    Through the great strike we will follow
    We will always be Victorious to the end.

6. If it's bloodshed we will follow
    In the footsteps of Bustamante
    With the Union as our Weapon
    We will follow BUSTAMANTE until he dies.

7. When he is dying we'll be crying
    In the graveyard we'll be singing
    In the dugout we'll be weeping
    We will follow our Leader to the last.

8. And the younger generation
    They will make a greener nation
    They are Cheering, Shouting, Singing,
    We will follow BUSTA footsteps till we die.

9. All Jamaica will remember
    That Bustamante was a Saviour
    May his dear name live forever
    In the hearts of generations yet unborn.

10. We will follow BUSTAMANTE
     We will follow BUSTAMANTE
     We will follow BUSTAMANTE
     We will follow BUSTAMANTE till we die.[121]

Many persons who lustily sang the "Bustamante Anthem" would abandon him in time. But in those heady years of 1938, 1939, 1940, and later, Bustamante was the leader for whom many said they would die, just as frequently as he said he would do the same for them. In the aftermath of Bustamante's first arrest in May 1938, St William Grant told an enthusiastic crowd: "We have the greatest leader that has ever been known in the shores of the West Indies and he is Alexander Bustamante and long may he live. . . . Remember that Bustamante said that he would die for the people of Jamaica. Well, you have seen that he was not faking. He was not lying. He means it and has proved that."[122]

The religious or Christian language that Bustamante's supporters used to describe him did not mean his deification. St William Grant told the cheering crowd at the Race Course that "Bustamante now is our God." He was quick to explain, however: "When I say God, I do not mean the creative [creator] God who changes day and night. But the Bible says we are in the likeness and image of God and if we are the image and likeness of God, Bustamante is a God from this point of view, of leading Jamaicans into perpetual freedom. . . . Long live Bustamante, God save Bustamante."[123]

Bustamante was prone to interpreting opposition to him in religious terms. His opponents, he said, were treating him in a way similar to that which Jesus Christ received as he faced His crucifixion. Invoking the scriptures, Bustamante alleged: "The perversion of the song 'We will follow Bustamante till we die' has been [due to] the chronic hate, jealousy, and ill will—the worm eating into the very soul of many who would give their lives if they could only get such a genuine and spontaneous love from the masses of this country. Significant it is, that it was just around this time, the season of Lent, when because thousands cried 'Hosanna to the Son of David,' the man Jesus was plotted against and his crucifixion arranged by a body of lawyers and high priests."[124] Pronouncements such as this one had an enormous resonance among Bustamante's admirers. But Jamaicans were too deeply steeped in Christian theology and eschatology to see Bustamante as anything other than a secular leader, even if some compared him to the Christian God or to Moses. In July 1939, for example, he was "baptized" at a public meeting in Kingston and renamed "Moses." "I call him Moses," said the man who served as his godparent, "because he is a great religious leader . . . just like the first Moses who led the children of Israel across the Red Sea." But he cautioned: "You all know that the Moses of old did not reach the promised land, and you mustn't expect this Moses, our Bustamante, to reach the promised land either. Like [the] Children of Israel, you must reach it all by yourselves."[125] Moses, to be sure, was not the messiah, but one who was leading the people to Him. Similarly, Bustamante was leading the Jamaican workers to the promised land of social and economic justice. This was an entirely secular mission.

The first anniversary of the founding of the Bustamante unions was the occasion for the pomp and pageantry that had made them simultaneously trade unions, sources of political education, and local entertainment. According to the *Daily Gleaner*, 20,000 "labourites and interested spectators" participated in a procession in Kingston, singing the BITU's anthem and marching to the strains of the music from a band. After a religious service, the colorful procession left the Kingston Race Course for its first destination: the Queen Victoria statue. The procession was led by about 100 cyclists, followed by a group "like the irregulars and skirmishers of a vast army, chiefly composed of the 'great unwashed,' for the most part boys and girls in their teens and all waving green branches." They were followed by union officials in cars and on foot. St William Grant walked with a "drawn sword at the head of his brown garbed band." Bustamante rode in a "brown tourer" with a "flag waving over his head." He "was half sitting, half standing" in the tourer, cutting a dramatic pose. There were over 100 Red Cross nurses in the procession, all marching behind their leader. Behind them came girl guides, boy scouts, guards marching four abreast, footmen, women and children, and "some five hundred cyclists." Lastly, "in a not exactly imposing rear guard were to be seen groups of ice cream vendors and pedlars like the stragglers of some great army." According to the reports of the event, Bustamante "harangued" the vast crowd at Queen Victoria's statue and laid wreaths in memory of those who had lost their lives in the revolts at Frome and Kingston a year earlier. Following a circuitous route, the marchers returned to the Race Course, where the labor leader gave "a fiery speech, punctuated by frequent pauses for effect and the applause of the assembled thousands."[126]

This was clearly a cultural performance, combining religion, hymn singing, music, fashion, oratory, drama, and so on. In fact, Bustamante's appeal rested in part on his understanding of the cultural pulls of the Jamaican working people, wrapping the marketing of his union in packages that resonated with his targets. Bustamante's genius was that he was able to dress his assaults on capital, his invocation of class conflict, and his promotion of worker solidarity in a garb that mirrored the cultural wellsprings of the people. Vernon Arnett, the secretary of the People's National Party, had famously likened Bustamante to Anansi, the sobriquet of the trickster in Jamaican lore. As Arnett explained, Bustamante

> has been put at the head of an organization by the people in the belief that he will serve them, and they cannot believe that he is merely serving his own interests. His cunning appeals to them that he is doing it to trick the employers and gain more power. The "nancy" complex of his is strong within us. For in the days of slavery when the slaves gathered together in the evenings, it was these tales of how the little anancy [spider] with his cunning could outwit the strong and powerful that they loved to hear. We must remember that in thinking of conditions today.[127]

This was an intriguing comparison. But Bustamante was a more complex and enigmatic figure, at once serious and controlled yet flamboyant and demagogic, sincere and passionate but bewilderingly inconsistent, rhetorically incendiary yet the apostle of restraint and nonviolence, the champion of social justice yet the defender of the political status quo, a victim of British official mistreatment yet a fervent admirer of the abiding purity of the conception and execution of the mother country's justice. The chief's weaknesses were as gigantic as his strengths. But there can be no doubt that he helped to force a morally ossified colonial society to see the hitherto invisible marginalized and oppressed people in its midst and to take steps to address their grievances.

Alexander Bustamante was not the architect of modern trade unionism in Jamaica, as he boasted. Unquestionably, he did more than anyone else to advance labor's cause. Despite his many personal imperfections and his erratic and dictatorial leadership style, Bustamante commanded the affection and loyalty of the workers in whose name he spoke. He had courageously embraced a cause larger than himself and kept faith with it throughout his political career. The labor leader was certainly Jamaica's most passionate voice in behalf of social justice for workers. This was at once his appeal and his enduring legacy.

SIX

Bustamante and the Politics of Power

"The position here is very difficult owing to the large number of persons who have nothing to do but attend mass meetings, listening to wild speakers, one of whom, Bustamante, has been guilty of utterances on which I am advised he can be arrested, but I do not desire to do so at the moment or until such utterances can be associated with any direct act of disturbance," Governor Edward Denham observed on May 8, 1938. His Excellency was writing to the secretary of state, Ormsby Gore, about potential disturbances in the island and his strategy for dealing with Alexander Bustamante. "Bustamante is challenging arrest," the governor said, "and no doubt all arrangements are made for the demonstration on his behalf if this occurred." But the governor thought it more judicious "to hold my hand for the moment but all steps are being taken to deal with any disturbances," he confessed. The governor stressed that it had "to be recognized that a West Indian mob gets completely out of hand and force has to be resisted by force." He knew that force "is the one thing they understand."[1]

Bustamante was arrested sixteen days later as the governor employed the state's power to crush the social unrest that he had predicted. Edward Denham's pejorative comments about Bustamante and the workers he led reflected the fears of the government and the island's elite, as well as the naive belief that "force" was an appropriate response to the social and economic ills that created the "mob." Bustamante's detention was short-lived, but the state's surveillance of his activities showed no abatement. Governor Arthur Richards, Denham's tough-minded successor, also awaited an opportunity to silence Bustamante, reduce his appeal to and power over the workers, and puncture the island's nascent nationalism.

Undoubtedly taking their cue from the administration, members of the police department seemed to delight in tormenting the labor leader. Inspector William Orrett pursued Bustamante relentlessly, beginning with his arrest during the rebellion of May 1938. Bustamante complained to the colonial officials about this apparent abuse of police power and also brought the matter to the attention of the Moyne Commission. The hostility manifested toward Bustamante by the police did not cease, generating more complaints on his part. Writing to the colonial secretary on August 17, 1939, Bustamante reported incidents of alleged police harassment of him, adding: "I will not alone attribute these incidents to just impertinence and ignorance, but it seems to me that there is a sinister motive to inflame and to cause public disturbance, for whilst I am willing to be arrested when I act in such a manner as to justify it, I do not intend to be made a victim of what I term a sinister motive with intent to humiliate and persecute. . . . I am determined not to have your police put their hands on me."[2]

Bustamante accused the police of acting in concert with his enemies and those of the BITU. He insisted that the police officers were trying to frame him on various charges. The police inspectors, he said, were endeavoring "to obstruct and foment trouble, and then if anything had occurred it would have been said I caused the trouble."[3] In a letter to Governor Richards, written on December 21, 1939, Bustamante accused "the government" of conspiring with J. A. G. Edwards, the former general secretary of the BITU, to frame him. Edwards's "gang" of conspirators, he alleged, included St William Grant and Hugh Buchanan, as well as "a well known legal man," presumably Norman Manley. "I know there is a move on foot to frame me in a criminal charge just to lose confidence in me," he told the governor, but "the whole police force, the legal man and all of them together will never succeed."[4]

J. A. G. Edwards was certainly working to effect Bustamante's political demise. In late fall 1939, Edwards and St William Grant "came to Inspector Orrett and reported a plot by Bustamante to kill Mr. Bradshaw and Mr. Manley," the commissioner of police informed the colonial secretary. Bradshaw was the chairman of the United Fruit Company, a major exporter of bananas. Apparently confident about the veracity of his charge, Edwards told an associate that "it won't be many days from this when an arrest will be made by government." He was certain that "the moment that takes place will be the moment the change for the better will start." Probably lacking convincing evidence, the police declined to arrest Bustamante, even allowing him to visit Cuba despite Edwards's claim that "it is felt that he is running away."[5]

The charge leveled against Bustamante by Edwards and Grant was preposterous. The record is silent on any evidence they may have presented to support it. In spite of Bustamante's deteriorating political relationship with his cousin, it is most unlikely that he was plotting to murder him. Ties of consanquinity stood in the way of such a horror, and Bustamante possessed a deep respect and affection for Norman Manley. It is unimaginable that he would have wished him dead or, worse, that he would have been the instrument of his cousin's assassination.

There were others who sought to destroy Bustamante's spell over the workers. Fearful of his spell over their employees, some employers hired people to disrupt his public meetings. Siding with capital and presumably concerned about the preservation of law and order, the police sometimes denied his request to hold these gatherings. When the inspector of police for the parish of St. Ann declined to grant Bustamante permission to conduct a public meeting in St. Ann's Bay in February 1940, the aggrieved labor leader complained to the colonial secretary. In response, the island's commissioner of police reminded the inspector that "it is for obvious reasons desirable . . . that labour should have the same facilities for holding meetings as is afforded to capital, provided that at such meetings order is maintained and traffic not unduly interfered with. It is also important that no action should be taken to lead the Bustamante Unions to think that they are being unfairly discriminated against."[6]

Bustamante remained the object of police suspicions and scrutiny. But he could give as good as he got, at least verbally. His invective against his tormentors was harsh, describing individual policemen to their face as "impertinent," "a damn fool," and so on. Bustamante expressed his defiance of the police in a telegram that he dispatched to Governor Richards in December 1939: "Whilst I cooperate with government not because I am frightened for I am not frightened of death[.] I am ready to die[.] A part of the police force does not demonstrate honour not even common decency like most Jamaicans of my colour. . . . [E]verything has been done . . . by the police department to prevent the people showing their goodwill towards me."

Bustamante's reference to people of "my colour" is tantalizing in its meaning. Did he mean brown-skinned Jamaicans? Bustamante was not a black Jamaican and since the terms "white," "brown," and "black" had specialized meanings in the racial psychology of the people, it is unlikely that the labor chief would have self-identified as "black." If Bustamante expected better decorum from people of "my colour," that would have constituted an unpardonable admission from one who was leading Jamaica's mostly black working population. Bustamante, however, defined himself as a white man when it was advantageous to do so. At a time when racial segregation was endemic in the United States of America and interracial marriages were prohibited in many states, Bustamante married a white woman in New York "by swearing that he was a white man born in Spain."[7]

The enigmatic labor leader, however, identified deeply with the poverty-stricken victims of police brutality, their color notwithstanding. He had, after all, been the object of police zealotry, but it was more than that. Bustamante was fiercely committed to the welfare of those at the bottom of the society and outraged at the abuse they suffered at the hands of an all-powerful police force. His was the lone voice denouncing police abuse. He assured Manley in February 1939: "I shall use everything that I have at my disposal to endeavour to have His Majesty's humble subjects defended whenever I believe that a confounded advantage is taken of them by anyone else who is more fortunate." He would later observe in a letter to the colonial secretary that "thousands are now refusing to sing the National Anthem for many things amongst which rank the excessive abuse of power that the people suffer at the hands of the police, and if these kinds of treatment continue, love will turn into hate for the flag." He wondered whether this abuse was occurring "because we are 'subjects' and not citizens." Bustamante also wondered why the people tolerated the abuse for "so long and I have reasons to say that there are hundreds of unfortunates behind the prison bars of this country today, whilst the authors of the provocation are enjoying freedom—the police."[8]

Bustamante said that "as a public man, I cannot close my eyes to the abuse and to the injustices which are measured out in this country." This passionate concern led him to proclaim: "[O]ne thing that this government should do, and which I am going to fight for, is to give legal aid to unfortunates who go before the Magistrates just like cows to the slaughter house, helpless and defenceless, because once the police say you have done something, God help the unfortunates. The words of the unfortunates mean nothing, the words of the witnesses mean less."[9] This was a devastating critique of the plight of poor people before an unfriendly judicial system. Bustamante would, before long, experience British justice in operation, Jamaican style.

Given his experiences with the police, Bustamante knew that he had to be careful about his own public utterances. But the labor leader was not given, in any case, to articulating harshly critical, consistent, and thoughtful positions on such volatile issues as self-government and British misrule of the colony. Governor Richards was not particularly angered by criticisms of the appalling standard of living of Jamaica's poor by Bustamante and others, but he became incensed when His Majesty's government was the target. Norman Manley, Kenneth Hill, Noel Nethersole, and other People's National Party (PNP) leaders had the capacity to unnerve the governor in this way, particularly with their bold talk of self-government to correct the ills of colonial rule. Bustamante was never feared by the governor as a direct threat to the colonial regime. He was dismayed, however, by Bustamante's "acrobatics," as he described his behavior in a letter to Manley in February 1940. "For sheer irresponsibility it would be hard to find his like," the governor wrote. He thought it was "a pity" that Bustamante "is in a position to play with other men's livelihood and lives." The real danger that Bustamante posed rested in his potential to provide Manley and the proponents of self-government with the shock troops they needed if a violent struggle erupted. But Manley never contemplated the use of violence, and Bustamante would not have been an accomplice in a cause he refused to embrace.

Governor Richards never appreciated the depth of Bustamante's fealty to the empire and the colonial regime and his inability to imagine a self-governing Jamaica, at least immediately. "It is better to have England with all her faults for one hundred years," Bustamante told a public meeting at the Conversorium on May 12, 1940, "than to have German rule for one day. . . . In this time of trouble, I shall never become a traitor to Great Britain. . . . Tonight I say from my heart that I am prepared, if it becomes necessary, not only to fight for England, but to die for her."[10] Bustamante was the governor's best ally in keeping the colony safe for Britain, but Richards failed, at first, to understand that reality. Fearing a Manley-Bustamante alliance in the cause of self-government, the governor had his security agents monitor Bustamante's speeches with a view to determining whether his language was seditious at a time when the mother country was at war. A policeman who was trained in the art of taking shorthand dutifully captured Bustamante's words, or so he reported.

Alexander Bustamante was not capable of restraining himself when he addressed his followers from a public platform. He was never given to self-censorship, and when he became excited, a torrent of words gushed from his mouth uncontrollably, as unpredictable in their subject as they were confusing and ambiguous in their meaning. Bustamante provided Governor Richards with the opportunity to silence him with a speech he delivered on September 7, 1940. After a two-year respite, labor unrest had returned to the waterfront, and as usual, Bustamante was involved on the side of the workers. The Shipping Association, the organization of employers on the wharf, had agreed to give the workers a bonus beginning on September 9. Bustamante rejected the bonus on the ground that it was inadequate and called a strike. Fearing a repetition of the 1938 rebellion, Governor Richards watched the developments rather closely and dispatched a policeman to take shorthand transcripts of the labor leader's speech at the Conversorium. Based upon the reported content of the speech, the governor ordered Bustamante's detention.

The policeman reported that about 1,500 persons attended the meeting. According to his account, Bustamante arrived "after the meeting was in full swing, tore off his coat, and walked up and down the platform shouting 'it will be bloodshed.'" He then proclaimed:

> There will be bloodshed. I expect everyone in this country to follow. We will let these employers respect us. We will take away their lands and give them to the workers. We shall fight with vengeance, we shall be ruthless with hate. From Kingston to Negrial [Negril?] shall be in the fight and if the government says we cannot keep meetings we will go in the forests, riverside, and bush. . . . We shall fight with vengeance and hatred. I shall preach hatred against them. We want our own government and it must be self government too. The niggers of this country shall rise. We do not want to go to war like a timid dog. There will be war. We want revolution in this country and before whites destroy us we shall destroy them. I am going to paralyse all industrial works in the country. There will be shedding of blood. The negro blood has been shedding for the past 102 years and the time has come when we shall shed theirs.

Continuing, the report quoted Bustamante as saying: "This time it is a race war. Down with the white man, down with capitalists. We want self government."

Governor Richards was outraged by these alleged statements by the labor leader. He reported to his superiors in London in the same letter in which he included the text of the speech that "vague national sentiments were enthusiastically applauded by large and increasingly excited audiences." Richards said the "sole idea of Bustamante is to keep the country in a constant ferment of unrest." Bustamante, the governor charged, "does not want peace and he is incapable of constructive effort." The "theme of bloodshed," that "has recently been running through his pronouncements is logical enough: the constant stirring up of hatred can have no other end." Richards was distressed that Bustamante's "influence over the mob" will continue "so long as he is at large to address them."

Faced with such impending peril, the governor sprung into action, ordering Bustamante's immediate detention on September 8. He acted, he said, under the terms of Defense Regulation 18, a measure that gave him the right to detain anyone who posed a threat to public order. Governor Richards said he had "no other course possible under local conditions in view of his [Bustamante's] platform and journalistic activities over some time past, culminating, despite personal warnings by me, in speech directly inciting to bloodshed, racial war, and revolution." Richards emphasized to the secretary of state that Bustamante's detention had "nothing to do with his activities as a trade union leader." He had tried "to help Bustamante as a union leader," but "this was a matter of some difficulty on account of the instability of Bustamante's character." He had detained Bustamante "entirely on account of his increasingly inflammatory utterances and influence over workers." This, he added, was the "only sure method of preventing outbreak of most serious disturbances in time of war."

Richards emphasized that despite "evidence to support a charge of sedition," he had decided to detain Bustamante under the Defense Regulations Act instead. This meant that he would not be required to provide Bustamante and the public with the reason for his action, and Bustamante would not be formally charged in court. The governor told the Colonial Office that a charge of sedition against Bustamante "would have involved immediate and protracted fights on the question of bail followed by lengthy magisterial and High Court proceedings lasting many weeks and accompanied throughout by the utmost publicity and state of extreme danger of public clashes." He said that his experience with local conditions led him to the conclusion that "ultimate conviction" of Bustamante was unlikely despite "whatever evidence adduced[,] and acquittal would have been a veritable triumph . . . resulting in greatly enhanced prestige" for Bustamante. This result, conjectured the governor, "would have been [predictable] even in the improbable event of conviction unless followed by long sentence which was unlikely." Richards was convinced that "the most practical step for public safety was obviously preventative action rather than punitive." He believed that "trouble would have been island wide and end incalculable." It was extremely difficult, the governor said, "to explain to anyone who does not know Bustamante, his peculiar influence over the people and utter impossibility of ever building anything permanent on such shifting foundations." Richards was certain that "constant publicity and excitement lie at the heart of his [Bustamante] success as mob leader." A "sensational" trial, Richards said, would have "flattered" Bustamante's "vanity" and would have made "maintenance of law and order exceedingly difficult." The situation demanded "swift and undramatic action," the governor asserted.

Bustamante, Richards added, "could not be kept in the penitentiary unless locked up separately." It would have been necessary to double the staff of wardens to cope with Bustamante's "inflammatory effect" on other prisoners, the governor emphasized.

Governor Richards never told Bustamante the reasons for his detention, although he probably had his suspicions. The governor, however, may have discussed them in general terms with Norman Manley, Bustamante's lead counsel. In his report to the Colonial Office, Richards cited Bustamante's speech at the Conversorium as the immediate cause, but he would later level three other allegations against the labor leader. Bustamante recalled that "the first time I had the slightest intimation of the charges against me was . . . fully sixteen months after I was detained."[11] Richards did not provide the detainee with the charges on his own volition. Rather, Bustamante received them only after he filed a petition for his release. The three additional charges were rather specious, reflecting Richards's zealot-like pursuit of the labor leader. Richards accused Bustamante of fomenting strikes on the waterfront, sending a threatening letter to the manager of the West Indies Sugar Company at Monymusk, and advocating violence to achieve self-government for Jamaica. Bustamante would have no difficulty in challenging these vacuous allegations.

Bustamante's sudden internment deprived the workers of the services of their leader. Writing to "the workers in Kingston and the Country" on September 11, he assured them that the union's managing executive committee, along with Norman Manley and Ross Livingston, would protect their interests during his absence. These people, he told the workers, would "make the best possible bargain with the different employers involved at any and all conferences held by the Labour Adviser . . . and take every precaution in safeguarding the interest and the job of each and every worker." He had authorized his team, he said, "to use their discretion . . . to instruct you to return to your work." If the workers returned to work after receiving such instruction, "you will be carrying out my wishes." In an additional communication to the workers, Bustamante enjoined them to accept his internment without protest.

Although he was detained and his visitors carefully monitored, Bustamante continued for a time to administer the affairs of his union. His most frequent visitor was Gladys Longbridge, the union's treasurer who also served as his private secretary, confidante, and companion. Miss Longbridge kept him abreast of the union's business and relayed his instructions to the officials still on the ground. But she was not the only visitor to the detainee's abode. Other union officials, including vice president H. M. Shirley, did so from time to time. These semiofficial visits went well enough for the first few months, although the conversations were not private, being overheard by the agents of the colonial regime. In January 1941, however, the governor prohibited Bustamante from discussing the affairs of the union with his visitors. According to Lord Moyne, the new secretary of state, Richards thought it "most undesirable" for Bustamante "to control" the business of the union from the internment camp.[12] His "control" of the union never ceased, although it was greatly diminished in succeeding months. Gladys Longbridge must have found ingenious ways to transmit information to him and then convey his instructions to his surrogates.

Bustamante's letters were also monitored, if not censored, while he was interned. His letters to Miss Longbridge, for example, were a study in emotional control, masking the tenderness that must have marked their personal relationship. Three decades his junior, the young woman was totally devoted to Bustamante as his selfless protector and defender. Bustamante reciprocated, acknowledging the crucial role she was playing in his life and the emotional toll his internment took on her. As one letter warmly affirmed:

My Dear Miss Longbridge:
   You have been so brave—so dutiful—so faithful so very true—so sincere so kind—any and everything you have done whatever way it turned good or bad—it was always meant for the best—for me you are faultless.
   I can see that you are slowly dying—don't fret too much over me—keep your chin up. See that you go home in the car in the evening—you know where money is[,] draw it to the last penny—if we ever meet again—and there is no money our meeting shall not be any less happy—not being able to see you—I know my personal business will go to greater ruin—Man was created to stand what comes—you are brave and honest—you have my esteem—so true.
   I am the same sincere Bustamante.[13]

Bustamante's admiration, love, and respect for Miss Longbridge are beautifully captured in this letter. It also demonstrated his concern for her financial well-being while he was interned. This was clearly one of his principal preoccupations, as a second letter reveals.

Dear Miss Longbridge,

As your safe guard—any money that you have been spending—and will spend—from funds of the loan and securities co[.]—which is mine—or from any other monies—you are under no obligation to give account to any person or persons regarding same—

All monies—that you have withdrawn from any of my bank accounts—and place it in joint accounts—between you and I have been athorized [sic] and sign by me—as a financial protection to you—

Alex Bustamante[14]

A third letter to Miss Longbridge seems to have been intended for her as much as for the censors, demonstrating his loyalty to the British Crown.

Miss Longbridge Dear[,]

You have proven yourself to be the most courageous woman in this Island—True to the core—keep your chin up. Their [sic] will be victory for England—she must win—Hitler will succeed for a time—but this tyranny will be smashed—and then things will again be normal as ever and will ever be.

Alex Bustamante.[15]

There can be no doubt that the Longbridge-Bustamante relationship was strengthened by the forced separation and the trauma of his internment. Miss Longbridge assumed the responsibility for Bustamante's affairs and gave him as much emotional support as circumstances allowed, thereby cementing a deeply genuine and loving commitment. She also kept a watchful eye on his medical condition, requesting in December 1941 that he be transferred to a sanatorium for proper medical care. Acting on the advice of the medical officer, the governor declined the request, noting that Bustamante "is in relatively good health." Bustamante's internment and isolation from the rough-and-tumble of his public life produced in him a degree of paranoia. On December 30, 1941, Miss Longbridge reported to the governor that "he has ceased taking advice from all and sundry including lawyers."[16]

The long months in confinement gave Bustamante time to think and reflect on the past, as well as on an uncertain future. He had declined, during his early months of confinement, to take his case to the local tribunal that had been created by the governor to hear appeals against his detention orders and to advise him accordingly. Bustamante doubted the importance of the tribunal, maintaining that the authorities were not required to accept its recommendation. In fact, all of its recommendations to the governor for release had been rejected. In addition, Bustamante maintained that since the government was privy to all the information about him, the tribunal's investigation would not uncover any additional evidence that would make a difference in his case.

Bustamante's strategy in internment was one of patient and watchful waiting. He never questioned the governor's right to deprive him of his liberty, charitably conceding that he would have acted similarly if he were in the governor's position. This was hardly an admission of guilt, but it was an acceptance of colonial authority regardless of how it was employed. Bustamante undoubtedly chafed under this overweening power, but he was a committed foot soldier for the empire, bearing the treatment meted out to him without much complaint.

If Bustamante declined to appeal personally to the local tribunal to hear his case, the union that he led was not so restrained. On February 17, 1941, the officers petitioned the secretary of state, Lord Moyne, to release their president "subject to such conditions and terms as may be thought necessary to be imposed in the interest of the future peace and good order of this country and the effective prosecution of the war." The signatories to the petition consisted of Norman Manley, the union's counsel; R. C. Livingston, its solicitor and member of the executive managing committee; H. M. Shirley, the vice president; S. Morais, the general secretary; and Gladys Longbridge, the treasurer.[17]

The petition, or "memorial" as it was called, was obviously a self-serving document sympathetic to Bustamante's cause. Its purpose was to convince Lord Moyne that Bustamante had been wronged and that his release did not pose a threat to public order. The memorial reviewed Bustamante's role in the establishment of the union and its ascendancy in the labor movement in the island. Reflecting some knowledge of the reasons for Bustamante's detention, the memorial argued that the police report that led to his arrest on September 8 may have contained "errors," particularly because Bustamante "is on occasion a very difficult speaker to report correctly." It noted that Bustamante had denied advocating bloodshed to achieve his objectives. His allusions to bloodshed, the document said, "were specific references to the fact that in the past on many occasions during strikes blood had been shed." Bustamante, it continued, "admits that he did state that the more he had preached industrial peace the more advantage had been taken by white employers of coloured labour, though he declares that he added that among the white employers and officials there were some who were better friends of labour than some of the coloured employers and officials."[18]

The memorial maintained that the power of detention "was only intended to be exercised in cases where either there was no possibility of resorting to the courts because there was no commission of any offense triable at law or in cases where the urgency of the matter was such that there was no time to resort to the courts." Bustamante's detention did not meet these criteria, the memorialists stressed. The document dismissed the argument that a Jamaican jury would not convict Bustamante, pointing out that in 1938 a jury had found one of his lieutenants guilty on a charge of sedition. Its argument was persuasive and powerful, most likely reflecting the legal talents of Norman Manley. "If it was thought," the document argued, "that no Jury would convict him it is further to be pointed out if he did say what he is alleged to have said in his speech he committed an offense triable before a Resident Magistrate alone and he could be proceeded against in the Court of the Resident Magistrate."[19]

Bustamante, the memorial stressed, was not a public menace, arguing that "there is no justification for thinking that if he was placed before the Courts his trial would lead to an outbreak of disorder." The document admitted that Bustamante's emotional outbursts and frequent intemperate language did not strengthen the argument for his release:

> It is well known that Alexander Bustamante is occasionally impulsive and on more than one occasion he has spoken more strongly than he himself would have done had he paused to reflect but the workers of Jamaica have never taken those strong outbursts at their face value because they understand his temperament, because they are steadily influenced by the infinitely more frequent inculcations of order and discipline which they have had from him and have always observed and because he himself if he has made strong utterances has almost invariably followed them by exhortations which have restored the idea of order and discipline which have been his ceaseless task to propagate and instill in the minds of the workers.[20]

This was an accurate characterization of the labor leader and his tendency to indulge in demagogic harangues. But such excesses were at once colorfully harmless and eerily threatening. "Almost everyone who understands general conditions would further admit that his supposedly violent statements are mere oratorical flourishes well understood as such by the mind of the people and very often necessary to rouse them to quite ordinary and moderate action on their own behalf," the memorial noted.[21] No one, however, could reliably predict that Bustamante's crowds would continue to show the restraint in their conduct that he was unable to do in his rhetoric. But on the other hand, the Jamaican working people knew a good theatrical performance when they saw one. Bustamante was nourished by the applause of the crowd and energized by its frenzy. His platform language simultaneously shaped, captured, and reflected the crowd's mood and pulse. The resulting paroxysms of excitement fed the chief's disposition to engage in rhetorical excess. This was his strength, and his weakness too—the remarkable capacity to excite a crowd, lead his listeners to the brink of violence, then pouring the metaphorical cold water on their anger, calming their fury and enjoining them to keep the peace. This uncanny ability to transmit mixed messages robbed Bustamante of the universal respect he desired, although it mattered little to the legions who saw him as their flawed champion, but champion nonetheless.

The memorial sought to convince the colonial secretary that Bustamante was an apostle of societal peace. It provided a long list of occasions on which he had intervened at the request of employers and the government to resolve disputes and maintain the peace. This included the "disturbances" in the island in May and June 1938. On the night that he was released from custody in 1938, the memorial recalled, Bustamante "travelled to Mandeville and journeyed on to the Parish of St. Elizabeth preaching peace and order and quelling threatened disturbances of a grave nature. He restored calm and order in Kingston among all classes of workers within forty-eight hours. He then proceeded to pay repeated visits to the Parish of St. Mary where very serious disturbances were feared and he toured the Parish day and night and invariably pacified the people and sent the crowds home without trouble of any sort taking place."[22]

It was true enough that Bustamante helped to calm emotions in these and many other instances. He was guided, the memorial said, by his "real desire that order should be kept and that the best interests of the workers should be safeguarded." Bustamante had also served the colonial state by traveling across the island to build support for the war, the memorial emphasized. Bustamante, the document said, "is willing to give assurances in regard to his future conduct including an assurance that he will not in any way advocate a resort to violence and is further willing to submit to reasonable conditions to secure that his assurances are observed."[23]

Ironically, the governor had accused one of the Crown's most loyal subjects—one upon whom he himself had depended to promote the cause of the war—of subversion. Since Bustamante had been detained under the Defense Regulations Act, the memorialists seemed to have believed that the charge had some merit, hence their efforts to underscore his patriotism, perhaps in the fear that he would be interned for the duration of the war. "There would be consternation throughout the whole of Jamaica in the working classes," the memorial asserted, "if it was thought for a moment that government was minded to keep him under detention for an unknown and indefinite period likely to be measured only by the duration of the war."[24]

The memorial had no effect on the government's plans because it had its own agenda. By the fall of 1941, however, Bustamante was ready to appeal to the local tribunal for a hearing on his release. On December 30, 1941, Miss Longbridge wrote to the governor informing him that Bustamante had not yet been notified "as to the grounds on which he should appeal."[25] The information was evidently conveyed to him shortly thereafter because the hearing took place on January 10, 1942. Mr. Justice D. T. Sherlock served as the chairman, and the other two members of the committee were Sir Charlton Harrison, a Jamaican-born colonial official who had served in India, and J. G. Kieffer, a businessman. At the outset, the chairman told Bustamante that the hearing was occurring at the governor's request "as an act of grace." Bustamante was granted leave to present a statement in response to the allegations that had been made against him.[26]

In his lengthy statement, Bustamante dismissed the charge that he had threatened the manager of the West Indies Sugar Company at Monymusk, saying that he had no recollection of the contents of the letter. He denied fomenting any "discontent" on the waterfront between June and September 1940, detailing his role in resolving various other labor disputes. Bustamante rejected the allegation that he was stimulating racial prejudice and violence in the island. "For years in almost every speech of mine," the statement declared, "I have made it my duty not alone to denounce colour prejudice but to make the workers realize that I am not fighting for any race but workers." He could not, he said, respond to the report of his speech at the Conversorium because "the particulars are too vague." He remembered urging the workers "not to carry any kind of weapons, sticks or stones." Bustamante described the charge that he advocated violence to achieve self-government "as a pure and undiluted fabrication." He said that "never in all my life have I ever advocated violence and the most generous thing

I can say is that the truth was not honoured when this charge was leveled against me."²⁷

Bustamante elaborated on these issues under questioning from members of the tribunal. In its report, the tribunal observed that he "was making a considerable effort to appear calm and collected, but it was quite clear that it would have taken very little to excite him. He appeared to be very temperamental."²⁸ Already interned for sixteen months and recognizing the importance of the hearing for his freedom, Bustamante was probably very nervous and agitated. His reputation as a temperamental person was well known, haunting him even on occasions such as this one.

Bustamante, in his testimony, repeated the denials he had included in his statement. When Justice Sherlock read the letter he had written to the manager of the West Indies Sugar Company at Monymusk, the labor leader admitted that it was "not a proper one and that it was not meant to be acted on."²⁹ The letters he wrote were designed "to compel action on the part of the employers." Bustamante had long employed such coercive tactics in his dealings with employers, so this was hardly a surprising revelation.

The labor leader was troubled by the accusation that he advocated violence in the cause of self-government. Such an allegation, he said, "was entirely without foundation" because he "had never breathed such a thing and [he] could never have advocated the shedding of blood to achieve self-government as in his opinion it was not worth shedding." He recalled saying at North Parade, however, that "if anybody's blood was to be shed, it must be his, not the workers." It is unlikely that Bustamante was being deliberately mendacious. His carelessly worded and contradictory messages on platforms sent mixed messages to his listeners. As Bustamante's principal lieutenant, H. M. Shirley, said in his testimony before the Committee, "[W]hen Mr. Bustamante was excited he did not quite know what he was saying."³⁰

Bustamante also sought to distance himself from the cause of self-government and the People's National Party, one of its principal advocates. "I am not mad for self-government," he testified. "[I]f Manley wants self-government, he must get it by himself." He denied being a member of the Communist Party and the PNP. His union, he said, was "associated" with the PNP, but "the day I get out [of internment] I intend to break off that association." When the tribunal asked him if he were prepared "to give an undertaking not to address any open air meetings, political, or industrial," he pledged: "I shall never address one word to the People's National Party. I have been double crossed. I will be quite willing to give an undertaking not to speak publicly for the duration of the war, and should I want to speak at a meeting of any sort at any time, I would first ask His Excellency the Governor for permission to do so, and tell him the subject I wanted to speak on."[31]

Bustamante's willingness to break with the PNP was exactly what the governor wanted to hear. His claim that he was double-crossed by the party was a direct reference to his belief that it was co-opting the workers during his internment, thereby diluting the strength and power of the union and weakening his leadership. The crafty Bustamante knew that the governor wanted to destroy any relationship between the union and the party in order to prevent their uniting to demand self-government. By announcing that he would sever the union's links with the party, Bustamante made it unnecessary for the governor to demand it as the quid pro quo for his release. There was no need for the labor leader to have revealed his intentions at the hearing unless he expected the governor to release him in return. The implied quid pro quo gave both the governor and the labor leader the space to deny that a deal had been struck.

Gladys Longbridge's testimony supported Bustamante's claim that he did not advocate violence. She said she attended all of his meetings but could not recall any one at which he "urged people to shed blood." She remembered, however, that he had frequently said that "there was never conquest without shedding of blood or success without pain." H. M. Shirley testified that Bustamante gave "a long speech in his usual manner" at the Conversorium. Bustamante, Shirley said, "might have said there would be shedding of blood; reference was made to revolution, but in what sense he could not recollect." Shirley said he did not approve of any "amalgamation" of the union with the PNP since a trade union should be "separate and distinct from any other organization." He did not believe that Bustamante's release would cause any "fuss or trouble," although there would be "rejoicing." In response to a question as to whether Bustamante "would keep any understanding," he said the labor leader was "very excitable," and he was "not certain how he would act." This was not a ringing endorsement of Bustamante's strength of character, but Shirley said nothing that was not already public knowledge.[32]

Bustamante's speech at the Conversorium was the immediate occasion for his arrest. It had been taken down in shorthand by Corporal Rowe of the Central Intelligence Department. Bustamante had questioned the reliability of the transcript, claiming that the corporal was not within earshot of his speech. As he explained:

There was no Police at that meeting which was held in a Hall (7th September) when I spoke. When I arrived in the hall there were three police, one Detective Sgt. Vassell, a black Detective I know as Golden and another I believe (shorthand writers). I at once asked the Police who were sitting in the audience to come on the platform where they could be seated comfortably and where they would be unmolested; for owing to the wicked treatment of the Police (with exceptions of course) to the Public they are not very much liked, and due to my frame-up in 1938. That's my reason for always asking them to the platform, out of all danger and which invitation they always accepted. But that night they did not accept my invitation. I told them to leave the hall then, which they did. I have definite evidence that they stayed at a distance from the hall out in the street where I know that even if they had the sensitive hearing of a deer they could not take down my speech correctly. I have no definite knowledge of course that it was the Police who made the report of such a speech, but I have my strong suspicion and I am sanguine of one fact that whosoever it was they made their own speech, wrote it down themselves out of their own petrified, sordid, and depraved minds, for reasons unknown to me. But I strongly suspect, and I link it with Sugar.[33]

The authorities maintained that the shorthand writer was in a room adjacent to the Conversorium and that he could hear Bustamante's speech. Corporal Rowe testified that he could hear the speech "perfectly" and "was prepared to swear to the accuracy of his notes."[34] The racially strident tone of the speech, as reported, was out of character with Bustamante's previous utterances. Its ferocious appeal to violence was also a departure from Bustamante's customary rhetorical style. The labor leader had consistently accused the police of intimidation and harassment of himself and the workers he led. It was therefore conceivable that Corporal Rowe's transcript of Bustamante's speech was inaccurate or entirely fallacious. There was precedent for officers of the law distorting the content of the speeches they monitored. Evon Blake, who served as a policeman in the 1930s, was assigned to "take notes" at meetings where Garvey, Coombs, and Bustamante spoke. He admitted that he "doctored the speeches when they were dangerous.... I either deleted or doctored" them. While Blake was protecting these men from prosecution by the authorities, Rowe may have wanted to see Bustamante interned.[35]

Norman Manley was one individual who complained that he was a victim of selective reporting by note-taking police officers who monitored his speeches. Writing to Inspector Higgins of the Central Intelligence Department on March 22, 1941, he said: "I have on a previous occasion called attention to the important necessity of having the whole of the speech taken if any report is to be taken because otherwise what will be sent in will of necessity create a wrong impression." Manley thought that "this matter is the more important because these speeches are not being taken because it is supposed that anybody is committing a legal offence but are being taken for political reasons and I suppose for matters connected with the Defence of the Realm Regulations."

This was a chilling observation about the government's intimidation of the voices of protest and dissent in the island. Manley's account of his own experiences and the potential for the distortion of the speeches that were given in the island continued in his letter to Higgins.

> I raise this question again because on the night of Friday the 21st [1941] I was in St. Thomas and addressed three large public meetings at all of which the police were present. The object of these meetings was to announce the result of the settlement of the Strike and to request the workers to return to work in a peaceful and satisfied frame of mind. I took the precaution of taking with me a Short-hand writer and I also caused some observations to be made at the manner in which the police took notes. At Seaforth it was ascertained that those who were taking the notes were not able to keep up with what was being said and as a result had to omit a great deal. What was much worse was the discovery of the fact that whenever anything was said which was an exhortation to good behaviour and order, to going back to work in a spirit of friendliness[,] those remarks were not taken down at all. To what extent this went I cannot say.
>
> I am perfectly sure that if an address to workers is reported in that spirit it will create a complete misconception of the whole tenor and object of the speech. One cannot address workers without reminding them of their struggles though that may be a comparatively minor part of a peace-making speech but if nothing is recorded of peace and goodwill then the speech might indeed easily appear to be almost inciting.[36]

This extended excerpt from Manley's letter helps to cast some doubt on the credibility of Corporal Rowe's transcript of Bustamante's speech. The truth cannot now be ascertained, but the corporal's uncorroborated transcript would not have been sufficient to convict Bustamante in a court of law. But the hearing was not a judicial proceeding; it was designed primarily for the internee to appeal the grounds on which his confinement was based. It had, in this instance, the effect of exposing in retrospect the weakness of the case against Bustamante. Governor Richards had confined him for seventeen months, not because there was convincing and incontrovertible evidence that he posed a serious threat to the survival of the colonial state but because he was deemed to be an incorrigible troublemaker, acting in the service of his constituency of workers.

Having heard the evidence that supported Bustamante's internment and his defense, the tribunal recommended that he should be released. The report was sharply critical of him, however, and skeptical of his future conduct. "Mr. Bustamante in our opinion," it said, "is not quite normal." He was, it continued, "very calm and reasonable before us, but it is obvious that he is quite a different person on a platform addressing a public meeting. His outstanding characteristics are vanity and a desire for power. He without doubt has great influence over the members of his Union, and appears to be quite sincere in his assertion that he has at heart the interests of what he indifferently describes as 'the masses,' 'the toilers,' 'the workers,' 'the people.'"

The tribunal was satisfied that the reports by the police of Bustamante's speeches "are substantially accurate" and that "there are amply sufficient grounds for the Detention Order made against him." It thought that his detention "in all probability has had a steadying effect on him," and that his willingness "not to address public meetings or do anything to create disorder of any kind and solely devote himself to legitimate Trade Union affairs" justified his release.[37] Bustamante, although he expected to be released, was never told the date and time. According to Gladys Longbridge, the governor invited him to Kings House on February 7 to discuss the terms of his imminent freedom. As she recalled, "I went with Busta that morning and, in my presence, Bustamante told the Governor that, while he would respect the terms of his release, he would continue to fight for the cause to which he had dedicated himself." Making a thinly veiled reference to the governor, Bustamante said that "those who had the authority to investigate his detention and did not do so, were dishonest and that he would see to it that such persons were made to leave the country."[38] It is clear that Bustamante was nurturing a controlled rage against the colonial officials and a sense that he had been wronged. It would take him some time to heal psychologically and bury the hatchet.

Bustamante's release occurred on the 8th of February, the day after he met with the governor. According to the newspaper account of the event, "[N]ear 12 noon, an officer asked the Labour leader to accompany him for a ride.... [W]hen they were outside the Camp, Mr. Bustamante was told he was free." Bustamante confessed: "I did not manifest any emotion when I was told to go, just as I had said nothing when I was taken 17 months ago to Camp." The *Daily Gleaner* described him as "perhaps a bit thinner, very dignified, with much more silver in his hair" and speaking in "a voice more than usual soft." The *Gleaner* thought he was rather subdued. "There was not the slightest trace of bitterness in either remark or gesture," the newspaper reported. Bustamante did not betray any rancor at his internment, recognizing that that was a moment to demonstrate a generosity of spirit. "I have nothing against the government," he said, "when I was interned I went without a word and after seventeen months internment I still have nothing against them. I realize my loss of freedom is the price which every leader must pay."[39] The labor leader was being uncharacteristically restrained and diplomatic. But he was seething with rage against the colonial authorities and those he called his enemies in the labor union. His internment, however, had made him a martyr for labor's cause.

Although Bustamante viewed his internment as an act of gross injustice, he never questioned the governor's right to deprive him of his liberty. But this did not mean that he accepted his treatment passively or dissuaded his allies from their efforts to free him. The union and Manley were in the forefront of these initiatives, sending petitions and letters to the governor and to the Colonial Office, pleading with sympathetic members of parliament such as Arthur Creech Jones and David Adams to take up his cause. Sir Walter Citrine, the general secretary of the Trades Union Congress in England, was also requested to intervene with the colonial authorities on Bustamante's behalf.

Bustamante belittled these efforts upon his release, accusing Norman Manley and the union's officials of being lethargic and negligent in promoting his cause. He was convinced that it was to their political advantage to keep him interned. Bustamante denounced Manley for allegedly waiting at least eleven weeks to prepare an appeal on his behalf. He asked rhetorically:

> Isn't it a fact that I gave you [Manley] and Mr. Livingston [the union's solicitor] instructions to have my appeal filed, and that Mr. Livingston said it would take three weeks, and that I waited for 11 weeks and yet nothing was done? Isn't it a fact that after I saw no appeal paper

come after those 11 weeks, I asked Miss Longbridge to furnish you with information regarding my activities over the country, so that a letter could be sent to the House of Parliament on my behalf? Isn't it a fact that Miss Longbridge came to you for four weeks straight or more and asked you to see the Governor in my case and each time you refused, and then afterwards you told Miss Longbridge and myself that you had gone, to which I had no proof? Isn't it a fact that although many communications were sent to England and after some months had elapsed only one replied, and neither you nor Shirley bothered to write to find out if the other letters had been received?[40]

Clearly, Bustamante distrusted both his principal legal advocate, Manley, and Shirley, the man who was leading the union in his absence. There is no independent corroboration of Bustamante's allegations about the delay in filing the petition; his chronic tendency to exaggeration and verbal excesses make it difficult to accept his charges at face value. There is some evidence, however, that Manley made inquiries about the receipt of his communications with interested parties in England.

Manley was restrained and essentially accurate in his responses to Bustamante's allegations: "I am not going to tell the long story of the thousand and one things we did to try and get him out—of the dozens and dozens of visits I paid to him; from going to the Governor to plea for him, to writing to members of parliament, to sending petitions, to having personal interviews with Mr. G. Hall, the Undersecretary of State for the Colonies; from getting private doctors to see him when he was ill; whatever he wanted I did and did gladly."

The extant records support Manley's claims. Norman Manley probably did not visit Bustamante "dozens and dozens" of times but his surviving papers contain several requests for permission to see his interned cousin. In response to the wishes of the officials of the BITU, he met with Governor Richards two months after Bustamante's interment to plead for his release. In asking for the meeting, Manley told the governor that he believed Bustamante "would submit to any conditions you might impose" if he were released. Manley reported that Bustamante "tells me that he would like to be allowed to leave Jamaica for a few months." The governor was not particularly enthusiastic about such a meeting with Manley. In approving the request, he cautioned Manley: "I cannot . . . hold out much prospect of a favourable reply to any proposal for his [Bustamante's] release in the immediate future." He saw "no harm," however, in discussing the matter.

"Bustamante is so mercurial a character to deal with," the puzzled governor added. The meeting, predictably, achieved nothing.[41] The governor did not give much weight to Bustamante's offer to go into temporary exile, a proposal that would have astonished the workers in the union had they known about it.

Confined for seventeen months in an internment camp, Bustamante must have felt at times abandoned by his allies in the emotionally difficult moments that he undoubtedly experienced. Miss Longbridge revealed that he had come to trust no one, with her and possibly Edith Nelson as the exceptions. Separated from the union, his aides, and the adulation of his supporters, Bustamante must have become impatient and despondent as the months passed and as he awaited the resolution of his appeal. It is also understandable that he would harbor the belief that his legal team and union colleagues were not being sufficiently aggressive in advancing his case and securing his release. But Bustamante never seemed to appreciate the slow pace at which such matters often moved and the depth of Governor Richards's determination to keep him away from the workers. Norman Manley was never his enemy. "I never spoke for fifteen months," Manley recalled, "that I never denounced his detention as an act of injustice, and I still say it was an act of injustice. It was wrong to have detained him, and it never can become right. Justice is justice, and it does not alter from one day to another." The developing antagonism between the two men was misdirected; the real conflict should have been between the colonial state and the owners of capital on the one hand and Bustamante, Manley, and the workers on the other.

Approximately ten months after his release, Bustamante began a campaign to be exonerated of the charges that had been leveled against him. Writing to the secretary of state on December 22, 1942, he requested that he "cause the governor of Jamaica to make investigations into charges placed against me leading to my recent detention and continued detention for seventeen months." He stressed that the request was being made "in the interest of my honour and my always well guarded and unblemished name, but also in the interest of public good, and public security and in the interest of British Justice in which I believe." Bustamante said he could prove, with the requisite evidence, "that every charge that was placed against me was a most wicked fabrication of vicious and unbelievable lies."

Bustamante's detailed letter asserted his innocence, contested the charges against him, and affirmed his patriotism. He was not satisfied with the government declaring that "your sentence or your term in detention prison has been suspended." Bustamante said the "suspension" in his case was "similar to an innocent man who was convicted of a murder which he never committed, then some good governor comes along and says 'I reprieve you from death and you are commuted to life sentence'—for an act he did not commit." His language dripped with sarcasm in his reference to "some good governor." Its tone was accusatory, stressing: "Unless justice is done under the British flag then I cannot see what good this war would achieve by England having rushed to defend peoples of Europe over whom the British flag did not fly and does not fly today, and at the same time fighting for permanent Democracy for all of us."[42]

Bustamante said he was unable to see "how you can be fighting for justice and fairplay for all of us . . . and at the same time one of us is being crucified under the same British flag—and a loyal British subject at that." Although Bustamante did not name him, he was clearly referring to Governor Richards when he asserted that "government has a moral responsibility to all those over whom they govern and a responsibility to see that British justice is untainted, and that if it has been marred through the acts of Government's Agents and can be proven, then those agents who caused British justice to be scarred should be removed for public safety, public good, and for the upholding of the true essence of British Justice."

Bustamante, the fervent admirer of all things British, was experiencing an epiphany. He was beginning to question his belief in the efficacy of British justice and the probity of colonial officials and "those who have come from abroad." As he charged, somewhat incoherently:

> And now, the Governor of Jamaica: he is far removed from us. He is not associated with the common things of life, nor naturally, the common minds that would descend to those loathsome things, even though big employers may be amongst these common minds he as governor not alone [sensitive] to the ways of Jamaicans but also to the common minds that some of those who come from abroad, now enjoying the fruits of our land, possess. Of course he must listen to someone but there is a glaring fact facing the Governor, yourself sir, myself, my people and the justice of the British Empire that I do not alone say that I was framed on tissues of black lies but that I now assure you that I can prove it to the last word with such evidence as would make you shudder to believe that such acts, could not alone be perpetrated under His Majesty's Flag but cause a prison term or detention, the loss of man's most precious heritage and those things

England says we are entitled to, Justice, Liberty, Freedom, and the denial of a fair trial to one whose loyalty has not alone been proven but stood the acid test and has remained loyal in spite of injustices not once, but more.[43]

The rawness of the text and its unedifying style suggests that Bustamante wrote it unaided by a lawyer. It is likely that Gladys Longbridge, who served as his principal typist and editor, was the only other person who read it before it was dispatched to the governor for transmission to the secretary of state. Bustamante's sharp critique of British justice in the text went beyond anything he had uttered in public. He accused the government of being complicit in a "frame up" against him in 1938 when he was arrested and in 1940 when he was detained. "I was surprised when I was released," he complained, "not as an innocent person as I still am, but under a suspension order with restrictions as if I were guilty of some crime, as if I had committed some offence, when I had committed no offence. Whatever offence was committed, I did not commit any against the State but an offence was committed, and committed against me as it was in 1938. I never committed any offence against the state in 1938 either, but an offence was then committed against me." Characterizing the charges against him as "an ugly frame up," he said that "the most serious part of it is, those I believe who took part in framing me are still doing public duty; that is the grave part of it." The police officer "who framed me in 1938 and 1940," Bustamante claimed, "has been promoted, I suppose over the glorification that someone succeeded in putting me behind bars, thereby getting me out of the way for some time."[44]

Bustamante's letter exonerated policemen from England or Ireland for any involvement in the "frame up." He said he felt sure that when the investigation he requested was undertaken, "it will be found that no police from the other side has any connection with it, what I mean is that no Irish or English police born on the other side has anything to do with these things." The labor leader, on the other hand, was not equally charitable to the Jamaican-born police officers. "It will be proven," he asserted, "that it is our own Jamaicans, that is why I have such a high regard for the Police that are sent here from abroad, for it is seldom we find this kind of low mentality and destructive mind amongst them; it is sad to say so for I am a Jamaican."[45] This was certainly not an expression of confidence in the fair-mindedness of Jamaican police officers from a man who believed he had been seriously wronged by them.

Bustamante, the consummate colonial subject, was astonished that the authorities had accused him of advocating self-government for Jamaica through the use of force. "At that time," Bustamante wrote, "I had so little interest in self government that I was not even a member of the People's National Party known to be advocating self government." He repeated many of the arguments he had used when he appeared before the local tribunal in January 1942. Addressing the issue of his advocacy of violence, he asked rhetorically: "Can you imagine anyone who is so interested in Self Government as to advocate Self Government by force (meaning by military rebellion) and not even to be a member of this Self Government stuff particularly when my personal membership in this Self Government business would bring at least six hundred thousand members in it, and perhaps more? Can you imagine anyone so insane in a tiny island as Jamaica—unarmed, defenseless, and peaceful people with the mighty British Navy, the Army, and the Air force advocating Self Government by force?"[46]

Bustamante, to be sure, was exaggerating his influence in the island. His union, at its peak, may have had a membership of 50,000. He assured the secretary of state that if he so desired, he could "convert" one-half of the island's population, or 600,000 persons, to the cause of self-government, since "the very, very great majority of the people follow my dictates, and so I do not allow my ambition to guide me but my heart and my conscience." If he "were mad for Self Government," he said, "and [if] I did not want to unite myself with the tiny negative minority who calls themselves Self Government seekers, I would have launched out for Self Government myself for I have the people behind me, the middle, the low, and some of the high, in any case the very vast majority, more than any man or any group, or all other groups combined. I have not much desire nor no itch for Self Government now, nor any desire whatsoever for the time being to be so separated from England." Bustamante, in this comment, was conflating self-government with independence. Few Jamaicans at the time, including Manley, advocated independence. "I have never in my life advocated immediate self government," Bustamante boasted, "neither in secret nor in public, and I do nothing in secret; my life is like an open book." He said he was "the most consistent and determined opponent of Self Government now," since "at least for the time being it would be dishonest on my part to mislead my people just for my political aggrandizement or perhaps financial gain." He was founding a political party, the Jamaica Labour Party, "in which Self Government is not included." He supported "a wider and broader constitution" for the island, "which means we should have more say over our country in our own affairs." Bustamante had an "idea," he confessed, "that England and the English people, have a particularly soft spot in their heart for Jamaica. This feeling naturally brings one very near to England for I say those who are not with us are against us, and those who are with us we are with them."[47]

Bustamante was tied umbilically to the mother country and was, at the time, psychologically and intellectually unable to accept Jamaicans governing themselves. The text of his letter reveals a psychological dependence on the colonial power, and he was always a proud defender of the British empire in all of his utterances. Still, he was shaken by his internment, and his belief in the purity of British justice and the abiding rectitude of those who administered it weakened. Bustamante's feeling that a grievous wrong had been committed against him permeated his letter to the colonial secretary. "If I made utterances that had legitimately taken me to Detention prison," he wrote, "I would have done so in what I believe would be the interest of my people and I would be man enough to admit that I did it, to write that I did it, to sing that I did it and let the matter alone." He had vigorously denied making any such utterances and inciting violence in the speech he gave at the Race Course in Kingston. Bustamante recalled telling the crowd that "if anybody's blood is to be spilt, let mine be spilt" (meaning my . . . blood, not the workers)." He believed that "even if I uttered these words I should be commended for wanting only my blood to be spilt and not the blood of others."[48]

There is no evidence that Bustamante shared with his associates the information that he was asking the colonial secretary to order the Jamaican government to carry out a "public investigation" of his case. He did, however, seek the assistance of David Adams, a Labour member of Parliament sympathetic to his cause. The two letters that he wrote to Adams were read by the local censors but were released because they were deemed innocuous. Adams had become Bustamante's last hope since the colonial secretary had rejected his application for an investigation, declaring that there was no reason to "question the action the Governor took."[49]

Bustamante's two letters to Adams, written in April 1943, show a marked evolution in his thinking. He had begun to blame the colonial state for persecuting him for his work on behalf of the dispossessed. "I quite realize the position I have placed myself into by fighting for my downtrodden people," he noted. Bustamante emphasized that his request for an investigation into his case "cannot be sidetracked, unless what we preach about British justice is purely meant as a camouflage," quickly adding: "I do not believe [this] is the case." Bustamante was beginning to invoke the specter of racialism, pointing out that "coloured colonials are entitled to the same justice as others." The formerly uncritical admirer of Britain was now entertaining the view that "if one has influence with one's people it is considered a crime and Jamaicans have no leader, we are just colonials, we are not entitled to leadership."[50]

Bustamante had criticized the barons of capital in the past, but he possessed an enormous reverence for the Crown, the empire, and its officers. His internment and his sense that a profound injustice had been done to him, however, were changing his rhetorical tone, if not his loyalty to England. He was quick to reassure Mr. Adams that in spite of the wrongs he described, "we adore our flag, the very, very great majority of us, and we trust and hope for cleaner days in Jamaica, less persecution, more justice." He wanted Adams, "as a labour man[,] to live in Jamaica for about three months without mixing with plutocrats and visit certain places and see how the unfortunate are treated."[51]

Bustamante's communication with British officials reveals the continuing pain of his incarceration and a sense of betrayal by the pristine imperial justice he thought he understood. Although his faith in the integrity of the empire he worshipped and of which he was a proud member was shaken, Bustamante could not bring himself to renounce his affection for it and to embrace self-government for his people. There was no epiphany, no sharp, sudden, life-altering confrontation with the political beliefs that he had embraced and championed for so long and their perverted actualization.

Bustamante fought vigorously to clear his name upon his release from the detention camp. But he had other scores to settle as well. During Bustamante's internment, Gladys Longbridge had kept him fully informed about the developments in the union, warning him that his leadership was in jeopardy. Norman Manley, the union's general counsel, had brought several of his associates in the PNP to assist in the union's work. They included such party stalwarts as Kenneth Hill, Frank Hill, Winston Grubb, Noel Nethersole, Richard Hart, Arthur Henry, and Osmond Dyce.

Manley and these men realized that the PNP's electoral success depended significantly on its ability to attract the workers to its fold, particularly when universal adult suffrage was achieved. They viewed Bustamante's conservative stances, especially on the question of self-government, with anathema. Nor did they possess much respect for his intellectual ability. Bustamante's autocratic leadership style and his volatile and unpredictable temperament were not qualities they admired, complicating any prospects of a productive collaboration with him. Still, these prominent members of the PNP looked enviously at Bustamante's sway and influence over the workers. They knew they could not supplant his appeal, but they recognized that an organic union between the PNP and Bustamante would redound to the benefit of both. The PNP would obtain the mass base it lacked, and Bustamante would have politicians on his side working to advance labor's cause.

Bustamante was never comfortable with a potential marriage with the PNP. He was suspicious of the party's intentions and rejected its anticolonial rhetoric. Bustamante was exceedingly proud of his blood ties with Manley but felt threatened by him, harboring the thought that Manley was competing with him for the affection of the workers. This was largely a product of Bustamante's imagination; Manley knew that the workers' hearts resided with his cousin. "I have constantly said that I am not a labour leader," Manley declared, "and I don't pose as a Labour leader, I lead a political party whose duty it is to work for the cause of labour." He had been very sensitive to the need to maintain the autonomy of the union while Bustamante was interned, recognizing that boundaries should exist between the PNP and the BITU. When Robert Harding, the secretary of the BITU's branch in Lucea, invited Manley to intervene in a labor dispute in February 1941, his response reaffirmed his support for the independence of the union: "I have to say that whilst I am anxious to help in any way I can, communications of this sort should be sent direct to your Union who want all the information they can get and whose duty it is to receive and consider it. My help is given through the Union itself and much more good will be done if you communicate directly with them and leave them to communicate with me where they want my help."

Manley's PNP associates may not have been as scrupulous in respecting the boundaries between the two organizations, but the party leader was not complicit in any such transgressions. The PNP and the BITU seemed to have cooperated quite effectively at the local levels to advance their mutual interests. Concerned about the potential cessation of the collaboration of the two organizations in Montego Bay, the officials of the BITU wrote to Manley in April 1941 asking for his intervention:

> Concerning the great successes achieved by the Union we must congratulate you for the stern and ardent support of your organization the PNP. . . . As you know Mr. L. W. Rose of the B.I.T.U. and O. Dyce

of the P.N.P. [have] been with us since the past weeks[,] well they have been called in Kingston today which is remorseful grief on our part. Their campaign has proven to be a complete success which adds a quota of nine branches. If at this moment they should be omitted from us their marvelous works would be completely smash so Sir we are asking you to help us by interviewing Mr. Shirley on the matter that he can send them back as quick as possible to carry on this marvelous campaign.[52]

It is not known if the two men returned to Montego Bay. Manley, of course, was acutely cognizant of the role that unions should play in society and of the power the workers could exercise if they were allied with a political party.

> I say and I have always said that the first and most important task today is to build up stable trade unions. . . . You are only fit for Self-Government when the lower classes, the workers, the downtrodden, the humbler people are building up the power to show that they can create leadership with principle. Unions led from above are worthless. . . . How can [universal] adult suffrage be useful without a strong labour organisation to marshall and organize all the workers of this country? We want them to stand in their own organisations solidly organized to use their political power for their own development and their own prosperity in their own country. . . . It is the duty of a progressive political party to fight and to make any sacrifice for the progress of the union movement in a country.[53]

Manley expressed his determination to help the unions "in times of crisis," but when the crisis "is over I am prepared to walk out and leave them alone to run their own job." Bustamante never quite believed Manley's lofty expression of disinterest in a leadership role in the trade-union movement, but the barrister was being sincere. Bustamante's distrust of Manley's motives was a critical factor in the acrimonious dispute between the two men, but it was also fed by Bustamante's willingness to serve the interests of a colonial governor anxious to see a split between the political party and the labor movement.[54]

Bustamante left the internment camp in February 1942 determined to break with the officers of the union who had exercised power in his absence. Nursing many grievances, the leader vowed to remove them and to reassert his authority over the organization he had founded. Shortly after his release on February 8, Bustamante received an invitation to a reception in his honor organized by the union's managing executive committee. This invitation provided him with an opportunity to reveal his feelings and level charges at the officials, insulting them in the process. Rejecting the invitation, Bustamante accused the officials of betraying him, attempting to delay his release from detention, and besmirching his character. "There are certain officers right in the office," he wrote, "persons whom my blood has almost been depleted in order to provide them legitimate employment, whose conduct has helped materially to hinder, obstruct, and delay my release from detention." Displaying his characteristic rhetorical flamboyance, he continued: "More than once, plots have been formulated by certain persons in my own office and circulated throughout this country not alone to destroy my irreproachable and honourable name and defame my character, but also the unimpeachable integrity and honour of trusted and loyal aides of mine who passed through the baptism of fire in my office during my absence and who also passed through tribulation and sufferings equally with me in the infancy of this movement while traitors came, went and will go."[55]

These remarks reflected Bustamante's addiction to hyperbole, but they contained ominous threats, especially in relationship to the "traitors" who "will go." The trusted aides to whom he referred undoubtedly included Gladys Longbridge and Edith Nelson. Bustamante also targeted Norman Manley and the other members of the People's National Party who had become involved in varying degrees in the union's affairs while he was detained. "To aggravate matters," Bustamante wrote, "there has been and still exists an unholy combination of certain persons with political ambition whose objective is that of destroying me and then to assume control of the Union as a political machine and to serve their own big friends."[56] This allegation, although grossly exaggerated, contained some truth. But the machinations of the PNP's officials to which he referred were not as Machiavellian as they were framed by Bustamante.

Bustamante implied that the union represented the poor and the vulnerable, while the PNP promoted the interests of the elites. "This organization," he affirmed, "was formed for the interest of the masses and not in the interest of any particular officer or any other organization or any group or group of persons who can well take care of themselves because they possess intelligence, influence, or wealth." He knew that the "tens of thousands of the lowly, humble, grateful masses" were "deeply appreciative of the great sacrifices I have made without grumbling." The chief ended on a note of defiance. "Rest assured," he said, "that the man who was born in a little thatched house in the wilds of Hanover will, with the aid of Almighty God, the workers, and the loyal officers, break this plot asunder and bring it to earth, not for any material benefit for myself but for the benefit of the workers of the country whose sacred trust I enjoy and whose trust I will never betray."[57]

Bustamante lost no time in keeping his threat to reassert his power over the union. Shortly after his release, he visited the union's headquarters determined to sever ties with those whom he believed were planning to usurp his authority, effect a closer alliance with the PNP, and lead the union along a more democratic path. Chastising those leaders who were present when he arrived, the angry founding president declared: "I want you all to understand that this organization was built on my blood and the suffering of the workers, . . . [Y]ou will not be allowed to smash it." Identifying the principal offenders, he summarily fired them, "pointing at them individually," recalled Gladys Longbridge. "Shirley, you are fired," he said. "Morais, you are fired! Hamilton, you are fired! McBean, you are fired! Chambers, you are fired! Nelson, you are fired!" When the victims of Bustamante's notorious temper and impetuosity yelled, "[Y]ou can't fire me! More than one coffin will come out of here today," Bustamante chased them from the room brandishing a chair, breaking it on the back of one of the hapless men. Bustamante would later pay a fine in court for his violent display.[58]

Bustamante's unilateral dismissal of the officials demonstrated the dictatorial power that he wielded. The Bustamante Industrial Trade Union was unquestionably his organization; he was the jefe maximo who thought he possessed untrammeled authority and power, but times had changed since his detention, so his intemperate firing of the officials would most certainly be challenged. Norman Manley, whose influence in the union had risen during Bustamante's absence, led the charge. Manley probably had anticipated that Bustamante's return to the helm of the union would precipitate problems owing to his dictatorial management style and his well-known inability to work amicably and cooperatively with subordinates. There was also the added complication that Manley probably did not welcome a diminution in the influence he had exercised in the union during Bustamante's internment.

Norman Manley had developed a good working relationship with H. M. Shirley while Bustamante was interned. The affairs of the union were more democratically managed, and there seemed to have been a greater degree of collegiality and collective responsibility than under Bustamante's leadership. Gladys Longbridge and Edith Nelson, the assistant general secretary, probably felt marginalized because of their personal closeness to Bustamante, and everyone knew that Miss Longbridge, in particular, kept him fully informed about the activities of the men in charge. A month before Bustamante's release, and anticipating the break with him, Manley attended a public function at the Conversorium honoring H. M. Shirley for his performance as leader of the BITU during the president's confinement. He praised Shirley's "guts," adding that "during the past year I have been associated on many platforms all over the island with the officers of the Bustamante Industrial Trade Unions. I have been proud to be with them. I have never felt happier than when I have been standing shoulder to shoulder with men whom I know will fight and fight to the end and so long as we can go forward with the speed that has been shown in the past year, the progressive movement in Jamaica cannot fail in this island."[59]

Many other speakers praised Shirley's accomplishments during his tenure as leader of the union. In response, Shirley thanked several individuals and organizations for their support, including the People's National Party. Given Bustamante's anathema to the party, he must have been incensed when he heard about, or read, Shirley's speech. Conceivably, he may have seen the praise accorded Shirley as an indirect criticism of his leadership and accomplishments. Bustamante was also not one to tolerate any challenge, real or imagined, to his leadership. But although he had announced Shirley's dismissal along with the others, he had no constitutional authority to dismiss the vice president since his was an elected position, unlike the others, who were appointed and subject to the leader's whims. Regardless of whether or not Bustamante lacked the authority to dismiss Shirley, his tenure as an official in the union had effectively ended.

Manley viewed Bustamante's conduct with consternation, recognizing that he was really the principal target of the union leader's vituperation. Manley chose a public meeting at Edelweiss Park on February 16, 1942, to level what the *Gleaner* described as "sensational charges" against the labor leader. The meeting was held under the auspices of the PNP, and the speakers included Shirley, Noel Nethersole, and William Seivright. But it was Manley who created the most excitement at the meeting with his attack on Bustamante. Believing that he was putting his life at risk by attacking Bustamante, the barrister declared: "They can kill me this time, but I am not keeping my mouth shut. I am going to speak the truth about this iniquity."[60]

This "iniquity" included a number of serious allegations. Manley revealed that Bustamante had admitted to him in August 1941 "that he had been taken from the Detention Camp and in the presence of a high official was asked to sign a paper promising to denounce the PNP as a condition for his relief [sic] from detention." As if this were not bad enough, Manley voiced his resentment at Bustamante's charge that the union's officials had been engaged in a conspiracy against him, detailing his own role in the struggle to get him released.

> I can go on back to 1941 when the People's National Party used to hold weekly meetings at the Race Course, and I have time and again with Mr. [H. M.] Shirley, Mr. [Leslie] Rose and the rest of them denounced the government for the injustice of his detention. When he was detained, the Union officers asked me to draw up a petition for them to send . . . [to the authorities] and I did it . . . and it was signed by tens of thousands. They asked me to interview the Governor on their behalf and I did it, and I pleaded the justice of his case for release. They asked me to draw up a petition for the Secretary of State . . . and it went to England . . . and I sent it to the Labour Committee of the Labour Party in England.

Manley listed other efforts he made on Bustamante's behalf. He took particular umbrage at the labor leader's assault on the union's officials and the claim that they wanted to "hinder and delay" his release. "Can any worker in Jamaica believe a wicked, bloody lie like that?" Manley asked the crowd. The "great throng," according to the *Gleaner*, responded with a unanimous "no." "I did not believe," Manley confessed, "that I would ever live to see a leader in this country turn on his own people who have sweated their guts out for him, who have never stood on a platform without mentioning his name, who have kept that name fresh and strong and vigorous in the eyes of the people and stoop to accusing them of so foul a crime in order to curry favour with police and government." Then he added with an unmistakable reference to Bustamante: "Vanity, self-aggrandisement, wishing to stand alone, as king, will not bring prosperity [to] the unfortunate masses of this country." Manley then accused Bustamante of receiving a salary of £2,000 per annum from the union, as well as an entertainment allowance. This salary, he lamented, was "drawn from the pennies put up by the workers." Manley would later charge that in contrast to Bustamante's salary, the union's vice president, H. M. Shirley, received £3.10 per week, or £165 per annum. He further alleged that Bustamante hired his car to the union at the rate of one shilling per mile.[61]

Predictably, an angry Bustamante denied the allegations made against him. On February 21, five days after Manley gave his speech, Bustamante issued a statement claiming that he had been "scandalized and libeled."[62] In succeeding weeks, the public was treated to the unseemly spectacle of the two titans making vicious charges and countercharges, diminishing themselves in the process. The public took sides, depending on their emotional or political attachment to either of the men. Both men distorted the facts, obfuscated the issues, and questioned the probity of his antagonist. Unlike the lawyerly Manley, Bustamante digressed in his statements and remarks, often employing the clever turn of phrase that cheapened the discussion or debate. The truth was not readily obvious, but there is enough in the historical record to permit plausible speculations.

There is some indication in the records that Manley discussed with Bustamante the question of his release on September 13, 1941, and not in August, as Manley recalled. This was a minor discrepancy, probably the result of a faulty memory. Manley's brief notes of the meeting include such headings as "Gov[ernor] refuses [to] consider Busta's release"; "Denunciation of PNP"; "Colsec [colonial secretary] had documents"; "He [presumably Bustamante] wrote on back [of] proposals, 'will be no party to dishonourable proposals'"; "Colsec said nothing except 'we have no malice against you.'"[63]

It is apparent from these tantalizingly sketchy notes that Bustamante had a discussion with the colonial secretary, presumably to explore the conditions related to his potential release. The issue of the "Denunciation of PNP" arose probably as a quid pro quo. Bustamante, as Manley's notes suggest, said he declined to accept that condition. Based upon an informed interpretation of the notes, it seems plausible that Manley's account of the September meeting with Bustamante was substantially accurate.

Six days after Bustamante's release from internment and soon after he began his attack on his former colleagues, Manley wrote him a letter that sheds additional light on the alleged deal with the government. This important letter deserves to be reproduced fully.

Dear Bustamante,
I have read the *Daily Worker* and I now see that the plot that I suspected all the time has been made. You have come out to attack the P.N.P. and others who worked faithfully while you were away for you and the cause including your own best and most loyal officers.

I do not forget that you told me, last year September, that funny story about how you were sent for by the Colonial Secretary and promised your release if you would attack the P.N.P. I knew at the time that you were trying to fool me [by not admitting that you accepted the deal] but it let me know what you really had in mind to do and now you have made the deal and lined up yourself against those who helped your Union when you were away and defended you and worked for you all the time.

Well it's not the first time you have done this. For the sake of the progress of the country I have shut my mouth for three and a half years about you. I have borne all your attacks in silence. I have been stoned at your request—I have seen you try to break up the [labor?] movement for no reason except your personal interest.

I told you when I last saw you only a few weeks ago in Camp that I was sure you would soon come out (I was right) and that you would find the Union stronger than ever and your own name fresh in all the workers' minds and you were glad and thanked me for all I had done.

You could be at the top of a united movement for progress and everyone would recognize your position if you had not chosen to make this deal and carry out this plot.

I have all the facts and all the evidence. I have knowledge of many things that some people think hidden. Some people are going to be surprised.

I am not sitting down and keeping quiet any longer. If it is war, it is your choice. I offered you help and friendship and you took it and now join my enemies to stab me in the back as you have done before. This time I am going to see that the truth is publicly told from one end of Jamaica to the other.[64]

This letter reveals an angry Norman Manley denouncing Alexander Bustamante for allegedly being in collusion with the government against the PNP and presumably the workers. Manley was threatening to go public with the information he said he possessed, deepening the feud that Bustamante had clearly started. Not surprisingly, Bustamante rejected Manley's allegation. In his February 21 statement, Bustamante denied having had conversations with Manley regarding any deal with the authorities for his release. As he explained, "Mr. Manley [said] . . . that I was asked to sign a document with Government to attack his party, yet Government did not release me until I had appeared before the Advisory Board . . . almost six months later. Does that appeal to the belief of even an imbecile?" Returning to the matter on Saturday, February 26, Bustamante admitted that he would have signed any document disassociating his union from any political party had he been presented with one. He confessed that "if government had approached me—which they did not—telling me that one condition of my release should be that the Union be kept from association with any political party; that, in my opinion would have been perfectly alright."[65]

Manley insisted that Bustamante had discussed with him the government's request that he sign a document severing his ties with any political party. "I say it as a fact," Manley emphasized, "that he told me that a high government officer saw him out of camp and tried to get him to sign a document promising to attack the PNP if released." He elaborated:

> I am not saying that any Government official asked him to sign the document. There is no evidence of that, except Bustamante's word, which I for one would not accept. What I say is that he told me so when I asked him if it was true that certain base fellows had suggested to him to sign a paper to attack the PNP. His answer showed me that such a paper did exist and that he had the idea in his mind. His conduct on release proves that I read his mind right. . . . I can call many persons to prove that I mentioned it months ago, and forecast that he would take the line of attack that he has taken. I say categorically that it is a fact and that he has told me so not once but several times even describing in detail the document in question.[66]

The two leaders related diametrically opposed stories. Manley was as adamant in claiming that Bustamante told him about the government's proposed deal as Bustamante was in denying it. It must be recalled, however, that Bustamante had told the local tribunal that heard his appeal on January 10 that he planned to break with the PNP. In volunteering this information, Bustamante was seeking to influence the appeal in his favor. Since he had been interned on a charge of sedition, his union's association with a political party was an irrelevant matter, unless he knew that a break with the PNP was the price he had to pay for his release. In fact, Governor Richards had stressed that Bustamante's detention had nothing to do "with his activities as a trade union leader." It is noteworthy that Bustamante never revealed to the public that he had told the tribunal of his intention to break with the PNP, confining himself to denying Manley's charges of collusion with the governor. Manley was a brilliant barrister, but he was not a clairvoyant. He could not have known with certitude that the government had a special interest in Bustamante's severing of his ties with the PNP, an issue that was unrelated to the charge of sedition. That information could only have come from Bustamante. Given the negative implication for Bustamante's reputation of any acknowledged quid pro quo with the government, Manley taunted: "Of course, I do not expect Bustamante to admit it. He dare not."[67]

Engineered by Bustamante, the split between the two men dramatized the success of the governor's policy. "I will say this, without any boast," Bustamante had said before his internment, "that there is no greater power in this country than the combination of Manley and Bustamante. I intend to cooperate with the party [PNP] for the benefit of the masses."[68] But he retreated from this position in order to obtain his liberty. When Colonel Stratton of the Colonial Office visited the island in June 1942, he was able to report that "Sir Arthur Richards's recent release of Bustamante from internment had been based on the hope that Bustamante's rivalry with Mr. Manley would divide the forces of opposition." The colonel noted that "Bustamante and Manley were certainly at logger heads at present," but he cautioned that "there was always the risk of a combination between the two which would add the full strength of the Trades Unions to the People's National Party." Governor Richards also held the same position, admitting in a letter to the Colonial Office in June 1942 his motivation for Bustamante's release. "Nuisance, though Bustamante is," the governor wrote, "there is no doubt that had he not been released or had he gone in with Manley the situation [threat of social unrest] would be far more serious than it is. However, there is never absent the possibility that if Bustamante finds himself being beaten he may make terms with the People's National Party in spite of the unforgivable things that he and Manley have said about each other. Political memories are short."[69] The feared political rapprochement between the two rivals did not occur, reflecting the triumph of Richards's machinations and Bustamante's active collaboration with the agents of colonial rule.

The feud between Bustamante and Manley intensified when the latter continued to question the handling of the BITU's finances. Allan Coombs, it may be recalled, had publicly raised the question of financial impropriety in the organization as early as August 1938. There had been, in subsequent months, much gossip and innuendo about official malfeasance in it. An undated flyer that circulated in 1939, for example, accused Bustamante of stirring up "colour and class" prejudices and of "robbing" the people. The allegations were ugly and inflammatory, and they may even have been libelous. The flyer proclaimed:

> What fools you are
>   Bustamante is a brown man and Livingston a Jamaica white.
>   Both are middle-class men yet they are trying to stir up colour and class
>   Go to the Race Course meeting and make Bustamante make fools of you
>   He has collected over £20,000 from your pennies
>   Remember how [J. A. G.] Edwards stole the U.N.I.A. money?
>   That's what is happening now
>   BUSTAMANTE IS ROBBING YOU
>   [ROSS] LIVINGSTON IS ROBBING YOU
>   EDWARDS IS ROBBING YOU AGAIN
>   LORD! YOU FOOL!
>   Bustamante was going to England with your money—but [St William] Grant stopped him.[70]

A document that the Jamaican government submitted to the Colonial Office in 1942 echoed these innuendos. It had been seized by the body that had been appointed to censor the mails during wartime. Addressed to "Fellow Comrades," the document bemoaned the fact that in spite of the thousands of pounds that its members had contributed to the BITU, it owned no property. "Is it not a burning shame and distress," the document asked, "that up to now we have nothing to show for it, no building no Hall no Property, must we not now conclude that something is definitely wrong?" After denouncing the union's "rotten Dictator Constitution," it continued its scathing criticism.

> We now admit that we have been fools and babes, by allowing Bustamante to elect himself President for life, to appoint and disappoint whoever he pleases to run the union as his own private property, he certainly had guts. Here again he has stooped so low, he appoints his dear lady friend who is his private secretary [Gladys Longbridge], yes, private at that, to be Treasurer of our union funds, if this is not a scandal and a most barefaced disgrace, then we all should be kicked, take the assistant general secretary [Edith Nelson], in fact take these

two honourable ladies, holding high appointments, what are their influence their integrity, we will not answer at this time.[71]

Norman Manley accorded some credibility to these innuendoes and allegations when he attacked Bustamante's salary and his entertainment allowance in his February 16, 1942, speech at Edelweiss Park. Although Manley did not directly accuse Bustamante of malfeasance, he was raising serious questions about how the union's funds were being spent. His charge that Bustamante received £2,000 per annum in salary was one of the most contentious that he had made. "You [Bustamante] go into a poor struggling organization collecting pennies out of the sweat and blood of the workers and then you turn around and draw a salary of over £2,000 a year," Manley declared. His indictment of his cousin was nothing if not harsh. "I say that this hypocrite who pretends to be making great sacrifices for labour, and to have lost thousands of pounds for labour, thousands that are as big a fiction as half of what he talks, I say the sacrifice was to go into this thing not when it was strong and established, but in the early days just after the suffering and bloodshed of May 1938, and saddle the organization with the crushing burden of this huge salary."[72]

Bustamante denied that he had ever "drawn £2,000 in any one year" from the union, adding that even if the union paid him £5,000 per annum, "it could not repay me for the loss of my own financial business [usury] which I have to close down, much more for my health, the effort and energy I have expended, the night and day work I have had to do."[73]

Manley's information regarding Bustamante's salary must have come from Shirley or other officials of the union. The two leaders issued figures that seemingly supported their claims, complicating the question of ascertaining the truth in the absence of the union's financial records. It is true that the union's executive managing committee voted Bustamante a salary of £2,000 per annum in 1938, but he never drew the full amount in any one year. The union's finances were inadequate to bear such a burden. Bustamante drew the handsome salary of £512 between June 1, 1940, and September 7, 1940, a period of approximately three months. In addition, he received £113 for renting his car to the union, making a total of £675 for the period. Manley extrapolated from these figures to support his argument that Bustamante earned in excess of £2,000 annually. This was a distortion of Bustamante's actual earnings. Still, at various times, Bustamante drew £30 per week in salary and an additional £10 in entertainment allowance, leading Manley to inquire whether Bustamante was entertaining himself.

Bustamante, despite the declining coffers of the union, accepted a salary of £10 per week during his detention. Allan Wayte, who was hired to audit the union's accounts in 1942, was particularly scathing in his assessment of Bustamante's use of the union's resources in this way. He observed:

> If this man who poses as so fabulously rich, as the friend of the poor, downtrodden labourers, who declared before them that it was his intention to go on hunger strike until released, who declaims to high heaven that he is willing to give his last drop of blood for the workers (but who will not part with one copper of his own money for them) had been genuinely and sincerely their friend, wouldn't he have relieved them of his support while in Camp?.... His best friend cannot in justice consider him the people's friend. He was just a sucker, sucking the blood of the people.[74]

H. M. Shirley, the BITU's former vice president, voiced the same sentiment. In a statement to the *Gleaner* on March 14, 1942, he attacked Bustamante's conduct mercilessly: "Anyone who has followed his career must have realized how little is his knowledge of Trade Unionism and his ideas of protecting the funds of the Union for the benefit of the people. What rich man stoops so low that out of their pitiful pennies the half-fed and half-naked workers, out of a desire to better their lot and the lot of their children, must pay for his motor car, must pay for gas and oil, tyres, repairs, must pay for chauffeur's clothes, chauffeur's wages and for every mile of roadway covered."[75]

These were damaging allegations. Given the economic plight of the workers, Bustamante should have been more circumspect in his financial arrangements with the union he led. Miss Longbridge, the union's treasurer, received £5 per week and drew an additional £1 in sick pay when she took a six-month leave of absence during Bustamante's internment. In contrast, the union's secretary earned £2.10 per week. Although Bustamante claimed that H. M. Shirley, as vice president, earned £7.10 per week, he did so only after November 1940, when he assumed the leadership of the union in Bustamante's absence. Prior to that month, his salary was £3.7 weekly. Manley was being deliberately misleading when he created the impression that Shirley's salary always remained at £3.7, even after he became the acting leader.

Manley's allegation that the union paid Bustamante one shilling per mile for the use of his car was accurate. Bustamante dismissed the allegation as "a lie" but produced no credible evidence to the contrary. "Even if I did this," Bustamante said in his defense, "it would be the legitimate price which obtained before the war."[76] Such a financial arrangement with the union was ethically questionable. Bustamante used his power to get the union to use his car for general purposes as opposed to the cars the organization owned. This was clearly a conflict of interest and a veritable abuse of power. In condemning the arrangement, and speaking as a lawyer, Manley said that the union "can recover every farthing drawn by Bustamante for hireage of his motor car." He emphasized that "it is a principle of law that persons engaged in the management of an organization cannot trade in that organization in the manner that Mr. Bustamante has done."[77]

As the row between the two men progressed, Bustamante proposed a highly creative resolution. Accusing Manley of lying about him, he challenged him to a wager. According to its terms, Bustamante would put up £2,000 against £500 by Manley "if he has got it." The challenge was that Manley would be required to prove the charges or forfeit his £500. "Prove them now," Bustamante thundered, "or forever hold your peace or go back into oblivion from which I emerged you." Manley readily accepted the wager, observing: "I am afraid Bustamante is finding the strain even more than he can bear." But Manley was certain that Bustamante would not make good on his challenge. "You watch what he will say," Manley declared. "He has not put up his £2,000. He never will." Bustamante failed to put up the £2,000 and the matter thereby ended, eventually fading from the public's consciousness.[78] It was a charade, comic in its conceptualization and predictably childish in its aborted execution. A classic Bustamante theatrical tease, it did him no lasting harm but provided fodder for those who saw him as mere bluster and little substance.

The allegations of fiscal misconduct notwithstanding, there is no incontrovertible evidence to support them. The president and the treasurer were overpaid, however, when their salaries are compared with that earned by school principals and physicians in the island. The treasurer's annual salary was £260, or £5 per week. In contrast, the salary of the head teachers of primary schools ranged from £96 to £200 per annum. Physicians employed by the government received about £500 per year, depending on their years of service. Set at £2,000 per annum, Bustamante's salary was excessive.[79]

There is much evidence that the union's finances were subjected to sloppy bookkeeping, and there was inadequate oversight of expenditures. The president spent funds without any accounting, and receipts were not required for expenditures of less than £5. The books were frequently not up to date. The treasurer, Gladys Longbridge, lacked the requisite experience and training to manage the resources of such a large organization. She had been a cashier for a brief period at the Arlington House Hotel and Restaurant, hardly the preparation necessary for the major responsibilities she was being asked to undertake on behalf of the union. "I believe that she was given much more than she was able to carry," declared H. M. Shirley.[80]

The public brawl between Bustamante and Manley cast an unwelcomed searchlight on the governance of the union. In the aftermath of the abortive general strike that Bustamante called in February 1939, Manley and the Trades Union Advisory Council had tried to get Bustamante to democratize his unions, but the exercise was a failure. Three years later, the chief still controlled the BITU, an anachronism in a modern Jamaica that was responding to democratic impulses. The union's constitution still named Bustamante the president for life and gave him the authority to appoint its principal officers—with the notable exception of the vice president—and they served at his pleasure. The appointed officers comprised the managing executive committee, namely, the treasurer, the general secretary, the assistant secretary, and the union's solicitor. The president served as its chairman, effectively dominating the committee since he appointed its members. The constitution also gave the president sole control over the union's finances. The day-to-day activities of the union were supervised by a "brain trust" consisting of the president, the treasurer, and the assistant secretary. Allan Wayte, a former auditor for the union, observed uncharitably: "Alexander Bustamante, the man who had been to jail for the workers, the man who had thousands of money to devote to the cause of the workers and did not need a penny of their money, was appointed the first President. A President for life, a protector and trustee for the pennies of the workers. What a prospect for both sides! On the one side, thousands of pounds to be scattered by this rich gentleman, and on the other side . . . ? I am wondering now whose mouth watered more."[81]

Norman Manley was the most prominent critic of the union's constitution and its modus operandi, vowing to "wipe out the farce that was masquerading as decent union administration." He was joined in his public criticism by some of its dissident members and workers of the Machado Tobacco Company. Meeting on February 23, 1942, "the full membership of factory workers numbering 300 odd and workers from other factories" passed a resolution denouncing the "dictatorial" constitution. The resolution charged that the constitution did not serve "our interest" and demanded that the "dictatorial powers" of the president be abrogated. If this did not occur, the resolution said, "we are not prepared to continue as members" of the union. Fourteen days later, on March 6, "a largely attended" meeting of workers at the Ward Theatre denounced Bustamante's "despotic leadership." The motion was moved by Coombs, Bustamante's rival and former colleague. It said that Bustamante "lacks the necessary qualities as a leader," noting that "it will be extremely dangerous to the interest of the workers" to keep Bustamante as their leader. The resolution called upon workers to "take united action" against Bustamante with a view "to overthrowing his leadership."[82]

In spite of the negative publicity that he received from this dispute, Bustamante retained his strong support among the workers. It seemed to have made little or no difference in their affection and admiration for him. Predictably, the managing executive committee of the union adopted a resolution on February 25 expressing its "undying and unswerving loyalty to our leader . . . standing shoulder to shoulder with the leader, who, in time will vanquish all his foes." In early March Bustamante undertook a triumphant tour of the parishes of Westmoreland, Hanover, St. Elizabeth, St. James, and Trelawny. "Mr. Bustamante was acclaimed by thousands of workers who flocked to every centre to get a glimpse of him," declared one of his principal supporters, Leslie W. Rose. St William Grant, Bustamante's erstwhile associate, attended a huge meeting held by the union on March 15 to declare his support for his former embattled leader. C. M. Mallette, one of the speakers at the meeting and a worker at the Myrtle Bank Hotel, declared: "I am proud to see such a large gathering. . . . There is no power on earth that can prevail against Alexander Bustamante." A few weeks later, Bustamante was crowned "King of Labour" at a function held at St. George's Hall. The *Gleaner* reported that the crown was "silver papered," observing that the workers "extolled in fervid language their leader's work and worth."[83]

Such ceremonies were good theater, but in a deeper sense they were heartfelt expressions of affection for, and loyalty to, the leader. A bewildered elite could not understand the wellsprings of such a deep emotional connection with Bustamante. Allan Wayte, who was no admirer of Bustamante, observed that his henchmen were always reminding the people that he was arrested in 1938. "They are constantly pumping it into their minds," he said, and declaring "wat if him tek a thousand pounds. This man went to prison for us."[84] Bustamante, in their eyes, could do no wrong, or if he did, they would grant him penance.

In the bitter war of words between the "two giants," as Florizel Glasspole, a union colleague, characterized them, Manley emerged as the superior advocate. Focused and to the point, Manley marshaled his evidence to make his points with telling effectiveness. Bustamante's statements were usually rambling digressions interspersed with an endearing folksiness but lacking the intellectual impact of Manley's more sophisticated language. Bustamante was certainly accurate in observing that Manley was using "clever tactics" in his statements, but the two men were competing for the public's support using their own weapons.[85] Bustamante was a natural performer, while Manley was the more cerebral antagonist. But in any contest for the affections of the Jamaican worker, Bustamante faced no serious challenge from Norman Manley at the time. When Manley questioned why Bustamante needed £10 per week as an entertainment allowance, the wealthy labor leader derided the successful barrister as someone who consorted with and worked for the capitalist elite. "Mr. Manley wants to know who I have entertained with the Union's allowance," he taunted. "Perhaps he believes I have entertained the Jamaica Telephone Company of which he is chairman, the West Indies Sugar Company for which he is lawyer, all big business trusts in the country with which he is connected."[86] Bustamante was portraying himself as the genuine friend of the workers and Manley as the untrustworthy ally and a member of the island's business and social elite. Manley was accustomed to Bustamante's frequent derision, insults and attacks and their negative impact on the workers. "I have been stoned more than once," he joked. "But it has been very amusing, because these people do not aim straight."[87]

The team that managed the BITU's affairs during Bustamante's internment brought a degree of sophistication, sobriety, and skill to the bargaining table that the chief was not capable of doing. H. M. Shirley won high praise from Manley and others for his quietly competent management of the union's business. He had successfully negotiated, with the assistance of Manley and others, thirteen new labor contracts with such employers as the Sugar Manufacturers Association, the Shipping Association, the Kingston Ice making Company, the Jamaica Shirt Factory, the Match Factory, and others.

The most important agreement, to be sure, was signed with the Sugar Manufacturers Association in March 1941. It was the product of a slow but successful negotiation conducted under the auspices of the Sugar Industry Advisory Board, which had been created by the Advisory Board Regulations Act of 1940. The advisory board consisted of three representatives from the

Sugar Manufacturers Association, three from the Bustamante Industrial Trade Union, and one from the Jamaica Agricultural Society, the island's largest organization of farmers. Reaching an agreement proved elusive, and there were rumors that the union was considering an industry-wide strike. Eventually, the labor adviser, F. A. Norman, announced a settlement on March 21, providing for a wage increase for the workers. Significantly, the agreement was to last for two years, and wages were to be linked to the cost-of-living index. This was the first time in the brief history of unionism in the island that workers received automatic increases in their wage based upon the cost-of-living index. It was a landmark agreement, one that set a precedent that neither the unions nor capital could ignore.[88] Bustamante was not pleased with the agreements that were signed in his absence. He denounced Shirley for signing "many illegal documents, signing away the workers' rights for arbitration for better conditions for three years, and even until the expiration of the war." He remained silent on the merits of the cost-of-living increases, preferring to announce on his own volition a new regulation for the conduct of the union's negotiations. "No persons, the executive managing committee of this organization, nor any officer," he pronounced, "can sign any agreement for workers for longer than three months."[89] This was a repudiation of much of what the BITU had accomplished during the leader's internment, an act of profound shortsightedness and pique.

Bustamante also condemned the agreements as "shocking and appalling." He ridiculed them as "really victories for themselves [the officials] and not for the workers for they got a fair pay from the Union and their stomachs were filled." Bustamante accused the union's officers of staging "presentations and Victory Dances licking up the floor with their 'La Conga,' while the workers' hearts were filled with sorrow and their eyes with tears."[90] This was Bustamante's customary rhetorical noise, more a manifestation of sour grapes and less a careful assessment of the nature of the contracts. By winning significant benefits such as cost-of-living increases for the sugar workers, Shirley had enhanced his prestige in the union, much to Bustamante's chagrin.

Encouraged by the support he received from some of the workers and PNP officials after Bustamante "fired" him, Shirley decided to found his own union. He announced the decision at a public meeting that he held in Kingston on March 3, 1942. Shirley declared that the new organization would operate along democratic lines, in contrast to the BITU. He named it the Jamaica United Workers Union (JUWU) and invited the workers in all sectors of the economy to join, waiving the membership fees for three months for members of the Bustamante union. "I call upon every worker in Jamaica to put his faith in the Jamaica United Workers Union," he exhorted. "Let our cry be: Down with Dictatorship." He said he had received messages of support from workers in Westmoreland, St. Elizabeth, St. Mary, Trelawny, and St. James. "Tonight," Shirley proclaimed, "we have to choose between the smashing of the workers' movement and the salvation of it."[91]

This was easier said than done. Shirley faced the daunting challenge of attracting members from the BITU and sustaining their élan. Several hundred workers initially flocked to the new union, but most remained fervent supporters of the labor chief. Bustamante and other BITU officials denounced Shirley's union as a creation of the chief's enemies, the People's National Party, and the employers. The PNP merely wanted their votes, Bustamante said, "but when it got them nothing would be done to help the workers." It was in the interest of the employers, Bustamante told the workers, to have two unions so the workers "would be divided and could do nothing." The aim of his "adversaries," Bustamante charged, was to "deprive" the workers "of their power of bargaining."[92]

The hostile relationship between the supporters of the two unions became violent in various parts of the island. "The battles were not confined to verbal pyrotechnics," wrote a contributor to the *Daily Gleaner*, "but actually descended to physical displays . . . and the men handled were literally put to flight." One BITU official reported that S. Morais, the BITU's former secretary who had joined the JUWU, "was in Golden Grove [St. Thomas] but we chase him away." Another dispatched a telegram to the BITU's head office in Kingston, reporting that several prominent JUWU members were "flogged" in Dalvey and had "to fly like birds." A third telegram confirmed that Shirley and Kenneth Hill were "driven out of Grange Hill and other parts of Westmoreland last night."[93]

Bustamante's foot soldiers disrupted Shirley's attempts to hold public meetings, intimidating his supporters. When Shirley arrived in Port Antonio to conduct a meeting in mid-April 1942, for example, he was "greeted with choruses in praise of Bustamante, and loud jeers." Shirley and his team "were not afforded the opportunity to speak and the crowd was getting in an angry mood when the police quieted them down." The visitors had to beat a hasty retreat. As if to pour salt on Shirley's wounds, the BITU held "a successful meeting" after his departure. Such hostile tactics, repeated throughout the island, seriously impeded Shirley's organizational efforts.[94]

The JUWU trudged along, however, competing mostly unsuccessfully with the better-organized and more-entrenched BITU. It boasted a mere 700 members in 1943, eventually disappearing in 1945 from the trade-union scene. The violent attacks by workers on their peers who supported the JUWU showed that a healthy working-class consciousness, empathy, and solidarity were still emerging. The fact that some workers showed a preference for the JUWU over the BITU would not have been the occasion for violence directed against them if a vibrant working-class consciousness had existed and trumped other loyalties. It is entirely conceivable, however, that some of this violence was stimulated and orchestrated by the leaders of the BITU, who wanted to destroy their pesky rival.

The months immediately following Bustamante's release from the internment camp had not been the best of times for him. He had initiated the imbroglio with the union's officials, Manley, and the PNP, tarnishing his image among some Jamaicans. Although the labor leader attacked in the press those whom he deemed his adversaries, he could not do so from a public platform, given the restrictions that the governor had imposed upon him. Unhappy with the restrictions, Bustamante telegraphed the governor on March 16, 1942, urging their abrogation. "I am being persecuted by government," Bustamante charged. Continuing, he complained that "now my lips are sealed. My hands are tied by restrictions so that the People's National Party and its leader can plot, conspire and lie against me." Resorting to his customary braggadocio, he declared: "I cannot be destroyed, but [they aim] to destroy the people I love so much—who are the masses, for whom I suffer so much." He pleaded with the governor to have the "restrictions lifted so that I can speak and so that righteousness shall destroy iniquity."[95]

Bustamante saw his fight as an apocalyptic struggle of "good" versus "evil," a claim that many of his supporters would have endorsed. Governor Richards never subscribed to such self-serving sentiments, believing that incipient movements such as the one led by Bustamante should be crushed by the coercive power of the state. In spite of his autocratic tendencies and his desire to make Jamaica safe for the British Empire, however, Richards could be a pragmatic administrator. He had belatedly come to recognize that Bustamante would serve colonial interests more effectively if he could speak freely. Richards's principal objective was to divide the labor movement from the pro-self-government forces as represented by Manley and the PNP. Bustamante had fulfilled his promise to break with them, and he could use the political platform to promote his cause, intensify the dispute with Manley, and help separate the workers from the PNP. Accordingly, on April 14 the governor lifted the restrictions against Bustamante's addressing of open-air or indoor public meetings or participating in marches and processions. He was also no longer required to submit to the censors any article that he wrote prior to its publication. The governor said he acted "without prejudice to my power to reimpose such conditions or to impose any other conditions in lieu thereof, or in addition thereto."[96] Bustamante was forbidden to address any public meeting or participate in a procession that was prohibited by the government. He was now serving the cause of labor as he saw it and the interest of the colonial state as Richards defined it. The two were never in harmony.

Although he wanted the restrictions lifted, Bustamante was surprised when he received the unexpected good news. He was having lunch in a restaurant when two police officers approached him, one bearing a letter from Governor Richards. Bustamante gave one of them, Sergeant Vassal, a welcoming smile. According to a newspaper report, Bustamante was handed the letter by Hamilton, the second officer. "As he glanced through the pages," the *Jamaica Times* reported, "all signs of happiness left his face. It now wore a frown. He had seen 'Restrictions' mentioned. That was enough. He flew into a rage." Engaging in his usual rant, Bustamante screamed: "[I]t is a threat, nobody can intimidate me." He then directly referred to his committing suicide by fasting, thundering: "It is painful, but 20 days of fasting will end it all. No sacrifice is too great for me to make for the workers."[97]

Possessing a much calmer disposition, Gladys Longbridge began to read the letter. "At first her expression was one of anxiety," the newspaper said, "but at the end of the first page she sighed in relief." Turning to the chief, Miss Longbridge exclaimed: "Busta, you haven't read it properly. It isn't so bad." Reading the document a second time, Bustamante did so more slowly and carefully. His mood changed dramatically as he absorbed the letter's contents more thoroughly. "This time his eyes did not merely pick out a misleading word," the newspaper observed. His reaction softened, and "then surpassing even his rage of a few minutes back was his jubilance at what the documents said. At last he was free."[98] Bustamante's rhetorical explosion revealed his continuing anger at the governor's treatment of him and the degree to which he chafed under the restrictions he endured. His threat of suicide was another one of his characteristic outbursts, reflecting the heat and disappointment of the moment, with the anger that drove it dissipating as quickly as it came.

Although Bustamante regained his freedom to speak, the union's newspaper, the *Jamaica Worker*, remained under censorship. According to Governor Richards, the paper had been placed under an order of censorship on September 9, 1940, "because of the inflammatory nature of articles published after Bustamante was interned." On June 18, 1942, a large gathering of workers meeting at the Conversorium passed a resolution demanding an end to the censorship. The text, and a subsequent one, bore Bustamante's fingerprints with its colorful language and its expression of fealty to British "principles." The resolution maintained that the paper's censorship was "in grave conflict with the established principle of Freedom of the Press, and oft expressed desire of the Imperial Government to foster, develop, and encourage the growth of the Trade Union Movement." The paper, the resolution charged, "is being hindered, obstructed, and chafed by the unnecessary restrictions and censorship thus imposed, while anti-Government, Anti-British, and other unsavoury publications are allowed to go untrammeled and unabridged." It denounced "this infringement upon our rights as British Citizens," calling for the removal of "this Dictatorial policy which is un-British" and "contrary to the principles for which the Empire and the U.S.A. are at war." Writing to the Colonial Office in August 1942, Richards defended the retention of the censorship order. Although the governor thought "the tone" of the paper had "improved," he did not "consider that the removal of censorship at the present time would be conducive to the maintenance of public order." Bustamante, he said, wrote the majority of the articles, "and, even under censorship[, he] is inclined towards incitement."[99]

The opponents of the censorship of the *Jamaica Worker* returned to the subject in December 1942. They submitted a resolution to the governor, extolling freedom of the press as "an indispensable jewel of British policy at home and in the colonies." It depicted the paper as "the only true and genuine Labour Paper in this country" and one that was "neither anti-government, anti-Imperialist nor anti-British." The paper, the resolution claimed, "has never written or entertained in its pages any seditious or libellous articles." It characterized the censorship imposed on the paper as a "most unwarranted, uncalled for, monstrous, and provocative discrimination." The resolution bemoaned the fact that "no other press in this country is subjected to such humiliating impositions and inconvenience—although it is known that there are anti-Government and anti-British Press still uncensored and allowed unbridled sway."[100]

Since most issues of the *Jamaica Worker* have not survived, it is difficult to determine why the governor imposed censorship on it. The surviving issues reveal a paper focused on matters relating to the BITU and its officials, particularly Bustamante. As a fervent admirer of the British Empire, the labor leader would not have allowed the publication of articles deemed to be seditious or even critical of the mother country. *Public Opinion*, the PNP's unofficial organ, posed a greater threat to the status quo given the political tone of the articles it consistently published. It was harshly critical of the government, unabashedly anti-imperialist, and aggressively pro-self-government in its editorial policy. Richards feared the potential power of working people who were united, politically conscious, and in control of what they read—hence the censorship of the only paper that was aimed at them.

Governor Richards also declined to lift the requirement that Bustamante notify the authorities of his address at all times and of his destination if he left the jurisdiction of the Kingston and St. Andrew Corporation. At a meeting held at the Conversorium in Kingston on June 28, 1942, "thousands of workers" forwarded a resolution to the governor to "raise this most humiliating, unjustified, and obnoxious imposition, which indeed is not creating that feeling which should exist between Government and the people." The resolution explained: "Government in spite of the irreproachable and unimpeached character of the said Alexander Bustamante as a private citizen and Leader of the People, has placed on him an Infra dig and highly humiliating, Degrading, Unwarranted, undue and unjustifiable restriction only applicable to Habitual Criminals of the most dangerous and incorrigible type."[101]

Twenty-eight months after the governor imposed the censorship on the *Jamaica Worker* and almost eleven months after Bustamante had restrictions placed on his movements, the governor was prepared to act again. Bustamante had adhered to the terms of his release, broken with Manley and the PNP, and repeatedly expressed his support for the war and his loyalty to Britain and her empire. Accordingly, the censorship of the paper and Bustamante's restrictions were "rescinded" on December 24, 1942.[102] This Christmas gift exacted a price. A chastened Alexander Bustamante became more rhetorically subdued in public, holding much of his signature fire and affirming an exaggerated patriotism. He was never to be the firebrand of 1938 again; his passion for the cause of the workers had not cooled, but he now fought for them looking over his shoulders and with his hands tied behind his back.

Bustamante was not destroyed politically by the colonial state's persecution. In fact, it enhanced his reputation among the workers as the intrepid champion of their cause, a leader who was unjustly treated because he was the threatening voice of labor. Governor Richards, however, had made of Bustamante a compliant defender of the political status quo. His behavior upon his release from internment did nothing to reassure his detractors that he was a responsible agent of change in the island. The split between Bustamante and Manley was as unfortunate as it was harmful to labor's interest and that of the Jamaican people as a whole. It divided labor's ranks and weakened it, at least in the short run. By drawing their daggers against each other more ferociously than they did against the barons of capital, Manley and Bustamante were undermining labor's cause. Still, the energies that were unleashed by the rebellion of 1938 could not be vanquished by this colossal failure of leadership.

SEVEN

Challenging Power and Facing the Consequences

"Despite the great heat in the Hall," the *Daily Gleaner* reported, "men and women of all classes listened attentively for close over three hours." The large crowd of some 2,000 persons had gathered in the St. George's Hall in Kingston to protest against the government's abuse of the power it acquired under the aegis of the Defense Regulations it had received from the Colonial Office. The meeting was presided over by the prominent attorney Leslie Ashenheim. He was the acting chairman of the recently founded Jamaica Council of Civil Liberties, which was modeled after its English counterpart, the National Council of Civil Liberties. Ashenheim said its raison d'etre was "to watch over and to guard over the civil liberties of the people of this country—not those of one class alone, but of every class." Observing the size of the audience in St. George's Hall on that June evening in 1941, Ashenheim characterized the meeting as "one of the historic occasions in the history of Jamaica." He urged his listeners to "look around" and "observe the completely representative character of the people present here, the richest and the poorest joined together. And we are determined that for this evening we are Jamaicans and Jamaicans only."

The *Gleaner* listed the names of some of the "notables" in attendance. It included legislators, civic leaders, and members of the professions. There was no mention of anyone who was not a "notable," of the people who were the fulcrum of the labor rebellion and the social movement in progress. Ashenheim had, however, celebrated the classless nature of those who had come to peacefully petition their monarch, to contest the colonial state's incursions into the sanctuaries of their lives. H. M. Shirley, the acting president of the BITU and one of the speakers at the meeting, declared that he was representing "the greater portion of the inarticulate masses throughout the length and breadth of Jamaica." Still, it was for the most part a gathering of elites who were nursing nationalist sentiments and suspicious of any expansion of the power of the state.[1]

The colonial authorities, predictably, attempted to disparage those members of the elite who participated in the meeting or who were members of the Jamaica Council of Civil Liberties. Speaking in the Legislative Council, Colonial Secretary A. W. Grantham denounced what he considered to be their hypocrisy, charging: "What is more curious is to see some of the persons who are now donning the robes of the apostles of liberty—people whom we know are opposed to giving the elected members of the Council a majority of members in the Council, and who favour the most rigid form of Crown Colony Government—it being understood of course that they will have the ear of the Government—these people get up today and talk about the liberty of the subject."

The *Gleaner* was not pleased with this scathing assault on segments of the Jamaican elite, wondering why the colonial secretary "should so sweepingly and indiscriminately indulge in this sort of censure of others, of all and sundry, without justification." The colonial secretary was clearly stung by the criticism of the Defense Regulations and the manner of their enforcement. But he had transgressed a colonial etiquette that looked askance at such rhetorical abuse of His Majesty's subjects by the officers of the administration. The *Gleaner*'s editorial writer confessed that he read Grantham's remarks "in sorrow."[2]

The Defense Regulations that stirred such emotions on both sides had been promulgated in England, and were made applicable in the colonies, by the Neville Chamberlain government in 1938. In their original form, the regulations allowed the arrest and detention of individuals who allegedly engaged in acts prejudicial to public safety or the security of the realm. It also prescribed a similar treatment for enemy aliens. The press was subject to censorship, particularly in reference to its coverage of matters relating to the conduct of a military conflict. The government also imposed restrictions on the publication of "enemy propaganda" or anything that might damage public morale. The accused persons were denied the right to trial in the courts and could be detained indefinitely. Outraged by this flagrant violation of the right to a court trial afforded British citizens accused of crimes, the House of Commons repudiated some of the regulations, characterizing them as "obnoxious" and "undemocratic." The offending regulations, however, were dispatched to the colonies in 1939 en toto and were being implemented by Governor Richards in Jamaica. Five persons had become victims of the regulations by June 1941.

Governor Richards gave himself considerable latitude in the interpretation and enforcement of the Defense Regulations. He could, for example, detain someone "preventively." The governor, as Leslie Ashenheim said, has the power "to detain . . . a person to prevent him from doing something and before he has done anything at all." As Ashenheim also accurately observed, "the circumstances under which such power may be used are wholly undefined and depend on nothing whatever except the Governor being satisfied of the necessity for the detention." Consequently, Ashenheim continued, "the liberty of the subject is entirely at the mercy of the Governor and without any safeguards at all."[3] This was unlike the situation in England, where someone could be detained only if he were of "hostile origin or associations" or engaged in acts that threatened national security.

Governor Richards did not hesitate to detain foreign nationals, particularly Germans, under the terms of the regulations. These detentions were not greeted by any public outcry in the island, given the strength of the prevailing anti-German bias. But it was decidedly another matter when Jamaicans were the victims of the governor's exercise of his new powers. After all, Jamaicans were being recruited to serve in the war, and many were volunteering to fight for the king and the empire with unbridled enthusiasm. England's fortunes, however, were hardly promising in the early stages of the conflict, although she did beat back Germany's attempt in 1940 to bomb the nation into submission. By 1941 Germany was in control of much of Europe, and England's prospects of ultimate victory were nothing if not uncertain. Under the circumstances, Governor Richards saw it as his duty to snuff out any dissent in the Caribbean island, albeit one far removed from the theater of the conflict and where pro-Allied sentiment was both strong and pervasive.

Jamaicans, in general, did not question the need for some restrictions in wartime. Norman Manley, however, condemned the "war hysteria" that drove their high-handed enforcement, calling for "cool heads, and confident hearts." Criticizing the government for preventing Jamaicans from knowing what "other countries are allowed to know," Manley noted that "it goes back to this ridiculous fear which is largely based upon a misunderstanding of the people or contempt for them."[4] The outcry against aspects of the Defense Regulations Act produced some modifications of them in August 1941, such as allowing detainees to know the charges leveled against them so that they could more effectively prepare an appeal. The change tempered the Star Chamber–like regulations that had denied detainees information about their alleged misdeeds.

Acting under the aegis of the Defense Regulations Act, Richards began to immunize Jamaicans from what he thought were subversive ideas and publications. In 1940, for example, the Legislative Council passed the Undesirable Publications Act, which prohibited the importation of printed material deemed to be promoting subversive activity. By October 1941 a long list of publications had been placed on the prohibited list. The titles, in most cases, reveal nothing about the contents of the book, pamphlet, newsletter, or article. But some of them suggest, generally speaking, the subject matter. Several titles refer to India, presumably its struggle for independence. Others deal with Russia, workers, trade unions, socialism, and so on. Richards and his advisers who may have read these publications considered their contents to be too incendiary for the Jamaican people. The official list of banned publications provides some indication of the reach of colonial censorship as well as the ideas from which Richards wanted to protect the colonized Jamaicans.

1. "World News and Views."
2. "International Trade Union information."
3. "Information Bulletin of the I.S.H."
4. "International of Seamen and Harbour Workers Post, Box 480. Antwerp. (Postal packets printed in Chinese or Japanese and identifiable as issued by the above.)
5. "Pan Pacific Worker."
6. "What Is the International Trade Unions Committee of Negro Workers?" by George Padmore.
7. "The Negro Worker."
8. "The Draft Platform of the Communist Party of India."
9. "Hindusthan." Printed in Bristol.
10. "Hindusthan Gahr," published in Indian vernacular.
11. "Indian Front News Bulletin."
12. "Indian United Front."
13. "United India, or Hind. [Hindi?]"
14. "The Indian War of Independence of 1857," by an Indian Nationalist.
15. "Information and Press Service of the I.S.H."
16. Volume I, no. 1 of Publication of Aftermath and Leaflet entitled "Aftermath—Preliminary Statement."
17. Saoirse Eireann Wolfe Tone Weekly. News from Germany, published by H. R. Hoffman, head of Propaganda Bureau of the German Foreign Office in Munich.
18. A four-page printed leaflet in English commencing "Dear Sir, you know that newspapers today . . . and signed "A Friend of Anglo-German Co-Operation and Understanding."

19. A folded postcard with two maps portraying the Polish Corridor and a hypothetical corridor between Liverpool and Hull.

20. Any publication emanating from the Anglo-German Information Service.

21. "Daily Worker."
22. "Action."
23. "The Week."
24. "Russia Today."
25. "Russia Today Newsletter."
26. "Challenge."
27. "Inside the Empire."
28. "The New Propellor."
29. "Action News Services."
30. "Peoples Post."
31. "Headline."
32. "Free Press."
33. "Angles."
34. "The British Union Quarterly."
35. "Moscow News."
36. "Die Welt."
37. "Labour Monthly."
38. "Vema."
39. "Kypriakar Nea."
40. "Colonial Informatist Bulletin."
41. "Enemies."
42. "Light."
43. "Model Study No. 2."
44. "God and the State." Nos. 41–44, published by Watchtower Bible and Tract Society Incorporated, International Bible Students Association, Brooklyn, New York, United States of America.

45. "Spicy Detective" (published by Culture Publications Incorporated of Wilmington, Delaware, in the United States of America).

46. "Socialist Appeal" (Official Organ of the Socialist Workers Party, Section of the Fourth International published by the New International—116 University Place New York City, U.S.A.)

47. "International News" (Organ of the Provincial International Contact Mission, 1904 Division Street, Illinois, U.S.A.).

48. "Fighting Worker" (Organ of the Revolutionary Workers League of the United States of America).

49. "Workers Age" (published in the United States of America).[5]

The Jamaican literati did not welcome this attack on their freedom to read whatever they wanted, even if many of them were not inclined to read much of the banned material. It was the principle that mattered. But not all Jamaican leaders opposed the governor's policing of what they read. Alexander Bustamante, for example, seemed ambivalent on the matter. As Bustamante reported to the governor on May 3, 1940, he was incensed when he received several copies of a flier that proclaimed:

Beware!
Be Ready to protect our
civil liberties
No one man has the right to decide
what books we should read.
We have the right to read what we like.
There is a Bill before the Council which
will give the Governor power to
prohibit the importation of literature.
Band together and resist this assault.
Are you a member of a friendly
society, lodge, trade union, political
or civil organization, religious
body, club?
Pass resolutions of protest in your
district.[6]

In submitting the flier to the governor, Bustamante complained that he had been asked to help distribute it throughout the island. His indignation was clear as he promised: "I will of course have nothing to do with these things, for whilst I believe in full liberty, lots of these literary trash which is being imported in this country, and being printed here only tend to deteriorate further the minds of our so-called intelligent, and ignorant people.... [W]hen the enemies or these political parasites have what they term their grievance, they use every means to drag me into it."

Bustamante condemned "this element" as belonging to "a Communistic group," accusing them of causing "an enormous amount of disloyalty to the British empire, and they have seized the war as an opportunity to propagate their viciousness." Continuing, Bustamante named two individuals who he thought were being disloyal to the Crown. "On Wednesday night of this week," he reported,

> I drove along North Parade and saw about forty ragged looking people standing there, a half intelligent fellow black whose name I think is Lindsay, and an Indian named Beckford, and these two fellows who are well known as pernicious communists were trying to convince the others that it would be a glorious day for us, if Germany wins the war, because Russia would be a dominant power in the world, and then we would have economical equality. Just what they mean I do not know, but I do know this kind of teaching to the ignorant people is breeding disaster.

Bustamante suggested that the police force should keep such people under surveillance. "If our detectives had the right instinct in detecting," he observed, "they could do lot of good work by mingling with every little such group they see around and if there is one man in this country that should be brought to justice to prevent him instilling pernicious seeds in the minds of the ignorant, he is Beckford (this Coolieman)."[7] Ironically, Bustamante was himself the object of surveillance by the government, but he was probably unaware of the intensity of the scrutiny of his speeches and associations. The labor leader also reported the two men to the government's Criminal Investigation Department, but he failed to produce any witnesses as requested. Consequently, the commissioner of police said that since he doubted Bustamante's "genuine sincerity with regard to this matter," the investigation could be "carried no further." He assured the colonial secretary that Bustamante's remarks "with reference to Communistic Groups and the spreading of disloyalty etc is [sic] quite true and, as you are aware, has been fully reported on."[8]

Bustamante was not the stereotypical informant. He was genuinely offended by the comments made by Beckford and Lindsay and sought no political or financial advantage for providing the information about them. Bustamante was a patriot who disliked criticisms of the imperial government and its officers. He would later, for example, assure the governor that he had been "using my voice and my influence to eradicate the evil seeds that are being sown against the king in this island . . . also the seed of hate that is being sown against the English, particularly the Governor, the Colonial Secretary. . . . and all other people born over the seas."[9]

Still, a definitive judgment on Bustamante's conduct and motivation cannot be easily rendered. Nine days after he mailed the flier to the governor, denounced the "literary trash" being imported into the island, and seemingly endorsed Richards's role in prohibiting such literature, Bustamante publicly reversed himself. At a public meeting held at the Conversorium on May 12, he said that the governor should not be "the sole person determining what people should read," calling such a situation "a form of dictatorship."[10]

Gleaner columnist G. St. C. Scotter was a different case. As a journalist, he had the time to reflect on what he wrote, unlike Bustamante, who made extemporaneous utterances, usually from a political platform. Scotter, given his job as a writer for a newspaper, should normally have been expected to endorse the unrestricted circulation of books and ideas. The columnist, however, openly ridiculed the People's National Party for its opposition to the governor's restrictions on the importation of certain books and journals. "Pity the poor PNP," he wrote, "now wailing up and down the country because his Excellency proposes to ban the importation of undesirable literature into this island during war time . . . but . . . if the PNP were to be deprived for the duration of their Fabian flapdoodle, their Marxian muck, that would be just too bad."[11] Governor Richards, an equal opportunity persecutor, would shortly intern Scotter for his critical views on the war in progress.

The ban on publications failed to protect Jamaicans from the virus of their presumed contents. In fact, the rhetorical assaults on the colonial regime continued unabated, keeping the security forces busy and on the offensive. Not only did the governor pursue an aggressive policy of policing what Jamaicans read, but he also introduced a law in June 1939 giving him the right to prohibit public meetings. It was known as the "Public Meeting Law, 1939."

The governor justified the law on the grounds that "meetings were being held at street corners and other public places, at which those listening to the speaker or speakers would get worked up into a state of excitement." He said that on a number of occasions, the meetings ended "by the crowd proceeding either as one body, or else breaking up into several groups, to loot Chinese grocery stores." The governor explained that the law was designed to put a stop to such disorder and to prevent the potential loss of lives. It empowered him "to prohibit in certain circumstances, meetings and processions, in the interests of good order and the public safety." This could be done "in any area, or in any parish, district, village, or town in the island" and was applicable "in any public place." The attorney general said the law was also designed "to give additional powers to the police in times of civil unrest."[12]

Although the majority of the elected members of the Legislative Council supported the measure, it elicited strong protest from the members from Kingston and Clarendon. They declared the Public Meeting Law "an infringement on the right of freedom and of free speech." They were not persuaded that such a bill was needed, and they opposed the expansion of the power it gave to the police. "It cannot be right," they submitted, "to pass a law applicable to the whole of Jamaica when what is complained of is confined to Kingston." They thought that the passage of the law would telegraph to the world "that the people of this colony are people of general lawless behaviour."[13]

Other critics saw more-sinister motives behind the introduction of the bill. The *Jamaica Standard* noted that the law "*could* be used, and might be used to check some militant person acting within his ordinary legal rights." The paper called the law "political blackmail," noting that it "illustrates a tendency to take advantage of public alarm to strengthen the executive power to an unnecessary degree." It observed that the "concentration of power in the hands of the executive has long been going on in a way which suggests deliberate policy." The paper regretted this development, since the governor and his counselors "are not responsible to the people whose rights are at stake."[14]

The PNP also voiced strong opposition to the bill. It organized, along with other organizations, a massive protest at St. George's Hall on July 6. Viewing the bill as an attack upon the democratic liberties of the people, Norman Manley declared that "no one can say that there has been, in the past history of this country, any persistent tendency to aggravated disorder. On the contrary, compared with countries of the advanced social order which exist in the United States, France, or even Great Britain herself, Jamaica must be among the paragon of all countries for the observance of order."

Manley argued that the bill constituted an assault on the least powerful members of the society. They were the ones who either held or attended street meetings. "The better class people," Manley said, "don't hold meetings of that sort, because they don't feel grievances of that nature." W. Adolphe Roberts, president of the Jamaica Progressive League, asked the audience at St. George's Hall a number of rhetorical questions. "Is there in existence in the island of Jamaica a state of affairs bordering on revolution?" he inquired. "Are mobs marching through the streets or threatening to march?" Continuing, Roberts posed the question: "Is there any danger to life and property . . . anything that calls for military or police action?"[15]

The Jamaica Progressive League issued a statement criticizing the bill, finding it "wholly unnecessary, unduly repressive and flagrantly violative of the elementary and fundamental rights and privileges of the people of the Island of Jamaica, namely the long established and sacred rights of free speech and free assembly." It condemned and denounced "the spineless and unpatriotic" behavior of the elected members of the Legislative Council who "yielded to the dictatorial demands of the governor" and supported the bill.[16] The Whitfield Chapter of the Universal Negro Improvement Association reminded the governor that the "Negro people of the colony, have got a right to free speech Politically and Religiously." The loss of that right, the chapter declared, "would cause a great hatred to be stirred against the British Empire." In what appeared to be a prediction that poor Jamaicans would find it difficult to serve if war were declared, the chapter noted that "it would not be the Capitalists of this country that would be called to go to the front, but the poor Negro worker."[17]

The Public Meeting Law was passed, opposition to it notwithstanding. There was widespread distrust of the governor's motives and his ability to respect the civil rights of the Jamaican people. Under the circumstances, the government compromised, and the bill was given an expiration date of one year. The governor was sensitive to the criticisms leveled at the law and enforced it in a balanced fashion, diluting the opposition to it. When it was being considered for its successful renewal a year later, the *Gleaner* observed that "more meetings are now held in reputable places than ever before, and all orders of the people attend these meetings."[18]

Governor Richards also took an interest in the potential use of the postal service to promote subversive activity, especially during wartime. He issued the Postal Censorship Order in 1941 requiring that all envelopes bear on the outside the name and address of the sender. Compliance with this requirement allowed the government's censors to monitor the mails, identifying those persons who were considered security risks. The order required that the postal authorities forward all letters that contravened the rule to the chief censor "to be disposed of in such manner as he may think fit."[19] In practice, the censorship authorities returned these letters to the post office for transmission to the intended address if they were judged to be innocuous. In other instances, they were sent to the security authorities for additional review, kept for a period of time, or destroyed.

The order incurred the opposition of the PNP, particularly its requirement that inland letters bear the name and address of the sender on the envelope. Vernon Arnett, the party's secretary, had no objection to letters mailed to foreign countries being subjected to this requirement. He thought, however, that as far as local correspondence was concerned, the order constituted "an unjustifiable abuse of their [the people's] rights as well as a most annoying and meaningless inconvenience to put them to."[20] Governor Richards, not unexpectedly, strongly defended the Postal Censorship Order, underscoring its importance as a security measure, particularly in an island "whose facilities for watching etc a subject are not as complete as they are in England."[21]

The Colonial Office took an active interest in the matter, subjecting it to considerable internal debate. Officials sought the advice of England's security and censorship personnel to determine whether it was necessary for internal letters to bear the address of the sender. They were advised that such a requirement was unnecessary and did not exist in the mother country. Consequently, Richards was ordered to rescind the measure, and he did so in November 1942. The governor was also told that letters should never be destroyed by the censorship authorities.[22] The overzealous Richards had introduced, once again, wartime regulations that were more stringent than those existing in England. The censors remained active throughout the war, opening and reading the mail of all and sundry. In one two-week period in 1943, they read 17,000 letters.[23]

Governor Richards did not appreciate the value of street gatherings or soapbox utterances in the parks to those who had no other means of ventilating their unhappiness with their condition and life chances. These people, mostly from the underclass, had no access to the halls of power, were denied the right to vote, and nursed a variety of grievances. The vibrant political and social theater of the streets and the parks unnerved those who feared that disorder came in its wake. A colonial regime, increasingly intolerant of the motions from below, would use its power to suppress these assemblies, much to the chagrin of those persons who wanted to protect the civil liberties of all Jamaicans.

The coercive reach of the authorities was as broad as it was elastic. In August 1939, for example, the police banned all street gatherings in Victoria Gardens in downtown Kingston and in areas contiguous to it. The ban was directed at "gatherings for singing and drum beating . . . with cult leaders in the front line," according to the news report. The "cult leaders" included the black-nationalist Rastafarians. According to the *Gleaner*, policemen were dispatched to the areas in question each evening "to see that self constituted preachers and park politicians are not given a chance even to assemble much more to pursue their calling." The news reporter was pleased by "the vigilance of the police" because they did not allow "four, five, or half a dozen men . . . who should otherwise be on relief work, or arranging to go upon the land under the extensive land settlement scheme of the government to meet in the Park. As soon as they assemble, comes the enquiry: 'What is your business?' with an order to 'move on.' And off the men go—no back answers to the police either."[24]

Such power, to be sure, could be abused, and its exercise was not prompted solely by the desire to maintain law and order. The authorities opposed the discussion of the "color question" at these gatherings because they believed it would exacerbate social tensions. They even banned the customary street processions in Kingston commemorating Emancipation Day on August 1.[25] The government's critics also ran the risk of being harassed or arrested by the police on spurious grounds. In September 1940 the police arrested well-known critics of the administration Richard Hart, Arthur Henry, and Leopold Grant for allegedly participating in an unauthorized procession. The prosecution made the ludicrous claim that the three men, and a fourth who was not arrested, formed a procession. On dismissing the case, the magistrate observed that "four men walking as these Defendants were walking did not themselves form a procession."[26]

These were the petty actions of a state that was becoming increasingly repressive. Alexander Bustamante complained to the governor in September 1938 that the police were harassing him and other officials of his union. The police, he alleged, took notes "wherever we go to give labour meetings." Bustamante reported: "[W]e are heeled by secret service men taking down notes. This irritates instead of pacifying." Bustamante charged that "this kind of foolish tactics by government endeavouring to imprison us should we slip does not tend for better peace and order." He thought that the "tax payers money could be used more effectively by spending your money to catch thieves and burglars." When the surveillance did not cease, the labor leader complained to the governor again in February 1939, vowing to contest any attempts to "humiliate or destroy" him.[27]

Norman Manley and other officials of the PNP and the various trade unions were similarly harassed. Their meetings, particularly those held in Kingston and St. Andrew, were attended by police officers, and the content of their speeches was reported to the relevant authorities. Their presence intimidated the attendees. "The police wagon is sometimes parked right in front of the only entrance to the meeting place," Manley complained, "with the result that people get scared and do not come in." He thought that the government had "a deliberate" policy to discredit the organizations concerned. The speakers, Manley said, were made "to feel that they are working in an atmosphere of hostility." He thought that such intimidation by the police was "all part and parcel of the terrible decay in this country of normal ideas of civil liberties such as obtain in England." Manley was not being overly sensitive and accusatory; Jamaicans were experiencing a troubling assault on their freedoms.[28]

Norman Manley, by 1939, was emerging as the most effective and consistent defender of the civil liberties of Jamaicans in the face of the government's ferocious assault on them. Outraged by the crude attempts to suffocate criticism and dissent ostensibly during wartime, Manley risked internment by denouncing them. "For our country to progress," he told the Western Federation of Teachers assembled in Montego Bay, "there must be freedom of thought, freedom of action, and not this immoral restraint." He was aware, he said, that "intense pressure" is being put on teachers "to abjure all political interests in this country." He knew that their political views had a great influence on their careers. Still, he enjoined them to "fight at all costs and always every attempt by force, by threat, or by favour to restrain or suppress [your] legitimate freedoms."[29] The distinguished Labour MP Arthur Creech Jones was also disturbed by the assault on the civil liberties of the Jamaican people. Writing to Secretary of State Malcolm MacDonald, he said the Public Meeting Law constituted "the adoption of desperate measures in a situation allowed to deteriorate without any adequate measure to arrest it." Creech Jones complained that "civil liberty is brushed on one side and it is hoped that trouble is averted by this kind of repression."[30]

The exigencies of wartime security, and Governor Richards's distaste for critics of the colonial administration and those who advocated self-government for the island, led him to preside over a nascent police state. His administration kept a vigilant eye open for those who were espousing these ideas, keeping them under surveillance. Norman Manley, for example, was placed on the Security List.[31] That the island's most eminent son and a respected officer of the courts was seen as constituting a security threat and placed under surveillance indicated Richards's mistrust of local leadership and the extent to which he would go to destroy it.[32]

There were, to be sure, pockets of dissent in the island, people who were not reluctant to openly criticize the behavior of the colonial state. But this carried considerable risk. In July 1938, for example, the government arrested Stennet Kerr Coombs and Hugh C. Buchanan, the publishers of the recently founded *Jamaica Labour Weekly*. Buchanan was the secretary of the Bustamante unions and served as editor of the four-page weekly paper. Coombs was the owner of the printing press. The news article that offended the government had appeared on June 18 under the caption "Police Terror in St. James." The two men were charged with seditious libel for publishing it.

The article had appeared about four weeks after the labor unrest in Kingston. The island was still recovering from the turmoil, and a nervous government sought to protect the people from what it deemed inflammatory language. An avidly prolabor newspaper, the *Jamaica Labour Weekly*'s article charged that "innocent people" were "beaten and shot" in St. James. The parish, it said, was "under martial law," and the government was "determined to kill every working man or woman in the parishes of St. James, Hanover, Trelawny, and Westmoreland who dare to raise their voices in defence of labour." The article alleged that "special constables composed mostly of the habitual criminals and officer [?] workers have been armed and given orders to shoot and kill." The superintendent of police "has left off his duties, and become chief of the band of ruffians who are terrorizing the people," it added.[33]

These were allegations that Buchanan and Coombs could not substantiate. Norman Manley, their defense attorney, argued that the men were utilizing their right to free speech and had reported the truth, since people had been "beaten and shot" during the unrest of May and June. The learned counsel maintained that "if any person intended to be seditious such statements would have been accompanied by the most inflammatory appeals and comments that would have excited the ordinary man. But the proprietors were careful to avoid the use of strong adjectives . . . and confined themselves strictly to statements of facts."[34]

The jury was unpersuaded by these and other arguments, finding the men guilty. The judge sentenced them to six months in prison.[35] Applauding the conviction, the *Daily Gleaner* concluded that the men "had written certain statements that were malicious, untrue, defamatory and calculated at the time to have most unpleasant consequences." This organ of the elites felt that if the men went unpunished, people would feel that if they disturbed "the peace and order of a community," the government "should not seek to restore order if that meant firing upon a disobedient and turbulent mob."[36] This was an exaggerated response to an article published by two inexperienced journalists who were unfamiliar with the ethics of their adopted profession.

Arrested on a charge of sedition in December 1938, Altamont Reid and his case demonstrated the government's insecurity and tendency to use the judicial system to intimidate and silence critics. Reid, a thirty-three-year-old Rastafarian, street orator, and self-appointed president of the Kingston Division of "The King of Kings" Salvation Mission, was picked up after addressing a crowd of some 300 persons at North Parade. Presenting the case on behalf of the Crown, T. Henry Mayers accused Reid of inciting the crowd to racial strife and murder. Testifying, Detective James B. B. Smith said he took notes at the meeting, hearing Reid say: "If there be no shedding of blood, there can be no redemption. God says a white man's neck must be cut off." Continuing, Smith quoted Reid: "[Y]ou must kill, first Lizard, then frogs, then fowls and then practice to kill the white man. . . . Black men sharpen your machetes, back and front, and be ready to kill." Continuing to exhort his audience, Reid allegedly said: "The white man is thoroughly against the black man. . . . The Chinese, the Syrians, the white man, every man is going to get his neck cut off." Reid denied saying the words attributed to him and reportedly made "a stirring plea" to the jury to acquit him. The jury was unable to agree, forcing the judge to declare a mistrial.[37]

Some jurors may have thought that Reid's statements were innocuous, probably the rambling utterances of a troubled mind. Others may have believed that he posed no serious threat to the colonial state rhetorically, much less physically. But an insecure administration was very sensitive to the invocation of a racialized language against it, forbidding the newspapers to carry stories relating to racial strife anywhere. But race stood at the center of Jamaican life in wartime as much as it had in the island's history since Christopher Columbus revealed its existence to Europeans in 1494.

Governor Richards wept as his ship sailed from Suva Harbour in Fiji for Jamaica in July 1938. The people he had served for less than two years as their governor presented him with a whale's tooth as a gift the previous evening, an artifact that symbolized health and integrity. Richards would need both as he confronted the new challenges in Jamaica. According to his biographer, Richards demanded that the Colonial Office give him a free hand in the discharge of his responsibilities. He would receive a letter from Permanent Under-Secretary Sir Cosmo Parkinson assuring him that "while they all at the Colonial Office knew that he would never tell them what he was proposing to do, the least they could ask was that he would tell them what he had done."[38]

This was a carte blanche that gave the Colonial Office considerable deniability and cover if the new governor committed grievous wrongs against the Jamaican people. It also granted Richards much discretion in the discharge of his duties, thereby creating the likelihood of the abuse of his powers as governor. Richards understood, however, that while his power was almost untrammeled, he could not govern the island successfully if coercion was the weapon of first and last resort. He needed local allies, or at least the sympathetic understanding of prominent Jamaicans such as Norman Manley.

Arthur Richards and Norman Manley enjoyed a mutually respectful relationship during the first two years of the governor's tenure. Richards wrote "personal and confidential" letters to "My dear Manley," signing them simply, "A. A. Richards." Manley reciprocated, using the more formal "Your Excellency" as the salutation and signing such letters "N. W. Manley." The two men observed the conventions governing the difference in their status in the manner in which they greeted one another in these letters, and their families never seemed to have interacted socially. Social intimacies would have transgressed the colonial and racial etiquettes. The governor was the all-powerful white man, the representative of His Imperial Majesty. Norman Manley was the subject, an inferior being contaminated by his partial African racial ancestry. Such disabilities aside, the two men felt comfortable enough with one another for the governor to borrow a book from Manley's library.[39] Richards made critical comments about Bustamante and others in his letters to Manley, secure in the knowledge that his confidence would not be betrayed.

Manley was, however, not a sycophant of the imperial overlord. Although Richards benefited from his advice from time to time, Manley protected his independence. When Richards publicly denounced the government's critics as "traitors" in May 1940, for example, Manley was quick to take umbrage. "I resent bitterly the charge of traitor made by implication against myself and the people I am associated with," he complained to the governor.[40] Richards responded immediately, assuring the colonial leader:

> You are, I am sure, aware that there is no one in Jamaica who has more sincerely and consistently believed in you personally and defended your name in private and in public, than myself. If my judgment is correct we stand, in our different ways, for so many of the same things. I have rejected, and still reject, all suggestions which

reflect upon your loyalty. You have fought for the Empire and, in my opinion, would fight again if you could. No mention of traitors which I make can ever have the slightest reference to you. I do not think that it is in your nature to play such a part and I never have thought so.

Richards absolved Manley of any disloyal conduct. He noted, however, that "there are traitors in our midst [as] you probably know, as most of us do know it." He was cognizant of the "wave of disloyalty passing through the Kingston and St. Catherine areas." The governor told Manley that "one must take note of, though one may discount its importance to some extent, the widespread seditious talk, the putting up of notices Long Live Hitler; 'Down with the British Empire,' etc and the cheering of German Troops by certain sections of the audience in Kingston cinemas. Nor can one entirely ignore the seditiously inflammatory effect of certain printed papers."

Governor Richards observed that "disloyal" Jamaicans "profess to be members of the P.N.P. whose name inevitably suffers in consequence." He understood Manley's plight as leader of the party, noting that "there is no man in Jamaica who is more entitled than yourself to say, 'Heaven defend me from my friends.'" Richards assured Manley that he could not ignore threats to the political order. "I shall find it impossible," he said, "to stretch tolerance beyond certain limits, nor could it be any comfort to me to find you on my side in a cataclysm which either of us, had we been wiser, might have done much to avert." Speaking candidly to Manley, Richards expressed his desire "to preserve freedom of speech and writing." But, he added, "there must come a time when persons must be restrained who cannot relate the inopportune exercise of such licence to the circumstances of a life and death struggle for the existence of every ideal we possess." Jamaica, Richards explained to Manley, had "a coterie" of people, namely, "Communists, Anarchist, call it what you will, whose only desire is disorder, who are seething with malice and hatred of all established order. They have nothing to lose but their hopes, have no constructive aims and indeed have nothing but a sense of malignant frustration."[41] Richards was clearly describing and maligning Manley's colleagues. He may even have expected Manley to help temper their criticisms of the empire and encourage them to affirm their loyalty to it. If that was the governor's intention, Manley never obliged.

Writing in June 1942, Governor Richards described Jamaica's problems as he saw them, giving his impression of the island's people and its leaders. It was an extraordinary letter to H. F. Downie of the Colonial Office, and it provides a window into the thinking of a colonial governor who had little respect for the people he governed and who was out of step with their strivings. Richards began his letter by observing that the "the laboring classes" in Jamaica had never been so "well-off" as in the previous year. Although they were enjoying "plentiful" work at good pay, there was "unrest . . . in the air." Jamaicans shared, the governor said, a "general half-unconscious anxiety about the war and the unsettlement of the minds of a very ignorant people by inability to grasp the vastness of it." Jamaicans blamed the hardships necessitated by the war "on a careless and incompetent government." The *Daily Gleaner*, the governor complained, "contains never a good word for government or any of its works but is given over to malicious misrepresentation and vindictive invention." The governor was bristling at the newspaper's occasional criticism of the administration's policies. The *Gleaner*, however, was widely recognized as the voice of the elite groups in the society, expressed a conservative political philosophy, and looked askance at any fundamental change in the political status quo. Richards misrepresented the ideological position of the newspaper, betraying his sensitivity to criticism of any sort.

The colonial governor reserved his most scathing criticism for *Public Opinion*, the two afternoon newspapers, and the People's National Party. As he expressed it:

> Weekly in *Public Opinion*, daily in two small evening papers (corresponding elsewhere to the vernacular press), and hourly in conversation for the past two years the People's National Party led by Manley and Nethersole and the associated subversive groups have preached the iniquity and incompetence and bad faith of Government. For two years every conceivable perversion of motive and fact has been instilled into the people. No effort has been spared to stir up unrest and to discredit authority and a skein of racial hatred has been skillfully woven into the pattern of the incompetent Englishman in selfish and autocratic control for his own good and the people's detriment. The chickens are now coming home to roost. I doubt whether even Manley could now, if he wished which apparently he does not—stop them. You cannot teach the gospel of hate with such unscrupulous passion for years to a very ignorant and emotional people without reaping some of the inevitable results of such work.

Comments such as these once again reflected the governor's tendency to equate criticism with subversion. His ferocious assault on Manley and the

PNP demonstrated his misunderstanding of the people's quest for political autonomy. Baffled by the criticisms of the status quo, Richards dismissed the Jamaican people as "constitutionally of an envious, jealous and spiteful nature [who have] always listened with avidity to abuse of Government." The governor was contemptuous of Bustamante, characterizing him as "a damned nuisance" who was "first and last out for Bustamante and Bustamante's credit." He did not believe the labor leader to be "fundamentally anti-Government," but his activities were "sporadic and incoherent."

Governor Richards's description of Norman Manley, his personality, and his leadership style was an exercise in lofty condescension tempered by a guarded admiration for the eminent Jamaican. Richards reported that he had recently met with Manley, who turned in "a brilliant performance." He was, the governor said,

> a very complex personality and he talks on such occasion with all the ascetic aloofness of an Indian Saint. The highest principles and the loftiest motives, with no mundane flaws to stain their radiance. He can side-step a direct question or elude a difficulty with greater ability than anyone I have ever met. Talking to him it is difficult to feel anything but admiration for the self-less patriot who has given up everything that makes life worth living, books, art, music—all that leisure means to culture—for the sake of the call. No wonder he fascinates all comers. Apart from the political scene there is no one whom I would sooner make a friend of and have as a companion than Manley. But all this bears no relation to his daily conduct and less than no relation to the activities of his Party, which tend to be purely pernicious, despite the many good causes mixed up with their aspirations. It is more than doing evil that good may come. The instruments Manley works with are bad.

The governor clearly admired the man but despised his politics. He accused Manley of not accepting responsibility for the "trouble" in the island that he saw on the horizon:

> He denies that the steady undermining of respect for authority, the incessant misrepresentation of Government and its motives can have only one result. He speaks of the need of fearless propagation of the truth, disregarding the fact that it is only too often not the truth. He urges upon me that the really great man is impervious to abuse and

criticism and misrepresentation and should unfalteringly pursue his impartial path notwithstanding and so on and so on. But in the next breath he complains bitterly of the way in which he has been abused and falsely critiized [sic] and misrepresented. All with brilliant obscurity, not crudely as I have put it.

Governor Richards, to be sure, was hardly Manley's intellectual equal and probably lost many a private debate with him. But he was generous enough to observe that his antagonist was "not a hypocrite" and was "in many aspects passionately sincere." Manley was "a sort of auto-intoxication intellectual parthogenesis," a characterization whose meaning cannot be easily discerned. The governor observed that many members of the PNP "worship" Manley "as something approaching a god and he, being after all human, grows more impatient of opposition with the years." The governor mused that "dictatorship emerges easily in an atmosphere of adulation."

Still, Richards recognized Norman Manley's outstanding intellectual gifts and considerable talents as a leader. "He is no ordinary problem," the governor observed. He was "potentially a great leader, for good or ill, of a caliber that I have not met in any other Colony," Richards grudgingly conceded. The governor said that "like most idealists," Manley had "an infinite power of self-deception." He needed the help of "an organizer and someone to supply the practical ability he lacks" in order for him to "go far." Richards concluded that "for the moment," Manley "has left a brilliant future behind him and bids fair to perish in the deuce of the present mess." He confessed that he and Manley differed "as to whose funeral the mess will be."[42]

Governor Richards was profoundly ambivalent in his attitude to Manley, but he had considerably less patience with Englishmen who supported the political aspirations of the Jamaican people. In 1938, for example, the board of directors of Tate and Lyle Co. approved the appointment of the young nephew of Sir Leonard Lyle, its chairman, as the new managing director of the West Indies Sugar Company. Robert L. M. Kirkwood was thirty-eight years old when he accepted the assignment. He undertook his duties with undisguised gusto, demonstrating a commendable understanding of the plight of the workers and earning the well-deserved reputation as a reformer. He began his career in the island by strongly supporting Governor Richards and his administration. "Here in Jamaica you have today a fearless governor," he told an audience at Vere in August 1939. Richards was "a just and good man who is out to help the under dog and the poor men in Jamaica in every way possible.... [He] is a fine man who is out to do everything he can to help you."[43] Probably gratified by such a vote of confidence, Richards appointed Kirkwood to the Legislative Council. The governor also wanted to give him political experience, expecting that the government could count on his legislative support since he was a nominated member. Kirkwood, however, seemed to have experienced epiphanies the longer he stayed in the island, and he never felt obligated to support the government in the Council, much to the disappointment of the governor. He sought to bridge the existing political divide in the legislature, establishing friendships with two of the administration's most persistent critics: Dr. E. E. Campbell, the member for Kingston, and J. A. G. Smith, the member for Clarendon. A strong supporter of the cause of self-government for the island, Kirkwood collaborated with Norman Manley and others in advancing that effort.

Not surprisingly, Kirkwood's political positions and associations elicited the governor's ire. Responding to Kirkwood's criticism of the deplorable living conditions of poor Jamaicans, Richards said that he "is not honest or sincere; he is merely playing the old game of begging the plaudits of the poor and ignorant by inflaming their passions. This mental diabetic has much sugar in the blood." Accusing Kirkwood of "playing with fire," Richards declared that the young man possessed "unbounded energy" but "only moderate brains, inordinate vanity and a complete indifference to the value of money never having had to earn it." Evidently puzzled by Kirkwood's expressed sympathies for the poor and not for his own social class, Richards dismissed him as a charlatan, adding: "I have also known he is an unscrupulous egotist concerned only with his own ambitions and prepared to let other people pay any price for their gratification. He has always been a defeatist and with each turn of the war he has trimmed his future plans to the prospective wind. Any ideology will do as long as he is on the winning side. . . . He has been a bitter disappointment on [the] Legislative Council—one of my mistakes. His craving for publicity and popularity has led him very low."

Continuing his tirade against Kirkwood, the governor reported that "his own name here among respectable people is nil." This group, presumably, was the white elite. Richards wished that Leonard Lyle would recall Kirkwood from Jamaica but conjectured that he was "less a nuisance to Lyle in Jamaica than he would be in London." The governor predicted that Kirkwood "will end by destroying the Sugar Manufacturers Association." Kirkwood, he stressed, "is almost a menace here. To have a man in his position behaving as a political mountebank and playing down to a black gallery will in due course react on the West Indies Sugar Company."[44]

Robert Kirkwood was subverting the prevailing social, racial, and class etiquette in the island, much to the distaste of the sitting governor. Not only was he embracing the cause of self-government, but he also was promising to get the governor dismissed and promoting racial equality. Addressing a meeting organized by the Universal Negro Improvement Association, Kirkwood proclaimed:

> We will speak together with a voice that is unanimous and we will ask for a new constitution and a new deal which have the ideals for which young Jamaicans long. Liberty, equality, equal opportunities for all and a recognition that men of all colours are brothers and equals, equals in skill, brain, activity, imagination, enthusiasm, personality, and idealism. Equal in heart and soul. Equal in some and everything, every characteristic which man entertains and which makes man evidence of God's creatures. We shall appeal to the Mother Country, Parliament, and I can assure you that we shall not appeal in vain. And when that time comes, you Jamaicans here and your brothers and your children's children shall say it matters not, I am master of my faith, I am the captain of my soul.[45]

These were subversive ideas in a colony characterized by racial, social, and economic inequalities as well as political control by an imperial power. Kirkwood was not the first or only Englishman in the colony to espouse them, but he was the first representative of capital to do so unabashedly and with such harsh criticism of the class he represented. Earning the affection of many black Jamaicans, Kirkwood even flirted with the idea of seeking an elected seat in the Legislative Council when J. A. G. Smith died in early 1942.

Continuing to be perturbed by the behavior of the seemingly renegade child of white privilege, Richards dispatched a letter of complaint to Sir Leonard Lyle, Kirkwood's uncle. The letter was an eloquent and bitter denunciation of Kirkwood's behavior. Richards had no tolerance for a white representative of capital betraying his class and race by criticizing his heritage and impugning the integrity of the colonial administration. Referring directly to Kirkwood, the governor wrote:

> It is so terribly easy for the loose-tongued demagogue to gain a facile popularity by denouncing conditions for which he has no sane remedy and for reducing discussion of the petty done, the undone vast,

and the frank but temperate admission of responsibilities imperfectly fulfilled, which in the main characterizes a Parliamentary Debate, to the rabble rousing abuse so certain to earn a cheap popularity in Jamaica. That is what I deplore most in Kirkwood. It tickles the mob immensely to hear a wealthy capitalist denouncing all bankers and financiers *et hoc genus omne* as men who cheated the people at the end of the last war and who must be prevented from similar betrayal of the cause of liberty at the end of this one. What a nemesis he is piling up for the West Indies Sugar Co. and Tate and Lyle in the future.

Richards continued in his rhetorically brutal fashion, describing Kirkwood as "a spoilt product of the silver spoon." Kirkwood's criticisms of the administration had resonance, Richards said, because "to the vast majority of Jamaicans purity of motives, honesty of purpose and personal and official integrity are unthinkable concepts." The colonial governor evidently could not help being contemptuous of the Jamaican people, an attitude that characterized his tenure as head of government. He found it "despicably mean" and "contemptibly easy" for "[Kirkwood] who represents, whether he likes it or not big finance to foul his own nest and to throw mud at the pillars which uphold his own position. . . . [F]or the moment the tinsel glitter of his new found popularity attracts Kirkwood, and he is all for the Negro brother—at other people's expense."[46]

The Colonial Office declined to intervene in the dispute between the governor and the representative of big capital. One official, concluding that it would be inappropriate to do so, said "we had better leave Mr. Kirkwood alone," adding: "Anything that looks like a Colonial Office intrigue against him will do more harm than good." Amidst all of this turmoil, Kirkwood was recalled to London in late 1942 to meet with the board of directors of the West Indies Sugar Company. In a meeting at the Colonial Office, one official reported that "he expressed himself . . . particularly about what he called the Fascist tendencies of the present [Richards] regime, especially in its resentment of any kind of criticism." The official confessed that in the dispute between Richards and Kirkwood, he was "of the opinion that the major part of the blame rests with the Governor."[47]

Although the details of Kirkwood's discussion with Leonard Lyle and his board of directors are not known, Kirkwood returned to Jamaica a chastened man. He seemed to have been admonished to effect a modus vivendi with the governor or face dismissal. Kirkwood remained silent on many issues, curbed his criticism of the administration, distanced himself from Manley and the PNP, and adopted a lower public profile. Echoing the sentiments of the Colonial Office, he even publicly lectured Manley and the PNP to accept the new constitution that the mother country was then offering. The rejection of the constitution, he said, would mean that the PNP would be "a party to spreading suspicion of Britain and things British." He denounced the "small band of irresponsible left wing fanatics and faddists" who he said were "directing PNP policy from well deserved obscurity behind the scenes."[48] This was a marked *volte-face* in Kirkwood's political stance. The Kirkwood of old would never have used such language publicly to describe members of the PNP.

The dispute between Richards and Kirkwood was one between two representatives of the white colonial elite. Richards reacted angrily to criticisms from the young, ambitious voice of capital who was throwing stones at his privileged heritage. While he could understand why Norman Manley wanted a different future for Jamaica, he had no empathy for Kirkwood's embrace of self-government and other reforms in the island, believing it to be exercises in hypocrisy. Kirkwood's change in political tone after his return from England gave some credence to Richards's position. Faced with the prospect of losing his job or muting his professed beliefs, Kirkwood chose the latter option, thereby joining a long list of individuals for whom principled political behavior was a cruel hoax.

Manley's increasingly pugnacious espousal of a Jamaican nationalism was particularly galling to the colonial governor. Arthur Richards would become the exemplar of the intolerant, autocratic, and overbearing colonial administrator who had little understanding of, or sympathy with, the nationalist stirrings of the Jamaican people. "There is in Jamaica," Richards wrote to the Colonial Office, "a considerable and growing subversive element now hardly troubling to conceal its real aim, the overthrow of all order and honest government and its replacement by some fantastic form of local administration independent financially and otherwise of the United Kingdom, labeled 'self-government' so as to delude the less unbalanced members of the People's National Party which is responsible for it." Clearly, the governor equated a call for self-government with subversive activity. The alarmist Richards charged that the People's National Party "has members in many Government Departments who act as spies and help to spread its pinchbeck doctrines which are readily and uncritically accepted by ignorant but otherwise harmless people, particularly those in the humbler walks of life, whose minds were sedulously poisoned during the past few years by the steady output of antigovernment propaganda." Richards accused the members of the PNP of "using and contriving every opportunity for spiteful misrepresentation of every act of the Government." Norman Manley, the governor wrote, "has now discarded any pretension to be other than the implacable opponent of this administration and has identified himself with the forces of disorder or has become too weak to resist them." *Public Opinion*, the weekly newspaper sympathetic to the PNP, was, in the governor's opinion, wielding an "evil influence." He lamented that "nothing can be done to change the outlook of the warped and conceited fanatics who direct it."[49]

Writing to the secretary of state in June 1942, Richards blamed "the unhealthy tone throughout Jamaica" largely on "the activities of the People's National Party during the past two years." He accused the party of preaching "distrust" of the government and "disrespect for authority with passionate and venomous persistence, one section in blind disregard of the inevitable end and the other with deliberate intention, the disorder by which they hope to profit."[50] The party was stimulating chaos in the island, the governor charged, expecting to reap political rewards from the ensuing instability. The governor's demonization of the PNP, its leader, and *Public Opinion* demonstrated his distance from the pulse of a rising nationalism in the island. The tragedy, however, was that colonial policy was sometimes formulated on the basis of such ignorance, and the governor could persecute with impunity those who were criticizing the status quo and imagining a different future for their country.

The governor based his venomous diatribes on the reports he was receiving from his security forces. Reporting to him in November 1942, for example, the security officials at Up Park Camp emphasized that the PNP had fallen "under the influence and control and domination of a group of men with avowed revolutionary aims." The report concluded that the "constitutional demands towards Dominion Status and ultimate complete self government represent the aspirations of the bulk of the liberal minded Jamaica conscious Jamaicans. The association of the P.N.P. with this program is illusory, and expressed democratic aims serve as a facade for subversion and revolutionary activities." Accepting this characterization of the PNP as a subversive organization and believing that there were many people of a similar disposition in Jamaica, Richards ordered the Criminal Investigation Department to keep the suspects under surveillance, compile a security list, record their speeches by shorthand, invade their offices to search for incriminating evidence, and view them as enemies of the colonial state.⁵¹ To contemplate different power arrangements in Jamaica was considered to be a subversive act, a pernicious construction that symbolized the pathology of the colonial experience. The advocacy of the cause of political self-determination was criminalized; the king's subjects in Jamaica were not to be encouraged to follow the example of the Canadians, the Australians, and the New Zealanders in claiming themselves. These former colonies had set precedents and had been exemplars of the journey from colony to nationhood.

Richards's continuing paranoia was worsened by the diet of misinformation he was fed by his subordinates. In May 1942, for example, Inspector P. Long of the Criminal Investigation Department reported that "unintelligent press reporting, resulting in misrepresentation, and intelligent misreporting resulting in misunderstanding, greatly assist in spreading uneasiness" in the island. He identified the *Daily Gleaner*; the *New Negro Voice*, the organ of the Universal Negro Improvement Association; and *Public Opinion* as being among the principal offenders. The Propaganda Committee of the People's National Party, the Universal Negro Improvement Association, and the Negro Workers Educational League were described as "systematically working up mistrust and lack of confidence in the Government amongst the people." The PNP, the report claimed, wanted to maintain "unrest and apprehension" in the island since "the public are easier to lead in this state." The party was a haven for "communistically minded persons." The people were being convinced by the party that they were "oppressed" and "starving," which were the first steps "toward public unrest." Manley was unable to control "the more leftist persons" in the party and was in an "unbalanced state," the report asserted.⁵²

The men and women who challenged the colonial status quo in the 1930s and the 1940s were shaped by several ideological and intellectual currents. As colonial peoples, the ideology of self-determination was receiving a receptive ear in Jamaica as it did in other colonies. The nationalist stirrings in India, Burma, and Malaysia had a profound resonance among young Jamaican intellectuals who began to assert their claim to self-government. Adolf Hitler's espousal of an ugly racism in Germany invited a negative reaction in the island and a concomitant desire to cleanse it of British-inspired racial prejudice. Above all, the struggle for social justice by the workers in several islands, particularly their own, energized them to demand fundamental changes in the social, political, and economic structures.

Arthur Richards had been hastily dispatched to the island in the wake of Governor Edward Denham's death. His first challenge was to control domestic unrest, a job that was soon complicated by the outbreak of World War II in 1939. His most controversial weapon in his crusade against critics of the war was the arrest and detention of those whom he accused of subversion. But his definition of what constituted subversion was rather elastic, including anyone who condemned imperialism, criticized the war and the colonial administration, or advocated self-government for the island, the cause of the dispossessed, and social justice.

Richards was using his power to detain to silence the voices of change, but he produced instead a climate of fear. It was a type of fear, though, that did not paralyze but invited an aggressive response. The formation of the Jamaica Council of Civil Liberties and the holding of protest meetings across the island constituted the most effective reaction. Unperturbed, Richards was embracing the illusion that the decapitation of a movement or the persecution of its leaders would lead to its demise and the death of the ideas that gave it birth.

The first person to be caught in Richards's dragnet was G. St. C. Scotter, the English-born columnist for the *Daily Gleaner*. He was not a purveyor of sedition, nor did he oppose the war's objectives. But he questioned its prosecution and expressed a deep pessimism about the prospects of an Allied victory. Richards was concerned that Scotter's attitude might have a deleterious effect on war morale in Jamaica, impeding the recruitment of troops. He detained him in May 1940.[53]

Richards was particularly exercised by critics of the political and economic status quo in the island. His targets for detention, with the exception of Scotter, were people focused on the construction of a new Jamaica and a more-just society. Alexander Bustamante was detained in September 1940 for allegedly inciting a race war. He was followed by W. A. Williams, an organizer for the Bustamante Industrial Trade Union. In March 1941 the governor detained Samuel C. Marquis, the propaganda officer of the People's National Party. The grounds for his detention, according to a Colonial Office minute, "were that he had for many months been consistently making seditious and inflammatory speeches."[54] The record is silent on the content of these speeches. Marquis appealed his detention, but the advisory committee that heard it declined to intervene, holding that "any revocation, suspension or variation of the Detention Order would be detrimental to public safety and Defence of the Realm."[55]

Bustamante's detention created a great outcry among his supporters, requiring him to issue an appeal for order. The detention of Wilfred Domingo in June 1941 elicited much consternation among the elite groups in the island, members of the People's National Party, and the growing number of nationalists. Born in Jamaica, Domingo was fifty-five years old in 1941 and resided in New York. Domingo was a founding member of the Jamaica Progressive League and was serving as one of its vice presidents. He was a prominent supporter of the cause of self-government for Jamaica, and Manley invited him to take up a temporary assignment in Jamaica, furthering the work of the PNP. Domingo arrived at Port Royal on the SS *Vevaqua* on June 17, 1941, but he was arrested before the ship docked and was taken to the internment camp.

The American and Jamaican governments had been monitoring Domingo's activities for some time and also reading his mail. The Americans believed he was a communist, but that pejorative appellation was usually applied very loosely. J. Edgar Hoover, the director of the Federal Bureau of Investigation, reported that "it is said that he [Domingo] was sent to Moscow, Russia for training in 1931 and he and other members of his organisations are felt to be definitely communistic in their sympathies."[56] There is no independent confirmation of Hoover's allegation of Domingo's visit to Moscow and its purpose. The two organizations to which Domingo belonged—the Jamaica Progressive League and the West Indies National Council—were decidedly nationalist in their inspiration.

Hoover reported to the Department of State that Domingo had subversive literature in his possession when he was detained in Jamaica. This included "a picture of Lenin" and such publications as "the manifesto of the Communist Party," "The Next Emancipation," "Do we have a stake in the war," "Britain's Prisoners," "Thomas Paine," "Colonies[:] what Africa Thinks," and "The Decline and Fall of the British Empire." Presumably, the possession of these works meant that Domingo was a communist. Hoover noted, however, that when Domingo appealed his detention in September 1941, he stated "that he was not and never had been a Communist, but admitted that he was associated with various public bodies, some members of which held communistic views."[57]

The evidence advanced to justify Domingo's detention was not only weak but spurious. In making his case, Richards charged that

> from September, 1939, until immediately before he left the United States of America for Jamaica . . . Mr. Domingo conducted a protracted correspondence with persons taking an active part in politics, including Messers. M. L. Campbell, N. W. Manley, E. V. [V. L.] Arnett and E. E. A. Campbell of such nature as

a) To promote and foster Anti-British sentiments and to embarrass and impede the policy of the imperial and local governments in relation to the war effort.

b) To foster defeatist sentiments.

c) To excite opposition to the policy of United States to establish defence bases in Jamaica, and to embarrass and delay the rapid execution of plans for establishing such bases.

d) To promote and foster among the Colonial population of Jamaica feelings of colour prejudice and racial animosity in particular by alleging the existence of such feelings among officers and men of the United States Forces, likely to be stationed in Jamaica.

The governor quoted from Domingo's letters to M. L. Campbell, Norman Manley, and V. L. Arnett to show his position on American racism, the questions of self-government for Jamaica, American bases in Jamaica, and the rights of Puerto Ricans. None of these statements indicated disloyalty to the empire or posed any threat to the security of Jamaica. The fact that they resulted in the loss of a British citizen's freedom for almost two years suggested Richards's narrow interpretation of the Defense Regulations, his little respect for the rights of Jamaican subjects, and his overweening intolerance. The parts of Domingo's letters that so offended the governor deserve to be examined.

Writing to Campbell on March 13, 1941, Domingo expressed his concern that the American who would be in charge of the naval base in Jamaica came from the South. He feared the introduction of racial segregation, American style, in the island, warning that Jamaica could become "another India." India was then engaged in an aggressive campaign for its independence. "I had noticed the head of the American invaders is from the South," Domingo wrote to Campbell. "I share your fears regarding them on the island." Continuing, he issued a threat to the mother country. "If England wants another India, this time at the door of the United States," Domingo observed, "then we should be prepared to let her have it." Returning to his concern about American racial contamination, he warned that "with Americans in their Country, Jamaicans had better unite." These comments were hardly the stuff that should have invited official attention and persecution. Domingo's letter to Norman Manley was equally innocuous. "Self government must give us the power to defend ourselves against the Americans in Jamaica," he had written to Manley on January 24, 1941. Richards was not amused by this assertion of Jamaican nationalism.

Domingo's letter to the secretary of the PNP, V. L. Arnett, also opposed the American presence in Jamaica. He expressed the hope that the PNP "will take immediate action to offset any riots by Americans in Jamaica." Domingo reminded Arnett that the "majority of the men in the American Army and Navy are from the Southern States and they regard any person with the slightest drop of Negro blood as a person without rights to be respected by them."[58] Given the existence of a rabid form of racial segregation in the American South at the time, Domingo was not crying wolf. Nevertheless, Governor Richards used the letters to accuse him of promoting and fostering feelings of racial animus in the island. The colonial governor was living in a fool's paradise: black Jamaicans were already very familiar with the virus of racial prejudice, albeit British style.

Although Domingo was harshly critical of imperialism, he supported Britain's war effort. As a man of African descent, he could hardly have supported the Nazis and their assertion of an unrepentant and ferocious racism. But his criticism of imperialism led people such as Richards who had no deep understanding of the pulse of colonial peoples to question his loyalty to England. The matter was more complex. On December 17, 1939, for example, Domingo participated in a debate in New York, arguing for the affirmative on the question, "Should British Colonial Negroes Support the British Empire in the Present War"? Writing to Jamaican journalist Frank Hill, he explained: "You probably learned of the debate I had with a Communist friend of mine as to the attitude British Colonial Negroes should take in the present war between Great Britain and Germany. I took the affirmative that we should support the former, not because we love her but as between the two evils—British imperialism and Nazism—we should prefer the former to win."

Domingo stressed that he was opposed to "all imperialisms," and that he supported Russia unconditionally since she was "the only anti-imperialistic country in the world." To him, Russia was "the hope of all oppressed colonial peoples, especially those of the colonial races."[59] Sentiments such as these, to be sure, did not endear Domingo to Hoover or Richards.

The injustice of Domingo's internment generated protests in Jamaica, the United States, and England. Prominent Jamaicans founded the Jamaican Council of Civil Liberties. Letters and telegrams protesting against the internment were dispatched to Richards by the Jamaica Progressive League in New York; the National Negro Congress in Washington, D.C.; American socialist and politician Norman Thomas; the West Indies National Council in New York; and a host of other organizations and individuals. Dr. H. B. Morgan, a Labour member of the British Parliament, predicted that the Domingo case "is going to cause trouble in Jamaica for years to come. It will leave a legacy of repugnance and hatred for years." The MP thought the "whole history of his original highhanded (if not illegal) arrest and his persistent imprisonment is worthy of a Hitlerian regime." Morgan saw Richards's treatment of the black Jamaican as "a dreadful exhibition of anti-negro prejudice, tinged with malice, over officially unpopular but truly democratic views. He wants the West Indies to be governed by West Indians under British suzerainty, and really so do I."[60]

Upon his hearing of Domingo's detention, a concerned Norman Manley wrote to the governor asking to meet with him to discuss the matter. He explained to Richards that he had invited Domingo to Jamaica to assist in the organization of the BITU and to work for the PNP. Domingo was expected to remain in the island for one year "as a paid employee" of the two organizations. Manley assured the governor that Domingo was not a communist "or a sympathizer with their doctrines." He was "a staunch anti-Nazi and in no shape or form a defeatist or anti war." Manley noted that Domingo took "strong but sensible" positions on "racial questions." Domingo, he said, supported the PNP's policy on constitutional reform and endorsed "proposals that do not go as far as responsible Govt." Manley admitted to Richards that "nothing was further from my thoughts than the notion that he [Domingo] would have been regarded as an undesirable."[61]

Governor Richards was unpersuaded by Manley's attempt to depict Domingo as posing no threat to the colonial state. He refused to meet with Manley to discuss the case, a rebuff that enraged the barrister and led to a break between the two men. Richards's letter to Manley explained his reasons for declining to see him: "I have been into the case of Domingo with the officers concerned and the conflict of opinion between your estimate of him and theirs is very marked. I am bound to say that after studying their side of the case I should not be justified in acting on the assumption that Domingo's activities here were intended—by Domingo himself—to be harmless. Nor do I see how—with the best will in the world—you could hope to control him in such activities seeing that his whole outlook on life seems to be permeated with racial hatred."

Richards regretted that Manley had not informed him earlier about Domingo's visit and its purpose. "It might have been possible," the governor wrote, "to nip in the bud the whole proposal for his return."[62] The governor gave no credence to Manley's arguments, thereby losing his goodwill and guarded understanding. Manley severed his personal relationship with the stubborn and imperious governor. The breach would not be repaired until after a year had elapsed.

W. Adolphe Roberts, the president of the New York branch of the Jamaica Progressive League, shared Manley's outrage at Domingo's detention. Writing to Manley on July 14, 1941, he accepted some responsibility for it: "I feel as great a responsibility as you do in the matter. For the suggestion to you that he be asked to return to Jamaica to work for the P.N.P. came from me. And I used my influence with him to sacrifice his business interests in New York and leave as soon as possible. Not that he needed much urging. He saw it from the viewpoint of pure patriotism and was proud of the opportunity." As Manley did in his letter to Richards, Roberts emphasized Domingo's patriotism. "There is no Negro leader anywhere in the empire," he wrote, "more wholeheartedly pro-British where the war is concerned than Domingo, or more fiercely anti-Nazi." Roberts appreciated the difficulties that Manley faced in securing Domingo's release, noting "the almost insufferable concentration of power, which leaves you helpless except to present arguments."[63]

The outrage over Domingo's arrest failed to achieve his release. The Colonial Office defended the governor's action, and a compliant Advisory Committee rejected Domingo's appeal in September 1941, maintaining that "evidence is available that indicates that Domingo has been engaged in defeatist and antiwar propaganda, including propaganda designed to stimulate opposition on racial grounds to the establishment of United States Bases in the West Indies."[64] This was a distortion of Domingo's positions, particularly of his stance on the war.

The American consul general, Hugh H. Watson, was aware that Richards's detention of British subjects caused "a great deal of anxiety" in the island. Watson reported to his government that none of those interned, "so far as is known, is in any way pro-German; probably none of them is anti-British in the broad sense of the term; all of them are bitter critics of the present Government of Jamaica." This was an accurate observation, as was his additional comment that many people think "that the Government is using a power given for a specific purpose under the Defense Regulations to accomplish ends for which it was never intended and which could not be accomplished under civil law."[65]

Although Consul General Watson probably never told the governor that he was perverting the Defense Regulations, he spoke the truth. His observation on the governor's misreading of the pulse of dissent in Jamaica was devastatingly perspicacious. He observed that "the question of 'disloyalty' in Jamaica arises in large part from confusion of thought. Practically speaking there is no pro-German feeling; there is relatively little anti-British feeling; of opposition to the government set up and maintained in Jamaica by the British Colonial Office there is much. The labeling of the pro-Jamaica policy of the better types of Jamaicans as unpatriotic, anti-British and even pro-German is not born out of the facts."[66]

Despite the protests on his behalf, Domingo remained interned until February 19, 1943. The *Gleaner* reported that he "seemed very tired and worn out" when he regained his freedom. The PNP celebrated his release at a large public meeting a few days later at Edelweiss Park.[67] Domingo's release did not go unnoticed in London, and it was the subject of questions in the House of Commons. Labour MP David Adams inquired of the secretary of state the reason for Richards's action. This was the unenlightening dialogue:

> COLONEL STANLEY: Mr. Domingo has been released without restriction. He was detained under Jamaica Defence Regulations, because the Governor was satisfied that his detention was necessary with a view to preventing him acting in a manner prejudicial to public safety and defence.
>
> MR. ADAMS: Does the Minister not consider it a remarkable thing for a person to be charged with an offence which he has not committed but which he might commit, and to be interned for a long period?
>
> COLONEL STANLEY: He was not charged with an offence. This is a similar procedure to the procedure here under 18b. He was detained to prevent him acting in a manner prejudicial to public safety.
>
> MR. SILVERMAN: What information has the Governor had to induce him to change his mind? He was satisfied at one moment that the detention was necessary, and satisfied very much later that the detention was not necessary.
>
> COLONEL STANLEY: Like my right Hon. Friend when he is dealing with 18b cases, I cannot go into details. The Governor was satisfied that the detention was no longer necessary.
>
> MR. RILEY: When the Right Hon. and gallant Gentleman says that Mr. Domingo was released without restriction, does that mean that he will be allowed to remain in Jamaica and do the work of the People's National Party?
>
> COLONEL STANLEY: The answer is that he was released without restriction.

DR. MORGAN: Was Mr. Domingo's release made on the recommendation of the local advisory committee, or was it the Governor's decision, by himself?

COLONEL STANLEY: I would like to confirm this, but I understand that it was the Governor's decision, by himself.[68]

The internment of Domingo and the other men was an intolerant and uncomprehending response by the governor to social and political ferment in the island. It was hard work policing the thought of those Jamaicans who were reading Karl Marx, denouncing imperialism, expressing support for nationalists in other colonies, and demanding self-government for their country. Most identified with the economic plight of the workers and were busy organizing them and forming trade unions. The People's National Party became their political sanctuary after its founding, and Norman Manley was their political, if not intellectual, leader. These men included Noel Nethersole, Richard Hart, the brothers Kenneth Hill and Frank Hill, Winston Grubb, and Arthur Henry. Richards had dossiers compiled on the men, ready to be used when the occasion warranted. By early 1942 Richards was convinced that they were subversives who should be deprived of their liberty.

There was no persuasive evidence that any of these men were engaging in plots against the government. They were articulating the gospels of political and social change, but not the cathartic value of violence. The power of ideas was their weapon; the righteousness of the cause was their justification. Frank Hill, who was described by Richards as "a leading member of the Metropolitan Group of left wing PNP," had one of the more extensive dossiers compiled on him. Richards reported that throughout the war, Hill "has been an untiring exponent of most extreme views, and has been known to be unceasingly engaged in anti-British and Racial propaganda." Hill, Richards continued, had been using "the difficulties of local war conditions to hamper the war effort in every way, and to incite disaffection." The governor produced no evidence to support these serious allegations. They were really official lies, concocted to justify any steps he might take against Hill. "I have long desired for the public safety to curb this man's activities," Richards told his superiors, "and information now at my disposal shows that it is imperative to exercise control over him before he has further opportunity of disseminating such dangerous opinions amongst the ignorant masses here, who are unusually receptive to such propaganda."

Richards submitted what he said were extracts from Hill's speeches and writings to prove that he was a dangerous subversive and a threat to public order. Rather, they reveal a Jamaican nationalist harshly critical of British imperialism and advocating independence for the island. The first excerpt was from a resolution that Hill offered at a meeting of the Metropolitan Group. It expressed his unhappiness with the impact of the war on the island and the sacrifices Jamaicans were making. Hill's resolution expressed a profound mistrust of the motives of the imperial government and demanded Jamaica's independence.

> Whereas our people are suffering strangulation of trade because the geographical natural trade routes have been closed by our Imperial rulers, and whereas our people can no longer bear these needless sufferings and wanton waste of our precious lifeblood and whereas the British government cannot be trusted to frame a constitution for our people, the British Government's record in India right up to the present time furnishing further evidence of the little faith that colonial peoples can have in the honest intensions of British Imperialism, be it resolved that the P.N.P. in the name of the people of Jamaica demand a declaration by the British Government of Jamaica's independence.

Two excerpts from his writings indicate Hill's opposition to colonialism and his view that the colonial peoples were being manipulated to fight in a war not of their making:

> We want public mass feeling aroused. All that wealth of anti-Imperialist feeling bred by years of British evil rule: for this is not our war, it is Tory England's war. It is evident that as time goes on the illusion may be shattered but the main illusion remains that our Imperial masters, having drenched their empire in blood and filth and oppression all these years, have suddenly seen the error of their ways. That is the illusion that supposedly intelligent men and women who are fighting for the liberation of their country from British Imperialists are believing. Does not it sound like a huge farce?

These words dripped with a vitriol unacceptable from the mouth of a colonial subject. Hill saw the war as shattering the "illusion" of Britain's "power and greatness": "Hitherto whatever loyalty or sentimental attachment these people felt towards Britain was due to the illusion of her power and greatness. I am sure you will agree with me in saying that such an illusion has been mercilessly exposed by international events of the past year, and that the middle class takes little pains to hide ridicule, and even contempt for British people. This is easily understandable."

Frank Hill also urged the PNP to condemn British imperialism more strongly, noting: "Our party must declare openly that the British Empire is an evil system at the core . . . that at the present stage it is decadent and incompetent, and can only maintain its hold on the subject peoples—by far the majority—by such acts of violence and repression that are indistinguishable from Fascist terrorism."

Hill used very acerbic language to predict more social unrest in Jamaica and the demise of the British Empire: "We are at the beginning of a gigantic upheaval which may well make 1938 look like a picnic party. Let us be reasonable. British imperialism has shot its bolt. It is breaking up with a vengeance on its past misdeeds—nothing can save it, nor anyone for that matter. Who would want to? Not the millions who suffer under its tyranny. And it cannot save itself. . . . It can call on its instruments of terror, taunt the countryside with those instruments as it started to do last week in the hope that bullets will fill the bellies that ache for food."

These and other harshly critical comments incurred the wrath of Governor Richards, who was itching to silence him. None of the supposedly incriminating evidence revealed Hill advocating physical attacks on the colonial state. His was a rhetorical assault on an imperial regime that had enslaved his people, denied most of them the full rights of citizenship after emancipation, and embraced and practiced the ideology of white supremacy.[69]

Governor Richards was equally troubled by Kenneth Hill's activities. The younger brother of Frank Hill was a prominent member of the PNP and was serving as its third vice president. The governor reported that he had been appointed by the Metropolitan Group to convert "the masses to P.N.P. self-government policy." He was "assigned to hooliganism in country parishes for this campaign, together with the task of training country agents, these being activities in which he is shown by various committees and meeting reports to have particularly distinguished himself in the past." The governor did not explain what he meant by "hooliganism" or why its practice would be efficacious in promoting the cause of self-government. Richards admitted that he could not provide examples of Hill's political views as he has "always exercised extreme caution" in his behavior. He knew, however, that since 1939, this man has been a most pernicious influence, and still is, a most vicious and untiring troublemaker. He has always been extremely skillful in covering his tracks, and in ensuring that no documentary evidence is ever available, so that the only persons incriminated are subordinates, carrying out, sometimes unconsciously, his policy and objects. No man has been more consistent in subterranean activities against Imperial and local war efforts, and in promoting disaffection, and he is probably the most dangerous subversive agent in Jamaica. His success in avoiding detection, over a period when the nature of his activities has been so notorious, is a measure of his cleverness.[70]

This venomous assault on Kenneth Hill was not supported by any evidence. The governor clearly feared the influence of the young politician and trade unionist. But more than his unsubstantiated words were needed to make a credible and effective case against the Jamaican. Had Richards made his allegations publicly, Hill would have had the grounds for a libel suit. Acting with the power of the colonial state behind him, the governor had no compunction in making damaging allegations about the conduct of colonial subjects whose politics he abhorred.

Richards manifested a similarly callous attitude toward Noel Nethersole, a prominent attorney and first vice president of the People's National Party. Born in 1903, Nethersole was a Rhodes Scholar, talented cricketer, and socialist who was elected president of the National Reform Association in 1937. Richards described Nethersole as "an inveterate trouble-maker, who throughout the war has persistently worked to undermine authority and to promote unrest and dissatisfaction." Nethersole, who also was an elected member of the Kingston and St. Andrew Corporation, was described by the governor "as an extreme radical and . . . a bitter opponent of the Imperial and Local governments [who] exploits every war-time difficulty for their embarrassment and for the furtherance of his own political views." Continuing his disparagement of Nethersole, Governor Richards said "his method is to use the illiterate peasants and workmen as his tools and trade unionism is his chief political weapon." He depicted the attorney as "the type who stays in the background and incites others to violence and remains comfortably at home when the rioting begins and the arrests are made." Nethersole, he said, "has always been far too wary to put himself within the reach of the law."[71]

There was nothing in the public record to support such accusations. But Richards seemed unable to resist attributing the worst motives and behavior to his Jamaican critics, especially those who belonged to the PNP. Richard Hart, a young solicitor, "was an extreme and violent revolutionary," the governor charged, "who has unceasingly engaged since the outbreak of war in subversive activities of a most dangerous character." Hart "is strongly anti-British and anti-government" and "now appears to be implicated in a conspiracy to promote revolution and violence."[72] Another member of the PNP, A. L. Henry, was depicted by the governor as "a notorious agitator and inciter to disorder and a political journalist of extreme ant-white and anti-British views." Henry, the governor observed, "has shown a tendency to become the instrument of cleverer men."[73]

Richards specialized in the denigration and silencing of colonial subjects who were rejecting and challenging the status quo, but he also wanted to employ state power to control the hordes of unemployed subjects. When he visited Jamaica in early 1939, Lord Olivier, the highly respected former governor, reported that "proposals were being discussed of [for] providing labour concentration camps" for the mass of the unemployed. Richards "said to me that he would like to round them up into into labour camps and make them work." Astonished, Lord Olivier reminded Richards that that "had been the idea of the British Poor Law of 1839; that the labour camps were then called 'workhouses,' and, by William Cobbett 'Bastiles,' and that that method had now been long improved on by intelligent British statesmanship." This was a strong critique of the governor's thinking and his political style. Richards's lingering affection for coercive mechanisms to address contemporary ferment did not serve him well in Jamaica.[74]

Governor Richards had an opportunity to silence the critics of the empire and the administration when the railway workers formed a union in mid-1942. Richard Hart, Noel Nethersole, and Arthur Henry had played crucial roles in its organization. Hart was elected the president, Nethersole the vice president, and Henry the secretary. Named the Jamaica Government Railway Employees Union, it was officially registered on June 23, receiving the government's recognition as a bona fide body shortly thereafter. The Richards administration was not enamored of the union's leadership and kept them under surveillance. It informed the union on September 26 that its recognition was being withdrawn because its principal officials were not employees of the railway. The union, in response, rejected the justification for the decision, inaugurating a bitter dispute with the Richards administration.[75]

The union's solicitor appealed to the labour adviser on October 7, charging that a trade dispute existed as defined by the existing Defense Projects and Essential Services Order. These regulations allowed trade disputes that could not otherwise be resolved to be submitted to an Industrial Defense Tribunal by the governor upon the recommendation of the labour adviser. Six days later, the government emphatically informed the union that no trade dispute existed, taking the matter out of the hands of the labour adviser.[76] This legally questionable decision seems to have been orchestrated by the governor and ultimately led to the intervention of the Colonial Office.

The governor sought to strengthen his position by issuing additional defense regulations on October 21, empowering him to implement them in an emergency to maintain "essential services and supplies." The new regulations applied to the railways and to the postal and telegraph departments. They were designed, in the governor's words, "to exclude all non-employees of the department from membership or office in [a] departmental trade union." The regulations directly targeted Hart, Nethersole, and Henry, who, the governor charged, "are notorious agitators, whose main object is political friction." These leaders, he said, all belonged to the Metropolitan Group, whose views "are frankly revolutionary communism with extremely anti-British and anti-American bias." The governor denounced the group as "obsessed with racial hatred, and self government means to them, taking advantage of war conditions to secede altogether from Britain with South American Republic[s] whose support they propose to discard when Jamaican independence is secured." This was a fantasy employed by the governor to legitimize his high-handed behavior. He further reported that "subversive" literature had been discovered in the union's offices, "including books by Lenin with marked passages as to the need for operating through trades unions by means of specially trained revolutionaries." Consequently, he was faced "with the alternative of doing nothing at all, or of using every means in my power to check organized subversion disguised as genuine trade unionism."[77]

In order to procure evidence supporting claims that the leaders were engaged in subversive activities, the police searched the residence and office of some of them. They were undoubtedly acting under instructions from the governor, or most certainly with his approval. The police searched the residences of Frank Hill, Richard Hart, Osmond Dyce, Richard Fox, and a Mrs. Brown, identified as a member of the PNP. They also searched the Railway Union's office, as well as Frank Hill's printing and publishing office. The police officers seized books, letters, writings, typewriters, and personal notes in these incursions. The police reportedly had in their possession "a considerable number of forged documents," purportedly composed by the accused men. These documents, Manley said, "pretended the existence of a conspiracy to organise an uprising or disorders" in Westmoreland and St. Thomas. They "were delivered to the police for monetary reward," Manley alleged. The police had not taken any steps "to prosecute the forgers for forgery, for conspiracy to injure and or defraud or for acting to the Public Mischief," the party leader charged.[78]

The behavior by the police reflected the Richards administration's anti-PNP fervor more than it did any opposition to trade unions. The assault on the Railway Union was a proxy for the animus that the governor displayed toward the political party and its pesky leaders. But it was a fight that Richards was not likely to win. His superiors in London saw the conflict as an attack on unionism and firmly defended the rights of the workers that were entrenched in British law and practice. By masking the real reason for his assault on the union, Richards made a tactical error. The Colonial Office would not condone an attack on organized labor, although it might have cast a blind eye on any blows the governor delivered to the PNP. Arthur Richards's obfuscation of the real issue that drove the dispute was clearly unhelpful to his objective.

The governor's actions were the subject of considerable discussion in the Colonial Office. These officials could find no precedent in trade-union law in England for refusing to recognize a union because its leaders were not practitioners of the occupation or trade to be unionized. The Colonial Office received a strong protest against the governor's behavior from Sir Walter Citrine, the general secretary of the British Trades Union Congress. He urged the secretary of state "to request the governor to refrain from persisting in the arbitrary action which he appears to have taken as this unwarranted violation of the right of freedom of association may have serious consequences."[79]

A zealot-like Richards complicated matters by issuing an order under the Defense Regulations interning Frank and Kenneth Hill, Richard Hart, and Arthur Henry on November 3. The PNP quickly condemned this "latest move in the series of improper acts which began when government made its first attack on the Railway Union." A pained Norman Manley was characteristically reflective. "I suppose it is typical of our times," he ventured, "that people must suffer for their opposition and suffer for having the courage to do what is right. But the last judgment has yet to be delivered on these matters and I think I know what History will say." Three days after interning the men, Richards issued an order restricting the movements of seven members of the PNP and the Metropolitan Group for allegedly engaging in subversive activities. The accused men included Samuel Hinds, W. A. McBean, Walter C. Bethune, Roy Woodham, Richard Fox, Cecil Nelson, and Osmond Dyce. "These men are trained agents of the four detainees for propaganda work in Kingston and the country districts," the governor explained. The men could not leave their parishes without permission, had to report to the police each week and notify the authorities if they changed their addresses, and were prohibited from addressing public meetings, doing political work, or contributing articles to newspapers.[80]

The internment of the four men and the restrictions placed on the others constituted a frontal assault on the PNP designed to cripple if not to destroy the party. The Hill brothers and Henry held important leadership positions in the PNP, and the men placed under restrictions were its principal fieldworkers and organizers. Manley condemned the government's attacks on the party and its leaders, saying that they were not "deserved or warranted and ... are designed to hamper or destroy the Party and its work and constitute an unjust and unjustifiable use of the powers given by the Defence Regulations and involve the harm and oppression of persons whose conduct and intentions were in no manner whatever such as to bring them within the scope of the Regulations involved." Manley's denunciation of the government's conduct was accompanied by a damaging but uncorroborated accusation against Bustamante. Manley said that he had been "informed that Bustamante had admitted making communications to Government stating that the Party was planning an uprising in the Country and that secret meetings were being held with that in view." Manley declared that "these statements, if they were made, were wholly untrue." This was an astonishing story. The PNP's executive took it seriously enough to discuss it. But Manley's guarded comment seemed to suggest that he entertained some doubts about the story's veracity.[81]

Richards succeeded, at least temporarily, in decapitating the union and wounding the PNP by interning some of their leaders. Although the Colonial Office agreed with Richards that "persons of approved subversive tendencies should not occupy positions where they can influence vital services," it was not "satisfied as to [the] method adopted." It was particularly opposed to the use of the Defense Regulations to resolve what was essentially a legal dispute. Consequently, it ordered the governor to issue a statement and to deliver a broadcast stating that there was no connection between the men's detention and the fact that they held positions in the Railway Union. He was to reaffirm the government's support for the trade-union movement. Governor Richards acquiesced to this request on

November 9. This was a calculated deception and a public-relations exercise because there was undoubtedly a link between the detentions and the men's leadership roles in the union.[82]

The Colonial Office had no stomach for Richards's use of his power to alter the traditional rules governing the trade-union movement. On November 17 the secretary of state ordered him to recognize the Railway Union and to withdraw the orders he had issued under the aegis of the Defense Regulations. "My strong desire has been to give you my support," the secretary explained,

> in the difficult situation which you are facing, but for reasons of high policy I have reached the conclusion with much regret that I must ask you to withdraw the regulation and to renew your recognition of the Railway Union. I suggest that your announcement should give reasons for your action in passing the regulation, which should be based on the fact that you had knowledge of subversive activities amongst some of those concerned which, in present circumstances of war, could not be tolerated. You should repeat your assurances that your action was not aimed at Trade Unions as such, and should give some indication that you are in sympathy with trade union movements. You should add that as your original object has been achieved, you have decided to withdraw the regulation and renew recognition of the Union.[83]

The governor did as he was instructed, and the union was recognized with no change in its leadership. But two of its officers, along with the Hill brothers, still languished in the internment camp, despite continuing public protest. Kenneth Hill dispatched letters to Arthur Creech Jones and Sir Walter Citrine to intercede with the Colonial Office on their behalf. He also wrote to Sir Stafford Cripps, asking him to "give some of your valuable time to our cases." He assured Sir Stafford that the accusation of "subversive activity" leveled at them was "utterly untrue." He affirmed the "all-out support of the war" of all the organizations to which the detainees belonged. Hill stressed that the trade unions with which he was associated were committed to making "the fullest use of and exhaust the machinery of conciliation and arbitration in our negotiation with employers." He told the English parliamentarian that "we have had only one desire, which we shall carry into the future with us, and that is to assist constructively in the social, economic and political development of our people, within the framework of the Party and the Unions . . . and by constitutional means."[84]

Hill's letter was dispassionate in tone and framed in such a way as to elicit Cripps's sympathetic understanding. Sir Stafford recalled meeting Hill when he visited Jamaica in September 1938 and gave the keynote address at the launching of the People's National Party. He forwarded Hill's letter to the colonial secretary, describing him as "a very nice young negro . . . with whose ability I was much struck." Hill, Sir Stafford added, "is exactly the type of man that good sensible handling can make a real asset to Jamaica, whereas shutting him up will only make him bitter and vengeful and won't do any good." Recalling that Hill was once allied with Bustamante, Cripps said that he knew that "Ken Hill's honesty got across Bustamante's crookedness at one time" and hoped that that had nothing to do with his internment.[85] This was an ambiguous comment. Did Sir Stafford mean that Hill was being punished because he criticized and broke with the labor chief, and that the governor was doing Bustamante's bidding? This would have been a preposterous construction of what was transpiring. Bustamante, it should be noted, said nothing during the Railway Union's conflict with the governor, probably because of his antipathy to Manley and the PNP.

The Colonial Office duly considered Sir Stafford's intervention, but not before using Governor Richards's negative assessment of Hill to counter his description of him as "a nice young negro." These officials hoped, however, that the governor would be favorably disposed to releasing the detainees since he, according to another official, was now embarking upon "a liberal and conciliatory policy, i.e. friendship with Manley, release of Domingo, constitutional reforms." The same official admitted that he had "grave doubts as to whether their activities were really subversive." Any optimism that the Colonial Office entertained about an imminent release of the detainees was tempered by the reality that Richards "has always been the most reluctant of all Colonial Governors to show liberality in relaxing detention orders."[86]

Responding to the pressure from the Colonial Office and to Jamaican opinion, Richards lifted the restrictions on the movements of the seven men in question in January 1943. On March 18 he unexpectedly released the four detainees unconditionally. The four jubilant men immediately issued statements thanking their supporters. They had been interned for four-and-a-half months on spurious grounds. Governor Richards kept his silence, but his decision to release the men was a most popular one. The internment of the men and their release concluded another unhappy chapter in Jamaica's march to self-determination. A governor who could not and did not understand their political aspirations saw their quest as subversive and used his power to crush them. But state power was inadequate to the task of silencing or destroying nationalist sentiments.

Jamaica's intellectuals did not constitute a large group, but they were becoming increasingly vocal and noisy in the wake of the workers' revolt of 1938. Most, such as Philip Sherlock, W. A. Domingo, Frank Hill, Roger Mais, were Jamaican born, but others, like E. H. J. King, H. P. Jacobs, and Henry Fowler, hailed from England. Men such as King, Hill, and Mais found an intellectual home in the pages of *Public Opinion*, the most fiery of the organs of opinion. Governor Richards and his intelligence and security personnel monitored the writings of these people, looking for seditious language in the context of the war. Although Richards left the island for Nigeria in 1943, the security machinery that he had created remained in place. The new governor, John Huggins, was more tolerant of criticism and was less confrontational in style. Still, one of the most controversial attacks on one of the island's prominent intellectuals occurred quite early in his tenure in office.

Roger Mais at the time was a playwright, poet, short-story writer, and painter. As a columnist for *Public Opinion*, he had published an article on July 11, 1944, entitled "Now We Know." The government promptly arrested him on a charge of seditious libel. Mais was accused of a breach of the Defense Regulations Act of 1940 for attempting to influence the public in a manner likely to be prejudicial to the effective prosecution of the war. The prosecution maintained that the article would have a negative effect on the campaign to recruit Jamaican soldiers then in progress. The newspaper and its editor, O. T. Fairclough, were similarly charged. The accused were defended by the prominent solicitor H. O. A. Dayes and the popular barrister Norman Manley. The attorney general, T. Henry Mayers, presented the case for the Crown.

The case was followed with great interest in Jamaica and by some members of the Labour Party in England. In his article "Now We Know," Mais condemned the imperial government for not granting a new constitution to the island that included provisions for self-government and the introduction of an Executive Committee that would operate like a quasiministerial system. He criticized Prime Minister Winston Churchill for his defense of imperialism and the domination of "alien races." Mais supported the war against the Nazis, but as the descendant of enslaved Africans, he reserved his harshest criticism for a British Empire that he said rested on the exploitation of other peoples, and he sneered at England's hypocritical embrace of democratic principles. It was a bitter denunciation of the mother country, one destined to invite a coercive retaliation by the colonial state. "Now We Know" spoke some harsh truths and represented the most eloquent attack on the colonial experience ever made by a Jamaican.

> Now we know why the draft of the New Constitution has not been published before. The authors of that particular piece of hypocrisy and deception are the little men who are hopping about like mad all over the British Empire implementing the real official policy, implicit in statements made by the Prime Minister from time to time.
>
> That man of brave speeches has told the world again and again that he does not intend the old order to change; that he does not mean to yield an inch in concessions to anyone, least of all to people in the colonies. Time and again he has avowed in open parliament that, in so many words, what we are fighting for is that England might retain her exclusive prerogative to the conquest and enslavement of other nations, and she will not brook competition in that particular field from anyone.
>
> For it is not the non-dissolution of the Empire that is aimed at—there are free dominions within the Empire—but it is the non-dissolution of a colonial system which permits the shameless exploitation of those colonies across the seas of an Empire upon which the sun never sets.
>
> That the sun may never set upon aggression and inequality and human degradation; that the sun may never set upon privilege and repression and exploitation . . .
>
> That the sun may never set upon the putting of one man's greed before the blood and the sweat of a million . . .
>
> That the sun may never set upon urchins in rags and old men and old women in rags, prostrate with hunger and sores upon the sidewalks of cities and upon straw pallets among vermin in poor-houses and prisons and homes.
>
> That the sun may never set upon the groaning of people of alien races who have been brought the blessings of empire; of famine and plague and the sword . . .
>
> That the sun may never set upon the insolence and arrogance of one race toward all others; and especially to those whose manhood they hold in eternal bondage through their own straw-bosses and quislings and cheap jim-cracks and all the scabs and blacklegs and

yes-men and betrayers of their own whom they can buy for a piece of ribbon to wear on their coats or a medal to wear on their coats or some letters to come after their names or for the privilege of calling some big-wig by his first name "Hello Bill!" "Hello, Charlie, how's the boy!" or with a sinecure of office with access to travelling expenses or with other such scraps which fall unnoticed from the full table where the unholy feast is devoured by their lords and masters.

For such things as these Colonials from all parts of Empire are fighting . . .

For such things as these our young men have added their names to the roll of honoured dead with their mothers and wives and sisters and sweethearts present at the unveiling and proud to honour their dead . . .

For such things . . .

That the sun may never set upon the great British tradition of Democracy which chains men and women and little children with more than physical chains; chains of ignorance and the apathy of the underfed and the submissiveness which is a spiritual sickness in the thews and sinews of a man; chains them in dungeons of gold mines and silver mines and diamond mines and upon sugar plantations and rubber plantations and tea plantations.

For the great idea of Democracy which relegates all "niggers" of whichever race to their proper place in the scheme of political economy:

That we Colonials may ever sing in our schoolrooms those rousing songs like "There'll always be an England" and "Rule Britannia" and the rest . . .

That we might take an equal pride with all English-men in the glory of the Greatest Empire upon Earth; that we may rejoice we are privileged to serve it seeing it couldn't exist without us.

That we may take pride if we are no more that the great hunks of red meat upon which the noble Lion feeds that he might have the great sinews and the fierce blood and the mighty roar to afright his enemies . . .

That we may rise dutifully to our feet and sing with the rest "God Save the King" before we take our seats in the cinema, or after the show . . .

That we might rejoice in our bonds and join in sneering at the great socialist republics which comprise the greatest states upon earth . . .

That we might rejoice in our poverty and degradation and sickness and ignorance and sores; for it is accounted more blessed to be poor.

For such things as these we are fighting side by side with others in the good cause.[87]

When Mais was cross-examined in court by his solicitor, Dayes, he outlined his positions on the Nazis, imperialism, and self-government. These were the issues that animated his thinking, and his opinions on them had made him the target of official attack.

MR. DAYES: When you wrote this article on the Sunday morning, why did you write it?
MR. MAIS: As a protest.
MR. DAYES: What is your attitude towards Nazism and Fascism?
MR. MAIS: I am opposed to those forms of government.
MR. DAYES: What is your attitude to the war? Do you think we should fight it?
MR. MAIS: Oh yes.
MR. DAYES: How important would you regard our victory?
MR. MAIS: It would be a matter of major importance.
MR. DAYES: Do you desire a victory?
MR. MAIS: Of course. I want to say it would be a matter of the greatest importance.
MR. DAYES: Now, is that just an attitude of today, or has it been an attitude against Nazism and Fascism from when?
MR. MAIS: From their inception.
MR. DAYES: What is your attitude, Mr. Mais, towards imperialism?
MR. MAIS: I am opposed to it.
MR. DAYES: To only one kind, or all kinds?
MR. MAIS: To all kinds.

Continuing his evidence, Mais said that imperialism had to lead to "complete self-government."[88]

The opposition to imperialism was considered a subversive act at a time when serious cracks were appearing in the British imperial wall in India and nationalists were ubiquitous in many of the other colonies. Jamaica was no exception, and Mais was one of those who promoted a self-governing island. In delivering his judgment, His Honour, J. L. Cundall, dismissed Mais's "interpretation" of imperialism as appearing "to be a highly imaginative one."

Mais, the judge said, "while indulging in one of his higher flights of fancy, genuinely believed that the motives which prompted him to write and publish the article were good motives, but he has endeavoured to influence public opinion, and to do so in a manner likely to be prejudicial to the war effort." Mais was misguided, the judge concluded, and had been led astray by his reading of "propaganda" he did not understand. Lecturing the brilliant Jamaican, the learned judge said: "You appear to be a great reader, but you seem to be lacking of sufficient mental stability and practical experience to enable you to assimilate and to assess at its true value all that you do read. You have allowed yourself I think to be influenced by a mass of propaganda that you do not properly understand."

This assessment did not lead Judge Cundall to dismiss the case against the muddleheaded accused, as seen through his imperious judicial optic. He sentenced Mais to six months in prison and fined City Printery, Ltd., £200 for publishing the offending column.[89]

When he heard about Mais's arrest, Henry Brinton, a British Labour MP, brought the matter to the attention of Clement Attlee, the party's leader. "I have no doubt," Brinton wrote to Attlee, "that in typical Jamaican manner, Mais wrote something excessively childish and silly. I doubt, however, whether British justice is greatly enhanced or the Prime Minister's [Churchill] reputation increased, by a spiteful and legally dubious prosecution for a show of bad taste under great provocation." Mais was evidently the victim of the educational system, the parliamentarian suggested, albeit sarcastically. "After all," Brinton wrote, "the Imperial government ought to be tolerant of the effects of defective education since it is their business to see that education is not defective." Brinton told Attlee that life in Jamaica in wartime "is anything but pleasant or safe for any politically conscious person." This had been borne out by Governor Richards's assault on political dissent and his affinity for the detention camp. Brinton wanted Jamaican politicians, "who after all are only learning the game, to be treated with courtesy or their views listened to with respect." The colonial administrators, he alleged, "will not admit natives to their club." Governor Richards, he reported, "would slang local politicians like a fish wife but interned anyone who replied 'tu quoque' [you, too]".[90] Attlee did not intervene; Mais was convicted, lost his appeal, and served four months of his time.

Governor Richards did not succeed in silencing dissent, although his actions undoubtedly created an unhealthy climate in the island. His most influential critic, Norman Manley, somehow escaped his coercive net. Manley's internment would have been a veritable coup for the governor, but it would have provoked an island-wide outrage or worse. The Englishman and the Jamaican nationalist sang in different choirs and listened to different ideological orchestras. They held divergent views about Jamaica's future. While Richards was a paid employee of the Crown, working under the terms of a five-year contract, Manley was a Jamaican who had no such escape hatch. Richards was the outsider whose job it was to keep Jamaica stable and safely ensconced in the British Empire. Manley, on the other hand, was a nationalist who was then contemplating self-government and eventually independence for his homeland. The two competing visions of Jamaica's future were irreconcilable.

The two men enjoyed a fragile modus vivendi after their reconciliation. But the guarded trust that had characterized their earlier relationship was never restored. Richards became more strident in his criticism of Manley in his letters to the Colonial Office, and Manley kept his distance from the governor. When Richards was promoted and posted to Nigeria in mid-1943, Manley hastened to offer him his good wishes, assuring the departing governor that Jamaica had seen its worst days. Responding, Richards said he welcomed the "new sphere," noting that "at least it will be free from the damnable inheritances which I found accumulated here." He wished that he could agree with Manley that "the worst of our troubles are past." Emphasizing his doubts, Richards cautioned Manley to "make the sign of the Cross every time you look to your left."

Richards could not resist taking a parting shot at Jamaicans and at Manley. "How hard it is in this happy land," the governor lamented, "to do anything sensible in the interests of the public." He continued to be bothered by the criticism of his administration. "The technique of malicious misrepresentation perfected by the *Gleaner* over two generations and not entirely disdained by the PNP is so easily acquired and is now a distressing and almost universal complaint," Richards alleged bitterly. The governor seemed relieved that he was leaving the island and its problems.

> Personally, as I survey the embattled charlatans and listen to the huckster cries of the Roys [Roy Lindo?] Bobbies [Robert Kirkwood] and Bustas [Bustamante] I think of Pyrrhus. You remember his parting comment—How wonderful a field I am leaving to the Romans and the Carthaginians. In any case, the prayers of the congregation are invited for my successor—the unknown warrior? or the victim of

the sacrifice? Though I must admit I hazard a guess that the sacrificial honours are reserved for you, but I suppose you would perversely insist upon a preference for the martyr's crown over a saintly halo. You have always made a virtue of discomfort.[91]

This was a teasing jab at Manley's political modus operandi. But it was also a tantalizingly ambiguous rhetorical end to the complex relationship between the colonial governor and the seemingly defiant and incorrigible subject.

The people who contemplated a better future for their island homeland challenged the political status quo, frequently using very harsh language. The colonial regime tried to silence them using the coercive power at its disposal. It attempted to destroy the People's National Party by persecuting some of its leaders, hoping thereby to snuff out its nationalist ideology. Governor Richards, in particular, had no tolerance for the voices of protest and dissent. But the empire could not and did not win these confrontations over the long haul. The ideas that promoted and fertilized dissent and nationalist sentiments could not be eradicated by persecution and punishment. Ultimately, the men who suffered internment and the loss of their liberty for their ideas would be absolved at the bar of history.

EIGHT

Constitutional Change

"We are imperialists," the *Daily Gleaner* exulted in an editorial comment on May 5, 1941. "We love the word as well as the thing. We believe in the British Empire . . . and of course imperialism goes with Empire as salt fish goes with ackee, and as avocado pear goes with roasted bread fruit." The *Gleaner* was not engaging in a moment of levity. The newspaper was defending the British Empire from assaults by its critics and proudly proclaiming its endorsement of, and devotion to, imperialism. Jamaica had become a Spanish colony in 1494 and remained so until the English seized it in 1655. Almost three centuries later, the *Daily Gleaner* was expressing its gratitude, and that of many other Jamaicans, for being a part of the British Empire.

It was an extraordinary homage to the empire. In its celebration of the ecstasy of the imperial connection, the *Gleaner* linked it to the Jamaican culinary delights of salted codfish and ackee and avocado pears and roasted bread fruit. This was an intriguing analogy, but many of the newspaper's readers would have found it ludicrous in light of the socioeconomic conditions that produced the rebellion of 1938 and the continuing inequities over which the imperial government presided. Still, the *Gleaner*'s tribute to Britain undoubtedly resonated with the privileged members of the society. Robert Kirkwood, himself a child of privilege, ridiculed the people who former governor Lord Olivier called "the Plutocrats." "Their religion," Kirkwood said, "is the old type of Imperialism, and England is their god, except in such matters as sugar quotas and citrous [citrus] preferences to the U.S.A."[1]

The existing Jamaican constitution was an anachronism at a time when many peoples in the colonial worlds were beginning to demand a greater degree of control over their affairs. This was the case in India, Malaya, Indonesia, and elsewhere. Although the 1938 Moyne Commission was not empowered to address issues of constitutional change specifically, it was generally expected that such matters could not be ignored in the much-anticipated report. Appointed in mid-1938, governor Arthur Richards was sensitive to the rumblings for constitutional change and began to solicit the opinions of the elected members of the legislature on the issue shortly after he assumed his duties. Richards made his request on September 7, 1938, but, as he reported to the Colonial Office, no legislator had responded by February 24, 1939.[2]

The governor was not optimistic that he would receive more than one or two responses, even if he pressed the matter. These legislators had, with the possible exception of J. A. G. Smith, the member for Clarendon, shown scant interest in the constitutional future of the island. Richards was aware, however, of "the inchoate yearnings" for constitutional change among some Jamaicans "and the vote-catching generalities demanding manifold varieties of change which range from an unofficial majority in [the] Legislative Council to complete self government."[3]

Despite his brief tenure in the island, Richards had become very familiar with the weaknesses in the government's administrative structure. His travels throughout the colony exposed him to the grievances of the people and allowed him to form his impressions of them, their aspirations, and their needs. A stern administrator often given to intolerance, Richards was sent to the island in the aftermath of the rebellion to reassert the authority of the imperial regime and to restore the respect of the people. Seen through the optic of the Colonial Office, he was the perfect man for the job. He was fiercely protective of British interests, entertained no criticism of imperial behavior, and was an indefatigable worker. Richards wore the garb of the Colonial Official and believed he knew what was best for His Majesty's subjects, deluging his superiors with recommendations that sometimes reflected his flawed understanding of the people he governed and their political pulse. Despite his sense of superiority and his confidence in his infallibility, Richards welcomed the advice of at least one local personage. He sought out Norman Manley, as we have seen, for advice on constitutional and other matters, but the two men soon developed an almost irreconcilable conflict when Richards began to detain critics of the regime.

But that was all in the future. Richards's first report to the Colonial Office on constitutional matters included a memorandum from Manley "prepared specially at my request." He praised Manley as "the most successful and the ablest barrister in Jamaica," admitting: "I have had many discussions with him during the past six months."[4] Notably, Richards kept his distance from Alexander Bustamante, although both men believed Jamaica was not ready for self-government and that it should not occur for several years. Manley was Richards's intellectual superior, but the two men were able to establish a common ground. Bustamante and Richards had little in common.

Richards held Manley, the exceptional Jamaican, in high regard. But he found "the people of all classes" in the island "extremely vocal and extremely ignorant." The members of the economic elite—the large merchants, estates owners, and the country gentry—were apolitical, in the governor's opinion. "These classes," he wrote, "may think differently on most other subjects [but] are united in a wish to return to full Crown Colony Government." Richards understood these people very well, recognizing that they feared for their future under self-government. The governor showed no such insight into the political moorings of the workers. He concluded, erroneously, that they had no interest in the political life of the island. "The bulk of the labouring classes and many of the middle classes," he wrote, "would like to be left alone." He saw them as being susceptible to the wiles of agitators. Richards identified a third group that he said included clerks, teachers, and professional politicians, as well as "labourers who have been to Cuba, Panama and America, professional agitators with a foreign training, and a sprinkling of educated idealists, fanatics, and men with a colour complex." The governor could not conceal his disdain for "this small group [that] clamours for self government, by which of course it means government by their own group."[5]

This was a caricature of Jamaicans, perhaps an easy way to diminish those who were only seeking to govern themselves. Richards was harshly critical of the previous administrations in the island, particularly of the inefficiency of the Parochial Board system. In Jamaica, Richards complained, "there is no district administration in the ordinary Colonial sense and, and so far as I know, the history of general administration in Jamaica is one of neglect." He claimed that "this is no new condition. It has always been so. Designed under the pseudo-democracy of the Parochial Board system, camouflaged under the cries of elected members, the administration of Jamaica is, and always has been a sham."[6]

This was a stinging indictment of the colonial administration in Jamaica. It was bold, courageous, and factual. Richards stated emphatically that "the problem which faces Jamaica, apart from the economic difficulties and the social chaos indicated by its [high] percentage of illegitimacy, is a complex overhaul and reconstruction of its system of administration." He attributed much responsibility to the government for the 1938 rebellion. Richards was convinced "that an ultimate analysis of the recent unrest . . . would reach beyond economic stress, beyond the facts of hunger and poverty, to a subconscious feeling. That government is possibly too unwilling or indifferent but is certainly unable to look after the interests of the common people." Richards took a long view of the colonial record in the island. "The present state of Jamaica is the logical result of the last hundred years of administration," he declared. "It would be futile to complain," he added, "of the harvest we are now reaping but at least we can try to effect a revolutionary change in our future crop." Richards assured the secretary of state that he did not think it was right "to conceal from you my grave dissatisfaction with the present system by merely attempting to make the best of it."[7]

The governor's description of the Jamaican people and the inefficiency of the local administration had a deep resonance in the Colonial Office. It reinforced in some officials the view that Jamaicans were unprepared for the responsibilities of self-government. Expressing his reaction, one official noted: "The governor says that the people of all classes are extremely vocal and extremely ignorant; that the curse of Jamaica is insularity accentuated by an even narrower parochial outlook, largely fostered and stimulated by the politician for his own ends; and that reckless misrepresentation is the substitute for serious thought and is the common currency of Jamaican politics. I regret that I must agree with this view."[8]

The official accepted the governor's assessment in toto, leading him to adopt an imperious tone.

> It is from such people as these that comes the clamour for a further measure of participation in government. Their excuse for failure to contribute anything to the common welfare is that they have no real power and that their advice remains unheeded, and that this discourages them from all effort. Give us, they say, some actual power in the management of our own affairs and you will see how well we can and will do. An effective answer would be to point to the internal administration of the Island [Parochial Boards] where these people have real power, and where they have shown they have neither the will nor the ability to conduct public business properly. Until they have shown themselves "faithful over a few things" they ought not to expect to be made "ruler over many things."[9]

This was an offensive rationalization for delay on the question of constitutional change. Richards would not have disagreed with such sentiments were he safely ensconced in London. But as the principal colonial administrator in Kingston, he had to be more pragmatic. "My own view, detached from any considerations of present expediency or future policy," he told the secretary of state, "is that the present constitution is quite workable and that it represents as great an advance on the road of democratic control as is warranted by the state of development, political and educational, of the people." His crystal ball had told him, however, that there would be trouble if the island did not take "a direct step forward on the path of self-government before the small circle of dreamers, anti-imperialists and semi-seditious agitators are able to say that the British government has once more given in to fear what it refused to concede to reason." Richards was convinced, he said, that those who were demanding self-government would increase in number and "in violence of demand." He predicted that "in the course of—say—the next fifteen years political relations between the Government and the people will be likely to deteriorate unless a sincere attempt is made to train the Jamaican to take and to make a proper use of responsibility."[10]

The governor's concern for the longevity of the imperial presence in the island led him to recommend constitutional changes that would give Jamaicans more responsibility for the conduct of their affairs. He had discussed such matters with Norman Manley over a period of six months, admitting that "my proposals for reform closely resemble his own." To some extent, the governor noted, "we have doubtless modified each other's views."[11]

The governor proposed a Legislative Council composed of twenty-nine elected members, one from each of the fourteen parishes and five from each of the three counties. The Council would include three ex officio members: the colonial secretary, the attorney general, and the island treasurer. In addition, the governor would nominate eight members, one representing each county and five on general grounds. The proposal provided for the appointment of an "unofficial" president of the legislature by the governor. The elected members would possess the right to initiate legislation on all matters except those directly relating to finance. Significantly, the governor retained the power of the purse, could veto legislation with which he disagreed, and could certify any measure that the legislature rejected. The governor also retained the right to dissolve the Council and call a new election.

The governor's proposal included the retention of a Privy Council. It would comprise four ex officio members consisting of the officer in charge of the troops, the colonial secretary, the attorney general, and the treasurer. The Privy Council would also have five unofficial members who would be nominated by the governor. At least two of these people would be chosen from the ranks of the elected members of the Legislative Council. The governor would preside over the ten-member Privy Council. Governor Richards recommended that if the extended powers accorded to the Jamaicans under the proposed new constitution were "well used," over the next decade they should be granted further responsibilities "on the road to self government."[12]

The governor's proposals represented nothing more than a baby step on the march to political autonomy for Jamaicans. The power of the office of the governor remained essentially unchanged, despite an increase in the number of the elected members of the Legislative Council and their ability to initiate legislation, except those relating to financial matters. Norman Manley's "Memorandum on Constitutional Change for Jamaica" that Richards submitted to the Colonial Office did not depart in any significant way from the governor's proposals. The two men agreed on the composition of the Legislative Council, the role of its members, and the governor's powers. There were two relatively minor disagreements. The governor wanted the legislative term to be five years, while Manley preferred four. Secondly, Richards proposed that the constitution be changed after ten years if it worked well, while Manley suggested four or eight years. As far as membership on the Privy Council was concerned, Manley speculated that the elected members "might be given the right to name three members" to that body. On the other hand, Richards proposed that the governor should have the power to name at least two of the elected members to the Privy Council.[13]

Neither Norman Manley nor Arthur Richards believed at the time that Jamaica was ready for self-government. It is surprising, however, that Manley would have settled for a new constitution that granted so little power to the elected representatives of the people. He reiterated his support for universal adult suffrage, something he had first publicly expressed before the Moyne Commission. Governor Richards proposed the retention of the property qualifications for the suffrage for men until age twenty-five. Women would be accorded the franchise at twenty-five without any restrictions. Manley admitted in his memorandum that he was articulating his own views and not those of the People's National Party. In fact, it is not known whether his party colleagues knew of his discussions with the governor or if he had shown them the memorandum. Many members of the PNP, especially those associated with the Metropolitan Group in Kingston, were demanding immediate self-government. They would never have endorsed their leader's proposals.

As did Richards, Manley warned of dire consequences if the Jamaican people were denied self-government in the future. He recognized, however, that not everyone supported the idea. The "white element," he said, and "the coloured persons who are closely associated with it in interest and sympathy, were definitely averse and hostile" to self-government. On the other hand, there were Jamaicans who supported it on "grounds of natural justice" but who were "skeptical as to the reality of the desire of the Imperial Authority to see Self-Government realized by the subject peoples." Then he asserted that "the few in Jamaica who really know the extent to which resentment, suspicion and class and colour consciousness live beneath the superficial surface of loyalty and good will, realize that a deliberate thwarting of inevitable and proper ambitions will do a harm that may well prove impossible to eradicate."[14]

The Colonial Office seemed favorably disposed to the Richards-Manley proposals because they did not portend a fundamental transfer of power to the Jamaican people. But it preferred to await the Moyne Commission's report before making a decision on a new constitution for the island and its provisions. The problem became more complicated when the Legislative Council voted to consider the question of constitutional change for the island. It passed a resolution on April 11, 1939, establishing a committee to prepare and draft "a political constitution" for the colony, instructing it to bear in mind the precedent of the representative government that existed prior to 1865.

The committee was chaired by J. A. G. Smith, the senior elected legislator, and included all of the Council's fourteen elected members and three of the nominated ones. It held five sessions and presented a majority and two minority reports. The first document—and the one that was adopted by the Council, becoming known as the Smith Constitution—proposed a House of Assembly composed of fourteen elected members. It provided for a second chamber, a wholly nominated Legislative Council consisting of ten members and presided over by the governor, who would possess a casting vote. This document also proposed the creation of a ten-member Executive Committee, with the governor as chairman. Five members of the Executive Committee were to be chosen by the House of Assembly from among its members. The governor would appoint the remaining five members, three of whom were to be officials of the government, and two "non officials." This important committee would assist the governor in preparing the estimates and in levying and disbursing public funds, as well as in general administration. In addition, the committee would advise the governor on all matters submitted to it. It was recommended that the committee "shall be the official organ of intercommunication" between the governor and the two legislative chambers. The proposed constitution accorded the governor the right to refuse assent to any resolution or bill that he thought was not in the country's best interest. The measure had to be submitted, however, to the colonial secretary for his adjudication.[15]

The second document, signed by six members, recommended a House of Assembly with twenty-eight members, two from each parish. The third document endorsed a unicameral legislature of forty members, twenty-six of whom would be elected. Each of the fourteen parishes would elect one member, and the remaining twelve seats would be divided among the three counties. The fourteen nonelected members would include the four principal officers of the government, and the other ten would be nominated by the governor. One of the ten elected members should be appointed by the speaker of the House of Assembly.[16] The committee made no recommendation on the question of universal suffrage, justifying its silence on the ground that the matter was already being considered by the Colonial Office. This was a disingenuous dodge since the elected members' public support for such a measure concealed their private misgivings and their fear that an enlarged electorate would probably mean their electoral demise.

The long-anticipated Moyne Commission's report gave the Colonial Office the cover it needed to stymie any demands by Caribbean peoples for greater control over their affairs. The commission declined to support "the grant of immediate and complete self government based on universal suffrage." It did not believe that a government controlled by the colonized peoples could manage the increased resources that it was recommending for the territories. "At the current stage," the commission maintained, "we attach more importance to the truly representative character of Legislative Councils than to any drastic change in their functions." Accordingly, it recommended that "consideration should be given to the adoption of a Committee system on an advisory basis to give elected representatives an insight into the practical details of government." Since the commission believed that "the elected element" in the Legislative Councils should be "as truly representative as possible," it emphasized that "the object of policy should be the introduction of universal adult suffrage."[17]

Although the *Daily Gleaner*, at times, recognized the inevitability of some kind of constitutional change, it was not enthusiastic about the prospect. It was particularly horrified that self-government might be a possibility. "From complete Self-government for Jamaica, Good Lord deliver us," proclaimed the newspaper on June 20, 1938. Alarmed that such a change could be considered in the wake of the labor rebellion, the influential newspaper asserted that "an advanced Political Constitution, particularly Self-Government, is entirely out of the question when but a few weeks ago the capital of Kingston was threatened by mob rule."[18]

The *Gleaner* evidently believed that by singing the praises of the British Empire, it could dilute the strength of any demand for self-government. "As to the British Empire," one editorial declared, "we firmly believe in its Imperialism; we see no reason whatever why it should be ashamed of the name 'British Empire,' we see every reason why it should be proud of that name."[19] Ignoring the fact that Jamaica was a Crown colony administered almost dictatorially by the governor, the *Gleaner* described the British Empire as "a great and democratic congeries of people steadily moving upward and onward, it stands for what is desirable in human life." Jamaica, the newspaper exulted, was organically linked to Britain "and would not appreciate any radical change." It emphasized that "materially and spiritually the whole set of this island, the trend of its mind and feeling, materially and economically, is Britainward."[20]

The *Gleaner* was oblivious to the impact of African cultures, and to some extent those of India, China, and elsewhere, on the island's cultural and ethnic landscapes. "The fact is that we the natives of Jamaica," the newspaper boasted rather incredibly, "do not regard ourselves as a subject population, but rather as free Britishers, proud of our long connection with the British Empire." H. G. Delisser, the editor, was a white Jamaican and the voice of a small but powerful minority in the island. Some Jamaicans who were unfamiliar with their history of a racialized slavery and colonialism would have agreed. But others would have rejected the *Gleaner*'s claim that they revered England and "her virtues and her traditions with a religious fervour, dissecting often, section from section—not according to colour or creed but according to views and ideas—but determined to assist in the working out of our own future as a constituent part of the great empire to which we all belong."[21]

The *Gleaner* was sanitizing a history that had racism and human exploitation at its core and taking comfort from an imagined empire free from these ills. The newspaper was never sympathetic to any nationalist sentiment in the island. Its fear of self-government for Jamaica informed its position that the legislators should "leave the Constitution issue to be fully and honestly dealt with after the war."[22] This was a recipe for delay, but it did not work. In August 1941 the prime minister of England and the president of the United States issued what became known as the Eight Points. The third point affirmed the respect the two countries had for "the right of all peoples to choose the form of government under which they will live." The *Gleaner* was quick to deny the applicability of the principle to Jamaica, arguing that "the word 'peoples' as used in the sentence . . . could not refer to established colonies: the presumption is that such colonies are already part of and are satisfied to be and to remain constituent elements of the larger whole." The newspaper conceded that it may be wrong in its claim, but "the fact remains that Jamaica has not only been British for three hundred years but has every desire and intention of remaining so."[23] The venerable newspaper was simply out of touch with the sentiments of a sector of the population that it served. It was the ghostly voice of the past.

The elected members of the Legislative Council were certainly aware that the labor rebellion had challenged the status quo and altered the island's priorities. Elected by the miniscule number of persons who enjoyed the franchise, they knew that electoral reforms would follow in the wake of the rebellion, probably threatening their individual electability. An expansion of the franchise was expected to be one of the demands of the workers who were becoming politicized. Acting largely in response to the imperative for self-preservation and not principle, the elected members considered the question of universal suffrage on December 13, 1938. The member for Clarendon, J. A. G. Smith, moved a motion stating "that in the opinion of this Council, the law should be amended so as to provide for universal suffrage." The motion was deliberately vague and did not indicate when universal suffrage was to be implemented. Nor did it say whether any conditions should be attached to its award. One colonial official observed that the motion was loosely worded so that members "could vote for it without doing violence to their real opinion."

The debate on the motion was an exercise in pedestrianism. No one invoked any high-minded principles to justify the granting of universal suffrage, probably because the motion was inspired by the politics of hypocrisy. Harold Allan, the member for Portland, supported a gradual introduction of the franchise. He did not believe "there should be any problem whatever in arranging it in stages." The member for St. Ann, C. A. Little, agreed. Nominated member Sir William Morrison said he was prepared to support the motion "on the understanding that we do not rush it." The government's spokesperson, the colonial secretary, stressed that "government is not at present convinced that a far reaching constitutional change like the one that is covered by this resolution should yet be implemented." Of the twelve elected members present, eleven supported the motion. The member for St. Andrew, Sir George Seymour Seymour, declined to vote. One nominated member, Sir William Morrison, voted in the affirmative, while his colleague, Dr. Lawson Gifford, was the sole negative vote. The other nominated and official members declined to vote.[24]

Reviewing the debate, one colonial official observed rather accurately that he did not "perceive any marked enthusiasm for the proposal." He thought it was "probably all window-dressing."[25] The *Gleaner* was gratified that many of the motion's supporters urged a gradual introduction of the measure. "We are satisfied," the *Gleaner* admitted, "that most if not all of them perceived the inadvisability of anything like universal suffrage at once; and we think they realize that no such change is going to be made in Jamaica." It thought that the elected members voted for the motion because they feared the electoral consequences of a negative vote. Such a vote, the newspaper argued, would provide their opponents with "a formidable if fallacious argument against them."[26]

The hypocrisy that informed the affirmative vote for universal suffrage was confirmed in a private conversation that Governor Richards held with J. A. G. Smith shortly after the measure was passed. "I frightened the life out of J. A. G. Smith the other day . . . by referring to the approaching days of universal suffrage, in private conversation," Richards reported to the Colonial Office. "He looked at me and said, 'But you could never allow that. It would not work and the people are not ready for it.' I replied, 'But look at your own motion in Council, unanimously supported by your colleagues.' 'Ah yes,' he said, 'I did not mean that it could be done at once.'"[27]

The proposed new constitution that the Legislative Council adopted was limited in its vision for a changing Jamaica and retrogressive in its conceptualization. Its principal architect, exponent, and defender was J. A. G. Smith. An indefatigable worker, he lacked Norman Manley's intellectual depth and political foresight. Smith wanted Jamaica to return to the constitution that it possessed in 1865, before it was replaced by the existing one that granted it Crown colony status. Based on an extremely limited franchise, the pre-1865 constitution had provided for a two-chamber legislature, a wholly elected lower chamber, and a nominated upper chamber. The governor possessed the right to veto any legislation to which he was opposed, as well as to "certify" or implement any measure that the legislators rejected. Barbados, Bermuda, and the Bahamas still enjoyed such a constitution, a fact to which Smith constantly referred in justification of the document the Legislative Council was proposing.

Smith was hankering for a constitution that had been in operation seventy-five years earlier. But the island and its needs had changed; some Jamaicans were beginning to demand a greater degree of control over their internal affairs. Although he was an eminent barrister, Smith appeared to equate a return to representative government with the acquisition of power over their own affairs by the Jamaican people. Norman Manley, whose view of the kind of constitution the country needed was still evolving, reminded an audience in Kingston that the constitution the existing one replaced "gave no responsibility whatever to Jamaicans." That constitution, Manley observed, "had been a compromise, an abortion, which gave—and rightly so—no responsibility to the people who then had political power, a narrow little class composed of wealthy men." Manley argued that "anybody who goes back to those days and tries to apply it to the Jamaica of today is living in dreams." He continued:

> What we are aiming at today is not the creation of a small clique of financially strong tyrants to dominate the life of this country. What we are aiming at today is opening the political gates to everybody, and letting the multitudes come in. Why? Because it is only then that the real life of the people, the real heart and soul of the people will find expression.... What is the sense, I ask, of going back to a former generation with its dead problems? To a constitution that was corrupt and stinking before it was destroyed and asking us to seek salvation in that?[28]

These were very harsh criticisms of the Smith constitution, and its architect did not take them kindly. He denounced the reckless statements of the members of a "certain party" and urged Jamaicans to "beware of these false prophets."[29] By 1941 Manley and the PNP had embraced self-government for the island, so they found anathema the Smith constitution's accommodation to colonialism and the governor's retention of a veto power over measures passed by the legislatures. Smith was not a convert to self-government, hence his strong defense of the constitutional proposals that bore his name. The adoption of his proposed constitution would have been largely a retrogressive step.

Governor Richards was careful not to take a public position on any constitutional provisions for the island. But he shared his opinions with the Colonial Office from time to time. The governor's consistently negative view of the Jamaican people and of their leaders did nothing to help their case for constitutional reform in the Colonial Office. In a letter to the secretary of state, Richards identified the "difficulties" that impeded the "gratification" of "some of the craving for a closer share in the work of Government." The first obstacle was "the deep seated mistrust felt by all Jamaicans for each other as well as for government." Jamaicans, the governor said, "are individualists and have not the team spirit.... [T]hey can only combine to destroy and find it hard to cooperate in any constructive effort." Such defects, Richards said, were exacerbated by "the shallow loquacity of the population and the melancholy fact that there is scarcely anyone qualified by experience or fortified by study to discuss constitutional questions." Jamaicans are not given to "serious study" of any issue, the governor complained. "I think it must be harder to talk sense in Jamaica than in any other country in the World," he reported. Richards quoted approvingly a pejorative comment about Jamaicans made by a visitor to the island in 1866. The visitor regretted that "two centuries of British rule had produced few persons of an intellectual standard which, at its maximum point, could be classed much higher than that of a somewhat ill-informed [English] village schoolmaster. At the same time, however, they had acquired just that superficial acquaintance with the shibboleths of Western political thought and practice which can be so irritating." These words, governor Richards declared, "might have been written yesterday. The exceptions are only too few."[30] Governor Richards did not blame British colonial rule and its educational system for these alleged deficiencies.

Richards clearly intended to demonstrate that Jamaicans were not yet ready to control their internal affairs. He singled out two of their most prominent leaders for particular abuse. J. A. G. Smith, he said, was "impervious to reason." He "will oppose anything other than his own proposals" in the legislature and "will employ a life time's practice in the arts of obstruction and misrepresentation to prevent the acceptance of any other proposal." The governor also held an uncharitable view of Norman Manley as a responsible leader. Manley, he said, "controls the People's National Party completely when its activities have a destructive direction, in other words when his desire to lead coincides with their desire to follow."[31] By denigrating Smith, Manley, and the Jamaican people in the eyes of the

Colonial Office, the island's governor was the acerbic voice of a ruling elite distrustful of change but increasingly unable to arrest or contain it.

Governor Richards was never a part of the cheering gallery for Jamaica, instead specializing in abusing the people in his official communications. But his perceptions of the Jamaican people and their leaders, however flawed, were important in shaping colonial policy. The Colonial Office, following Richards's lead, showed no enthusiasm for granting greater political autonomy to the Jamaicans. It did not respond to the Smith constitutional proposals for two years, allowing its architect to accuse the secretary of state of "discourtesy to our Island legislature."[32]

The Colonial Office began to demonstrate greater interest in the question of constitutional change in the island when Lord Moyne became the secretary of state in 1941. He had headed the commission that studied the social and economic conditions in the West Indies in the aftermath of the labor rebellions. Consequently, he brought some understanding of the realities in these islands to his office. In March 1941 he proposed the introduction of universal adult suffrage, admitting that he saw "no reason why this should not be embodied as an integral part of the needed changes." He recommended, in contradistinction to the Smith constitution, a single-chamber legislature with a majority of elected members. It would include nominated members as well as three officials of the government, namely, the colonial secretary, the treasurer, and the attorney general. Lord Moyne proposed granting to the governor the absolute power to veto any measure passed by the legislature to which he was opposed. The governor could also implement any bill that was rejected by the legislature.[33] Lord Moyne clearly did not support any significant devolution of power from the governor to the island's legislature.

J. A. G. Smith was troubled by the proposals that gave the governor absolute control of the legislative process. He denounced Lord Moyne for "treating Jamaicans as if they were very young children." He condemned the proposals as being "repugnant to our intelligence," urging that they "be rejected unanimously." In order to ascertain the public's reaction, the governor asked the elected members of the Legislative Council to convene meetings with their constituents to discuss the proposals. This exercise in direct democracy was not a striking success since the meetings were sparsely attended. The consensus that emerged was that the Moyne proposal should be rejected in its existing form and the Smith constitutional proposals adopted. Accordingly, the Legislative Council rejected Lord Moyne's proposals in August 1941, thereby reaffirming its support for the Smith alternative.[34]

Lord Moyne was hardly pleased by this unusual display of independence by the elected members of the Council. In a dispatch to Governor Richards on January 7, 1942, he expressed his "great disappointment" at the Council's action, conceding that "serious misapprehensions" existed in the island regarding the nature of the "officially sponsored proposal" and "the limits within which I feel bound . . . to confine any scheme of constitutional reform." Fortified in his belief in the efficacy of his proposals, Lord Moyne refused to make any significant concessions to Jamaican opinion. He was aware, he said, of the divisions in the island on "the question of the form and direction which constitutional development should assume." He was referring to such divisions as those concerning a bicameral versus unicameral legislature and representative government as opposed to responsible or self-government. Lord Moyne was emphatic in his reiteration of imperial authority in the island, admitting: "I am unable to entertain any proposals which would have the effect of obscuring the vital distinction between responsible and representative government: the supreme executive authority of the governor must therefore be preserved and it is essential that he should have the necessary powers of 'certification' and of 'veto.'" The secretary of state also rejected proposals from the People's National Party "for the conversion of elected members into Ministers with executive powers and for the limitation of the Governor's powers in respect of legislation."[35]

The secretary of state's uncompromising stance fed suspicions that the Colonial Office was planning to introduce a new constitution by issuing an Order in Council. Accordingly, on March 10, 1942, the Legislative Council approved a resolution asking the Colonial Office to revisit the disputed proposals. It also requested the immediate introduction of an Executive Committee consisting of ten members, of whom five were to be elected members of the Legislative Council and five were to be nominated members. This committee, chaired by the governor, would assist him in the governance of the island.[36]

Jamaica lost one of its principal advocates of constitutional change when J. A. G. Smith died unexpectedly in early 1942. But the country's interest in the question intensified, particularly when the elected members of the Legislative Council, the People's National Party, and the Federation of Citizens' Association agreed to work jointly to achieve a new constitution.

The representatives of these three groups agreed on several main proposals, including:

> a) That the veto power ought not to be in the hands of the governor at all, or if in his hands ought to be limited and controlled by explicit provisions in the constitution and by provision for an appeal to His Majesty in Council.
> b) That any and every power of certification is obnoxious and contrary to the principles of Representative and Responsible Government.
> c) That a progressively increasing responsibility for the conduct of executive affairs ought to be provided for so that a measure of Responsible Government should be provided from the moment the New Constitution comes into force.[37]

The three groups also endorsed a bicameral legislature and the creation of an Executive Committee, "which shall be the principal instrument of policy and shall have power to initiate all laws financial or otherwise." This committee would be responsible for the preparation of the annual budget and all supplementary budgetary expenditures. Ultimately, it would evolve into a Council of Ministers "and shall have plenary powers in local affairs as the Executive Centre of the Constitution of the Colony."[38]

Norman Manley was the principal architect of these proposals, which went far beyond any that had been previously advanced. The political pulse of the island was also changing in the direction of a more-radical constitutional change. The collaboration between the three aforementioned groups made it more difficult for the Colonial Office to ignore local opinion and to introduce a new constitution by fiat. There was also a perceptible change in the Colonial Office, a greater readiness to imagine the Jamaican people exercising more control over their affairs. In contrast, Governor Richards was still showing little respect for the Jamaican people and demonstrating an appalling insensitivity to their aspirations. A memorandum written in mid-1942 in the Colonial Office urged the promotion of "harmony between Jamaicans and their British Government. This cannot be done by impugning the good faith of leaders of Jamaican opinion; by taking careful steps to conceal matters of policy from the Legislature; by accusing Jamaicans of 'unwillingness to cooperate,' 'unconstructive criticism,' and so forth; while at the same time taking great care that the critics are neither given a chance to 'cooperate,' or to prove their worth in any executive or administrative capacity."[39]

This was an unvarnished criticism of Governor Richards and his contemptuous attitude toward Jamaicans. The internal memorandum recommended that the colonial administration should consult with the Jamaican people "and endeavour to take at any rate a decent measure of their advice; and, above all, where that advice must be rejected for reasons of high policy, we should at least use great tact and discretion in so doing."[40] Such an attitude presaged a willingness to accord some weight to Jamaican opinion and not to be as dismissive of it as the sitting governor was wont to do.

Psychologically, the Colonial Office was beginning to realize that the empire's days were numbered. The officials sensed that if they could not contain the rising nationalist tide, they had better work with it. Governor Richards did not experience any such epiphany and was still clinging to the politics of abuse and suspicion. "If we really intend to 'educate' Jamaicans for full Self-Government, it is essential that Jamaicans be permitted to take an active part in charting their own destiny," urged the Colonial Office's internal memorandum. Jamaicans, it maintained, "cannot learn to govern themselves by watching other people at work.... [I]t is only by responsibility that they will learn the sobering effect of power." The memorandum was harshly critical of Jamaica's existing constitution and the proposed Moyne constitution. "Constitutions which, like the Moyne Constitution and the present constitution," it argued, "give Elected Members ample opportunity to obstruct, but no opportunity to construct, are bound to create friction and hinder reform." The memorandum suggested that "the continuance of such procedure is alike contrary to British political principles and the oft-repeated pledges of the Imperial Government that we will 'educate' the Colonial peoples to govern themselves."[41]

The memorandum did not advocate granting the governor the power to veto legislation submitted to him. It feared that since the members of the legislature would be elected on the basis of adult suffrage, "the veto would possibly be required so often as to bring that form of constitution into contempt." The best "brake" on the excesses of the elected legislators, it suggested, would be "that applied by the more conservative, educated Jamaicans upon their own people, by means of a Second, or Upper, Chamber to the Legislature."[42] This was a new idea; no official had hitherto suggested the elimination of the governor's power of the veto in a colony that lacked self-government. But it was one indication of a changing sentiment in the Colonial Office on the question of the governance of colonial peoples.

This new mood was reflected in another internal memorandum written in November 1942. It urged the introduction of a new constitution in Jamaica without delay.

> Such is the internal political condition of Jamaica that I doubt whether the position can be held there much longer without some serious trouble if we proceed as we are doing at present. In addition to the factors working in the island, there are outside influences being brought to bear on the question. The recent statement by President Roosevelt [on the right to self-determination] and the continual allusions to reform in the B.W.I. [British West Indies] in both Houses of Parliament, in the Press and elsewhere, make it desirable for us to show our good faith and not give the impression that we are taking cover under a smoke screen of dilatory improvement of the administrative machine.[43]

The "smoke screen" to which the memorandum referred related to the contemplated reorganization of the local administration in the fourteen parishes. The Parochial Boards had been characterized by their inefficiency, and Governor Richards was advocating reforms. Some officials had argued that constitutional changes should await their adoption. The memorandum rejected procrastination: "If we proceed vigorously towards a new constitution we shall proclaim our good faith to the world, and to the American world in particular, we shall be able to assess the actual strength of the PNP; we shall to some extent avoid the perpetual references to Jamaica in both Houses of Parliament, references which are so disturbing to good government in that island; and we shall at least appear to give some constitutional advance willingly instead of having it dragged out of us as has so often been the case in other constitutional advances elsewhere."[44]

This was an exercise bereft of any larger principle. The needs of the Jamaican people were notably absent from the narrative. But the imperial government's act of benevolence would not go unnoticed, it conjectured. "We may even get some credit for good intentions," the document said reassuringly. "But, above all," it continued, "we may be able to clear the political air in Jamaica and to remove to some extent that curious sense of frustration which appears to be predominant among the most advanced elements in that country." The proponents of constitutional change would have been astonished to hear their frustration described as "curious." But they would have been pleased by the memorandum's conclusion that the awarding of a new constitution "will be the right and proper thing to do." The writer of the memorandum admitted that he had consulted with a colleague who agreed with his conclusions but who made "the very relevant quotation" that "in every political crises it is pace more than principle that I find we have to consider."[45] Jamaica's eventual acquisition of a new constitution would represent the triumph of pragmatism over principle, despite the justice of the island's claim. The pace of the movement toward constitutional change quickened in the fall of 1942. Lord Moyne had been replaced as colonial secretary by Colonel Oliver Stanley, who brought a greater degree of energy and passion to an issue that had increasing resonance in the island.

"One of the greatest stories in the world," the *Gleaner* reported in its issue of February 24, 1943,

> is about the child who on reaching the age of understanding suddenly said to her mother: "I was present at your wedding." The mother as a test replied, "Then will you tell me Dear, what was the most remarkable feature of it?" "I remember," said the child, "that I sat next to Daddy before you arrived and everybody kept staring at me." The mother collapsed because the fact was that at her wedding the seat beside the groom remained vacant, and the groomsman, for no apparent reason, never took it. Everyone remarked on the vacant chair. Several persons stared at a vacant chair in the Legislative Council yesterday. It was the seat of the senior Elected Member, now held by the Hon. Dr. Gordon Veitch who suddenly fell ill. Up to April last year this seat belonged to the Hon. J. A. G. Smith, K.C. deceased, the man whose labours, more than others, created the form of constitution which the Secretary of State has largely approved. Was it coincidence that at the Special session at which the triumph of the Smith Constitution was to be announced, the seat he held in Council should be the vacant one? Was J. A. G. Smith there?[46]

This question cannot be answered definitively, but it is certain that many Jamaicans spent days discussing the intriguing event. A strongly held belief in the existence of spirits and their living presence in society would have lubricated and informed such discussions and speculation. Smith's presence, albeit in the form of a spirit, would not have been unwelcome, given the role that he had played in making such a momentous occasion possible.

The occasion was both serious and festive. "Never has the Legislative Council of Jamaica shown a finer spirit of good will and gratification, almost approaching jubilation," the *Gleaner* gushed. The visitors' seats and the public gallery "were crowded with scores of well known citizens," the newspaper reported as it proceeded to name some of them. Prominent members of the PNP, such as Norman Manley, Vernon Arnett, and Noel Nethersole, were present. Alexander Bustamante, who had played no role in constructing the constitution, was notably absent. Governor Richards was in fine oratorical form. "The problems of the future loom large enough and need no shadows from the past to darken them," he told the gathering.[47]

The day for such jubilation was Tuesday, February 23, 1943. The people had come to the Legislative Council to hear the governor read the text of the secretary of state's dispatch on the draft constitution for the island. They would hear that he had accepted the substance of the 1939 Smith draft constitution that had been rejected by Lord Moyne. The Smith constitution had constituted the basis of a joint memorandum that had been sent to the Colonial Office by the elected members of the Legislative Council, the People's National Party, and the Federation of Citizens' Associations.

The constitution provided for a two-chamber legislature with a House of Assembly, or lower house, of at least twenty-four members, elected on the basis of universal adult suffrage. The Legislative Council, or upper house, would consist of fifteen nominated members, a majority of whom should be unofficial. There would be an Executive Committee of ten members, five of whom were to be members of the House of Assembly, three would be unofficial members of the Legislative Council, and two should be government officials. The governor was to act as the chairman, possessing a casting vote. The Executive Committee was to serve as the principal instrument of policy, having the power to initiate all laws, financial and otherwise. It was accorded the power to prepare the budget and all supplementary budgetary provisions. The Privy Council, which traditionally served in an advisory capacity to the governor, would be eliminated.

The proposed new constitution gave the governor the power to certify—that is to say, to approve—any bill, law, or resolution rejected by the two legislative chambers. He could only do so, however, on the advice of the Executive Committee. The governor retained the power to veto any measure passed by the legislatures. The constitution was to enjoy an experimental period of five years, after which it would be reviewed and further advances to self-government granted, if warranted.[48]

The secretary of state invited the elected members of the Legislative Council, the People's National Party, and the Federation of Citizens' Associations to review the draft constitution and to submit their responses to it. The Colonial Office was particularly interested in the views of Norman Manley, the Jamaican the officials held in the highest regard. They believed that Manley's support for the constitution's provisions would influence other Jamaicans to accept them. On February 16, a week before the governor revealed the details of the new constitution, the Colonial Office inquired whether he had "disclosed to Manley any particulars of the proposals and if so what was his reaction." Replying two days later, Richards said he had not done so since he thought it would "be very undesirable to favour him with special advance information."[49] Imbued with a sense of superiority over the colonized subject, no matter how eminent, Richards would never have taken Manley into his full confidence on such a consequential matter.

In order to ensure Manley's endorsement of the constitutional provisions, the Colonial Office solicited the assistance of distinguished socialist and Labour MP Sir Stafford Cripps. A friend of Manley's, Sir Stafford had given the keynote address when the PNP was founded in September 1938. Moreover, he was supportive of the party's quest for self-government. In spite of these credentials, Sir Stafford agreed to do the bidding of the Colonial Office, guaranteeing Manley's acceptance of the constitution. He drafted a letter to Manley that the Colonial Office dispatched to him by telegram. Sir Stafford told Manley that he regarded the proposals "as a very progressive and marked advance along the right road," adding: "I may say for your private and confidential information that it is not (repeat not) put forward as a basis for any bargaining but as the maximum to which the government is at present prepared to go. I believe it goes as far as the people of Jamaica can step in a single stride. I trust that you and all my friends in Jamaica will accept this genuine offer of the government which has my fullest approval and for which I have been working as you know."[50]

Manley's response was immediate. "Reasonably certain constitution will be accepted on all major points," he telegraphed Sir Stafford.[51]

The Colonial Office must have congratulated itself for securing Sir Stafford's support for the constitution and in helping to mute Manley's criticism of it. By writing to Manley and endorsing the constitution, he was letting Manley know that he could not expect his support should he criticize or, worse, reject the constitution. Sir Stafford was doing his duty for his king and his country. But Manley did not know that his esteemed friend and the Colonial Office were speaking with one voice.

Norman Manley was not particularly enthusiastic about the provisions of the new constitution because they did not go far enough in the direction of self-government. But he held his tongue. The elected members of the Legislative Council and the Federation of Citizens' Associations had more-limited goals, hence their more-favorable reaction to the proposals. Members of the Council welcomed the new responsibilities but were humbled by the challenges they thought the country would confront. Dr. E. E. Campbell, the member for Kingston, believed that universal adult suffrage posed "the greatest danger to the successful working of the new constitution. . . . [T]he danger lies in the fact that illiteracy being so high as it is at the present time, emotion and sentiment may overwhelm sound judgment." Others cheered its implementation as a positive development for the society. Dr. Oswald Anderson, the new member for St. Andrew, was worried about the country's future in the British Empire. "Our aim is to bind us nearer to the heart of the British empire," he said, and to "help us to manifest our worthiness of being considered an integral part of the British empire."[52] Jamaica was on the path to self-government and independence, but Anderson was still psychologically tethered to the empire.

The governor's possession of the power of certification and veto bothered some legislators, but others saw it as an imperial right. The member for Trelawny, the Reverend J. W. Maxwell, agreed that "the power of certification should rest with the Governor, since he is ultimately responsible to the Secretary of State for the good government of the country." On the other hand, the member for St. James, A. B. Lowe, complained that "at this time of our existence when we are fighting for Democracy, it was most inopportune and undesirable that more power should be given to any one man, whatever his position might be." Alexander Bustamante did not express an opinion on the new constitution, at least not publicly.[53]

There are a number of extant candid and unedited comments from other members of the public. These were taken from the correspondence of Jamaicans with overseas friends and family members. In the two weeks following the announcement of the provisions of the constitution, Jamaican censors opened 17,000 letters that were mailed to overseas addresses. This was a power the government had accorded itself as a security measure during wartime. The censors duly copied excerpts from these letters that commented on the new constitution, forwarding them to the administration. They found a number of references to the constitution, dividing them into "enthusiastic comment," "favourable opinions," and "negative comments." These comments, the censors' report said, "emanated mainly from persons who are known to be actively connected with political parties in Jamaica, and who would, ipso facto, pass an opinion on the New Constitution."

The comments that are reproduced here provide an optic into the pulse of a group of Jamaicans on the constitutional issue. They capture their support for it, their fears, and even their criticisms of the Colonial Office. Notably, some critics were dismayed by Bustamante's potential political ascendancy, facilitated by the provisions of the new constitution, particularly the granting of universal adult suffrage.

ENTHUSIASTIC COMMENT

"We are of course delighted to have got this five-year trial Constitution, for it is a step towards what we are striving for, and those of us who really love JAMAICA have got to pull together and try to make our trial period one of success, to prove that we have got men capable of governing the Island."

FAVOURABLE OPINIONS

"The proposed NEW CONSTITUTION is the topic of the day! Whatever may be the defects or insufficiencies of it, there is no doubt that it is a big step in advance and will require of JAMAICANS much sane thought and action during the five years of probation, or experiment."

"The new constitution has received more than a favourable, almost ballyhoo press. . . . There appears on all sides to be a genuine determination to use it with constructive good-will and in the best interests of JAMAICA and of good relations between Government and people and JAMAICA and GREAT BRITAIN."

"I suppose you've heard over the radio of the proposed New Constitution for Jamaica. Public opinion is in favour of it, and, on the whole, I think the attitude of the Colonial Office is much more sympathetic and considerate towards us now, than it was up to even a year ago."

"We have been let go of half-way up the hill, and it remains to be seen, whether we roll down again, or bravely struggle on, under our own steam, until we reach the top. Personally, I am not very optimistic about it."

"Everybody is excited about our new Constitution and conjecturing what the outcome of so much liberty will be."

NEGATIVE COMMENTS

"There are the usual clique who are smirking over the whole thing and predict the crawling on our bellies at the end of the five years, begging for the old regime."

"Our great Colonial Office, who do not understand WEST INDIAN things a bit, give them enough encouragement to make them bold."

"In a colony like JAMAICA, where slavery has only been abolished for the last 100 odd years and the majority of our people are still hopelessly illiterate and ignorant, they are not fit for self-government, but still want careful nursing."

"[T]he men who should engage in politics will not stir themselves, so the power will fall into the hands of the rabble. BUSTAMANTE is going to run for Council Member and has put up his two girl assistants [Miss Longbridge and Miss Nelson] to do the same."

"We have a marvelous new Constitution here now and the result theoretically is UTOPIA, practically the only change is a large number of extra 'jobs' and enormously increased salaries of all the top-notchers."

"BUSTAMANTE is priceless, he is going to put up his 2 devoted women secretaries [Miss Longbridge and Miss Nelson] and himself and other duds from his crazy trade union gang. The tragedy is that he can still sway the masses in the country parts and if his bunch of imbeciles got in, the whole show would be wrecked at once, as there isn't one with the brain of a rabbit among them."

The promulgation of the new constitution scaled a major hurdle when the Colonial Office announced on June 2, 1943, the acceptance of thirteen of the fourteen amendments that had been proposed by the elected members of the Legislative Council, the People's National Party, and the Federation of Citizens' Associations. The one remaining issue to be decided was the name of the upper house. The Colonial Office had disagreed with naming it the Senate. The amendments were relatively inconsequential, such as the renaming of the Executive Committee as the Executive Council and the House of Assembly as the House of Representatives.

There would, however, be a final but major dispute between the Colonial Office and the Jamaican political parties that left bruised feelings in the island. By mid-1944, the Colonial Office had decided to retain the Privy Council in the new constitution and reconsidered the role of the Executive Council. Its function was not to be defined in the constitution, allowing the governor to use that body as he determined. The council would not serve as the principal instrument of policy, although the governor was required to consult it in its formulation. The governor was not bound by the council's advice, however. Outraged by this volte-face, Manley denounced it as "a breach of promise." It "is most unpleasant business," he declared. "I for one am not surprised. The lessons of Imperialistic history are there for all to learn whose eyes are not blinded and whose ears are not deaf." The PNP later submitted a formal protest to the Colonial Office, and so did the Jamaica Labour Party, which had been founded the previous year.[54]

The new governor, Sir John Huggins, tried to mollify critics by pointing out that the instructions accompanying the final draft of the constitution would be consistent with what was included in the draft constitution announced on February 23, 1943. This was an exercise in obfuscation. Norman Manley was absolutely accurate in his condemnation of the final draft.

> Now the truth of the matter is that the new constitution contains no provision at all whereby the Executive Council will be the principal instrument of policy for Jamaica. They have gutted out of it all we fought for in five years. What have they done? They promised that the Privy Council should disappear and another body, which would be assisted by the Government, would take its place. And right on the first page, of the [final] draft Constitution, the heading is Privy Council and . . . the duties to be performed by the Privy Council were the same as the duties which were to be performed by the Executive Council, which we suggested should take its place.[55]

The Colonial Office had won. Governor Richards may have played a role in effecting the volte-face, but this remains a suspicion. He was never a strong advocate of any devolution of power to the Jamaican people. Accepting the revised constitution as a bitter fait accompli, Manley urged his party to work for its success. "Let us work together so that the future will establish our claims for a higher and better thing," he advised. "We would be putting down everything we stood for if we did not support it fully. I am confident that the whole party will accept the New Constitution in that spirit and will work for it in the confidence that it will succeed."[56]

Jamaica's new constitution was promulgated on Monday, November 20, 1944. The governor did so before a vast crowd of some 40,000 persons assembled at South Parade and representing "the masses and the classes" of the island, according to the *Daily Gleaner*. "The enthusiasm of the tremendous crowd," the newspaper reported, "knew no bounds." The island's dignitaries were present, and the politicians were cheered as they took their reserved seats. Norman Manley, the most prominent advocate of self-government and the man whose views carried the most weight at home and in the Colonial Office, was not seated with the other luminaries. He was probably trying to put a symbolic distance between himself and the nature of the constitution that was being promulgated. Manley, according to the *Gleaner*, "received the widest acclaim, for unlike other persons of prominence, he went to the top of the [Kingston] Parish Church clock tower overlooking the entire scene and waved his hand to the vast crowd below. His presence was quickly observed and his greeting responded to by thousands with vociferous and prolonged applause."[57]

This was a gracious tribute to Manley. Along with the crowd's enthusiasm that the *Gleaner* observed, it noticed at times "an atmosphere of subdued thanksgiving and uncertain hopefulness."[58] This mood was understandable; it was the first fledgling step on a journey that would not end until August 1962, when Jamaica became an independent nation.

It was nothing if not a grand occasion. The Right Honorable Oliver Frederick George Stanley, the secretary of state for the colonies, was visiting Jamaica to open the legislature consequent upon the grant of a new constitution. Arriving in Kingston by plane from the Bahamas on January 3, 1945, the eminent representative of the imperial government was greeted by 20,000 cheering Jamaicans, who packed King Street and its environs for his momentous entry into the commercial heart of the city. They had begun to assemble early in the morning by the hundreds, swelling to thousands by one o'clock. People waited on the sidewalks and on rooftops to cheer the visiting dignitary. Buildings had been painted, stores decorated, shrubs planted, and streets swept clean for the occasion.

The crowd warmly applauded the politicians as they arrived for the welcoming ceremony, reserving special excitement for Alexander Bustamante, who "smilingly bowed his acknowledgment." Three weeks earlier, the political party that he founded had won the first election held under the aegis of universal adult suffrage. Accordingly, he would be the most important and powerful member of the new legislature. Ironically, Bustamante had played no role in the initial movement for constitutional change in the island that ultimately led to self-government and independence. As late as January 1943 he was telling the American diplomat Paul Blanshard: "I don't want independence for the island. I don't want to throw the British out. I could be Prime Minister if the people got the vote. But I don't want to take that office. I want more power for the people under the constitution, but I don't want to cut off Jamaica from Britain." But such comments were of little import on this special occasion. The *Gleaner* described the scene when Stanley and Bustamante met:

> All eyes were turned on Colonel Stanley as he shook hands with Labour Leader Bustamante. The two men were conspicuously tall: Colonel Stanley was a Crown taller than his Excellency [the governor] who is considered a very tall man. Both the Secretary of State and the Labour Leader have hair that has turned white; when they met, however, Alexander Bustamante after catching Col. Stanley's hand in a firm grip, bowed to his waist, a sweeping bow that left Colonel Stanley towering above him. If anything the smile of the Secretary of State was broader and more infectious than before and he raised his voice as he spoke to Mr. Bustamante, returning with interest the cordiality of the handshake he had received: then he passed on, and Mr. Bustamante straightened up, a look of appreciation on his face.[59]

The welcome that the Jamaicans accorded the visiting official was as enthusiastic as it was heartfelt. That 20,000 persons greeted him was a testimony to their fealty to the Crown and the excitement that Colonel Stanley's visit engendered. Bustamante's bow to the secretary of state invites comparisons with Cudjoe's reportedly kissing the feet of the British official upon the signing of a peace treaty in 1739. Cudjoe, the leader of the Maroons in Accompong, St. Elizabeth, led a series of military conflicts with the British overlords, fighting them to a standstill. Cudjoe, it is said, concluded the signing of the peace treaty by an extraordinary act of obeisance: the kissing of the feet of the Crown's representative, Colonel Guthrie. Bustamante "bowed to his waist, a sweeping bow" when he greeted Colonel Stanley, making, as did Cudjoe, a symbolic gesture of respect and obeisance. Neither Colonel Guthrie nor Colonel Stanley reciprocated the gestures, thereby maintaining the boundaries of superior and subordinate that lubricated and legitimized the colonial relationship.[60]

The effusion of fervor for the imperial connection continued at a civic reception for Colonel Stanley that was held at the Ward Theatre a day after he arrived in the island. "Never a welcome so sincere and fervid, never a response as universally appealing and satisfactory to a population as were enjoyed in a thronged Ward Theatre—and by thousands who listened over the radio," exulted the *Daily Gleaner*. Once again, thousands of Jamaicans gathered to welcome the imperial visitor, following the proceedings in the Ward Theatre by loudspeakers. The civic address that was read to Colonel Stanley affirmed the colony's loyalty to the Crown. "The people of this ancient Colony," it read, "are very proud of its traditional loyalty to the British Crown and its readiness to respond to the mother country's call in any hour of need." When Colonel Stanley traveled to the legislature to officially open it on January 9, he was once again greeted by thousands of Jamaicans who "thronged the roadways."[61]

Colonel Stanley was the first secretary of state for the colonies to pay an official visit to Jamaica. By 1944 Jamaica had been a British colony for approximately 290 years. It had begun to take its first tentative steps on the path to self-government, but most Jamaicans were still psychologically tied to the British empire. The struggle to obtain a new constitution had been waged by a small group of intellectuals, some members of the Legislative Council, the People's National Party, the Federation of Citizens' Associations, and a few others. But it lacked a deep and pervasive popular appeal and emotional resonance. "This thing to me is a religion," Norman Manley had said of self-government. But he was not yet speaking for the majority of Jamaicans.[62]

Most people had not yet made the psychological leap from being "Britons" to defining themselves as Jamaicans, if the latter appellation were accorded a national, in contradistinction to an ethnic, meaning. H. S. McGrath of Charlemont captured this profound and continuing identification with the empire and the pride in being a "Briton," especially in time of war:

Rally, Britons round the Banner
Of our Empire's fair renown,
Tho' it waves o'er many nations
One its cause and one its Crown
Over Continent and Ocean.
Let your plaudits loudly ring,
British hearts and British voices
Have one watchword, "God save the king."

Rally, round the dear old Banner
In the hour of storm and grief.

Union is the balm of sorrow,
Loyalty is war's relief
Foes may envy and insult us,
Proudly back their sneers we fling.
Earthly powers can never harm us
If our cause is "God and King."

Rally, Britons, round the Banner
Emblem of the Free and Brave
Rise the swords of might and Empire
Only to protect and save;
Countless swords for freedom flashing,
Myriad loyal hearts will sing,
One our cause and our watchword
For the right of "God and King."[63]

By itself, the new constitution could not create in any Jamaican a new national identity in opposition to that of being a Briton. Bustamante's dramatic act of obeisance to Colonel Stanley was not an aberration. Still, the construction of a Jamaican nation and a vibrant and abiding sense of Jamaicanness was in progress.

NINE

Party Politics

"I am not a labour leader," Norman Manley declared to the large crowd that assembled to hear him on May 26, 1938. The barrister had volunteered to mediate the labor-inspired rebellion on the waterfront in Kingston. Hitherto, Manley was not identified with labor's cause, but he had stepped in to fill the vacuum created in the leadership of the nascent labor movement by the arrest of Alexander Bustamante. Experiencing an epiphany, Manley became deeply immersed in the workers' struggle for social justice. Two days after his declaration that he was not a labor leader, Manley was able to say that "now is the golden opportunity for forming a Labour Party in Jamaica."[1] The planning to create such a party was under way, he announced.

Norman Manley, to be sure, was not apolitical. He was, for example, president of the Jamaica Welfare League, an organization of middle-class people founded in the 1930s to promote social and civic reforms in the island. Manley had eschewed any interest in electoral politics, however, preferring to concentrate on his very active and successful professional career. In 1937 he rejected an invitation to stand as a candidate for a seat on the Kingston and St. Andrew Corporation. As he told his colleague O. T. Fairclough, "The problems of Jamaica, my dear Fairclough, are social and economic, not political." The labor rebellion and his role in helping to resolve it sensitized him to the need to be more actively engaged in the political life of the country. As Manley admitted in 1942, "I had no previous political experience but my work for labour in the 1938 troubles convinced me of the need for organized political action devoted to the interest of the working class and small peasant." Hitherto, Manley confessed, he "was a theoretic socialist handicapped by middle class reflexes."[2]

A Fabian socialist, Manley was an admirer of the British Labour Party, using it as a model for the one he wanted to found in Jamaica. Marcus Garvey had formed the short-lived People's Political Party in 1929, but the island had no functioning political party in 1938. The members of the

Legislative Council and the Parochial Boards of the parishes contested elections as individuals, not as candidates representing a political party.

The first major public step on the road to founding a new political party occurred on August 10, 1938. The occasion was "a crowded meeting" at Collegiate Hall in Kingston convened by the National Reform Association. Several prominent individuals attended, including Alexander Bustamante, Kenneth Hill, H. P. Jacobs, and Mrs. Mary Morris Knibb, a well-known social worker. Manley, the guest speaker, explained his involvement in the meeting: "I am not a professional politician. I have never, myself, taken any active part in politics as they exist in Jamaica today. But I am speaking as a Jamaican to Jamaicans. I am speaking as one who believes in the future of this country and as one who has watched and thought over it for many years. I have not myself any axe to grind; but I have ambitions for the thousands who, I know are more alive than ever today for the need for unity in this country."[3]

Despite Manley's disclaimer, this was really his first foray into Jamaica's political arena. Unlike those Jamaicans who wanted to minimize the significance of the labor rebellion and saw it as the work of agitators, he believed it was "symptomatic of a great awakening and a real feeling in the people which, though without knowledge, or aim, or direction, sprang from a deep sense of wants, and from a deep longing for a greater unity and a greater share in belonging to a people as a whole."[4]

Manley believed that some people had "witnessed the awakening of a moral sense, a moral energy and a moral desire to do something." A political party, he argued, would promote unity and collective action to address the country's problems. The party that he contemplated was "a party of the people, a party of the basic elements of the country out of which the future of the country must be built up."[5]

Jamaica's first truly modern political party was launched at a meeting held at the Ward Theatre on September 18, 1938. Alexander Bustamante was on the platform, along with the prominent attorney Noel Nethersole; C. A. Little, the member of the Legislative Council for Manchester; H. Anglin Jones of the Jamaica Union of Teachers; and others. The keynote address was delivered by Sir Stafford Cripps, the renowned socialist, parliamentarian, and member of the British Labour Party. Manley and Cripps, reported the *Gleaner*, spoke to "a gathering sufficient to fill the theatre and crowd [in] North Parade and Victoria Gardens, thrilled to the most vital analysis of present conditions that has ever been offered to our community."[6]

Manley was at his rhetorical and inspiring best, as befitting the moment. The People's National Party, as the new party was named, was destined to play an important role in Jamaica's history. "It is called the People's Party," Manley said, "because it will unswervingly aim at all those measures which will serve the masses of the country." It is true, Manley declared, "that there is a common mass in this country whose interest must predominate above and beyond all other classes because no man is democratic, no man is a sincere and honest democrat who does not accept the elementary principle that the object of civilization is to raise the standard of living and security of the masses of the people."[7]

Explaining the presence of the word "national" in the party's nomenclature, Manley said that "if this country, if this little island of ours is to be consolidated together and bettered, it must be by developing the idea of Jamaica as a national whole. And the party is pledged to the development of that national spirit." The party was conceived in the aftermath of the May and June rebellion, Manley said, because it was clear that "the institutions of this country had long ceased to lead public opinion or to inspire confidence in any quarter in this island." He had noticed the growth of a nationalist spirit, "the most hopeful thing in Jamaica today." Jamaicans confronted the challenge of "the hard road of political organization, facing the hard road of discipline, developing your own capacities, your own powers and leadership and your own people to the stage where they are capable of managing their own affairs."[8]

The PNP would be "modeled on strictly democratic lines," Manley announced. It was going to create independent party groups throughout the island, and they would be entitled to representation in all of its councils and conferences. The party planned to educate the people regarding "the true position they should occupy and to what they should expect of their democratic institutions." It wanted to see the emergence of an informed electorate that was not subject to the influence of demagogues. Manley said he knew the party faced much opposition, but

> if we never desert our own principles, if we believe in what we are aiming at, if we appreciate those who regard this country as their home, those who believe that a real civilization is possible for people of mixed origin, if we never allow people to deflect us from our course, those who would like to continue to live in the feeling that Jamaica is the grandest little country to make their living in, and the nicest country in the world to have a holiday in—if we can do those things and be true to what we believe in, true to the ideals that we have started, and if we can combine that with hard work and practical

intelligence, and with a readiness to do that work and show that intelligence in our own affairs, then I believe we will have launched tonight a government which as nothing else started in Jamaica, will make of this country a real place that our children and our children's children will be proud to say "we come from Jamaica."[9]

Although the PNP was a nationalist party, Manley did not think "that Jamaica is today ripe for self-government, but I claim that we must start a movement working which will help us to become ripe for it." There was no revolutionary content in Manley's speech. The PNP was committed to improving the condition of the poor and to a gradual march to self-government, objectives that were neither utopian, politically injudicious, nor subversive. Still, they would generate opprobrium from the defenders of the status quo.

Sir Stafford Cripps electrified the audience by reminding it that

> the whole administration of a colony as things exist today must always be determined primarily by the imperial needs of the Empire. That is why self government is withheld in so many cases especially where the numerical majority of the people are not white in colour. And when that is so, the interests of the Jamaican people must naturally give way, as long as the present system of colonial government rules in our Empire. . . . [H]owever humanitarian the administration of the colony may be in any particular instance, they are not run as a charity by the Mother Country. They are run because certain vested interests make a very good thing out of them.[10]

These were strong words emanating from a respected member of the British Parliament, words far more critical than anything Manley dared to say unless he wanted to be charged with sedition. Sir Stafford hoped that the PNP would work to achieve "the happiness and prosperity of the common people." He urged harmony between "industrial and political organizations," namely, the unions and the political parties. But Sir Stafford warned that they should "possess two different lines of approach" and "a different personnel in charge of each." Although he did not urge the granting of self-government to the island, Sir Stafford spoke approvingly of the need by human beings for economic and political freedom. "It is essential," he stressed, "that the policies of the government should be based exclusively upon Jamaican interests and upon those Jamaican interests that affect the common people." The visiting parliamentarian said he had "no desire to flatter," but he had not "come across any more experienced, wiser, better equipped, more honest or a more able a leader than you have in Mr. Manley in Jamaica."[11]

The PNP's constitution explained its founding objectives. The party was created, it said, "to secure and extend the liberties, to protect the interests, and to develop the national life and prosperity of the people of Jamaica as a whole." It wanted to promote "the organization of Jamaica into a country of small settlers, farmers and workers" and "the development of a planned policy for the social and economic future of the colony." The party was dedicated to achieving "political self determination and responsibility" for the island "as a national unit." The constitution did not formulate a program for the achievement of its objectives, but Manley explained that in keeping with the party's democratic principles, a policy statement would come only after its membership had met and developed one. Along with Noel Nethersole, H. P. Jacobs, and others, Manley undertook a speech-making campaign to educate Jamaicans about party politics, the PNP, and its plans for the country. He recalled that "the real work of the first year was conveying the idea of the need for a Party and what party politics implied. . . . I think I addressed about 200 meetings that year, all on the same topic."[12]

Norman Manley's corpus of speeches illuminates the ways in which the party leader tried to foster a national consciousness in Jamaica. It was hardly an easy task, given the fact that the island's peoples were socialized into being British and members of the British Empire. A sense of Jamaicanness, if one existed at all, was secondary to the two larger identities. To many, Jamaica was the place where they lived, not a signifier of a national identity, because the island had no independent political existence; it was owned by the British. England, the Crown, and the empire demanded the people's fealty; together they provided the wellsprings of the colonial people's affection and identity. Manley recognized the salience of these identities when he addressed a meeting at Lacovia in December 1938. He explained that "the reason why some people did not like the idea of self government was that they did not feel themselves to belong to Jamaica. They were the sort of Jamaicans who said they were 'going home' when they meant they were going to England. Any man who got on a train [plane?] outward bound from Jamaica and said he was 'going home' was not a national of this country."[13]

Manley obviously had a valid point, and therein resided one of the fundamental challenges that the newly formed nationalist party confronted.

How could it influence such people and others like them to begin to think of themselves as Jamaicans and be proud of that self-definition?

Understanding that Jamaicans needed to develop a national consciousness, Manley had included the word "national" in the party's nomenclature. The speeches that he gave in the aftermath of its founding urged the cessation of debilitating suspicions and divisions among the Jamaican people. He wondered whether "the time will ever come in this country of ours when we will put aside these jealousies and these suspicions and be prepared to stand together as a united people and really work as a group for our own salvation and our own destinies. . . . I think every thinking man realizes in this country that until we can achieve unity among the people to whom this country belongs we cannot go forward along the proper road of our own destiny; we cannot achieve our fullest development as a people."

Manley understood the factors that impeded the creation of the national spirit that he desired. He identified interclass and intraclass divisions as major obstacles. These difficulties had to be surmounted because "if there was a national spirit in a country, the humblest man from the poorest class, and the greatest man from the highest class were all nationals of one country and regarded each other as such."[14]

Led by Manley, the PNP initially maintained that Jamaicans were not yet ready to undertake the responsibilities of self-government. Manley's first detailed statement on the question came in a letter that he wrote to the Reverend Ethelred Brown, the secretary of the Jamaica Progressive League of New York, on September 15, 1938. "I believe," Manley wrote, that

> a) Jamaica should definitely aim at achieving responsible government. It is necessary to start working for that aim immediately.
>
> b) I believe that in the existing state of political development and consciousness in the Island it could not now accept that responsibility and has no chance of getting it conceded.
>
> c) I believe that there should be an intensive development of the political education and life of the country through the medium of a political party so that a foundation for the future may be laid and I believe that that foundation can be laid in the existing circumstances.[15]

Manley assumed the principal responsibility for this political education of the Jamaican people. Addressing the biannual meeting of the St. Mary Federation of Citizens' Associations held at Port Maria in November 1938, he declared: "I have said it before and I will say it again that aiming at self government the People's National Party does not pretend to say that we are, at this very minute, ripe for self government. We are not ripe for it because we have not learnt unity, and discipline, and organization. We are not fit for such a government until we sweep away the stupid class prejudice and until we can unite in a common platform and until we can get cleaner and more honest politics and cleaner and more honest politicians."[16]

The PNP's position on the timing of self-government evolved throughout 1938 and 1939. Unlike the PNP, the Jamaica Progressive League, the acknowledged principal organized voice of Jamaican nationalism, advocated the immediate acquisition of self-government and Dominion status for the island. The Jamaica branch of the League was established in 1937 and became an affiliate of the PNP when it was founded almost a year later. Speaking at a public meeting in January 1939, W. Adolphe Roberts, the president of the New York branch, observed that "the Party is by no means committed to immediate self government, but in advocating its own more radical policy, the League is by no means disloyal to the party." In his address to the meeting, Manley confessed that when Roberts had discussed the question of self-government with him a year earlier, he "had not seen it." But he "had travelled in his own mind a long way in 12 months," doing so "with the country and not away from it." The PNP, he said, wanted the development of an organization as "the forerunner of self government." The PNP and the Jamaica Progressive League, Manley stressed, possessed the same "aims and ambitions" for the island.[17]

Manley was certainly educable on the question of self-government for the island, but he was an opponent of immediate Dominion status and independence. Seeking to remain on good terms with Governor Richards, he assured him: "I am not an imperialist. I have never disguised my views on that. At the same time I am not a believer in independence for Jamaica. . . . [I]t is utterly and childishly impracticable." Manley and the PNP, however, continued their evolution on the question of self-government, and by January 1941 the process was complete. "The great and overwhelming reason why Self-Government is imperative for a people," Manley told a huge gathering at the Ward Theatre on January 15, 1941, "is that without it, it is impossible to achieve real unity and impossible for the people of the country to grow into manhood." The audience applauded when he declared that "the only test of the fitness of a people for Self-Government is their own demand for it, their own willingness to accept the responsibilities of it." Jamaicans, Manley said, "were tired of being preached at, they were tired of being insulted in their own country."[18] Several months later, the PNP adopted its stirring anthem, "Jamaica, Arise!" The lyrics both reflected and shaped the party's nationalist orientation and spirit.

> The trumpet has sounded
> My countrymen all!
> So awake from your slumbers
> And answer the call.
> The torch has been lighted
> The dawn is at hand.
> Who joins in the fight
> For his own native land?
>
> Land of my birth, I pledge to be
> Loyal and faithful, true to thee.
>
> Oh! The toll will be heavy,
> And the campaign long,
> The road will be dreary,
> The barriers strong.
> Our progress may falter,
> And energies wane,
> But steadfast in spirit,
> Our goal we will gain.
>
> Land of my birth I pledge to be
> Loyal and faithful, true to thee.
>
> In steadfast assurance
> That God will look down,
> And give us His blessing
> Our efforts to crown.
> Let us all be united
> To build by His grace,
> A nobler Jamaica,
> A loftier race.
>
> Land of my birth I pledge to be
> Loyal and faithful, true to thee.

The PNP's membership grew steadily throughout its first year. Fifteen months after the party's formation, Manley was able to report to its first national convention that 157 groups had been established. This was a remarkable achievement, but he was not satisfied with the overall support the party was receiving. "It is astonishing how difficult it is to get people to come forward to help," Manley wrote to Sir Stafford Cripps in November 1938. "There is a sort of stupor everywhere. The people don't want to be moved or roused or set to work for high aims." He remained optimistic, however. Manley was "full of hope" that the situation would change. "We have worn down the initial opposition and abuse," he reported, "and now there is a touch of the patronizing in press comments which has to be hit aside."

Manley was cognizant of the daunting task of effecting fundamental changes in the island. "It is particularly difficult to see what to do in the given social and economic framework with little countries like this," he admitted to Sir Stafford. "We are completely at the mercy of world economic forces," he observed, and "in the given system, no internal effort can provide the means to do more than make ripples in the surface of our deep troubles." He expressed his desire to continue working with Bustamante and hoped that Sir Walter Citrine "can succeed in getting Bustamante to see his task from [a] new angle." Manley said he had managed "to avoid any rupture" with Bustamante, and "better collaboration is a possibility" even if Bustamante was not yet ready to join the PNP. In October 1938 Manley had asked that the party be "given a chance." The long-awaited decision came in January 1939 when Bustamante formally became a member, exhorting "the masses of this island" to follow his example.[19]

Norman Manley enthusiastically welcomed Bustamante into the PNP's fold. The labor leader brought his mass base, potentially, into the party. Manley genuinely wanted his party to have a mutually beneficial relationship with the labor movement. "If the party cannot make contact with the masses of the country," Manley said, "it is better that it had not been born."[20] In a letter that he wrote to Manley about two months after he joined the PNP, Bustamante explained the role he was playing as a party member: "I am just as much interested in the People's National Party, of which you are President, just as anxious to see it continue making a great hit, as I am about the Union of which I am President, and I make it my point of duty not alone to bring it vividly before the public, but to instruct my officers from Head Office that wherever they go they must bring the People's National Party to the attention of the people."[21]

Pleased to receive Bustamante's support, Manley quickly expressed his gratitude. "I am very sensible of the assistance you and all your organisers are giving to the Drive for the Party," he wrote to Bustamante on March 24. He reminded the labor leader that he "had always cherished the hope that the P.N.P. would be and remain a political instrument for the Labour Unions as well." Manley emphasized his view that the party and the union should collaborate to their mutual advantage. "It is logical and right that that should be so if we are to regard ourselves as a Progressive Party. I think both movements have a great deal to gain from each other."

Bustamante, at the time, endorsed these sentiments. He was grateful for Manley's help in saving trade unionism in the island after the disastrous general strike that he had called in February. Bustamante supported the Trade Union Advisory Council that had been created at Manley's instance to bring some degree of rationality to the practice of trade unionism in the island. In affirming his support for the PNP, Bustamante thanked Manley "for the very sincere manner in which you and Mr. Nethersole [secretary of the Trade Union Advisory Council] are cooperating with our union." His deep respect for Norman Manley's rectitude was clear. "I should not really say sincere," he wrote in his letter to Manley, "for a person of your type will either co-operate sincerely or have nothing to do with a matter." He described Nethersole as "certainly a gem, honest to the core."

Given Bustamante's high regard for Manley and Nethersole and their support of the labor movement, it is hardly surprising that he would join the PNP. But the political marriage was short-lived. Temperamentally ill-equipped to working well with his colleagues and fearful of any competition for the affection of the workers, Bustamante soon began to denounce Manley and the party he led. Tensions arose between the two men when Manley refused to condemn an article in *Public Opinion* that was critical of Bustamante and his union's autocratic constitution. The article appeared under the pseudonym "Philosopher," someone Bustamante identified as an official of the PNP. Bustamante's letter of protest to Manley was angry and threatening in its tone, as it denounced "the attack leveled at our Union":

> This is not the policy that is adopted by any of the officers of this union towards the People's National Party, and we are not going to accept any attack from one of your officers without retaliation. If there is going to be a fight, let there be an open fight. If there is going to be unity, let there be unity. It is a daring and unwarranted attack upon

the Constitution of this Union, and whilst there are fights and fights in the P.N.P., whilst I too could make several attacks on its policy . . . I look at the whole incident in the Press with regret; that is how much I am interested in the P.N.P.

Despite his affirmation of loyalty to the party, Bustamante went on to declare that unless the attacks on his union ceased, he was "going to fight back."

Bustamante overreacted to the criticism of "Philosopher." The writer had said nothing new, but the labor chief always lost his balance when he was criticized. Replying to Bustamante's letter, Manley disclaimed any responsibility for the offending article. He admitted that he was "disturbed" by what Bustamante had written, adding: "I have no control whatsoever over the author of the article in question and I have never sought to influence journalists in any way in regard to what they may conceive to be fair criticism. The person in question is, I believe, a member of the Party but he holds no Executive office at all and has never taken an active part in anything to do with the Party. He is as free to criticize the party as he is to criticize Trade Unions. I have no objection to criticism as long as it is honest."

This was an eloquent endorsement of the efficacy of free speech in an island where it would be attacked time and time again. Manley also seized the opportunity to reaffirm his support for the trade-union movement and the need for the PNP's collaboration with it: "I believe in the Union movement and I know that it is a necessary and proper development in Jamaica. I will never attack that movement and that stands whether my Movement is attacked or not. When you attacked the P.N.P. I did not retaliate by attacking Labour unions. I continued as I have already done to support [them] with every means that lay in my power. I do not make friends today and enemies tomorrow. Once I have made up my mind about the righteousness of a cause I stick to it."

These were high-minded and principled assertions. Norman Manley never wavered in his support for the advancement of labor's cause throughout his political career. Bustamante's letter, however, opened a wound in his relations with Manley and the PNP, and the blood would continue to ooze. By September 1939 Bustamante was gloating that he had destroyed the PNP in the rural areas. This was an exaggeration, but he had punctured the party's potential popularity among the workers, characterizing it as communist inspired and therefore a subversive organization inimical to the interests of Jamaicans.[22]

Writing in a letter to the *Daily Gleaner* in June 1939, Bustamante linked Manley to communism. "It is unfortunate," he wrote, "that the present Founder of the People's National Party has allowed himself to be hood winked and surrounded with so much of the Philosophy of Communism, not realizing that however much intelligence he may possess, however much trained he may be in a certain line, that he like all of us are Novices in certain things and are at the mercy of a dangerous Science which has destroyed and distorted governments of a greater magnitude than that of Jamaica, leaving it [sic] in a pitiful and sorrowful condition."

The letter was a confused diatribe, but it smeared Manley and the PNP. Bustamante was clearly referring to Manley when he charged that "persons of intelligence" were being destroyed by this "illogical Science."

> The sad part is that we do not know enough of the Science of Communism, we Novices find ourselves playing with fire, and by the time we realize the magnitude of the conflagration we shall have been left destitute and destroyed by these dangerous Scientists. Russia is a striking EXAMPLE, but the most sad aspect of the whole affair is that the Men who are generally destroyed through this illogical Science are frequently persons of Intelligence and honesty of purpose, who if they could only have realized that they were merely a doll in the hands of these Communists and International World Workers, they would get rid of any such destructive elements from amongst their body.

Much of the letter defies rational analysis, but since Bustamante tarred Manley with a communist brush with telling effectiveness, it is important to view the ideology through his distorted optic.

> Whilst the ethical principles of Socialism are good, I maintain that COMMUNISM is a source of danger, and these Communists realize how pernicious this philosophy is. That is why right here in Jamaica they are working surreptitiously. Indeed, we find in this Country that Communism is much hidden in "LEFTS"[?] and "RIGHTS"(?) just to cover up the trail of Communism, for they realize too well that if these "LEFTS"(?) and "RIGHTS"(?) are called by their correct names, the public would look upon them not just with suspicion, but with scorn, and the strong arm of the law would bring its soul down and smite the enemies of Society, the State, the Church, and the Proletariat group to whom so many false Prophets have appeared.[23]

Having written his treatise on communism and outlined its evils, Bustamante said he "could say much more" but did not, mercifully sparing the *Daily Gleaner*'s readers from additional confusion. He hoped, however, that his letter would serve as a "warning" to the PNP "to purge itself before it is too late." Manley did not respond publicly to Bustamante's politically and personally damaging accusation. But the allegation of communist contamination would stick, forcing the PNP to address it more forcefully in later years.

Bustamante's allegations that the PNP was a communist organization was a gross exaggeration. There were some Jamaicans who shared Bustamante's point of view, and the party as a whole smarted from such attacks. Manley admitted that he learned, probably in 1940, that Frank Hill and Richard Hart, both founding members of the party, "belonged to a very small set of theoretic communists." He observed, however, that "it was easy in these days in a British Colony to pin the label 'Communist' on anything political that was not shoddy compromise or ante deluvian [sic] antics. The presence in the Party of three or four alleged Communists became magnified beyond reality. Bustamante made great play of it for his own ends."

Manley said he "took no action" against the "Hart-Hill Group" because "firstly I considered them too few to matter, secondly I felt they supplied a necessary spur to action for the mild and sometimes sleepy centre, and last and principally because it was and is my view that extremism in youth is a good thing and that it only becomes a danger if it is denied outlet in action and driven to underground channels."

Better organized and more ferociously committed to their ideological convictions, those associated with the party's "extreme left," as Manley described them, drove its agenda. "It is a hard fact," Manley observed, "that the reformist will not make the sacrifices the work demands." He noted that "the sympathisers with the extreme left" were "the only people prepared to do continuous political work—organization and political education which are our workers' main tasks." Concerned about the increasing influence of that faction in the party, Manley said that the 1941 annual conference "issued a sharp warning in a resolution affirming that the Party had a body of opinion of its own and that members who sought to propagate another body of opinion must resign or would be expelled."

These internal tensions were contained but never resolved. The party confronted a major crisis in September 1942 when Frank Hill announced his intention to move a motion at the annual conference demanding independence for the island. Manley and his moderate allies threatened to decline office in the party if the motion were approved. Faced with a potentially disastrous split in the party's ranks and the loss of Manley's leadership, Hill and his associates dropped the idea, despite being "exceedingly upset," as the party leader recalled. Still, the Hill-Hart group, as Manley called them, dominated the conference and won an overwhelming majority of the seats on the party's council, the body from which the Executive was elected. Manley reported that O. T. Fairclough, H. P. Jacobs, "and other moderates were axed and when finally the Executive was formed it was completely comprised of themselves [the Hill-Hart group] and their own."

Manley was not pleased by these developments, but he could do little to prevent them. The PNP, after all, was a democratic organization packed with bright and independent-minded individuals. Manley was their elected leader, but he did not command much affection or support from the extreme left. Manley admitted that he preferred to distance himself from the internecine disputes. "I have always kept clear," he said, "of all inter-party [intraparty] groupings and have formed no bloc of my own." He was "powerless," he confessed, to prevent the "extreme left's" domination of the 1942 convention, "and indeed [I] had no fear at all of my ability, aided by circumstance and the sobering effects of executive work, to keep a balance between haste and discretion." Manley really had no stomach for these disputes, remaining detached and above the fray.

Such a strategy did not work. Manley had to act as an arbiter between the two competing factions from time to time, often satisfying neither one. Writing to Manley in March 1943, Henry Fowler, a member of the party's Executive, was brutally frank: "As long as you had to stand as mediator between sections of the party, arriving at decisions as to how to preserve the balance of the Party, and getting those decisions translated into actions without offending one group or another, each grouping watched you; and because it was in the nature of the situation that you could not deal openly with the situations that arose they felt there was something sinister in your actions. Each side sought to strengthen their hold on the Executive so as to control you by numerical force."

This was a credible assessment of Manley's leadership, the challenges he faced, and the consequences of his actions. The internal divisions in the party gave Manley the space to act independently or to temporize, much to the resentment of the two factions. Henry Fowler pointed out to his leader that "you have found it necessary, owing to the cleavages in the Party, to decide what is reasonable and correct, and force that policy through without a frank discussion of the issues. Almost invariably you have been right, and the public prestige of the Party is due to your ability to hold the balance. But within the Party it has led to both 'left' and 'right' regarding you with suspicion."

Not only did Manley face the problem of balancing the ideological divides in the PNP, but he also had to soothe the war weariness and disenchantment of some of its stalwart members. By mid-1940, the party had contested two by-elections in Kingston, losing both. Noel Nethersole, the party's first vice president, confided his unhappiness with the pace of change in the island, predicting a new rebellion. Writing to the party's leader in July 1940, he emphasized that "an economic and financial revolution is a basic ingredient of any progress in this country." But he recognized that "in this regard we are faced with at present insuperable obstacles. We face opposition from the Colonial Office, [from] Local Financial Advisers, from Banking Interests, and from Local Vested Interests. We have not the influence, the material nor the opportunity to withstand such a combination."

Nethersole complained that the PNP had been "persistently and effectively misrepresented by a strongly vocal section of the community with press and other sources of propaganda." This was an accurate charge, the truth of which Manley was entirely familiar. Nethersole was certain that the PNP would be asked to help "quell" the "outburst" he saw coming. He recommended that the party refuse such an invitation; he knew that "personally I should refuse." The PNP "shall be accused of fomenting" the rebellion, he predicted.

> [T]he result will be a desperate condition. Many persons will be shot and imprisoned and no immediate benefit will accrue to anyone. We [the PNP] shall rightly lose the confidence of the masses and with it our bulwark of strength. We shall be held up to obloquy as subversive persons and so forth and worst of all we and those for whom we stand will be at the mercy of the gang of opportunists who maintain their hold by the use of the savage and beastly weapon of colour under the pretence of helping the working class when their real design is to replace one form of domination with another.

Nethersole declared that he could not participate in anything that was not in the interest of the working people. Under the circumstances, he had decided "to abstain from Party activities." He planned to "resume the right of personal and I hope legitimate criticism of Government." Nethersole's potential withdrawal from the front lines of the PNP presented

Norman Manley with one of his greatest challenges as its leader. Nethersole was, arguably, the most prominent member of the party after Manley, and his departure from the active political scene would have been a grievous loss to the party that he helped to found. Manley seemed to have moved quickly to soothe Nethersole's fears and pain, and he never left the party's fold. But the episode revealed one of the many fault lines in the PNP.[24]

Manley was never able to unite the PNP or to maintain the élan that accompanied its founding. Its ideological differences were too wide, but remarkably, its internal squabbles did not produce a public split in its ranks, at least not in the 1940s. The PNP muddled along, however, politically handicapped at times but not disabled.

Bustamante's break with the PNP was as impetuous as was his brief rapprochement with it. Not wanting to alienate the workers who loved and supported Bustamante, and perhaps because of his more-reserved temperament, Manley avoided public brawls with his antagonist, usually declining to personalize their disputes. The PNP, to be sure, needed Bustamante and his legions of supporters more than the reverse. Bustamante must have come to realize, in his more thoughtful moments, that his union's partnership with a political party redounded to the advantage of both. The union brought a mass base to the party, and the PNP could potentially protect and advance labor's interests in the halls of the legislature.

The rapprochement between the People's National Party and the Bustamante Industrial Trade Union (BITU) occurred on Labour Day 1940. Seeking to bury the hatchet in the interest of labor, the two organizations held a joint meeting at the Majestic Theatre in Kingston. As he rose to address the gathering, Bustamante invited representatives of the PNP to stand on his right. Proceeding to blame others for the split between the two organizations, the labor leader declared: "For some time there has been a certain section that has been doing their best to separate my organization from the organization of the PNP. I suppose it is for obvious reasons and because it is known that the best way to rule is to divide."[25] Bustamante was constructing a narrative that was not in accord with the facts. The break had been of his own making. But he was now committed to working with the PNP, confessing: "For some months I have made up my mind not to allow anything whatever again to separate me and the Bustamante Industrial Union from the People's National Party. I have definitely decided that if in the future there is any trouble between us, that trouble will be settled in some office and that trouble will not be the business of the public."[26]

Continuing to the cheers of the audience, Bustamante vowed to "join hands and heart with Mr. Norman Washington Manley on my left here and with the other members of the PNP on my right to work in friendship so that we will achieve something if not today, tomorrow, worthwhile for the masses." This dramatic reconciliation was not destined to endure. Approximately ten weeks later, Governor Arthur Richards interned Bustamante. When he was released from detention after seventeen months, he effected his final break with Manley and the PNP.

At its first annual convention, held in December 1939, the PNP decided against pursuing constitutional changes for the island during wartime. This was a pragmatic decision, designed to convince the colonial state that the party was a patriotic organization willing to "abstain from its agitation for constitutional reform."[27] This was an act of self-abnegation to which the party did not adhere particularly after the Moyne Commission's report became the subject of vigorous discussion in the island in 1940 and in subsequent years. The PNP had not taken its decision lightly in December 1939, but it could hardly have remained silent when the country was becoming focused on its constitutional future.

Despite its muted stance on constitutional issues in 1939, the PNP unveiled its objectives on other questions. Its policy, the party said, was circumscribed by what could be achieved in wartime. The policy that it announced was reformist in its conceptualization and content but realistic in its assessment of what was practical and achievable in the island. In order to alleviate the economic condition of the rural poor, the party advocated the compulsory acquisition of land for food production, the planned development of land-settlement schemes, and the provision of credit for farmers. It recommended "the intensification of the development of the resources of the country to provide work," an increase in wages, and the implementation of a minimum-wage bill. The party urged the development of industries "allied to agricultural production." It supported an increase in projects "assisting education and social advancement" and the introduction of an old-age pension scheme.[28] These were not radical ideas, but they drew attention to the island's challenges, even if they lacked specific policy details.

Although Manley was the acknowledged principal founder of the PNP, his was not its only ideological voice. As a Fabian socialist, Manley was associated with the moderate wing of the party, a restraining influence on those who were demanding a more-radical systemic change in the social-economic structures of the country. His principal allies included O. T. Fairclough, the editor of *Public Opinion*; Wills O. Isaacs, a commission agent from Kingston; and H. P. Jacobs. Those who supported more-radical stances by the party consisted of Noel Nethersole, its vice president; Vernon Arnett, the secretary; and the journalists Frank and Kenneth Hill, among others. These men were all active members of the Kingston-based Metropolitan Group of the PNP, the most radical of the party's groups in the island. The Reverend Oswald G. Penso of the Duke Street Christian Church served as the chairman.

Reverend Penso was a self-proclaimed socialist, and so were many other members of the Metropolitan Group. But the PNP had not declared itself a socialist organization when it was founded in September 1938. In fact, it would do so only after its membership had discussed the issue and the party felt confident enough to define itself as socialist in an island largely ignorant of its meaning and political practice. Speaking in late October 1938, Reverend Penso reflected the views of many of the PNP's adherents when he admitted: "Personally, I am a socialist. Personally, I believe the majority or even all the leaders of the party are socialists. That is why I am a member. But we cannot say at present that we are a socialist group. Not until after a conference of delegates from the several groups can a definite policy or program be stated."[29]

That moment came in August 1940. The occasion was the second annual conference of the party, held at the Coke Memorial Hall. The conference considered and approved a statement explaining the ideological change and listened to a speech by Manley defending it. The statement admitted that the party's original program was "reformist," but "world events" had altered the "outlook for the future," necessitating a change in its philosophy. The Moyne Commission, the statement said, had recommended structural reforms, and this had confirmed the PNP in its view that "Jamaica's hopes would depend on Jamaica's own efforts" and that "the party would have to move forward in our policies or perish." In order to address the island's problems, the party "must frankly proclaim its faith in the Socialist cause; must test all policies by their consistency with and tendency to foster that cause. The Party must realize that no tolerable solution exists for us under any other social system. The Party must seek to propagate the ideas of socialistic justice and economic equality and must demonstrate how those ideas could be translated into practical effect on the lives of the men and women of the country."[30]

The statement indicated that the PNP had reconsidered and abandoned its earlier decision not to demand self-government while the war was being conducted. The party knew that only a socialist government in England would be sympathetic to the cause it was promoting. Evidently not expecting this to occur soon, the PNP recognized that "any real programme for the development of the country is dependent upon our being responsible for our own government."[31]

In his speech to the convention and ultimately to the larger public, Manley sought to dispel negative understandings of socialism. The socialism that the PNP proposed, Manley affirmed, was neither revolutionary nor antireligious. Seeking to reassure the predominantly Christian population in the island that it should not fear socialism, Manley declared: "Indeed there is a very strong body of people who call themselves Christian socialists because they actually affirm that socialism is the only Christian principle of social organization that has ever been devised. . . . Any genuine pretence of democracy must allow religious liberty."[32]

Manley assured his listeners that "you are not being committed either to revolution or to godlessness [but] . . . to accept a policy which will search both your hearts and minds, your courage and your understanding, if it is to develop and prosper in the island."[33] The PNP's unapologetic embrace of socialism represented a watershed moment in its young life. There was no compelling need for the party to invite an ideological label given the realistic expectation that its enemies would accuse it of communism, equating it with socialism. In an island with Christian traditions and a population largely unfamiliar with either ideology, this was a calculated risk for the infant party. The party chose honesty in announcing its ideological stripe, reflecting the triumph of principle over obfuscation and deception.

The PNP's new ideology elicited much public reaction. The *Daily Gleaner* wanted to know "which brand" of socialism would be introduced in the island. It attempted to scare its readers by claiming that socialism meant that the people's land would be taken over by the state since land was the most important means of production in the island. "Our peasant proprietary system," the *Gleaner* pointed out, "is the antithesis or opposite of a socialist system. . . . [C]ertainly we do not see the Jamaican peasantry or yeomanry or plantocracy agreeing willingly to farm their lands in common, to surrender their properties to the Government." This was an inflammatory claim, threatening in its implications for anyone who owned land in the island. The PNP was never completely successful in refuting it.[34]

The *Gleaner* articulated secular objections to socialism, but others voiced their opposition in religious terms. Father Charles Judah, a prominent Roman Catholic priest, gave a highly publicized lecture entitled "Can Christians Be Socialists?" Declaring that he was presenting the Catholic point of view and the "Catholic philosophy of the State," Father Judah stressed that socialism was "founded upon a doctrine of human society peculiarly its own, which is opposed to true Christianity." "Religious Socialism" and "Christian Socialism," the priest said, "are expressions implying a contradiction in terms. No one can be at the same time a sincere socialist and a true Christian." Father Judah maintained that since socialism "cannot be brought into harmony with the dogmas of the Catholic church ... we must oppose it with all our might."[35] The *Gleaner* published the lengthy speech in its entirety, and its claims were undoubtedly the subject of heated discussion throughout the island among Christians of all denominational stripes. It must have presented to many people the painful dilemma of choosing between their party and their Christian faith.

The PNP was subjected to withering criticisms from its founding. As one prominent Englishman noted in early 1939, "The People's National Party is regarded with the gravest suspicion by those who normally have the ear of government." Some critics accused the party of promoting dictatorship and being dominated by revolutionaries. "There are no revolutionaries in the party," Manley said in a defiant response. "It is said they are the people behind me. Well I know all the people behind me and if I have any complaint to make about them, it is that they are not red and revolutionary enough. No! It is not that they are too revolutionary, but just the reverse." Miss May Farquharson, a white woman and member of the island's social and economic elite, condemned the "anti-British sentiments and statements" of the PNP, as well as "the hatred and bitterness shown in so many of the speeches and publications of those who are advocating democracy." She saw the emphasis on the development of a "national" spirit as "definitely a backward, and not a forward move towards a genuine world civilization."[36] May Farquharson, and those who shared her views, had no empathetic understanding of the nascent nationalism in the island and the desire of many Jamaicans to govern themselves.

The PNP also faced the opposition of the Federation of Citizens' Associations. Norman Manley was not a member of any of these associations, but he realized that the PNP could benefit from working with them. The party could draw upon their membership, and in fact, Manley invited representatives from the federation to participate in writing a constitution for the

PNP. When he addressed the inaugural meeting of the party in September 1938, he also invited the various associations to become affiliates of the PNP. The response to this invitation was not a particularly positive one. Representatives of the federation, fearing that the PNP was a competitor for its membership, launched personal attacks on Manley. They charged that the party intended to absorb the citizens' associations and that it aspired to establish a dictatorship in the island. These attacks led Manley to repudiate his invitation to the associations, although he said the party still welcomed the support of individual members. "I am not out for power," an angry Norman Manley declared. "And I am not out to help myself, but to help Jamaica and my fellow countrymen, and I believe the time has come when people like me should come forward and offer that help without being abused by these ignoramuses that care nothing for the country."[37] Such name calling hardly cooled the aroused passions, and although the breach was never completely healed, the PNP eventually worked with the Federation of Citizens' Associations to carve out a new constitution for the island. The PNP survived over the long haul, but the federation became moribund.

The most sustained and effective opposition to the PNP came from the wealthy ethnic minorities, particularly Syrians, Jews, and the locally and foreign-born English. These groups had become psychologically unhinged by the labor rebellion, the PNP's assertion of an increasingly strident Jamaican nationalism, and the party's embrace of socialism. They feared the potential power of an enfranchised black majority and any resultant assaults on their economic and social privileges. The *Daily Gleaner* was their mouthpiece, and the powerful Jamaica Imperial Association was the advocate and defender of their economic interests. Founded in March 1943, the Jamaica Democratic Party became their political voice and the beneficiary of their generous funding.

Manley knew that much of this opposition to the PNP was based on racial prejudice. "Every minority group and most conspicuously the rich minorities, Jews and Syrians have joined solidly anti-PNP," he wrote in a personal note to the editor of the *Daily Gleaner* in December 1943. "Here is a movement [the PNP] that rallies to it the hopes of coloured people conscious of the disabilities of colour all over the world. Here in Jamaica are groups of whom some sympathy might be expected. In fact the most bitter and remorseless opponents are these very people."

Manley thought that it was "no accident" that "not one single one of these groups has joined the local movement." He strongly defended the

PNP's commitment to racial justice, condemning those Jamaicans who were aligned in opposition.

> For years the PNP has steadily announced that its policy is four-square for racial equality. It is prepared to fight publicly and has done so, on that issue. But for years it has been accused of stirring up racial strife. And now it sees racial groups line up solidly against it. I know that the reason is that these groups are dominated by a philosophy of commercialism. It is so here in Jamaica more clearly than elsewhere. In other lands all racial groups have contributed a quota, large or small, to the general movement left or right or centre. Jamaica is unique in the solidarity of these groups.

Manley recognized that "we on our side are up against the combined forces of money-power." He was not, however, prepared to respond to this opposition "by letting loose other dangerous and deplorable things." He was dedicated to taking the high road in the contest with these opponents, to assert a moral superiority over them. "I have been through two or three very tough years," Manley wrote, "but I have come through to some sort of integration of my life that leaves the worthwhile pieces intact." Manley's distancing of himself from the ugly underside of the developing political discourse and practice in the island was not a hypocritical pose. That was the measure of the man, a defining characteristic of his public life. Manley brought decency and moral rectitude to Jamaica's political culture to a degree unmatched by any of his contemporaries.[38]

Governor Arthur Richards did not welcome any criticism of England, its empire, or the local administration over which he presided. Normally, he confined his distaste for the PNP and his criticism of it to his official communications with his superiors in London. In December 1940, however, Richards made a particularly scathing assault on the government's critics. He did not mention Manley and the PNP by name, but it was clear that they were the targets of his venom. Speaking at the opening of an Anglican school at Bull Savannah, the governor denounced the "would be leaders of the people, who say government is a failure and who draw a caricature of government as they misunderstand it and then demand control should be handed over to those whose chief qualification is an itch to govern, combined with a lack of training for the task." They were "political quacks," the governor charged, "whose voices are so loud that one might think that government had only to wave a wand to make the desert blossom like the rose."[39]

The governor's intemperate outburst did not go unanswered. Speaking at a public meeting at the Race Course, Manley criticized those who had led the island over the last century. "You talk about how to govern this country," he exclaimed. "All government is difficult, all government needs understanding and all government needs experience." Then he ridiculed the caliber of the colonial administrators by confessing: "I look back on a hundred years of Jamaican history and what do I find? That on the average every twenty years they [Britain] have had to send a Commission to Jamaica to find out what is wrong with it. I seem to say to myself: these people that are governing Jamaica cannot be so very sensible, because they cannot keep straight for twenty years."[40] Norman Manley was in a jovial mood. His audience laughed at that comment. But the Jamaican leader knew that he had spoken an ugly truth.

Governor Richards did not stand alone in his criticism of the political inexperience of the PNP's leaders. One critic, a prominent civil servant, thought that the party's "continuous and acid criticism of everything the [government] . . . says or does" was "killing" its chances with the electorate. This criticism, he said, "even if merited is tactless and fills the heart of the people who are by nature conservative, with fear, fear that the party stands only for destruction." The critic thought the PNP had been injudicious in assuming the socialist mantle. "The Bolshie [Bolshevik] bogey has been so successfully exploited by capitalists throughout the world," he noted, "that one would have thought that the PNP would have avoided playing right into the hands of the exploiters who desire no change." The PNP's open identification with socialism was a principled act, but it probably brought it more criticism than support in an island that was suspicious of both socialism and communism and fearful of the two ideologies. As E. D. Carberry, the aforementioned critic, said, "there is no genuine admiration for the Soviets" in Jamaica. Manley had blundered, he alleged, but "the worst of it is that I don't think he realizes it even now."[41] The result of the forthcoming elections would determine the wisdom of the party's actions.

Alexander Bustamante had severed the ties between the BITU and the PNP immediately upon his release from detention in February 1942. It was an acrimonious parting, diminishing both Manley and Bustamante in the process. The PNP's leaders gave their support to the competing union founded by H. M. Shirley. Bustamante bided his time, but by July 1942 he had decided to found his own political party. He had begun to test the political waters earlier that year when he publicly endorsed two candidates who were contesting by-elections for the Legislative Council. The candidates, R. O. Terrier in Clarendon and Roy Lindo in St. Mary, won the contests. Encouraged by these results, Bustamante began planning to found a political party that would represent the interests of labor in the legislature.[42]

Bustamante first publicly promoted the concept of a labor party on August 9, 1942, at a meeting attended by a "large crowd" at the Race Course. He assured the crowd that he, and presumably the potential new party, "neither hated nor intended to preach hatred for the rich or the propertied classes." He was only setting out "to curtail the length of the rich man's pockets." Bustamante left no doubt that he would be the absolute leader of the party. "I will be the boss of my party," he shouted. "If any member goes to the [Legislative] Council and deceives me he shall have a hot time; for I will be boss. I will direct you how to vote and for whom to vote."

The founder and party leader designate intended to control the organization much the same way that he administered the affairs of the BITU. It was not to be conceived as a democratic organization; Bustamante, as we have noted, was temperamentally incapable of functioning in an environment where the principles of democracy prevailed. In fact, when the new party was founded, its constitution institutionalized and enshrined Bustamante's autocratic control. It allowed, for example, "a Managing Executive Committee, the personnel of which shall be nominated by the Leader and Founder of the party . . . and elected by the general membership of the party." Bustamante had the sole right to nominate the members of this important committee, thereby exercising absolute control over the party. The constitution also specified that "the founder and leader of the party . . . shall be responsible for the choice and selection of candidates of the party for the House of Representatives, the K.S.A.C. [Kingston and St. Andrew Corporation] and Parochial Boards."[43]

The *Daily Gleaner* was appalled by the absolute power that the constitution allowed Bustamante to wield in the party. It observed that "one-man control of this type is essentially a principle of Fascism and not of Democracy, and we cannot help thinking the Labour Party must have committed an oversight in their constitution." Bustamante wanted to dominate the party, but he did not aspire to have total control of the Legislative Council. "The Labour Party will endeavour to have 75 percent of the seats," he said.

The remainder should be held by capital. "The trouble with this island," Bustamante averred, "is that one set of people has all the say. I do not wish that to continue. I will see that Capital also have a voice."[44]

Bustamante told the August 1942 meeting at the Race Course that he was not "aiming at self-aggrandizement," nor would he use the party as a stepping stone to becoming "prime minister or anything of the kind." His focus was on the economic condition of the workers and the measures that were needed to improve it. This was both the strength and the weakness of the objectives of the projected party as Bustamante outlined them. The overriding concern for the welfare of the workers was defensible in the platform of a labor party. But Bustamante was silent on the needs of other sectors of the society and on its general requirements, such as economic growth, education, health, housing, and extensive agrarian reform. Nor was there any mention of constitutional change, one of the most highly discussed issues of the time. There was no articulation of any principle that would guide the party's behavior in office.[45]

The political platform of the party Bustamante anticipated consisted of eight planks. They included financial aid from the government for all expectant mothers before and for a few months after delivery, medical examination of all prisoners before the start of their incarceration, the provision of legal assistance for all accused persons, and the introduction of an old-age pension scheme. The additional planks consisted of the implementation of a land-settlement scheme, an eight-hour day for all workers, a workmen's compensation law, and a minimum-wage law. Bustamante also promised to promote the election of many of the "common boys" to political office. He told his audience at the Race Course that he would not share the additional planks of the party's platform because "he did not believe any party should disclose all its aims and objects [objectives]." This was an incredible statement, suggesting that Bustamante did not understand the protocols of party politics, including the imperative to announce detailed platforms or manifestoes, animating objectives, and ideologies. Bustamante's model was the labor negotiating table, where both sides guarded their strategies. He had not begun to make the transition from labor leader to potential political chieftain.[46]

The PNP and the proposed labor party constituted a study in contrasts. Led by the cerebral Norman Manley, the PNP declared itself socialist, advocated universal adult suffrage and self-government, and envisioned a fundamental social and economic transformation of the society. Democratically organized, the party appealed primarily to the middle class, lacking a strong emotional connection with the working people. On the other hand, Bustamante's labor party was the child of the trade union he founded and was committed to capitalism. Bustamante was expected to exercise supreme authority in the party as he did in the union, rejecting immediate self-government and advocating policies that primarily reflected the interests of his labor constituency.

There were Jamaicans, however, who thought that their interests were not represented by either the PNP or the labor movement and the political party to which it was giving birth. The conservative business and propertied elite did not find a home in either party and were receptive to the emergence of one that was sympathetic to their needs. The representatives of privilege had yearned for such a party prior to Bustamante's announcement regarding the formation of a labor party in August 1942. Labor, they argued, was represented by the PNP and the BITU, but capital lacked an organized political voice. Writing to the *Gleaner* on March 3, 1942, T. H. Sharp, a large landowner from the parish of Manchester, proposed the creation of a new party. It would be a party representing those people who "stand on middle ground," eschewing extremism. He volunteered to be the leader of such a party, launching "a trial balloon."[47]

Sharp's proposal for a new party was endorsed by *Gleaner* columnist G. St. C. Scotter. He preferred, however, that an "Agricultural" party be formed since the "best hope for the island's future lies not in political systems or constitutional changes, but rather in full and fair development of the island's land and agriculture." Dr. Winston Lyon thought that if the party were "a judicious mixture of liberal thought and conservative action, I feel sure that it would have the support of many thousands of thinking people in Jamaica."[48] The idea for a new party gained strength, and the Jamaica Democratic Party (JDP) was founded at a meeting held in Kingston at the Ward Theatre on March 17, 1943. The meeting was attended by many prominent representatives of business, the plantocracy, members of the Kingston and Andrew Corporation, and members of the Legislative Council. It attracted a number of hecklers, as well, who tried unsuccessfully to halt the proceedings.[49] The JDP, despite T. H. Sharp's claim to its presidency, did not elect a national leader, preferring to create a more decentralized structure of parish leaders.

The JDP was the refuge of the Jamaican elite who feared the socialism of the PNP and the prolabor bias of the proposed labor party. Its policy objectives were remarkably vague. The party's three "basic principles" included "increasing the production and the income of the island and ensuring a fair distribution." The second was "the obtaining of the kind of constitution most likely to bring us happiness and contentment." The party's third principle was "the elimination of inequalities, injustices, and grievances wherever and whenever found." Specifically, the JDP endorsed the "principles" of universal suffrage, "with self government as the ultimate aim to be reached in progressive terms." It proposed a "retention of our status as British citizens—a part of the British empire." Unlike the PNP, the JDP endorsed "the system of Private enterprise."[50]

The JDP's founding was quickly followed by that of the Jamaica Labour Party (JLP). This occurred at a meeting held at the Ward Theatre on July 8, 1943. It was, reported the Gleaner, attended "by the masses . . . and representatives of many public bodies." Addressing the meeting, party leader Bustamante vowed to fight for "a 'New Deal' for labour in this country," telling the audience: "I expect you to vote for every man and woman I put forward for the House of Representatives and I expect you to help me to pack Labour members in that House." Those in attendance passed a resolution pledging to work "unceasingly for the progress, expansion, and growth, and the successful accomplishment of the ideals and principles," of the party. The resolution expressed its "full and implicit confidence" in Bustamante, "who for a considerable number of years in all vicissitudes of life in sunshine and in storm has been a rock to lean upon and a fortress for the working people of this country, whose untiring zeal, sacrificial devotion and courage to the cause of Labour is a tradition and model worthy of emulation."[51] Bustamante, the unchallenged "boss" of the party, invited this kind of worshipful adulation from his associates, but it was not an asset for the party and the country. It laid the foundation for the kind of personalist leadership that would become an unhealthy feature of Jamaica's political culture.

Jamaica boasted three major political parties by the middle of 1943. The ideologically socialist PNP had been in existence for five years. Formed in March 1943, the JDP was described by the Daily Gleaner as "the conservative party of Jamaica, having a policy intended to appeal at the same time to business and to labour, to planter and to peasant." The JLP was the third major party, characterized by the Gleaner as "Mr. Bustamante's party" and "therefore . . . assured of a numerous following, regardless of its programme, because of the personality of its leader."[52] The three parties presented the electorate with clear choices. Their existence reflected the developing vibrancy of party politics in the country, and this was also manifested by the formation of several other parties, albeit ones of more limited appeal. They included the Jags Smith Party, led by Mrs. Amy Ashwood Garvey, the first wife of Marcus Garvey. Founded in October 1943, the party was named after the deceased legislator from Clarendon.[53] Other minor and short-lived parties included the Negro Party, the United Rate Payers Party, the Liberal Party, and the Jamaica Small Settlers Party.[54]

The most astute observer of the rough-and-tumble of party politics in the island was Paul Blanshard, an American who served as a consultant to the Anglo-American Caribbean Commission. Established in 1942 as a joint American and British venture, the commission was designed to promote the improvement of the socioeconomic conditions prevailing in the Caribbean islands. Reporting to the Department of State in September 1943, Blanshard said he had noticed "the temporary subordination of imperialism V. [versus] self government as an issue in local politics." The introduction of a new constitution in the island, he said, had muted criticism of the imperial government, except for "asides" in *Public Opinion*, the unofficial organ of the PNP. Blanshard reported that the major political parties wanted the constitution to work, but "the extreme rightists" wanted the experiment to fail "if success means the capture of the government by socialists." Similarly, the "extreme leftists" would welcome failure "if success means the continuation of the present economic set up." Blanshard believed the "right" was "the more dangerous because of its greater resources and because it draws strength from the considerable group of upper-class citizens who sincerely opposed more self government . . . and who now sincerely believe that the local black population cannot govern itself wisely."[55]

The communists, Blanshard said, constituted a very small group. They were collaborating with the PNP "as an inner but not altogether welcome nucleus." Blanshard noted quite accurately the unwillingness of any party to define itself as conservative. "All the parties," he wrote, "would like to be considered parties of the masses." Given the fact that 90 percent of Jamaicans were of African descent, with most of them having been denied the franchise in the past, the parties knew "that any party is doomed which allows itself to be jockeyed into the position of 'representing' the small white aristocracy." Any party that was seen as the voice of "white or light-brown business interests" would be "buried under a landslide of working class, black votes."[56]

Bustamante's "weird personal vehicle, the Jamaica Labour Party," was the beneficiary of these fears, Blanshard argued. He was going to receive "considerable support from conservative business interests who fear the combination of his pro-labor economics and pro-capitalist politics less than they fear the socialistic program advocated by the PNP." Bustamante was becoming more acceptable to the business interests, appearing "as a bitter opponent of all forms of public ownership." He had recently signed a letter in the press to that effect, "which was obviously produced by some conservative research organization." Bustamante, Blanshard added, "is too nearly illiterate to compose a reasoned discussion of economic issues without help." If Bustamante's party won the election, Blanshard opined, "he would ostensibly represent labor, but his record thus far indicates that he would be a pliant tool for shrewd business manipulators in handling complex problems of government."[57]

Although the JDP provided a hospitable home for the propertied and business interests, it lacked a mass base that would ensure its victory at the polls. Blanshard thought that the JLP "was moving towards an alliance" with the JDP, producing a united front against the PNP.[58] A formal alliance did not materialize, but the two parties worked out a modus vivendi, aiming their rhetorical fire at the PNP and not at each other. The two parties would never have been able to work together amicably. Bustamante may have been malleable in the hands of the astute representatives of capital, but he would never have abandoned labor's cause entirely. Blanshard's assertion that Bustamante was not equipped to address the "complex" problems of the country was not without foundation. But what Bustamante lacked in academic preparation he compensated for in the fervor of his advocacy of the workers' welfare and the sincerity of his commitment. These qualities were evident in a personal letter that he wrote to Mr. S. J. H. West of Glasgow, St. Ann, on August 20, 1943. There was a by-election in progress to fill a seat in the Legislative Council for the parish of St. Ann. Dr. Ivan Lloyd, a physician, was representing the PNP, and Bustamante opposed him aggressively.

Responding to a letter from West about the election, Bustamante reaffirmed that the JLP existed "for the country on [sic] a whole but to particularly protect the small man and the workers." The party's policy, he said, "is definitely to reduce the hunger, nakedness and landlessness and many hundreds of other things, to make laws, and to increase pay and to reduce taxation on the small man." Implying that Dr. Lloyd was providing the people with "free medicine" in return for their votes, Bustamante emphasized that "a little free medicine is very good, but that can't put food into the people's stomach, pay their rent, buy clothing, get them land etc. The people must be placed in a position so that they will be able to buy their own medicine and be independent. . . . I don't expect to get one big employer's vote, I am not seeking their votes. I am not out to destroy them either, I am out to help the small man."⁵⁹

Bustamante's letter was intended for West's eyes only. But he was displaying his empathy with the pain of the dispossessed, dramatizing in this personal note why he would resist the blandishments of the elite and not desert those who had given him legitimacy and potential political power. A member of the economic elite, Bustamante had become a passionate advocate of the incremental betterment of the conditions and life chances of the working people, but not the destruction of, or even the introduction of fundamental reforms to, the social order of which he was a privileged part.

Jamaica's first election under the aegis of universal adult suffrage was scheduled for December 14, 1944. As the date approached, the three major parties—the PNP, the JDP, and the JLP—began competing for the votes of the 663,069 people on the official voters list. It is instructive to examine the conduct of the campaign. Although it was generally acknowledged that the PNP and the JDP functioned as parties with an organizational structure and in accordance with democratic principles, the JLP operated as a dictatorship. Paul Blanshard concluded that "although Bustamante calls his political party a Labor Party, its form or organization is a dictatorship in which Busta himself nominates all candidates and names all members of the party's executive board." "Yes," Bustamante admitted to Blanshard, "I named the candidates. The Executive of my party wanted to name the candidates and I knew that it would have been more democratic. But I knew the people in the country [rural areas] and I chose the candidates instead."⁶⁰ Bustamante also alluded to his domination of the party when he wrote to S. J. H. West, telling him that "if the people do not believe in my honesty and sincerity after five years of sacrifice to this country, then they must not vote for the candidate I put up, for the candidate will not be able to do as he please[s] in the Council." Bustamante went on to say that the elected official "must abide by the policy of the Party."⁶¹ This was a meaningless comment, since Bustamante was the sole author of the JLP's policy. A month before the elections, the *Gleaner* observed in an editorial column that "the so-called Labour Party is not a political organization." The island's most highly respected newspaper was still maintaining that the JLP "is and should be called a Trade Union Party as its interests are confined to those of the various Trade Unions with whom Mr. Bustamante is connected. Its appeal is purely personal and owes nothing to political considerations or to any policy put forward other than that of obtaining higher wages and better working conditions for the members of the Unions concerned."[62]

The *Gleaner* had made an accurate assessment, but this was of little or no import to the JLP's political base. The country's history with party politics was very short, and in many cases the personality of the party's leader rather than its ideology determined the support it received. There was also a considerable number of people who were expected to vote for independent candidates. Some contemplated doing so because they rejected the three major parties or admired someone who ran on an independent ticket. Others intended to boycott or subvert the election. A *Gleaner* editorial of November 29 noted the existence of "a fantastic idea" that "was quite prevalent amongst people who had no special interest in politics." These people reasoned that if they abstained from voting, "the electorate, thus deprived of their guiding wisdom, will put such ridiculous people in the House of Representatives that Britain will cancel the constitution. . . . [S]ome of them even threaten to vote for the candidate they like least so as to make doubly sure that the constitution will be a failure."[63]

This obstructionist attitude was the last political gasp of the reactionary members of the elite. It did not prevail because it was malevolently retrogressive and was rejected as a viable strategy by most of the other opponents of constitutional change and progress in the country.

Campaigning aggressively for the support of the electorate, the three major parties held public meetings and wrote and published their manifestoes. The PNP reaffirmed its commitment to socialism, promising to "give to everyone equal opportunities to live a full and decent life." It proposed a program of land distribution, industrial development, a public-works initiative, full employment, universal education, a minimum-wage law, and a variety of other social-welfare programs. The party pledged to work for the success of the new constitution and the achievement of Dominion status.[64]

The well-financed Jamaica Democratic Party advertised its program rather extensively in the newspaper. It repeated its devotion to private enterprise and pledged to initiate a program for full employment, the development of "non agricultural industries," and "the creation of a new and more varied economy." The party opposed socialism, warning the voters that if Jamaica "became a socialist state," the people would be denied freedom of speech, of the press, and of worship. Such a political regime meant that Jamaicans "would have no free choice in the matter of what work" they did and "could own no property: all property must be in the form of collective property.... [O]ur children, like yourself are slaves of the state." Accordingly, "dictatorship [was] inevitable."[65]

Such scaremongering had a negative impact on the PNP's reputation but, ironically, the JLP was the beneficiary at the polls. Unlike the PNP and the JDP, the JLP's manifesto emphasized the personality of its leader in its appeal to the voters. Its manifesto included a letter from Bustamante.

> The voice of the man who has always been with you—Bustamante—vows to Almighty God and to you, to work diligently and unswervingly for your upliftment and for the country's progress and when that voice can be heard no more, hundreds and thousands will be heard to say: "when we were in dire need for leadership, when we had almost given up hope of finding a friend with a heart that had our understanding, the man BUSTAMANTE voluntarily came forward, offered his services to us: he led we followed and brought for us and our children improvements as never before."[66]

Bustamante ordered the workers to "shun" their "new overnight friends" and to remember that his "efforts have put more money in the pockets of every working man and woman throughout the country." Defining itself as the party of labor, the JLP promised "substantial wage increases," "lands for all people who want to cultivate," the reduction of market fees, unemployment insurance, the erection of schools in the remote parts of the island, and several prolabor programs. As was the case with the JDP's manifesto, the JLP was silent on the issue of Dominion status for the country.[67]

The governor selected November 29 as the date for the nomination of candidates for the election. The electoral contest attracted 130 candidates for the thirty-two available seats. The JLP nominated twenty-nine candidates, the PNP nineteen, and the JDP nine. The newly founded Jamaica Liberal Party and the United Rent Payers Party each nominated one candidate. The remaining seventy-one candidates consisted of independents.[68] Nomination day passed peacefully, although the candidates were greeted by enthusiastic supporters as they handed in their papers. Bustamante's detractors poked fun at him for allegedly seeking the assistance of Frank Pixley, the JLP's nominee for the Central Kingston constituency, in completing his papers. As the story was told and retold, some embroidered it by declaring that "Busta can't sign him name, unless Pixley hold him hand." When the nomination ceremony ended, one woman reportedly approached Kenneth

Hill, Bustamante's opponent in the constituency of Western Kingston, "with outstretched arms": "God bless you, me son! she said. Ah see Busta have to call Pixley to sign him name, and how you flash you pen. Ah say to meself. H'm, Busta can't represent us, me son, we will have to put in Ken Hill." One commentator had some perverse fun with the incident, observing that "there are thousands of other persons in Jamaica who cannot write. Why people should be about expecting 'the Chief' to be able to write, I cannot for the life of me find out."[69]

This was a moment of levity in an otherwise serious electoral contest sprinkled with violence, personal attacks, and untruths. Members of the PNP and the Jamaica Progressive League had long complained that the police cast a blind eye on attacks on their meetings allegedly by Bustamante's supporters. The independent observer, Paul Blanshard, supported these allegations, accusing the police of "pretending that the disturbances are two-way brawls, and looking the other way." In retaliation, Blanshard said, the PNP organized "a guard for its meetings and successfully fought off the Busta gangsters." Bustamante did not calm the people's mood when he dramatically beat an effigy of Manley with a cane at a public meeting, urging the audience to give his opponent a similar treatment at the polls.[70] This was a symbolically ugly performance. Jamaica's fragile political culture was being constructed, and incidents such as this one were legitimizing the violence that would become one of its pervasive and negative features. Still, the roots of politically inspired violence in Jamaica have had many parents. Slavery and colonialism, for example, depended upon institutional coercion and violence for their sustenance, defined the ethos of the society, and left an indelible imprint on the texture of social and political interactions.

The candidates representing the three parties hurled personal invectives at one another and at the competing organizations as well. Independent candidates may have behaved in a similar fashion, but they ran as individuals, having no party to defend. Many stood on their record of service to a particular constituency or parish, depending on their reputation to marshal electoral support. Others were newcomers to the public sphere, relying on their rhetoric, charisma, political program, or personal appeal to win support. A few published their manifesto in the newspaper.

These candidates, understandably, promoted a variety of causes. C. H. Murray, who was standing in Eastern St. Thomas, advocated "increased land settlement, improved educational facilities and a better standard of living for all." Albert Robinson, who was running in the same constituency, proposed free education for every child, "scientific soil research" to aid the development of agriculture, improvements in medical care, and a "progressive system" of land settlement, among other social and economic reforms. Mrs. Mary Morris Knibb, who was contesting the Eastern St. Andrew seat, appealed for support from women voters, emphasizing that "the blow for full freedom will be struck by the women of my constituency." The Reverend C. A. Wilson, who wanted to represent Southern St. Elizabeth, announced that he had been "called by God to serve." Among other objectives, he proposed "the abolition of poverty and unemployment."[71]

Lacking the support of an organized party, independents used their own funds to promote their candidacies. Desmonds M. Hall, a candidate for the Northwestern Clarendon seat, published a detailed manifesto in the *Daily Gleaner*, for which he must have paid a considerable sum. Hall was a resident of rural Jamaica and probably had little more than an elementary-school education. He was a loyal citizen of the empire and proud of that relationship. Although he invited the voters to vote "Desmonds" for "independence," it is not clear what he meant by the term, given his expressed devotion to Britain as reflected in one stanza of a poem his manifesto contained:

> Lift your hearts to Britain
> For the wondrous gift she's given
> May she early rule the world
> And reach the goal she's striven
> Three cheers for the Red, White, and Blue
> To Britain we'll be true
> The Constitution's now in sway
> This is the happier day
> Onward then Jamaica
> Sing "God save the King"
> Dear Britain gives a freedom!
> Let the Anthem ring.

This paean to Britain's benevolence in granting Jamaica a new constitution reflected the sentiments of most of the Jamaican people. It ignored the reverberations of the 1938 rebellion and the efforts of the PNP, the Jamaica Progressive League, and other organizations and individuals. But the independent candidate had been socialized into his worshipful view of Britain and her administration of the empire. Hall's manifesto, despite its simplicity and seeming incomprehension, was close to the ground, and it provides a window into the thinking of one candidate who was taking advantage of the opportunities provided by the new constitution. In its own way, it addressed some of the major issues with which Jamaican society was grappling.

MANIFESTO

RE THE NEW CONSTITUTION EDUCATION

a) A West Indian University to the faculty of Law, Medicine, Engineering, Divinity, Arts and a touch of Military Philosophy with an Addendum.

b) A thorough education of the masses. Let the masses taste the Holy Rosary of Universal Advancement.

c) Housing and salary of our school teachers. Let the elementary teachers demonstrate in practical life—Education (i.e. The supine of the Latin verb Educo regarding the elementary schools as the poor Man's University.

d) To eradicate the system of co-education in elementary schools (of the sexes).

INDUSTRIAL EDUCATION

To solve domestic and local problems of economy.

LAND SETTLEMENT

A comprehensive land settlement.

TAX

a) General Head Tax to relieve our burdened small settlers and settlers on the whole.

b) A graduated tax of lands: i.e. from revenue of the lands in proportion to the revenue from natural source.

c) General review of taxation to relieve distress of settlers.

d) Let us live on earth in peace and comfort.

AGRICULTURE

A Progressive Policy.

MEDICAL

a) Perfection of the present system.

CONSTITUTION

A scheme of research.

RELIGION

a) (Remedial): To prepare the path for the incoming souls.
b) To regard existing man as agent for the incoming souls, so that babies yet unborn, ten, twenty, and the many more years hence may sing "Praise God!" and "God save the King" when they shall have come.
c) To regard this world as God's gift to man.
d) Let Theologians lead us by the principles of biology and cease bothering the outgoing souls.
e) To build the nation for happiness and peace, and let man die as how he lives.

SOCIALISM

a) Jamaica for Jamaicans.
b) Supplication to Authorities and Capitalists to mitigate undue sufferings of the lesser classes. Jamaica the Pearl of the Antilles Rich in Resources? Why then undue poverty and distress?
c) Let us save our people from the prisons through this petty offence—larceny.

LAWS

To repeal at once the Civil Laws in support of success re the new Constitution.

GOVERNMENT

Administration of justice to all.[72]

Hall did not win the election, obtaining only 360 votes and placing last in a field of six candidates. The worker-driven rebellion of 1938 had not only given Desmonds Hall and people like him the franchise, but it also allowed them to run for the legislature. It had taken the descendants of the enslaved peoples 106 years to achieve this degree of political equality. Hall was as free to test his fortunes at the polls as were Norman Manley, Alexander Bustamante, or O. Alphonsous Malcolm, a prominent educator in the constituency who also contested the election. This right had been a long time in coming, and it constituted a political revolution in 1944. Hall lost the election, but he was a victor in a larger sense. This descendant of the enslaved peoples and the beneficiary of the rebellion of 1938 could now claim his country and his place at its center. Desmonds Hall, with all of his educational wrinkles, was one of the faces of the new Jamaica in formation.

Unlike Desmonds Hall, Isaac Barrant won his election. Nominated to contest the constituency of Eastern St. Thomas by the JLP, Barrant received 8,161 votes to 715 for his principal opponent. He had been the supervising secretary of the BITU in the parish, earning Bustamante's trust and respect. Of lowly social origins, Barrant received only a primary-school education and held a number of jobs, including that of a headman on the roads, a linesman on the Pringle Estates in St. Thomas, and a sideman on a truck. Gladys Longbridge said Barrant "knew the meaning of 'hard life' and the hunger of the poor and the obstacles they faced in struggling for betterment."

Making good on his promise to elevate the "common boys," Bustamante also selected other working people to contest the 1944 election, including Leslie Rose, a shoemaker who was elected in St. Catherine; Leopold Lynch, a tailor who won a seat in Portland; and John Regeorge Henry, a cultivator who was also successful in St. Catherine. Barrant, Rose, and Lynch won reelection in 1949, and Barrant was later named the minister of agriculture. Gladys Longbridge, a partisan, described him as "perhaps the best Minister of Agriculture the country ever had." This was a charitable assessment, but Barrant chafed under the derision of his detractors. W. A. Domingo reported on a speech that Barrant delivered in New York City: "So Barrant, after disclaiming any knowledge of science seemed determined to prove that he was not illiterate demonstrated that he could spell at least three words, for he spelled out MAN—HONEST—CONQUER, claiming that regardless of his lowly origin he was a man, that he was honest and that his party would conquer. For unknown reasons he repeated the five vowels—a e i o u." Domingo's summary of Barrant's speech may have been a caricature. There is no doubt that Barrant confronted educational challenges, as seen in a handwritten letter that he sent to Norman Manley in July 1941:

> Mr. N. W. Manley
> Barister [sic] at Law
> Duke Street
>
> Dear Sir,
> With the greatest amount of respect and pleasure we are extending to you this invitation to a Panamanian Queen Carnival to be held on the 25th August 1941 at Morant Bay. Yourself along with Mr. H. M. Shirley and Mr. Ross Livingston are asked to take part in our Cornation Ceremony. We the Workers through our commettee do humbly asked that you will accept our invitation and be prepared to give our thousands an address. Please reply.

Barrant was probably not an inspired choice for the important position of minister of agriculture. Despite his declining health, he discharged his responsibilities with seriousness and good sense, earning the admiration of even those who derided him. As Gladys Longbridge observed in her memoir, Barrant "had a vision and the energy to make plans work and he had proven his worth through union representation." His educational deficiencies notwithstanding, Barrant possessed, as did Bustamante, the earthy wisdom of the masses of the people. When Barrant died in 1956, Norman Manley described him as "a man who won the regard of every person who believed in the capacity of our people to overcome difficulties and achieve high office and hold it with merit." The rebellion of 1938 created the space for Barrant to reach beyond his boundaries, to show what Freedom's Children could accomplish if given the opportunity. Jamaica's new leaders would continue to face the daunting challenge of giving practical expression to the exhilarating promise of freedom.[73]

Hall, and minor candidates like him, were largely ignored by those representing the major parties as they attacked one another. Resurrecting the allegations that Bustamante had profited financially from the union that he led, the PNP and *Public Opinion* mercilessly assaulted his integrity. Stung by these accusations, Bustamante called them "malicious" and "socialistic-communistic." Promising to protect his safety, Bustamante issued a public challenge to Manley to attend "a mass meeting" of the JLP to substantiate the charges of fiscal malfeasance that the PNP was making against him. This was political grandstanding, and Manley ignored the challenge. The accusations did not cease, and as late as one day before the election,

Bustamante's opponent in Western Kingston, Kenneth Hill, repeated some of the charges in an advertisement in the *Gleaner*.

The corruption issue was the ubiquitous ghost that haunted the campaign. Blanshard reported that Bustamante "was suspected of receiving a large bribe, but he apparently escaped prosecution by paying it back." There were rumors, according to Blanshard, that Harold Allan, the independent candidate in the constituency of Western Portland, paid Bustamante £200 "not to Run a Labour Party candidate against him." Norman Manley reported in a document that was received by the Caribbean Commission that "it is believed that some of these persons [JLP candidates] paid substantial sums of money to Bustamante for the privilege of standing 'for labor.'" He confessed: "I cannot vouch this as a fact. . . . [It is] probably true but only in a few instances."[74] These serious and salacious charges cannot be uncritically elevated to the level of truth since their dramatic and harsh force is tempered by the absence of incontrovertible evidence. The incidence of corruption and charges of complicity leveled by the political parties at one another, particularly at election time, became pernicious features of the Jamaican political culture.

These accusations did little to damage Bustamante's credibility among his supporters. Nor did attacks on his intellectual preparation affect the ardor of his appeal. "I have real ability," his opponent Kenneth Hill boasted, "but one has only to meet Bustamante for five minutes and talk to him on any serious question, or discuss with him any matter affecting labour, where facts and figures are involved, to discover that he was politically illiterate and is only a loud mouthed fellow who had for a time captured the imagination of the masses."[75] It was common knowledge that Bustamante had not received much formal education, a deficiency that his admirers found of little consequence. Bustamante was probably more troubled by the rumor that he had an incurable sore on his foot. Dramatically removing his shoes and socks and rolling up his trousers to just above his knee, the flamboyant labor leader revealed his leg before a crowd that had gathered at the Casa Grande Hotel on Spanish Town Road. "When the crowd saw the fair unbroken skin," the *Gleaner* reported, one woman shouted, "'[W]hat beautiful legs.'" The chief "was evidently pleased with the compliment," the newspaper noted.[76]

Norman Manley was also the victim of personal assaults. He was demonized as a communist by Bustamante and by his other opponents and critics. Some conflated communism and socialism, accusing the PNP's leader and his colleagues of simultaneously promoting the two ideologies. Others damned Manley as an atheist, a particularly serious charge in an island with deep Christian beliefs and traditions. Manley was, some said, a proponent of dictatorship and an apostle of intolerance. He seemed to have been particularly stung by the accusation that he was promoting racial prejudice in the island, presumably directed at people of European descent and those who were phenotypically black. He was, according to the baseless charge, a proponent of "brown man" rule. This was an incendiary allegation; most Jamaicans had black skin, and any such suggestion was guaranteed an adverse reaction.

Manley's election campaign was certainly damaged by these serious allegations. In order to refute them, he took out an advertisement in the *Gleaner* two days before election day. Entitled "I Deny and I Affirm," Manley denied that he had said "things indicating race and colour prejudice." The PNP's leader stressed: "I hate and I fight against any form of racial intolerance. I believe that Jamaica has room for the gift of all her citizens irrespective of race or colour." He affirmed his belief in "the rights of the individual" because "civilization depends on finding how best the rights and opportunities of the individual can be enlarged within and as a part of the Community itself."[77] This exercise in damage control probably came too late in the campaign to be effective, and in any event, Manley's reputation had been already tarnished.

The JDP and the JLP were markedly more critical of the PNP than they were of each other. The PNP was the fearsome enemy; the island had to be spared the demonic power of its socialist or communist ideology. Although Bustamante denied it, the two parties seemed to have had a tacit understanding to support each other whenever either one was in a straight contest with the PNP. Bustamante said any talk of such "an alliance" between the two parties by Manley was designed "to convey to the people that I have sold Labour out to the employers." It was more "socialistic-communistic mischief," the JLP leader charged.[78]

The PNP and the JLP were both capable of engaging in political mischief. Bustamante and his party repeatedly minimized Manley's role in mediating the rebellion of May 1938, deriding his valid claim to be a friend of labor. In response, the PNP compiled a history of Manley's contribution to the labor movement since 1938, publishing it as an advertisement in the *Gleaner*. It was, save for some embellishment, an accurate account. The PNP blundered, however, when it published an advertisement in the same newspaper entitled "The Truth about Manley's Great Fight for Labour in May,

1938." It was a compilation of headlines taken from the *Gleaner* and brief excerpts from the stories, highlighting Manley's activities during those tumultuous days. The stories were doctored by the addition or deletion of certain words, and in one case a headline was completely manufactured.[79]

The advertisement was an exercise in deception. The JLP pointed out the distortions in "The Whole Truth," an advertisement it published in the *Gleaner* on November 18. Three PNP officials—William Seivright, H. O. A. Dayes, and W. E. Foster Davies—defended the party's advertisement a few days later. It was an unpersuasive defense of an unethical act. There is no evidence that Manley had seen and approved the offending advertisement. That must remain a matter of speculation, but the advertisement damaged his image and that of the party he founded and led. Paul Blanshard characterized the campaign as "vituperative, vindictive, and vulgar." The newspapers were not impartial in their coverage, he correctly alleged. The *Daily Gleaner*, the diplomat said, "preserved the fiction of impartiality" by declining to endorse candidates but "printed columns of editorial contributions centering on criticism of the P.N.P., and sparing Bustamante."[80]

As election day approached, Bustamante stood almost alone in predicting a clean sweep by his candidates. The voter turnout exceeded all expectations, as 389,109 persons, or 58.7 percent, cast their ballots. Of this number, 34,982 ballots, or 10.3 percent, were rejected or deemed to be invalid. These ballots were improperly marked, undoubtedly an indication of the high rate of illiteracy in the island. The JLP trounced its opponents, winning twenty-two seats, or 41.4 percent of the ballots that were cast. The independent candidates received 30 percent of the votes, electing five candidates. Surprisingly, the PNP polled only 82,029, or 23.5 percent, of the votes, winning five seats. Despite its lavish spending on advertisements, the JDP's nine candidates obtained only 4.1 percent of the votes, failing to win any seats. Alexander Bustamante won 68 percent of the votes in his constituency, while Kenneth Hill, his vigorous opponent, received an embarrassingly low 32 percent. Norman Manley was narrowly defeated in his constituency of Eastern St. Andrew, receiving 4,756 votes to the victor's 5,079. Of the twelve former members of the Legislative Council who contested the election, only four were elected. Two of them, Harold Allan of Portland and Roy Lindo of St. Mary, ran as independents. The other two, F. G. Veitch of Hanover and Ivan Lloyd of St. Ann, represented the JLP and the PNP, respectively. The two major parties each nominated one female candidate. The JDP did not nominate any women as candidates, and only one woman ran as an independent. Iris Collins, the JLP candidate in Northwestern

St. James, became the first woman elected to a Jamaican legislature. Edith Dalton James, who contested the constituency of Western St. Andrew on the PNP's ticket, was handily defeated by E. R. Dudley Evans of the JLP.[81]

The Jamaica Labour Party's overwhelming victory reflected the triumph of the working class that had begun to emerge during the rebellion of 1938. Norman Manley was one of the first Jamaicans to recognize the enormity of the transfiguration that the working people experienced during the election campaign and on election day. In the aftermath of the voting, Manley wrote:

> As it was, in the last week the labor vote, comprised of the uneducated and socially depressed mass, hardened and a sudden miracle of class conscious solidarity was wrought. "Vote labor" became a magic slogan. It ran like a fire thru the Island and cast a spell on all the poor-laborers and small farmers alike. The mass vote, unconscious of its own betrayal was governed by a sagacity on the political plane that would be beyond praise but for its emotional origin, and its final dependence on a blind acceptance of the orders of "The Leader."[82]

The election gave the workers their first real opportunity to act collectively on an island-wide scale. Their votes were cast predominantly for Bustamante, their acknowledged leader, voice, and advocate. The JLP's victorious candidates owed their success principally to their association with him; a vote for them was a vote for Bustamante. The JLP was Bustamante's creation, having no independent existence. Bustamante and his candidates were elected to be the enablers of Jamaica's newly minted working class in the locus of representative political power and to keep faith with the promise of the 1938 rebellion.

Manley also noticed a revolution of another sort. "By and large," he wrote, "Adult Suffrage has wrought a political Revolution. A new and for Jamaica unprecedented political awakening has occurred. It permeates all classes." It was for "the common man," Manley argued, "a great discovery of freedom to have voted for a 'cause' rather than a man and as happened in a few cases for a man of his own type and class because he stood for the cause. The circumstances are unfortunate but a deep and ancient inferiority complex has been broken for once by a sudden swift blow. The results must in the long view be significant."[83]

Most of the individuals elected to be the voice of labor in the House of Representatives, however, did not hail from the working class. They included two physicians, two lawyers, two ministers of religion, six teachers, and several businessmen and planters. Four of the elected members, in addition to Bustamante, were members of the BITU's executive committee. At least fifteen of them boasted a secondary-school education or higher. Acknowledging the support he received from labor, Bustamante declared that "the great majority of voters in this country belong to labour which includes the small cultivators and the small businessmen who faithfully promised me throughout the country that they would stand beside the Labour Party and myself. They have done so." Bustamante was grateful for this support, but he maintained that he would not "act in any way or form which would destroy any section of the country, for I realize that in any country that wishes to progress there must be Capital and Labour."[84]

Bustamante also enjoyed significant support from the wealthy, conservative business elite. Some of this affection derived from their fear of socialism, and Bustamante was expected to pursue business-friendly policies. Paul Blanshard observed that there was "a moral alliance between the conservatives and Busta." He saw the seeds of fascism in this relationship between the labor leader and the island's elite group. His rhetoric represented a devastating assault on Bustamante and his political style.

> Bustamante himself resembles the fascist stereotypes in many particulars. He is a dictator who uses mass slogans skillfully; he is antisocialist but sufficiently pro labor to escape the suspicion that he is an agent of the rich; he is more acceptable to the rich than a genuine revolutionist because he does not propose to change the class structure of the society. Those are the typical requisites of a fascist dictator in Europe, and the reaction of the upper class of Jamaica to Bustamante is quite similar to the early reaction of the European upper class to Hitler and Mussolini. . . . The conservatives think that they can control him and protect their own position in society at the same time.[85]

Although Blanshard feared that Bustamante's "incipient alliance with the upper classes" could be transformed into a fascist dictatorship, he thought that the British "traditions and safeguards for freedom of speech" made such an outcome unlikely. In addition, most English residents in the island did not welcome black rule, regardless of its ideological stripe. In fact, some of them admitted to Blanshard that they only supported Bustamante because "they think he will make 'nigger government' ridiculous."[86]

Bustamante demonstrated with some alacrity signs that he was beginning to understand the new responsibilities the voters had entrusted to him and the JLP. "My party has taken on its shoulders a very grave responsibility," he said. He seemed to have been preparing for his new role as a legislator during the campaign. "I was fighting this election with great confidence," Bustamante confessed, "and despite the fact that I realize that I am of a highly temperamental nature, I remained absolutely calm and carried through my campaign with real and true dignity of which I am proud."[87] This exercise in introspection was rare for Bustamante, but his campaign was not as high-minded in tone as he implied. Bustamante was still smarting, however, from the harsh criticisms he received during the election campaign. He complained in an interview that "the PNP have done everything humanly possible to hurt my public life and my irreproachable and unimpeachable character. The thing that hurts me most is that they did everything possible and in their organ 'Public Opinion' [to claim] that I stole £1,200, when the balance sheets in Spanish Town which every honest person could scan and show that these things are untrue."[88]

Understandably, Norman Manley was disappointed by the results of the election. Six years after its founding, the PNP did not obtain as much as one-fourth of the votes cast. It must be recalled, however, that the PNP contested only nineteen seats to the JLP's twenty-nine. This disparity helps to explain the size of the PNP's total vote, but it does not obscure the fact that the party was rejected in fourteen of the nineteen constituencies that it contested. As its leader, Manley lacked Bustamante's appeal to the workers and the small farmers who constituted the majority of the electorate, hence the party's poor showing. Frank Gordon, who witnessed the 1938 rebellion in Kingston, observed that the people "liked Norman Manley Q.C. [sic] Barrister-at-law, but they didn't like Manley, the politician." Manley would have agreed. He knew that he was not a gifted politician. "I am not a politician by instinct," he confided to Governor Richards. "I prefer honesty to tactics."[89] Paul Blanshard offered one credible explanation for Bustamante's victory. He recalled that former governor Richards "was quite frank in saying to friends that he feared Manley more than Bustamante and that he released Bustamante during the war in order to cancel the growing influence of Manley." Blanshard concluded that "the present ascendancy of Bustamante over Manley is a triumph of Machiavellian colonial policy."[90]

There were many Jamaicans, however, who grieved Manley's electoral loss, offering words of comfort. Writing to Manley from Port Antonio, L. L. Nunez, a young man, assured him that "the vast majority of thinking young Jamaicans share my unshaken and abiding faith in your wisdom and trustworthiness." He blamed Manley's defeat on "the shoddy methods of wicked men upon an ignorant electorate." William Seivright, Manley's party colleague, wrote to his leader and told him "how much the more in a monstrous defeat we love, admire, and still look up to you for leadership in what may be the country's time of its greatest danger."[91] Rather than being crippled by disappointment or consumed by the attribution of blame for the relatively dismal results, however, Jamaica's most visionary leader focused on the positive meanings of the electoral results. Four days after the election, the PNP issued an official statement vowing to continue the task of political education in the country, the struggle for self-government, and its support for the labor movement.[92] Manley elaborated on these themes when he addressed the party's annual conference on January 7, 1945.

In his address to the convention, Manley praised the voters of the country for their rejection of "whatever they thought stood for the old order." This was an undisguised reference to the JDP. "Those who voted Labour [the JLP] voted for what they believed was progress, those who voted for our party voted for what they knew was progress," Manley declared. Manley, who was committed to institutionalizing party politics in the country and deemphasizing personalities, was gratified that the lesson was "partly learnt." He admonished the gathering to "draw encouragement from the fact that we have by our leadership wrought a political revolution in this country. We have spent six years teaching Jamaicans to vote for causes, not for men. The lesson is partly learnt . . . and if we go firmly we will finally teach them the lesson and lay the foundations of a sound political development for the people by the people." Manley's genius resided in his ability to imagine and promote a different future for Jamaica, one that transcended narrow individual and partisan interests. He reminded his audience that "our job is not one of self, or position, or opportunity; it is one of working together for the good of our country for if we fail I say what will happen to Jamaica will be failure in the true sense of the word. If we succeed, Jamaica will make not only a foundation for herself for future prosperity, but a lasting and permanent contribution to the development of Colonial peoples. Our task is as big as that and it is the service we give that will uplift our country and uplift our people."[93]

Abe Issa, a prominent businessman and one of the leaders of the JDP, reaffirmed his party's intention to work for the island's self-government through "a gradual and orderly process." He knew, he said, that voters distrusted his party, believing "of our party that we fought not just for ourselves but for the Labour Party." Issa did not deny the allegation, but it hardly mattered. His party had been vanquished in the election and was on its way to oblivion.[94]

As the leader of the majority party in the House of Representatives, Bustamante had to nominate a speaker and five members of the Executive Council, as provided for by the new constitution. The council consisted of five elected members of the House of Representatives and five members nominated by the governor, who had a casting vote. This body was akin to an embryonic cabinet under the Westminster model of governance. The governor's appointees were chosen from the island's conservative wealthy elite, choices that blatantly ignored the wishes of the Jamaican who voted for the JLP and the PNP. One of the appointees, R. B. Barker, was the only member of the previous legislature to oppose the sending of a delegation to London to discuss the question of constitutional change in the island. With the support of his appointees and his possession of the casting vote, the governor could effectively control the business of the Executive Council.

Surprising his detractors, Bustamante demonstrated a capacity for growth, impressing the public with his seriousness and restraining his generally loose tongue. Writing to the Colonial Office three months after the House of Representatives was convened, Governor John Huggins reported that there had been "difficult moments" in the Executive Council "when Bustamante's excitable temperament might easily have got the better of him but, on the whole, a good start has been made." The governor was concerned, however, that the majority party had not brought forward any proposals "to implement the somewhat wild promises" that its candidates had made during the election campaign. Bustamante had not given much thought to governing the country, had produced no program, and had listed no legislative priorities. Recognizing that the majority party had no "clearly defined programme," Huggins was certain that it was "not likely to evolve one in the immediate future."

This was not a promising legislative start; Bustamante and his party were demonstrating their unpreparedness for the responsibilities of government. The governor's candid assessment of the elected members of the Executive Council provides us with some insights into the character and performance of Jamaica's newly elected leaders. Huggins's description of Bustamante was interesting though not particularly surprising. Bustamante had assigned himself the job of the executive councillor for communications, although he had no apparent qualifications for that post. In addition, he functioned as leader of the majority party in the legislature.

The governor reported that Bustamante was "clearly trying to learn his job and is obviously doing his best to restrain his natural impetuosity until he has found his feet."

Governor Huggins described Bustamante as "a shrewd, likeable individual with decent instincts, but entirely unpredictable." Bustamante, he said, "is of the dictator type who prefers to play a lone and spectacular hand." He was showing, however, "a very welcome tendency in Executive Council to listen to advice." Still, the governor worried that "even out of the clearest sky," Bustamante could "fly off the handle" and assume "a dramatic and spectacular stand, which he may quickly regret, but from which his vanity will not allow him to recede."

Huggins had much respect for Harold Allan, the executive councillor for finance and general purposes. Allan had been a member of the old legislature and now sat in the House of Representatives as an independent member. The governor considered him to be "an experienced and able Councillor and a clear and constructive thinker." Allan, he said, "had a steadying influence on Bustamante," who "places very considerable confidence in his opinion." The governor was less charitable in his description of E. R. Dudley Evans, the executive councillor for agriculture. He dismissed Evans, a solicitor, as knowing "nothing about agriculture" but said he was "making a determined effort to acquire a working knowledge of the subject." Huggins thought, however, that Evans would not "find this easy . . . because he is not overburdened with brains . . . [and] appears to be a very slow worker." J. A. McPherson, the executive councillor for education, Huggins observed, "is trying very hard and is willing to learn, but is clearly out of his depth." On the other hand, the governor saw Frank Pixley, the executive councillor for social services, as possessing "a good brain." The speaker, F. G. Veitch, was "performing moderately well," Huggins said, "but he will certainly never be an outstanding success." Veitch, he added, "is far too inclined to fortify himself with rum and may at times find it difficult to keep awake in the afternoons."[95]

Bustamante and his team did not compile a particularly notable record during their first term in office. Bustamante lost considerable popularity, even in his own constituency of Western Kingston. Facing defeat in the 1949 elections, he fled to Clarendon, where he found a more hospitable political environment and constituency. Norman Manley was elected to the House of Representatives in 1949, but the JLP retained its majority status, albeit a reduced one. In 1952 the PNP faced a bitter internal crisis when it expelled four of its leading members who were identified as communists. Norman

Manley's handling of the imbroglio invited the tender praise of his second son, Michael, then a young man of twenty-eight. "Dad," Michael's letter to his father began, "may I say, humbly, that there could not have been a finer chapter in your life than the last six months." He then admonished: "Do not cease till we have built Jerusalem."[96]

Approximately thirty months after Michael's touching tribute to his father, the PNP won Jamaica's third general election held under universal adult suffrage. Many workers and small farmers had shifted their party allegiance and would do so time and time again. Party politics was becoming imbedded in the island's psychology and culture. Norman Manley, its principal architect, understood the continuing fragility of his creation. Writing in 1968 to his former nemesis Arthur Richards, now Lord Milverton, he shared his fears about his homeland's future. "Here in Jamaica we are passing through difficult times," Manley wrote. "If the two-party system can survive then we will come through safely, but if not, I wouldn't like to prophesy what will happen."[97] The two-party system has continued to survive, but Jerusalem is still under construction.

CONCLUSION

It had been a century since property in persons had officially ended in Jamaica. But the passage of the Act of Emancipation in 1833 and the formal end of slavery in 1838 could not destroy the habits of thought and behavior that had nurtured and fertilized the institution of African slavery in the island since its introduction by the Spaniards in 1511. Their English successors had expanded and strengthened it, continuing the psychological maiming of the society and all of its people. Emancipation did not exorcise the invisible demons of slavery; they were too pervasive, ubiquitous, and entrenched.

Jamaican society was not static in its century of freedom. A minority of the descendants of the enslaved had inched their way into the middle class, and some even sat in the Legislative Council. There was a glass ceiling, however, and black Jamaicans could not aspire to fill the top positions in the colonial administration. The changes that would have created a dominant space for the majority of Jamaicans in the political and economic systems of the island did not occur. Marginalized and battered by the brutish circumstances of their lives, these people made the most of their situation, surviving as best they could. The enslaved peoples in Jamaica had a tradition of resistance, and that rebellious spirit continued in freedom. Occurring in 1865, the Morant Bay Rebellion was one dramatic example of violent protest. But resistance took other forms as well. The society had grown accustomed to the landless occupying other people's property, work stoppages, sabotage at the workplace, verbal attacks on employers, and so on. Unlike the more-privileged members of the society who employed their rhetoric, pen, typewriter, and votes as sites of opposition to conditions they disliked, the working people used their bodies as the vehicles of resistance. Underneath the society's veneer of calm for long periods existed a rage that awaited an igniting spark to destroy the old order.

Discontented workers rebelled in May and June 1938. Their actions were spontaneous outbursts, the product of the accumulated grievances of a people upon whom life had not smiled too brilliantly. Angry and atomized, these workers did not yet possess a well-defined class consciousness. Their primary loyalties were to family, boss and workplace, church, local affiliations, and home district. Deeply suspicious of differences, most workers did not share a larger consciousness and an identity with those who labored at similar jobs in another village, town, or city. Employers used these atomized workers as strikebreakers and encouraged competition among them in order to pay lower wages. The rebellion produced a series of epiphanies among them as they came to recognize that they shared similar experiences, travails, and challenges. Jamaican workers began to forge a common consciousness as they appreciated the efficacy of collective action. Their searing experiences in the struggles of 1938 made of them an embryonic working class, anxious to become members of modern trade unions and supporters of the political parties in formation.

Long the victims of race, color, and class prejudices, Freedom's Children assaulted the physical and symbolic exemplars of their oppression during the rebellion. Their long-term victory over these forces cannot be measured only by the usual tangible criteria, such as improvements in wages and working conditions. Their victory fueled the process of changing the zeitgeist of their homeland. This troubling and shuffling of the social and racial status quo would be slow, painful, and frequently frustrating, but the process could not be contained and remains in progress.

Alexander Bustamante emerged as the principal voice of the workers, although he had not come from their ranks. A member of the privileged colonial elite by color and self-proclaimed wealth, Bustamante had embraced the cause of the workers before May 1938, but with modest success. Bustamante did not stimulate the rebellion in Frome. Nor was he its architect on the Kingston waterfront. The heroes of the island-wide rebellion were the workers and their unemployed allies. Bustamante hurried to Frome after the outbreak of the revolt, and he was invited by workers on the Kingston waterfront to lead them after they had begun their protest. They shouted their decision to strike when Bustamante asked their intentions on May 22. The newly minted leader was not the proponent of this course of action. He had not been a worker on the waterfront or anywhere else, so he lacked the moral authority to recommend such a potentially life-altering act.

But the developing rebellion became Bustamante's moment. Accepting with gusto the invitation to lead the workers on Kingston's wharves, he electrified them with his speeches, increasing the tempo and ferocity of the protest. Bustamante, however, did not articulate a coherent series of demands for the workers he was leading or a leadership strategy. The workers had made Bustamante their voice, an expression of belief in his sincerity and in his capacity to advocate and represent their cause. It was a gigantic leap of faith because Bustamante had yet to prove his mettle as a labor leader.

Bustamante's arrest conferred martyrdom on him. In its telling and retelling, the labor leader's behavior at the time of his arrest in May 1938 reached mythical proportions. The seemingly intrepid Bustamante had lost his freedom briefly in labor's cause, a sacrifice that assured him the affection of the workers and a lasting place in the island's labor lore. Bustamante's release from jail led to a resolution of the crisis in Kingston, but the rebellion continued in many parts of the island for at least another two weeks. Moving quickly to marshal the energies of the workers, Bustamante began to form labor unions, achieving a much greater degree of success than Allan Coombs, the founder of modern trade unionism in the island, could ever have imagined.

Intolerant of criticism of the colonial administration, particularly during wartime, Governor Arthur Richards ordered Bustamante's internment in September 1940. Bustamante was accused of advocating violence and fomenting a race war. It was a spurious charge, driven largely by the imperative to destroy the nascent movement for self-government. Hoping that Bustamante's internment would deny the movement the mass support of the workers, the governor used the power of the colonial state to silence him. Bustamante's release after seventeen months was ostensibly a quid pro quo for his decision to sever his union's ties with the People's National Party and the struggle for self-government.

Bustamante's internment raised his stock among the workers. But his ugly brawl with Norman Manley after his release damaged the cause of unionism in the island. Although Bustamante's emotional connection with the workers remained strong, he was chronically unable to work well with his colleagues. Nor did he embrace democratic principles in his union or in the Jamaica Labour Party that he founded in 1943. These disabilities and allegations of fiscal impropriety in the Bustamante Industrial Trade Union did not seriously tarnish his image or undermine his support among the workers. His erratic management style and unfamiliarity with the etiquette of the negotiating table were hardly assets to the union. His personal limitations notwithstanding, Alexander Bustamante contributed more than anyone else at the time to the growth of trade unionism and the struggle for social justice in Jamaica.

If the workers called Bustamante into service, they also created the space for Norman Manley to enter the political arena. The successful barrister had volunteered to mediate the rebellion on the waterfront in May 1938, placing his considerable legal talent and prestige at the disposal of the workers. Hitherto, Manley had confined himself to the practice of the law and the welfare of wealthy clients such as the West Indies Sugar Company. The rebellion on the waterfront was Manley's epiphany. Heeding a call to public service, he proposed the formation of a political party to promote and safeguard the workers' interests. Upon Bustamante's release from jail, the two men traveled together to restore calm in the island. It was an uneasy partnership, as they possessed different temperaments and intellectual backgrounds, as well as competing ambitions.

Norman Manley supported Bustamante's efforts to unionize the workers, but he declined to describe himself as a labor leader. In early 1939 he played a defining role in helping unionism to survive in the island when Bustamante called an ill-conceived general strike. Manley gave Bustamante legal assistance when he was interned in 1940, although Bustamante later maintained, albeit erroneously, that Manley's efforts were neither aggressive nor effective.

Manley's public trajectory changed fundamentally as a consequence of the labor rebellion. It sensitized him to the plight of the workers, introducing him to a world far removed from that of the privileged, of whom he was a part. Manley's founding, along with others, of the People's National Party in September 1938 was a function of the epiphany he had experienced. His promotion of the causes of socialism, constitutional change, and self-government reflected his political evolution. Manley lacked Bustamante's rapport with the workers, but he was unquestionably the principal architect of party politics and the movement for self-government in the island.

Bustamante and Manley dominated the political life of Jamaica between 1938 and 1944, and they would do so for the subsequent two decades. Apart from their cooperating briefly on the cause of trade unionism and Bustamante's brief membership in the PNP, the two men held different visions of the country's future. Manley proclaimed himself and the PNP socialists, while Bustamante affirmed his devotion to capitalism. Bustamante opposed Manley's demand for immediate self-government, emphasizing his deep loyalty to the British Empire. His indefensible internment for seventeen months did little to temper his support for colonialism, although it shook his faith somewhat in the purity of British justice. Manley was the supreme political visionary of the time, bold and imaginative in his thinking and a fearless advocate of self-government and the democratic rights of all Jamaicans. Between 1938 and 1944, Bustamante did not demonstrate any leadership on such important questions as universal adult suffrage, constitutional change, and self-government. He was a labor leader, passionately committed to improving the condition of Jamaica's workers. But being unschooled and inexperienced in the modus operandi of modern trade unions, Bustamante frequently damaged the labor movement by his unsteady and undisciplined leadership style as much as he helped it.

Bustamante, Manley, and their respective lieutenants were the progeny of the labor rebellion. They were the elite voices of Jamaica's workers, leaders that the people trusted to represent them around the negotiating table with the barons of capital and in the halls of political power. The thousands of men and women whose rebellion shook the island like an earthquake in May and June 1938 were planting the seeds of a new Jamaica. They rudely awakened the colonial state to the wrongs of economic exploitation and deprivation, racially based privilege, and the denial of basic political rights to the vast majority of the people. A century after slavery's end, the workers of the island had forced a new beginning. Some people gave their lives, others faced bayonets with courage and resolve, and still others became the daring and resolute foot soldiers in service of a sustained and meaningful societal change. They were the true progenitors of modern Jamaica.

Jamaica became a sovereign nation in 1962, twenty-four years after the labor rebellion. A half century later, the island has acquired the trappings of a modern society, a strong middle class has emerged, and there have been significant improvements in its infrastructure and in the provision and delivery of social services. But Jamaica is also a fertile ground for political corruption, a site of an entrenched personalism in politics, a violent society with a monstrous crime rate and an appalling disrespect for human life. It boasts a pervasive and crippling poverty, manifesting the stark reality that for many citizens, a tenacious hope is a cruel illusion. Colorism has not disappeared from the cultural landscape, and an acute bigotry against gays and lesbians is ubiquitous, often clothed in a vulgar Christian rhetoric.

Jamaica's political leaders, with some exceptions, have been deficient in espousing lofty visions for the society, and mediocrity has been elevated to a principle in the nation's secular and political lives. Their challenges have been exacerbated by the structurally created economic weaknesses inherited from colonialism and the impact of harsh global conditions on the fortunes of a small and relatively poor island. The island is still haunted by the ghosts of slavery and colonialism, ugly spectres that must be exorcised before the people can move forward with a healthy sense of self and confidence, commanding a future unburdened by the demons of the past. The creative energies of Jamaicans have not been stilled; they remain vibrant and ready to be harnessed and channeled into new and positive directions. The descendants of Freedom's Children still await, for the most part, the fulfillment of the tantalizing promise of 1938.

NOTES

Abbreviations

BM Bustamante Museum, Kingston, Jamaica
CO Records of the Colonial Office, Commonwealth and Foreign and Commonwealth Offices, British National Archives, London
DG *Daily Gleaner*, Kingston, Jamaica
JA Jamaica Archives, Spanish Town, Jamaica
NA-DS National Archives, U.S. Department of State, Record Group 59, College Park, Md.
NMP Norman Manley Papers, Jamaica Archives, Spanish Town, Jamaica

Introduction

1. For a discussion of Bustamante's genealogy and early life, see George Eaton, *Alexander Bustamante and Modern Jamaica* (Kingston: Kingston Publishers Limited, 1973), 1–16.

2. Norman Manley's early life is also discussed in Rex Nettleford, ed., *Manley and the New Jamaica: Selected Speeches and Writings, 1938–1968* (London: London Caribbean Limited, 1971).

3. "Lecturer Outlines Problems of History," *DG*, January 24, 1957, 9. Augier was one of my mentors at the university.

Chapter One

1. "Down the Union Jack, up the Black, Gold, and Green," *DG*, August 8, 1962, 1.

2. A useful summary of Jamaica's constitutional development is found in "History of the Constitution of Jamaica," CO 137/847/7.

3. O. Nigel Bolland, *On the March: Labour Rebellions in the British Caribbean, 1934–39* (Kingston: Ian Randle Publishers; London: James Currey Publishers, 1995), 7.

4. Arthur Richards to the Secretary of State for the Colonies, February 24, 1939, CO 137/834/7.

5. Arthur Richards to the Secretary of State for the Colonies, April 22, 1939, CO 137/834/7.

6. Ibid.

7. Ibid.

8. Ibid.

9. "The Jamaica People," editorial, *DG*, March 13, 1939, 12.

10. *Eighth Census of Jamaica and Dependencies* (Kingston: Government Printer, 1945), LXIX. See also, "What the Census Tells," *DG*, February 10, 1944, 1, 4.

11. *Eighth Census of Jamaica and Dependencies*, 3.

12. See "The National Income of Jamaica, 1942," a bulletin prepared by Frederic Benham and located in CO 137/865/5.

13. "Report by Orde Browne," July 18, 1939, CO 137/835/2. See also "Major Orde Browne's Report on Conditions in Jamaica," *DG*, August 9, 1939, 18, 19; and "Major Orde Browne's Report," DG, August, 16, 1939, 8.

14. "Report by Orde Browne."

15. "Report on Unemployment in Jamaica," April 20, 1936, CO 137/811/13. The commission reported that 12,721 Jamaicans were "repatriated" to the island between 1930 and 1934. They came principally from Cuba, Panama, and Costa Rica. In addition, 15,500 persons returned voluntarily during the same period. The two groups of returnees brought 3,000 children with them. Finding it difficult to obtain employment on the island, many of these people participated in the 1938 labor rebellion.

16. Editorial, *DG*, January 5, 1938, 10.

17. "Report on Unemployment in Jamaica." For a very detailed analysis of the working population of Jamaica in 1943, see *Eighth Census of Jamaica and Dependencies*, 148–212. See also James Carnegie, *Some Aspects of Jamaican Politics, 1918–1938* (Kingston: Institute of Jamaica, 1973), 21.

18. Patrick E. Bryan and Karl Watson, eds., *Not for Wages Alone: Eyewitness Summaries of the 1939 Labour Rebellion in Jamaica* (Mona: University of the West Indies Press, 2003), 64.

19. Ibid., 138–39

20. Ibid., 122.

21. Ibid., 112.

22. Ibid., 109.

23. *Eighth Census of Jamaica and Dependencies*, XCI–CII.

24. Ibid.

25. Bryan and Watson, *Not for Wages Alone*, 130.

26. For a discussion of Robert Rumble's role in the search for land, see Ken Post, *Arise Ye Starvelings: The Jamaican Labour Rebellion of 1938 and Its Aftermath* (The Hague: Martinus Nijhoff, 1978), 248–49. For a fine discussion of land settlement schemes in Jamaica, see Marleen A. Bartley, "Land Settlement in Jamaica, 1923–1949," in *Jamaica in Slavery and Freedom: History, Heritage, and Culture*, ed. Kathleen Monteith and Glen Richards (Kingston: University of West Indies Press, 2002), 324–39.

27. Abigail B. Bakan, *Ideology and Class Conflict in Jamaica* (Montreal and Kingston: McGill-Queens University Press, 1990). See also Post, *Arise Ye Starvelings*, 6.

28. See Bakan, *Ideology and Class Conflict in Jamaica*, and Post, *Arise Ye Starvelings*.

29. For the text of the Declaration of Rights of the Negro Peoples of the World, see William L. Van Deburg, ed., *Modern Black Nationalism: From Marcus Garvey to Louis Farrakhan* (New York: New York University Press, 1997), 23–31. See also

Tony Martin, *Race First: The Ideological and Organizational Struggles of Marcus Garvey and the Universal Negro Improvement Association* (Westport, Conn.: Greenwood Press, 1976).

30. Carnegie, *Some Aspects of Jamaican Politics*, 55.

31. Van Deburg, *Modern Black Nationalism*, 29–30.

32. For an insightful discussion of Ethiopianism, see Wilson Jeremiah Moses, *Afrotopia: The Roots of African American Popular History* (New York: Cambridge University Press, 1998). For a discussion of the rise of the Rastafarian movement, see Post, *Arise Ye Starvelings*, 163–74. The impact of the Italo-Ethiopian war on African Americans and their responses are discussed by Joseph E. Harris, *African American Reactions to War in Ethiopia, 1936–1941* (Baton Rouge: Louisiana State University Press, 1994); and William R. Scott, *The Sons of Sheba's Race: African Americans and the Italo-Ethiopian War, 1935–1941* (Bloomington: University of Indiana Press, 1993).

33. Carnegie, *Some Aspects of Jamaican Politics*, 96–127.

Chapter Two

1. "P. W. Labourers to Get 25 Percent Increase in Wages," *DG*, May 31, 1938, 1, 7. Ken Post has written the most detailed account of the labor rebellion of 1938. See his *Arise Ye Starvelings: The Jamaican Labour Rebellion of 1938 and Its Aftermath* (The Hague: Martinus Nijhoff, 1978), and *Strike the Iron: A Colony at War*, vol. 1, *Jamaica, 1939–1945* (Atlantic Highlands, N.J.: Humanities Press, 1981).

2. "Since Retirement, Reflections by Sir Alexander Bustamante," undated, uncataloged, BM, 1.

3. For a good discussion of Underhill's letter, see Abigail Bakan, *Ideology and Class Conflict in Jamaica* (Montreal and Kingston: McGill-Queens University Press, 1990), 70–75.

4. 439 black persons lost their lives during the rebellion, and another 354 were executed after questionable court proceedings.

5. Bustamante to George Griffiths, January 26, 1938, CO 137/825/12.

6. Ibid.

7. Bustamante to Clement Attlee, February 11, 1938, CO 137/825/12.

8. Bustamante to Clement Attlee, March 16, 1938, in ibid. For a discussion of the unrest in Trinidad, consult Kelvin Singh, *Race and Class Struggles in a Colonial State: Trinidad, 1917–1945* (Alberta: University of Calgary Press; and Kingston: University of the West Indies Press, 1994).

9. "Call for a Commission of Enquiry," Bustamante to the Editor, *Manchester Guardian*, April 6, 1938, filed in CO 137/825/12.

10. Governor Denham to the Secretary of State for the Colonies, April 17, 1938, CO 137/825/12.

11. Ibid.

12. Governor Denham to the Secretary of State for the Colonies, May 8, 1938, CO 137/826/9. See also Governor Denham to the Secretary of State, April 17, 1938, CO 137/825/12. Run along the lines of the Borstal School in England, industrial

schools were institutions where boys were taught agriculture, carpentry, and tailoring and girls were taught domestic subjects.

13. These press clippings are found in CO 137/825/12.
14. "Children without Clothes," *DG*, April 21, 1938, 1.
15. "Tate and Lyle Probably Spend £500,000 in Westmoreland This Year," *DG*, March 26, 1938, 1. See "Report to the Governor," October 15, 1938, CO 137/826/9.
16. *Report (with Appendices) of the Commission Appointed to Enquire into the Disturbances Which Occurred in Jamaica between the 23rd May and the 8th June 1938* (Kingston: Government Printer, 1938).
17. Governor Denham to the Secretary of State for the Colonies, May 8, 1938, CO 137/826/9.
18. "Five Shots Were Fired," *DG*, May 2, 1938, 1; "1,000 Labourers Halt Tate and Lyle in Westmoreland," *DG*, May 2, 1938, 1.
19. Ibid.
20. Patrick E. Bryan and Karl Watson, eds., *Not for Wages Alone: Eyewitness Summaries of the 1938 Labour Rebellion in Jamaica* (Mona: University of the West Indies Press, 2003), 61
21. "1,000 Labourers Halt Tate and Lyle," 1.
22. "The Workers Side in Westmoreland Fatal Riot Issue," *DG*, May 4, 1938, 7.
23. "The Harangue That Added Fire to Fury," *DG*, May 3, 1938, 1.
24. "4 Dead, 9 in Hospital, 89 Arrested," *DG*, May 3, 1938, 1.
25. "Report re Strike at Frome," O'Donoghue to the Inspector General, undated, CO 137/826/9; Report by Inspector S. Huggins, May 3, 1938, CO 137/826/9.
26. "Riot Ended," *DG*, May 4, 1938, 1; Bryan and Watson, *Not for Wages Alone*, 62.
27. "Governor's Strong Warning to Agitators," *DG*, May 4, 1938, 1.
28. Governor Denham to the Secretary of State for the Colonies, May 21, 1938, CO 137/826/9.
29. "The Management States," *DG*, May 2, 1938, 1.
30. "To Provide Work for Unemployed in Kingston," *DG*, May 4, 1938, 1.
31. "British Parliament Hears about Westmoreland's Riots," *DG*, May 5, 1938, 1.
32. "London Journal and Duty Cast on Tate and Lyle," *DG*, May 6, 1938, 1.
33. Ibid.
34. "Cheap Sugar in UK Caused Sweated Labour in W.I.," *DG*, May 7, 1938, 1, 6.
35. "Lord Olivier Comes out Again in Defence of West Indian Labour," *DG*, May 11, 1938, 1.
36. "Governor Denham to the Secretary of State for the Colonies," May 21, 1938, CO 137/826/9.
37. Ibid.
38. "Promised Work Today and They Are Out to Get It," *DG*, May 12, 1938, 1; "Labourers Want Work Cost It What It Will," *DG*, May 13, 1938, 1.
39. "Angry Unemployed Again Stop Work at Trench Pen," *DG*, May 18, 1938, 1.
40. "Unrest on the Waterfront," *DG*, May 20, 1938, 1, 10; "Rates of Pay on Wharves of Metropolis," *DG*, May 20, 1938, 1, 10.
41. Bryan and Watson, *Not for Wages Alone*, 70.

42. Ibid., 173.
43. Ibid.
44. Ibid., 70.
45. Ibid.
46. Ibid., 70–72.
47. "Since Retirement," 4.
48. Bryan and Watson, *Not for Wages Alone*, 72.
49. Ibid., 34.
50. Ibid., 172.
51. Ibid.
52. Ibid., 33–34.
53. Ibid., 148.
54. Ibid.
55. Ibid.
56. Ibid., 138.
57. Ibid., 168.
58. Ibid., 63.
59. Ibid., 175.
60. Ibid., 170.
61. Ibid., 33–34.
62. "Since Retirement," 5.
63. "Sunday's Dawn Brings Strike to No. 2 Pier," *DG*, May 23, 1938, 10.
64. Ibid.
65. "Highlights of City Labour Trouble Seen Yesterday," *DG*, May 23, 1938, 11. Campbell was elected a member of the Legislative Council in a bye election in 1939.
66. This brief summary of the events of May 21 and May 22 are taken from various reports in the *Daily Gleaner*. See "City Dock Hands Stick out in Strike for Higher Wages," *DG*, May 23, 1938, 1; "Weekend Labour Troubles," *DG*, May 23, 1938, 10; "Labour Leader Tries Hard to Settle Strike," *DG*, May 23, 1938; "Case of the Workers," *DG*, May 23, 1938; "'Fighting Barrister' Booed as He Tried to Calm Discontent," *DG*, May 23, 1938, 11; "Sunday's Dawn Brings Strike to No. 2 Pier," *DG*, May 23, 1938, 10; "Situation at Grace Wharf Is Unchanged," *DG*, May 23, 1938, 11; "Sailors Show Sympathy with Local Longshoremen's Strike," *DG*, May 23, 1938.
67. "5 Given Prison Terms for Taking Part in 'Mob' Day Disorders," *DG*, June 15, 1938, 10.
68. Bryan and Watson, *Not for Wages Alone*, 132.
69. Ibid., 68.
70. The best account of the rebellion of May 23 and May 24 is found in "Two Killed, One Seriously Wounded as Police Fire to Drive Back Mob," *DG*, May 25, 1938, 1, 7; "Mother and Two Small Sons Shot down in Matthews Lane; Two of Three Killed Instantly," *DG*, May 25, 1938, 1.
71. Bryan and Watson, *Not for Wages Alone*, 74.
72. Ibid., 48.
73. "Since Retirement," 6.

74. "Bail Refused for Bustamante and Grant," *DG*, May 25, 1938, 1.
75. "Since Retirement," 7
76. Ibid.
77. Bryan and Watson, *Not for Wages Alone*, 141.
78. "Mr. Manley Pledges Himself to Advocate Labour's Cause," *DG*, May 25, 1938, 1, 7.
79. Ibid.
80. Ibid.
81. "Special Power Given Governor in Emergency," *DG*, May 26, 1938, 1. The governor's comment on Manley is found in O. Nigel Bolland, *On the March: Labour Rebellions in the British Caribbean, 1934–39* (Kingston: Ian Randle Publishers; London: James Currey Publishers, 1995), 140.
82. "Manley Busy as Mediator in Strike Case," *DG*, May 26, 1938, 1, 7; "Statement to Ship Labourers by Mr. Manley," *DG*, May 26, 1938, 1.
83. "Conciliation Board Starts Its Labours," *DG*, May 28, 1938, 1; "Further Strikes," *DG*, May 28, 1938, 1, 7; "Trouble at Caymanas Estate Yesterday," *DG*, May 28, 1938, 7; Commission Report, November 15, 1938, 7 CO 137/826/9; "Spanish Town Mob Meets Police with Bricks and Revolver Shots," *DG*, May 27, 1938, 1.
84. "Has Labour Won?," *DG*, May 27, 1938, 7.
85. "Labour's Big Chance to Have Its Just Claims Recognised," *DG*, May 27, 1938, 1.
86. "Ready to Form Union: But Jailed Leaders Must First Be Freed," *DG*, May 28, 1938, 1; "No Work, We Want Bustamante," *DG*, May 28, 1938, 1.
87. "Bustamante and Grant out Saturday," *DG*, May 30, 1938, 1, 7; "Dock Strike Settled Saturday Afternoon," *DG*, May 30, 1938, 1, 7; "Mr. Bustamante Sees Better Day for the Toilers," *DG*, May 30, 1938, 1.
88. "Dock Strikers Welcome Labour Leader after Release," *Jamaica Standard*, May 30, 1938, 3; "Bustamante Will Stand for Legislature in 1940," *DG*, June 14, 1938, 1. Aggie Bernard, a woman who cooked on the wharf and sold food to the men, deserves credit for organizing the feeding program for the strikers. See Bryan and Watson, *Not for Wages Alone*, 75–76, 174.
89. See *Report of the Commission*.
90. Marcus Garvey to the Secretary of State for the Colonies, May 26, 1938, CO 137/834/7.
91. P. W. Peat to the Secretary of State for the Colonies, June 1938 (exact date not clear), CO 137/834/7.
92. Glanville Richards to the Secretary of State for the Colonies, June 7, 1938, CO 137/834/7.
93. James Gibb to the Secretary of the State for the Colonies, June 6, 1938, CO 137/834/7.
94. These resolutions are located in CO 137/834/7.
95. "Stern Warning to Hooligans and Roughs," *DG*, June 2, 1938, 3.
96. "Bustamante Appeals to All to Maintain Law and Order," *DG*, June 7, 1938.
97. "Minimum Rates for Classes of Agricultural Labour in St. Mary," *DG*, June 2, 1938, 1.

98. "£500,000 for Land Settlement and to Lessen Unemployment," *DG*, June 6, 1938, 1.
99. *Report of the Commission*.
100. Ibid.
101. Norman Manley to the editor of the *DG*, June 21, 1947, NMP 4/60/2B/12
102. "To the People of Jamaica," *DG*, November 17, 1944, 7.
103. Bryan and Watson, *Not for Wages Alone*, 109.

Chapter Three

1. A copy of this letter is located in the Norman Manley Papers. It was dated April 12, 1939, and an informed analysis of it suggests that it was written by Robert Kirkwood. Manley's copy was unsigned, so its author will probably remain a matter of speculation. See NMP 4/60/2B/5. For a discussion of British racial attitudes to African peoples, see Philip D. Curtin, *The Image of Africa: British Ideas and Action, 1780–1850*, 2 vols. (Madison: University of Wisconsin Press, 1964); and Winthrop Jordan, *White over Black: American Attitudes toward the Negro, 1550–1812* (Chapel Hill: University of North Carolina Press, 1968).
2. Dr. Anderson to Dr. Moody, July 5, 1938, CO 138/435/2.
3. Una Marson, "Racial Feelings," *Public Opinion*, July 17, 1937, 3.
4. Ibid.
5. Una Marson, "Coloured Contributions," *Public Opinion*, July 3, 1937, 11.
6. George Seymour Seymour to Norman Manley, July 4, 1938, NMP 4/60/2B/2.
7. Patrick E. Bryan and Karl Watson, eds., *Not for Wages Alone: Eyewitness Summaries of the 1939 Labour Rebellion in Jamaica* (Mona: University of the West Indies Press, 2003), 121.
8. Ibid., 125.
9. Ibid., 135.
10. Curtin, *The Image of Africa*.
11. Davies's unsolicited letter can be found in CO 137/849/7.
12. Ibid.
13. Mrs. Hyatt-Shortt's letter is located in CO 137/849/7.
14. Ibid.
15. Josiah Oldfield to Lord Cranbourne, undated, CO 137/849/7.
16. Ibid.
17. Oldfield to Manley, May 27, 1947; and Manley to Oldfield, June 21, 1947, NMP 4/60/2B/12.
18. "No Servant Problem in Jamaica," *DG*, February 2, 1939, 19.
19. Ibid.
20. Ibid.
21. Ibid.
22. Ibid. See also "Witchcraft in Jamaica," *DG*, January 16, 1939, 18.
23. "Bishop's Secretary Gives Her Impressions of Jamaica and Jamaicans," *DG*, August 29, 1939, 9.

24. "Bishop Sara Disassociates Himself from Statements Supposed to Have Been Made by Miss Mary Luke, His Secretary," *DG*, October 23, 1939, 3.
25. Ibid.
26. "Bishop Sara Resigns as Assistant Bishop," *DG*, October 13, 1939, 1.
27. "Impressions of Jamaica," *DG*, February 6, 1939, 17; also "Impressions of Jamaica," *DG*, February 24, 1939, 19.
28. Pease to Secretary of State, 1939, CO 137/827/1.
29. Ibid.
30. "Minister Writes on Jamaica," *DG*, November 4, 1938, 11.
31. "Loyal "Children' of the Empire," *DG*, November 1, 1938, 17.
32. Ibid.
33. Ernest Platt to Creech Jones, December 5, 1942, CO 968/68/5.
34. Ibid.
35. See Eric Williams, *British Historians and the West Indies* (New York: Charles Scribner's Sons, 1966).
36. "Resentment over Terms of Advertisement," *DG*, July 1, 1938, 1.
37. Ibid.
38. "That Medical Advertisement," *DG*, July 6, 1938, 7; "London Again Hears about This Colony," *DG*, July 5, 1938, 1,; "Late News from Great Britain," *DG*, August 16, 1938, 17.
39. Anderson to Moody, July 5, 1938, CO 318/435/2.
40. Ibid.
41. "Mayor's Cable," editorial, *DG*, July 7, 1938, 12.
42. Ibid.
43. "Discrimination in Stores," letter to the editor, *DG*, December 3, 1938, 12.
44. Marson, "Racial Feelings," 3.
45. Bryan and Watson, *Not for Wages Alone*, 64.
46. Ibid., 109.
47. "Situations Vacant," advertisement in the *Jamaica Standard*, September 23, 1938, 18.
48. Bryan and Watson, *Not for Wages Alone*, 152.
49. Ibid., 127.
50. "Discrimination in Stores," 12.
51. "Faced with Censure Motion, Mayor Resigns," *DG*, July 12, 1939, 7.
52. Ibid.
53. Ibid.
54. Ibid.
55. Ibid.
56. Ibid.
57. Ibid.
58. Ibid.
59. "Thousands Ask Dr. Anderson to Stand Again," *DG*, July 16, 1938, 1.
60. "People's Request," editorial, *DG*, July 14, 1938, 12.
61. "Kingston Citizens Association Meeting and Dr. Anderson's Resignation," *DG*, July 14, 1938, 20; "Colour Discrimination?," letter from Rupert Meikle, *DG*,

July 15, 1938, 12; "Jamaicans Abroad Approve Action of Dr. Anderson in Resigning as Mayor," *DG*, August 6, 1938, 3; "Jamaicans in New York Irked by Advertisement for Doctor Here," *DG*, July 19, 1938, 7; "A Man with a Golden Heart," letter from Edgar Bradshaw, *DG*, July 18, 1938, 17; "The Resolution of Censure," letter from O. Alphonsous Malcolm, *DG*, July 16, 1938, 12.

62. "Ability Not Colour," editorial, *DG*, July 16, 1938, 12.

63. "Dr. Anderson's Resignation," letter from "Rate Payer," *DG*, July 16, 1938, 12; "Why Foster Race Hatred?," letter from "Thoughts of a Reader," *DG*, July 8, 1938, 17; "Why Foster Race Hatred?," letter from "Anti-Humbug," *DG*, July 18, 1938, 17.

64. "Dr. Anderson Again on Corporation Council," *DG*, August 4, 1938, 1.

65. Bryan and Watson, *Not for Wages Alone*, 152, 25, 153.

66. Norman Manley to Dr. Wilfred Rankin, May 31, 1946, NMP 4/60/2B/11.

67. H. C. Buchanan to N. W. Manley, May 26, 1943, NMP 4/60/2B/7.

Chapter Four

1. "Who's Who in the W.I. Royal Commission," *DG*, October 13, 1938, 23.

2. Ken Post, *Arise Ye Starvelings: The Jamaican Labour Rebellion of 1938 and Its Aftermath* (The Hague: Martinus Nijhoff, 1978), 249.

3. See the advertisement, "Notice," *DG*, June 24, 1938, 2; "Timely Warning," editorial, *DG*, June 15, 1938, 12.

4. "Peasants Think They Will Get Free Lands Emancipation Day," *DG*, June 28, 1938, 8.

5. "Elected Members Asked to Dispel Land Claim Delusion among Tenants in Country," *DG*, July 15, 1938, 17.

6. "Text of Message to Acting Governor on Rumored Emancipation Day Disturbances," *DG*, July 26, 1938, 16.

7. These sentiments are found in messages from the Hon. A. B. Lowe, *DG*, July 30, 1938, 33; Alexander Bustamante, *DG*, July 30, 1938, 27; centenary sermon, "Lest We Forget," *DG*, August 16, 1938, 13.

8. "England and Emancipation," *DG*, July 30, 1938, 26. For a discussion of slavery in Africa, see Suzanne Meiers and Igor Kopytoff, eds., *Slavery in Africa: Historical and Anthropological Perspectives* (Madison: University of Wisconsin Press, 1977).

9. "England and Emancipation," 26.

10. "Peasants Think That They Will Get Free Lands," 8.

11. For a discussion of the Sam Sharpe rebellion, see Mary Turner, *Slaves and Missionaries: The Disintegration of Jamaican Slave Society, 1788–1834* (Urbana: University of Illinois Press, 1982).

12. "History of Emancipation," *DG*, July 30, 1938, 38. William Knibb was a revered Baptist missionary in the island.

13. Ibid.

14. Ibid.

15. E. L. Allen, letter to the editor, *DG*, June 27, 1938, 10. Allen later became the island's minister of education.

16. "Timely Warning," editorial, *DG*, June 24, 1938, 12.

17. "Bloodshed Disappointment," editorial, *Jamaica Labour Weekly*, August 6, 1938, 1.

18. "Emancipation Day," letter to the editor, *DG*, June 25, 1938, 12.

19. "Perfect Peace," by E. F. Williams in *Jamaica Labour Weekly*, August 13, 1938, 4.

20. "Message from the Hon. C. C. Woolley, *DG*, July 30, 1938, 25.

21. "Mack and Fippence Is Their Cry," *DG*, October 24, 1938, 17; "Britain's Overseas Responsibilities," *DG*, October 24, 1938, 17.

22. "Royal Commission Appointed [to] Investigate W. I. Conditions," *DG*, July 29, 1938, 1.

23. "West Indies Commission: A Native Member Suggested," *DG*, August 16, 1938, 18.

24. "The Royal Commission," editorial, *Jamaica Labour Weekly*, October 5, 1938, 1.

25. "Empire Day," editorial, *Jamaica Labour Weekly*, May 24, 1938, 1.

26. "The Royal Commission," letter to the editor, *DG*, October 14, 1938, 12.

27. "The Commission," editorial, *DG*, August 18, 1938, 12.

28. "Commission Starts Work," *DG*, November 4, 1938, 1.

29. "Commissioners Tour Slum Areas of City," *DG*, November 7, 1938, 1, 7.

30. "Poverty and Squalor of Rural Jamaica Seen by Royal Commissioners," *DG*, November 7, 1938, 7.

31. Ibid.

32. *Eighth Census of Jamaica and Dependencies* (Kingston: Government Printer, 1945), 226, 227.

33. "The Commission," editorial, *DG*, November 5, 1938, 12.

34. "Whitened Sepulchres," letter to the editor, *DG*, November 8, 1943, 12.

35. "Why No Records Are Kept at Hospitals," *DG*, November 8, 1938, 17.

36. "Royal Commission Continues Taking of Evidence," *DG*, November 8, 1938, 8.

37. Ibid.

38. Ibid.

39. "Bustamante before Royal Commission: Workers Crowd in Hundreds to Hear Leader," *DG*, November 17, 1938, 1.

40. Ibid.

41. Ibid.

42. These figures are taken from "Memorandum of the Jamaica Imperial Association to the West Indies Royal Commission," CO 950/80.

43. This extended discussion of the memorandum of the Bustamante unions and Bustamante's testimony before the commission is based on "Bustamante Unions Memorandum to Commission," *DG*, November 18, 1938, 21; and "Leader Gives Evidence before Royal Commission," *DG*, November 17, 1938, 16.

44. "Coombs Memorandum to the Royal Commission," CO 950/135.

45. Coombs's testimony before the commission is found in "Beating of Banana Labourers Still Continues," *DG*, December 3, 1938, 1.

46. Noel Nethersole and Lewis Ashenheim were prominent solicitors, Philip Sherlock and H. P. Jacobs were public intellectuals, and Edith Clarke was a professional sociologist.

47. Manley's testimony is reproduced in "Manley on Degeneracy and Gross Corruption of Our Quasi-Democratic Institutions," *DG*, November 15, 1938, 16.

48. The letter is found in "Existing Jamaica Law Real Obstacle to Formation of Proper Trade Unions," *DG*, November 15, 1938, 18.

49. "Dominion Status Sought in Memorandum to Royal Commission," *DG*, November 2, 1938, 6; "Evidence on Education to be Given by the Jamaica Union of Teachers," CO 950/82; "Chinese and the Royal Commission," *DG*, November 29, 1938, 19; "Memorandum of the Jamaica Imperial Association," CO 950/80.

50. Robert Kirkwood to the Secretary of State, April 12, 1939, NMP 4/60/2B/5.

51. "Royal Commission's Recommendations," *DG*, March 5, 1940, 8.

52. "Government's Decision Not to Publish Report on West Indies Sharply Criticised," *DG*, February 21, 1940, 1.

53. For the full text of the report, see *Report of the West India Royal Commission [the Moyne Commission]* (London: His Majesty's Stationery Office, 1945). See also "Recommendations of Royal Commission to the West Indies," *DG*, February 21, 1940, 1.

54. "Verdict, No Evidence," *London Daily Express*, February 21, 1940, 8; "Decisions," editorial, *DG*, February 21, 1940, 10; "Mr. Manley on the Royal Commission's Report," March 9, 1940, 8, 11.

Chapter Five

1. Alexander Bustamante to the Secretary of State, December 22, 1942, CO 968/68/7.

2. George Eaton, "Trade Union Development in Jamaica," *Caribbean Quarterly* 8, nos. 1 and 2 (1962): 45–53, 69–75.

3. The Officer Administering the Government of Jamaica to the Secretary of State, June 8, 1938, CO 137/826/9.

4. "Mr. Alexander Bustamante Forced to Seek Police Aid at Port Antonio," *DG*, October 23, 1937, 1.

5. Ibid.

6. Ibid.; "How Labour Leaders Met Port Antonio Opposition," *DG*, October 25, 1937, 3; "Labourers of Portland and Workers Body," *DG*, November 17, 1937, 11; "Labour Leaders Give Their Side of Story," *DG*, October 5, 1937, 23.

7. "Banana Strike Situation in St. James Tense," *DG*, October 7, 1937, 1.

8. "St. Thomas District in Restive Mood as Estate Labourers Strike," *DG*, January 6, 1938, 1.

9. "13 Tried for Intimidation," *DG*, January 13, 1938, 1.

10. Ibid.

11. Although sixty-four men were arrested, only sixty-three faced the judge; One man was sent to the hospital when he fell ill. For the judge's verdict and his admonition, see "3 Sent to Prison as St. Thomas Strike Trial Ends," *DG*, January 15, 1938, 1, 15.

12. "The Workers' Union: A Peep behind Closed Doors," letter to the editor from A. G. S. Coombs, *DG*, November 18, 1937, 12.

13. Letter to the editor, undated and uncataloged, BM; Bustamante to Coombs, November 18, 1937, uncataloged, BM; Bustamante to Coombs, October 5, 1937, uncataloged, BM. Bustamante provided one example of the deception in which some officers of the JUTU were engaged. As he wrote in a letter to *DG*:

> One of the officers in an executive meeting previous to the one when I was elected president told the committee that he had promised the people sick and death benefits, but he knew that this would have been impossible, however he was certain that when the time came for the people to receive these benefits, they would all be in arrears with their subscription and even if they were not in arrears, when they became sick they being so poor, he is sure, they would not have any money to pay a doctor to obtain a doctor's certificate, and without such certificate they would get no benefit. I felt that my blood had passed through my arteries one thousand times quicker than it should at such a high-handed scheming, and I made it known in no uncertain words.

For the full text of Bustamante's letter, see Bustamante to the Editor, November 18, 1937, uncataloged, BM.

14. Bustamante to Coombs, October 5, 1937, uncataloged, BM.

15. "A Word to Unionist: Stop These Little Strikes," Alexander Bustamante letter to the editor, *DG*, November 5, 1937, 10.

16. "Organisation of Workers," Alexander Bustamante, letter to the editor of *DG*, December 22, 1937, 12.

17. *Trade Unionism in Jamaica, 1918–1946* (Kingston: Central Bureau of Statistics, 1946), 11.

18. "Plans Underway to Form Five Labour Unions," *DG*, June 23, 1938, 1, 7. The two additional unions were the Artisans and the Commercial and Industrial Clerks.

19. Ibid.

20. "Meeting at Papine," *DG*, June 23, 1938, 7.

21. Ibid.

22. Bustamante to Manley, April 6, 1940, NMP 4/60/28/4; "Bustamante and His Officers," *DG*, September 10, 1938, 12.

23. Patrick E. Bryan and Karl Watson, eds., *Not for Wages Alone: Eyewitness Summaries of the 1939 Labour Rebellion in Jamaica* (Mona: University of the West Indies Press, 2003), 109.

24. Ibid., 121–22.

25. Ibid., 75–76.

26. Ibid., 38–39.

27. Ibid., 174.

28. Ibid., 39.

29. *Eighth Census of Jamaica and Its Dependencies 1943* (Kingston: Government Printer, 1945), 164–65.

30. "Domestic Servants," letter to the editor, *DG*, October 24, 1941, 6.
31. "Servants' Wages," editorial, *DG*, October 20, 1941, 6; "Servant Question," editorial, *DG*, October 30, 1941, 6; "This Question," editorial, *DG*, November 5, 1941, 6.
32. "Today," G. St. C. Scotter, *DG*, October 21, 1941.
33. Bryan and Watson, *Not for Wages Alone*, 121–22.
34. Ibid.
35. "Bustamante Defies Capitalists at Port Maria Mass Meeting," *DG*, September 24, 1938, 7.
36. Ibid.; "Buste's [*sic*] Boast," *DG*, September 20, 1938, 7.
37. "Alexander Bustamante," *DG*, November 2, 1938, 13.
38. "What Is Labour's Program?," *DG*, September 9, 1938, 1.
39. "Bustamante and/or Unionism," *DG*, August 26, 1938, 11.
40. "Why I Want Power," *DG*, August 31, 1938, 3.
41. G. St. C. Scotter, "One man[?] The One Man Union," *DG*, September 1, 1938, 5.
42. "Mr. Bustamante Declares for Industrial Peace," *DG*, September 2, 1938, 5.
43. "Bustamante and His Aspirations," *DG*, August 30, 1938, 24.
44. Ibid.
45. Alexander Bustamante's Memorial to the Secretary of State, August 1940, CO 137/846/15.
46. Ibid.
47. "The Rights of the Working Man," *DG*, March 10, 1941, 8.
48. "Problems Ahead," *DG*, July 7, 1939; "Bustamante Rechristened Moses," *DG*, August 28, 1939, 19.
49. "Fall of Bustamante Seen by Businessman," *DG*, September 2, 1938, 11.
50. Minute by G. Orde Browne, October 14, 1940, CO 137/846/15.
51. "Schism in the Bustamante Labour Camp," *DG*, August 15, 1938, 1.
52. "Bustamante at Parting of Ways," *DG*, August 16, 1938, 1.
53. "Grant Now Contrite," *DG*, August 18, 1938, 1.
54. "Grant Is Fired," *DG*, August 18, 1938, 1.
55. "Labour Meeting at Montego Bay," *DG*, August 18, 1938, 1.
56. "Bustamante Union Rift Widens as Chiefs Talk," *DG*, August 17, 1938, 3; St William Grant Still Out of Labour Union," *DG*, August 25, 1938, 3.
57. "Disruption in Labour Union," *DG*, April 18, 1939, 18.
58. "Transport Workers Back Mr. Ken Hill in Action," *DG*, April 24, 1939, 5; "More Resignations from Bustamante Industrial [Trade] Union," April 24, 1939, 3.
59. "Leader Tells Why Officers Resigned," *DG*, April 30, 1939, 1.
60. "Bustamante "Fires' Chief Aide–Then Resigns from Unions," *DG*, August 21, 1939, 1.
61. "Union Officers Back Answering Bustamante," *DG*, October 16, 1939, 10.
62. "Coombs Criticizes Bustamante Unions," *DG*, September 5, 1938, 24.
63. "Grant Suspended, Seeks Reform in Bustamante Union," October 28, 1939, 6.
64. Ibid.
65. "Rift in Ranks of Bustamante Union Widens," November 4, 1939, 5.
66. "Labour Union Purge," November 1, 1939, 1.
67. "Local Forces Mobilized," *DG*, January 4, 1939, 1.

68. See "Strikes Called Off," *DG*, January 5, 1939, 1; "Workers Overrule Bustamante," *DG*, January 7, 1939, 1; "Bustamante Lashes Outlaw Strikers," *DG*, January 7, 1939, 7; "Arbitration Board," *DG*, January 9, 1939, 1; "Bustamante to Crush Unauthorized Strikes," *DG*, January 9, 1939, 1; "Bustamante's Dramatic Speech," *DG*, January 5, 1939, 1.

69. "Clash in Victoria Park," *DG*, January 5, 1939, 1.

70. "Bustamante to Crush Unauthorized Strikes," 1; "Bustamante Lashes Outlaw Strikers," 7.

71. "Island Sick of Labour Strife in City," *DG*, January 13, 1939, 1; "Unemployed March Again," *DG*, January 24, 1939, 1.

72. "Bustamante Denies That He Was Booed," *DG*, July 4, 1938, 1.

73. "No Union with Crooks Declares Bustamante," *DG*, December 17, 1938, 1, 3.

74. "Mr. Coombs and Mr. Bustamante," *DG*, December 21, 1938, 3, 7.

75. Bustamante to Manley, August 24, 1938, NMP 4/60/2B/2.

76. Manley to Bustamante, August 29, 1938, NMP 4/60/2B/2.

77. "Bustamante Threatens a General Strike," *DG*, September 19, 1938, 1.

78. Ibid.

79. Kirkwood to the Secretary of State, April 12, 1939, NMP 4/60/2B/5.

80. Ibid.

81. "Bustamante Calls Strike at Montego Bay," *DG*, February 15, 1939, 1, 18.

82. This account of developments in the strike is taken from "Police Open Fire," *DG*, February 15, 1939, 1; "State of Emergency," *DG*, February 15, 1939, 1; "No Negotiation Till Strike Is Called Off," *DG*, February 17, 1939, 1; "The Governor's New Powers," *DG*, February 15, 1939, 1; "Notice," *DG*, February 15, 1939, 1.

83. Kirkwood to the Secretary of State, April 22, 1939, NMP 4/60/2B/5; "State of Emergency," 1; "No negotiations," 1.

84. "Country Workers Make Kingston Wharves Busy and Bustling," *DG*, February 18, 1939, 1, 7; "Strike Ends," *DG*, February 18, 1939, 1; "Recent General Strike," *DG*, February 24, 1939, 12.

85. "How Shipping Companies Dealt with the Port Strike," *DG*, February 18, 1939, 1, 6.

86. Ibid.

87. Kirkwood to the Secretary of State, April 12, 1939.

88. "The PNP and Labour Unions in Jamaica," *DG*, June 10, 1939, 3–4; "Advisory Council Will Decide Union's Policy," *DG*, February 21, 1939, 1; "Unions' Council Members Named," *DG*, February 23, 1939, 1, 13.

89. "Unions' Council Members Named."

90. "Trades Union Council Set up," *DG*, February 27, 1939, 1.

91. "Alexander Bustamante's Letter to the Workers in the Aftermath of the Abortive General Strike of February, 1939," NMP 4/60/2B/4.

92. "No Amalgamation Says Mr. Coombs," *DG*, April 11, 1939, 8; "Coombs and Bustamante Again at Variance," *DG*, April 8, 1939, 19.

93. This discussion of Coombs, his finances, and the Manley-Bustamante correspondence is based on Bustamante to Manley, February 21, 1939, NMP 4/60/2B/3; Manley to Bustamante, March 24, 1939, NMP 4/60/2B/3; Bustamante to Coombs,

March 25, 1939, NMP 4/60/2B/3; and Bustamante to Coombs, March 31, 1939 NMP 4/60/2B/3. See various related letters in NMP 4/60/2B/4. The Colonial Office was aware of the allegation that Coombs was dishonest. When it came to the officials' attention that the funds of the JWTU were being misused, one official observed: "Mr. Coombs seems to have the same idea as other W. I. labour union leaders as to the best method of using the Union's funds." Minute by J. Emmens, 4/6/38, CO 137/827/1.

94. "No Amalgamation"; "Coombs and Bustamante again at Variance."

95. "Union Chief Fined for Not Tendering Financial Returns," *DG*, November 15, 1939, 1, 13.

96. See "The PNP and Labour Unions in Jamaica," *DG*, June 10, 1939, 3.

97. Ibid.

98. "Group Urges Reforms in Bustamante Unions," *DG*, March 31, 1939, 9.

99. "Bustamante Out," *DG*, April 28, 1939, 1; "Bustamante Might Purge Trade Council," *DG*, May 1, 1939, 1.

100. "New Trades Union Council Is Formed," *DG*, May 6, 1939, 1.

101. "H.S.B. Lunches with Bustamante and Discusses People's National Party," *DG*, September 20, 1939, 9.

102. "To the People of Jamaica," *DG*, November 17, 1944, 7.

103. This discussion of the Bustamante-Penso feud is found in "Bustamante Resigns as Union Head," *DG*, April 15, 1940, 1; "Feud in Labour Union," *DG*, March 29, 1940, 1; "Suit Is Filed against Union Chief and Aide," *DG*, April 6, 1940, 1; "Judge's Criticisms of Solicitor's Work," *DG*, April 18, 1940, 1; and Bustamante to Manley, April 6, 1940, NMP 4/6/2B/4.

104. "Busha Slips Bustamante," *DG*, May 15, 1939, 12.

105. Ibid.

106. Copy of report by Mr. J. G. Young, January 1939, JA 1B/5/77/55.

107. Bustamante to Miret, August 21, 1942, CO 137/852/2.

108. Bustamante to Fletcher, October 6, 1942, CO 137/852/2.

109. Bustamante to R. F. Robison, January 25, 1943, CO 137/855/11.

110. Bustamante wrote letters to Powell on March 8, 17, and 20, 1943. Some of his other letters are undated. See CO 137/855/11. Also see W. E. Powell to the Secretary of State, May 4, 1943, CO 137/855/11.

111. "From the Governor, Notes of My Interview with Bustamante, 2/9/38, JA 1B/5/77.

112. See "Says Jamaicans Look upon Bustamante as Man of Hour," *DG*, June 6, 1938, 9.

113. "Bustamante Will Stand for Legislature in 1940," *DG*, June 14, 1938, 1.

114. Bryan and Watson, *Not for Wages Alone*, 135–36.

115. For the report on Bustamante's speech, see "1,500 Hear Labour Chief at Duckenfield," *Jamaica Times*, April 23, 1942, 5, 11.

116. See Ken Post, *Strike the Iron: A Colony at War*, vol. 1, *Jamaica, 1939–1945* (Atlantic Highlands, N.J.: Humanities Press, 1981), 159–60; Norman Manley to Peter Blackman, April 29, 1941, NMP 4/60/2B/5.

117. See "1,500 Hear Labour Chief."

118. "The Manley-Bustamante Dispute," *DG*, March 24, 1942, 6.
119. See, for example, Abigail B. Bakan, *Ideology and Class Conflict in Jamaica* (Montreal and Kingston: McGill-Queens University Press, 1990); Paul Blanshard, "The Government of Jamaica," General Records of the Department of State, Decimal File, 1945–49, February 1, 1945, Box 6052, NA-DS.
120. *Jamaica Labour Weekly*, August 20, 1938, 4.
121. *Jamaica Labour Weekly*, February 18, 1939, 4.
122. "Bustamante Is Our God Says Grant at Race Course," *DG*, May 30, 1938, 19.
123. Ibid.
124. "Bustamante Lashes Out at Mr. Manley," *DG*, February 26, 1942, 8.
125. "Bustamante Rechristened Moses."
126. "Bustamante Has Huge Procession in Metropolis," *DG*, May 25, 1939, 19.
127. Vernon Arnett as quoted in Ken Post, *Arise Ye Starvelings: The Jamaican Labour Rebellion of 1938 and Its Aftermath* (The Hague: Martinus Nijhoff, 1978), 252.

Chapter Six

1. Denham to the Secretary of State, May 8, 1938, CO 137/826/9.
2. Bustamante to the Colonial Secretary, August 17, 1939, JA 1B/5/77/55.
3. Bustamante to the Colonial Secretary, February 23, 1940, JA 1B/5/77/55.
4. Bustamante to Governor Richards, December 21, 1939, JA 1B/5/77/55.
5. The Commissioner of Police to the Colonial Secretary, January 1, 1940, JA 1B/5/77/55; J. M. Edwards to Comrade Gunter, November 18, 1939, JA 1B/5/77/55.
6. Inspector of Police, St. Ann, to the Commissioner of Police, February 22, 1940, JA 1B/5/77/55. See also Inspector of Police, St. Ann, to the Commissioner of Police, March 23, 1940, JA 1B/5/77/55; and Commissioner of Police to the Inspector of Police, St. Ann, March 13, 1940, JA 1B/5/77/55.
7. Bustamante to Governor Richards, December 1939, JA 1B/5/77/55; Paul Blanshard, "The Government of Jamaica," General Records of the Department of State, Decimal File, 1945–49, February 1, 1945, Box 6052, NA-DS.
8. Alexander Bustamante to N. W. Manley, February 7, 1939, NMP 4/60/2B/4; Bustamante to the Colonial Secretary, August 17, 1939, JA 1B/5/77/55.
9. Bustamante to the Colonial Secretary, August 17, 1939.
10. "Labor Leader Avows Fealty to Great Britain," *DG*, May 15, 1940, 9.
11. Bustamante's Petition, December 24, 1942, CO 968/68/7. For the report on Bustamante's speech and the governor's letter, see Governor Richards to the Secretary of State, September 13, 1940, CO 137/840/5.
12. Lord Moyne to Sir Walter Citrine, undated, CO 137/852/1.
13. These letters are undated and are located in the Bustamante Museum (uncataloged). The social conventions of the time prevented the couple from publicly acknowledging the intimacy of their relationship. Bustamante's description of Ms. Longbridge as his private secretary was a euphemism. He was also still married to a woman who lived overseas, and as an ardent Catholic, he refused to divorce her. When Bustamante's wife died, he married Miss Longbridge in 1962.
14. Ibid.

15. Ibid.

16. J. Barnes to Miss Longbridge, December 22, 1941, uncataloged, BM; Gladys Longbridge to Sir Arthur Richards, December 30, 1941, uncataloged, BM.

17. "The Humble and Respectful Memorial of the Bustamante Industrial Trade Union," February 17, 1931, CO 137/852/1.

18. Ibid.
19. Ibid.
20. Ibid.
21. Ibid.
22. Ibid.
23. Ibid.
24. Ibid.

25. Gladys Longbridge to Governor Richards, December 30, 1941, uncataloged, BM.

26. "Statement of Alexander Bustamante to the Detention Advisory Committee," January 10, 1942, CO 968/68/7.

27. Ibid.
28. Ibid.
29. Ibid.
30. Ibid.
31. Ibid.
32. Ibid.

33. Bustamante to Oliver Stanley, December 22, 1943, CO 968/68/7.

34. "Statement of Alexander Bustamante."

35. Patrick E. Bryan and Karl Watson, eds., *Not for Wages Alone: Eyewitness Summaries of the 1939 Labour Rebellion in Jamaica* (Mona: University of the West Indies Press, 2003), 171.

36. N. W. Manley to Inspector Higgins, March 22, 1942, NMP 4/60/2B/5.

37. "Statement of Alexander Bustamante."

38. Gladys Bustamante, *The Memoirs of Lady Bustamante* (Kingston: Kingston Publishers Limited, 1997), 131.

39. "Bustamante Released from Detention," *DG*, February 9, 1942, 1.

40. "Documents in Issue," *DG*, February 21, 1942, 8; "Labour Leader Hurls Accusations at Head of People's National Party," *DG*, February 27, 1942, 11; Norman Manley to Governor Richards, undated copy of the letter, NMP 4/60/2B/4; Norman Manley to My Dear Governor, undated copy of letter, NMP 4/60/2B/4; Governor Richards to N. W. Manley, October 30, 1940, NMP 4/60/2B/4; Governor Richards to My Dear Manley, October 30, 1940, NMP 4/60/2B/4.

41. "Mr. Manley Tells How He Helped Mr. Bustamante and His Union," *DG*, February 26, 1942, 8. See NMP 4/60/2B/5 for Manley's application for permits to visit Bustamante and the letters he wrote on Bustamante's behalf to various organizations. Manley seems to have exaggerated the number of times he visited Bustamante, although he did so quite frequently in 1941.

42. Bustamante to the Secretary of State, December 22, 1942, CO 968/68/7.

43. Ibid.

44. Ibid.
45. Ibid.
46. Ibid.
47. Ibid.
48. Ibid.
49. W. Flinn to Bustamante, April 10, 1943, CO 968/68/7.
50. See Postal and Telegraph Censorship, 26/5/43, CO 968/68/7.
51. Ibid.
52. This discussion of the relationship of the BITU and the PNP during Bustamante's internment is based on "Mr. Manley Urges Loyalty," *DG*, March 3, 1942, 11; Norman Manley to Robert Harding, February 6, 1941, NMP 4/60/2B/5; and Local Officers of the BITU in Montego Bay to N. W. Manley, April 16, 1941, NMP 4/60/2B/5.
53. "Mr. Manley Urges Loyalty," 11.
54. Ibid.
55. "Documents in Issue," *DG*, February 21, 1942, 8.
56. Ibid.
57. Ibid.
58. Gladys Bustamante, *The Memoirs of Lady Bustamante*, 135. The Nelson who Bustamante fired was not Edith Nelson but a male with that surname.
59. "Vice President of Bustamante Unions Praised," *DG*, January 12, 1942, 8.
60. "Sensational Charges against Bustamante," *DG*, September 17, 1942, 8.
61. "PNP's Leader's Bitter Denunciation of Labor Union Head," *DG*, September 17, 1942, 8; "Labour Leader Charges Libel," *DG*, February 21, 1942, 8.
62. "Labor Leader Charges Libel," 8.
63. "Notes by Norman Manley," September 13, 1941, NMP 4/60/2B/5.
64. Norman Manley to Alexander Bustamante, February 14, 1942, NMP 4/60/2B/5.
65. "Statement by Mr. Manley," *DG*, February 28, 1942, 8; "Labour Leader Charges Libel," 8.
66. "Labour Leader Charges Libel."
67. "Statement by Mr. Manley."
68. "Labour Leader Avows Fealty," 9.
69. Colonial Office Minute, June 29, 1942, CO 137/854/14; Richards to H. F. Downie, June 1, 1942, CO 137/854/14.
70. Ca. 1939, uncataloged, BM.
71. Mail and Telegraph Censorship, November 23, 1942, CO 968/68/7.
72. "Mr. Manley Hits Hard and Straight at Mr. Bustamante," *DG*, February 26, 1942, 3.
73. Labour Leader Charges Libel."
74. "Inside the Bustamante Racket," *Public Opinion*, April 4, 1942, 9.
75. "No Time Should Be Lost in Looking after Workers," *DG*, March 16, 1942, 9.
76. "Statement by Bustamante," *DG*, February 23, 1942, 8.
77. "Mr. Manley Raps at Constitution of Bustamante Union," *DG*, March 2, 1942, 9.

78. "Mr. Manley Accepts," *DG*, February 24, 1942, 6; "Mr. Manley Confident Union Chief Will Not Put up Wager," *DG*, February 25, 1942, 8.

79. For salaries in Jamaica, see *Report of the West India Royal Commission [the Moyne Commission]* (London: His Majesty's Stationery Office, 1945), 167–68; *Eighth Census of Jamaica and Dependencies* (Kingston: Government Printer, 1945), 214–25. When he became the chief minister of Jamaica in 1953, Bustamante received an annual salary of £2,500. The ministers were each paid £2,000. See "About Ministers' Pay, Allowance," *DG*, July 22, 1954, 1.

80. "Mr. Shirley Comments on Issue," *DG*, February 26, 1942, 6; "The Manley-Bustamante Controversy Proceeds," *DG*, February 23, 1942, 12; "Manley-Bustamante Fight Waxes," *DG*, February 24, 1942, 6.

81. "Inside the Bustamante Racket," 9.

82. "Mr. Manley Raps at Constitution of Bustamante Union," 9; "BITU Members Call for Change in Constitution, *DG*," February 24, 1942, 4; "Meeting Calls on Mr. Bustamante to Quit Labour Leadership," March 6, 1942, 8; "Call for Formation of New Trades Union," *DG*, March 2, 1942, 5.

83. "BITU Committee Supports Bustamante," *DG*, February 28, 1942, 8; "Bustamante Back in City, Reports All Workers Loyal," *DG*, March 17, 1942, 8; "King of Labour," *DG*, May 28, 1942, 4; "St William Grant Sides with BITU," *DG*, March 17, 1942, 7.

84. "Inside the Bustamante Racket," 10.

85. "Mr. Bustamante Claims Mr. Manley Is Side Tracking Main Issue," *DG*, February 26, 1942, 6.

86. "Mr. Bustamante Lashes Out at Manley," *DG*, February 26, 1942, 6.

87. "Mr. Manley Tells How He Helped Mr. Bustamante and His Union," *DG*, February 26, 1942, 8.

88. "Sugar Wage Dispute Settled," *DG*, March 22, 1941, 10.

89. "Mr. Bustamante's observations on Mr. Shirley's Statement," *DG*, March 5, 1942, 11.

90. Ibid.

91. "New Labour Organisation," *DG*, March 4, 1942, 8.

92. "1,500 Hear Labour Chief at Duckenfield," *Jamaica Times*, April 25, 1942, 5.

93. "Matters of Moment: Trade Union Civil War Continues Unabated," *DG*, March 2, 1942, 6.

94. "Noisy Welcome for Shirley at Port Antonio," *Jamaica Times*, April 18, 1942, 1; Ken Post, *Strike the Iron: A Colony at War*, vol. 1, *Jamaica, 1939–1945* (Atlantic Highlands, N.J.: Humanities Press, 1981), 234–38.

95. Telegram to the Governor, *DG*, March 17, 1942, 5.

96. The Suspension of Detention Order against Bustamante, April 14, 1942, CO 868/68/7.

97. "Bars on Labour Chief Lifted," *Jamaica Times*, April 18, 1942, 1.

98. Ibid.

99. Richards to the Secretary of State, August 4, 1942, CO 875/13/3; Resolution, June 28, 1942, CO 875/13/3.

100. "Re Censorship of the Jamaica Worker," December 13, 1942, CO 968/68/7.

101. Resolution, June 28, 1942, CO 968/68/7.
102. W. H. Flinn to the Secretary of State, January 23, 1943, CO 968/68/7.

Chapter Seven

1. "City Mass Meeting," *DG*, June 25, 1941, 1.
2. The Colonial Secretary's comment and the *Daily Gleaner*'s response are found in "A Mistake," editorial, *DG*, June 28, 1941, 12.
3. "The Defence Regulations: Powers of Detention," *DG*, June 30, 1941, 3.
4. "Critical of Government's Policy," *DG*, September 27, 1941, 9.
5. The list of prohibited publications is found in Governor Richards to the Secretary of State, October 22, 1941, CO 333/847/2. As of October 1941 no one had been charged with violating the law, the governor reported to the Colonial Office. See his letter in ibid.
6. Alexander Bustamante to Governor Richards, May 3, 1940, JA 1B/5/77/140.
7. Ibid.
8. The Commissioner of Police to the Colonial Secretary, May 22, 1940, JA 1B/5/77/140.
9. Alexander Bustamante to the Colonial Secretary, August 10, 1942, JA 1B/5/77/140.
10. "Labour Leader Avows Fealty to Great Britain," *DG*, May 15, 1940, 9.
11. Column by G. St. C. Scotter, *DG*, May 15, 1940, 3.
12. See Governor Richards to the Secretary of State, January 15, 1940, CO 137/838/10; Report on a Law to Empower the Governor by Proclamation to Prohibit in Circumstances Meetings and Processions in the Interests of Good Order and the Public Safety, July 22, 1939, CO 137/838/10.
13. "Statement by Smith and Campbell," undated, CO 137/838/10.
14. "This Latest Law," editorial, *Jamaica Standard*, June 23, 1939, copy located in CO 137/838/10.
15. "Protest Public Meetings Law," *DG*, July 7, 1939, 1, 6.
16. Resolution by the Jamaica Progressive League, undated, CO 137/838/10.
17. Whitfield Chapter of the UNIA to Governor Richards, June 29, 1939, CO 137/838/10.
18. "Public Meetings," editorial, *DG*, September 29, 1941, 8.
19. Governor Richards to the Secretary of State, March 23, 1942, CO 968/66/9.
20. V. L. Arnett to the National Council for Civil Liberties, January 27, 1942, CO 968/66/9.
21. Governor Richards to the Secretary of State, undated, CO 968/66/9.
22. Colonial Office Minutes, various dates, CO 968/66/9.
23. Report by Imperial Censorship, Jamaica, August 10, 1943, CO 137/849/8.
24. "Police Order against Street Gatherings," *DG*, August 11, 1939, 20.
25. "No Street Procession on August 1," *DG*, July 15, 1939, 1.
26. "Hart and Others Dismissed under Defense Regulations," *DG*, December 16, 1940, 1.

27. "Bustamante Threatens and Appeals," *DG*, September 9, 1938, 3; "Mr. Bustamante Complains to the Government about Police," *DG*, February 8, 1939, 10.
28. "Party Object to Conduct of Police," *DG*, June 2, 1941, 5.
29. "Policy of Pressure on Teachers Deplored," *DG*, April 29, 1941, 9.
30. Arthur Creech Jones to the Secretary of State, July 17, 1939, CO 137/835/2.
31. Postal and Telegraph Censorship, January 27, 1942, CO 968/66/9.
32. "Sent to Circuit on a Charge of Sedition," *DG*, August 31, 1938, 1, 10.
33. Ibid.
34. "Buchanan and Coombs on Trial in Circuit for Seditious Libel," *DG*, October 4, 1938, 19.
35. "Buchanan and Coombs Sent to Prison," *DG*, October 25, 1938, 1, 7.
36. "The Sentence," editorial, *DG*, October 25, 1938, 12.
37. "North Parade Orator Faces Sedition Charge," *DG*, March 3, 1939, 13; "Jury Unable to Agree on Sedition Verdict," *DG*, March 9, 1939, 18.
38. Richard Peel, *Old Sinister: A Memoir of Sir Arthur Richards* (Cambridge, UK: F. and P. Piggott Limited, 1985), 67, 71.
39. Richards to Manley, May 8, 1940, NMP 4/60/2B/4.
40. Norman Manley to Governor Richards, May 24, 1940, NMP 4/60/2B/4.
41. Governor Richards to Norman Manley, May 24, 1940, NMP 4/60/2B/4.
42. For Richards's comments about Manley, see Governor Richards to H. F. Downie, June 1, 1942, CO 137/854/14.
43. "Mr. Kirkwood Defends Governor," *DG*, August 24, 1939, 13.
44. Governor Richards to H. F. Downie, undated, CO 137/854/14.
45. Speech to the Universal Negro Improvement Association, July 20, 1942, CO 137/850/4.
46. Governor Richards to Leonard Lyle, July 18, 1942, CO 137/850/6.
47. Colonial Office Minutes, September 9, 1942, and October 10, 1942, CO 137/850/4.
48. "Mr. Kirkwood and the PNP Leaders," *DG*, October 2, 1943, 3.
49. Governor Richards to the Colonial Office, October 29, 1942, CO 137/854/15.
50. Governor Richards to the Secretary of State, June 1, 1942, CO 137/854/14.
51. "Note on the Political Situation, Jamaica," November 11, 1942, CO 968/68/5.
52. "Report from the Criminal Investigation Department," May 20, 1942, CO 137/854/14.
53. Ken Post, *Strike the Iron: A Colony at War*, vol. 1, *Jamaica, 1939–1945* (Atlantic Highlands, N.J.: Humanities Press, 1981), 177.
54. Colonial Office Minute, undated, CO 137/854/16.
55. Ibid.
56. Central Decimal File, 1940–44, Box 5062, NA-DS.
57. "Communist Activities in Jamaica," J. Edgar Hoover to Adolf Berle, June 23, 1942, in ibid. This was a lengthy report on the Domingo case.
58. Ibid.
59. Ibid.
60. Ibid.; Dr. Morgan's letter was dated November 11, 1942. See CO 968/68/9.
61. Norman Manley to Governor Richards, June 18, 1941, NMP 4/60/2B/5.

62. Governor Richards to Norman Manley, June 19, 1941, NMP 4/60/2B/5.
63. W. A. Domingo to Norman Manley, July 14, 1941, NMP 4/60/2B/5.
64. "Domingo Detained for Duration," *DG*, October 8, 1941, 1.
65. "Political Developments in Jamaica," July 16, 1941, Central Decimal File, 1940–1944, Box 5062, NA-DS.
66. Ibid.
67. "Domingo Released," *DG*, February 20, 1943, 1.
68. "Domingo's Case," *DG*, April 20, 1943, 3. Section 18b of the regulations governed the circumstances under which individuals could be detained.
69. Governor Richards's indictment of Frank Hill is found in Governor Richards to the Secretary of State, November 6, 1942, CO 137/845/15.
70. Governor Richards to the Secretary of State, November 8, 1942, CO 137/845/15.
71. Governor Richards to the Secretary of State, undated, CO 137/845/15.
72. Ibid.
73. Ibid.
74. Lord Olivier to the Secretary of State, July 14, 1939, CO 137/835/2. William Cobbett (1763–1835) was an English journalist, farmer, and reformer.
75. "Chronological Table of Events," undated, CO 137/845/15.
76. Ibid.
77. Governor Richards to the Secretary of State for the Colonies, October 26, 1942, CO 137/842/15; Governor Richards to the Secretary of State for the Colonies, October 31, 1942, CO 137/842/15; Governor Richards to the Secretary of State, November 1, 1942, CO 137/842/15.
78. For a discussion of these issues, see the memorial that Norman Manley prepared but evidently did not send to the secretary of state. See "Memorial Submitted by the People's National Party of Jamaica," undated, NMP 4/60/2B/8.
79. Walter Citrine to the Secretary of State for the Colonies, November, 2, 1942, CO 137/845/15.
80. "4 Labour Union Officials Detained," *DG*, November 4, 1942, 1; "PNP Statement on Detention Order," *DG*, November 4, 1942, 1; "Mr. Manley on the Men Just Interned," *DG*, November 5, 1942, 4; Governor Richards to the Secretary of State, November 8, 1942, CO 137/845/15.
81. "Memorial Submitted by the People's National Party of Jamaica."
82. "Chronological Table of Events"; Governor Richards to the Secretary of State for the Colonies, November 9, 1942, CO 137/845/15.
83. The Secretary of State for the Colonies to Governor Richards, November 17, 1942, CO 137/845/15.
84. Kenneth Hill to Sir Stafford Cripps, December 27, 1942, CO 137/854/16.
85. Sir Stafford Cripps to the Secretary of State, March 3, 1942, CO 137/854/16.
86. Colonial Office Minutes, February 2, 1943, and February 18, 1943, CO 137/854/16.
87. For the text of "Now We Know," see CO 137/859/16.
88. "Roger Mais Sentenced to Six Months; City Printery Ltd. Fined £200," *DG*, November 25, 1944, 1, 9.

89. Ibid.

90. Henry Brinton to Clement Attlee, October 11, 1944, CO 137/859/16.

91. Governor Richards to Norman Manley, July 7, 1943, NMP 4/60/2B/7. Roy Lindo was an elected member of the Legislative Council, representing the parish of St. Mary. A large landowner, he was, at times, a critic of the administration. Norman Manley's letter to Richards has not been located.

Chapter Eight

1. "We Imperialists," editorial, *DG*, May 5, 1941, 8. See copy of a letter presumably written to the secretary of state, Malcolm MacDonald, on April 12, 1939, NMP 4/60/2B/5.

2. Governor Richards to the Secretary of State, February 14, 1939, CO 137/834/7.

3. Ibid.

4. Ibid.

5. Governor Richards to the Secretary of State, April 22, 1939, CO 137/834/7.

6. Ibid.

7. Ibid.

8. Colonial Office Minute, October 10, 1939, CO 137/834/7.

9. Ibid.

10. Governor Richards to the Secretary of State, February 24, 1939, CO 137/834/7.

11. Ibid.

12. Ibid.

13. Ibid.

14. Ibid.

15. See "Report of the Select Committee of the Legislative Council Appointed to Prepare and Draft a Political Constitution," undated, CO 137/849/8.

16. Ibid.

17. "Why Suggestion for Two Houses Was Rejected by Secretary of State," *DG*, August 13, 1941, 1.

18. "Self Government," editorial, *DG*, June 22, 1938, 12.

19. "Imperialism," editorial, *DG*, September 10, 1940, 8.

20. "The Future," editorial, *DG*, September 10, 1940, 8.

21. "We the Natives," editorial, *DG*, September 25, 1941, 8.

22. "Constitution," editorial, *DG*, August 18, 1941, 8.

23. Ibid.

24. For a report on the motion and the debate, see "Council Accept Motion for Provision of Universal Suffrage," *DG*, November 14, 1938, 18.

25. Colonial Office Minute, January 23, 1939, CO 137/834/7.

26. "Gradualness," editorial, *DG*, December 14, 1938, 12.

27. Governor Richards to the Secretary of State, undated, CO 137/834/7.

28. "Unite for Political Advancement, Mr. Manley's Call to Jamaica," *DG*, September 6, 1941, 9.

29. "Mr. Smith Returns to Constitution Issues," *DG*, October 10, 1941, 7.

30. See Governor Richards to the Secretary of State, April 8, 1942, CO 137/849/7, for these observations.

31. Ibid.

32. "Government Told Legislative Council's Reply," *DG*, August 14, 1941.

33. "Wide Changes in Constitution," *DG*, March 13, 1941, 1; "Proposals before Country for a Change in Political Constitution," *DG*, July 12, 1941, 6.

34. Ibid.

35. "Lord Moyne's Fiat: Jamaica Must Carry through Constitutional Reforms on the Lines That He Suggests," *DG*, February 11, 1942, 1.

36. Memorandum by N. W. Manley, May 6, 1942, CO 137/849/5.

37. Ibid.

38. Ibid.

39. Colonial Office memorandum, undated, CO 137/849/7.

40. Ibid.

41. Ibid.

42. Ibid.

43. Colonial Office memorandum, October 16, 1942, CO 137/849/7.

44. Ibid.

45. Ibid.

46. "Was J. A. G. Smith There?," *DG*, February 24, 1943, 7.

47. "Book of Jamaica History Is Open at a New Page," *DG*, February 24, 1943, 1.

48. "New Constitution for the Island Sent out in Momentous Dispatch from the Secretary of State," *DG*, February 24, 1943, 1.

49. The Secretary of State to Governor Richards, February 16, 1942, CO 137/849/8; Governor Richards to the Secretary of State, February 18, 1942, CO 137/849/8.

50. Sir Stafford Cripps to Norman Manley, February 22, 1943, CO 137/849/8.

51. Norman Manley to Sir Stafford Cripps, February 23, 1943, CO 137/849/8.

52. "Member for Kingston Accepts Proposed New Constitution," *DG*, April 16, 1943, 7; "Legislators Begin Debate on Proposed New Constitution," *DG*, August 15, 1943, 8.

53. "Views on Constitution Issue," *DG*, February 26, 1943, 4.

54. For reports on this dispute, see "Manley Not Surprised," *Public Opinion*, June 25, 1944, 10; "Memorandum Submitted by the PNP," July 3, 1944, CO 137/859/18; Governor Huggins to the Secretary of State, July 25, 1944, CO 137/859/16; and "Mr. Manley Charges Breach of Promise in Respect to Constitution," *DG*, July 25, 1944, 3.

55. For this and other comments by Manley, see "Manley Not Surprised."

56. "PNP Leader Urges Party to Work for Success of Constitution," *DG*, January 10, 1945, 5.

57. "Governor Proclaims New Constitution," *DG*, November 21, 1944, 1.

58. Ibid.

59. "Secretary of State for Colonies in Jamaica," *DG*, January 4, 1945, 1, 13.

60. The meaning of Cudjoe's kissing of Colonel Guthrie's feet has been the subject of scholarly controversy. For a good discussion of the Maroon wars, see Mavis C. Campbell, *The Maroons of Jamaica, 1655–1796* (Trenton, N.J.: African World Press, Inc., 1990).

61. "Colonel Stanley Pledges to Work within His Power for Constitution's Success," *DG*, January 5, 1944, 1; "The Civic Address," *DG*, January 5, 1944; "Jamaica's Historic Day," *DG*, January 5, 1944.

62. "Mr. Manley Answers 'Popular' Arguments against Home Rule," *DG*, December 23, 1942, 6.

63. "Christmas within the Empire," *DG*, December 23, 1942, 6.

Chapter Nine

1. "Time for Labour Party in Jamaica Says Manley," *DG*, May 30, 1938, 1, 7.

2. Ken Post, *Arise Ye Starvelings: The Jamaican Labour Rebellion of 1938 and Its Aftermath* (The Hague: Martinus Nijhoff, 1978), 220; Manley to Stannard, December 21, 1942, NMP 4/60/2B/6.

3. "Unite in One Political Party, Urges Manley," *DG*, August 11, 1938, 7.

4. Ibid.

5. Ibid.

6. "Theatre Packed at Launching of People's Party," *DG*, September, 19, 1938, 1, 7.

7. Ibid.

8. Ibid.

9. Ibid.

10. Ibid.

11. Ibid.

12. J. Edgar Hoover to Adolf Berle, Central Decimal File, 1940–44, Box 5062, NA-DS; Manley to Stannard, NMP 4/60/2B/6.

13. "Masses of This Country Have No Political Rights at All," *DG*, December 14, 1938, 21.

14. "Mr. Manley Withers National Party Politics," *DG*, October, 28, 1938, 16.

15. Norman Manley to Ethelred Brown, September 15, 1938, NMP 4/60/2B/2.

16. "Mr. Manley Withers," 18.

17. "Self Government for Jamaica Stressed at Welcome to Progressive League Leaders," *DG*, June 9, 1939, 21.

18. The copy of Manley's letter to Governor Richards is undated, but it was most likely written in 1940. See N. W. Manley to My Dear Governor, NMP 4/60/2B/4; "Call Sounded at Ward Theatre Mass Meeting for Change in Island's Constitution," *DG*, January 17, 1941, 9.

19. Norman Manley to Sir Stafford Cripps, November 27, 1938, NMP 4/60/2B/3; "Mr. Bustamante Is for People's Party," *DG*, October 25, 1938, 18; "Bustamante Joins PNP," *DG*, January 24, 1939, 25.

20. "Text of Mr. Manley's Speech at PNP Parley," *DG*, December 22, 1939, 13, 19.

21. A. Bustamante to N. W. Manley, March 21, 1939, NMP 4/60/2B/3.

22. The preceding discussion of the relationship between Bustamante, Manley, and the PNP is based principally upon letters that were exchanged between the two men. See N. W. Manley to Alexander Bustamante, March 24, 1939, NMP 4/60/2B/3; Alexander Bustamante to N. W. Manley, April 1, 1939, NMP 4/60/2B/3; N. W. Manley to Alexander Bustamante, April 4, 1939, NMP 4/60/2B/3; and "Interview with Alexander Bustamante," *DG*, September 20, 1939, 9.

23. "Mr. Bustamante and the PNP," letter to the editor from A. Bustamante, *DG*, June 15, 1939, 12. The preceding comments on the divisions in the PNP are found in a report that Norman Manley prepared for English journalist Harold Stannard in December 1942. See NMP 4/60/2B/6; and Henry Fowler to N. W. Manley, March 20, 1943, NMP 4/60/2B/7. For Noel Nethersole's letter, see N. N. Nethersole to N. W. Manley, July 2, 1940, NMP 4/60/2B/4.

24. The preceding comments are found in a report that Norman Manley prepared for Harold Stannard in December 1942, NMP 4/60/2B/6; Henry Fowler to N. W. Manley, March 20, 1943, NMP 4/60/2B/7.

25. "Labour Day Marked in Jamaica," *DG*, May 28, 1940, 10.

26. Ibid.

27. "Policy of the PNP Party Is Outlined," *DG*, December 23, 1939, 1, 19.

28. Ibid.

29. "Metropolitan Group of PNP Meets," *DG*, November 1, 1938, 21; see also "Mr. Nethersole Addresses Metropolitan Group of National Party," *DG*, November 1, 1938.

30. "PNP Now Socialist," *DG*, August 30, 1940, 6.

31. Ibid.

32. Ibid.

33. Ibid.

34. "Socialism," editorial, *DG*, September 24, 1940, 8.

35. "Can Christians Be Socialists?," *DG*, February 11, 1941, 9, 14.

36. The Englishman was probably Robert Kirkwood. See the unsigned letter to Malcolm [MacDonald], April 12, 1938, NMP 4/60/2B/5; "The Platform of the PNP," *DG*, August 6, 1939, 20.

37. "Mr. Manley Withers," 18, 9; "Text of Mr. Manley's Speech at PNP Parley," 13.

38. For Manley's account of this opposition, see N. W. Manley to Duckie, December 21, 1943, NMP 4/60/2B/5. The letter was probably not mailed since the extant copy is marked "not sent." Whether it was sent or not, the letter addresses Manley's reaction to the opposition of the ethnic groups in question.

39. "Governor Attacks Political Quacks," *DG*, December 14, 1940, 17.

40. "The Future of Jamaica," *DG*, December 16, 1940, 6.

41. This letter was intercepted by the censors who operated during the war. E. D. Carberry to Dr. H. B. Morgan, April 25, 1942, CO 137/854/14.

42. "Bustamante to Enter Political Arena," *Jamaica Times*, July 18, 1942, 1; "Mr. Bustamante Aims to Be a Political Boss," *DG*, August 11, 1942, 3.

43. "Is This Fascism," editorial, *DG*, August 18, 1943, 4.

44. Ibid.; "Mr. Bustamante Aims to Be a Political Boss," 3.

45. "Mr. Bustamante Aims to Be a Political Boss," 3.
46. Ibid.; "Bustamante to Enter Political Arena."
47. "A New Political Party Here Suggested," letter to the editor from T. H. Sharp, *DG*, March 3, 1942, 7.
48. "Today," column by G. St. C. Scotter, *DG*, March 4, 1942, 3; "A New Political Party," 6.
49. "JDP Gets Mixed Reception at Ward Theatre Meeting," *DG*, March 18, 1943, 1.
50. "Democratic Party Sets out Its Aim in Draft Policy," *DG*, March 16, 1943, 3.
51. "Jamaica Labour Party Launched at Great Meeting at Ward Theatre," *DG*, July 9, 1943, 3; "Labour Party Launched in Metropolis," *DG*, July 10, 1943, 10.
52. "Labour Party," editorial, *DG*, July 10, 1943, 6.
53. "Launching of Jags Smith Political Party," *DG*, October 11, 1943, 6.
54. J. Edgar Hoover to Adolf Berle, July 2, 1943, Central Decimal File 1940–44, Box 5062, NA-DS.
55. "The Political Situation in Jamaica," memorandum prepared by Paul Blanshard, September 20, 1943, Central Decimal File, 1940–44, Box 5062, NA-DS.
56. Ibid.
57. Ibid.
58. Ibid.
59. Bustamante to S. J. H. West, August 26, 1943, uncataloged, BM.
60. Blanshard, "The Political Situation"; Paul Blanshard, "The Government of Jamaica," General Records of the Department of State, Decimal File, 1945–49, February 1, 1945, Box 6052, NA-DS.
61. Bustamante to S. J. H. West.
62. "The Reason Why," editorial, *DG*, November 15, 1944, 6. Bustamante would later attribute his victory at the polls to the fact that "I had personality and the people like me more than Manley. I had done something for labor and the people knew it." See Blanshard, "The Government of Jamaica."
63. "Nomination Day," editorial, *DG*, November 29, 1944, 6.
64. "A Plan for National Prosperity," *DG*, November 30, 1944, 4.
65. "If Jamaica Became a Socialist State," *DG*, December 4, 1944, 9.
66. "Jamaica Labour Party's Aims and Objects," *DG*, December 11, 1944, 16.
67. Ibid.
68. "130 Nominated for 32 Seats in New House," *DG*, November 30, 1944, 10.
69. "The Hand," *Public Opinion*, December 1, 1944, 1, 4; "Walk down King Street," *Public Opinion*, December 2, 1944, 3.
70. Blanshard, "The Political Situation."
71. "To the Electors of Eastern St. Thomas," *DG*, December 11, 1944, 17; "Vote for Albert Henry Robinson," *DG*, December 11, 1944, 17; "Mary Morris Knibb," *DG*, December 11, 1944, 19; "Vote for Rev. C. A. Wilson," *DG*, December 11, 1944, 19.
72. Desmonds Hall, "Fellow Electors of Northwestern Clarendon," *DG*, December 11, 1944, 7.
73. This brief discussion of Isaac Barrant's life is based upon Gladys Bustamante, *The Memoirs of Lady Bustamante* (Kingston: Kingston Publishers Limited,

1997), 143–45; W. A. Domingo to O. T. Fairclough, June 22, 1954, NMP 4/60/2B/16; "Preliminary Figures," *DG*, December 16, 1944, 11; and I. W. A. Barrant to Norman Manley, July 1, 1941, NMP 4/60/2B/5; "Isaac Barrant Is Dead," *DG*, August 19, 1956, 1; "We Shall All Miss Him," *DG*, August 19, 1956, 1. Candidates who had little money campaigned as befitting their economic condition. Leopold Lynch, a JLP candidate, successfully campaigned on a bicycle in Eastern Portland; and Fred L. B. Evans, an independent candidate, rode a donkey in Eastern Westmoreland and won the seat.

74. "To the People of Jamaica," *DG*, November 7, 1944, 7; "Challenge to Manley," *DG*, November 17, 1944, 5; "Advertisement by Ken Hill," *DG*, December 13, 1944, 9; Blanshard, "The Government of Jamaica."

75. "Election Meetings," *DG*, October 13, 1944, 7.

76. "Bustamante Bares Legs at Election Meeting to Give Lie to Rumour," *DG*, November 4, 1944, 8.

77. Manley was never able to dispel the distrust based upon his skin color, although Bustamante seemed to escape it. Perhaps Bustamante's personal relationship with the somewhat darker-skinned Gladys Longbridge served to temper such prejudice. Manley's wife, Edna, was identified as white by many Jamaicans, a charge that complicated the situation. As late as July 1955, Mrs. Manley was forced to declare that she was "Coloured and proud of it." Writing to Manley in August, 1947, W. A. Domingo told him that "a strong argument" used against him in New York by Jamaicans was "the brown man stuff." Responding, Manley observed that "it only shows how deep seated these irrational things are." See "Manley, I Deny and I Affirm," *DG*, December 12, 1944, 9; W. A. Domingo to N. W. Manley, August 25, 1947, NMP 4/60/2B/12; N. W. Manley to W. A. Domingo, October 2, 1947, NMP 4/60/2B/12; "Mrs. Manley: Coloured and Proud of It," *DG*, July 20, 1953, 1.

78. "To the People of Jamaica," 7.

79. "The Truth about Manley's Great Fight for Labour in May, 1938," supplement to the *DG*, November 4, 1944.

80. "The Whole Truth," *DG*, November 18, 1944, 7; "A Fraud Exposed," *DG*, November 25, 1944, 9; Blanshard, "The Government of Jamaica."

81. For a breakdown of the election results, see "Bustamante Landslide," *DG*, December 16, 1944, 1; *General Election 1944: Report of the Chief Electoral Officer* (Kingston: Government Printer, 1945); "Preliminary Returns for the Election," *DG*, December 16, 1944, 1.

82. Blanshard, "The Government of Jamaica."

83. Ibid.

84. "Will Seek to Cooperate with All Peoples for Good of the People," *DG*, December 16, 1944, 1.

85. Blanshard, "The Government of Jamaica."

86. Ibid.

87. "Will Seek to Cooperate."

88. Ibid.; American Counsel to the Department of State, December 16, 1944, Central Decimal File, 1940–44, Box 5062, NA-DS.

89. Patrick E. Bryan and Karl Watson, eds., *Not for Wages Alone: Eyewitness Summaries of the 1939 Labour Rebellion in Jamaica* (Mona: University of the West Indies Press, 2003), 146; N. W. Manley to Governor Richards, undated but written in 1940, copy in NMP 4/60/2B/4.

90. Blanshard, "The Government of Jamaica." Bustamante's widely acknowledged appeal to the working people was dramatically reflected in his explanation for the victory of F. G. Veitch in Western Hanover. He told Blanshard that "at Lucea . . . it looked as if Veitch was losing to Thomas of the P.N.P. and I went out there and made 25 speeches in two days, some of them without a microphone. I said: I am not asking you to vote for Veitch; I am telling you to vote for Veitch. And they did. They will do what I say whether it is right or wrong." This may have been an apocryphal account, but it captured the narrative of Bustamante's relationship with the working people. Bustamante's memory may also have failed him as he recounted the story. The PNP did not contest the constituency of Western Hanover that Veitch won, and there was no candidate named Thomas. See Blanshard, "The Government of Jamaica," for Bustamante's comment.

91. L. L. Nunez to Norman Manley, December 27, 1944, NMP 4/60/2B/9; William Seivright to Norman Manley, December 15, 1944, NMP 4/60/2B/9.

92. "PNP to Go Steadily ahead with Its Policies," *DG*, December 18, 1944, 1.

93. "PNP Leader Urges Party to Work for Success of Constitution," *DG*, January 10, 1945, 5.

94. "JDP Determined to Work for Success of New Constitution," *DG*, December 16, 1944, 1.

95. This account of the JLP's early months in office is taken from Governor Huggins's report to the Colonial Office. See Huggins to the Secretary of State, April 22, 1945, CO 137/859/17.

96. Michael Manley to Norman Manley, July 3, 1952, NMP 4/60/2B/15. Michael Manley became Jamaica's fourth prime minister in 1972.

97. Quoted in Richard Peel, *Old Sinister: A Memoir of Sir Arthur Richards* (Cambridge, UK: F. and P. Piggott Limited, 1985), 92.

SELECTED BIBLIOGRAPHY

Primary Sources

This study is based significantly on manuscript sources located in Spanish Town, Jamaica; Kingston, Jamaica; London, UK; and College Park, Maryland. I consulted manuscripts housed in the Jamaica Archives at Spanish Town and at the Institute of Jamaica and the Bustamante Museum in Kingston. In addition, I used the manuscripts located in the British National Archives at Kew Gardens, London, and in the National Archives at College Park.

Manuscript and Archival Material

COLLEGE PARK, MD.
    National Archives of the United States

KINGSTON, JAMAICA
    The Bustamante Museum
    The Institute of Jamaica

LONDON, UK
    British National Archives
        Records of the Colonial Office, Commonwealth and Foreign and Commonwealth Offices
    Records of the Prime Minister's Office

SPANISH TOWN, JAMAICA
    Jamaica Archives
        Norman Manley Papers

Government and Official Publications

Eighth Census of Jamaica and Its Dependencies, 1943. Kingston: Government Printer, 1945.

General Election 1944: Report of the Chief Electoral Officer. Kingston: Government Printer, 1945.

Report of the West India Royal Commission [the Moyne Commission]. London: His Majesty's Stationery Office, 1945.

Report (with Appendices) of the Commission Appointed to Enquire into the Disturbances Which Occurred in Jamaica between the 23rd May and the 8th June 1938. Kingston: Government Printer, 1938.

Report (with Appendices) of the Commission Appointed to Enquire into the Disturbances Which Occurred on Frome Estate in Westmoreland on 2nd May 1938. Kingston: Government Printer, 1938.

Newspapers

Daily Gleaner
Jamaica Standard
Jamaica Times
Jamaica Worker
Public Opinion

Selected Secondary Sources

Bakan, Abigail. *Ideology and Class Conflict in Jamaica*. Montreal and Kingston: McGill-Queens University Press, 1990.

Basdeo, Sabadeo. "Walter Citrine and the British Caribbean Workers Movement during the Moyne Commission Hearing, 1938–1939." In *Politics, Society, and Culture in the Caribbean*, edited by Blanca Silvestrini, 239–55. San Juan: University of Puerto Rico, 1983.

Bell, Wendell. *Jamaican Leaders: Political Attitudes in a New Nation*. Berkeley: University of California Press, 1964.

Bolland, O. Nigel. *On the March: Labour Rebellions in the British Caribbean, 1934–1939*. Kingston: Ian Randle Publishers, 1995; and London: James Currey Publishers, 1995.

———. *The Politics of Labour in the Caribbean*. Kingston: Ian Randle Publishers, 2001.

Brenner, Aaron, Robert Brenner, and Cal Winslow, eds. *Rebel Rank and File: Labor Militancy and Revolt from Below in the Long 1970s*. London and New York: Verso Press, 2010.

Brodber, Erna. *The Second Generation of Freemen in Jamaica, 1917–1944*. Gainesville: University of Florida Press, 2004.

Bryan, Patrick. *The Jamaican People, 1880–1902: Race, Class, and Social Control*. London: Macmillan, 1991.

Bryan, Patrick, and Karl Watson, eds. *Not for Wages Alone: Eyewitness Summaries of the 1938 Labour Rebellion in Jamaica*. Mona: University of the West Indies Press, 2003.

Bustamante, Gladys. *The Memoirs of Lady Bustamante*. Kingston: Kingston Publishers Limited, 1997.

Campbell, Mavis C. *The Maroons of Jamaica, 1655–1796*. Trenton, N.J.: Africa World Press, Inc., 1990.

Carnegie, James. *Some Aspects of Jamaican Politics, 1918–1938*. Kingston: Institute of Jamaica, 1973.

Clarke, Colin G. *Kingston, Jamaica: Urban Development and Social Change, 1692–1962*. Berkeley: University of California Press, 1975.

Cross, Malcolm, and Gad Heuman, eds. *Labour in the Caribbean: From Emancipation to Independence*. London: MacMillan, 1968.

Cumper, George E. "Labour Demand and Supply in the Jamaican Sugar Industry, 1830–1850." *Social and Economic Studies* 2, no. 4 (1954): 37–86.

Curtin, Philip D. *The Image of Africa: British Ideas and Action, 1780–1850*. 2 vols. Madison: University of Wisconsin Press 1964.

———. *Two Jamaicas: The Role of Ideas in a Tropical Colony, 1830–1865*. New York: Atheneum, 1970.

Eaton, George. *Alexander Bustamante and Modern Jamaica*. Kingston: Kingston Publishers Limited, 1975.

———. "Trade Union Development in Jamaica." *Caribbean Quarterly* 8, nos. 1 and 2 (1962): 45–55, 69–75.

Eisner, Gisela. *Jamaica, 1830–1930: A Study in Economic Growth*. Manchester: Manchester University Press, 1961.

Frucht, Richard. "A Caribbean Social Type: Neither 'Peasant' nor 'Proletarian.'" *Social and Economic Studies* 16, no. 3 (1967): 295–300

Hall, Douglas. *Free Jamaica, 1838–1865*. New Haven, Conn.: Yale University Press, 1959.

Hart, Richard. *Rise and Organise: The Birth of the Workers and National Movements in Jamaica, 1936–1939*. London: Karia Press, 1989.

Harris, Joseph E. *African American Reactions to War in Ethiopia, 1936–1941*. Baton Rouge: Louisiana State University Press, 1994.

Haverty-Stacke, Donna T., and Daniel J. Walkowitz, eds. *Rethinking U.S. Labor History: Essays on the Working-Class Experience, 1756–2009*. New York: The Continuum International Publishing Group, 2010.

Heuman, Gad. *The Killing Time: The Morant Bay Rebellion in Jamaica*. London: MacMillan, 1994.

Hill, Frank. *Bustamante and His Letters*. Kingston: Kingston Publishers Limited, 1976.

Holt, Thomas. *The Problem of Freedom: Race, Labour, and Politics in Jamaica and Britain, 1832–1938*. Baltimore: Johns Hopkins University Press, 1992.

James, Winston. *Holding aloft the Banner of Ethiopia: Caribbean Radicalism in Early Twentieth-Century America*. London: Verso, 1999.

Jones, Ken. *Bustamante: Jokes, Quotes, Anecdotes*. Kingston: Kenneth Jones, 2009.

Knight, Franklin. *The Caribbean: The Genesis of a Fragmented Nationalism*. 2nd ed. New York: Oxford University Press, 1990.

Laurence, Keith. *Immigration into the West Indies in the Nineteenth Century*. Barbados: Caribbean Universities Press, 1971.

———. *A Question of Labour: Indentured Immigration into Trinidad and British Guiana, 1875–1917*. Kingston: Ian Randle Publishers; and London: James Currey Publishers, 1994.

Le Guerre, John Gaffar. "The Moyne Commission and the Jamaican Left." *Social and Economic Studies* 31, no. 3 (1982): 59–94.

Lewis, Gordon. *Main Currents in Caribbean Thought*. Baltimore: Johns Hopkins University Press, 1983.

Manley, Michael. *A Voice at the Workplace: Reflections on Colonialism and the Jamaican Worker*. London: André Deutsch, 1975.

Martin, Tony. *Race First: The Ideological and Organizational Struggles of Marcus Garvey and the Universal Negro Improvement Association*. Westport, Conn: Greenwood Press, 1976.

Moore, Brian, and Michele A. Johnson, eds. *"Squalid Kingston," 1890–1920: How the Poor Lived, Moved, and Had Their Being*. Mona: University of the West Indies, 2000.

Moses, William Jeremiah. *Afrotopia: The Roots of African American Popular History*. New York: Cambridge University Press, 1998.

Munroe, Trevor. "The People's National Party, 1938–44: A View of the Early Nationalist Movement in Jamaica." Unpublished M.A. thesis, University of the West Indies, Mona, 1966.

———. *The Politics of Constitutional Decolonization: Jamaica, 1944–1962*. Jamaica: Institute of Social and Economic Research, 1972.

Nettleford, Rex, ed. *Manley and the New Jamaica: Selected Speeches and Writings, 1938–1968*. London: London Caribbean Limited, 1971.

———. *Mirror, Mirror: Identity, Race, and Protest in Jamaica*. Jamaica: Collins and Sangster, 1970.

Peel, Richard. *Old Sinister: A Memoir of Sir Arthur Richards, GCMG: First Baron Milverton of Lagos and Clifton in the City of Bristol, 1885–1978*. Cambridge, UK: F. and P. Piggott Limited, 1985.

Phelps, O. W. "Rise and Fall of the Labour Movement in Jamaica." *Social and Economic Studies* 9, no. 4 (1960): 417–68.

Post, Ken. *Arise Ye Starvelings: The Jamaica Labour Rebellion of 1938 and Its Aftermath*. The Hague: Maritinus Nijhoff, 1978.

———. "The Politics of Protest in Jamaica, 1938: Some Problems of Analysis and Conceptualization." *Social and Economic Studies* 18, no. 4 (1969): 374–90.

———. *Strike the Iron: A Colony at War*. Vol. 1, *Jamaica, 1939–1945*. Atlantic Highlands, N.J.: Humanities Press, 1981.

Ranston, Jackie. *From We Were Boys: The Story of the Magnificent Cousins Manley and Bustamante*. Jamaica: Bustamante Institute of Public and International Affairs, 1989.

Ryan, Selwyn D. *Race and Nationalism in Trinidad and Tobago: A Study of Decolonisation in a Multiracial Society*. Toronto: University of Toronto Press, 1972.

St. Pierre, Maurice. "The 1938 Jamaica Disturbances: A Portrait of Mass Reaction against Colonialism." *Social and Economic Studies* 27, no. 2 (1978): 171–96.

Scott, William R. *The Sons of Sheba's Race: African Americans and the Italo-Ethiopian War, 1931–1941*. Bloomington: University of Indiana Press, 1993.

Seaga, Edward. *Edward Seaga: My Life and Leadership*. Vol. 1, *Clash of Ideologies (1930–1980)*. London: MacMillan, 2009.

Shearer, Hugh. *Alexander Bustamante: Portrait of a Hero*. Kingston: Kingston Publishers Limited, 1978.

Singh, Kelvin. *Race and Class Struggles in a Colonial State: Trinidad, 1917–1945*. Alberta: University of Calgary Press; and Kingston: University of the West Indies Press, 1994.

Stolberg, Claus F., ed. *Jamaica 1938: The Living Conditions of the Urban and Rural Poor—Two Social Surveys*. Mona: University of the West Indies Press, 1990.

Van Deburg, William L., ed. *Modern Black Nationalism: From Marcus Garvey to Louis Farrakhan*. New York: New York University Press, 1997.

Williams, Eric. *British Historians and the West Indies*. New York: Charles Scribner's Sons, 1966.

Wilmot, Swithin. "Emancipation in Action: Workers and Wage Conflict in Jamaica, 1838–1848." In *Caribbean Freedom: Economy and Society from Emancipation to the Present*, edited by Hilary Beckles and Verene Shepherd. Kingston: Ian Randle Publishers, 1993.

INDEX

Page numbers in *italic* type indicate illustrations, maps, and tables.

Act of Emancipation of 1833, 357
Adams, David, 198, 204–5, 262
Advisory Board Regulations Act of 1940, 222–23
Advisory Council. *See* Trades Union Advisory Council
Africa, 24, 25, 26, 64, 66, 68–70, 89
"Africa for the Africans" (slogan), 24
African Americans, 26, 65
African-descent Jamaicans. *See* Black Jamaicans; Skin color
Agriculture. *See* Farms and farmworkers
Agriculture minister (Jamaica), 345, 346
Aitken, P. A. (Madam DeMena), 153
Allan, Harold, 39, 289, 347, 349, 355
Alves, Alexander Bain, 115
Anansi (trickster), 177
Anderson, Oswald E., 77–87; as Advisory Council member, 153; on colonial race hatred, 65, 77, 83; constitutional change and, 304; critics of, 84–85; resignation/mass meeting support for, 83; winning of by-election by, 85, 86
Anglicans, 73–74, 89
Anglo-American Caribbean Commission, 336
Annotto Bay, 33
Antigua, 22
Armitage, James A., 134
Arnett, Vernon, 177–78, 239–40, 257, 258, 259, 299, 326
Artisans' Union, 115
Ashenheim, Leslie, 230, 232
Ashenheim, Lewis, 108
Aspinall, Mrs. (English resident), 72–73
Assembly. *See* House of Assembly
Atheism, 348
Atlantic slave trade. *See* Slavery

Attlee, Clement, 30–31, 277
Attorney general, 15
Augier, Roy, 6

Bahamas, 22, 291
Bailey, Amy, 79, 80, 84
Banana industry, 75, 155, 157, 180; Bustamante-called general strike and, 148–51; economic problems of, 105; Maritime Union and, 124; Panama disease effects on, 105; strikes, 9, 55, 57, 59, 60, 116; unionization and, 117, 118; women workers and, 127
Bank jobs, 79, 80
Bank of Nova Scotia, 80
Baptists, 29, 75, 91
Barbados, 22, 93, 291
Barker, R. B., 354
Barrant, Isaac, 345–46
Bedward, Alexander, 23–24
Bedwardite movement, 24
Beggars, 30
Bermuda, 291
Bernard, Aggie, 127
Bethune, Walter C., 270
Bible, 25, 173
Bicameral legislature, 295, 296, 299, 303, 305. *See also* House of Representatives
Bigenot, S., 174; "Bustamante Anthem," 174–75
BITU. *See* Bustamante Industrial Trade Union
Black Jamaicans: anthem of, 25; at bottom of shade hierarchy, 58, 84; challenges to status quo by, 66–67; cultural impact of, 288; demographic dominance of, 14, *14*; discontent of, 9, 64, 68; discrimination against (*see* Racial discrimination);

399

English misinformation about, 72–74; ethnic Jamaicans' prejudice against, 329; first political party for (*see* United Negro Party); Garveyism and, 23–27, 42, 43, 45, 46, 65–66, 86, 120; government-sponsored miscegenation program proposed for, 71; improved conditions after 1938 for, 85–86; inferior status of, 14, 23, 68, 70, 71, 357; labor rebellion of 1938 and (*see* Labor rebellion); leadership roles and, 44; legacy of slavery and, 64, 88–90, 102, 341, 362; loyalty to British Crown of, 75, 89, 91; of mixed-race ancestry, 13, 26, 44, 45; party politics and, 329, 336, 348, 351; political equality and, 345; population growth of, 13–14, 25; postemancipation generation of, 23–24; racial consciousness and, 23–25, 43, 65–66; relations with white Jamaican residents of, 85; resentment of Chinese entrepreneurs by, 49, 57, 60; Richards's unjust treatment of, 260; rising middle class among, 23, 26, 73, 357; stereotypical constructs of, 29, 64–65, 68–77; strikers' demands and, 142; Universal Negro Improvement Association impact on, 45–46. *See also* Race; Racism; Skin color

Blacklock, Mary, 93

Black pride movements, 23–27, 45, 65–66

Blake, Evon, 43, 44, 46, 127, 195

Blanshard, Paul, 305–6, 336–37, 338, 341, 347, 349, 351, 352

Board of Conciliation. *See* Conciliation Board

Bradshaw, Edgar, 84

Bradshaw, Thomas, 147–48, 180

Brinton, Henry, 277

Britain: Bustamante complaint letters to, 9, 29–31, 32, 204–5; Bustamante's internment and, 198, 199, 211; Domingo's internment and, 259, 260, 262–63; free expression tradition of, 227, 351; Jamaican labor rebellion reactions in, 39–40, 57, 63; justice system of, 201–2, 203, 204–5, 360; Labour Party in, 30, 204, 211, 242, 260, 262, 273, 277, 310; low sugar prices in, 40, 105; nineteenth-century workhouses of, 267; Parliament of (*see* British Parliament); per capita income in, 15; racial views and, 29, 64–77; trade unionism in, 93, 198, 269; Trade Union Law (1919) of, 98, 116, 269; World War II and, 183, 201, 232, 259, 261, 264, 307–8

British Empire: Bustamante's loyalty to, 183, 188, 200–205, 228, 235–36, 305–6, 360; colonialism's cardinal principle and, 113; colonial secretary for (*see* Secretary of state for the colonies); Crown colony status and, 9–10, 282, 288, 290; *Daily Gleaner* defense of, 280, 287–89; Defense Regulations of, 185, 192, 230–40, 258; independence movements and, 233, 255, 258, 276, 280; Jamaican constitutional change proposals and, 296–98, 307–8; Jamaican grievances and, 5, 11–13, 28, 29–31, 40–41, 91–93, 182–83, 246, 264–65; Jamaican independence from (1962), 7, 305, 361; Jamaican national identity vs., 308, 313, 314; Jamaican racial discrimination and, 65, 77–78, 83, 205, 259, 357; Jamaican self-government proponents and (*see* Self-government); Jamaicans' loyalty to, 75, 89, 91, 301, 306–8, 313, 334, 342; Jamaica's new constitution (1944) and, 5, 63, 299–304, 336, 339, 342, 354; Jamaica's takeover (1655) by, 7, 8, 280; Mais critique of policies of, 273–77; Richards's defense of, 330–31; self-determination ideology and, 255, 258, 280, 289; stereotypes of black Jamaicans and, 29, 64–65, 68–77; World War II and, 259, 261, 264. *See also* Colonial Office; Royal Commission

British Guiana, 13, 22, 93, 114

British Honduras, 22, 93

British Medical Journal, 77

British National Archives, 4

British Parliament, 31, 32, 198, 260, 297. *See also* House of Commons

British West Indies, 5, 40; emancipation centenary and, 23, 27, 41, 87; English racism and, 71–72; reform and, 297; Royal Commission mission and, 87, 93; special yearly grant to, 113; wave of protests and strikes (1930s) in, 22, 31; worker conditions and, 58

Bronstorph Ice Company, 145

Brown, Ethelred, 314

Brown, F. L., 97–98

Brown, Sir Henry, 39

Brown skin, 79, 80; Bustamante's lightness

and, 3, 44, 45, 50–51, 108, 181, 358; political parties and, 336, 348
Buchanan, Hugh, 86, 120–21, 124, 125–26, 167; arrest for seditious libel of, 243; Bustamante's charges against, 180; resignation from Bustamante unions of, 137–39
Buff Bay, 118
Builders and Allied Trades Union, 154
Burma, 255
Burns, Hugh S., 55
Bus operators' strike, 52
Bustamante, Alexander, 2–6, 15, 16, 28–33, 83, 89, 272, 278, 281, 282, 358–61; "agitator" reputation of, 32, 132, 134, 179; arrest/jailing (May 1938) of, 28, 50, 51, 56, 62–63, 175, 179, 191, 221, 309, 359; arrogance of, 120–21, 123, 131, 132, 160–61; background and occupations of, 2, 28, 29, 45, 108, 181, 358; British loyalty of, 183, 188, 200–205, 228, 235–36, 305–6; business interests and, 333, 334, 336, 337, 351; changed surname of, 2; characteristic stance of, 133, 142; charisma of, 2, 5, 44–45, 169–70, 172, 173; Christian vocabulary of, 173–74; colonial government's subduing of, 228–29, 236; confrontational rhetoric of, 105–6, 124, 125, 129–30, 134, 138–39, 142, 146, 147, 149, 166–67, 168, 171–72, 183, 184, 185, 190–91, 195, 208, 223; constitutional change and, 299, 301, 303, 305–6, 333, 361; contradictions of, 168–69, 178; Coombs feud with, 2, 43–45, 120, 123, 126, 137, 140, 143–45, 147, 150, 155–58, 159, 172, 184, 221; critics of, 33, 125, 131–32, 134, 138–41, 346–47, 352; critique of colonial policies by, 9, 29–31, 98–107; crowned "King of Labour," 221; denunciations of Manley and People's National Party by, 318–21; election (1944) and, 343, 345, 346–47, 348, 349, 350–52, 354–55; fiscal impropriety charges against, 158, 211–12, 215–20, 346–47, 352, 359; general strike called by, 145–54, 161, 318, 360; Grant conflict with, 135, 136–37, 139–41; hyperbolic language of, 136, 199, 206, 208; internment (1940–42) of, 5, 115, 170–72, 184–200, 207–8, 211, 212–14, 215, 218, 225, 228, 256, 325, 332, 352, 360; as Jamaica's first prime minister, 7; labor commitment of, 337–38, 361; labor negotiating style of, 164–67; labor organizing strategy of, 126, 358–59; labor philosophy of, 120, 121–24, 130–31; labor rebellion (1938) role of, 3, 5, 38, 42, 43–44, 46–49, 50, 51, 55, 56, 61, 62, 142, 179, 191, 221, 358–59; leadership style of, 56, 120, 123–24, 132, 137, 138, 139–40, 142, 145, 147, 155, 159–60, 161, 178, 206, 209, 216, 224, 332, 334, 338, 351, 354–55, 359, 361; letters to Longbridge of, 187–88; lifting of speech restrictions on, 225–26; light skin color of, 3, 44, 45, 50–51, 108, 181, 358; Manley's public attack on, 5, 210–18; messianism and, 172–73, 176; paranoia of, 172, 180; personal limitations of, 161, 205–6, 359; physical appearance of, 44–45, 50; police harassment of, 179–80, 241; political conservatism of, 105–6, 130–32, 182, 205, 229, 235–36, 320–21, 359, 360–61; political party founding by (see Jamaica Labour Party); popularity loss of, 355; race and class uplift speeches of, 67–69; revised recollections (1944) of, 161; Richards's characterization of, 248; Royal Commission testimony of, 98–107, 109, 110; self-invention/reinvention of, 2, 161, 181; showmanship of, 46–47, 133, 136, 177; Stanley's meeting with, 306–7, 308; tarnished image of, 225; temperament of, 47, 120, 121, 129–32, 139, 142, 146, 147, 161, 163, 168–69, 177, 178, 190, 193, 206, 209, 226; theatrics of, 163–64, 170, 171–72; trade union founding by (see Bustamante Industrial Trade Union; Bustamante unions); wealth and privilege of, 2, 108, 116, 168, 172; "Why I Want Power" article by, 131–32, 358; women workers and, 128; worker adulation of, 71, 129, 154, 169–70, 172–78, 181, 185, 206, 221, 224, 228–29, 319, 335, 340, 358–59; as workers' spokesman, 28–29, 55, 59, 107, 109, 133, 134
"Bustamante Anthem" (Bigenot), 174–75
Bustamante Industrial Trade Union (BITU), 3, 15, 146–68, 171, 193, 194, 205–7, 214, 324–25; Bustamante's and Longbridge's resignation letter and, 162–63; Bustamante's complaints about, 180, 198–99, 207–9, 223; Bustamante's control of, 137–40, 155, 159–63, 207–9, 216–21, 224, 318, 332,

359; Bustamante's salary/entertainment allowance from, 211–12, 217–19, 222, 346; censorship of newspaper of, 227–28; Coombs-Bustamante dispute and, 156, 158; critics of Bustamante's leadership of, 137–40, 155, 159–63, 216–21; dominance in Jamaica of, 168; first anniversary procession of, 176–77; fiscal impropriety allegations about, 140, 158, 162, 215–20, 359; general strike (February 1939) called by, 146–52; internal turmoil and, 161–63, 168, 180–81; internment of organizer for, 256; Jamaica Labour Party ties with, 334, 338–39, 351; Jamaica United Workers Union conflict with, 224–25; leadership during Bustamante's internment of, 186–87, 189–92, 198–200, 205–6, 207–10, 218, 222–23; Manley as counsel to, 126, 146, 186, 189, 205–6, 209–10; membership (1943) of, *169*; negotiation approach of, 164–67; new labor contracts of, 222–23; officers of, 189, 220, 345; People's National Party severed ties with, 324–25, 331–32, 359; police harassment of, 241; registration (January 1939) of, 124; strike problems and, 145–47; Sugar Manufacturers Association agreement with, 222–23; Trades Union Advisory Council and, 153, 154, 155, 156, 159–61; undemocratic constitution of, 162, 220; worker loyalty to, 224

Bustamante Museum, 4

Bustamante unions (June 1938–January 1939), 3, 96, 124–41, 359; first anniversary of founding of, 176–77; labor reform requests to Royal Commission from, 99–107; lack of program of, 99, 106, 130–31, 134–35; leadership instability of, 135–37; membership recruitment/composition of, 125–27; organization of, 124–26; reorganization of (*see* Bustamante Industrial Trade Union); seven components of, 3, 5; women's limited representation in, 126, 128, 129

Butler, Uriah, 31

Byfield, Donald, 63, 79

Campbell, Erasmus E. A., 48, 55, 152, 153, 250, 257, 301

Campbell, M. L., 257, 258

Campbell, T. A., 117

Capitalism, 129, 133, 134, 142, 146, 152, 164, 335, 339; Bustamante and, 333, 334, 336, 337, 351, 360

Carberry, E. D., 330

Cargill, S. R., 80–81, 82

Caribbean colonies. *See* British West Indies

Carpenters, Bricklayers, and Painters Union. *See* Artisans' Union

Caymanas Sugar Estate, 55

Censorship, 216, 226, 227, 228, 231, 237; of mail, 239–40, 257, 258, 301–2; Undesirable Publications Act and, 233–35

Census (1943): female workers, 128; overcrowded housing conditions, 95; race classification, 13–14, 67; workforce classification, 19

Central Intelligence Department, 194–95, 196

Chamberlain, Neville, 231

Child labor, 33, 107

Children's dire conditions, 30, 31, 32–33, 41

Chinese in Jamaica, 13, 15, 96, 111; black Jamaicans' resentment of, 49, 57, 60

Chisholm, J. C., 85

Christianity, 173–76, 327, 328, 348, 361

Churchill, Winston, 273, 274, 277, 288–89

Citrine, Sir Walter, 143–45, 198, 317; Hill brothers' internment and, 271–72; as Royal Commission member, 93, 96–98, 101–4, 106, 108, 112; as worker social justice advocate, 112, 269

City cleaners' strike, 52

City Printery, Ltd., 277

Civic organizations, 26, 27

Civil liberties, 230–32, 235, 238, 239, 241; defenders of, 242, 243, 257, 259; Richards's surveillance measures and, 254–55

Civil service, 79

Clarendon Parish, 15, 22, 250, 289, 332, 342, 355; landholding and, 87–88; opponents of Public Meeting Law in, 238; strikes in, 57

Clarke, Edith, 108

Clarke, William Alexander. *See* Bustamante, Alexander

Class: Bustamante rhetoric and, 106; challenges to existing social order and, 68; divisions in, 314; prejudices and, 67, 216,

402 | Index

358; race conflated with, 65; social hierarchy and, 57, 65, 67, 70, 79. *See also* Elite; Middle class; Underclass; Working-class consciousness
Class conflict, 64, 91, 133, 177
Clerks, 55, 79, 80, 128, 132, 133, 282; exclusion from workmen's compensation of, 97; union members, 169
Cobbett, William, 267
Coconut Producers Association, 165–66
Collective bargaining, 116
Collins, Iris, 349–50
Colonial Development Fund, 113
Colonialism: cardinal principle of, 113; legacy in Jamaica of, 362. *See also* British Empire; Imperialism; Self-determination ideology; Self-government
Colonial Office, 5, 9, 16–17, 53, 262, 354; Bustamante Industrial and Trade Union fiscal irregularities and, 216; Bustamante-Manley rivalry and, 215; Bustamante's complaints and, 29, 31, 33; Bustamante's internment and, 198; constitutional change and, 281, 285, 290, 292–305; financial assistance and, 113; Hill brothers' internment and, 271–72; Kirkwood-Richards dispute and, 252–53; labor rebellion reactions and, 57, 58, 59–60; Labour Adviser to, 133–34, 135; land settlement rumors and, 88; Manley and, 300, 305, 331; plight of Jamaican workers and, 96–97; Postal Censorship Order and, 240; racial policies and, 64–65, 77, 78, 83, 205, 259, 357; Richards's relationship with, 185, 244–45, 253, 261, 269, 270–72, 281, 283, 295–96; Royal Commission report and, 112, 113, 114, 287; trade unionism and, 168, 268
Colonial secretary. *See* Secretary of state for the colonies
Colorism. *See* Skin color
"Coloured" people (census definition), 67
Columbus, Christopher, 7
Commission of Enquiry, 39, 60–61
Communism, 132, 134, 138–39, 160, 161, 235, 236, 330; Bustamante's accusations of, 319–21; Domingo alleged link with, 257; Manley/People's National Party alleged ties with, 255, 268, 319–21, 327, 336, 347–48

Communist Party, 58, 193, 257; People's National Party expulsion of members of, 355–56
Conciliation Board, 54, 55, 59; Bustamante's critique of, 145–46; members of, 60
Conservatives, 247, 336–37, 339, 351, 354
Constant Spring Hotel (Kingston), 94, 98, 110; strike, 141
Constitution (1663–1865), 8–9, 290; reforms (1854), 8
Constitution (1895), 9–10, 11, 105, 296
Constitution (1944), 5, 63, 299–304, 336, 339, 342, 354; Manley's view of, 301, 304, 305; promulgation of, 304–7; provisions of, 299; responses to, 301–3
Constitutional change, 203–4, 253, 274, 280–308, 325, 335, 342, 360; Bustamante's aversion to, 299, 301, 303, 305–6, 333, 361; Moyne's proposals for, 293, 296; Richards's proposals for, 284–85; Smith's proposals for, 286–87, 290–94, 298–99
Construction workers' strikes, 57
Conversorium, 237; Bustamante speech at, 186, 192, 194–95; Shirley honors and, 210; workers' anticensorship resolution at, 227
Coombs, Allan George St. Claver, 128, 195, 215; background of, 26, 116; Bustamante's feud with, 2, 43–45, 120, 123, 126, 137, 140, 143–45, 147, 148, 150, 155–58, 159, 172, 184, 221; labor rebellion and, 38, 59; Royal Commission testimony of, 107–8, 109; significance to trade unionism of, 2, 115. *See also* Jamaica Workers and Tradesmen Union
Copra-Dryer Morant Bay strike, 165–66
Corruption, 361
Cost of living: per capital weekly income compared with, 15–16; wages linked with index of, 223
Council of Ministers, 295
Cowell Lloyd, F., 75
Craft guilds, 115
Creech Jones, Arthur, 75–76, 113, 198, 242, 271–72
Crime, 76
Criminal Investigation Department, 254–55
Cripps, Sir Stafford, 130–31, 271–72, 300–301, 310, 317
Crowdy, Rachel, 93
Crown Agents, 79

Crown colony status, 9–10, 282, 288, 290
Cuba, 2, 22, 58, 120, 180, 282
Cudjoe (Maroon leader), 306
Cundall, J. L., 276–77

Daily Dispatch (newspaper), 75
Daily Gleaner (newspaper), 4, 10–11, 73, 75, 77, 89–90, 91, 95, 128, 172, 218, 221, 224, 240–41, 310; on Bustamante and People's National Party, 160–61; Bustamante-Coombs feud and, 123; Bustamante letters to, 121–23, 131, 320–21; on Bustamante's general strike, 148; on Bustamante's "intemperate" allegations, 32–33; on Bustamante's political party, 332; on Bustamante's release from internment, 198; on Bustamante's speeches, 133; on Bustamante-Stanley meeting, 306–7; on Bustamante unions, 124, 136, 141, 176–77; conservative politics of, 247; on crowd's response to new constitution, 304–5; on crowd's response to Stanley's visit, 306–7; defense of British Empire by, 280, 287–89; Defense Regulations abuses and, 230–31, 237; on domestic servant conditions, 128–29; on Domingo's release from internment, 262; election (1944) and, 342–45, 347, 348–49; ethnic minorities and, 329; on independence celebration, 7; on Jamaican people, 13; land giveaways rumors and, 88, 91; on Manley charges against Bustamante, 210, 211; objections to socialism of, 327–28; on political parties, 332, 334, 335, 338–39; on Port Antonio unrest, 117–18; on Public Meetings Law effects, 239; on racial discrimination charges, 78–79, 81, 82, 83, 84–85; on reception to draft constitution, 299; Richards's policies and, 247, 255, 256, 278; on Royal Commission, 96, 98, 108, 114; on rural migrants to Kingston, 95–96; on seditious libel conviction, 243–44; as self-government opponent, 287–88, 289; on Smith's empty seat, 298; on spreading strikes, 55, 56–57; on sugar workers' rebellion (1938), 36–37, 38, 63; on unemployment demonstration, 42, 141–42; on unemployment factors, 19, 78–79; on waterfront labor rebellion (1938), 47, 49, 54, 56
Daily Herald (British newspaper), 39–40

Daily Telegraph (British newspaper), 92–93
Davies, Frederick, 68–69
Davies, W. E. Foster, 349
Dayes, H. O. A., 273, 276, 349
Declaration of Rights of the Negro Peoples of the World, 24
Defense Projects and Essential Services Order, 267–68
Defense Regulations Act, 185, 192, 230–40; essential services added to, 268; Mais arrest and, 273–77; prosecutions under, 243–44, 256; protest against abuses of, 230–32; Richards's misuse of, 258, 261–62, 268, 269–71. *See also* Internment
Delisser, H. G., 288
Demographics, 7, 13, 19; by race and sex, 13–15, *14, 15*
Denham, Edward, 18, 30, 31–32, 33, 88, 179; Conciliation Board and, 54, 145; death of, 41, 60, 255; sugar workers' rebellion and, 36, 38, 39, 40–41; waterfront workers' rebellion and, 53, 54, 59–60
Depression (1930s), 1, 19–20
Detention. *See* Internment
Dillon, J. T., 91
Discrimination. *See* Racial discrimination; Sex dixcrimination
Disease, 134
Dissent, suppression of, 5, 185, 192, 196, 230–40, 273–78
Dockhands. *See* Waterfront labor rebellion; Waterfront workers
"Dollar a Day, A" (workers' rallying cry), 37–38
Domestic servants, 20, 72, 97, 107, 127; harsh conditions/low wages of, 128–29
Domingo, W. A., 151–52, 153, 273, 345; internment of, 256–63, 272
Dominion status, 111, 254, 315, 339, 340
Doorly, Sir Charles, 39
Downie, H. F., 246–47
Duckenfield estate (St. Thomas), 119, 170, 171–72
Dung Hill (Kingston slum), 94
Durham, Vivian, 44, 46–47, 127, 129
Duval, T., 81
Dyce, Osmond, 205, 206–7, 268, 270

East Indian workers, 13, 96

East Queen Street Baptist Church, 75
Economic conditions. *See* Socioeconomic conditions
Edelweiss Park meeting (1942), 210
Education. *See* Schools
Edwards, J. A. G., 141, 147, 151–52, 155, 165, 216; charges against Bustamante, 180–81
Edwards, J. M., 125
Eight Points, 289
Election (1944), 338–55; as first under universal adult suffrage, 5, 305, 338; independent candidates and, 341–45, 347, 349; Jamaica Labour Party's victory in, 305, 350–51, 354; Manley's loss in, 349, 352–53; political mischief and, 348–49; violence and, 341; voter turnout for, 349
Election (1949), 355
Election (1955), 355–56
Electrical Trades Union, 93
Elite: Bustamante's connection with, 168, 172, 338, 351, 358, 361; callousness to dispossessed by, 41, 77, 91–92, 120; conservatism of, 336, 339; demonization of Bustamante by, 33; election obstructionism and, 339; Executive Council appointees and, 354; fears of worker unrest and, 179; Jamaica Democratic Party and, 334–35; Manley as counsel to, 3, 43, 53, 222, 360, 361; protest against Defense Regulations abuses and, 230–31; Richards-Kirkwood dispute and, 253; status quo protection and, 91, 280, 282, 336; testimony before Royal Commission by, 108, 111–12; wealthy ethnic minorities and, 329; white population's power as, 8–9, 14–15, 23, 29, 64, 65, 67, 78, 265, 288
Elliott, V., 138
Emancipation (1838), 1, 6, 7, 13; centenary of, 23, 27, 41, 87; challenges in century following, 41, 96, 357; postcentenary conditions and, 87; rumor of land bequests and, 88. *See also* Black Jamaicans
Emancipation Day (August 1), 87, 88–92, 241
Emergency Powers Law of 1938, 149–50
Emigrant returns, 2, 19, 22
Empire Day, 49–50
Employment: intermittent, 16–17, 18, 21; positive changes in, 85–86; skin color discrimination in, 79, 80, 84; women's limited options and, 20, 80, 126–27. *See also* Workers
Enemy aliens, 230
England. *See* Britain
Escaped slave colony, 8, 306, 357
Ethiopia/Ethiopianism, 25–26
"Ethiopia, Thou Land of Our Fathers" (anthem), 25
Ethnic minorities, 96, 111, 329; black Jamaican resentment of, 49, 57, 60
Ethnocentrism, 64
European peoples, 15; stereotypical views of Africa and Africans and, 64, 66, 68–70. *See also* White population
Evans, E. R. Dudley, 81, 350, 355
Executive Committee, 9, 294, 295, 299
Executive Council, 303–4, 354, 355
Eyre, Edward, 29

Fabian socialism, 309, 325–26
Factory Workers Union, 124
Fairclough, O. T., 273, 322, 326
Farms and farmworkers, 19, 223, 334; exemption from workmen's compensation of, 97–98, 101; general strike threat and, 146–47; government land settlement plan for, 60; People's National Party objectives for, 325; Royal Commission recommendations for, 113; statistics (1943), 21; union for, 124; women's hard jobs, 128. *See also* Sugar estates
Farquharson, May, 328
Fascism, 43, 102–4, 265, 276, 332, 351
Federal Bureau of Investigation (U.S.), 257
Federation of Citizens' Associations, 26, 328–29; constitutional change proposals and, 294–96, 299, 300, 301, 303; People's National Party and, 328–29
Fletcher, S. G., 165–66
Fletcher, Stuart, 92–93
Four Paths School, 33
Fowler, Henry, 273, 322–23
Fox, Richard, 268, 270
Franchise. *See* Suffrage; Universal adult suffrage
Franchise Act of 1859, 9
Francis, Roderick, 50
Free assembly, restraints on, 237–39, 240–41, 243

Freeholds. *See* Landholding
Free press, 227, 246
Free speech, 238, 239, 243, 246, 319, 351
Frome sugar estate worker rebellion (May 1938), 2, 33, 36–42, 52, 61, 62, 177, 358

Garvey, Amy Ashwood, 336
Garvey, Marcus, 24–25, 26, 44, 65, 66, 195, 336; background of, 24; on Jamaican poverty, 57–58; People's Political Party founding by, 24, 309; as unifier of black people, 45, 46, 86
Garveyism, 42, 43, 120
Gender: Bustamante union members and, 126–27, 128; population classification by, *14*; suffrage rights and, 4, 9, 10, 285; wages and, 17; work opportunity and, 20. *See also* Men; Women
General strike (February 1939), 145–54, 161, 219, 318, 360; failure of, 151–52, 154
General Workers Union, 124
Germany, 232, 236, 246, 255. *See also* Nazism
Gibb, James, 58
Gifford, Lawson, 290
Glanville Richards, R. F., 58
Glasspole, Florizel, 221–22
Gordon, Frank, 20, 52, 352
Government, 8–13; black Jamaicans' glass ceiling in, 357; blindness to workers' dire conditions of, 29–31; Bustamante charges against, 102–4; of individual parishes, 11; land-settlement scheme of, 22; new constitution (1944) and, 295, 296, 299, 303–4; relief programs of, 32; Richards's indictment of, 282–83; suppression of critics of, 5, 196, 241, 261; white minority elite hold on, 14–15; widespread opposition to, 262; worker abuse by, 107–8. *See also* Colonial Office
Governors, 9–13, 15, 29, 33, 40; Conciliation Board and, 60; Executive Council nominees by, 354; powers of, 9, 285, 288, 290–91, 293, 296, 299, 301, 304; public vs. private racial views of, 65. *See also* Denham, Edward; Huggins, John; Richards, Arthur
Grant, L. A., 37, 39
Grant, Leopold, 241
Grant, St William, 42–43, 44, 46, 50, 124, 126; arrest and imprisonment with Bustamente of, 51, 55, 56, 137; on Bustamante's greatness, 175–76; Bustamante unions and, 124, 126, 135–37, 139–41, 177; charges against Bustamante and, 180–81; general strike and, 147
Grantham, A. W., 96–97, 98
Great Britain. *See* Britain; British Empire
Griffiths, George, 29–30, 126
Gross national income (1942), 15, *17*
Grubb, Winston, 20, 205, 263
Guild system, 124
Gunter, Reuben, 118
Guthrie, Colonel, 306

Haile Selassie (emperor of Ethiopia), 25–26
Haitian revolution (1790s), 68, 76
Half-Way Tree, 85–86
Hall, Desmonds M., manifesto of, 342–45, 346
Hall, Lucius, 79
Hanover Parish, 243, 349; as Bustamante's birthplace, 2; Bustamante's triumphant tour of, 221
Harrison, Sir Charlton, 192
Hart, Richard, 205, 241, 321–22; Richards's campaign against, 263, 267, 268, 269, 272
Headquarters House (Kingston), 42
Health officer advertisement, 77–78, 79, 82
Henry, Arthur, 205, 241, 263, 267; Richards's campaign against, 268, 269, 270, 272
Henry, John Regeorge, 345
Higgins, Inspector (Central Intelligence Department), 196
Highgate (St. Mary Parish), 155, 172
Hill, Frank, 205, 259, 273, 321–22, 326; Richards's campaign against, 263–65, 268, 269, 270, 271; Richards's release of, 272
Hill, Kenneth, 26, 83, 125, 138, 151–52, 310, 326; Bustamante Industrial Trade Union and, 205; Bustamante dispute with/resignation of, 163; election (1944) and, 341, 347, 349; Jamaica United Workers Union and, 224; Richards's campaign against, 263, 265–66, 269, 270, 271; Richards's release of, 272
Hinds, Samuel, 270
Hitler, Adolf, 142, 147, 246, 255, 351
Hoover, J. Edgar, 257, 259

Hospital workers' strike, 55
Hours of work, 33–34, 39, 133, 134; maximum, 100, 334
House of Assembly (Jamaica), 9, 239, 240–41, 299; renamed House of Representatives, 303
House of Commons (Britain), 29, 39, 77, 231, 262–63
House of Representatives (Jamaica), 4, 332, 339, 350–51, 354–55; Bustamante's leadership in, 354–55
Houses of Parliament. *See* British Parliament
Housing, 36, 94–95, 107, 110
Howell, Leonard, 25
Huggins, John, 273, 304, 354–55
Hunter, J. H., 172
Hyatt-Shortt, Helen P., 69–70, 71
Hymns, 174, 177

Illiteracy, 14, *16*, 105, 301, 303, 349
Imperialism, 259, 273, 276–77, 280. *See also* British Empire; Colonialism
Income: as franchise requirement, 9, 10, 11; gross annual, *17*; gross national, 15, *17*; per capita weekly, 15. *See also* Wages
Indentured labor, 13
Independence (Jamaica): Bustamante's opposition to, 306; celebration (1962) of, 7, 305, 361; Hill's advocacy of, 321–22; Manley's view of, 315; self-government vs., 203
India: independence movement in, 233, 255, 258, 276, 280; workers in Jamaica from, 13, 96
Indonesia, 280
Industrial Defense Tribunal, 268
Intellectuals, 273–79, 307
International African Service Bureau, 93
Internment, 4, 5; basis of government power of, 185, 190, 192, 231; Bustamante exoneration campaign and, 200–205; Bustamante hearing (1942) and, 192–97; Bustamante release from, 197, 198, 215, 325, 352, 360; Bustamante release terms and, 211, 212–14, 228, 332, 360; Richards's targets for, 115, 170–72, 184–201, 218, 231–33, 256–63, 269–73, 277
Interracial marriage, 181
Isaacs, Wills O., 326

Islington, 57
Issa, Abe, 353–54
Italo-Ethiopian War (1935), 25–26
Itinerant laborers, 19

Jacobs, H. P., 60, 108, 153, 273, 310, 313, 322, 326
Jags Smith Party, 336
Jamaica: African slave emancipation in (1838), 1, 6, 7, 13; African slave population of, 7, 8–9; American naval base in, 258–59, 261; British takeover of (1655), 7, 280; Bustamante's vs. Manley's view of future of, 360; colonial history of, 7–27, 280; conditions in 1938 in, 7–27; critics of British administration of, 11–13, 34, 40; Crown colony government of, 9–10; Dominion status proponents for, 111, 254, 315, 339, 340; ethnic minorities in, 13, 15, 49, 57, 60, 80, 96, 111, 320; fault lines in society of, 85; first elected legislature of, 4; importation of indentured laborers to, 13; independence celebration (1962) of, 7, 305, 361; map of parishes of, *8*, 11; modernization of, 4, 6; motto of, 7; nascent nationalism and, 5, 179, 249–50, 253, 313 (*see also* Self-government); personalist political leadership and, 335, 361; political deficiencies in, 361–62; racial consciousness and, 5, 25–27, 244, 251, 288; racial diversity of, 13–14; survival of two-party system in, 356
Jamaica Agricultural Society, 223
Jamaica Archives, 4
"Jamaica, Arise!" (anthem), 316
Jamaica Banana Producers Association, 148, 157
Jamaica Biscuit Factory, 174
Jamaica College, 3
Jamaica Council of Civil Liberties, 230, 256, 259
Jamaica Democratic Party (JDP): election (1944) and, 338, 339–40, 348, 349, 353; ethnic minority members of, 329; founding and basic principles of, 334–35, 337
Jamaica Federation of Labour, 115–16
Jamaica Government Railways Employees Union: formation of, 267–71; membership (1943), *169*

Index | 407

Jamaica Hotel Employees Association, 116, 123
Jamaica Imperial Association, 26, 96, 111, 329
Jamaica Labour Party (JLP), 3, 203, 304, 332–34, 336–37; Bustamante's style of leadership of, 332, 334, 338, 340–41, 350, 359; election (1944) and, 305, 338, 340, 345–51, 354; founding of, 3, 335; leadership in House of Representatives of, 354–55; platform of, 333; trade union ties with, 334, 338–39
Jamaica Labour Weekly (newspaper), 91, 93–94, 243
Jamaica Liberal Party, 336, 340
Jamaican Union of Teachers, 111
Jamaican United Clerks' Association, 154
Jamaica Planter (ship), 48
Jamaica Printers and Allied Workers' Union, membership (1943), *169*
Jamaica Progressive League, 96, 111, 153, 238, 239, 257, 315, 340, 342
Jamaica Progressive League (New York), 58, 84, 259, 261, 314, 315
Jamaica Shirt Factory, 222; strike (1942), 164–65
Jamaica Small Settlers Party, 336
Jamaica Standard (newspaper), 80, 238
Jamaica Telephone Company, 222
Jamaica Times (newspaper), 32, 170, 172, 226
Jamaica Union of Teachers, 88, 96, 310
Jamaica United Clerks Association, 116; membership (1943), *169*
Jamaica United Workers Union (JUWU), 223–25; membership (1943), *169*, 225
Jamaica War veterans and Small Planters Trades and Labor Unions, membership (1943), *169*
Jamaica Welfare League, 26, 108, 309
Jamaica Worker (BITU organ), 227–28
Jamaica Workers and Tradesmen Union (JWTU): Bustamante's leadership role with, 116–17; Bustamante's split with, 120–21, 123, 158; Coombs founding and presidency of, 2, 26, 28, 56, 107, 116, 146, 359; general strike and, 147–48, 149, 150; internal disputes and, 123; membership numbers of, 123; Port Antonio public meeting (1937) of, 117–18; Trades Union Advisory Council and, 154, 155, 156
James, C. L. R., 93
James, Carmelita, 68, 169–70
James, Edith Dalton, 350
JDP. *See* Jamaica Democratic Party
Jews in Jamaica, 329
JLP. *See* Jamaica Labour Party
Jones, H. Anglin, 310
Jones, Morgan, 112
Josephs, Euphey, 67–68, 68, 80
Judah, Charles, "Can Christians Be Socialists?" lecture, 328
JUWU. *See* Jamaica United Workers Union
JWTU. *See* Jamaica Workers and Tradesmen Union

Kennedy, Joseph, 45–46
Kenya, 93, 113
Kenyatta, Jomo, 93
Kerr-Coombs, Stennet, 85, 243
Kieffer, J. G., 192
King, E. H. J., 273
"King of Kings" Salvation Mission, 243
King's Counsel (Jamaica), 3, 240
Kingston, 60, 94, 241, 301, 326; ban on street gatherings in, 240–41; Bustamante general strike and, 148, 150, 151, 152–53; Bustamante unions first anniversary procession in, 176–77; as capital city and nominal parish, 11; domestic servant numbers/conditions in, 128; government construction program in, 39; government of, 24; Jamaica Shirt Factory strike in, 164–65; march of unemployed persons in, 42; mayoral charges of racial discrimination and, 65, 77, 80, 83; opponents of Public Meeting Law in, 238; plight of unemployed in, 30, 31; population distribution, 15; promulgation of new constitution and, 304–7; racial consciousness meetings and, 26; Royal Commission slum investigation in, 94–95; rural migrants to, 22, 95, 128; strikes in, 2, 3, 42–56, 59, 141, 142–43; unemployed adults in, 17–18, 19, 141–42. *See also* Waterfront labor rebellion
Kingston and St. Andrew Corporation, 42, 77, 80–87, 153, 228, 309, 332, 334; Garvey's election to, 24; Nethersole as elected

member of, 266
Kingston Citizens Association, 83–84
Kingston Ice Making Company, 222
Kingston Race Course: Bustamante speech (August 20, 1939), 139; Bustamante speech (June 12, 1938), 124; Bustamante speech (February 1939), 152–53
Kirkwood, Robert, 15–16, 64, 112, 147, 150, 151, 249–53, 278, 280
Knibb, Mary Morris, 310, 342
Knibb, William, 90

Labor force, 19, 20–22, 127, 128. *See also* Workers
Labor law, 96–98, 101, 107, 109, 113–14, 116, 269, 333
Labor movement. *See* Trade unionism
Labor rebellion (May–June, 1938), 1–6, 28–63, 64, 154, 357–59, 361, 362; aftermath of, 59–63, 91, 281, 358; analyses of causes of, 57–58, 64, 78, 282–83; British reaction to, 39–40; Bustamante's commemoration of, 177; Bustamante's involvement with, 3, 5, 38, 42, 43–44, 46–49, 50, 51, 55, 56, 59, 61, 62, 142, 175, 179, 191, 221, 309, 358–59; cathartic effect on participants of, 68; causes of, 5, 21–33, 60, 280; centenary of emancipation coincident with, 23, 27; Commission of Inquiry and, 39, 60–61; Conciliation Board and, 54, 55, 59, 60, 145; condemnations of, 58–59; deaths from, 50, 60; Frome as signifier for, 41–42 (*see also* Frome sugar estate worker rebellion); grievances and, 37; leaders of, 37, 42–43, 53; Manley's mediation of, 3, 5, 52–54, 55–56, 59, 61, 63, 145, 309, 348–49, 360; outbreak of, 2, 33, 36–42; racial consciousness developed by, 26, 86; rallying cry of, 37–38; Royal Commission inquiry and (*see* Royal Commission); significant consequences of, 39, 63, 229, 273, 289, 310, 342, 344–45, 346, 350, 361; social change resulting from, 4, 60, 85–86; spontaneity of, 27; tandem strikes and, 52–53, 54–55, 56–57, 61; violence and, 37, 38, 42, 48–50, 54, 55, 57, 59, 60, 243; waterfront workers and (*see* Waterfront labor rebellion); white fears stirred by, 68–69; women participants of, 59, 127

Labor unions. *See* Trade unionism; *specific unions*
Labour Adviser, 133–34, 135
"Labourers' Psalm, The" (Williams), 173
Labour Party (Britain), 30, 204, 211, 242, 260, 262, 273, 277, 310; Manley's admiration for, 309
Labour Party (Jamaica). *See* Jamaica Labour Party
Landholding: distribution statistics (1938), 22; fears of socialist takeover and, 327; land-settlement scheme proposals and, 22, 60, 105, 109, 325, 333, 342; pleas for small parcels of, 76; rumored land giveaways and, 87–88, 91; "squatter" seizures of land and, 21–22; as suffrage and political office requirement, 9, 10. *See also* Farms and farmworkers
Land hunger, 21–22, 76, 91, 105
Lazarus, F., 172
League of Coloured Peoples (London), 78
League of Nations Society (Oxford University), 50
Leeward Islands, 93, 97
Legal aid, 101–2
Legislative Council, 9–12, 39, 54, 60, 89, 116, 310, 334, 357; black Jamaican members of, 357; Bustamante's planned candidacy for, 132; constitutional change and, 281, 286–87, 290–91, 294–96, 298–99, 300, 301, 303; critics of elected members of, 10–12; election (1944) and, 349; Garvey's failed bid for, 24; general strike emergency meeting of, 150; individual election contestants and, 310; Jamaica Labour Party and, 332; Kirkwood's appointment to, 250, 251; lack of power of, 11, 109; political divide in, 250; public meeting suppression by, 238, 239; racial issues and, 25, 66–67; Richards's proposal for, 284, 285; St. Ann by-election and, 337–38; Smith's vacant chair in, 298; Undesirable Publications Act and, 233–35; universal adult suffrage and, 287, 289–90, 299
Legislature. *See* Bicameral Legislature; House of Representatives
Lindo, Roy, 332, 349
Little, C. A., 289, 311
Livingston, N. B., 81

Livingston, Ross, 63, 125, 141, 153, 158, 163, 167, 186, 198, 216
Lloyd, Ivan, 337–38, 349
Lloyd George, David, 92
Loftman, J. H., 88
London Daily Express (British newspaper), 168
London Daily Herald (British newspaper), 93
London Express (British newspaper), 114
London Scots Self-Government Committee, 58
Long, P., 255
Longbridge, Gladys, 20, 43–44, 67, 226, 303; on Barrant, 345, 346; Bustamante's internment and, 170–71, 186–88, 192, 194, 197, 199, 200, 202, 205, 210; critics of, 216–17; devotion to Bustamante of, 187, 208, 210; lack of financial experience of, 220; marriage to Bustamante of, 127; union roles of, 16, 126, 129, 140, 160, 161, 162, 186–87, 189, 209; union salary of, 218; on women participants in labor rebellion, 127
Longshoremen. *See* Waterfront workers
Longshoremen's Union No. 1, 115
Longshoremen's Union No. 2, 115, 116
Lowe, A. B., 89, 301
Lowe, Sylvia, 92; "History of Emancipation," 89–90
Low Leighton estate (Kingston), 95
Luke, Mary, 73–74
Lyle, Sir Leonard, 40, 249, 250, 251–52
Lynch, Leopold, 345
Lyon, Winston, 334

MacDonald, Malcolm, 64, 242
Machado Tobacco Company, 220–21
Mail, monitoring of, 239–40, 257, 258, 301–2
Mais, Roger, 273–77; "Now We Know," 273–77
Malaya, 280
Malaysia, 255
Malcolm, O. Alphonsous, 84, 96, 345
Mallette, G. M., 221
Malnutrition, 30, 32–33, 41
Manchester Guardian (British newspaper), 31, 93
Manchester Parish, 19, 60, 310; as Manley's birthplace; strikes in, 57
Mandeville, 60, 75–76, 191

Manley, Edna, 56, 127
Manley, Michael, 356
Manley, Norman Washington, 6, *54*, 133, 253, 269, 328–31, 345–46, 360–61; background and career of, 3, 4, 52–53, 360; basis of genius of, 353; British insults to, 71; brown skin of, 3, 86; Bustamante contrasted with, 352, 360; Bustamante-Coombs feud mediation and, 143; Bustamante's accusations/break with, 5, 198–99, 210–18, 221–22, 225, 226, 228, 229, 270, 317–21, 324, 325–26, 341, 352, 359; Bustamante's blood ties with, 3, 206; on Bustamante's general strike threat, 146; Bustamante's internment release and, 171–72, 189–92, 198–200, 201, 211, 325; Bustamante's relations with, 5, 52, 56, 61–63, 158–61, 162, 171–72, 180–81, 206, 207, 208; on colonial administration, 331; colonial officials' high regard for, 300; constitutional change and, 291, 295, 299, 300–301, 304, 305, 360; as counsel to Bustamante Industrial Trade Union, 126, 146, 186, 189, 205–6, 209–10; on dangers of messianism, 173; defense of civil liberties by, 242, 243; defense of People's National Party by, 328–29; on Defense Regulations enforcement, 232; Domingo's internment and, 257, 258, 260; election (1944) and, 341, 345, 346, 347–49, 350, 352–53; election (1949) win of, 355–56; elite clients of, 3, 43, 52, 222, 360, 361; "I Deny and Affirm," 348; intellectual depth of, 290, 333; Jamaica Welfare League founding by, 26, 309; as labor rebellion mediator, 3, 5, 52–54, 55–56, 59, 61, 63, 145, 309, 348–49, 360; as Mais defense counsel, 273; "Memorandum on Constitutional Change for Jamaica," 286; police harassment and, 196, 241–42, 269; political ideology and, 309, 320–21, 325–26, 347–48, 360–61; political leadership and, 3, 263, 310, 313–15, 317, 322–23, 355–56, 359–60; praise and respect for, 53, 61, 305; protest against Public Meetings Act and, 238; Richards's relationship with, 245–49, 253, 254, 260–61, 270, 278–79, 281–82, 284–88, 292–93, 300, 315, 352, 356; Royal Commission testimony of,

108–10; security surveillance of, 242; self-government position of, 109, 182–83, 193, 203, 207, 225, 250, 253, 278, 285, 286, 301, 312, 314–16, 315, 360; speech on socialism of, 326; Trades Union Advisory Council and, 151–52, 153, 154–56, 158–59, 161. *See also* People's National Party
Maranga Lane (Kingston slum), 94
Maritime Union, 124
Markinnon, Sir Perry, 109–10
Maroons, 8, 306, 357
Marquis, Samuel C., 256
Marson, Una, 65–66, 79
Marxism, 120, 263
Match Factory, 222
Maxwell, J. W., 301
Mayers, T. Henry, 244, 273
McBean, W. A., 270
McDonald, Malcolm, 39
McGrath, H. S., 307–8
McKenzie, Lawrence, 45
McLaughlin, E. E., 83
McPherson, J. A., 355
Mechanics Union of Trade Associations, 115
Meikle, Rupert, 84
Men: Bustamante unions' predominance of, 126–27; population statistics, *14*; suffrage restrictions for, 9, 10, 285. *See also* Universal adult suffrage
Messianism, 173, 176
Metropolitan Group (People's National Party), 263, 264, 265, 268, 269–70, 285, 326
Middle class, 29, 282; African-descent members of, 23, 26, 73, 357; Bustamante detractors among, 131; emergence in Jamaica of, 361; People's National Party and, 333–34
Minimum wage, 96–97, 99, 325
Miret, Francisco, 164–65
Miscegenation: proposed government-sponsored program of, 71; U.S. interracial marriage ban and, 181
Mixed-race ancestry, 13, 26, 44, 45
Montego Bay, 57, 60, 137, 147, 206–7; Bustamante general strike in, 148, 149, 150, 151; Coombs Royal Commission testimony in, 107, 108
Montego Bay Clerks Association, 154

Moody, Harold, 78
Morais, S., 189, 209, 224
Morant Bay, 33, 69
Morant Bay rebellion (1865), 9, 29, 85, 357
Morgan, H. B., 260
Morrison, Sir William, 289, 290
Moyne, Lord, 93, 94, 95, 99, 100, 101–2, 105, 108; Bustamante's internment and, 187, 189–92; constitutional change and, 293, 294, 296, 299; replacement of, 298
Moyne Commission. *See* Royal Commission
Municipal Workers Union, 124
Murray, C. H., 341
Mussolini, Benito, 43, 142, 147, 351

National Archives of the United States, 4
National Council of Civil Liberties (Britain), 230
National identity, 308, 313, 314
Nationalism, 5, 179, 254, 255, 257, 258, 263, 279. *See also* Self-government
National Negro Congress (Washington, D.C.), 259
National origin, race conflated with, 13
National Reform Association, 26, 266, 310
Nazism, 255, 259, 261, 262, 273, 276
Negro Party, 336
Negro Workers Educational League, 255
Nelson, Cecil, 270
Nelson, Edith, 129, 200, 208, 210, 216–17, 303
Nethersole, J. M., 59
Nethersole, Noel, 108, 153, 154, 159, 160, 162, 163, 205, 318; charges against Bustamante and, 210; constitutional change and, 299; distinguished background of, 266; People's National Party and, 310, 313, 323–25, 326; Richards's charges against, 263, 266–67, 268; self-government advocacy and, 182–83
New Negro Voice (UNIA organ), 255
Newspapers. *See* Press; *specific names*
New York, 2, 24, 28, 42, 58, 257
Nigeria, 113, 273, 278
Norman, F. A., 334
Northern Longshoremen's Union, 154
Nunez, L. L, 352–53

Occupational safety laws, 97, 101

O'Donoghue, L., 38
Oil industry, 31
Old-age pensions, 325
Oldfield, Josiah, 70–71
Olivier, Sydney, Lord, 40, 267, 280
Orde Browne, G. St. J., 16–17, 135
Order in Council (1884), 9
Ormsby-Gore, David, 179
Orrett, William, 46–47, 50, 179–80
Oxford University, 3, 50

Padmore, George, 93
Panama, 2
Parish system: map, 8; population distribution, 15
Parkinson, Sir Cosmo, 244–45
Parliament. See British Parliament
Parochial Boards, 11, 12, 282, 297, 310, 332
Party politics. See Political parties
Passive resistance, 117
Pay scale. See Wages
Pear Tree Grove, 33
Pease, G. B., 74–75
Peat, P. W., 58
Penso, Oswald G., 162, 163, 326
People's National Party (PNP), 110, 151, 152, 159, 160–61, 177, 210, 259, 272, 310–31; Bustamante's membership in/break with, 5, 193–94, 202, 206–15, 224, 225, 317–22, 324–25, 331–32, 359, 360; communist sympathies and, 255, 268, 319–21, 355–56; constitutional change and, 294–96, 297, 299, 300, 303, 304, 325, 342; critics of, 328–29; critiques of colonial government by, 228; democratic organization/objectives of, 311–12, 338; Domingo's internment release and, 262; election (1944) and, 338, 339, 340, 341, 346–49, 350, 352, 354; election (1955) win of, 356; founding (1938) of, 5, 300, 310–12, 360; ideological development of, 321–24, 325–30, 333, 335, 336, 337; internal crises of, 355–56; "Jamaica, Arise!" anthem of, 316; Jamaica Labour Party contrasted with, 333–34; leaders of, 263–66, 270; membership growth of, 317; objectives of, 312–14, 325–26, 333–34, 353–55; organ of (see *Public Opinion*); People's Democratic Party and, 334, 335; police harassment of, 241–42; political ideology development of, 325–30, 333–37, 339, 360; radical wing of (see Metropolitan Group); Richards's campaign against, 253–56, 261, 263–70, 278, 279, 292, 359; self-government and, 182–83, 193, 202, 225, 228, 265, 285, 312, 315, 326, 333, 353–54, 359; wartime restrictive measures and, 237, 238, 239–40; worker support for, 205–6, 319, 324–25
People's Political Party, 24, 309
Personalist politics, 335, 340–41, 361
Phenotypical prejudice. See Shade prejudice
Picketing: disallowance of, 98, 101, 116; legalization of, 113
Pixley, Frank, 340–41, 355
Plantation system, 7
Platt, Ernest, 75–76
PNP. See People's National Party
Police: expanded power of, 238, 240–42; general strike violence and, 149; harassment by, 46–47, 104, 124, 179–81, 194–96, 202, 241–42, 269; Jamaican-born, 202; labor rebellion (1938) and, 38, 39, 46, 49, 50–51, 60; note-taking of political speeches by, 181, 183, 184, 194–96, 244; political violence and, 341; searches by, 268–69; street gatherings ban and, 240–41; strikes and, 31, 57, 59, 119; surveillance by, 235; worker abuse by, 107–8, 182; worker unrest and, 117–22
Political autonomy. See Self-government
Political parties, 3, 5, 86, 263, 309–56; absence in 1938 of, 309; challenges facing, 313–14; characterization of, 336–37, 338; constitution (1944) and, 301–3, 304, 305; corruption charges and, 346–47; first election and, 338–41, 345–53; labor ties with, 206–7, 358; Manley and, 3, 263, 328–31, 359–60; minor and short-lived, 336; personalist leadership and, 335, 340–41, 361; three major, 333–38; violence and, 341. See also Jamaica Democratic Party; Jamaica Labour Party; People's National Party
Poll tax, 9, 10
Poor Law of 1839 (Britain), 267
Poor Man's Improvement Land Settlement and Labour Association, 22, 87–88
Port Antonio, 60, 95, 224, 352; Bustamante

general strike and, 148, 149, 150, 151; Jamaica Workers and Tradesmen Union meeting, 117–18
Portland Parish, 19, 39, 57, 289, 345, 347, 349
Port Maria, 33, 60, 129–30
Port Royal Parish, 11, 15
Port workers. *See* Waterfront workers
Postal Censorship Order (1941), 239–40
Poverty, 15, 23, 27–32, 57–58, 59, 91, 134, 250; Bustamente's campaign against, 28, 29–32, 170, 182; systemic factors and, 32, 41. *See also* Underclass
Powell, W. E., 166–67
Prejudice, 25, 68, 78–80, 216, 358; color of skin and (*see* Shade prejudice); ethnic minorities and, 49, 57, 60, 329. *See also* Racial discrimination; Racism
Press, 4, 29, 32–33; censorship of, 227–28, 231, 233–35; freedom of, 227, 246; racist views and, 71–72; Richards's critique of, 247, 254, 255; on Royal Commission report, 114; sugar estate labor rebellion coverage by, 36–40. *See also specific publications*
Price, Morvel, 37, 38
Prisons, 20, 31–32
Privy Council, 9, 284–85, 304
Property: as franchise requirement and, 9, 10, 11, 285; slaves as, 7, 8, 64. *See also* Landholding
Public Meeting Law of 1939, 237–42; protests against, 238–39, 242
Public Opinion (PNP unofficial organ), 228, 247, 254, 255, 273–74, 326, 336; attack on Bustamente's integrity, 346; critique of Bustamente union, 318–19
Public Works Department, 28
Purchasing power, 16–17, 33
Putnam, Philip, 74

Race, 64–86; capital vs. labor and, 142; census imprecise use of term, 13; as central to Jamaican life, 5, 244, 251, 288; challenges to existing social conventions of, 68; changes in Jamaican configuration of, 86; Garveyism and, 23–27, 43; Jamaican diversity of, 13; labor rebellion of 1938 and, 64, 78; language of uplift and, 65–67; literacy and, 14, 16; miscegenation proposed program and, 71; mixed ancestry and, 13, 26, 44, 45; politics and, 9, 14, 24, 26, 78; population classification by, 13, *14, 15*; reluctance of public discussion about, 78; resentment of Chinese entrepreneurs and, 49; Royal Commission members and, 93; as social and economic status determinant, 23, 79; street orators and, 240–41, 243. *See also* Black Jamaicans; Racism; Skin color; White population
Racial consciousness, 24
Racial discrimination, 5, 24, 79, 181, 192, 205, 259, 261, 357; British stereotypical constructs and, 29, 64–65, 68–77; discussion discomfort about, 25, 80–83; segregation and, 24, 65, 181, 258. *See also* Prejudice; Racism
Racial equality, 251, 329–30
Racial essentialism, 72
Racial uplift, 24, 26, 27. *See also* Black pride movements
Racism, 5, 69, 70–72, 76–77, 288; challenges to official sponsorship of, 86; Jamaican health officer advertisement and, 77–78, 79, 82; literature justifying, 64; Nazi Germany and, 255, 259; social hierarchies and, 67; in United States, 65, 181, 258–59
Rae, Ernest, 80
Railway workers, 124, 268; strike, 55, 116. *See also* Jamaica Government Railways Employees Union
Rankin, Jeremiah, 174
Ras Tafari. *See* Haile Selassie
Rastafarians, 25, 26, 240–41, 243
Rebellion of 1938. *See* Labor rebellion
Reid, Altamont, 244
Reid, Charles Archibald, 60
Reid, George, 147, 148
Reid, Stanley, 21
Religion, 23, 25, 32, 173–74. *See also specific religions*
Rhodes Scholarship, 3
Richards, Arthur, 5, 6, 10–13, 207, 231–79, 297; arrival in Jamaica of, 244, 255–56, 281; assessment of Jamaicans by, 246–50, 253–54, 281–83, 292–93, 295–96, 300; Bustamente complaints to, 181–83; Bustamante general strike and, 146–47, 148, 149–50, 151, 153, 161; Bustamante Industrial Trade Union

and, 167–68; Bustamante-Manley split and, 215, 226; Bustamante's release from internment and, 197–98, 225, 352; characterization of Bustamante by, 248; climate of fear created by, 256; constitutional change and, 280–90, 292, 294, 299, 304; critics of colonial government and, 182–83, 228, 247–48, 278–79, 330–31; Defense Regulations implementation by, 185–92, 231–40, 261–62, 268, 269–71; departure for Nigeria of, 273, 278; efforts to silence Bustamante by, 179, 183, 184–85, 225, 228–29; internment policy of (*see* Internment); Kirkwood dispute with, 250–53; on labor rebellion causes, 60–61; Manley's relationship with, 245–49, 253, 254, 260–61, 278–79, 281–82, 284–88, 292–93, 300, 315, 352, 356; officially banned publications and, 233–35; personality of, 281; power/intolerance of, 244–45, 253–54, 256; pragmatic objectives of, 225–26; Public Meetings Law enforcement by, 239; Railway Union dispute with, 267–71; repressive measures of, 5, 231–43, 254–62, 263–66, 268–69, 273, 277–79, 281; self-government and, 225, 242, 254–55, 284, 285, 292–93, 315, 359; strike arbitration and, 142, 143

Roberts, W. Adolphe, 153, 238, 261, 315

Robinson, Albert, 341–42

Robinson, David, 149

Robison, R. F., 166

Roman Catholicism, 134, 328

Roosevelt, Franklin D., 288–89, 297

Rose, Leslie, 125, 206–7, 211, 221, 345

Rowe, Corporal (Central Intelligence Department), 194, 195, 196–97

Royal Commission (Moyne Commission), 5, 63, 78, 87, 93–114, 280, 286, 293; Bustamante testimony before, 98–107, 109, 110; chairman of, 93; Coombs testimony before, 107–8, 109; exclusion of poor workers and women from testifying before, 111; hearing of witnesses by, 96; interest group testimony before, 111–12; Jamaican doubts about, 93–94; Manley testimony before, 108–10, 285; members of, 87, 93; memorandum from workers in Spanish Town and, 110–11; mission of, 87, 93; Montego Bay testimony before, 108; on-site inspections by, 110; opening proceedings of, 94; report/proposals of, 112–14, 287, 325, 326

Rumble, Robert E., 21–22, 87–88

Rural-to-urban migration, 19, 22, 95, 128

Russell, Cecil, 119

Russia, 233, 236, 257, 259

St. Andrew Parish, 11, 15, 49, 66, 80, 95, 241, 290, 301, 342, 349, 350; domestic servant numbers, 128; skin shade prejudice, 67. *See also* Kingston and St. Andrew Corporation

St. Ann Parish, 25, 107, 181, 289, 349; by-election in, 337–38; as Garvey's birthplace, 24; strikes in, 57

St. Catherine Federation of Teachers, 68, 88

St. Catherine Parish, 55, 95, 345; strikes in, 57, 59, 141

St. Elizabeth Parish, 19, 107, 191, 224, 306, 342; Bustamante's triumphant tour of, 221; strikes in, 57

St. George's Hall (Kingston), 230, 238

St. James Parish, 107, 224, 243, 301, 349–50; banana workers in, 118; Bustamante's triumphant tour of, 221; Legislative Council representative from, 89; strikes in, 57, 59

St. Kitts, 23

St. Lucia, 22

St. Mary Federation of Citizens' Associations, biannual meeting (1938), 314–15

St. Mary Parish, 19, 107, 155, 172, 224, 332, 349; Bustamante's calming influence in, 191; strikes in, 57, 59

St. Thomas Parish, 25, 150, 269, 341–42, 345; Bustamante speech in, 170; land seizure in, 21; strikes in, 57, 118–19, 141; sugar estates strike plan in, 171

St. Vincent, 22

Salt Lane (Kingston slum), 94

Sangster, P. W., 94

Sanguinetti, S. T. B., 51

Sanitation workers' strike (1938), 52

Sara, E. G., 73–74

Schools, 30, 31, 32–33, 111, 343; teachers' political views and, 242

Scotter, G. St. C., 89, 129, 131–32, 237, 256, 334

Secretary of state for the colonies, 15, 31,

39, 40, 84, 88, 113, 187, 202, 203, 272, 299, 300, 301, 305; Bustamante complaints of police abuse to, 180, 181; Bustamante exoneration letter to, 200–204; constitutional change and, 293, 294, 296, 299; first official visit to Jamaica by, 307; Moyne as, 187, 293, 298; Stanley as, 115, 298, 305, 306–7; testimony to Royal Commission of, 96–97; universal suffrage and, 289–90

Security List, 242

Sedition, 170–72, 183, 185, 214, 215, 228, 244, 246, 273

Seditious libel, 243–44, 273

Segregation, 24, 65, 181, 258

Seivright, William, 210, 349, 353

Self-determination ideology, 255, 258, 280; African-descent peoples and, 24; British-U.S. leaders' statement on, 289; Jamaica Democratic Party and, 334; Richards's view of, 272–73, 285

Self-government, 5, 8, 58, 75, 105, 186, 249–51, 253, 255, 256, 259, 281, 284–88, 296, 312–16; advocates of, 75, 250, 251, 257, 258, 263, 265; Bustamante's objection to, 183, 193, 203–4, 205, 334, 360, 361; colonial movements for, 255; constitution draft of 1944 and, 301–5; Dominion status and, 111, 254, 315, 339, 340; Kirkwood's position on, 250, 251; Mais's views on, 276–77; Manley's position on, 109, 182–83, 207, 253, 278, 285, 301, 314–16, 360; opponents of, 70, 281, 282, 287–88, 289, 303, 336; People's National Party and, 182–83, 193, 202, 225, 228, 265, 285, 312, 315, 326, 333, 353–54, 359; Richards's policies and, 225, 242, 254–55, 284, 285, 292–93, 315, 359; Royal Commission report and, 113–14, 287; timing of, 315–16; trade unions and, 207. *See also* Constitutional change

Serge Island estate strike, 118–19

Seton, Claud Ramsay, 60

Sewell, Horace Somerville, 60

Sex discrimination, 79, 80

Sexual exploitation, 100–101

Seymour-Seymour, Sir George, 66–67, 290

Shade prejudice, 50–51, 65, 79–80, 84, 348, 358; acceptance of leaders and, 44; decline in, 86; economic barriers and, 58; hierarchy of color and, 58, 67, 84

Sharp, T. H., 334

Sharpe, Sam, 89

Sherlock, D. T., 192, 193

Sherlock, Philip, 108, 273

Shillingford, Mr. (director of prisons), 20

Shipping Association, 151, 163–64, 183–84, 222

Ship workers. *See* Waterfront workers

Shirley, H. M., 187, 189, 193, 194, 199, 211, 217, 222–25, 230, 332; attack on Bustamante by, 218; founding of own union by (*see* Jamaica United Workers Union); on Longbridge's lack of fiscal experience, 220; public event honoring, 209–10; union salary of, 211–12, 218

Shirt manufacturers' strike, 52

Shop assistants, 55, 79

Sick leave, 100–101

Single-chamber legislature, 293

Skin color: classifications of, 13; discrimination and, 5, 50, 78–83, 361; hierarchy of, 58, 67, 84; leadership and, 44, 45; lightness of, 44, 45, 50–51, 79, 80, 108, 181, 358; phenotypical prejudice and (*see* Shade prejudice); political parties and, 336; treatment of workers and, 102. *See also* Black Jamaicans; Brown skin; White population

Slave rebellion, 9, 29, 85, 357

Slavery, 7–8, 10, 89; escapees from, 8, 306, 357; formal end of (1838), 1, 6, 7, 13, 23, 357; forms of resistance to, 357; introduction into Jamaica of (1511), 7–8, 357; legacy of, 64, 88–90, 102, 341, 362. *See also* Emancipation

Slums, 94–95, 110

Smith, B. B., 244

Smith, J. A. G., 63, 250, 251, 281, 289, 336; constitutional change and, 286–87, 290–94, 298–99; death of, 294, 298

Smith Constitution, 286–87

Smith Village (Kingston slum), 94

Social hierarchy, 57, 65, 67, 70, 79

Socialism: communism conflated with, 347–48; Manley and, 309, 325–26, 360; opponents of, 327–28, 339–40, 351; People's National Party and, 325–30, 333, 334, 335, 336, 337, 339, 360

Index | 415

Social movements, 4, 26–27
Social unrest, 22–23, 31, 33, 52, 107–8, 123–24, 179. *See also* Labor rebellion; Strikes
Socioeconomic conditions, 5, 15–27, 41, 78, 280; Anglo-American Caribbean Commission and, 336; Bustamante's concerns about, 337–38; changes after 1938 in, 4, 85–86; colonial administration's prejudices and, 41, 67; colonial administration's response to, 179; Colonial Development Fund and, 113; colonial elite's blindness to, 41, 77, 91–92, 120; discontent with status quo and, 23–24, 29; for English expatriates vs. black Jamaicans, 65, 72–73, 85; growing unrest and, 179 (*see also* Labor rebellion); improvements since independence of, 361; Jamaica Democratic Party and, 334–35; Kirkwood's attention to, 250–52; People's National Party objectives and, 313, 325, 333–34; plight of underclass and, 29–31, 57–58, 182, 250, 280; political organizing and, 263, 317, 339–40; post-independence Jamaica and, 361–62; race and national origin and, 14, 15, 65; Richards's view of, 247; Royal Commission investigation of, 93–114; Royal Commission report documenting, 113; trade imports and exports and, 105; unstable labor market and, 22; women's status and, 129
Soulette, Spencer B., 80, 85–86
Spain, 7, 43, 161, 181, 280, 357
Spanish Town, 110; strikes in, 55
Spence, M. O., 128
Squatters, 21–22
Standard Fruit Company, 148, 157
Stanley, Oliver, 115, 298, 305, 306–7, 308
State Department (U.S.), 336
Steele, H., 172
Store employment. *See* Shop assistants
Stratton, Colonel (Colonial Office), 215
Street meetings and orators, prohibition of, 237–39, 240–41, 243
Strikebreakers, 149, 150, 151, 358
Strikes, 22–23, 31, 52–57, 66, 75, 118; Bustamante's view of, 102, 123, 142, 145–47, 152; colonial government's discouragement of, 98; employer legal action against, 116; government violence and, 102; January 1939 series of, 141–43; legal protection and, 113; in nineteenth century, 10; worker legal protection and, 101–2. *See also* General strike; Labor rebellion; *specific industries*
Stubbs, Sir Edward, 93, 94–95, 108
Subsistence farmers, 21
Subversive activity, 255–56, 257; opposition to imperialism as, 276; Richards's definition of, 263–66, 268–70, 272–73. *See also* Defense Regulations Act; Sedition
Suffrage: colonial restrictions on, 9, 10, 11, 111, *See also* Universal adult suffrage
Sugar estates: Bustamante general strike threat and, 148, 150; Bustamante unions and, 135, 145, 171, 222–23; Bustamante violence threats and, 163–64; economic problems of, 105; English low sugar prices and, 40, 105; export value increases and, 105; seasonal workers and, 22; slave trade and, 7; women employees of, 20, 126; workers' conditions and, 16, 20, 33, 58, 107, 133; workers' rebellion (May 1938), 2, 33, 36–42, 52, 55, 61, 62, 177, 358; workers' strike (January 1939), 141; workers' strikes (1867, 1868, 1878, 1901), 10, 116; workers' strikes (1937), 118–19; workers' unrest and, 31; workers' wages and, 16, 32–34, 40, 133. *See also* West Indies Sugar Company
Sugar Manufacturers Association, 171, 250; Bustamante Industrial Trade Union landmark agreement with, 222–23
Swaby, J. C., 89
Syrians in Jamaica, 13, 15, 80, 329

Tanganyika, 113
Tate and Lyle Co., 33, 39, 249, 252. *See also* West Indies Sugar Company
Taxes, 9, 10, 105, 342
Telephone operators, 128
Terrier, R. O., 332
Thomas, Daniel, 50
Thomas, Henry, 50
Thomas, Norman, 259
Thomas, Sarah, 50
Thomas, Stanley, 50
Thompson, C. V. R., 168–69
Thompson, Cpl. (Kingston police), 51

Thompson, R. A., 88, 89
Thomson, Ansel O., 119, 120
Trades Union Advisory Council, 152, 153–61, 219, 318; dissolution/reformation of, 160–61; members of, 153
Trades Union Congress (Britain), 93, 198, 269
Trade unionism, 4, 45, 115–78, 263, 358; Advisory Council formation for, 153–55; anthem of, 174–75; Britain and, 98, 116, 198, 269; Bustamante-Coombs feud effect on, 143–45, 148, 150, 155–56; Bustamante Kingston Race Course speech (June 1938) and, 124; Bustamante-Manley split effect on, 229; Bustamante's negative impact on, 147, 151–52, 359, 361; Bustamante's philosophy of, 121–23; Bustamante's role in founding, 3, 28, 44, 115, 116, 178, 359; colonial authorities dislike of, 98, 102; colonial government's support for, 270–71; Conciliation Board and, 54, 55, 59, 60, 145–46; Coombs's role in founding of, 2, 107–8, 115; early organizations in Jamaica of, 115–16; effect of squabbles among leaders on, 141; employer relations and, 116–17, 163–64; first Jamaican law for, 116 (*see also* Labor law); first modern union in Jamaican, 2, 26, 116 (*see also* Jamaica Workers and Tradesmen Union); general strike's imperilment of, 154; government-appointed mediation/arbitration and, 133–34, 142, 267–68; growing strength of, 123; leaders' lack of experience and, 55, 163; Manley's support for, 55, 151–52, 207, 318, 319, 348–49, 359–60; membership by union (1943), *169*; negotiation skills and, 163–67; occupational categories of, 124; opposition to, 116–17; picketing and, 98, 101, 113, 116; police harassment of, 241–42; political representation of, 207, 334, 350, 351; Richards's fears about, 225–26, 228; Royal Commission report and, 113–14; self-government advocates and, 207, 225; women's invisibility in, 126, 128, 129; worker ferment and, 141; worker loyalty to, 149; worker suspiciousness of, 116–17. *See also* Strikes
Trade Union Law of 1919 (Britain), 98, 116, 269
Trade Union Law of 1919 (Jamaica), 116

Tram cars, 52, 68
Tramways Transport & General Workers Union, membership (1943), *169*
Transport workers, 52, 97, 124; union membership (1943), *116*
Trelawny Parish, 60, 224, 243, 301; Bustamante's triumphant tour of, 221; strikes in, 57
Trench Pen (Kingston slum), 28, 42, 94
Trial, right to, 231
Trickster (Jamaican lore), 177–78
Trinidad and Tobago, 13, 22, 93, 112, 114; labor unrest in, 31; protective labor laws in, 97
23rd Psalm, 173

Underclass: Bustamante's championship of, 29, 106, 107; socioeconomic plight of, 29–31, 57–58, 182, 250, 280; street meetings and, 239–40. *See also* Poverty
Underemployment, 17, 22
Underhill, E. B., 29, 33
Undesirable Publications Act of 1940, 233–35, 237; list of publications, 233–35
Unemployed people, 17–21, 22, 30–32, 78–79, 107; colonial government's blindness to, 41; land settlement plan for, 60; pleas for work by, 76; Richards's proposed roundup into labor camps of, 267; as strikebreakers, 149, 151; as union members, 126; unrest among, 42, 141–42
UNIA. *See* Universal Negro Improvement Association
Unionization. *See* Trade unionism; *specific unions*
United Fruit Company, 42, 60, 147–48, 180
United Negro Party, 86
United Rate Payers Party, 336, 340
United States, 2, 257, 258, 280, 288–89, 297; Domingo's internment and, 259–60; first modern labor union in, 115; military base in Jamaica of, 258, 259, 261; racial segregation in, 65, 181, 258
Universal adult suffrage, 4, 6, 205, 333, 361; English opponents of, 70–71; first election under, 5, 305, 338–53; Jamaica Democratic Party support for, 334; labor organization and, 207; Legislative Council and, 287, 289–90, 299; Manley's support for,

Index | 417

109–10, 285, 350; as political revolution, 350; reservations about, 301; restrictions on, 285; Royal Commission support for, 114, 287; third general election under, 356
Universal Negro Improvement Association (UNIA), 26, 45–46, 66, 86, 216; founding of, 24, 25; Kirkwood's speech before, 251; protest against Public Assembly Law by, 239; Richards's charges against, 255
University College of the West Indies (later University of the West Indies), 6
Up Park Camp, 254
Urban areas, rural migrants to, 19, 22, 95, 128

Valentine, G. E., 153
Veitch, F. G., 298, 349, 355
Vernon, Stanley, 138
Victoria (queen of Great Britain), 87, 88, 89; Kingston statue of, 177
Victoria Gardens (Kingston), 240–41
Victoria Park (Kingston), 142
Violence: Bustamante's alleged advocacy of, 186, 192–93, 194, 195, 203; Bustamante's threat of, 163; Jamaican society and, 341, 361; labor rebellion (1938) and, 37, 38, 42, 48–50, 54, 55, 57, 59, 60, 243; between rival union members, 224, 225; worker grievances and, 118
Voting rights. See Suffrage; Universal adult suffrage

Wages, 15–17, 28, 340; banana workers' settlement, 59; cost-of-living index linked with, 223; domestic servants, 128–29; government increases in, 28; lowness of, 17, 22, 30, 101, 102, 107, 128–29, 133, 134; minimum wage laws and, 96–97, 99, 325; purchasing power of, 16–17, 33; sugar workers, 16, 32–34, *34*, *35*, 36, 39, 40, 133; sugar workers' agreement, 223; workers' estimated monthly minimum budget, *18*
Waiters, 128
Walker, C. G., 84, 85
Ward Theatre (Kingston), 206–7, 310, 315, 334, 335
Water Commission Workers' Union, membership (1943), *169*
Waterfront general strike (1939), 147, 148–52
Waterfront labor rebellion (1938), 3, 42–56, 59, 177, 358; arrests of Bustamante and Grant and, 50–51, 56, 359; Bustamante's speeches and, 47–48, 55, 56, 358–59; casualties of, 50; as catalyst for other strikes, 52–53, 54–55, 56–57; police fire and, 49–50; women participants of, 127; workers' objective and, 48
Waterfront workers, 33, 116; strike (1937), 36; strike (January 1939), 141, 142; unemployment and, 19–20; unions for, 115, 116, 124; unrest of (1940), 183–84, 186, 192; women as, 126
Watson, Hugh H., 261–62
Watson, Lucius, 19–20, 42, 46, 49, 50
Wayte, Allan, 218, 220, 221
West, S. J. H., 337–38, 339
Western Federation of Teachers, 242
Western Morning News (Plymouth newspaper), 72
West Indian Welfare Fund, 113
West India Regiment, 26
West India Royal Commission. See Royal Commission
West Indies. See British West Indies
West Indies National Council, 257
West Indies Sugar Company, 2, 16, 61, 64, 249–50, 252; Bustamante's alleged threatening letter to, 186, 192; cultivation rates, 34, *35*; improvement of worker conditions by, 33, 36, 38, 39; Manley's retainer with, 52, 222; worker pay scales, 33, *34*, 36, 39; workers' rebellion initiated at (1938), 2, 33, 36–42
Westminster model of government, 354
Westmoreland Parish, 33, 38, 107, 224, 243, 269; Bustamante's triumphant tour of, 221; strikes in, 57. See also Frome sugar estate worker rebellion
White population, 13; as apex of shade hierarchy, 84; Bustamante self-classification with, 181; concern about future in Jamaica for, 68–69; employment of, 79; expatriate superiority and, 72; growth in, 13–14; political parties and, 336; as power elite, 8–9, 14–15, 23–24, 29, 64, 65, 67, 78, 265, 288; privileged lives of, 65, 72–73; racial issues and, 26, 68–72, 79, 85
"Why I Want Power" (Bustamante article), 131–32

Wildcat strikes, 141, 149
Williams, E. F.: Emancipation Day poem of, 92; "The Labourers' Psalm," 173
Williams, W. A., 256
Wilson, C. A., 342
Windward Islands, 93, 97
Wint, D. T., 25
WISCO. *See* West Indies Sugar Company
Women: as domestic servants, 20, 72, 127, 128–29; as election (1944) candidates, 349–50; employer sexual exploitation of, 100–101; employment limitations for, 20, 80, 126–28; English misconceptions about, 72–73, 74, 75; hard physical labor of, 73, 102, 126, 128; labor movement's minimal representation of, 126, 128; as labor rebellion participants, 59, 127; low wages of, 17, 102, 128; multi-based discrimination against, 79–80; population statistics, *14*; Royal Commission's exclusion of testimony from, 111; as Royal Commission members, 93; subordinate societal status of, 111; suffrage limitations for, 4, 10, 111, 285
Woodham, Roy, 270
Woolley, C. C., 60, 91
Workers: Bustamante's championship of, 4, 5, 28–29, 32, 55, 59, 71, 107, 109, 122, 123, 129, 133, 134, 154, 169–70, 171–78, 181, 184, 185, 191, 206, 208–9, 221, 224, 228–29, 319, 335, 340, 350, 358–59; Bustamante's Royal Commission testimony and, 98; class consciousness development by (*see* Working-class consciousness); economic deprivation of, 15–19, 27, 29–30, 96–97; effect of rebellion of 1938 on, 63; employer relations with, 91–92; estimated monthly minimum budget, *18*; growing militancy of, 56–57; harsh conditions of, 29–31, 102, 107, 134; hours of work and, 33–34, 39, 100, 133, 134; intermittent employment of, 16–17, 18, 21; internal divisions among, 120; Manley's role with, 53, 55, 359–60; official inattention to plight of, 96–97; percentage engaged in agriculture (1943), 21 (*see also* Farms and farmworkers); police brutality toward, 107–8, 182; political organization and, 207; protective legislation and, 96–99, 101, 107, 109; racial consciousness development by, 26, 113–14; Richards's view of, 247, 282; rotational engagement of, 17, 42; Royal Commission hearings about, 96–97; safety measures and, 97, 101; seasonal employment of, 22; sick leave and, 100–101; skin pigment discrimination and, 79, 80, 84; unrest of, 22, 31, 52, 107–8, 116, 123–24, 183–84, 186, 192; wages and expenditures of, 16–17; women's limited options as, 20, 72, 73, 80, 102, 126–27, 127, 128–29. *See also* Employment; Labor rebellion; Trade unionism; Unemployed people
Workforce. *See* Labor force
Working-class consciousness: gradual formation of, 120, 142, 151, 167, 225, 358; as identity, 63; Jamaica Labour Party's election victory and, 350; leadership and, 45–46; workers' lack of, 357–58
Workmen's Compensation Act of 1937, 97–98, 101, 107, 109
World War II, 4, 113, 216; Britain and, 183, 201, 232, 259, 261, 264, 307–8; Bustamante's view of, 134, 183, 191–92, 194, 201, 228; Jamaicans and, 1, 232, 247, 258–59, 261–62, 264–65, 268, 273, 276, 277, 301, 307–8; Mais trial and, 276–77; People's National Party and, 325, 326; security measures, 5, 115, 184–85, 192, 196, 230–40, 242, 246, 254–55, 256, 273–78. *See also* Censorship; Defense Regulations Act; Sedition

Yeo, David, 75

www.ingramcontent.com/pod-product-compliance
Lightning Source LLC
Chambersburg PA
CBHW021114300426
44113CB00006B/144